The Best Test Preparation for the

NTE

NATIONAL
TEACHERS
EXAMINATION

CORE BATTERY

Earvin Berlin Aaron, Ed.D.
Chairperson of the Department
of Curriculum and Instruction
Texas Southern University, Houston, Texas

Betty Archambeault, Ph.D.
Assistant Professor of Education
Baylor University, Waco, Texas

Barbara L. Boe, Ph.D
Associate Dean of the Graduate Program
and Chairperson and Professor of Education
Carthage College, Kenosha, Wisconsin

Anita P.Davis, Ed.D.
Chairperson of Education Department
Converse College, Spartanburg, South Carolina

Russell G. Fitzgerald, Ed.D.
Chairperson of Education Department
Director of Teacher Education and Certification
Davis and Elkins College, Elkins, West Virginia

Nancy E. Kendall, Ph.D.
High School English Instructor
Oak Ridge High School, Orlando, Florida

Evalee Lasater, Ed.D.
Instructor and Student Teacher Supervisor
University of Missouri—Rolla, Rolla, Missouri

Vincent D. Mahoney, Ph.D.
Chairperson of Education Department
Iowa Wesleyan College, Mt. Pleasant, Iowa

Catherine E. McCartney, Ph.D.
Assistant Professor of Educational Psychology
Bemidji State University, Bemidji, Minnesota

Paul R. McGhee, Ph.D.
Chairperson of Elementary, Reading and
Special Education Department
Morehead State University, Morehead, Kentucky

Ruby Bostick Midkiff, Ed.D.
Assistant Professor of Education
Arkansas State University, State University, Arkansas

Murry Nelson, Ed.D.
Professor of Education, The Pennsylvania State University
University Park, Pennsylvania

Jacob L. Susskind, Ph.D.
Assistant Professor of Social Science and Education
The Pennsylvania State University,
Middletown, Pennsylvania

St
Ch
Ad
California Stat

RESEARCH & EDUCATION ASSOCIATION
61 Ethel Road West • Piscataway, New Jersey 08854

The Best Test Preparation for the
NATIONAL TEACHERS EXAMINATION (NTE)
CORE BATTERY

Printed in the United States of America

Library of Congress Catalog Card Number 94-67816

International Standard Book Number 0-87891-851-5

Research & Education Association
61 Ethel Road West
Piscataway, NJ 08854

REA supports the effort to conserve and
protect environmental resources by
printing on recycled papers.

ACKNOWLEDGEMENTS

We thank the following authors for their work on the NTE Specialty Tests:

Anita P. Davis, Ed.D., Chairperson of Education Department, Converse College, Spartanburg, South Carolina

Ellen Davis, M.A., English Instructor, Clear Lake High School, Houston, Texas

Russell G. Fitzgerald, Ed.D., Chairperson of Education Department, Director of Teacher Education and Certification, Davis and Elkins College, Elkins, West Virginia

Gene M. Hammitt, Ph.D., Professor of Modern Languages, Allegheny College, Meadville, Pennsylvania

Pnina Mohr Katz, M.Ed., Exercise Physiologist and Assistant Adjunct Professor of Biology, St. John's University, New York, New York

William D. Keller, Ed.D., Professor of Accounting, Ferris State University, Big Rapids, Michigan

Ann S. McChesney, Ed.D., R.D., C.H.E., Assistant Professor of Nutritional Sciences, Cook College - Rutgers University, New Brunswick, New Jersey

Linda Cregg Nielsen, M.A., Language Coordinator, Brandeis University, Waltham, Massachusetts

Donald E. Orlosky, Ed.D., Chairperson of Educational Leadership Department, University of South Florida, Tampa, Florida

Richard Pisacreta, Ph.D., Professor of Psychology, Ferris State University, Big Rapids, Michigan

Gavin Townsend, Ph.D., Assistant Professor of Art History, The University of Tennessee at Chattanooga, Tennessee

William C. Uhland, M.S., Research Scientist, Cooper Hospital, Camden, New Jersey

Tefera Worku, M.S., Instructor of Mathematics, State University of New York – Albany, Albany, New York

◆ ◆ ◆ ◆

We would like to thank the following people for their
writing and editing contributions to the book:

Alison D.H. Brennan, Ed.D.	J. Francisco Hidalgo, Ph.D.	Kathy L. O'Brien, Ed.D.
Gretchen Carr	Hans G. Jellen, Ph.D.	Mark Previte
Christine Caruso	Glen M. Kraig, Ed.D.	Stacey A. Sporer
Stephen Correia	Kenneth E. Lane, Ph.D.	Sandra Stauffer, Ph.D.
David Foster	Nancy J. Martin, Ph.D.	James Weaver
Charles P. Funkhouser, Ph.D.	Daniel Moran	Julie Weber
Richard K. Gordan, Ph.D.	Jeffrey L. McNair, Ph.D.	Melanie A. Yost, Ed.M.

CONTENTS

NTE STUDY SCHEDULE x

INTRODUCTION 1
    About Research and Education Association 1
    You Can Achieve a Top NTE Score 1
    About the Test Experts 2
    About the NTE Core Battery Test 2
    About the NTE Specialty Area Tests 3
    NTE Core Battery Test Format 3
    Scoring The Exam 4

NTE TEST TAKING STRATEGIES 8

    How to Beat the Clock 8
    Guessing Strategy 8
    Other Must-Do Strategies 8

THE TEST SECTIONS 8

    The Test of Communication Skills 9
        Listening 9
        Reading 13
        Writing 15

    The Test of General Knowledge 22
        Social Studies 22
        Mathematics 23
        Literature and Fine Arts 24
        Science 27

    The Test of Professional Knowledge 29

NTE — CORE BATTERY TEST 1 31

Communication Skills Answer Sheet 1 32
Test of Communication Skills 1 33
Answer Key 54
Detailed Explanations of Answers 55

General Knowledge Answer Sheet 1 71
Test of General Knowledge 1 72
Answer Key 109
Detailed Explanations of Answers 110

Professional Knowledge Answer Sheet 1 129
Test of Professional Knowledge 1 130
Answer Key 152
Detailed Explanations of Answers 153

NTE — CORE BATTERY TEST 2 173

Communication Skills Answer Sheet 2 174
Test of Communication Skills 2 175
Answer Key 195
Detailed Explanations of Answers 196

General Knowledge Answer Sheet 2 215
Test of General Knowledge 2 217
Answer Key 253
Detailed Explanations of Answers 254

Professional Knowledge Answer Sheet 2 274
Test of Professional Knowledge 2 275
Answer Key 297
Detailed Explanations of Answers 298

NTE — CORE BATTERY TEST 3 321

Communication Skills Answer Sheet 3 322
Test of Communication Skills 3 323
Answer Key 346
Detailed Explanations of Answers 347

General Knowledge Answer Sheet 3 363
Test of General Knowledge 3 365
Answer Key 404
Detailed Explanations of Answers 405

Professional Knowledge Answer Sheet 3....................................423
Test of Professional Knowledge 3 424
Answer Key 447
Detailed Explanations of Answers 448

NTE — CORE BATTERY TEST 4 469

Communication Skills Answer Sheet 4 470
Test of Communication Skills 4 471
Answer Key 497
Detailed Explanations of Answers 498

General Knowledge Answer Sheet 4 517
Test of General Knowledge 4 518
Answer Key 554
Detailed Explanations of Answers 555

Professional Knowledge Answer Sheet 4....................................574
Test of Professional Knowledge 4 575
Answer Key 594
Detailed Explanations of Answers 595

NTE — SPECIALTY TESTS 613

Answer Sheet for Specialty Tests 614

ART EDUCATION 615
Answer Key..622
Detailed Explanations of Answers 622

BIOLOGY AND GENERAL SCIENCE 625
Answer Key..630
Detailed Explanations of Answers 630

BUSINESS EDUCATION 633
Answer Key..637
Detailed Explanations of Answers 637

CHEMISTRY 642
    Answer Key.. 645
    Detailed Explanations of Answers 645

EARLY CHILDHOOD EDUCATION 648
    Answer Key.. 652
    Detailed Explanations of Answers 652

EDUCATIONAL LEADERSHIP:
ADMINISTRATION AND SUPERVISION 656
    Answer Key.. 661
    Detailed Explanations of Answers 661

EDUCATION OF MENTALLY RETARDED STUDENTS 665
    Answer Key.. 669
    Detailed Explanations of Answers 669

ELEMENTARY EDUCATION 672
    Answer Key.. 677
    Detailed Explanations of Answers 677

ENGLISH LANGUAGE AND LITERATURE 680
    Answer Key.. 686
    Detailed Explanations of Answers 686

FRENCH 688
    Answer Key.. 693
    Detailed Explanations of Answers 693

GUIDANCE COUNSELOR 695
    Answer Key.. 699
    Detailed Explanations of Answers 699

HOME ECONOMICS 701
    Answer Key.. 706
    Detailed Explanations of Answers 706

MATHEMATICS 709
    Answer Key.. 714
    Detailed Explanations of Answers 714

PHYSICAL EDUCATION 718
    Answer Key.. 721
    Detailed Explanations of Answers 721

SCHOOL PSYCHOLOGIST 724
    Answer Key... 728
    Detailed Explanations of Answers 728

SOCIAL STUDIES 731
    Answer Key... 735
    Detailed Explanations of Answers 735

SPANISH 738
    Answer Key... 743
    Detailed Explanations of Answers 743

SPECIAL EDUCATION 748
    Answer Key... 752
    Detailed Explanations of Answers 752

NTE Study Schedule

The following is a suggested six week study schedule for the National Teachers Examination. You may take certain sections of the NTE Core based on state examination requirements, so it is a good idea to adjust the schedule to your own personal needs.

This schedule is primarily for students planning to take the Core Battery as outlined in this book. In order for this schedule to benefit you the most, it is necessary that you follow the study activities carefully. You may want to condense or expand this schedule depending on how soon you will be taking the actual NTE. Set aside time each week, and work straight through the activity *without rushing*. By following a structured schedule, you will be sure to complete an adequate amount of studying, and you will be confident and prepared on the day of the actual exam.

Week	Activity
1	Acquaint yourself with the NTE by reading the Introduction, NTE Test Taking Strategies, and the Test Sections (pages 1 through 29). Keep a sheet of paper nearby as you are doing the examples for each section, and jot down any sections that are confusing or difficult for you. Locate reference sources to use for those portions of the exam. For instance, use your educational texts for the Professional Knowledge section.
2	Take Core Battery Test 1 as a diagnostic test in order to determine your strengths and weaknesses. After checking the answer key and the explanations, make a note of the questions that were difficult. Review the specific field of difficulty by using the appropriate textbooks, notes, course materials, etc., to prepare to take Test 2.
3	Take Core Battery Test 2. Read through all the detailed explanations carefully (not just those for your incorrect answers), and make a note of any sections that were difficult for you, or any questions that were still unclear after reading the explanations. Use sources of information, such as textbooks, notes, or course materials, to review those areas that need clarification.
4	Take Core Battery Test 3. Read through all the detailed explanations carefully (not just those for your incorrect answers), and make a note of any sections that were difficult for you, or any questions that were still unclear after reading the explanations. Use sources of information, such as textbooks, notes, or course materials, to review those areas that need clarification.
5	Take Core Battery Test 4. Read through all the detailed explanations carefully (not just those for your incorrect answers), and make a note of any sections that were difficult for you, or any questions that were still unclear after reading the explanations. Use sources of information, such as textbooks, notes, or course materials, to review those areas that need clarification.
6	Compare your progress between the exams. Note any sections where you were able to improve your score, and sections where your score remained the same or declined. Allow yourself extra study time for those areas that require added attention.

About Research and Education Association

REA is an organization of educators, scientists, and engineers specializing in various academic fields. REA was founded in 1959 for the purpose of disseminating the most recently developed scientific information to groups in industry, government and universities. Since then, REA has become a successful and highly respected publisher of study aids, test preps, handbooks and reference works.

REA's Test Preparation series extensively prepares students and professionals for the Medical College Admission Test (MCAT), Graduate Record Examinations (GRE), Graduate Management Admission Test (GMAT), Scholastic Assessment Test (SAT), Advanced Placement Exams, and SAT II: Subject Tests. Whereas most Test Preparation books present a limited amount of practice tests and bear little resemblance to the actual exams, REA's series presents at least four tests which accurately depict the actual exams in both degree of difficulty and types of questions. REA's tests are always based on the most recently administered exams and include every type of question that can be expected on the actual exams.

REA's publications and educational materials are highly regarded for their significant contribution to the quest for excellence that characterizes today's educational goals. We continually receive an unprecedented amount of praise from professionals, instructors, librarians, parents, and students for our published books. Our authors are as diverse as the subjects and fields represented in the books we publish. They are well-known in their respective fields and serve on the faculties of prestigious universities throughout the United States.

You can achieve a top NTE score

By reviewing and studying this book, you can achieve a top score on the NTE. The NTE tests knowledge which you have gained throughout your academic career, from college courses to outside supplemental reading. Most of the knowledge tested by the NTE Core Battery is covered in college or university teacher preparation programs. As the Educational Testing Service states, the NTE "aim[s] to measure in an objective and standardized manner academic knowledge and skills important for beginning teachers and other education professionals." While the test cannot ascertain other important aspects of teaching, such as dedication, rapport with students, and motivation, the test does assess basic skills relevant to the teaching profession.

The purpose of our book is to properly prepare you for the NTE by providing four full-length exams that accurately reflect the NTE in both the types of questions and degree of difficulty. The provided exams, based on the most recently administered NTEs, include every type of question that can be expected on the NTE. Following each exam is an answer key complete with detailed explanations and solutions. Designed specifically to clarify the material to the student, the explanations not only provide the correct answers, but also explain to the student why the answer to a particular question is more acceptable than any other answer choice. At the same time, the material most likely to be encountered on the actual NTE is reviewed. By completing all four exams and studying the explanations which follow, strengths and weaknesses can be discovered. This knowledge will allow you to concentrate on the sections of the exam you find to be most difficult.

About the Test Experts

To aid us in meeting our objectives for providing exams that accurately reflect the NTE, test experts in the relevant subject fields carefully prepared each and every exam section. Our authors have spent quality time examining and researching the mechanics of the actual NTE to see what types of practice questions accurately depict the exam and challenge the student. Our experts are highly regarded in the educational community, having studied at the doctoral level and taught in their respective fields at competitive universities and colleges throughout the United States. They have an in-depth knowledge of the questions they have presented in the book, and provide accurate questions which appeal to the student's interest. Each question is clearly explained in order to help the student achieve a top score on the NTE.

About the NTE Core Battery Test

The NTE Core Battery Test is required by most state boards of education for teacher certification. It is also used by colleges, universities, state departments of education and other educational organizations for a variety of purposes, from certification to graduate program admission. The exam tests communication skills (listening, reading and writing), general knowledge (social studies, mathematics, science, literature and fine arts), and professional knowledge (the process of teaching). The NTE Core Battery Test is given three times a year: in October, March, and June. The test is administered by the Educational Testing Service (ETS) under the direction of the Teacher Programs Council. Many states require only parts of the NTE Core Battery Test for certification. Contact your school counsel or local university for information on applying to take the test.

The NTE Core Battery Test contains three distinct sections broken down into the following areas:

1. The Test of Communication Skills: four thirty-minute sections containing listening, reading, and writing comprehension, and one written essay

2. The Test of General Knowledge: four thirty-minute sections which test science, mathematics, social studies, literature and fine arts

3. The Test of Professional Knowledge: four thirty-minute sections which test your knowledge of the teaching process. A trial section is included in this test but it is not counted toward your score.

Following this preface are test strategies, examples, and suggested study techniques which will help you to properly prepare for the NTE.

The NTE consists entirely of multiple choice questions, excepting the written essay, contained in twelve timed sections. Each question presents five choices (A through E), except for the Listening section, which presents four choices. Of the twelve sections, the actual test contains one trial Professional Knowledge section which is not counted toward your score; it is simply used for experimental purposes. For practical purposes, this book has omitted the trial section, presenting only the three counted and scored Professional Knowledge sections for each exam.

About the NTE Specialty Area Tests

In addition to the practice Core Battery tests which appear in this book, REA has provided sample questions and answer explanations, from the 18 most popular Specialty Area Tests. This section is located on page 613.

The Specialty Tests are required by many states, in addition to the Core Battery Test, for certification in specific areas of teaching. Other states require only the Specialty Area Test for certification in a specific field.

The following Specialty Area Tests are represented in this book:

Art Education	French
Biology and General Science	Home Economics Education
Business Education	Mathematics
Chemistry	Physical Education
Early Childhood Education	School Guidance Counselor
Educating the Mentally Handicapped	School Psychologist
Education Administration	Social Studies
Elementary Educatiuon	Spanish
English Language and Literature	Special Education

NTE Core Battery Test Format

Part	Section	Number of Questions	Minutes
Test of Communication Skills	Listening	40 items: statements and questions, conversations, and short talks	30
	Reading	30 items: reading comprehension passages and short statements	30
	Writing	45 items: usage, sentence correction, and composition strategies	30
	Essay	one topic relating to general situations in the classroom and in life in general	30

Test of General Knowledge	Social Studies	30 items: social and historical concepts	30
	Mathematics	25 items: basic and everyday mathematical and analytical skills	30
	Literature and Fine Arts	35 items: knowledge of humanities	30
	Science	30 items: understanding of physical, biological and earth sciences	30
Test of Professional Knowledge		140 total items: understanding of knowledge and skills necessary to teach; three sections plus one trial section (not scored)	30 min. each section

Total: 6 hours

Test of Communication Skills   = 115 questions + 1 essay
Test of General Knowledge   = 120 questions
Test of Professional Knowledge = 140 questions

TOTAL   375 questions + 1 essay

SCORING THE EXAM

The NTE Core Battery score is based upon the number of correct answers. The test does not deduct points for incorrect answers. (See "Guessing Strategy" for more information concerning this important fact.) The raw scores are calculated separately for each section, using particular formulas, and converted to scaled scores. The following formulas and charts will help you to compute your scaled score for each section.

Test of Communication Skills

1. Count the number of correct answers from the Listening, Reading, and Writing sections.

2. For the essay, which you cannot grade by yourself, a low, medium, and high score must be substituted into the computation. ETS graders use a scale of 0 to 12 (0 for essays which are not on the given topic, and 12 for the best essays). Choose three different grades for your essay and use them one at a time in your computations.

3. Multiply each score by the following numbers to obtain your raw scores:
    Listening: 2.3624   Writing: 1.000
    Reading: 2.6313   Essay: 3.8581
    Add up the raw scores to get your raw composite score.

4. Refer to the chart on the next page. Convert your raw composite score to the correct scaled score.

Test of Communication Skills
Conversion Table

Raw Composite	Scaled Score	Raw Composite	Scaled Score	Raw Composite	Scaled Score	Raw Composite	Scaled Score
0	600	33	611	66	622	99	634
1	600	34	612	67	623	100	634
2	601	35	612	68	623	101	634
3	601	36	612	69	623	102	635
4	601	37	613	70	624	103	635
5	602	38	613	71	624	104	635
6	602	39	613	72	624	105	636
7	602	40	614	73	625	106	636
8	603	41	614	74	625	107	636
9	603	42	614	75	625	108	637
10	603	43	615	76	626	109	637
11	604	44	615	77	626	110	637
12	604	45	615	78	626	111	638
13	604	46	616	79	627	112	638
14	605	47	616	80	627	113	638
15	605	48	616	81	628	114	639
16	605	49	617	82	628	115	639
17	606	50	617	83	628	116	639
18	606	51	617	84	629	117	640
19	606	52	618	85	629	118	640
20	607	53	618	86	629	119	640
21	607	54	618	87	630	120	641
22	607	55	619	88	630	121	641
23	608	56	619	89	630	122	641
24	608	57	619	90	631	123	642
25	608	58	620	91	631	124	642
26	609	59	620	92	631	125	642
27	609	60	620	93	632	126	643
28	610	61	621	94	632	127	643
29	610	62	621	95	632	128	643
30	610	63	621	96	633	129	644
31	611	64	622	97	633	130	644
32	611	65	622	98	633	131	644

Test of Communication Skills (cont.)
Conversion Table

Raw Composite	Scaled Score	Raw Composite	Scaled Score	Raw Composite	Scaled Score	Raw Composite	Scaled Score
132	645	165	656	199	668	232	679
133	645	166	656	200	668	233	679
134	646	167	657	201	668	234	679
135	646	168	657	202	669	235	680
136	646	169	657	203	669	236	680
137	647	170	658	204	669	237	680
138	647	171	658	205	670	238	681
139	647	172	658	206	670	239	681
140	648	173	659	207	670	240	682
141	648	174	659	208	671	241	682
142	648	175	659	209	671	242	682
143	649	176	660	210	671	243	683
144	649	177	660	211	672	244	683
145	649	178	660	212	672	245	683
146	650	179	661	213	672	246	684
147	650	180	661	214	673	247	684
148	650	181	661	215	673	248	684
149	651	182	662	216	673	249	685
150	651	183	662	217	674	250	685
151	651	184	662	218	674	251	685
152	652	185	663	219	674	252	686
153	652	186	663	220	675	253	686
154	652	187	663	221	675	254	686
155	653	188	664	222	675	255	687
156	653	190	665	223	676	256	687
157	653	191	665	224	676	257	687
158	654	192	665	225	676	258	688
159	654	193	666	226	677	259	688
160	654	194	666	227	677	260	688
161	655	195	666	228	677	261	689
162	655	196	667	229	678	262	689
163	655	197	667	230	678	263	689
164	656	198	667	231	678	264	690
						265	690

Test of General Knowledge

1. Count the number of correct answers from each section of this test.

2. Multiply each score by the following numbers to obtain your raw scores:
   Social Studies: 1.1688
   Mathematics: 1.2243
   Literature & Fine Arts: 1.000
   Science: 1.1666
   Add up your raw scores to get your raw composite score.

3. Refer to the chart below. Convert your raw composite score to the correct scaled score.

Test of General Knowledge
Conversion Table

Raw Composite	Scaled Score	Raw Composite	Scaled Score	Raw Composite	Scaled Score	Raw Composite	Scaled Score
0	600	35	623	69	646	103	668
1	601	36	624	70	646	104	669
2	601	37	624	71	647	105	669
3	602	38	625	72	648	106	670
4	603	39	626	73	648	107	671
5	603	40	626	74	649	108	671
6	604	41	627	75	650	109	672
7	605	42	628	76	650	110	673
8	605	43	628	77	651	111	673
9	606	44	629	78	652	112	674
10	607	45	630	79	652	113	675
11	607	46	630	80	653	114	675
12	608	47	631	81	654	115	676
13	609	48	632	82	654	116	677
14	609	49	632	83	655	117	677
15	610	50	633	84	656	118	678
16	611	51	634	85	656	119	679
17	611	52	634	86	657	120	679
18	612	53	635	87	658	121	680
19	613	54	636	88	658	122	681
20	613	55	636	89	659	123	681
21	614	56	637	90	660	124	682
22	615	57	638	91	660	125	683
23	615	58	638	92	661	126	683
24	616	59	639	93	662	127	684
25	617	60	640	94	662	128	685
26	617	61	640	95	663	129	685
27	618	62	641	96	664	130	686
28	619	63	642	97	664	131	687
29	619	64	642	98	665	132	687
30	620	65	643	99	666	133	688
31	621	66	644	100	666	134	689
32	621	67	644	101	667	135	689
33	622	68	645	102	668	136	690
34	623						

Test of Professional Knowledge

1. Count the number of correct answers from this test. This is your total raw score.
2. Refer to the table below. Convert your total raw score to the correct scaled score.

Test of Professional Knowledge
Conversion Table

Raw Total	Scaled Score	Raw Total	Scaled Score	Raw Total	Scaled Score	Raw Total	Scaled Score
0	600	27	623	53	646	79	668
1	601	28	624	54	647	80	669
2	602	29	625	55	648	81	670
3	603	30	626	56	648	82	671
4	603	31	627	57	649	83	672
5	604	32	628	58	650	84	673
6	605	33	629	59	651	85	674
7	606	34	629	60	652	86	674
8	607	35	630	61	653	87	675
9	608	36	631	62	654	88	676
10	609	37	632	63	655	89	677
11	610	38	633	64	655	90	678
12	610	39	634	65	656	91	679
13	611	40	635	66	657	92	680
14	612	41	635	67	658	93	680
15	613	42	636	68	659	94	681
16	614	43	637	69	660	95	682
17	615	44	638	70	661	96	683
18	616	45	639	71	661	97	684
19	616	46	640	72	662	98	685
20	617	47	641	73	663	99	686
21	618	48	642	74	664	100	687
22	619	49	642	75	665	101	687
23	620	50	643	76	666	102	688
24	621	51	644	77	667	103	689
25	622	52	645	78	668	104	690
26	623						

The average grades for the three sections of the NTE Core Battery test are:

Test of Communication Skills   659

Test of General Knowledge   656

Test of Professional Knowledge 656

You can compare your scores to these to see if you are above or below average.

NTE TEST TAKING STRATEGIES

How to Beat the Clock

Every second counts and you will want to use the available test time for each section in the most efficient manner. Here's how:

1. Memorize the test directions for each section of the test. You do not want to waste valuable time reading directions on the day of the exam . Your time should be spent on answering the questions.

2. Bring a watch to the exam and pace yourself. Work steadily and quickly. Do not get stuck or spend too much time on any one question.

Guessing Strategy

1. If you are uncertain about a question, guess at the answer rather than not answer at all. You will not be penalized for answering incorrectly, since wrong answers are not counted toward the final score. You should never leave a space on your answer sheet blank; be sure to fill in every space on the answer sheet. You will not be assessed a penalty for a wrong answer, but you will receive credit for any questions answered correctly by luck.

2. You can improve your guessing strategy by eliminating any choices recognized as incorrect. As you eliminate incorrect choices, cross them out. Remember that writing in test booklets is allowed, and that by crossing out incorrect choices, you will be better able to focus on the possibly correct answers.

Other Must-Do Strategies

1. As you work on the test, be sure that your answers correspond with the proper numbers and letters on the answer sheet.

2. If you are uncertain about a question, make your best guess using the guessing strategy described above, and circle your answer in the exam booklet. Do not leave it blank. If time runs out before you get to approach the question again, you will at least have it marked.

THE TEST SECTIONS

As mentioned above, the NTE Core Battery Test has three parts: Communication Skills, General Knowledge, and Professional Knowledge. The following explains these sections in detail and suggests helpful hints in selecting the correct answers. Also in this section are examples, with detailed explanations.

The Test of Communication Skills

The Test of Communication Skills tests your ability to use and understand written and spoken English. The questions in this section are broken down as follows:

40 Listening
30 Reading
45 Writing
1 Essay

The following material introduces each type of question asked in this section.

Listening

This section consists of multiple choice items which rely on audio taped statements, questions, dialogue, and short talks. You will hear a verbal message or exchange, and you will then have approximately twelve seconds to respond to questions about what you heard. There will be only answer choices in your test booklet.

Note: For this part of tests 1, 2 and 3, use the cassette which accompanies this book. The Listening section in Test 4 will be fully transcribed in the book. To practice, have a friend or family member read the spoken parts to you.

PART A

> **DIRECTIONS:** In this section, you will hear short statements and questions. When you hear a statement, select the answer which best restates or supports what you heard. When you hear a question, select the choice which best answers the question. The questions and statements are NOT written in your book. They will not be repeated.

EXAMPLES

1. *You will hear:* How much money did you bring?
   You will read:
   (A) I have $20 hidden in an envelope in my desk.
   (B) None, but I have a credit card.
   (C) There's some change in my car under the seat.
   (D) I spent my cash at the grocery store yesterday.

2. *You will hear:* The bus will leave promptly at 5:00 P.M. for the stadium and return after the game.
   You will read:
   (A) If you want to ride the bus, you need to be ready and waiting at the pick up point a few minutes before five.
   (B) The bus will return at 10:30 P.M.
   (C) No food or drinks are allowed on the bus but you can buy snacks at the stadium.
   (D) Forty people purchased tickets at $5.00 each to ride the bus to the game.

Suggested Techniques for Answering Listening Comprehension Statement/Question Items

- Listen carefully. Try not to move around in your seat or to let others' movements distract you.

- Practice listening at home. When you are watching TV or listening to the radio try to repeat in your head what someone has said.

EXPLANATIONS

1. **(B)** Answer (A) is incorrect because the speaker asks how much money you brought with you, not how much is in your desk. Answer (B) is correct because it directly responds to the question. Answer (C) is incorrect because it does not tell how much money you have with you. Answer (D) is incorrect because you were not asked how you spent your cash.

2. **(A)** This question asks you to respond to a statement concerning the time the bus leaves for the stadium. Answer (B) concerns the return time, which is not specified. Answer (C) is incorrect because food and drinks are not discussed. Answer (D) is incorrect because it adds new information and does not respond to the initial statement. Answer (A) is correct because it specifically responds to the information about the time the bus will leave

PART B

DIRECTIONS: In this section, you will hear short conversations between two people. After each conversation, a third person will ask you questions about what was discussed. When you hear a question, select the choice which best answers the question based on what you heard. The conversations and questions are NOT written in your test book. They will not be repeated.

EXAMPLES

Questions 1 through 3 are based on the following conversation.

Teacher: Why is your homework unfinished?

Student: I couldn't finish it because I was sick.

Teacher: That is the third time this week you have not finished an assignment.

Student: But I was busy.

Teacher: I thought you were sick. Finish this assignment and write a 100 word apology to me for being late with your homework.

1.   What can you conclude about the student?
   (A)   He seldom misses an assignment.
   (B)   He frequently does not finish his homework.
   (C)   He is on the basketball team and has practice everyday.
   (D)   He is often sick.

2.   What can you conclude about the teacher?

(A)   She is lenient.

(B)   She is strict.

(C)   She requires all students to finish homework assignments.

(D)   She dislikes this student.

3.   What is the student's excuse for not finishing the assignments?

(A)   He did not understand the assignments.

(B)   He was sick.

(C)   He was busy.

(D)   His excuse changes during the conversation.

Suggested Techniques for Answering Listening Comprehension Conversation Items

- Listen carefully. Try not to move around in your seat or to let others' movements distract you.

- When at home, practice remembering short conversations you have with family and friends. See if you can recall them as accurately as possible.

EXPLANATIONS

1.   **(B)**   The correct answer is (B), because the teacher states that the student has missed three assignments that week. Answer (A) is incorrect because it is the opposite of what the teacher says. Answers (C) and (D) are incorrect because, although he may be on the basketball team and he may often be sick, neither is indicated by the conversation.

2.   **(C)**   Answer (C) is correct because the teacher values homework and insists that students complete assignments. Answers (A), (B) and (D) are incorrect because the conversation lacks enough specific information to make such broad conclusions about the teacher's personality, or the students she dislikes.

3.   **(D)**   Answer (D) is correct because the student gives two different excuses. Answer (A) is incorrect because the student never suggests that he did not understand. Answers (B) and (C) are incorrect, because each individual excuse is incomplete.

PART C

DIRECTIONS: In this section, you will hear several short talks. After each talk, a second voice will ask questions about the talk. When you hear a question, select the choice which best answers the question based on what you heard. The short talks are NOT written in your test book. **They will not be repeated**.

Questions 1 through 4 are based on the following talk.

Maintaining beach front property is a never ending task. The spring begins with a thorough cleaning both inside and outside. Window frames need to be cleaned and repainted. Windows must be washed. The porch or patio must be swept and washed with water. Sometimes so much sand, grit and mold has accumulated on the outside walls and under the eaves, that it is necessary to wash the house with a pressure spray. Summer is a constant battle with dirt from rain and blowing sand. In the fall it is necessary to be on guard for hurricanes. Before winter arrives all the porch furniture must be stored. Pipes must be protected from possible freezing temperatures. Beach front property is wonderful, but the maintenance never ends.

1. What is the speaker's complaint?
    (A) Beach front property is expensive.
    (B) Beach front property is not worth the effort.
    (C) Hurricanes can cause a lot of destruction.
    (D) Maintenance never ends.

2. Which of the following is the major cause of maintenance problems?
    (A) Hurricanes   (C) Insects
    (B) Blowing sand and rain   (D) Freezing temperatures

3. With what does spring maintenance begin?
    (A) Thorough cleaning
    (B) Removing sand from porch
    (C) Removing mold from under the eaves
    (D) Protecting pipes

4. Which of the following is NOT a maintenance task for fall and winter?
    (A) Prepare for hurricanes   (C) Wash windows
    (B) Protect pipes   (D) Store porch furniture

Suggested Strategies for Answering Listening Comprehension Short Talk Items:

- Listen carefully. Try not to let others' movements distract you.

- Try to remember key phrases in the talk.

- Practice at home by having someone read a short passage to you and then ask you questions about it.

EXPLANATIONS

1. **(D)** Answer (D) is correct, because the speaker begins and ends with the statement that maintenance of beach front property never ends. Answer (A) is incorrect because the speaker never mentions expense. Answer (B) is incorrect because the speaker states that "beach front property is wonderful." Answer (C) is incorrect because although the speaker mentions hurricanes, the destruction they cause is not discussed.

2. **(B)** Answer (B) is correct because the speaker specifically names blowing sand and rain as the cause of maintenance problems. Hurricanes and freezing temperatures are

mentioned, but not as major problems, so answers (A) and (D) are incorrect. Answer (C) is incorrect because insects are not discussed.

3.   **(A)**   The correct answer is (A). The speaker begins by stating that "spring begins with a thorough cleaning…" Removing sand from the porch and cleaning the mold under the eaves are both mentioned, but those tasks are not first, so answers (B) and (C) are incorrect. Answer (D) is named as a task to prepare for winter, not spring.

4.   **(C)**   Answer (C) is correct. Washing windows was named as a maintenance task for spring. Answers (A), (B) and (D) are incorrect because preparing for hurricanes, protecting pipes, and storing porch furniture are all named as fall and winter maintenance tasks.

Reading

This section consists of thirty multiple choice questions which test your reading comprehension ability. This section is broken down into reading passages of about 100 to 200 words in length, as well as brief statements. You must read the passages and statements and answer questions about them.

> **DIRECTIONS:** Each passage is followed by questions based on its content. After reading the passage, choose the best answer to each question. Answer all the questions based on what is indicated or implied in the passage.

EXAMPLES

Questions 1 through 4 are based on the following passage.

It is a known fact that for the first time, a generation will not outstrip its parents' generation educationally, or economically. In fact, this generation of students won't even equal their parents' efforts.

1.   What is the main idea of this passage?
    (A)   Parents are economically and educationally better off than their children.
    (B)   Parents are ahead of their children economically.
    (C)   Parents are ahead of their children educationally.
    (D)   Parents and their children are about equal educationally.
    (E)   Parents and their children are about equal economically.

2.   Which of the following is an unstated assumption made by the author?
    (A)   This generation of students is lazy.
    (B)   This generation of students refuses to study.
    (C)   Parents are more industrious than their children.
    (D)   Parents are smarter than their children.
    (E)   Parents were more interested in school than their children are.

3.   Does the author adequately support his/her argument?
    (A)   The support is very adequate.

  (B) The support is somewhat adequate.

  (C) Marginally, the author's argument is supported.

  (D) The author's evidence is not appropriate at all.

  (E) The author provides no support for his/her idea presented in the passage.

4. Which of the following is a fact presented in the passage?

  (A) Parents are smarter than their children.

  (B) Parents are more industrious than their children.

  (C) Economically, parents are better off than their children.

  (D) The author believes that parents are educationally and economically superior to their children.

  (E) Educationally, parents are better off than their children.

Suggested Strategies for Answering Reading Comprehension Questions

- Look for main ideas in the passage, while following the development of the argument.

- Feel free to make notes in the margin, or to underline any sentences which will help.

- Read the passage for content, tone, and author's point of view.

- Skim some of the questions first before reading each passage. This will help you to gleam answers from the passage more easily.

- Try not to spend too much time deciphering the meaning of words and statements upon first reading the passage. It will be helpful to go back over specific parts of the passage for in-depth understanding, after each question has been read.

- Read all of the answer choices before choosing your answer.

EXPLANATIONS

1. **(A)** This question requires you to identify the main idea of this passage. Choices (B) and (C) are limited, because the passage indicates that parents outstrip their children both educationally and economically, as stated in choice (A). Choices (D) and (E) are inappropriate. The passage indicates that students will not even equal the educational and economic accomplishments of their parents.

2. **(C)** This question asks you to go beyond the facts that are presented in the passage. Choices (A) and (B) may be true, but the passage neither states, nor implies, anything that supports them. Also, just because this generation of students will not outstrip, or even equal its parents educationally or economically, this does not support the assumptions that parents are smarter than their children, or that parents were more interested in school than their children are today. It can be assumed, though, that parents are generally more industrious than their children, choice (C).

3. **(E)** A careful rereading of the passage will reveal that the author presents an idea, but no support for the idea. No empirical data is presented which clearly shows that parents are educationally and economically superior to their children. For example, in 1945, 85 percent of first-graders entering school graduated. In 1962, only 45 percent of the first-graders entering school graduated. Choice (E) is the correct answer. Choices (A), (B), (C) and (D) are not supported.

4. **(D)** This question requires you to determine which of the above statements is a fact. The passage contains no facts. Even though the passages begins with "It is a known fact that..." no evidence is presented; therefore, choices (A), (B), (C) and (E) are incorrect. However, choice (D) is a fact. The author does believe that parents are educationally and economically superior to their children.

Writing

This section consists of forty-five multiple choice questions which assess your language proficiency in grammar, sentence structure, and proper diction. Consulting a book in basic grammar and English will be helpful in preparing for this section. You will not be asked to identify specific parts of grammar. In the usage questions, certain words, phrases, or punctuation in a sentence will be underlined; one of the underlined items may be incorrect, or there may be no error at all. In the sentence correction part, some or all of a sentence will be underlined. You will have to choose the best way to rewrite the sentence, or to determine that it does not need rewriting at all. In the Composition Strategies section, you are to determine ways of improving or clarifying a short passage.

PART A: USAGE

DIRECTIONS: Each of the following sentences may contain an error in diction, usage, idiom, or grammar. Some sentences are correct. Some sentences contain one error. No sentence contains more than one error.

If there is an error, it will appear in one of the underlined portions labeled A, B, C, or D. If there is no error, choose the portion labeled E. If there is an error, select the letter of the portion that must be changed in order to correct the sentence.

1. To gain the most benefit from yoga, you must stretch muscles slowly with regular breathing
   A   B   C

and you hold each position. No error.
    D   E

2. The flooding was severe, and cars stall in the deep water near the school. No error.
      A   B   C   D   E

3. Judys friends and relations came to congratulate her on winning the contest and to admire
   A   B   C   D

her car. No error.
    E

4. The little boy approached the basketball coach timidly and ask for his autograph. No error.
    A   B   C   D   E

5. Your going to be late if you do not stop procrastinating and leave immediately. No error.
    A   B   C   D   E

Suggested Strategies for Answering Usage Questions

- Familiarize yourself with grammar. Even though you are not required to name specific elements of grammar, you should know about noun/verb agreement, possessives, proper punctuation, verb tenses, etc.

- Pay attention to what "sounds right."

EXPLANATIONS

1.   **(D)**   The error occurs at (D). "You" is used unnecessarily. The correct form would be "…you must stretch muscles slowly with regular breathing and hold each position."

2.   **(B)**   The error occurs at (B). The tense of "stall" does not agree with the tense of "was." The correct form should be "…and cars stalled…"

3   **(A)**   The error occurs at (A). "Judys friends" should be "Judy's friends" to show possession.

4.   **(C)**   The error occurs at (C). The tense of "ask" does not match the tense of "approached." The correct form would be "The little boy approached the basketball coach and asked…"

5.   **(A)**   The error occurs at (A). "Your" should be "you're" in this construction. "Your" means something belongs to you; it shows possession. "You're" means "you are."

PART B: SENTENCE CORRECTION

DIRECTIONS: In each of the following sentences, some portion of the sentence is underlined. Under each sentence are five choices. The first choice has the same wording as the original. The other four choices are reworded. Select the letter of the best choice which rewrites the sentence correctly.

EXAMPLES

1. Since the lost dog was returned to its owner everything turned out alright.

    (A)   its owner everything turned out alright.
    (B)   it's owner, everything ended alright.

(C) its owner, everything turned out alright.

(D) its owner everything turned out all right.

(E) its owner, everything turned out all right.

2. <u>Disgust at his own reaction,</u> Burt decided to begin working harder to achieve his goal of finishing by noon.

(A) Disgust at his own reaction

(B) Disgust at the reaction,

(C) Disgusting his reaction,

(D) Disgusted at his own reaction

(E) Disgusted at his own reaction,

3. Monroe and Allen never <u>knew if she angry or just joking.</u>

(A) knew if she angry or just joking.

(B) know if she get angry or just joking.

(C) knew whether she was angry or whether she was just joking.

(D) know if she is angry or just joking.

(E) knowed that she was angry or just joking.

4. <u>"The last bus" she said with a sigh "left ten minutes ago."</u>

(A) "The last bus" she said with a sigh "left ten minutes ago."

(B) The last bus left ten minutes ago.

(C) "The last bus," she said with a sigh, "left ten minutes ago."

(D) "The last bus left ten minutes ago." She said with a sigh.

(E) "The last bus," She said with a sigh, "Left ten minutes ago."

5. <u>The bright poster in Kim's room attracts the visitor's eye on the north wall.</u>

(A) The bright poster in Kim's room attracts the visitor's eye on the north wall.

(B) The bright poster on the north wall of Kim's room attracts the visitor's eye.

(C) The visitor's eye is attracted by the bright poster in Kim's room on the north wall.

(D) The north wall of Kim's room attracts the visitor's eye because of the bright poster.

(E) The bright poster in Kims' room attracts the visitor's eye on the north wall.

> **Suggested Techniques for Answering Sentence Correction Questions**
>
> - Concentrate on identifying errors and possible answers for the underlined part before reading the choices.
> - Choose (A) only if the given sentence seems correct and only after reading all of the other choices.
> - Focus on the clarity, structure and grammar of the sentence.
> - Determine how well each answer choice expresses the sentence.
> - It is helpful to substitute each choice in the underlined part of the given sentence, but avoid spending too much time on this process.

EXPLANATIONS

1. **(E)** The correct answer is (E). "Alright" is an incorrect spelling of "all right." Additionally, "since" indicates a subordinate clause which must be separated with a comma from the main part of the sentence. Only answer (E) corrects both problems.

2. **(E)** The correct answer is (E). The incorrect form of "disgust" is used in the original sentence. Past tense of the verb is required to agree with "decided." Answer (D) uses "disgusted" correctly, but the comma has been omitted. A comma is needed in this sentence for clarity and to separate the introductory clause from the remainder of the sentence. Answers (B) and (C) use inappropriate forms of "disgust." Answer (A) is identical to the original.

3. **(C)** The problem with this sentence is that it is awkward and uses illogical wording. Exactly what Monroe and Allen "never knew" is not clearly stated. The use of "if" sets up a conditional statement which does not logically match the meaning of the sentence. Answer (C) is correct because it clarifies the statement in a parallel form. Answers (A), (B), (D) and (E) do not clarify the original statement.

4. **(C)** The problem with this sentence is incorrect punctuation of the quoted statement. Answer (B) corrects the problem, but alters the meaning. Answer (C) uses correct punctuation. Answers (A), (D) and (E) all have punctuation errors.

5. **(B)** The problem with this sentence is that the phrases are illogically arranged. In the original sentence, the phrase "on the north wall" seems to describe where the "visitor's eye" is physically located. Answer (B) correctly uses "on the north wall" to modify "poster." Answers (C), (D) and (E) have problems with misplaced modifiers, similar to the original sentence. Answer (A) is identical to the original.

PART C: COMPOSITION STRATEGIES

> **DIRECTIONS:** Each of the passages below is followed by several questions or incomplete sentences. Under each question or sentence are five choices. Select the letter of the best choice and darken the corresponding oval.

EXAMPLES

(1) Polar bears, so named because they lived near the North Pole, are called "Nanook" by the Eskimo. (2) Living along the cold waters and ice floes of the Arctic Ocean, some polar

bears spend time along the coastal areas of northern Canada, Alaska, Norway, Siberia, and Greenland, although some bears live on the islands of the Arctic Ocean and never come close to the mainland. (3) Most of these areas lie north of the Arctic circle and about 85% of Greenland is always covered with ice. (4) To protect them from the arctic cold and ice, polar bears have water-repellant fur and a pad of dense, stiff fur on the soles of their snowshoe-like feet. (5) In addition, the bears have such a thick layer of fat that infrared photos show no detectable heat, except for their breath.

(6) Polar bears are the largest land-based carnivores. (7) Because their fur is white with a tinge of yellow, they are difficult to spot on ice floes, their favorite hunting ground. (8) Polar bears have a small head, a long neck, and a long body, so they make efficient swimmers. (9) Polar bears have no natural enemy except man. (10) Increased human activity in the Arctic region has put pressure on polar bear populations. (11) The Polar Bear Specialist Group was formed to conserve and manage this unique animal. (12) An increase in the number of polar bears is due to cooperation between five nations. (13) In 1965, there were 8,000 to 10,000 bears reported, but that population is estimated at 25,000 at the present.

1. Which of the following best expresses the author's intentions in the first paragraph?
    (A) To celebrate his/her fondness for polar bears
    (B) To describe some of the wildlife of Alaska
    (C) To provide a basic account of some of the polar bear's primary habits
    (D) To prove that mammals can live comfortably in unfavorable conditions
    (E) To show why polar bears are not suited to the Arctic region.

2. Which of the following sentences is not necessary to the first paragraph, and would be best eliminated?
    (A) Sentence 1   (D) Sentence 4
    (B) Sentence 2   (E) Sentence 5
    (C) Sentence 3

3. Which of the following sentences would best fit the writer's plan of development, and would fit between Sentences 6 and 7?
    (A) Full-grown polar bears may be about nine feet long and weigh between 1,000 and 1,600 pounds.
    (B) These bears have keen eyesight and are not sensitive to snow blindness.
    (C) In the winter the female polar bear enters a cave in an iceberg and gives birth to one or two cubs.
    (D) Polar bears can swim great distances with a speed of approximately six miles an hour.
    (E) Polar bears are often a popular attraction in city zoos; even Atlanta boasts a healthy polar bear.

EXPLANATIONS

1. **(C)** The passage basically describes some of the polar bear's basic traits. Its tone is detached and factual, like an entry in an encyclopedia. Therefore, the writer's personal feeling is not the issue as in choice (A). The paragraph is describing one example of Alaskan wildlife, so (C) is insufficient. (D)is inaccurate because the passage does not seem to set out to "prove" anything. Choice (E) contradicts the focus of the entire passage.

2. **(C)** Sentence (C) digresses from the main topic, which is the polar bear and its habits, to a geological account of the Arctic region in general. This is irrelevant to the progression of this passage, and would best be eliminated.

3.   **(A)**   Choice (A) is best because it continues the physical description of the polar bear. (B) is not wholly irrelevant, as it deals with the bears' eyesight, but it would be best placed elsewhere. (C) and (E) introduces new subjects. (D), like (B), is somewhat relevant, but would be best placed elsewhere.

Essay

This section consists of a thirty-minute essay which is evaluated holistically by ETS; that is, your essay will receive one grade based on overall quality. You will be presented with a topic that would apply in both the classroom, and life in general. Or, you may be asked to write an essay directed to a specific audience, such as the editor of a newspaper, your peers, or a future employer. These topics will not require specific knowledge of teaching theory. The judges will assess your skills by concentrating on your ability to focus on a central idea, knowledge of audience, consistency, strength of argument, persuasiveness, and proper diction and grammar.

DIRECTIONS: Plan and write an essay on the topic below. **Do not write on any other topic except the one given. Any other topics will be unacceptable.**

EXAMPLE

TOPIC: Many schools group students by ability. Are you in favor of this practice? Explain your position by discussing the positive or negative consequences of ability grouping for students and teachers.

Suggested Strategies for Writing an Essay

- Read the essay topic carefully. Be sure you understand exactly what it is asking.

- Organize your ideas. Use the first five minutes of this thirty-minute section to outline. This will help you to present a clear and cohesive argument.

- Stand by your argument. Do not stray into tangential areas that do not have anything to do with the original essay topic. Keep one main idea in mind as you write, and develop it as you go along.

- Write legibly.

- Avoid the passive voice, contractions, and clichés.

- Back up all generalizations with evidence. Do not assume your reader will know what you mean.

- Re-read your essay (if you have time) when you are finished. Correct misspellings and grammatical errors. An essay must be legible in order to receive a grade.

The following essay received scores at the highest end of the scale use in NTE essay scoring.

The practice of grouping students by ability in the elementary school has negative social and academic consequences for students. The negative effects of ability grouping overshadow the few positive benefits that may be derived from this practice. Grouping by ability may be appropriate for certain subjects such as reading, within a particular classroom as long as the group membership changes for instruction in other subjects. However, I feel that grouping by ability is an inappropriate practice at the elementary school level if all students remain in that group throughout the day.

One of the negative effects of ability grouping is that it contributes to the development of a poor self image for many students. Children of all ages are very adept at recognizing and correctly identifying high, middle and low ability groups. Assigning non-threatening names to the groups has no affect on children's ability to identify these groups. This is apparent when observing or talking with students in schools that use ability grouping. It does not matter whether the teacher calls the top group "Red Birds," "Group 3," "Triangles," or "Mrs. Smith's class," students are keenly aware of their membership in the group and the perceived ability of that group.

Students make comparisons between the ways teachers interact with different groups, the types of assignments groups receive and privileges different groups enjoy. Students in the high ability group may look down on other students and may refer to students in other groups as "stupid" or "dumb." Name-calling may result. Students in the low ability group may resent their placement in that group. Students in the middle ability group may feel ignored or may even resent being labeled "average." The naturally occurring friction between groups creates a climate in which teachers will have difficulty building positive self-images for all students.

Ability grouping also necessarily limits peer interaction both in and out of the classroom. Elementary students need to interact with many students to develop mature social and intellectual skills.

An additional negative effect of ability grouping is the stilted instructional environment that is created within the classroom. Teachers of high ability students are encouraged to feel privileged to teach this group and usually prepare creative, challenging lessons. Teachers of the low ability group usually provide many drill and practice worksheets and seldom assign text materials. Middle ability students may receive assignments based on the text, but these assignments are often accompanied by drill and practice worksheets. The result of these practices is that only the high ability students are challenged to work to their capacity.

The negative consequences of ability grouping are experienced by students of all ability levels. For those reasons, the practice of ability grouping in the elementary school should be abandoned.

EXPLANATION

This essay addresses the topic directly. The topic of ability grouping is narrowed in the first sentence to the use of this practice in elementary school. The author's point of view and the focus of the essay (the negative social and academic consequences) are also established in the first sentence. Specific negative effects are named and briefly discussed. The last paragraph restates the author's point of view.

Several sentences in the essay are wordy and seem to ramble. Some of the issues raised (peer interaction) are not fully discussed. The author mentions the "positive benefits" of ability grouping but does not specifically name or discuss the benefits. There are a few errors in punctuation and spelling. However, the author demonstrates the ability to clearly state a topic and present a specific point of view.

The Test of General Knowledge

This test assesses your knowledge of social studies, mathematics, science, literature, and fine arts. Each section will be described individually.

Social Studies

This section tests your knowledge of four major themes: development of the current state of human culture; understanding human behavior; universality and basic differences between cultures; and balanced perspectives on society. Combined with these themes are the topics covered in the section: United States history and culture; political institutions; characteristics of cultures and societies; economics; geography; and methods of social science. There will also be maps, graphs, charts and political cartoons which you will be required to interpret.

DIRECTIONS: Each of the following questions and incomplete statements is followed by five answer choices. Select the choice which best answers each question.

EXAMPLES

1. Select the most appropriate time period for the occurrence of the American Civil War.
   (A) 1700-1750　　　　(D) 1850-1900
   (B) 1750-1800　　　　(E) 1900-1950
   (C) 1800-1850

2. Which one of the following statements is most correct about people who live in similar habitats, but who are separated by a great distance?
   (A) Their cultures are likely to be almost identical.
   (B) They are always similar in their social characteristics.
   (C) They may have some culture traits that are alike.
   (D) They usually speak languages that are similar.
   (E) They satisfy their economic wants in the same ways.

3. The tools, means and methods through which we interact with our environment is a definition of
   (A) technology.　　　　(D) mass production.
   (B) television sets.　　　(E) automobiles.
   (C) computer software.

4. Which of the following fostered industrialization in the United States?
   (A) Slow growth of the domestic market
   (B) Distant foreign markets
   (C) Few raw materials
   (D) Surplus of labor
   (E) Lower wages for workers than in Europe

EXPLANATIONS

1.   **(D)**   This question requires you to place the Civil War in the correct half century. Choices (A), (B) and (C) are too early. Choice (E) is too late. Thus, the correct response is item (D), the second half of the 19th century.

2.   **(C)**   Since culture is a human construct, people who live in similar habitats do not necessarily have similar cultures. Thus, choices (A), (B), (D) and (E) are all incorrect. The most tentative response, (C), is the best answer.

3.   **(A)**   While aspects of choices (B), (C), (D) and (E) might be considered as tools, the best choice is (A) since it includes and encompasses the other items.

4.   **(B)**   At the time of the growth of industrialization in the United States, the domestic market was growing rapidly (A). America had plentiful raw materials (C) and labor was scarce (D). Wages for workers (E) were higher than in Europe. Since foreign markets were at some distance, choice (B) is correct.

Mathematics

This section tests general mathematical competency; that is, your ability to apply math in teaching and in everyday life. The questions involve more interpretation than computation. There are twenty-five questions in this section, covering number sense (decimals, fractions, etc.); practical applications; geometric, algebraic, and numerical relationships; measurement; deductive reasoning; and interpretation of graphic, symbolic, and verbal material. The difficulty level of this section is no higher than first year college mathematics.

> **DIRECTIONS:** Each of the following questions and incomplete statements is followed by five answer choices. Select the choice which best answers each question.

EXAMPLES

1.   Which of the following is NOT equivalent to 7/8?
     (A)   3/4   (D)   28/32
     (B)   14/16   (E)   21/24
     (C)   35/40

2.   A homeowner is ordering carpet for the living room. What essential data does he need to estimate the cost of carpeting the room?
     (A)   Carpet cost per square yard   (D)   (A) and (B)
     (B)   Room dimensions (length & width)   (E)   (C) and time payment plans
     (C)   Sale savings at local stores for carpet

3.   Which sentence below describes the graph?

-4 -3 -2 -1 0 1 2

(A)   X < -3 and X > -1   (D)   X ≤ -3 or X ≥ -1

(B)   -3 < X < -1   (E)   None of these.

(C)   X < -3 or X > -1

EXPLANATIONS

1.   **(A)**   You express other equivalent forms of a fractional number by multiplying it by expressions which are equal to one; e.g., 2/2, 3/3, 4/4, 5/5, etc. Thus 2/2 x 7/8 = 14/16, 3/3 x 7/8 = 21/24, etc. Accordingly, 14/16 is simply 7/8 times 2/2. Thus 7/8 and 14/16 are the same fractional number. In choice (C) 35/40 is produced by multiplying 7/8 by 5/5. Choice (D) is 7/8 multiplied by 4/4. Choice (E) is 7/8 multiplied by 3/3. Thus, all those choices name the same fractional number, 7/8. Choice (A) is not equivalent to any expression for 7/8. Choice (A) is the answer.

2.   **(D)**   You must know the area of the room (length x width). Also, you must know the cost per square yard you intend to spend. You calculate the cost by first changing the square footage (area of room) into square yards (divide by 27 square ft.). Then, multiply the cost per yard times the number of yards needed to get the cost of carpeting the room. Choice (D) is correct.

3.   **(C)**   You should first note that there is a gap in the graph (between -3 and -1) and that -3 and -1 are excluded from the plotted data. This is due to the open circles around the two numbers. The OR condition will be needed to describe values plotted. Either X will have a value below -3 OR a value above -1, but not including those numerals. Choice (A) includes values greater than -3 right on through, including -1. Choice (B) describes the interval that is the gap or unplotted part of the number line between -3 and -1. Choice (D) is wrong because it includes the points -3 and -1 with the equals part of the symbol, ≤ or ≥. Choice (C) is the correct answer. It describes what has been plotted.

Literature and Fine Arts

This section tests your knowledge of a) the basics of literature and art, b) your ability to integrate these basics into a larger whole, and c) your ability to relate these basics to the general environment. The questions cover such disciplines as art (painting, drawing, sculpture, photography, etc.), architecture, dance, literature (e.g., poetry, satire, drama), and the performing arts. All of the questions come from a variety of cultures and time periods. You need not be a liberal arts student to answer these questions; most of them involve what is observable from the visual provided with each question. For the literature part, it would be helpful to brush up on literary terms, such as simile, onomatopoeia, metaphor, and irony.

> **DIRECTIONS:** Each of the following questions and incomplete statements is followed by five answer choices. Select the choice which best answers each question.

EXAMPLES

LeCorbusier, L'Unite d'Habitation, Marseilles

1. The designer of the building pictured above seems to have been concerned with which
    of the following?
    (A) The amount of light available to the building's inhabitants
    (B) Building a modern skyscraper
    (C) Cylindrical shapes
    (D) Hidden staircases
    (E) Blending into the environment

Whilom ther was dwellynge at Oxenford
A riche gnof, that gestes heeld to bord,
And of his craft he was a carpenter.
With hym ther was dwellynge a povre scoler.

2. What can we assume about this passage?
    (A) It is probably a translation of some other language into English.
    (B) It is written in Middle English.
    (C) It is romantic in style.
    (D) It is written in Elizabethan English.
    (E) The speaker is a foreigner.

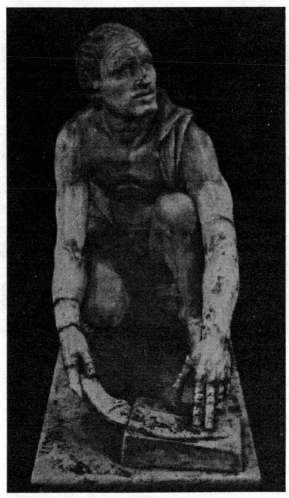

Knife sharpener, Galleria degli Uffizi, Florence

3. Which of the following does NOT lend credence to the conclusion that the above figure is a slave?

(A) Posture   (D) Muscle structure

(B) Clothing   (E) Attitude

(C) Action

EXPLANATIONS

1. **(A)** Le Corbusier's L'Unite d'Habitation (Union for Living) is an apartment house in Marseilles. Corbusier set out to build apartments vibrating with light. This is obvious from the many windows almost covering the side of the building. Thus, choice (A) is correct. The building is obviously not a skyscraper (B), since there are no more than eight floors. The building is structured around rectangular and linear shapes, rather than cylindrical (C). The staircase at left is not hidden, but in full view (D). As the building stands out in stark contrast to its surrounding environment, (E) is, obviously, not correct.

2. **(B)** This question tests your knowledge of the development of the English language. This passage is taken from one of Chaucer's *Canterbury Tales*, written in the late 14th century. This is evident from the highly "irregular" spelling of words such as "dwellynge" ("dwelling") and "povre" ("poor"). (A) is incorrect because a translation would be translated into standard, modern English. Choice (C) is wrong, because while the poem may be romantic, it is impossible to tell from this passage. Elizabethan English is completely different from Middle English, so (D) is incorrect, and (E) is wrong because it is impossible to tell from the passage whether or not the speaker is a foreigner. (B) is the correct answer.

3. **(D)** The squatting position of the figure is indicative of a low position, like that of a slave (A). Since he is wearing only a cloak thrown back over one shoulder, this, too, indicates the clothing of a commoner or a person of low status (B). The action, that of sharpening a knife, is a job which would be designated to a slave (C). However, the muscle structure of the figure would not really indicate social level, making (D) the correct choice.

Science

This section tests your general knowledge of scientific theories, principles and facts. There are thirty questions in this section which concentrate on nine themes: energy relationships; the operation of natural processes; the relationship between humans and the environment; aspects of Earth; atomic and molecular matter; forces (gravitational, electromagnetic, nuclear, and human); scientific method, and science's role in human life. These questions all involve significant themes in 20th century scientific thought, but they are not specifically technical.

DIRECTIONS: Each of the following questions and incomplete statements is followed by five answer choices. Select the choice which best answers each question.

EXAMPLES

1. Which of the following is the main difference between an organic and an inorganic compound?
   - (A) The former is a living compound, while the latter is a nonliving compound.
   - (B) There are many more of the latter than of the former.
   - (C) The latter can be synthesized only by living organisms.
   - (D) The latter can be synthesized only by non-living organisms.
   - (E) The former are those that contain carbon.

2. On the periodic table the symbol Pb represents which of the following?
   - (A) Iron
   - (B) Phosphorus
   - (C) Lead
   - (D) Plutonium
   - (E) Potassium

3. Which of the metric terms is closest to the measurement of a new piece of chalk?
   - (A) Meter
   - (B) Liter
   - (C) Gram
   - (D) Decimeter
   - (E) Kilometer

4.   Which of the following is a genetic disorder?

    (A)   Down's Syndrome (Mongolism)   (D)   Leukemia

    (B)   Syphilis   (E)   Emphysema

    (C)   Malaria

EXPLANATIONS

1.   **(E)**   Since the word *organic* means pertaining to or derived from living organisms or (in chemistry) a compound containing carbon (and in some cases oxygen), answer (A) (living and non-living compound) is inappropriate. Answer (B) is incorrect; there are more organic compounds than inorganic. Since inorganic compounds (C) can be synthesized in a laboratory, (C) is incorrect. (D) does not seem logical; dead organisms cannot synthesize a compound. (D) should not be selected. (E) is the correct answer. All organic compounds contain carbon.

2.   **(C)**   The symbol for iron is Fe. (A) is incorrect. Despite the fact that both phosphorous and the symbol Pb both begin with p, (B) is not the correct answer. The correct representation for this common element of lead is Pb. The correct symbol for lead is Pb; (C) is the correct answer. Even though plutonium and Pb both begin with p, (D) is not the correct answer and should not be chosen. Both potassium and Pb begin with p, but (E) is not the right choice.

3.   **(D)**   Since a meter is 39.37 inches, or about the height of a five-year-old child, (A) is not the best choice. A liter (B) is a measure of volume; it is slightly more than a quart. It is not the best unit by which to measure a piece of chalk. A gram (C) is about the weight of a paper clip; since a gram is a measure of weight (mass) and not length, gram is not the best unit to use. A decimeter (D) is one tenth of a meter; a personal reference for a decimeter is about the distance between the end of the thumb and the end of the middle finger. This distance is a little more than 3" in an adult—about the length of a new piece of chalk. (Since a meter is about 36", one tenth of 36" is a little over 3"—about the length of a new piece of chalk.) (D) is the right answer. A kilometer (E) is 1000 meters; since a meter is a little more than 3 feet, a measure of a little more than 3000 feet is not the best measure to apply to a new piece of chalk. (E) should not be chosen.

4.   **(A)**   Down's Syndrome (mongolism) is a genetic disorder; because of the fact that it is genetic, there is at present no treatment or cure for this disorder, which is characterized most often by stubby fingers, retarded physical development, "slanting" eyes, large tongue, and low mentality. Down's Syndrome results when the egg cell has a total of 24 chromosomes rather than the normal 23. (A) is the correct answer. Syphilis (B) is a sexually transmitted venereal disease; it is not genetically transmitted. (B) is not the correct answer. Malaria (C) is a disease transmitted by the infected Anopheles mosquito; since malaria is not genetic, (C) is not the best answer. Leukemia (D) is a disease characterized by the uncontrolled production of ineffectual white blood cells; it is a type of cancer. At present there is no evidence to suggest that it is genetic in origin. (C), therefore, is not the best answer. Emphysema (E) is a condition of the lungs in which they lose their elasticity. Environmental agents and smoking—not genetics—seem to bring about this disease. (E) is not the best answer.

The Test of Professional Knowledge

This test is broken down into four thirty-minute sections which consist of thirty-five questions each. One of the sections is experimental and is not counted toward your score. **For practical purposes, this section is excluded from the test in this book.** This test is designed to assess your understanding of the knowledge and skills necessary to teach, as well as the application of various classroom practices. The questions involve all aspects of teaching: these include planning, decision making, extraclassroom influences, methods of instruction, students' constitutional rights, evaluating student performance, and teaching ethics.

DIRECTIONS: Each of the following questions and incomplete statements is followed by five answer choices. Select the choice which best answers each question.

EXAMPLES

1. A well written instructional objective contains which of the following elements?

    I.   A statement of an observable, measurable behavior

    II.   A criterion of acceptable performance

    III.   The condition under which the student will demonstrate the behavior

    IV.   What the teacher will do to cause the students' behavioral change

    (A)   I and II only.

    (B)   I, II and III only.

    (C)   I, II and IV only.

    (D)   II, III, and IV only.

    (E)   I, II, III, and IV.

2. A student is asked to relate the contents of a graph to her classmates. This task is on which level of *Bloom's Taxonomy*?

    (A)   Knowledge

    (B)   Comprehension

    (C)   Application

    (D)   Analysis

    (E)   Synthesis

3. The principal of a high school may search the locker of a student under which of the following circumstances?

    (A)   The student has been misbehaving during the entire previous period.

    (B)   The principal has just spoken to the student body about substance abuse and wants to insure that there are no drugs on the school grounds.

    (C)   The principal has obtained a search warrant.

    (D)   The principal has reason to believe that there are drugs in the locker.

    (E)   The student was arrested the night before for dealing drugs and the principal wants to see if he is doing so at school, as well.

EXPLANATIONS

1.   **(B)**   Question one is based on the design of instruction. Answers (C), (D), and (E) can be eliminated from consideration since each of those includes IV, which is based on the

behavior of a teacher, rather than of a student. (A) can also be eliminated since it does not include a statement of the conditions under which the student will demonstrate the behavior. The best answer is (B), since it is expressed in terms of learner behavior, has a criterion of level of acceptable performance, and states the conditions under which the learner will exhibit the behavior.

2.   **(B)**   Question two is based on the design of instruction. *Bloom's Taxonomy* represents a hierarchy of learning tasks, each somewhat more demanding than the last. Knowledge level requires that the student present the information in the same format in which it was given him/her. Since the information is not being presented in the same format as given to the student, (A) is not a viable answer. Comprehension level involves the manipulation of some data, either translating it from one form to another or restating it in one's own words. In this situation the student must translate the material from a graphic representation to a verbal one. Hence, (B) is the best response. Application (C) requires that some rule must be selected by the student and used to solve the problem. Analysis (D) requires that some complex entity must be broken down to its constituent parts and examined to see how the parts work together to create the whole. Synthesis (E) would involve the creative meshing of elements to create a new and unique entity.

3.   **(D)**   Question three is based on the constitutional rights of students. In this instance, item (A) and item (E) can both be eliminated since there is no direct relationship indicated between the student's past behavior and the contents of the locker. Item (B) can similarly be eliminated since, again, this alone would not allow a school official to search the student's property without cause. A school official does not need a search warrant to search a student locker, while a police officer would. Thus (C) is not an appropriate answer. (D) is clearly the best response because the school official must have some reason to suspect that the student's locker contains an illegal substance in order to search it, although the rules are not as stringent as for a police officer, who must legally demonstrate due cause.

National Teachers Examination

CORE BATTERY

Test 1

NTE Test of Communication Skills

TEST 1 – ANSWER SHEET

Section 1: Listening

1. Ⓐ Ⓑ Ⓒ Ⓓ Ⓔ
2. Ⓐ Ⓑ Ⓒ Ⓓ Ⓔ
3. Ⓐ Ⓑ Ⓒ Ⓓ Ⓔ
4. Ⓐ Ⓑ Ⓒ Ⓓ Ⓔ
5. Ⓐ Ⓑ Ⓒ Ⓓ Ⓔ
6. Ⓐ Ⓑ Ⓒ Ⓓ Ⓔ
7. Ⓐ Ⓑ Ⓒ Ⓓ Ⓔ
8. Ⓐ Ⓑ Ⓒ Ⓓ Ⓔ
9. Ⓐ Ⓑ Ⓒ Ⓓ Ⓔ
10. Ⓐ Ⓑ Ⓒ Ⓓ Ⓔ
11. Ⓐ Ⓑ Ⓒ Ⓓ Ⓔ
12. Ⓐ Ⓑ Ⓒ Ⓓ Ⓔ
13. Ⓐ Ⓑ Ⓒ Ⓓ Ⓔ
14. Ⓐ Ⓑ Ⓒ Ⓓ Ⓔ
15. Ⓐ Ⓑ Ⓒ Ⓓ Ⓔ
16. Ⓐ Ⓑ Ⓒ Ⓓ Ⓔ
17. Ⓐ Ⓑ Ⓒ Ⓓ Ⓔ
18. Ⓐ Ⓑ Ⓒ Ⓓ Ⓔ
19. Ⓐ Ⓑ Ⓒ Ⓓ Ⓔ
20. Ⓐ Ⓑ Ⓒ Ⓓ Ⓔ
21. Ⓐ Ⓑ Ⓒ Ⓓ Ⓔ
22. Ⓐ Ⓑ Ⓒ Ⓓ Ⓔ
23. Ⓐ Ⓑ Ⓒ Ⓓ Ⓔ
24. Ⓐ Ⓑ Ⓒ Ⓓ Ⓔ
25. Ⓐ Ⓑ Ⓒ Ⓓ Ⓔ
26. Ⓐ Ⓑ Ⓒ Ⓓ Ⓔ
27. Ⓐ Ⓑ Ⓒ Ⓓ Ⓔ
28. Ⓐ Ⓑ Ⓒ Ⓓ Ⓔ
29. Ⓐ Ⓑ Ⓒ Ⓓ Ⓔ
30. Ⓐ Ⓑ Ⓒ Ⓓ Ⓔ
31. Ⓐ Ⓑ Ⓒ Ⓓ Ⓔ
32. Ⓐ Ⓑ Ⓒ Ⓓ Ⓔ
33. Ⓐ Ⓑ Ⓒ Ⓓ Ⓔ
34. Ⓐ Ⓑ Ⓒ Ⓓ Ⓔ
35. Ⓐ Ⓑ Ⓒ Ⓓ Ⓔ
36. Ⓐ Ⓑ Ⓒ Ⓓ Ⓔ
37. Ⓐ Ⓑ Ⓒ Ⓓ Ⓔ
38. Ⓐ Ⓑ Ⓒ Ⓓ Ⓔ
39. Ⓐ Ⓑ Ⓒ Ⓓ Ⓔ
40. Ⓐ Ⓑ Ⓒ Ⓓ Ⓔ

Section 2: Reading

1. Ⓐ Ⓑ Ⓒ Ⓓ Ⓔ
2. Ⓐ Ⓑ Ⓒ Ⓓ Ⓔ
3. Ⓐ Ⓑ Ⓒ Ⓓ Ⓔ
4. Ⓐ Ⓑ Ⓒ Ⓓ Ⓔ
5. Ⓐ Ⓑ Ⓒ Ⓓ Ⓔ
6. Ⓐ Ⓑ Ⓒ Ⓓ Ⓔ
7. Ⓐ Ⓑ Ⓒ Ⓓ Ⓔ
8. Ⓐ Ⓑ Ⓒ Ⓓ Ⓔ
9. Ⓐ Ⓑ Ⓒ Ⓓ Ⓔ
10. Ⓐ Ⓑ Ⓒ Ⓓ Ⓔ
11. Ⓐ Ⓑ Ⓒ Ⓓ Ⓔ
12. Ⓐ Ⓑ Ⓒ Ⓓ Ⓔ
13. Ⓐ Ⓑ Ⓒ Ⓓ Ⓔ
14. Ⓐ Ⓑ Ⓒ Ⓓ Ⓔ
15. Ⓐ Ⓑ Ⓒ Ⓓ Ⓔ
16. Ⓐ Ⓑ Ⓒ Ⓓ Ⓔ
17. Ⓐ Ⓑ Ⓒ Ⓓ Ⓔ
18. Ⓐ Ⓑ Ⓒ Ⓓ Ⓔ
19. Ⓐ Ⓑ Ⓒ Ⓓ Ⓔ
20. Ⓐ Ⓑ Ⓒ Ⓓ Ⓔ
21. Ⓐ Ⓑ Ⓒ Ⓓ Ⓔ
22. Ⓐ Ⓑ Ⓒ Ⓓ Ⓔ
23. Ⓐ Ⓑ Ⓒ Ⓓ Ⓔ
24. Ⓐ Ⓑ Ⓒ Ⓓ Ⓔ
25. Ⓐ Ⓑ Ⓒ Ⓓ Ⓔ
26. Ⓐ Ⓑ Ⓒ Ⓓ Ⓔ
27. Ⓐ Ⓑ Ⓒ Ⓓ Ⓔ
28. Ⓐ Ⓑ Ⓒ Ⓓ Ⓔ
29. Ⓐ Ⓑ Ⓒ Ⓓ Ⓔ
30. Ⓐ Ⓑ Ⓒ Ⓓ Ⓔ

Section 3: Writing

1. Ⓐ Ⓑ Ⓒ Ⓓ Ⓔ
2. Ⓐ Ⓑ Ⓒ Ⓓ Ⓔ
3. Ⓐ Ⓑ Ⓒ Ⓓ Ⓔ
4. Ⓐ Ⓑ Ⓒ Ⓓ Ⓔ
5. Ⓐ Ⓑ Ⓒ Ⓓ Ⓔ
6. Ⓐ Ⓑ Ⓒ Ⓓ Ⓔ
7. Ⓐ Ⓑ Ⓒ Ⓓ Ⓔ
8. Ⓐ Ⓑ Ⓒ Ⓓ Ⓔ

9. Ⓐ Ⓑ Ⓒ Ⓓ Ⓔ
10. Ⓐ Ⓑ Ⓒ Ⓓ Ⓔ
11. Ⓐ Ⓑ Ⓒ Ⓓ Ⓔ
12. Ⓐ Ⓑ Ⓒ Ⓓ Ⓔ
13. Ⓐ Ⓑ Ⓒ Ⓓ Ⓔ
14. Ⓐ Ⓑ Ⓒ Ⓓ Ⓔ
15. Ⓐ Ⓑ Ⓒ Ⓓ Ⓔ
16. Ⓐ Ⓑ Ⓒ Ⓓ Ⓔ
17. Ⓐ Ⓑ Ⓒ Ⓓ Ⓔ
18. Ⓐ Ⓑ Ⓒ Ⓓ Ⓔ
19. Ⓐ Ⓑ Ⓒ Ⓓ Ⓔ
20. Ⓐ Ⓑ Ⓒ Ⓓ Ⓔ
21. Ⓐ Ⓑ Ⓒ Ⓓ Ⓔ
22. Ⓐ Ⓑ Ⓒ Ⓓ Ⓔ
23. Ⓐ Ⓑ Ⓒ Ⓓ Ⓔ
24. Ⓐ Ⓑ Ⓒ Ⓓ Ⓔ
25. Ⓐ Ⓑ Ⓒ Ⓓ Ⓔ
26. Ⓐ Ⓑ Ⓒ Ⓓ Ⓔ
27. Ⓐ Ⓑ Ⓒ Ⓓ Ⓔ
28. Ⓐ Ⓑ Ⓒ Ⓓ Ⓔ
29. Ⓐ Ⓑ Ⓒ Ⓓ Ⓔ
30. Ⓐ Ⓑ Ⓒ Ⓓ Ⓔ
31. Ⓐ Ⓑ Ⓒ Ⓓ Ⓔ
32. Ⓐ Ⓑ Ⓒ Ⓓ Ⓔ
33. Ⓐ Ⓑ Ⓒ Ⓓ Ⓔ
34. Ⓐ Ⓑ Ⓒ Ⓓ Ⓔ
35. Ⓐ Ⓑ Ⓒ Ⓓ Ⓔ
36. Ⓐ Ⓑ Ⓒ Ⓓ Ⓔ
37. Ⓐ Ⓑ Ⓒ Ⓓ Ⓔ
38. Ⓐ Ⓑ Ⓒ Ⓓ Ⓔ
39. Ⓐ Ⓑ Ⓒ Ⓓ Ⓔ
40. Ⓐ Ⓑ Ⓒ Ⓓ Ⓔ
41. Ⓐ Ⓑ Ⓒ Ⓓ Ⓔ
42. Ⓐ Ⓑ Ⓒ Ⓓ Ⓔ
43. Ⓐ Ⓑ Ⓒ Ⓓ Ⓔ
44. Ⓐ Ⓑ Ⓒ Ⓓ Ⓔ
45. Ⓐ Ⓑ Ⓒ Ⓓ Ⓔ

NTE CORE BATTERY–Test 1
TEST OF COMMUNICATION SKILLS
Section 1: Listening

TIME: 30 Minutes
40 Questions

Part A

> **DIRECTIONS:** In this section, you will hear short statements and questions. For the purpose of this practice exam, insert audio cassette. When you hear a statement, select the answer which best restates or supports what you heard. When you hear a question, select the choice which best answers the question. The questions and statements are NOT written in your book. **They will not be repeated**.

1.   (A)   I have $20 hidden in an envelope in my desk.
      (B)   None, but I have a credit card.
      (C)   There's some change in my car under the seat.
      (D)   I spent my cash at the grocery yesterday.

2.   (A)   If you want to ride the bus, you need to be ready and waiting at the pick up point a few minutes before five.
      (B)   The bus will return at 10:30 P.M.
      (C)   No food or drinks are allowed on the bus, but you can buy snacks at the stadium.
      (D)   Forty people purchased tickets at $5.00 each to ride the bus to the game.

3.   (A)   It is raining outside.
      (B)   Everyone is nervous about the results of the test.
      (C)   The lunch bell rang two minutes late today.
      (D)   Many of my students also have the flu.

4.   (A)   Maybe we will have an early spring.
      (B)   The streets often flood at this time of year.
      (C)   We had a lot of snow this winter.
      (D)   I want to go fishing on Saturday.

5.   (A)   Three people who were invited did not attend.
      (B)   Thirty-two people attended the event.
      (C)   Joe was twenty minutes late.
      (D)   The party was to honor the recipient of the Scholar's Award.

6. (A) I understand now why the survey results are unreliable.
    (B) I think the survey is old.
    (C) Survey results don't make any sense.
    (D) I never liked surveys anyway.

7. (A) It's too bad make-ups are not permitted.
    (B) I'm glad I can make up my absences.
    (C) An absence in lab is really hard to make up.
    (D) Other lab instructors do not permit make-ups.

8. (A) My uncle always had a scholarship.
    (B) Tuition goes up $100.00 next fall.
    (C) My roommate has a job.
    (D) Student loans don't stretch very far.

9. (A) Immediately after work.
    (B) I will vote for McIntyre.
    (C) The sale tax is on the ballot again.
    (D) I can't believe it's Thursday already.

10. (A) I have never been to Oak River State Park.
    (B) My parents have a sailboat in Clearwater, Florida.
    (C) Spring break is in March this year.
    (D) Do you plan to camp out this summer?

11. (A) The fees charged by the health center will probably go up.
    (B) Students will appreciate the increased availability of health services.
    (C) I only saw a few students in the health center at the same time last Saturday.
    (D) The fees charged by the health center are too high.

12. (A) Health is being added to the curriculum next year.
    (B) Twenty new teachers will be hired.
    (C) Each school will have one additional temporary classroom.
    (D) School bus drivers will have longer hours next year.

13. (A) There is a hornet's nest in my garage.
    (B) Bees and wasps are both helpful and dangerous.
    (C) How many times has he been in a hospital?
    (D) Immunization treatments are very common for allergic reactions.

14. (A) Sandbags were not expected to slow the flooding.
    (B) More people were asked to volunteer.
    (C) Sandbags will be used to control the flooding.
    (D) Home owners near the river were evacuated.

15. (A) Campaign fraud is a serious crime.
     (B) That Congressman always was a thief.
     (C) No one should believe a Congressman.
     (D) Political campaigns require a lot of money.

Part B

DIRECTIONS: In this section, you will hear short conversations between two people. After each conversation, a third person will ask you questions about what was discussed. When you hear a question, select the choice which best answers the question based on what you heard. The conversations and questions are NOT written in your test book. **They will not be repeated.**

16. (A) It is an admission requirement at the university she wants him to attend.
     (B) It is required of the university he wants to attend.
     (C) He is going to major in physics in college.
     (D) He is very good in science.

17. (A) They are very close.
     (B) The mother is very weak.
     (C) The mother sometimes tells the son what to do.
     (D) The son always does what he wants regardless of what his mother says.

18. (A) He is not good in science.
     (B) He makes good grades.
     (C) He likes to stay out late at night with his friends instead of studying.
     (D) He does not see the need to prepare for more than one college.

19. (A) She seldom misses an assignment.
     (B) She frequently does not finish her homework.
     (C) She is on the basketball team and has practice everyday.
     (D) She is often sick.

20. (A) He is lenient.
     (B) He is strict.
     (C) He requires all students to finish homework assignments.
     (D) He dislikes this student.

21. (A) She did not understand the assignment.
     (B) She was sick.
     (C) She was busy.
     (D) Her excuse changes during the conversation.

22. (A) He has the proper shoes.
    (B) He feels better and has more energy.
    (C) He has not had any injuries.
    (D) He runs indoors.

23. (A) He prefers to walk, because jogging hurts his knees.
    (B) He prefers to walk because he does not have the proper shoes for jogging.
    (C) He cannot use an indoor track.
    (D) He wants to jog but does not know how to train.

24. (A) Jog on an indoor track and be certain to wear the proper shoes.
    (B) Always jog with a partner.
    (C) See a doctor before beginning to jog and have regular check-ups after you begin the jogging program.
    (D) Jog at least 30 miles a week to build up endurance.

Part C

DIRECTIONS: In this section, you will hear several short talks. After each talk, a second voice will ask questions about the talk. When you hear a question, select the choice which best answers the question based on what you heard. The short talks are NOT written in your test book. **They will not be repeated.**

25. (A) Beach front property is expensive.
    (B) Beach front property is not worth the effort.
    (C) Hurricanes can cause a lot of destruction.
    (D) Maintenance never ends. sand grit mold

26. (A) Hurricanes Fall   (C) Insects
    (B) Blowing sand and rain   (D) Freezing temperatures

27. (A) Thorough cleaning
    (B) Removing sand from the porch
    (C) Removing mold from under the eaves
    (D) Protecting pipes

28. (A) Prepare for hurricanes   (C) Wash windows
    (B) Protect pipes   (D) Store porch furniture

29. (A) To point out the hazards of camping
    (B) To discuss the importance of planning for a successful camping trip
    (C) To explain how enjoyable camping can be
    (D) To explain the best ways to cook outdoors

30. (A) Stay in motels   (C) Rent a recreational vehicle
    (B) Rent or borrow equipment   (D) Take the whole family

31. (A) Insect bites   (C) Sunburn
    (B) Poison ivy   (D) Food poisoning

32. (A) Food spoilage   (C) Expensive utensils
    (B) Burning food   (D) Lack of places to cook

33. (A) Students learn about measurement.
    (B) Students learn about different cultures.
    (C) Students learn about farming.
    (D) All of the above

34. (A) Reading   (C) Music
    (B) Math   (D) Science

35. (A) It is a valuable educational activity.
    (B) It is an interesting activity but lacks educational value.
    (C) The best part is the measuring of the flour.
    (D) It is a good activity for small groups.

36. (A) 1900-1910   (C) 1940-1950
    (B) 1920-1930   (D) 1970-1980

37. (A) Russia, Germany and Japan   (C) China and India
    (B) Cuba, Haiti and Honduras   (D) Canada, Mexico and the West Indies *(largest)*

38. (A) Revolution and political upheaval   (C) Hunger
    (B) Lack of opportunity   (D) Poverty

39. (A) Keeping illegal immigrants out of the country
    (B) Overpopulation
    (C) Ramifications of immigrants on governmental services
    (D) Health care for immigrants who do not speak English

40. (A) Immigration has started to decline.
    (B) The number of immigrants during the 1980s was double the number of immigrants of any other decade since 1900-1910.
    (C) Schools cannot absorb all the immigrants.
    (D) The majority of immigrants do not speak English and need special tutors and job training opportunities.

Section 2: Reading

TIME: 30 Minutes
30 Questions

DIRECTIONS: Each passage is followed by questions based on its content. After reading the passage, choose the best answer to each question. Answer all questions based on what is indicated or implied in that passage.

Questions 1-3 are based on the following passage.

The high school drop out rate remains high in many southern states. An average of 18% of the students who finish sixth grade in Texas, Mississippi, Louisiana and Alabama do not stay in school long enough to graduate from high school. Maintaining a precise count of the number of drop outs is difficult. Some students may still be listed as enrolled when in fact they have stopped attending school and do not plan to return. A slightly larger percentage of male students drop out of school than females. More students tend to leave school during the eleventh grade. Other times most frequently cited reasons for dropping out include failing grades, suspensions and expulsions, conflict with the school, pregnancy, marriage and economic hardship. Generally, students who are incarcerated are not counted in the total number of dropouts. Some school districts have implemented special programs to encourage teens to stay in school. These retention programs usually include tutoring, counseling and opportunities for part time employment at the school or in the neighborhood.

1. What is the main idea of the passage?
   (A) Everyone should graduate from high school.
   (B) More males drop out of school than females.
   (C) There are many reasons why students drop out of school.
   (D) Some southern states have large numbers of students who do not graduate from high school.
   (E) Many students would stay in school if they could work part time.

2. Which of the following is not stated in the passage?
   (A) Students in jail are not included in the total number of dropouts.
   (B) Some states have dropout rates of 18%.
   (C) Some students are labeled dropouts when they have moved out of the district.
   (D) Tutoring programs before and after school may be successful in encouraging some teens to stay in school.
   (E) Many students drop out in the eleventh grade.

3. Which statement best summarizes the author's attitude?
   (A) The drop out problem is of little importance to the author.
   (B) The author believes that teachers should spend more time encouraging students to stay in school.

    (C)   The author feels that the drop out problem is complex.

    (D)   Drop out prevention programs are a simple solution.

    (E)   The author has the attitude that anyone who drops out of school is stupid.

Questions 4-5 are based on the following passage.

Petrified trees are unusual artifacts of the Pliocene-Pleistocene Age. The petrification process began about 1.5 million years ago when a tree, often some type of hardwood, fell into a river and was washed into the sand or gravel bank. Water percolating through the sand or gravel deposited silica in the porous cells of the tree. Over time, the cells became a solid mass and the tree was petrified. Animal and plant fossils are often embedded in the tree.

4.   According to the passage, what conditions are necessary for trees to petrify?

    (A)   Water and sand or gravel   (D)   Heat, pressure and water

    (B)   Thick mud banks along a river (E)   Both (B) and (C) above.

    (C)   Heat and time

5.   Which of the following statements can be inferred from the passage?

    (A)   Petrified trees are very heavy.

    (B)   Petrified trees are interesting museum specimens.

    (C)   Petrified trees may have fossil evidence of other life forms.

    (D)   Scientists have difficulty dating petrified trees.

    (E)   Most petrified trees are found in southern and midwestern states.

Questions 6-10 are based on the following passage.

In medieval times, an almanac was a chart showing the movements of the stars over a period of several years. Eventually, almanacs were printed in book form and included information which was especially useful to farmers. In the sixteenth century, almanacs began to be issued every year and included predictions of the weather based on previous weather patterns. At about the same time, almanacs included elaborate calendars that listed church feast days. In the seventeenth century, almanacs included jokes and short accounts of humorous incidents. Benjamin Franklin continued this tradition with *Poor Richard's Almanac*, which was published from 1732-1758. In Germany, almanacs of the eighteenth century included sophisticated, contemporary poetry by serious authors. The almanacs printed in the United States from 1835-1856 were called "Davy Crockett" almanacs because they included many frontier tall tales based mainly on oral tradition.

6.   When did almanacs begin predicting the weather?

    (A)   Almanacs have always predicted the weather.

    (B)   In medieval times

    (C)   In the sixteenth century

    (D)   In the seventeenth century

    (E)   In the eighteenth century

7.   What was unique about the "Davy Crockett" almanacs?

    (A)   They were printed in Germany but sold in the United States.

    (B)   They included tall tales.

(C)   They included stories about Davy Crockett.

(D)   They were printed during the U.S. Civil War.

(E)   They predicted the weather.

8.   What was the purpose of the first almanacs?

(A)   To list church holidays   (D)   To chart the movement of the stars

(B)   To predict the weather   (E)   All of the above.

(C)   To print poetry and humorous stories

9.   Which of the following statements best describes the author's attitude toward almanacs?

(A)   Almanacs are an example of popular thinking in the sixteenth century.

(B)   Almanacs are archaic.

(C)   Almanacs made Franklin famous.

(D)   Almanacs are the only reliable source of weather predictions.

(E)   The purpose and content of almanacs has changed over time.

10.   Which of the following is NOT included in the passage?

(A)   Some almanacs included serious poetry.

(B)   Jokes were included in some almanacs.

(C)   Davy Crockett wrote almanacs in the 1800s.

(D)   Almanacs include calendars and make weather predictions.

(E)   Much of the information included in almanacs is useful to farmers.

Questions 11-16 are based on the following passage.

Six members of the local university basketball team walked off the court during practice last week. They later said they were protesting unfair treatment by the head coach. The day after walking off the court the players held a meeting with the university president to discuss their complaints. They met with the Director of Athletics two days later and expressed their concerns. They also met with the assistant coach. After refusing to practice for four days, the team apologized to the fans, returned to practice, and promised to play the next scheduled game that season. The players also stated that their opinion of the head coach had not changed, but that they thought the assistant coach was fair.

11.   What was the basketball players' complaint?

(A)   Unfair treatment by the coach

(B)   Too many practices

(C)   Practice was too long

(D)   No support from fans

(E)   No support from the university president

12.   Which of the following did the players not do?

(A)   Walk away from practice

(B)   Apologize to the fans

(C)   Meet with the Director of Athletics

(D)   Meet with the President of the University

(E) Agree to play for the team next year

13. Which of the following best describes the author's attitude?
    (A) The author believes the players' actions were humorous.
    (B) The author writes objectively about the players' actions.
    (C) The author condemns the players' actions.
    (D) The author believes the players are behaving childishly.
    (E) The author believes the players have damaged the university's reputation.

14. How long did the players protest?
    (A) One day   (D) Four days
    (B) Two days   (E) Seven days
    (C) Three days

15. Who met with the players to discuss their concerns?
    (A) The head coach   (D) The assistant coach
    (B) The university president (E) Answers (B), (C) and (D) only .
    (C) The athletic director

16. Which of the following best describes the team's protest?
    (A) A racial issue
    (B) Unequal player scholarship
    (C) Unequal privileges for some team members
    (D) A misunderstanding with the Director of Athletics
    (E) A conflict with the head coach

Questions 17-19 are based on the following passage.

My daughter, Marie, has two cats. The older cat is named Annie. She is white with large black spots. Annie has long hair and sheds constantly in warm weather. Cinnamon is a two-year-old male tabby. He loves to chase squirrels in the backyard, but he probably would be very surprised to catch one. Cinnamon prefers to stay outside all night unless it is extremely cold. In the morning, Cinnamon wants to come into the house and sleep. Annie seldom goes outside. She prefers to sit on the table or a chair where she can look outside through the windows. Marie has cared for both cats since they were kittens. She is very fond of both of them.

17. How old is Annie?
    (A) Two years   (D) One year
    (B) Five years   (E) Same age as Cinnamon
    (C) Not stated

18. According to the passage, which of the following is NOT true?
    (A) Annie chases squirrels.   (D) Annie has long hair.
    (B) Cinnamon stays outside at night. (E) Annie is a female cat.
    (C) Cinnamon is a male tabby.

19. According to the passage, which of the following statements is true?
    (A) Marie likes Annie more than Cinnamon.
    (B) Marie has cared for both cats since they were kittens.
    (C) Annie and Cinnamon often fight with each other.
    (D) Annie spends most nights outside.
    (E) Annie has had three litters of kittens.

Questions 20-21 are based on the following passage.

Many people are becoming more conscious of protecting their health by eating correctly and exercising regularly. Jane Fonda has made a fortune selling exercise videos. Richard Simmons gives advice to dieters and suggests aerobic exercises on a series of video tapes. Every major city in the United States has at least one health club and at least one weight reduction program. Membership fees in health clubs range from $50.00 a year to $100.00 or more a month. Participation in weight reduction programs costs as much as $75.00 a week. Clearly, exercise and diet programs are growing businesses. Only time will tell how much more the market can expand.

20. The author of this passage is most interested in which of the following?
    (A) The business side of exercise and diet programs
    (B) The value of exercise and diet for good health
    (C) The average cost of memberships in health clubs
    (D) The number of diet programs available
    (E) The value of Jane Fonda's exercise tapes

21. With which of the following would the author agree?
    (A) Jane Fonda has made too much money from her videos.
    (B) Richard Simmons should only give advice on dieting and leave exercise alone.
    (C) The future of health clubs and diet programs cannot be predicted.
    (D) Health clubs cost $75.00 a month on the average.
    (E) People should be concerned about their weight.

Questions 22-24 are based on the following passage.

The domestic oil industry continues to cut back its production, and the percentage of oil imported into the United States continues to increase. Increased dependence on foreign oil will have two results: first, foreign producers will raise prices, and we can be confident that U. S. importers will pay the higher price because of increased demand; second, more huge oil tankers will be needed to move the oil to the U.S. This increases the risk of oil spills and environmental damage to the U.S. shoreline. Domestic producers will be reluctant to increase production because they will benefit more from foreign oil price increases than from expanding their own capacities. Further, after the disastrous oil spill in Alaska, many domestic oil producers feel the need to "lay low" and let foreign oil producers take the blame for future price increases.

22. What is the author's purpose in this passage?
    (A) To explain the reasons for oil spills and environmental damage to the U.S. shoreline
    (B) To explain the reasons for decreased foreign oil production

(C)   To explain why more oil tankers are needed

(D)   To discuss ways to lower oil prices

(E)   To discuss the probable results of increased dependence on foreign oil

23.   According to the passage, what is the main reason domestic producers will not increase production?

(A)   They have more to gain by not increasing production.

(B)   Huge oil tankers are too expensive.

(C)   They are afraid of oil spills.

(D)   Foreign oil is falling in price.

(E)   All of the above.

24.   Which of the following is NOT given as a reason for higher prices?

(A)   Foreign producers will raise prices.

(B)   Domestic producers will cut production.

(C)   Domestic producers want to avoid publicity.

(D)   Increased cost of insurance for oil tanker ships after the recent Alaska oil spill.

(E)   More oil tankers will be needed.

Questions 25-27 are based on the following passage.

There is no explanation for personal taste in art. My Aunt Josephine collected expensive china figurines and beautiful antique Tiffany lamps. She also insisted that two brilliantly colored Picasso prints hang in a prominent place in her dining room. She always said she knew what she liked, and she did not need to explain her collection to anyone. I always marveled that Aunt Josephine would consistently pinch pennies in the grocery store, but spend hundreds to add to her collection, without blinking an eye.

25.   What best describes the author's attitude toward Aunt Josephine and her art collection?

(A)   The author is amused by Aunt Josephine's art collection.

(B)   The author is disgusted by Aunt Josephine's art collection.

(C)   The author thinks Aunt Josephine is stingy.

(D)   The author thinks Aunt Josephine is crazy.

(E)   The author is jealous of Aunt Josephine.

26.   What best describes Aunt Josephine's art collection, as a whole?

(A)   Eclectic and personal   (D)   Antique junk

(B)   Expensive and breakable   (E)   Answers (A) and (B) above.

(C)   Under-insured

27.   According to the passage, which of the following best describes Aunt Josephine?

(A)   Overweight and overbearing

(B)   Dependent on others' opinions

(C)   Independent of others' opinions

(D)   Very wealthy

(E)   Always interested in talking about art to anyone

Questions 28-30 are based on the following passage.

Housefires result in the deaths of dozens of people every year. Smoke inhalation is the cause of death in most cases. Tragically, most housefires could be prevented. Many more housefires occur during the cold winter months than during the summer. This is because many people use unreliable space heaters. Fireplaces are another cause of housefires, especially fireplaces that do not have screens to prevent sparks from igniting objects nearby. The third most common cause of housefires is untended pans cooking on the stove. A pan of food can burn dry in a very short period of time. This situation creates so much heat that the cabinets and surrounding objects can burst into flames.

28. According to the passage, which of the following is NOT a common cause of housefires?
     (A) Fireplaces
     (B) Faulty electrical wiring
     (C) Unreliable space heaters
     (D) Fires that begin in the kitchen
     (E) Sparks from fireplaces

29. According to the passage, which of the following is NOT true?
     (A) Smoke causes many deaths in housefires.
     (B) Housefires cause many deaths each year.
     (C) Space heaters cause some housefires.
     (D) More housefires occur during the winter than during the summer.
     (E) Sparks from a fireplace seldom ignite carpets.

30. According to the passage, which of the following should be recommended in order to avoid winter housefires?
     (A) Use screens on all fireplaces.
     (B) Avoid unreliable space heaters.
     (C) Keep doors and windows closed to avoid drafts.
     (D) Answers (A) and (B) only.
     (E) Answers (B) and (C) only.

Section 3: Writing

TIME: 30 Minutes
45 Questions

Part A

> **DIRECTIONS:** Each of the following sentences may contain an error in diction, usage, idiom, or grammar. Some sentences are correct. Some sentences contain one error. No sentence contains more than one error.
>
> If there is an error, it will appear in one of the underlined portions labeled (A), (B), (C), or (D). If there is no error, choose the portion labeled (E). If there is an error, select the letter of the portion that must be changed in order to correct the sentence.

1. Looking <u>fit</u> and alert after her recent heart attack and three-month hospital <u>stay,</u>
        A   B

<u>Grandma Taylor</u> entered the room, greeted those <u>present,</u> and <u>takes</u> her accustomed
                                                     C   D

place next to the window. <u>No error.</u>
                          E

2. <u>John's</u> <u>brother-in-law</u> became a <u>commercial airline pilot</u> after <u>serving in the Air</u>
     A   B   C   D

Force for seven years. <u>No error.</u>
                    E

3. Even seasoned <u>travelers, may</u> become distraught when <u>carefully</u> planned flight
                    A   B

connections <u>require last minute</u> changes due to inclement weather and <u>delayed</u>
                    C   D

departures. <u>No error.</u>
  D   E

4. The proliferation of <u>communications technologies,</u> and the resulting increased accessibility
                                     A

to information, <u>have</u> far-reaching social implications which are reminiscent of <u>Gutenberg's</u>
                B   C

invention of <u>movable type.</u> <u>No error.</u>
               D   E

5. Knowing that the backup diskettes were safe in his office was reassuring to Jack, as he
            A   B   C

viewed the damp and musty computer room still dripping with water from the broken
                                                  D

overhead sprinkler system. No error.
                          E

6. Mary was indignant when she realized that the salesman was ignoring her mother
            A   B   C

and she. No error.
  D   E

7. My family and me spent two weeks at Virginia Beach last summer. No error.
               A   B   C   D   E

8. Not only my aunt, but my uncle too, plays championship bridge in New York City.
   A   B   C   D

No error.
  E

9. The cold and wet children waited patiently in the rain for the school bus that never
       A   B   C   D

arrived. No error.
       E

10. In the last four years, I have had three different jobs, moved five times and learned patient.
              A   B   C   D

No error.
  E

11. The library clerk did not remove the book from the overdue list, even though I return it
                    A   B   C

on the due date. No error.
      D   E

12. My mother was the first person in her family to graduate from college and my father
          A   B   C

was the first person in his family to earn a Ph.D. No error.
                        D   E

13. <u>Although</u> my daughter has straight brown hair and brown <u>eyes</u> <u>my</u> son has curly
      A   B   C

<u>blond hair</u> and blue eyes. <u>No error.</u>
    D   E

whose

14. The book on submarine warfare was written by a man <u>who's</u> <u>hobby</u> <u>was</u> <u>building</u>
                                                A   B   C   D

<u>miniature sailboats.</u> <u>No error.</u>
               E

15. <u>Its</u> a recognized fact <u>that</u> any young man over seven feet tall <u>will</u> be recruited <u>to play</u>
  A   B   C   D

basketball. <u>No error.</u>
         E

16. Julius <u>Caesar</u> <u>was</u> born <u>in B.C. 100</u> and died in 44 <u>B.C.</u> <u>No error.</u>
     A   B   C   D   E

17. <u>20</u> <u>percent</u> of all students <u>enrolled</u> in the class <u>were</u> absent. <u>No error.</u>
   A   B   C   D   E

18. <u>After</u> her <u>8th</u> marriage ended in <u>divorce,</u> Julie <u>decided</u> never to marry again.
   A   B   C   D
<u>No error.</u>
  E

19. The fraternity <u>had hoped</u> to <u>have raised</u> enough money <u>to begin</u> construction <u>in June.</u>
                 A   B   C   D
<u>No error.</u>
  E

20. John and Harry <u>moved</u> to <u>Chicago,</u> where <u>he</u> <u>rented</u> an apartment on Michigan Avenue.
              A   B   C   D
<u>No error.</u>
  E

21. As the judge reviewed her case, Beverly told her that she had pulled out of a line
      A   B   C

   of slow-moving traffic and of her perfect driving record. No error.
                              D   E

22. Many politicians find it easier to speak in abstractions than grounding their
          A   B   C

  thoughts in reality. No error.
        D   E

23. Sharon was responsible for answering the telephone, typing letters, sorting the
            A   B   C   D

  mail, and ordering supplies. No error.
                      E

24. An ambulance finally arrived, but by that time we been taken to the hospital
             A   B   C

  by a friendly truck driver. No error.
        D   E

25. Nancy Rodriguez was first elected to the City Council in 1966, and has been
                        A   B   C

  reelected every year since then. No error.
         D   E

Part B

> **DIRECTIONS:** In each of the following sentences, some portion of the sentence is underlined. Under each sentence are five choices. The first choice has the same wording as the original. The other four choices are reworded. Select the letter of the best choice which rewrites the sentence correctly.

26.   During the training session for new employees, I was not only told what to do but also

    what to think.

    (A)   I was not only told what to do but also what to think.
    (B)   I was not told what to do but what to think.
    (C)   I was not only told what to do but what to think.
    (D)   I wasn't told not only what to do but what to think also.
    (E)   I was told not only what to do, but also, what to think.

27. It was obvious that the students liked the new teacher better than the principal.

    (A)   liked the new teacher better than the principal.
    (B)   liked the new teacher better than they liked the principal.
    (C)   liked the new teacher and the principal.
    (D)   liked the new teacher, and the principal.
    (E)   liked the new teacher's principal.

28. My present job is not as exciting as some of my friends.

    (A)   as exciting as some of my friends.
    (B)   as much excitement as my friend's job.
    (C)   as exciting as some of my friends' jobs.
    (D)   as far exciting as friend's jobs.
    (E)   as exciting as friend's jobs.

29. The committee had difficult decision on selecting a spokesperson.

    (A)   difficult decision on selecting a
    (B)   a difficult decision selecting as a
    (C)   difficulty deciding about selecting a
    (D)   difficult time to select a
    (E)   difficulty deciding on a

30. Everyone agreed library was closed too many hours on weekends.

    (A)   library was closed   (D)   that the library was closed
    (B)   the library had closed   (E)   that library remained close
    (C)   library was inconveniently closed

31. Intending to take advantage of the January sale Allison arrived before the store opened.

    (A)   January sale Allison   (D)   January sale so Allison
    (B)   January sale and Allison   (E)   January sale, and Allison
    (C)   January sale, Allison

32. Last summer we visited Hot Springs, Arkansas and St. Louis, Missouri.

    (A)   Arkansas and St. Louis, Missouri.
    (B)   Arkansas, and St. Louis, Missouri.
    (C)   Arkansas; and St. Louis, Missouri.
    (D)   Ark. and St. Louis, Mo.
    (E)   Arkansas and Saint Louis, Missouri.

33.   Senator Smith's expense accounts <u>are the scrutiny</u> by news media.

    (A)   are the scrutiny   (D)   are often the scrutiny

    (B)   are often scrutinized   (E)   are often questionable and reviewed

    (C)   are the scrutiny duty

34.   <u>My mother says that she never has and never will vote for a Republican.</u>

    (A)   My mother says that she never has and never will vote for a Republican.

    (B)   My mother has never voted for Republicans.

    (C)   My mother says that she never has voted, and never will vote, for a Republican.

    (D)   My mother has never and never will vote Republican.

    (E)   My mother says she has never and never would vote for a Republican.

35.   Joseph is <u>one of those individuals who tend</u> to follow the crowd.

    (A)   one of those individuals who tend

    (B)   one of those individuals who tends

    (C)   one of those individuals, who tend

    (D)   another individual who intend

    (E)   one of those individual people who tend

Part C

> **DIRECTIONS:** Each of the passages below is followed by several questions or incomplete sentences. Under each question or sentence are five choices. Select the letter of the best choice and darken the corresponding oval.

Questions 36-40 are based on the following passage.

(1) In 1840 Dickens came up with the idea of using a raven as a character in his new novel, Barnaby Rudge. (2) Soon, the word got out among his friends and neighbors that the famous author was interested in ravens and wanted to know more about them. (3) When someone gave a raven as a pet, he was delighted. (4) The raven was named Grip by Dickens' children and became a successful member of the family. (5) Grip began to get his way around the household, and if he wanted something, he took it, and Grip would bite the children's ankles when he felt displeased. (6) The raven in Barnaby Rudge is depicted as a trickster who slept "on horseback" in the stable and "has been known, by the mere superiority of his genius, to walk off unmolested with the dog's dinner." (7) _____

(8) Poe, however, was dissatisfied. (9) This was a comical presentation of the raven. (10) Poe felt that the large black bird should have a more prophetic use. (11) So, about a year after Barnaby Rudge was published, Poe began work on his poem, "The Raven." (12) _____ schoolchild can quote the famous line, "Quoth the Raven, 'Nevermore,'" but almost no one knows about Grip. (13) What happened to Grip? (14) Well, when he died, the Dickens family had become so attached to him that they had him stuffed and displayed him in the parlor.

36.   Which of the following indefinite pronouns should be used in Sentence 12?

    (A)   Any   (D)   One

    (B)   Each   (E)   Some

    (C)   None

37. What was the author's purpose in including Sentences 8-11?
    (A) To defend Poe's depiction of the raven.
    (B) To show ravens are not comical birds.
    (C) To highlight how some characters are unforgettable and others slip into obscurity.
    (D) To elicit sympathy for the raven.
    (E) To show that no discussion of ravens is complete without mentioning Poe's poem.

38. In the context of the sentences preceding and following which of the following is the best choice for Sentence 7?
    (A) So, you can get an idea of what life with Grip was like.
    (B) Therefore, the challenges of living with Grip must have been numerous and varied.
    (C) So, an idea of the life with Grip can be gotten.
    (D) So, life with Grip must have been entertaining.
    (E) These are some examples I have given of what life with Grip was like.

39. Which of the following is the best way to combine Sentences 8, 9, and 10?
    (A) Having dissatisfaction with the comical presentation of the big black bird, Poe felt it should be more prophetic.
    (B) As a result of dissatisfaction, Poe felt the big black bird should be presented more prophetically than comically.
    (C) However, Poe felt the comical presentation was not as good as the prophetic one.
    (D) Poe, however, dissatisfied with the comical presentation of the big black bird, felt a more prophetic use would be better.
    (E) Poe, however, was dissatisfied with this comical presentation and felt that the large black bird should have a more prophetic use.

40. In relation to the passage as a whole, which of the following best describes the writer's intention in the first paragraph?
    (A) To provide background information
    (B) To provide a concrete example of a humorous episode
    (C) To arouse sympathy in the reader
    (D) To evaluate the effectiveness of the treatment of the subject
    (E) To contrast with treatment of the subject in the second paragraph

Questions 41-45 are based on the following passage.

(1) Medieval literature and art, throughout the predominance of religious themes, was greatly varied. (2) In literature, for example, the chivalric tradition embodied in such works as the Arthurian legends, as well as the Anglo-Saxon epic Beowulf and the French epic Song of Roland, showed the richness of themes. (3) Originating in France during the mid-1100s, the Gothic style spread to other parts of Europe. (4) However, it was in Gothic architecture that the Medieval religious fervor best exhibited itself. (5) Gothic cathedrals were the creation of a community, many artisans and craftsman working over many generations. (6) Most of the populace could not read or write, so donating funds or working on the building and its

furnishings become a form of religious devotion as well as a means of impressing neighboring areas and attracting tourism. (7) The first Gothic structures were parts of an abbey and a cathedral. (8) _____ of Notre Dame in Paris, Westminster Abbey in England, and Cologne Cathedral in Germany.

(9) Gothic architecture strives to emphasize height and light. (10) Characteristic internal structures are the ribbed vault and pointed arches. (11) Thick stone walls give way to stained glass windows depicting religious scenes, and the masonry is embellished with delicate tracery. (12) Outside, slender beams called "flying buttresses" provide support for the height of the building. (13) Great spires complete the illusion of rising to the sky.

41. Which of the following would most appropriately replace "throughout" in Sentence 1?

    (A) beyond
    (B) until
    (C) despite
    (D) unless
    (E) under

42. Which of the following would improve and clarify the structure of the first paragraph?

    (A) Eliminate Sentence 5.
    (B) Place Sentence 3 after Sentence 7.
    (C) Reverse the order of Sentences 2 and 4.
    (D) Place the first Sentence at the end.
    (E) No change is necessary.

43. Which of the following words is used incorrectly in Sentence 6?

    (A) populace
    (B) donating
    (C) become
    (D) devotion
    (E) tourism

44. What would be the correct way to begin Sentence 8?

    (A) Later during the twelfth and thirteenth centuries, Gothic architecture reached its peak, in the great cathedrals
    (B) Later, during the twelfth and thirteenth centuries: Gothic architecture reached its peak in the great cathedrals
    (C) Later, during the twelfth, and thirteenth centuries, Gothic architecture reached its peak, in the great cathedrals
    (D) Later, during the twelfth and thirteenth centuries, Gothic architecture reached its peak in the great cathedrals
    (E) None of these.

45. Which of the following would best fit between Sentences 10 and 11?

    (A) Often, you can find gargoyles, grotesque demonic-looking creatures carved on the outside of the building.
    (B) Particularly impressive to me are the carvings of realistic animals and plants on the pulpits.
    (C) Tall, thin columns reach to the ceiling and help to support the roof.
    (D) These buildings were designed to impress everyone who saw them with the glory of God.
    (E) In the twelfth century, the Gothic style had reached its peak.

Section 4: Essay

TIME: 30 Minutes

> **DIRECTIONS:** Plan and write an essay on the topic given below. DO NOT WRITE ON ANY OTHER TOPIC OTHER THAN THE ONE SPECIFIED. AN ESSAY ON ANY OTHER TOPIC IS UNACCEPTABLE.

Many schools group students by ability. Are you in favor of this practice? Explain your position by discussing the positive or negative consequences of ability grouping for students and teachers.

TEST OF COMMUNICATION SKILLS

ANSWER KEY

SECTION 1: LISTENING

1.	(B)	11.	(B)	21.	(D)	31.	(D)
2.	(A)	12.	(A)	22.	(B)	32.	(A)
3.	(D)	13.	(D)	23.	(A)	33.	(D)
4.	(A)	14.	(C)	24.	(A)	34.	(C)
5.	(C)	15.	(A)	25.	(D)	35.	(A)
6.	(A)	16.	(A)	26.	(B)	36.	(A)
7.	(B)	17.	(C)	27.	(A)	37.	(D)
8.	(D)	18.	(D)	28.	(C)	38.	(A)
9.	(A)	19.	(B)	29.	(C)	39.	(C)
10.	(A)	20.	(C)	30.	(B)	40.	(B)

SECTION 2: READING

1.	(D)	9.	(E)	17.	(C)	25.	(A)
2.	(C)	10.	(C)	18.	(A)	26.	(A)
3.	(C)	11.	(A)	19.	(B)	27.	(C)
4.	(A)	12.	(E)	20.	(A)	28.	(B)
5.	(C)	13.	(B)	21.	(C)	29.	(E)
6.	(C)	14.	(D)	22.	(E)	30.	(D)
7.	(B)	15.	(E)	23.	(A)		
8.	(D)	16.	(E)	24.	(D)		

SECTION 3: WRITING

1.	(D)	13.	(B)	25.	(E)	37.	(C)
2.	(E)	14.	(A)	26.	(E)	38.	(D)
3.	(A)	15.	(A)	27.	(B)	39.	(E)
4.	(E)	16.	(C)	28.	(C)	40.	(A)
5.	(E)	17.	(A)	29.	(E)	41.	(C)
6.	(D)	18.	(B)	30.	(D)	42.	(B)
7.	(A)	19.	(B)	31.	(C)	43.	(C)
8.	(B)	20.	(C)	32.	(B)	44.	(D)
9.	(E)	21.	(D)	33.	(B)	45.	(C)
10.	(D)	22.	(C)	34.	(C)		
11.	(C)	23.	(E)	35.	(A)		
12.	(C)	24.	(C)	36.	(A)		

DETAILED EXPLANATIONS
OF ANSWERS
NTE CORE BATTERY–Test 1

TEST OF COMMUNICATION SKILLS
Section 1: Listening

Part A

1.   **(B)**   Answer (A) is incorrect because the speaker asks how much money you brought with you, not how much is in your desk. Answer (B) is correct because it directly responds to the question. Answer (C) is incorrect because it does not tell how much money you have with you. Answer (D) is incorrect because you were not asked how you spent your cash.

2.   **(A)**   This question asks you to respond to a statement concerning the time the bus leaves for the stadium. Answer (B) concerns the return time which is not specified. Answer (C) is incorrect because food and drinks are not discussed. Answer (D) is incorrect because it adds new information and does respond to the initial statement. Answer (A) is correct because it specifically responds to the information about the time the bus will leave.

3.   **(D)**   The statement lists flu symptoms. Answer (D) is an appropriate response because it directly supports the given statement. Answers (A), (B) and (C) introduce extraneous information.

4.   **(A)**   Answer (A) is correct because it is the only answer that mentions spring. Answers (B) and (C) discuss weather related issues but are not appropriate based on the statement concerning spring rain. Answer (D) is totally unrelated.

5.   **(C)**   The question specifically asks "who." Only answer (C) names a person. Answers (A), (B) and (D) discuss the party but do not name specific individuals.

6.   **(A)**   The speaker states that the survey results are distorted because different questions were used with some people. Answer (A) is an appropriate response because "unreliable" describes the survey results. Answer (B) is incorrect because there is no indication that the survey is old. Answer (C) is incorrect because it is not clear if this response refers to the same survey or to surveys in general. Answer (D) is not appropriate because you were not asked for your opinion.

7.   **(B)**   Answer (B) is correct because it directly responds to the availability of make-ups for absences. Answer (A) is incorrect because it contradicts the statement. Answer (C) is

inappropriate because the statement indicates it is easy, not hard to make up an absence. Answer (D) is inappropriate because the speaker does not say anything about other instructors' classes.

8.   **(D)**   Answer (D) is correct because it agrees with the speaker's statement that a student loan is not sufficient to pay all expenses. Answer (A) is incorrect because the speaker has not mentioned your uncle or scholarships. Answer (B) is incorrect because although the fee increase is relevant, it is not the best response. Answer (C) is inappropriate because your roommate's job is not relevant to student loans.

9.   **(A)**   Answer (A) is correct because the speaker asks "when" will you vote and only answer (A) specifies a time. Answer (B) is incorrect because you were not asked for whom you will vote. Answer (C) is incorrect because you were not asked what was on the ballot. Answer (D) is incorrect because it does not answer the question of "when" you will vote.

10.   **(A)**   Answer (A) is correct because this is the only answer that directly responds to the speaker. A sailboat in Florida is not related to white water rafting, so answer (B) is incorrect. Spring break might be related to rafting, but answer (A) is a better choice. Camping is also related to rafting, but it is not the best response to the speaker's statement.

11.   **(B)**   Answer (B) is correct because it responds directly to the statement without adding any new information. Responses (A) and (D) add information about fees although the statement never mentions payment of fees or amount of fees. Answer (C) suggests that few students used the health center which contradicts the information in the statement that students demanded longer hours.

12.   **(A)**   Answer (A) is correct. The speaker states that the addition of a health class is the reason why the school day will be lengthened. Response (B) may be correct but there is no indication in the original statement that new teachers will be hired. Responses (C) and (D) are incorrect because the speaker does not mention or imply that there will be a need for additional classrooms or longer hours for school bus drivers.

13.   **(D)**   Response (D) is correct. Responses (A), (B) and (C) each introduce new information. The speaker does not specify a particular insect or suggest that the reactions are so severe as to require hospitalization.

14.   **(C)**   Answer (C) is correct because the sandbags are being filled in anticipation of the flooding. Answer (A) is incorrect because there is no reason to fill sandbags if they are not expected to help. Answers (B) and (D) are incorrect because the speaker does not mention volunteers or evacuations.

15.   **(A)**   Answer (A) is correct because it responds directly to the speaker's statement. Answers (B) and (C) are incorrect because they are assumptions which have no basis in the speaker's statement. Answer (D) is true, but it does not respond directly to the statement.

Part B

16. **(A)**   Answer (A) is correct. The mother states that physics is an entrance requirement for the university in Texas that she wants her son to attend. Answer (B) is incorrect because it contradicts the son's first statement. Answers (C) and (D) are incorrect because there is no indication in the conversation of the son's academic interests or skills.

17. **(C)**   Answer (C) is the correct response because the mother is not willing to discuss the possibility of her son taking physics, she is insisting that he take it. Answer (A) is incorrect because there is no basis in the conversation for this conclusion. Answer (B) is incorrect because the mother is very forceful. Answer (D) is incorrect because the son appears to give in to his mother's wish.

18. **(D)**   Answer (D) is correct because the son is only interested in meeting the entrance requirements for the college he wants to attend. Answers (A) and (B) are incorrect because the conversation does not mention his personality or grades. Answer (C) is incorrect because the conversation does not indicate his personal habits.

19. **(B)**   The correct answer is (B) because the teacher states that the student has missed three assignments that week. Answer (A) is incorrect because it is the opposite of what the teacher says. Answers (C) and (D) are incorrect because although she may be on the basketball team and she may often be sick, neither is indicated by the conversation.

20. **(C)**   Answer (C) is correct because the teacher values homework and insists that students complete assignments. Answers (A), (B) and (D) are incorrect because the conversation lacks enough specific information to make such broad conclusions about the teacher's personality or the students he dislikes.

21. **(D)**   Answer (D) is correct because the student gives two different excuses. Answer (A) is incorrect because the student never suggests she did not understand. Answers (B) and (C) are incorrect because each individual excuse is incomplete.

22. **(B)**   Answer (B) is correct. The question asks "why." Only answer (B) responds to "why." Answers (A), (C) and (D) are all incidental issues to jogging, none names a specific reason for jogging.

23. **(A)**   The correct answer is (A) because the walker specifically says that he prefers to walk because jogging hurts his knees. Although answers (B), (C) and (D) are probable, there is no information in the conversation to indicate the walker lacks proper shoes, cannot use an indoor track or does not know how to train for jogging.

24. **(A)**   The jogger indicates in the first sentence that wearing the proper shoes and running on an indoor track or on grass can help prevent injuries. Answer (B) is incorrect because jogging with a partner is not mentioned in the conversation. Answer (C) is incorrect because having a physical check-up is not mentioned. Answer (D) is incorrect because the jogger never discusses the number of miles to run.

25. **(D)**   Answer (D) is correct because the speaker begins and ends with the statement that maintenance of beach front property never ends. Answer (A) is incorrect because the speaker never mentions expense. Answer (B) is incorrect because the speaker states that "beach front property is wonderful." Answer (C) is incorrect because although the speaker mentions hurricanes, the destruction they cause is not discussed.

26. **(B)**   Answer (B) is correct because the speaker specifically names blowing sand and rain as the cause of maintenance problems. Hurricanes and freezing temperatures are mentioned, but not as major problems, so answers (A) and (D) are incorrect. Answer (C) is incorrect because insects are not discussed.

27. **(A)**   The correct answer is (A). The speaker begins by stating that "spring begins with a thorough cleaning..." Removing sand from the porch and cleaning the mold under the eaves are both mentioned, but those tasks are not first, so answers (B) and (C) are incorrect. Answer (D) is named as a task to prepare for winter not spring.

28. **(C)**   Answer (C) is correct. Washing windows was named as a maintenance task for spring. Answers (A), (B) and (D) are incorrect because preparing for hurricanes, protecting pipes and storing porch furniture are all named as fall and winter maintenance tasks.

29. **(C)**   The correct answer is (C) because the speaker is discussing camping as an enjoyable experience. Answer (A) is incorrect because although the speaker mentions hazards, that is not the main purpose of the talk. Although the speaker discusses the importance of planning, that is not the purpose of the talk, so answer (B) is incorrect. Answer (D) is incorrect because the speaker barely mentions cooking outdoors.

30. **(B)**   Answer (B) is correct. This is a straight content question. Staying in motels will not minimize costs if you want to camp, so answer (A) is incorrect. Answers (C) and (D) are incorrect because they are not even mentioned in the talk.

31. **(D)**   Answer (D) is correct. This question asks you to identify a hazard not included in the talk. Answers (A), (B) and (C) are specifically named by the speaker.

32. **(A)**   The correct answer is (A) because the speaker states that food spoilage is a problem that can be avoided with careful planning. The speaker does not discuss burning food, expensive utensils or lack of places to cook.

33. **(D)**   The correct answer is (D) because students learn about measurement, different cultures and farming.

34. **(C)**   Answer (C) is correct because music is not mentioned by the speaker. Answers (A), (B) and (D) are included in the lesson according to the speaker.

35. **(A)**   The correct answer is (A). The speaker believes bread making has educational value for elementary students. Answer (B) is incorrect because it contradicts the speaker's statement. Answer (C) is incorrect because the speaker states that measuring is important, but he does not state that it is "the best part." Answer (D) is incorrect because it introduces a new idea not mentioned by the speaker.

36. **(A)**   The correct answer is (A). The speaker states that the number of immigrants during 1980-1990 was double the number since 1900-1910.

37. **(D)**   The correct answer is (D). The speaker specifically states that during the 1950s the majority of immigrants came from Canada, Mexico and the West Indies.

38. **(A)**   The correct answer is (A). Revolution and political upheaval are specifically mentioned as reasons why many immigrants left their native countries. Although poverty, hunger and lack of opportunity are reasonable answers, these were not mentioned by the speaker. Therefore, answers (B), (C) and (D) are incorrect.

39. **(C)**   The correct answer is (C). The speaker is concerned about the ramifications of large numbers of immigrants on schools, housing and governmental services. The speaker does not discuss illegal immigrants, overpopulation or health care, so answers (A), (B) and (D) are incorrect.

40. **(B)**   The correct answer is (B) because it restates the main idea of the first sentence. Answer (A) is incorrect because immigration has not declined. Answer (C) is incorrect because the speaker does not discuss the school's ability to absorb so many new students. Answer (D) is incorrect because it introduces several new ideas the speaker does not discuss.

Section 2: Reading

1. **(D)**   Although the author of the passage might agree with answer (A), this belief is not expressed in the paragraph. Answers (B) and (C) are both included in the paragraph but neither statement summarizes the content of the whole passage. Answer (E) refers to programs designed to keep students in school, but this is only a small portion of the entire passage, and therefore is not the main idea. The correct answer is (D) because it paraphrases the topic of the entire passage which is stated in the first and second sentences.

2. **(C)**   Answer (A) is specifically stated in the eighth sentence of the passage. Answer (B) is stated in the second sentence. Answer (D) is stated in the last two sentences. Answer (E) is stated in the sixth sentence. Answer (C) is correct because the paragraph does not discuss students moving out of the district.

3. **(C)**   This question requires you to determine the author's attitude although it is not specifically stated in the passage. Answer (A) is not appropriate because the entire passage discusses the drop out problem, and the topic must be of concern to the author. Answer (B) is incorrect because there is no mention of teachers in the passage. Answer (D) is possible because the author does discuss dropout prevention programs; however, the author does not state or imply that such programs are simple solutions to the problem. Although the author might agree with answer (E) there is no evidence of this in the passage. Answer (C) is the best answer because it refers to the main idea, and it can be inferred from the discussion that the author feels the drop out problem is complex and has many contributing factors.

4.   **(A)**   Answer (A) is correct because sand, gravel and water are specifically mentioned. Answer (B) specifies "mud" which is not in the passage. Answers (C) and (D) both include "heat," which is not mentioned.

5.   **(C)**   Question 5 asks you to infer information from the passage. Answer (A) is incorrect because the passage does not imply any information concerning the weight of petrified trees. Answer (B) specifies museums which are not mentioned. Answer (C) is correct because fossils are mentioned in the passage, and it can be inferred that these fossils provide evidence of other life forms. Answer (D) is not discussed. Answer (E) specifies the location of petrified trees which is not discussed in the passage.

6.   **(C)**   Answer (C) is correct. The time period when weather predictions were included in almanacs is specifically stated in the passage. Answer (A) is incorrect because early almanacs were charts of the stars and did not include other information.

7.   **(B)**   Answer (B) is correct. The only description of features of the Davy Crockett almanacs is in the last sentence of the passage. Answers (B) and (C) are incorrect because there is no mention in the passage of these almanacs being printed in Germany or being written about Davy Crockett. Since the U. S. Civil War was between 1861-1865 and the almanacs were printed between 1835-1856, answer (D) is incorrect. Answer (E) is probably true, but the question asks for a unique feature.

8.   **(D)**   According to this passage the purpose of almanacs has changed over time. However, early almanacs were charts of the movements of stars. Therefore, answer (D) is correct. Answers (A), (B) and (C) state items that were included in later almanacs.

9.   **(E)**   The entire passage discusses the changing content of almanacs over time, therefore, answer (E) is the best statement of the author's attitude. Answer (A) is incorrect because it ignores more recent almanacs. Answer (B) is incorrect because "archaic" means out of date, and this does not agree with the author's position. While the author may agree with answer (C), it does not summarize the author's attitude toward almanacs. Answer (D) is incorrect because the author does not discuss the reliability of almanac weather predictions.

10.   **(C)**   This question must be answered using the process of elimination. The information stated in answers (A), (B), (D) and (E) is specifically included in the passage. The passage does not specify who wrote the Davy Crockett almanacs. Therefore, answer (C) is correct.

11.   **(A)**   The second sentence of the passage states that the players were protesting unfair treatment, so answer (A) is correct. There is no information in the passage to support any of the other answers.

12.   **(E)**   This is another question that requires the process of elimination. Answers (A), (B), (C) and (D) are included in the passage. The players' plans for next year are not discussed, therefore answer (E) is correct.

13.   **(B)**   This question requires you to make a judgment concerning the author's attitude based on the information in the passage. There is no evidence to suggest that the author has a humorous attitude, or that the author condemns the players, or believes that they are

behaving childishly. The author may agree that the team has damaged the university's reputation, but this is not evident in the passage. Overall, the author writes objectively about the incident, so answer (B) is correct.

14.   **(D)**   This question requires you to do some careful reading because several time periods are included in the passage. However, the passage specifically states that the players returned after four days, so answer (D) is correct.

15.   **(E)**   Answer (E) is correct because the passage specifically states that the players met with the university president, the assistant coach and the athletic director. A meeting with the head coach is not discussed.

16.   **(E)**   Answer (E) is the best answer because the passage states that the team's protest concerned unfair treatment by the coach, but it does not specify the nature of the treatment. There is no evidence of a racial issue, so answer (A) is incorrect. Scholarships and team privileges are not discussed, so answers (B) and (C) are incorrect. The conflict was not with the Athletic Director, so answer (D) is incorrect.

17.   **(C)**   The correct answer is (C) because Annie's age is not included. The passage states that she is older than Cinnamon, so answer (E) is incorrect.

18.   **(A)**   This question requires the process of elimination. The passage states that Cinnamon stays outside at night and that Cinnamon is a male tabby. The passage also states that Annie has long hair and is a female cat. Cinnamon chases squirrels, but the passage does not state that Annie also chases squirrels. Answer (A) is correct.

19.   **(B)**   Answer (B) is correct. This information is stated in the next to the last sentence. There is no mention of Marie preferring one cat to the other, so answer (A) is incorrect. Cinnamon, not Annie, spends most nights outside, so answer (C) is incorrect. The passage does not discuss the cats fighting with each other, nor does the passage mention litters of kittens, so answers (D) and (E) are incorrect.

20.   **(A)**   The correct answer is (A). The last two sentences of the passage indicate that the author's interest is clearly the business aspect of exercise and diet programs. The author probably agrees that these programs are valuable, but that is not the main idea of the passage, so answers (B) and (E) are incorrect. Although the author does mention the cost of memberships and the large number of diet programs, neither topic is emphasized. Therefore, answers (C) and (D) are incorrect.

21.   **(C)**   Answer (C) is correct because this is a re-wording of the last sentence of the passage. The author acknowledges that Jane Fonda has made a lot of money from her exercise videos. However, it is not stated that this is "too much" money, therefore answer (A) is incorrect. The author states that Richard Simmons gives diet advice in his exercise video but does not discuss whether this is appropriate so answer (B) is incorrect. Answer (D) is incorrect because the average cost of health clubs is never discussed. Answer (E) is incorrect because the passage states that people are concerned; it does not state that they "should be concerned."

22.   **(E)**   In this question you are asked to infer a purpose from what the author has written.

Answer (A) is incorrect because the author only mentions environmental damage; the topic is not discussed at length. Answer (B) is incorrect because the passage clearly states that foreign oil production is increasing, not decreasing. Answer (C) is incorrect because, although this is discussed, it is not the main purpose for writing. Answer (D) is incorrect because the author does not discuss ways to lower oil prices. Answer (E) is correct because it summarizes the author's main idea, which is that the results of increased dependence on foreign oil can be predicted with relative certainty.

23. **(A)** This question asks you to determine why domestic oil producers will not increase production. The correct answer is (A) because this is specifically stated in the sixth sentence. Answer (D) states information that is opposite to what is stated in the paragraph. Although oil tankers are expensive and producers are afraid of spills, these are only contributing reasons to the problem. Therefore, answers (B) and (C) are incorrect.

24. **(D)** This question requires you to review the whole passage and eliminate answers. Answer (A) is stated in the third sentence. Answer (B) is stated in the first sentence. Answer (C) is a rewording of the last sentence. Answer (E) is in the fourth sentence. Answer (D) is correct because although the idea may be logical, insurance is never discussed in the passage.

25. **(A)** In this question you are asked to infer the author's attitude toward Aunt Josephine and her art collection. There are two clues in the passage. The first clue is in the third sentence when the author says that Aunt Josephine "insisted" on combining Picasso and Tiffany lamps. The author apparently feels that this is an unusual combination. The second clue is in the last sentence when the author "marveled" at her spending habits. Clearly, the author is amused and feels Aunt Josephine's behavior is quaint and perhaps eccentric. Answer (A) is the best answer. The author does not give any indication that he feels Aunt Josephine is "crazy" or "stingy" even though he admits she "pinches pennies." The author is neither disgusted, nor jealous, so answers (B) and (E) are incorrect.

26. **(A)** This question requires you to step back and view the art collection as an observer. Picasso prints are expensive, but not breakable, so answers (B) and (E) are incorrect. Answer (C) is incorrect because we have no information about insurance. Answer (D) is incorrect because Tiffany lamps and Picasso prints are not "junk." Eclectic means "choosing the best from diverse sources." This is exactly what Aunt Josephine has done, so answer (A) is correct.

27. **(C)** Answer (C) is correct. The passage does not discuss her weight or wealth, so answers (A) and (D) are incorrect. She is definitely not dependent on other people's opinions, so answer (B) is incorrect. She may be interested in talking with other people, but we do not know that this is true. Therefore, answer (E) is incorrect.

28. **(B)** This question asks you to use the process of elimination to determine an answer. The only answer not discussed in the passage is (B). All other answers are discussed. Answer (B) is correct.

29. **(E)** This question also asks you to determine which answer is not discussed in the passage. Answers (A), (B), (C) and (D) are specifically discussed. The correct answer is (E).

30. **(D)** Answer (D) is correct because screens for fireplaces and space heaters are both discussed in the passage. Keeping doors and windows closed is never discussed.

Section 3: Writing

Part A

1.   **(D)**   The error occurs at (D). The past tense of "take" is required to agree with the tense of "entered" and "greeted". There are no other errors in this sentence.

2.   **(E)**   There is no error in this sentence. The verb forms and punctuation are correct.

3.   **(A)**   The error occurs at (A). The comma separates the subject from the predicate of the sentence. It interrupts the flow of thought. There is no need for a comma here.

4.   **(E)**   No error.

5.   **(E)**   No error.

6.   **(D)**   The error occurs at (D). The correct pronoun is "her" not "she." "Her" is an objective pronoun, and "she" is nominative. To determine which pronoun to use in a compound subject or object, drop the noun or pronoun that occurs first and choose the correct pronoun as though the word would be used alone.

7.   **(A)**   The error occurs at (A). The correct pronoun is "I." To determine the correct pronoun in a compound subject, select the pronoun you would use if the subject were singular.

8.   **(B)**   The error occurs at (B). The correlative conjunction "not only" is always paired with "but also." The sentence should read "Not only my aunt but also my uncle plays championship bridge in New York City."

9.   **(E)**   No error.

10.   **(D)**   The error occurs at (D). The correct form is "patience." "Patient" is a person; "patience" is a personality trait.

11.   **(C)**   The error occurs at (C). The correct form is "returned." The past tense is required to agree with "did not remove."

12.   **(C)**   The error occurs at (C). A comma is required after "college." This sentence is composed of two independent clauses combined by the coordinate conjunction "and."

13.   **(B)**   The error occurs at (B). A comma is required after "eyes" because of the conjunction "although" which is used to subordinate the first clause.

14.   **(A)**   The error occurs at (A). The correct form is "whose." "Who's" means "who is."

15.   **(A)**   The error occurs at (A). The correct form is "it's." "Its" is the possessive form. "It's" means "it is."

16. **(C)** The error occurs at (C). The correct form is "100 B. C." The letters "B. C." always follow a year.

17. **(A)** The error occurs at (A). The number "20" should be spelled out because it is the first word in the sentence. Numbers over ten do not need to be spelled out unless they begin a sentence.

18. **(B)** The error occurs at (B). Numbers less than ten should be spelled out regardless of where they occur in the sentence.

19. **(B)** The error occurs at (B). The verb "raise" does not require a helping verb in this construction. The correct form is "The fraternity had hoped to raise..."

20. **(C)** The error occurs at (C). The pronoun "he" is unclear because it could refer to John or Harry. A possible correction would be "John and Harry moved to Chicago, where they..."

21. **(D)** The error occurs at (D). This sentence does not use parallel constructions. The clause, "that she had pulled out of a line of slow-moving traffic," requires another "that" clause, not the "of" in the original. A possible correction would be "As the judge reviewed her case, Beverly told her that she had pulled out of a line of slow-moving traffic and that she had a perfect driving record."

22. **(C)** The error occurs at (C). The comparisons are unbalanced. The phrase "than grounding" should be "to ground" to match "to speak."

23. **(E)** There is no error in this sentence. The verb phrase "was responsible" is correct. The phrases listing her responsibilities (answering the telephone, typing letters, sorting the mail, and ordering supplies) are parallel in form and are punctuated correctly.

24. **(C)** The error occurs at (C). The verb tense of "we been taken" is incorrect. A helping verb in the past tense is needed. The correct form is "we had been taken."

25. **(E)** There is no error in this sentence. There are two complete clauses which are correctly joined by a comma and coordinate conjunction. The verb tense is correct and parallel.

Part B

26. **(E)** The correct answer is (E). The problem in this sentence is that the verb "was told" is separated by "not only." Answer (B) changes the meaning of the sentence. Answer (C) does not have the complete con junction "not only. . .but also." Answer (D) separates the conjunction. Answer (A) is identical to the original sentence.

27. **(B)** The problem with this sentence is that it is unclear whether the students liked the new teacher better than they liked the principal, or if the students liked the new teacher better than the principal liked the new teacher. Correction (B) is the only answer that solves this problem without changing the meaning. Answers (C) and (E) solve the problem but the

meaning of the original sentence is changed. Answer (D) includes a comma error. Answer (A) is identical to the original.

28. **(C)** The meaning of this sentence is unclear. The sentence leaves the question of "what is less exciting than his job?" Answer (C) is correct because it specifies that "friend's jobs" are more exciting. Answer (A) is identical to the original. Answers (B) and (E) use an incorrect form of "excitement" for this sentence. Answer (D) is too wordy.

29. **(E)** The problem in this sentence is awkward wording. The best answer is (E). The verb form of "decision" is required to complete the main idea of the sentence that "the committee had difficulty deciding on a spokesperson. Answer (C) uses deciding, but "about" is redundant and confusing. Answers (B) and (D) do not use the correct form of "deciding" for this sentence. Answer (A) is identical to the original.

30. **(D)** In this sentence, the clause "library was closed" needs to be set off from the rest of the sentence by the word "that" in order to subordinate the clause. Answer (D) is correct. Answers (B) and (C) do not use "that." Answer (E) uses the present tense of "close" which is incorrect in this construction. Answer (A) is identical to the original.

31. **(C)** The correct answer is (C). This sentence is composed of an independent clause, "Allison arrived before the store opened," and a dependent clause "Intending to take advantage of the January sale." A comma is needed to separate the clauses.

32. **(B)** Answer (B) is correct. If cities and states are listed, as in this sentence, a comma must be used after the city and also after the state, unless the state is the last word in the sentence.

33. **(B)** The problem with this sentence is the incorrect use of "scrutiny." "Scrutiny" is a noun: "scrutinized" is a verb. Only answer (B) is correct since it uses the verb form which is required in this sentence.

34. **(C)** Answer (C) is correct. The addition of "voted" completes the thought and makes both parts of the verb parallel. Answer (A) is identical to the original. Answer (B) is correct but alters the meaning of the sentence. Answers (D) and (E) may be understandable, but they do not correct the error.

35. **(A)** The sentence is correct as it stands. The most common mistake would be to attribute "tend" to Joseph when in fact it goes with "individuals." Answer (B) uses the incorrect form of "tend." Answer (C) has a comma splice, (D) has an entirely different meaning and (E) is redundant.

36. **(A)** Choice (A) creates a situation that validates the author's belief that all school-children know about Poe's raven and not Dickens'. Choices (B) and (D) are correct grammatically, but do not fit in with the author's intention. (C) and (E) do not make sense grammatically.

37. **(C)** Sentences 8-11 provide a contrast between a well-known character and a more obscure one. The author of this passage uses the contrast as a transition into discussing the

final outcome of Grip. (A), (B), and (E) may all be correct, but they do not fit with the rest of the passage. There is no reference to the raven requiring sympathy.

38. **(D)** Choice (D) keeps the formal tone of the essay and avoids passive voice. Choice (A) and choice (E) both break the formal tone and use another voice: "you" and "I." Choice (B) is perhaps too formal and not straightforward. Choice (C) uses the passive voice.

39. **(E)** Choice (E) smoothly combines both major ideas as a cause-and-effect sequence. Choice (A) is the next best choice, but it is not as smoothly worded in the first half; also, this choice eliminates the idea of "use" in the second half. Choice (B) does not clarify the source of Poe's dissatisfaction. Choice (C) does not clearly present the idea that the prophetic use was Poe's, not Dickens'. Choice (D) has too many interruptions.

40. **(A)** Choice (A) is correct; the paragraph gives information on the origin of the bird. Although the paragraph gives one or two humorous incidents, choice (B) cannot be the main intention. Choice (C) is unlikely; the bird's biting is presented as more humorous than tragic. Choice (D) would be a more effective label for paragraph two. Choice (E) is partly correct, but the second paragraph returns to the Dickens' household.

41. **(C)** "Despite" best fits the relation between the religious and secular themes. Choice (A), "beyond" would be the next best choice, though it sounds a bit overzealous. Choice (B), "until" would be inappropriate since the rest of the passage does not suggest that the secular themes preceded the religious, but rather that they coexisted. "Unless" (D) and "under" (E) are nonsensical in this context.

42. **(B)** Sentence 3, as it stands, introduces a wholly new subject without transition. Sentence 4 best carries this transition, and should follow Sentence 2. Sentence 3 introduces the spread of Gothic style throughout Europe, and this point is directly supported in Sentence 8.

43. **(C)** "Become" should be in the past tense ("became") to accord with the rest of the passage.

44. **(D)** Choice (D) sets the clause off with commas, and best clarifies the sentence. Choice (A) uses commas to disrupt the main idea of the sentence. Choice (B) sets the clause off well, but the colon is inappropriate and should be a comma. Choice (C) employs too many commas; the second and fourth should be eliminated, as they disrupt the flow of the sentence.

45. **(C)** Choice (C) continues to describe the internal physical characteristics of Gothic cathedrals, and best fits between Sentences 10 and 11. Choice (A) switches to the external aspect of the building. Choice (B) introduces the author's opinion, which is not necessary at this part of the passage. Choice (D) is a relevant thought, but would best be placed elsewhere: it describes the purpose of the architecture, where Sentences 10 and 11 are describing the physical qualities of the interior of the buildings. Choice (E) is an unrelated, and possibly factually incorrect, statement.

Section 4: Essay

The following essay received scores at the highest end of the scale used in NTE essay scoring.

Essay A

The practice of grouping students by ability in the elementary school has negative social and academic consequences for students. The negative effects of ability grouping over-shadow the few positive benefits that may be derived from this practice. Grouping by ability may be appropriate for certain subjects, such as reading, within a particular classroom as long as the group membership changes for instruction in other subjects. However, I feel that grouping by ability is an inappropriate practice at the elementary school level if all students remain in that group throughout the day.

One of the negative effects of ability grouping is that it contributes to the development of a poor self-image for many students. Children of all ages are very adept at recognizing and correctly identifying high, middle and low ability groups. Assigning non-threatening names to the groups has no affect on children's ability to identify these groups. This is apparent when observing or talking with students in schools that use ability grouping. It does not matter whether the teacher call the top group "Red Birds," "Group 3," "Triangles," or "Mrs. Smith's class," students are keenly aware of their membership in the group and the perceived ability of that group.

Students make comparisons between the ways teachers interact with different groups, the types of assignments groups receive and privileges different groups enjoy. Students in the high ability group may look down on other students and may refer to students in other groups as "stupid" or "dumb." Name calling may result. Students in the low ability group may resent their placement in that group. Students in the middle ability group may feel ignored or may even resent being labeled "average." The naturally occurring friction between groups creates a climate in which teachers will have difficulty building positive self-images for all students.

Ability grouping also necessarily limits peer interaction, both in and out of the classroom. Elementary students need to interact with many students to develop mature social and intellectual skills.

An additional negative effect of ability grouping is the stilted instructional environment, that is created within the classroom. Teachers of high ability students are encouraged to feel privileged to teach this group and usually prepare creative, challenging lessons. Teachers of the low ability group usually provide many drill and practice worksheets and seldom assign text materials. Middle ability students may receive assignments based on the text, but these assignments are often accompanied by drill and practice worksheets. The result of these practices is that only the high ability students are challenged to work to their capacity.

The negative consequences of ability grouping are experienced by students of all ability levels. For these reasons, the practice of ability grouping in the elementary school should be abandoned.

Explanation of Essay A

This essay addresses the topic directly. The topic of ability grouping is narrowed in the first sentence to the use of this practice in elementary school. The author's point of view and the focus of the essay (the negative social and academic consequences) are also established in the first sentence. Specific negative effects are named and briefly discussed. The last paragraph restates the author's point of view.

Several sentences in the essay are wordy and seem to ramble. Some of the issues raised (peer interaction) are not fully discussed. The author mentions the "positive benefits" of ability grouping but does not specifically name or discuss the benefits. There are a few errors in punctuation and spelling. However, the author demonstrates the ability to clearly state a topic and present a specific point of view.

The following essay received scores in the middle of the NTE scoring scale.

Essay B

Most teachers prefer ability grouping. I know I would. Ability grouping allows teachers to plan assignments for specific groups of students. In this way, teachers can make assignments fit the needs of specific groups of students, instead of just making one assignment for everybody. Teachers can spend additional time helping slower students because the advanced group will be able to complete their assignments independantly. Teachers can also give the advanced students extra work or projects to keep them busy. This gave the teachers more time to work with students who really need help.

Schools that group by ability can plan smaller classes for slow students and larger classes for average and advanced students. This is better for the students because those who really need extra help have a better chance of receiving it. Smaller classes for slow students also helps the teachers give more attention to slow students.

Ability grouping is especially important is math and reading because these subjects give many students difficulty.

Explanation of Essay B

Although the essay is satisfactory given the thirty minute time limit, it is flawed for several reasons. The major error is the lack of a controlling central idea or theme. The topic stated in the first sentence, that most teachers prefer ability grouping, is never fully developed. Instead of developing this topic, the writer discusses the advantages of small classes for slower students. The last two paragraphs seem tacked on and are not smoothly connected to the first paragraph. In addition, there are several spelling errors and verb tense is inconsistently used.

The following essay received scores at the lowest end of the NTE scoring scale.

Essay C

Ability grouping is terrible. Its awful to be in the slow group because everybody in the whole school knows it. Average students don't like ability grouping either because teachers don't pay any attention to them. Only the smart kids receive any attention. Even then it only shows how different they are. Some kids in the slow class like it because they never have homework and the teachers don't expect them to finish assignments so they get lots of time in class to do everything.

I observed in a school that ability grouping and I would not want to teach there. They would probably assign a new teacher to the slow class.

Explanation of Essay C

This essay does discuss the topic, but the opinions stated are never developed. Although the writer gives several specific examples to support his point of view (that ability grouping is terrible) he does not develop any of these examples so that the reader can understand the reasons behind his conclusions. There are several punctuation errors. Several words are misspelled, and the writer has left out a word in the second paragraph.

NTE Test of General Knowledge

TEST 1 – ANSWER SHEET

Section 1:
Social Studies

1. Ⓐ Ⓑ Ⓒ Ⓓ Ⓔ
2. Ⓐ Ⓑ Ⓒ Ⓓ Ⓔ
3. Ⓐ Ⓑ Ⓒ Ⓓ Ⓔ
4. Ⓐ Ⓑ Ⓒ Ⓓ Ⓔ
5. Ⓐ Ⓑ Ⓒ Ⓓ Ⓔ
6. Ⓐ Ⓑ Ⓒ Ⓓ Ⓔ
7. Ⓐ Ⓑ Ⓒ Ⓓ Ⓔ
8. Ⓐ Ⓑ Ⓒ Ⓓ Ⓔ
9. Ⓐ Ⓑ Ⓒ Ⓓ Ⓔ
10. Ⓐ Ⓑ Ⓒ Ⓓ Ⓔ
11. Ⓐ Ⓑ Ⓒ Ⓓ Ⓔ
12. Ⓐ Ⓑ Ⓒ Ⓓ Ⓔ
13. Ⓐ Ⓑ Ⓒ Ⓓ Ⓔ
14. Ⓐ Ⓑ Ⓒ Ⓓ Ⓔ
15. Ⓐ Ⓑ Ⓒ Ⓓ Ⓔ
16. Ⓐ Ⓑ Ⓒ Ⓓ Ⓔ
17. Ⓐ Ⓑ Ⓒ Ⓓ Ⓔ
18. Ⓐ Ⓑ Ⓒ Ⓓ Ⓔ
19. Ⓐ Ⓑ Ⓒ Ⓓ Ⓔ
20. Ⓐ Ⓑ Ⓒ Ⓓ Ⓔ
21. Ⓐ Ⓑ Ⓒ Ⓓ Ⓔ
22. Ⓐ Ⓑ Ⓒ Ⓓ Ⓔ
23. Ⓐ Ⓑ Ⓒ Ⓓ Ⓔ
24. Ⓐ Ⓑ Ⓒ Ⓓ Ⓔ
25. Ⓐ Ⓑ Ⓒ Ⓓ Ⓔ
26. Ⓐ Ⓑ Ⓒ Ⓓ Ⓔ
27. Ⓐ Ⓑ Ⓒ Ⓓ Ⓔ
28. Ⓐ Ⓑ Ⓒ Ⓓ Ⓔ
29. Ⓐ Ⓑ Ⓒ Ⓓ Ⓔ
30. Ⓐ Ⓑ Ⓒ Ⓓ Ⓔ

Section 2: Math

1. Ⓐ Ⓑ Ⓒ Ⓓ Ⓔ
2. Ⓐ Ⓑ Ⓒ Ⓓ Ⓔ
3. Ⓐ Ⓑ Ⓒ Ⓓ Ⓔ
4. Ⓐ Ⓑ Ⓒ Ⓓ Ⓔ
5. Ⓐ Ⓑ Ⓒ Ⓓ Ⓔ
6. Ⓐ Ⓑ Ⓒ Ⓓ Ⓔ
7. Ⓐ Ⓑ Ⓒ Ⓓ Ⓔ
8. Ⓐ Ⓑ Ⓒ Ⓓ Ⓔ
9. Ⓐ Ⓑ Ⓒ Ⓓ Ⓔ

10. Ⓐ Ⓑ Ⓒ Ⓓ Ⓔ
11. Ⓐ Ⓑ Ⓒ Ⓓ Ⓔ
12. Ⓐ Ⓑ Ⓒ Ⓓ Ⓔ
13. Ⓐ Ⓑ Ⓒ Ⓓ Ⓔ
14. Ⓐ Ⓑ Ⓒ Ⓓ Ⓔ
15. Ⓐ Ⓑ Ⓒ Ⓓ Ⓔ
16. Ⓐ Ⓑ Ⓒ Ⓓ Ⓔ
17. Ⓐ Ⓑ Ⓒ Ⓓ Ⓔ
18. Ⓐ Ⓑ Ⓒ Ⓓ Ⓔ
19. Ⓐ Ⓑ Ⓒ Ⓓ Ⓔ
20. Ⓐ Ⓑ Ⓒ Ⓓ Ⓔ
21. Ⓐ Ⓑ Ⓒ Ⓓ Ⓔ
22. Ⓐ Ⓑ Ⓒ Ⓓ Ⓔ
23. Ⓐ Ⓑ Ⓒ Ⓓ Ⓔ
24. Ⓐ Ⓑ Ⓒ Ⓓ Ⓔ
25. Ⓐ Ⓑ Ⓒ Ⓓ Ⓔ

Section 3: Literature
and Fine Arts

1. Ⓐ Ⓑ Ⓒ Ⓓ Ⓔ
2. Ⓐ Ⓑ Ⓒ Ⓓ Ⓔ
3. Ⓐ Ⓑ Ⓒ Ⓓ Ⓔ
4. Ⓐ Ⓑ Ⓒ Ⓓ Ⓔ
5. Ⓐ Ⓑ Ⓒ Ⓓ Ⓔ
6. Ⓐ Ⓑ Ⓒ Ⓓ Ⓔ
7. Ⓐ Ⓑ Ⓒ Ⓓ Ⓔ
8. Ⓐ Ⓑ Ⓒ Ⓓ Ⓔ
9. Ⓐ Ⓑ Ⓒ Ⓓ Ⓔ
10. Ⓐ Ⓑ Ⓒ Ⓓ Ⓔ
11. Ⓐ Ⓑ Ⓒ Ⓓ Ⓔ
12. Ⓐ Ⓑ Ⓒ Ⓓ Ⓔ
13. Ⓐ Ⓑ Ⓒ Ⓓ Ⓔ
14. Ⓐ Ⓑ Ⓒ Ⓓ Ⓔ
15. Ⓐ Ⓑ Ⓒ Ⓓ Ⓔ
16. Ⓐ Ⓑ Ⓒ Ⓓ Ⓔ
17. Ⓐ Ⓑ Ⓒ Ⓓ Ⓔ
18. Ⓐ Ⓑ Ⓒ Ⓓ Ⓔ
19. Ⓐ Ⓑ Ⓒ Ⓓ Ⓔ
20. Ⓐ Ⓑ Ⓒ Ⓓ Ⓔ
21. Ⓐ Ⓑ Ⓒ Ⓓ Ⓔ
22. Ⓐ Ⓑ Ⓒ Ⓓ Ⓔ
23. Ⓐ Ⓑ Ⓒ Ⓓ Ⓔ
24. Ⓐ Ⓑ Ⓒ Ⓓ Ⓔ

Section 4: Science

1. Ⓐ Ⓑ Ⓒ Ⓓ Ⓔ
2. Ⓐ Ⓑ Ⓒ Ⓓ Ⓔ
3. Ⓐ Ⓑ Ⓒ Ⓓ Ⓔ
4. Ⓐ Ⓑ Ⓒ Ⓓ Ⓔ
5. Ⓐ Ⓑ Ⓒ Ⓓ Ⓔ
6. Ⓐ Ⓑ Ⓒ Ⓓ Ⓔ
7. Ⓐ Ⓑ Ⓒ Ⓓ Ⓔ
8. Ⓐ Ⓑ Ⓒ Ⓓ Ⓔ
9. Ⓐ Ⓑ Ⓒ Ⓓ Ⓔ
10. Ⓐ Ⓑ Ⓒ Ⓓ Ⓔ
11. Ⓐ Ⓑ Ⓒ Ⓓ Ⓔ
12. Ⓐ Ⓑ Ⓒ Ⓓ Ⓔ
13. Ⓐ Ⓑ Ⓒ Ⓓ Ⓔ
14. Ⓐ Ⓑ Ⓒ Ⓓ Ⓔ
15. Ⓐ Ⓑ Ⓒ Ⓓ Ⓔ
16. Ⓐ Ⓑ Ⓒ Ⓓ Ⓔ
17. Ⓐ Ⓑ Ⓒ Ⓓ Ⓔ
18. Ⓐ Ⓑ Ⓒ Ⓓ Ⓔ
19. Ⓐ Ⓑ Ⓒ Ⓓ Ⓔ
20. Ⓐ Ⓑ Ⓒ Ⓓ Ⓔ
21. Ⓐ Ⓑ Ⓒ Ⓓ Ⓔ
22. Ⓐ Ⓑ Ⓒ Ⓓ Ⓔ
23. Ⓐ Ⓑ Ⓒ Ⓓ Ⓔ
24. Ⓐ Ⓑ Ⓒ Ⓓ Ⓔ
25. Ⓐ Ⓑ Ⓒ Ⓓ Ⓔ
26. Ⓐ Ⓑ Ⓒ Ⓓ Ⓔ
27. Ⓐ Ⓑ Ⓒ Ⓓ Ⓔ
28. Ⓐ Ⓑ Ⓒ Ⓓ Ⓔ
29. Ⓐ Ⓑ Ⓒ Ⓓ Ⓔ
30. Ⓐ Ⓑ Ⓒ Ⓓ Ⓔ

Section 1 continued:

10. Ⓐ Ⓑ Ⓒ Ⓓ Ⓔ
11. Ⓐ Ⓑ Ⓒ Ⓓ Ⓔ
12. Ⓐ Ⓑ Ⓒ Ⓓ Ⓔ
13. Ⓐ Ⓑ Ⓒ Ⓓ Ⓔ
14. Ⓐ Ⓑ Ⓒ Ⓓ Ⓔ
15. Ⓐ Ⓑ Ⓒ Ⓓ Ⓔ
16. Ⓐ Ⓑ Ⓒ Ⓓ Ⓔ
17. Ⓐ Ⓑ Ⓒ Ⓓ Ⓔ
18. Ⓐ Ⓑ Ⓒ Ⓓ Ⓔ
19. Ⓐ Ⓑ Ⓒ Ⓓ Ⓔ
20. Ⓐ Ⓑ Ⓒ Ⓓ Ⓔ
21. Ⓐ Ⓑ Ⓒ Ⓓ Ⓔ
22. Ⓐ Ⓑ Ⓒ Ⓓ Ⓔ
23. Ⓐ Ⓑ Ⓒ Ⓓ Ⓔ
24. Ⓐ Ⓑ Ⓒ Ⓓ Ⓔ
25. Ⓐ Ⓑ Ⓒ Ⓓ Ⓔ

25. Ⓐ Ⓑ Ⓒ Ⓓ Ⓔ
26. Ⓐ Ⓑ Ⓒ Ⓓ Ⓔ
27. Ⓐ Ⓑ Ⓒ Ⓓ Ⓔ
28. Ⓐ Ⓑ Ⓒ Ⓓ Ⓔ
29. Ⓐ Ⓑ Ⓒ Ⓓ Ⓔ
30. Ⓐ Ⓑ Ⓒ Ⓓ Ⓔ
31. Ⓐ Ⓑ Ⓒ Ⓓ Ⓔ
32. Ⓐ Ⓑ Ⓒ Ⓓ Ⓔ
33. Ⓐ Ⓑ Ⓒ Ⓓ Ⓔ
34. Ⓐ Ⓑ Ⓒ Ⓓ Ⓔ
35. Ⓐ Ⓑ Ⓒ Ⓓ Ⓔ

NTE CORE BATTERY–Test 1
TEST OF GENERAL KNOWLEDGE
Section 1: Social Studies

TIME: 30 Minutes
30 Questions

DIRECTIONS: Each of the following questions and incomplete statements is followed by five answer choices. Select the choice which best answers each question.

President McKinley (the tailor) measures Uncle Sam for a new suit to fit the fattening results of his imperial appetite.

Puck, XLVIII, September 5, 1900, pp. 7-8.

1. The cartoon above refers to the results of which war?
    (A) War of 1812   (D) World War I
    (B) Civil War   (E) World War II
    (C) Spanish-American War

2. The study of interest groups, parties and constitutions would generally be included under the subject matter of

(A) political science.   (D) geography.

(B) economics.   (E) anthropology.

(C) sociology.

Reprinted by permission of Tribune Media Services.

3. What is the most likely conclusion the artist wants us to derive from the cartoon above?

(A) The antique store is open for business

(B) Americans love their old furniture

(C) Antique shops are often found in rural areas

(D) At some time ago, gasoline prices were low

(E) One person's junk is another's treasure

4. The primary objective of social scientists is to

(A) make humans happier.

(B) alter society.

(C) understand society and suggest alternatives to reach social goals.

(D) determine what social goals should be.

(E) find the origin of life.

5. The study of how the goods and services we want get produced, and how they are distributed among us is called

(A) history.   (D) geography.

(B) economics.   (E) sociology.

(C) political science.

6. Which of the following terms includes all of the others?
   (A) Capital goods
   (D) Workers
   (B) Natural resources
   (E) Entrepreneurs
   (C) Factors of production

THE UNITED STATES MUST NOT BECOME A "PITIFUL HELPLESS GIANT." – PRES. NIXON

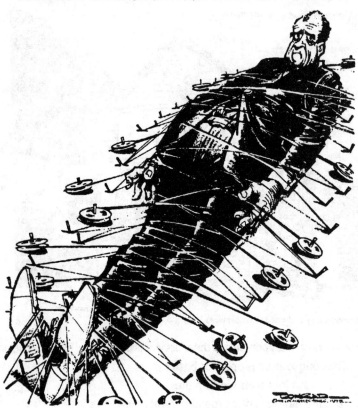

"Pitiful Helpless Giant" by Paul Conrad.
Copyright, 1973, Los Angeles Times.
Reprinted by permission.

7. In the cartoon above, what analogy does the artist draw upon?
   (A) *Giants of the Earth*
   (D) *Animal Farm*
   (B) *Gulliver's Travels*
   (E) *Brave New World*
   (C) *Jack and the Beanstalk*

8. Reproduction of the human species, physical care of the offspring, and providing affection and companionship are functions of which social institution?
   (A) Economy
   (D) Family
   (B) Government
   (E) Education
   (C) Religion

9. Which one of the following rarely adds much toward bringing about social change?

(A)   New ideas and ideologies   (D)   Established religious bodies
(B)   Climatic changes   (E)   Culture diffusion
(C)   Collective group action

10.   The five pillars of Islam do not include
      (A)   giving alms to the needy.
      (B)   performing set rituals of prayer five times daily. ✓
      (C)   giving to the Mosque each year the value of a goat.
      (D)   a pilgrimage to the Kaaba stone at Mecca. ✓
      (E)   the fast during Ramadan. ✓

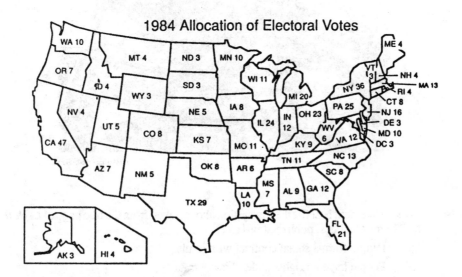

1984 Allocation of Electoral Votes

11.   The map above shows the 1984 allocation of electoral votes. What is the basis for the electoral vote?
      (A)   Number of representatives and senators
      (B)   Date of state's admission to the union
      (C)   Location of the state
      (D)   Tax contributions to the federal treasury
      (E)   The amount of revenue a state grosses per year

12.   Which of the following is not a problem faced by Puerto Ricans?
      (A)   Language difficulties   (D)   Lack of U.S. citizenship
      (B)   Lack of education   (E)   Lack of marketable skills
      (C)   Discrimination

13.   Which of the following was not one of the actions of the British government that the American colonies resented in the time preceding the Revolutionary War?
      (A)   The ban against trade with the French and Spanish West Indies
      (B)   Drafting troops for fighting in Europe

(C)   Enlist the colonists to support British troops in the colonies

(D)   The Stamp Act

(E)   The Townshend Revenue Act, including the duty on tea

The Granger Collection

14.   Which statement best fits the illustration above, taken from the title page of *Leviathan* by Thomas Hobbes, published in 1651?

    (A)   People form a social contract with a ruler

    (B)   People have no rights under this contract

    (C)   Symbols of power are relatively unimportant

    (D)   Anarchy results when the ruler is powerful

    (E)   A monarch's power does not depend on the people

15.   Which invention predated the others?

    (A)   Edison develops the electric light bulb

    (B)   Bell introduces the telephone

    (C)   Barbed wire for fences is first manufactured

    (D)   Whitney invents the cotton gin

    (E)   McCormick invents the reaper

16.   A company planning to invest in a foreign country would be deterred most by

    (A)   a large population.   (D)   low life expectancy.

    (B)   low national income.   (E)   low military expenditure per capita.

    (C)   unstable government.

17. Locate the country in which apartheid is the official government policy.

    (A) 1   (D) 4

    (B) 2   (E) 5

    (C) 3

18. Select the most appropriate time period for the occurrence of the American Civil War.

    (A) 1700-1750   (D) 1850-1900

    (B) 1750-1800   (E) 1900-1950

    (C) 1800-1850

19. Which one of the following statements is most correct about people who live in similar habitats, but who are separated by a great distance?

    (A) Their cultures are likely to be almost identical.

    (B) They are always similar in their social characteristics.

    (C) They may have some culture traits that are alike.

    (D) They usually speak languages that are similar.

    (E) They satisfy their economic wants in the same ways.

20. The tools, means and methods through which we interact with our environment is a definition of

    (A) technology.   (D) mass production.

    (B) television sets.   (E) automobiles.

    (C) computer software.

21. Which of the following fostered industrialization in the United States?

    (A) Slow growth of the domestic market

(B) Distant foreign markets

(C) Few raw materials

(D) Surplus of labor

(E) Lower wages for workers than in Europe

22. As a particular resource becomes scarcer, one can expect that
   (A) its price will rise.
   (B) use of the resource will increase.
   (C) exploration for the resource will diminish.
   (D) efforts will be made to find substitutes.
   (E) Both (A) and (D).

23. Demography is concerned with
   (A) the population in a geographical location
   (B) causes of population growth and decline
   (C) the distribution of population
   (D) All of the above.
   (E) Only (A) and (C).

24. According to Thomas Malthus, which of the following were "positive" checks on population growth?
   (A) War   (D) Voluntary sterilization
   (B) Disease   (E) Only (A) and (B).
   (C) Contraception devices

25. In the United States from about 1800, the long, almost uninterrupted decline in the birth rate resulted from
   (A) social and economic forces that prompted small families.
   (B) development of modern methods of birth control.
   (C) religious forces promoting the nuclear family.
   (D) government restrictions limiting family size.
   (E) Both (A) and (B).

26. Which of the following cities is expected to be the most populous in the year 2000?
   (A) Mexico City   (D) Calcutta
   (B) Cairo   (E) New York
   (C) Tokyo

27. A family which consists of a husband and wife and their dependent children is considered
   (A) extended.   (D) bigamous.
   (B) monogamous.   (E) Only (B) and (C).
   (C) nuclear.

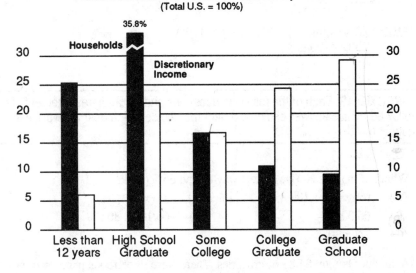

Education of Household Head

Percent Distribution of Households and Discretionary Income
(Total U.S. = 100%)

Educational Attainment

28. According to the graph, "Education of Household Head," which one of the following statements is true?

   (A) Households with some college education have about an equal percentage of discretionary income

   (B) The more education, the less discretionary income

   (C) The less education, the more discretionary income

   (D) There is no correlation between education and discretionary income

   (E) None of the above.

29. The advantage of the corporation form of business organization is that

   (A) it almost never operates at a loss.

   (B) ownership can be easily transferred.

   (C) it is subject to special government regulations.

   (D) it can be controlled by insiders.

   (E) Only (B) and (D).

30. Which of the following is the correct chronological order for the events in history listed below?

   I. The Social Security Act is passed

   II. The Congress of Industrial Organizations is formed

   III. The Great Depression starts with the stock market crash

   IV. Franklin D. Roosevelt is elected President

   (A) III, II, I, IV.   (D) II, III, IV, I.

   (B) IV, III, I, II.   (E) I, IV, III, II.

   (C) III, IV, I, II.

Section 2: Mathematics

TIME: 30 Minutes
25 Questions

DIRECTIONS: Each of the following questions and incomplete statements is followed by five answer choices. Select the choice which best answers each question.

---

1. Which of these is NOT a correct way to find 66% of 30?
   - (A) (66 x 30) ÷ 100
   - (B) 66.0 x 30
   - (C) 2/3 x 30
   - (D) .66 x 30
   - (E) 66/100 x 30

2. A shopper bought $4.83 of groceries. There were three foods purchased: potatoes, tomatoes, and green beans. The shopper purchased 2 lbs. of potatoes and 3 lbs. of tomatoes. What data do you need to determine cost per lb. of the green beans?
   - (A) Potatoes are 49¢/lb. and 2 lbs. green beans purchased.
   - (B) Tomatoes are 79¢/lb. and 2 lbs. green beans purchased.
   - (C) The change was 17¢ and 2 lbs. green beans purchased.
   - (D) $4.83; potatoes cost/lb; tomatoes cost/lb.
   - (E) Tomatoes cost/lb, potatoes cost/lb, number of lbs. of green beans, and grocery bill total.

3. Evaluate this expression:

   $$2X^2 - 9/Y \text{ When X is 6 and Y is 3.}$$

   - (A) 9
   - (B) 69
   - (C) 141
   - (D) 63
   - (E) 3

4. In the figure below, what is the area of the shaded region?

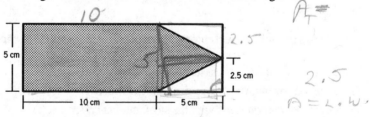

   - (A) 75 cm²
   - (B) 30 cm
   - (C) 40 cm
   - (D) 35 cm
   - (E) 62.5 cm²

5. Examine the elementary student's work below. Analyze what the error pattern is that the student is making. If the student worked the problem 88 plus 39, what incorrect answer would the student give (assuming the use of the error pattern exhibited below)?

74	35	67	56
+ 56	+ 92	+ 18	+ 97
1210	127	715	1413

(A)   127
(B)   131
(C)   51

(D)   117
(E)   1117

6. The needle on the dial points most nearly to which reading?

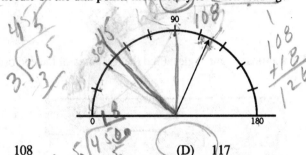

(A)   108
(B)   128
(C)   114

(D)   117
(E)   124

7. How many ten thousands are there in one million?

(A)   100
(B)   10
(C)   1,000

(D)   10,000
(E)   100,000

8. An owner of 2 twin siamese cats knows the following data:
    I.   Cost of a can of cat food
    II.   Volume of a can of cat food
    III.   Number of cans of cat food eaten each day by one cat
    IV.   The weight of the cat food in one can

Which of these data above can be used to determine the cost of cat food for 7 days for the 2 cats?

(A)   I and II only.
(B)   I and III only.
(C)   I and IV only.

(D)   III and IV only.
(E)   II, III and IV.

9. What are the coordinates of point W?

(A) (3,-3) (D) (-3,3)

(B) (0.3) (E) (2.5, -3.5)

(C) (3,0)

10. All angles in the figure are right angles. Find the total area of the enclosed region.

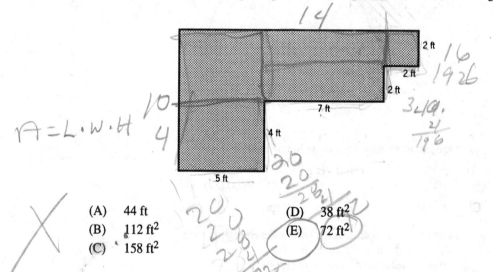

(A) 44 ft

(B) 112 ft²

(C) 158 ft²

(D) 38 ft²

(E) 72 ft²

11. The diagram below shows a path for electric flow. As the electrically charged particle flow moves through one complete circuit, it would NOT have to go through

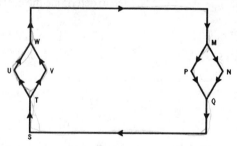

(A) V to get to W. (D) T to get to S.

(B) W to get to M. (E) Q to get to T.

(C) Q to get to T.

12. In each of the following drawings below, the solid bar represents $300,000. In which case does the striped bar most likely represent $750,000?

(A)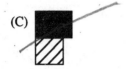

(B)

(C)

(D)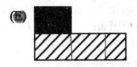

(E)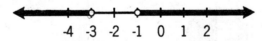

13. Which of the following is NOT equivalent to 7/8?

(A) 3/4   (D) 28/32
(B) 14/16   (E) 21/24
(C) 35/40

14. A homeowner is ordering carpet for the living room. What essential data does he need to estimate the cost of carpeting the room?

(A) Carpet cost per square yard
(B) Room dimensions (length & width)
(C) Sale savings at local stores for carpet
(D) (A) and (B).
(E) (C) and time payment plans.

15. Which sentence below describes the graph?

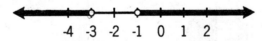

-4 -3 -2 -1 0 1 2

(A) X<-3 and X>-1   (D) X≤-3 or X≥-1
(B) -3< X<-1   (E) None of these.
(C) X<-3 or X>-1

16. Which of the following metric units would be the most appropriate unit with which to measure the length of a new pencil?

(A) Kilometer   (D) Dekameter
(B) Kectometer   (E) Centimeter
(C) Keter

17. In the figure below, all sides are at right angles. What is the perimeter of the enclosed area?

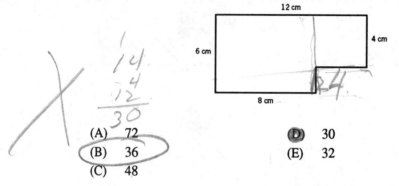

(A) 72

(B) 36

(C) 48

(D) 30

(E) 32

18. If a chair and couch cost a total of M dollars and the chair alone costs P dollars, which expression represents how much the couch alone costs?

(A) (M - P) dollars

(B) (P + M) dollars

(C) (P - M) dollars

(D) (M + P) dollars

(E) None of these.

19. A householder wants to represent monthly expenses on a circle graph. Rent (R) is about 32% of the monthly budget. Which circle graph best represents the rental expenses?

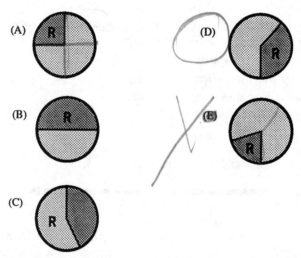

20. In the number below, which digit is in the hundred thousands place?

$$1825609.473$$

(A) 8

(B) 5

(C) 2

(D) 1

(E) 3

21. A stereo costs $350. The store reduces the price by $70. Which is the correct way to find what part the reduction is of the original price?

    (A)   70 x 350

    (B)   .70 x 350

    (C)   350 ÷ 70

    (D)   350 - 70

    (E)   70 ÷ 350

22. The ratio of faculty to students is 1 to 12 at a college. If the college has 1,500 students, how many faculty are there?

    (A)   100

    (B)   110

    (C)   125

    (D)   130

    (E)   145

23. Jill makes 48% of her first shots in basketball. She makes 60% of her second shots when she has made her first shot. What is the probability that Jill will make her first two shots?

    (A)   48%

    (B)   60%

    (C)   54%

    (D)   80%

    (E)   28.8%

    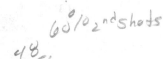

24. Jack paced the width of a field in 36 strides. John paced the width in 40 strides. Assuming that both boys counted correctly and took uniform strides, which statement must be true?

    (A)   Jack's stride must be smaller than John's stride.

    (B)   John has a longer stride than Jack.

    (C)   John's stride is 4 feet longer that Jack's.

    (D)   Jack has larger feet that John.

    (E)   Jack has a longer stride than John.

25. The graph below represents what numerical interval?

    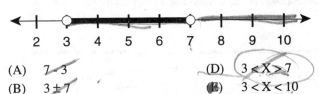

    (A)   7-3

    (B)   3 ± 7

    (C)   3 ½ to 6 ½

    (D)   3 < X > 7

    (E)   3 < X < 10

    $$3 < X < 7$$

Section 3: Literature and Fine Arts

TIME: 30 Minutes
35 Questions

DIRECTIONS: Each of the following questions and incomplete statements is followed by five answer choices. Select the choice which best answers each question.

my fate. Re-mem-ber me, but ah! _____ for-get my_ fate!

1. Which of the following is true about the above music?

   (A) It is written in three flats.
   (B) The time signature is obvious.
   (C) There is a repetitive bass pattern.
   (D) The bass clef rests for three measures in this segment.
   (E) It is written for two voices.

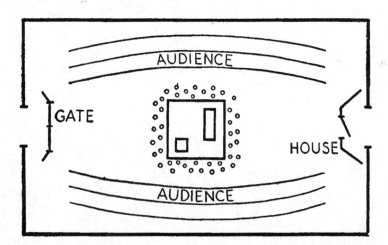

2. The picture on the previous page is an example of which of the following types of staging?

    (A) Thrust
    (B) Proscenium
    (C) Theatre-in-the-Round
    (D) Central
    (E) Open

Questions 3-5 refer to the following poem.

> My mistress' eyes are nothing like the sun;
> Coral is far more red than her lips' red;
> If snow be white, why then her breasts are dun;
> If hairs be wires, black wires grow on her head.
> I have seen roses damasked, red and white,
> But no such roses see I in her cheeks;
> And in some perfumes is there more delight
> Than in the breath that from my mistress reeks.
> I love to hear her speak, yet well I know
> That music hath a far more pleasing sound;
> I grant I never saw a goddess go;
> My mistress, when she walks treads on the ground.
> And yet, by heaven, I think my love as rare
> As any she belied with false compare.

3. This poem is different from other sonnets in that

    (A) it is Shakespearean.
    (B) it is Italian.
    (C) it describes the appearance of a beloved woman.
    (D) it does not describe the woman as beautiful.
    (E) it does not follow the proper sonnet conventions.

4. The last two lines of the poem

    (A) reaffirm the argument held throughout the poem.
    (B) start a new topic.
    (C) refute the argument held throughout the poem.
    (D) are a continuation of the ideas introduced in the poem.
    (E) use extensive metaphors.

5. The poem can best be described as

    (A) witty and satirical.
    (B) intense.
    (C) sarcastic.
    (D) brooding.
    (E) sentimental.

6.   From which of the following structures is the above picture taken?

(A)   Notre Dame Cathedral   (D)   Versailles Palace

(B)   The Parthenon   (E)   The Taj Mahal

(C)   The Sistine Chapel

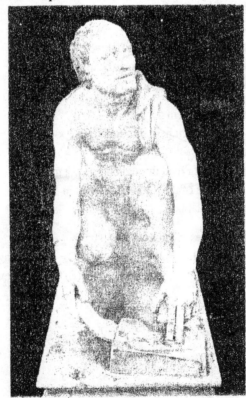

Galleria degli Ufizi, Florena.

7. The figure pictured on the previous page was most likely which of the following?

    (A)   A slave or menial servant   (D)   A farmer

    (B)   A knight's page   (E)   A carpenter's apprentice

    (C)   A religious novice

> Whilom ther was dwellynge at Oxenford
> A riche gnof, that gestes heeld to bord,
> And of his craft he was a carpenter.
> With hym ther was dwellynge a povre scoler.

8. What can we assume about this passage?

    (A)   It is probably a translation of some other language into English.

    (B)   It is written in Middle English.

    (C)   It is romantic in style.

    (D)   It is written in Elizabethan English.

    (E)   The speaker is a foreigner.

Tomb of Nakht, Thebes.

9. All of the following can be construed from the print above EXCEPT

    (A)   The three figures portrayed are musicians.

    (B)   The art work conveys a strong sense of depth.

    (C)   The drawing is representative of Egyptian tomb paintings .

    (D)   The artist was not concerned with modeling the figures in three dimensions.

    (E)   The artist employed a standardized figure type.

10. Which of the following best describes the statue pictured above?

    (A)   Comic   (D)   Imposing

    (B)   Tragic   (E)   Introspective

    (C)   Ornate

Questions 11-13 refer to the following passages.

    (A)   That's my last duchess painted on the wall,

           Looking as if she were alive. I call

           That piece a wonder, now: Fra Pandolf's hands

           Worked busily a day, and there she stands.

    (B)   <u>Nov. 24</u>. A rainy morning. We were all well except that my head ached a little and I took my breakfast in bed. I read a little of Chaucer, prepared the goose for dinner, and then we all walked out. I was obliged to return for my fur tippet and Spenser it was so cold.

    (C)   There were times in early autumn--in September--when the greater circuses would come to town--the Ringling Brothers, Robinson's, and Barnum & Baily shows, and when I was a route-boy on the morning paper, on those mornings when the circus would be coming in, I would rush madly through my route in the cool and thrilling darkness that comes before the break of day, and then I would go back home and get my brother out of bed.

(D)   This American government--what is it but a tradition, though a recent one, endeavoring to transmit itself unimpaired to posterity, but each instant losing some of its integrity? It has not the vitality and force of a single living man; for a single man can bend it to his will. It is a sort of wooden gun to the people themselves; and, if ever they should use it in earnest as a real one against each other, it will surely split.

(E)   Miniver Cheevy, born too late,
    Scratched his head and kept on thinking;
Miniver coughed, and called it fate,
    And kept on drinking.

11.   Which of the above passages creates a mood of strange excitement? *C*

12.   Which of the above passages is most likely taken from a dramatic monologue? *A*

13.   Which of the above passages uses a metaphor to make a point? *D*

Rijk Museum, Amsterdam.

14.   From this picture, one can assume that the music being played and sung is
    (A)   an opera.
    (B)   a sad, serious melody.
    (C)   a dirge.
    (D)   a light, boisterous tune.
    (E)   a hymn.

L'Unite d'habitation, Marseilles.

15. The designer of the building pictured above seems to have been concerned with which of the following?

(A) The amount of light available to the building's inhabitants

(B) Building a modern skyscraper

(C) Cylindrical shapes

(D) Hidden staircases

(E) Blending the building into its setting

16. King: Take thy fair hour, Laertes; time be thine,

      And thy best graces spend it at thy will!

      But now, my cousin Hamlet, and my son,—

Hamlet: (*Aside*) A little more than kin, and less than kind.

In the above lines, what does the stage direction "(*Aside*)" mean?

(A) The actor steps aside to make room for other action on stage.

(B) The actor directly addresses only one particular actor on stage.

(C) The actor directly addresses the audience, while out of hearing of the other actors.

(D) The previous speaker steps aside to make room for this actor.

(E) The actor speaks to someone off stage.

17. The building pictured above suggests which of the following?

(A) Undulating waves of water   (D) A massive mountain

(B) A congested city street   (E) A tree with spreading branches

(C) A chambered nautilus

Questions 18-20 refer to the following passage.

(A) Fair is foul and foul is fair.
Hover through the fog and filthy air.

(B) Weary of myself, and sick of asking
What I am, and what I ought to be,
At this vessel's prow I stand, which bears me
Forward, forward o'er the starlit sea.

And a look of passionate desire
O'er the sea and to the stars I send:
"Ye who from my childhood up have calmed me,
Calm me, ah, compose me to the end!

(C) There were a king with a large jaw and a queen with a plain face, on the throne
of England; there were a king with a large jaw and a queen with a fair face on
the throne of France. In both countries it was clearer than crystal to the lords of
the state preserves of loaves and fishes, that things were in general settled for
ever.

(D) no thats no way for him he has no manners nor no refinement nor no nothing
in his nature slapping us behind like that on my bottom because I didnt call him
Hugh the ignoramus doesnt know poetry from a cabbage thats what you get for
not keeping them in their proper place
Ulysses by James Joyce. Copyright © 1984 by the Trustees of the Estate of James Joyce. Reprinted
with permission of Penguin Books, USA, Inc.

93

(E)   The worthy woman bustled off, and I crouched nearer the fire; my head felt hot, and the rest of me chill; moreover I was excited, almost to a pitch of foolishness, through 1my nerves and brain. This caused me to feel, not uncomfortable, but rather fearful (as I am still) of serious effects from the incidents of today and yesterday.

18.   Which passage describes a person seeking personal insight and solace?

19.   Which passage uses the "stream of consciousness" technique to mimic the workings of the human mind?

20.   Which passage contains examples of alliteration?

21.   The Director of Companies was our captain and our host. We four affectionately watched his back as he stood in the bows looking to seaward. On the whole river there was nothing that looked half so nautical. He resembled a pilot, which to a seaman is trustworthiness personified.

The above is an example of

(A)   prose.   (D)   a non sequitur.

(B)   unrhymed iambic pentameter.   (E)   free verse.

(C)   an elegy.

22.   A group of townspeople stood on the station siding of a little Kansas town, awaiting the coming of the night train, which was already twenty minutes overdue. The snow had fallen thick over everything; in the pale starlight the line of bluffs across the wide, white meadows south of the town made soft, smoke-colored curves against the sky.

This passage is most likely taken from which of the following?

(A)   The conclusion of a short story   (D)   The dénouement of a short story

(B)   The beginning of a short story   (E)   None of these.

(C)   The climax of a short story

(A)

(B)

(C)

(D)

(E)

23. Which of the examples pictured does not share cultural heritage with the others?

24. In which example does the composition set up a circular motion within the picture's borders?

25. Which example tends most strongly to represent human features as a composite of stylized, abstracted forms?

The curfew tolls the knell of parting day,
  The lowing herd wind slowly o'er the lea,
The plowman homeward plods his weary way,
  And leaves the world to darkness and to me.

26. Which of the following sounds is NOT referred to in the above lines?
    (A) Bells
    (B) Wind through the trees
    (C) Footsteps
    (D) Cows
    (E) A man walking

We think our fathers fools, so wise we grow;
Our wiser sons, no doubt, will think us so.

27. Which is the best paraphrase of the above lines?
    (A) As we grow older, we think our fathers wiser.
    (B) As we grow older, we think our fathers are fools, and our sons will probably think the same of us.
    (C) Sons always believe their fathers are fools, but fathers always think their sons are wise.
    (D) Fathers always think they are smarter than their sons.
    (E) Fathers and sons are always trying to prove that they are wiser than each other.

Chartres Cathedral.

28.   Which of the following best identifies the medium of the work above?

(A)   Oil painting on canvas   (D)   Mosiac tile inlay

(B)   Stained glass window   (E)   Woven wool tapestry

(C)   Marble sculpture

> Gallants, attend, and hear a friend
> Trill forth harmonious ditty:
> Strange things I'll tell, which late befell
> In Philadelphia city.

29.   Judging from the first stanza of this poem, which of the following is true?

(A)   The poem has a serious tone.

(B)   The poem has no predictable rhyme scheme.

(C)   The poem may be satirical or humorous.

(D)   The rhyme scheme will be a-b-a-b.

(E)   The rhyme scheme will be a-a-b-b.

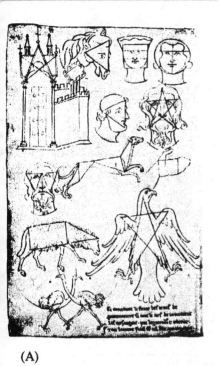

(A)

Questions 30 through 32
are based on the
following works of art

(B)

(C)

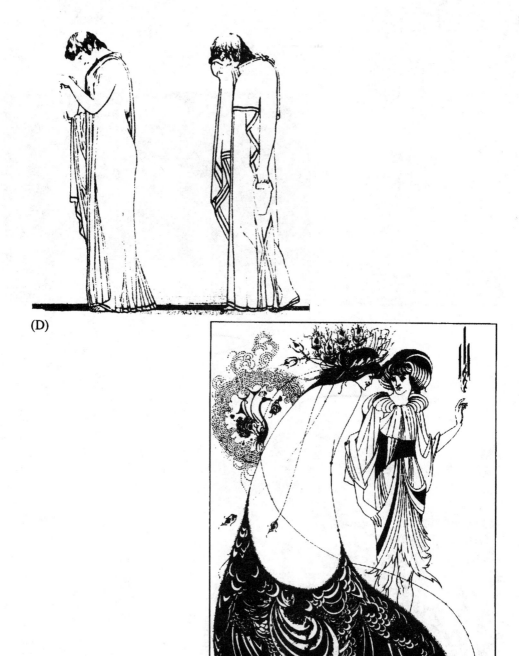

(D)

(E)

30.   * Which example depends most heavily on the decorative contrasts of black and white?

31. Which example seems to use coarse texture to emphasize an expressive effect?

32. In which example do the contents seem most like unrelated, documentary notations

Musée Barbier-Muller, Geneva

33. The mask above represents which of the following cultural traditions?
   (A) African
   (B) Greek
   (C) Roman
   (D) Dutch
   (E) Persian

'Twas on a lofty vase's side,
Where China's gayest art had dyed
The azure flowers, that blow;
Demurest of the tabby kind,
The pensive Selima reclined,
Gazed on the lake below.

Her conscious tail her joy declared;
The fair round face, the snowy beard,
The velvet of her paws,
Her coat, that with the tortoise vies,
Her ears of jet, and emerald eyes,
She saw; and purred applause.

101

34. What is the subject of the stanzas on the previous page?
    (A) A snake
    (B) A turtle swimming in a lake
    (C) A vase
    (D) A dog watching a cat
    (E) A cat

35. The shore was fledged with palm trees. These stood or leaned or reclined against the light and their green feathers were a hundred feet up in the air. The ground beneath them was a bank covered with coarse grass, torn everywhere by the upheavals of fallen trees, scattered with decaying coconuts and palm saplings. Behind this was the darkness of the forest proper...
    The Lord of the Flies by William Golding. Copyright © 1954 by William Golding. Reprinted with permission of Putnam Publishing Group.

    The above passage can best be described as
    (A) surrealistic.
    (B) expressionistic.
    (C) realistic.
    (D) romantic.
    (E) Gothic.

Section 4: Science

TIME: 30 Minutes
30 Questions

DIRECTIONS: Each of the following questions and incomplete statements is followed by five answer choices. Select the choice which best answers each question.

1. Which of the following is the dominant source of all or nearly all of the Earth's energy?

   (A) Plants

   (B) Animals

   (C) Coal

   (D) Oil

   (E) The Sun

2. Which of the following is true?

   (A) Energy may be converted from one form to another.

   (B) Energy may not be converted from one form to another.

   (C) The energy that a moving object possesses because of its motion is correctly known as potential energy.

   (D) Objects which possess energy because of their position are said to have kinetic energy.

   (E) Most scientists readily agree that energy from nuclear fission will be the chief source of energy by the year 2000.

3. Which of the following situations might cause harm to an embryo?

   (A) The father is RH-positive; the mother, RH-negative.

   (B) The mother had German Measles during the first trimester of pregnancy.

   (C) The father is RH-negative; the mother, RH-positive.

   (D) (A) and (B) only.

   (E) (B) and (C) only.

4. Heavy infections of *Trichinella* in people may cause a disease called trichinosis; such a situation may best be described as which of the following?

   (A) Parasitism

   (B) Mutualism

   (C) Commercialism

   (D) Benevolent

   (E) Benign

5. Which of the following is the main difference between an organic and an inorganic compound?

   (A) The former is a living compound, while the latter is a nonliving compound.

   (B) There are many more of the latter than of the former.

   (C) The latter can be synthesized only by living organisms.

   (D) The latter can be synthesized only by nonliving organisms.

   (E) The former are those that contain carbon.

6. On the periodic table the symbol Pb represents which of the following?
   (A) Iron
   (B) Phosphorus
   (C) Lead
   (D) Plutonium
   (E) Potassium

7. Which of the metric terms is closest to the measurement of a new piece of chalk?
   (A) Meter
   (B) Liter
   (C) Gram
   (D) Decimeter
   (E) Kilometer

8. Which of the following is a genetic disorder?
   (A) Down's Syndrome (Mongolism)
   (B) Syphilis
   (C) Malaria
   (D) Leukemia
   (E) Emphysema

9. A litmus test conducted on HCL would have which of the following results?
   (A) There is no effect on the color of the litmus paper.
   (B) The litmus paper disintegrates.
   (C) The litmus paper turns blue.
   (D) The litmus paper turns red.
   (E) The carbonation causes oxygen bubbles to rise to the top.

10. Water is which of the following?
    (A) A base
    (B) An acid
    (C) A compound
    (D) All of the above.
    (E) None of the above.

11. When is the Earth closest to the Sun?
    (A) During the summer
    (B) During the fall
    (C) During the winter
    (D) During the spring
    (E) During the spring and summer

12. What causes day and night?
    (A) Tilt of the Earth on its axis.
    (B) Rotation of the Earth about the Sun.
    (C) Revolution of the Earth about the Sun.
    (D) Rotation of the Sun about the Earth.
    (E) Revolution of the Sun about the Earth.

13. Scurvy is the result of which of the following?
    (A) Insufficient sunshine
    (B) Insufficient calcium
    (C) Insufficient Vitamin C
    (D) Insufficient Vitamin B
    (E) A viral infection

14. Which statement about cells, the basic building blocks of everything that is living, is true?

    (A)   Animals, unlike plants, have cells.

    (B)   Plant cells, unlike animal cells, have a nonliving cell wall.

    (C)   Chlorophyll is found only in the cells of plants.

    (D)   Animal cells, unlike plant cells, contain the DNA molecule used to carry genetic information.

    (E)   The cells of fungi are rich in chlorophyll, which aid in their manufacture of food.

15. Which of the following facts about elements is true?

    (A)   Elements are found in nature; nonelements are made by scientists.

    (B)   Elements are made by scientists; nonelements are found in nature.

    (C)   Some elements are found in nature, but others are made by scientists.

    (D)   There are 107 presently-known atoms, so there are 214 identified elements.

    (E)   Steel, brass, and water are common elements.

16. Biologists use a classification scheme to classify living things; which of the following schemes is correctly ordered?

    (A)   Kingdom, class, order, phylum, family, species, genus.

    (B)   Kingdom, order, class, family, phylum, species, genus.

    (C)   Genus, species, family, order, class, phylum, kingdom.

    (D)   Kingdom, phylum, class, order, family, genus, species.

    (E)   Genus, species, family, order, phylum, class, kingdom.

17. Which of the following resources are renewable?

    (A)   Coal, oil, gas   (D)   Freshwater, coal, vegetation

    (B)   Metals, minerals, coal   (E)   Oil, soil, vegetation

    (C)   Soil, vegetation, animals

18. Almost all interactions of matter result from the operation of which of the forces listed below?

    (A)   Gravitational force   (D)   All of the above.

    (B)   Electromagnetic force   (E)   None of the above.

    (C)   Nuclear force

19. Order the following into the steps in the scientific method.

    I.   Form the hypothesis.   IV.   Collect the data.

    II.   State the problem.   V.   Communicate the findings.

    III.   Test the hypothesis.

    (A)   I, II, III, IV, V.   (D)   II, I, III, IV, V.

    (B)   I, II, III, V, IV.   (E)   II, IV, I, III, V.

    (C)   II, III, IV, V, I.

20. Which of the following statements is incorrect?
    (A) Data is the information the scientist collects.
    (B) An hypothesis is an explanation which will account for the interrelations found in the data.
    (C) A principle or law is an accepted theory.
    (D) If the summary of relationships pertains to more than a very narrow field, and if the explanation for the correlated data is detailed, it may constitute an outline so well-supported as to be termed a theory.
    (E) A single valid fact that completely contradicts a theory is not sufficient to overthrow the theory.

21. Which of the following is/are characteristics of mammals?
    I.   Body hair
    II.   Young born alive
    III. Young fed on milk
    IV.   Warm blooded
    V.   Spinal cord

    (A) All of the above.
    (B) I, II, III, IV only.
    (C) I, II, III, V only.
    (D) I, III, IV, V only.
    (E) None of the above.

22. Which of the following lists contains an organ which is NOT a part of the digestive system?
    (A) Pancreas, small intestine, large intestine
    (B) Gall bladder, stomach, rectum
    (C) Esophagus, stomach, small intestine
    (D) Spleen, stomach, small intestine
    (E) Mouth, liver, salivary glands

23. Which of the following contains an item that is NOT a function of all living things?
    I.   Food getting, transporting
    II.   Assimilating, respirating
    III. Responding to environmental stimuli, reproducing
    IV.   Communicating, digesting
    V.   Producing food, excreting

    (A) I and IV.
    (B) II and III.
    (C) III and IV.
    (D) IV and V.
    (E) I and V

24. The rhythm of the tides on the Earth are the result of which of the following?
    I.   The gravitational pull of the moon
    II.   The rotation of the Earth
    III. The pull of the planets
    IV.   Nuclear fission
    V.   Condensation and evaporation

(A) All the above.   (D) V only.

(B) None of the above.   (E) II and V only.

(C) I and II only.

25. Which of the following is NOT a part of the molecular theory of matter?

(A) Matter is composed of exceedingly small particles called molecules.

(B) Each different kind of matter is made up of its own particular kind of molecules.

(C) Molecules are in rapid and ceaseless motion.

(D) Molecules attract each other.

(E) When molecules of water are split (perhaps with the aid of an electric current), the result is even smaller particles of the water.

26. Most scientists would agree with all the following statements about the routine use of pesticides EXCEPT which one?

(A) As a result of the widespread use of DDT, a new type of housefly emerged.

(B) Pesticides tend to become progressively less effective as the organisms become immune.

(C) Chemical control of pests should be used routinely, since it may result in the evolution of exciting new types of organisms.

(D) Application of chemical substances endanger both foes and friends (like honeybees) so routine use of chemicals seems inadvisable.

(E) A pesticide may kill not only the intended insects but also the birds which feed on them.

27. All these statements illustrate recycling in nature EXCEPT which one?

(A) Carbon dioxide (a waste from respiration) is recycled by plants as a raw material for food production.

(B) Nitrogen found in plant and animal waste may be reclaimed by the soil and used by plants in manufacturing protein.

(C) Tin-coated steel cans rust away and disappear into the environment.

(D) Aluminum cans are nonbiodegradable.

(E) Some bacteria that live deep in marshes, mud, and soil can live and grow in the absence of oxygen; these microbes (anaerobic bacteria) decompose organic matter.

28. To determine the amount of heat energy needed to raise the temperature of 50 grams of water at 50°C to water at 90°C, one must use which of the following factors?

I. The heat needed to melt a gram of ice.

II. The heat needed to change a gram of water to gas.

III. The heat needed to raise by 1° the temperature of a gram of water.

IV. The heat needed to raise by 1° the temperature of a gram of ice.

(A) I and III only.   (D) III only.

(B) II and IV only.   (E) I only.

(C) I, II, and III only.

29. Which of the following is FALSE?
     (A) The apparent motion of stars each night is due to the turning of the Earth.
     (B) The apparent brightness of a star depends on several factors: distance from Earth, size, temperature.
     (C) The Milky Way is the galaxy of the universe.
     (D) The Sun is a star.
     (E) Constellations are patterns of stars.

30. Which is NOT true of protein?
     (A) All proteins are identical in their chemical makeup.
     (B) Proteins are made up of smaller units called amino acids.
     (C) A variety of protein from different sources is required in a good diet to provide the essential amino acids.
     (D) Some amino acids cannot be synthesized by humans and are known as the essential amino acids.
     (E) Proteins of animal origin have the highest nutritious value for humans.

TEST OF GENERAL KNOWLEDGE

ANSWER KEY

SECTION 1: SOCIAL STUDIES

1.	(C)	9.	(D)	17.	(A)	25.	(E)
2.	(A)	10.	(C)	18.	(D)	26.	(A)
3.	(D)	11.	(A)	19.	(C)	27.	(E)
4.	(C)	12.	(D)	20.	(A)	28.	(A)
5.	(B)	13.	(B)	21.	(B)	29.	(B)
6.	(C)	14.	(A)	22.	(E)	30.	(C)
7.	(B)	15.	(D)	23.	(D)		
8.	(D)	16.	(C)	24.	(E)		

SECTION 2: MATHEMATICS

1.	(B)	8.	(B)	15.	(C)	22.	(C)
2.	(E)	9.	(A)	16.	(E)	23.	(E)
3.	(B)	10.	(E)	17.	(B)	24.	(E)
4.	(E)	11.	(A)	18.	(A)	25.	(D)
5.	(E)	12.	(E)	19.	(D)		
6.	(D)	13.	(A)	20.	(A)		
7.	(A)	14.	(D)	21.	(E)		

SECTION 3: LITERATURE AND FINE ARTS

1.	(C)	10.	(D)	19.	(D)	28.	(B)
2.	(D)	11.	(C)	20.	(A)	29.	(C)
3.	(D)	12.	(A)	21.	(A)	30.	(E)
4.	(C)	13.	(D)	22.	(B)	31.	(B)
5.	(A)	14.	(D)	23.	(B)	32.	(A)
6.	(B)	15.	(A)	24.	(D)	33.	(A)
7.	(A)	16.	(C)	25.	(B)	34.	(E)
8.	(B)	17.	(D)	26.	(B)	35.	(C)
9.	(B)	18.	(B)	27.	(B)		

SECTION 4: SCIENCE

1.	(E)	9.	(D)	17.	(C)	25.	(E)
2.	(A)	10.	(D)	18.	(D)	26.	(C)
3.	(D)	11.	(C)	19.	(E)	27.	(D)
4.	(A)	12.	(B)	20.	(E)	28.	(D)
5.	(E)	13.	(C)	21.	(A)	29.	(C)
6.	(C)	14.	(B)	22.	(D)	30.	(A)
7.	(D)	15.	(C)	23.	(D)		
8.	(A)	16.	(D)	24.	(C)		

DETAILED EXPLANATIONS OF ANSWERS
NTE CORE BATTERY–Test 1

TEST OF GENERAL KNOWLEDGE
Section 1: Social Studies

1.   **(C)**   The question deals with the growth of the United States during President McKinley's tenure. President Madison was in office during the War of 1812. President Lincoln headed the government during the Civil War. President Wilson led the country in World War I. President F.D. Roosevelt was the leader in World War II. Thus, the correct answer is (C).

2.   **(A)**   This question calls for you to understand the subject matter included in several social sciences. The correct answer is (A). Choice (B) deals with the productive and distributive use of resources. Answers (C) and (E) are behavioral sciences. Answer (D) deals with humans' relations with the earth.

3.   **(D)**   While answers (A), (B), (C) and (E) have some measure of truth and may seem plausible, they are not the cartoonist's concern. This cartoon was created in the late 1970's and reflects the steep increase in gasoline prices which occurred when the OPEC oil cartel met and demanded higher prices for their product. The correct response is (D).

4.   **(C)**   This question helps you to understand the function social scientists play in our society. Though a by-product of their work may be answers (A) and (B), those are not primary objectives. Answer (D) is the responsibility of all citizens in a democratic society. Choice (E) is of no or little interest to social scientists. Therefore, choice (C) is the correct one.

5.   **(B)**   What are the definitions of the social sciences and history is the subject of this question. Choice (A) deals with the past. Answer (C) is the study of power and its allocation in the society. The study of humans' relations with the earth is item (D). Answer (E) deals with group behavior. So, choice (B), the "dismal science," economics, is the correct response.

6.   **(C)**   This question requires you to find the broadest term, the most inclusive term. Choice (A) refers to those goods which produce more goods. Item (B) refers to such things as raw materials, trees, coal, gold and the like. Items (D) and (E) are the people who make something using items (A) and (B). Thus, the term which includes all the others is choice (C).

7.   **(B)**   This question deals with political and literary history. A sophisticated knowledge is required to reject answers (A), (C), (D), and (E) as incorrect. The artist shows President Nixon, during the Watergate crisis, as a giant tied down by puny bits of tape. The President would not release the tapes, claiming executive privilege (the Watergate Scandal).

The analogy is to Jonathan Swift's satire, *Gulliver's Travels* (B), in which Gulliver gets tied down during his voyage to Lilliput.

8.　**(D)**　Here, the respondent is required to know the functions of several social institutions. Choice (A) deals with the production and distribution of goods and services. Item (B) is about the structure and allocation of power in the society. Choice (C) deals with philosophical questions about the origins of life and death. Item (E) is about the transmission of culture. The best response is choice (D), family.

9.　**(D)**　Items (A), (B), (C) and (E) all possess the potential for bringing about social change. Choice (D) is correct because it wants to preserve the status quo and does not seek to alter society.

10.　**(C)**　The religion of Islam was founded by Mohammed, who claimed no divinity. The sacred book of Islam is the Koran, which contains the revelations of the prophet Mohammed. This religion was influenced by Judaism and Christianity. The five pillars of Islam state the religious duties of a believer. Choice (C) is not one of those duties and thus, the correct answer.

11.　**(A)**　Since 1790, the United States counts the people living in the country at the time of the decade year. This census forms the basis for the allotment of representatives to each state. The electoral vote is derived from the total number of representatives and senators in each state, therefore item (A) is the correct answer.

12.　**(D)**　Choices (A), (B), (C), and (E) are all problems faced by Puerto Ricans who decide to live on the mainland. The correct response is choice (D), because in 1917, the Jones Act granted Puerto Ricans United States citizenship and manhood suffrage.

13.　**(B)**　The Navigation Acts listed goods that could be shipped only to England from the colonies. The Quartering Act required local civil authorities to provide quarters and supplies for British troops. The Stamp Act, which called for a tax in the form of stamps affixed to newspapers and other papers, was much hated. Choice (E), an external tax, was passed to levy duties on the colonial imports of lead, paint, paper, glass and tea. The correct response, (B), was not contemplated by the British.

14.　**(A)**　Responses (B), (C), (D), and (E) are incorrect. Hobbes wrote about the social contract between the people and the ruler, thus answer (A) is correct.

15.　**(D)**　This question in the history of technology, tests the respondent's knowledge of chronology. Choice (A) is the most recent development. Choices (B) and (C) were introduced in 1876. Choice (E) was invented in 1831. The correct response (D) was invented relatively early in the Industrial Revolution, 1814.

16.　**(C)**　Governmental stability is the greatest desiderata for a firm intending to invest abroad. If the government is unstable it may topple, causing disruption in business and possible nationalization of foreign-owned companies. Therefore, the best answer is (C).

17.　**(A)**　Answer (B) represents Egypt. Answer (C) refers to Nigeria. Answer (D) stands for Ethiopia. Choice (E) represents Morocco. The correct answer is (A), which stands for South Africa.

18. **(D)** This question requires you to place the Civil War in the correct half century. Choices (A), (B), and (C) are too early. Choice (E) is too late. Thus, the correct response is item (D), the second half of the nineteenth century.

19. **(C)** Since culture is a human construct, people who live in similar habitats do not necessarily have similar cultures. Thus, choices (A), (B), (D), and (E) are all incorrect. The most tentative response, (C), is the best answer.

20. **(A)** While aspects of choices (B), (C), (D), and (E) might be considered as tools, the best choice is (A) since it includes and encompasses the other items.

21. **(B)** At the time of the growth of industrialization in the United States, the domestic market was growing rapidly (A). America had plentiful raw materials (C) and labor was scarce (D). Wages for workers (E) were higher than in Europe. Since foreign markets were at some distance, choice (B) is correct.

22. **(E)** This question deals with the economic problem of scarcity, such as the problems associated with the resource of oil. Choices (B) and (C) are incorrect, since these actions will not solve the problem. The correct choices are both (A) and (D), thus (E) is the best possible answer.

23. **(D)** The question requires the respondent to know the content of demography, literally writing about people. Answer (E) is partially correct. Since demography deals with items (A), (B), and (C), the most precise answer is (D).

24. **(E)** Malthus's theory that population tends to outrun the means of subsistence has been influential in understanding demography. He did not write about choices (C) or (D). He included malnutrition and famine as "positive" checks on population growth. Also, he listed choices (A) and (B), thus choice (E) is the best answer.

25. **(E)** This question tests the respondent's knowledge of the causes of population trends in the U.S. Choice (C) is wrong because religious bodies may promote the nuclear family, but this does not account for the decline in the birth rate. In our country, family size is a matter of private choice, not government edict, thus making item (D) wrong. Choices (A) and (B) are both contributive to the decline of the birth rate, and so choice (E) is the best.

26. **(A)** By the year 2000, all of these cities will have increased in population. Choices (B), (C), (D), and (E) will not, however, grow as fast as choice (A), which is correct. Mexico City is expected to reach 26 million by the year 2000.

27. **(E)** An extended family (A) may include other members besides those listed, so this choice is wrong. Item (D) is incorrect because it includes more spouses than one husband and wife. Both (B) and (C) are descriptive of the family, so the best possible answer is (E).

28. **(A)** This question tests the respondent's ability to read and interpret a graph. Choices (B), (C), (D), and (E) are incorrect. The best response is choice (A), because the dark bar and the light bar are between 15% and 20%.

29. **(B)** The corporation is usually created by a charter. It is owned and controlled by shareholders indirectly. It is directly run and managed by the board of directors. In the law, the corporation is a legal person. This form of business organization has several advantages: limited liability, ease of raising capital, permanence and ease of transfer of ownership. Thus, (B) is the best answer.

30. **(C)** The Social Security Act was passed by Congress in 1935. The CIO of 1938 was based on vertical or industrial unionism, with the objective of organizing the mass production industries of the United States. The stock market crash occurred in 1929. FDR was first elected President in 1933. Thus, the correct order is choice (C).]

Section 2: Mathematics

1. **(B)** The choices illustrate various ways to express 66%; e.g., .66, 66/100, 2/3. Thus choices (C), (D), and (E) are correct. Choice (A) is correct, since percent is based on 100. You multiply the whole numbers and divide by 100 to locate the decimal point in the answer. The answer actually is not equal to 20, unless rounded off. Choice (B) is the wrong expression for 66%. Thus, the best answer is (B). Choice (B) is incorrect because 66% cannot be expressed as 66.0. Also, if you multiply 66 by 30, you obtain a very large answer, which makes no sense, since 66% is a fraction of the 30. Thus a reasonable answer must be less than 30.

2. **(E)** You multiply the cost per lb. times the number of lbs. purchased for each of the items: potatoes and tomatoes. Add these products and subtract from the $4.83. This gives the amount of money spent on green beans. Divide by 2, since 2 lbs. were purchased. Thus, all the data listed in choice (E) is what you need:

$$.49 \times 2 = .98 \text{ potatoes}$$
$$.79 \times 3 = \underline{2.37} \text{ tomatoes}$$
$$3.35$$
$$\$4.83 - 3.35 = \$1.48$$
$$\$1.48 \div 2 = \$.74/\text{lb. for green beens}$$

3. **(B)** You must substitute the appropriate values of X and Y into the expression and calculate the value of each term before subtracting the Y term from the X term.

$2X^2$ is $2(6)^2$ or $2(36)$ or 72. 9/Y is 9/3 or 3. Thus $72-3 = 69$.

Choice (B) is correct. The other choices result from incorrect sequences of performing the term evaluations.

4. **(E)** First, you should note that you want area, not perimeter. Next, you can imagine the figure divided into a rectangle 10 cm by 5 cm or 50 square centimeters of area. The triangle can be computed in several ways. The easier way is to note that the shaded triangle is one half of the square, which is 5 cm by 5 cm or 25 square centimeters. Thus, the shaded triangle is 12.5 square centimeters. The total shaded area is 50 plus 12.5, or 62.5 square centimeters. Thus Choice (E) is correct. Choice (C) would be discarded immediately, since it is not in square units of area. It is in fact the perimeter of the total rectangle (15 + 15 + 5 + 5 or 40 cm). Choice (A) is the area of the total rectangle (15cm by 5cm or 75 square cm). Choices (B) and (D) are not close to the shaded area, but rather, are closer to the perimeter of the shaded area. Choice (E) is the correct area for the shaded part of the figure, 62.5 square centimeters.

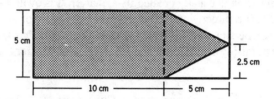

5.   **(E)**   You should note that the student is failing to carry in both the ones and tens places. Eg., 56 + 97

6 + 7 = 13 Record the 3 ones and carry the one ten.

5 + 9 = 14 plus the one ten is 15, thus, 153, not 1413.

Choice (A) is the standard answer. It is eliminated, since there is no error pattern. Choice (C) exhibits switching from addition to subtraction (9 – 8 = 1) and (8 – 3 = 5). Also, the child subtracts the top number from the bottom one on the first step. In Choice (B) the child subtracts 8 from 9, and also 3 from 8, and then adds to the 8 in the tens place. In Choice (D) the child forgets to add the one ten carried. Only Choice (E) illustrates the pattern of recording the sum and not carrying. The correct answer is (E).

6.   **(D)**   You should first count the number of spaces on the dial. There are 10 spaces. Five spaces equals 90 units. 90 divided by 5 is 18 units. Each space is worth 18 units. The needle points to, most likely, about halfway between the marks numbered 6 and 7. Thus, one half of 18, plus 6 times 18, is 117. Choice (D) is the correct reading.

7.   **(A)**   You know that ten thousand contains 4 zeros, or 10^4 in place value. One million contains 10^6, or six zeros. Thus 10^6 divided by 10^4 is 10^2 or 100. You may divide out 10,000 into one million, but that is the laborious way to solve this. Choice (A) is correct.

$$\begin{array}{cc} 100 & 100 \\ 10{,}000 \overline{)\ 1{,}000{,}000} & \text{or} \quad 1 \overline{)\ 100} \\ 10^4 \quad 10^6 & \\ \dfrac{1{,}000{,}000}{10{,}000} = \dfrac{10^6}{10^4} & 10^{6-4} = 10^2 \end{array}$$

In dividing exponents, you subtract them. Thus 10^4 becomes 10^{-4} and is subtracted from 10^6.

8.   **(B)**   You are challenged to analyze which data you would need to calculate the cost of feeding 2 cats for 7 days. If you calculate the cost for one cat for 7 days, then double the answer, you would have an approximate cost for 2 cats. Total cost is cost of a can of food, times the number of cans of food eaten each day by one cat, times 7 days. Thus choice (A) is incorrect. You do not need to know volume of food, unless maybe you wish to feed the cats according to their weight. Choices (C), (D), and (E) are incorrect because you either have unneeded information (C) IV, or incorrect data for problem solving [(D), IV and (E), II & IV]. Thus Choice (B) is correct.

9.   **(A)**   You read coordinates of a point in pairs. The X position or horizontal direction is read first. It is always the first number in the pair of numbers representing the point plotted. The Y position is read second. This is the vertical direction, either up or down on the

coordinate plane. The Y position is always the second number in the pair of numbers representing any point in the plane.

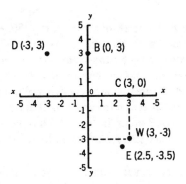

Thus Choice (A) is correct. The X position is 3 units to the right along the X axis. The Y position is -3 units downwards along the Y axis. Where the two lines intersect from +3 and -3 is where the point is located (3,-3). Choices (B), (C), (D) and (E) are plotted below for you to compare their locations in the plane with the correct answer, (A).

10. **(E)** You can construct rectangles in numerous ways to cover the total area. One approach is illustrated below for you. You have three rectangles and one square covering the shaded area. Find the areas of each figure and add the areas for the total area. Rectangles 1 and 2 are each 5 ft by 4 ft^2, yielding 20 ft^2 plus 20^2 ft, or 40 ft^2. Rectangle 3 is 7 ft by 4 ft, giving 28 ft^2. The square is 2 ft by 2 ft, or 4 square feet. The sum is 40 plus 28 plus 4, or 72 square feet. Choice (A) is the perimeter of the total figue (5+4+7+2+2+2+12+8=44 ft). Choice (B) is the area of a rectangle: 14 ft by 8 ft, or 112 square feet. This area is too large, since it ignores the stepwise figure removed, or not shaded, in the original problem. Choice (C) has no numerical connection to the area dimensions. Choice (D) is the area of rectangle 3, plus one half of either rectangle 1 or 2 (28 ft^2 plus 10 ft^2). Thus, Choice (E) is the correct answer, 72 ft^2.

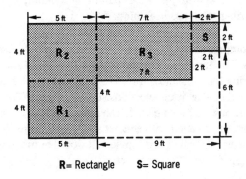

R= Rectangle   S= Square

11. **(A)** You should note that the particle flow divides at 2 points, T and M. At these points the flow has two paths to reach either point W or point Q. Thus, the correct choice is

(A). Particle flow can reach point W by going through point U, rather than V. It would have to flow through all other points listed in order to make a complete circuit or total clockwise path.

12.   **(E)**   You should note, that the ratio of $300,000 to $750,000 is one to 2.5. That is, the $750,000 is 2 and one half times larger than the $300,000 ($300,000 plus $150,000). Thus you should search for a drawing that has the lower bar 2.5 times as long as the upper bar. Note all the upper bars in each of the drawings are the same length to represent the $300,000 or the 1 in the ratio. Choices (C) and (D) are not large enough multiples of the top bar. Thus, they can be eliminated immediately. Choice (A) is a little short of 2.5, namely 2 times the top bar, and Choice (B) is a little too long, 3 times the top bar. Thus by visual estimation of lengths, the correct representation is Choice (E). It shows a ratio of 1 to 2.5.

13.   **(A)**   You express other equivalent forms of a fractional number by multiplying it by expressions which are equal to one; e.g., 2/2, 3/3, 4/4, 5/5, etc. Thus, 2/2 x 7/8 = 14/16; 3/3 x 7/8 = 21/24, etc. Accordingly, 14/16 is simply 7/8 times 2/2. Thus, 7/8 and 14/16 are the same fractional number. In choice (C) 35/40 is produced by multipling 7/8 by 5/5. Choice (D) is 7/8 multiplied by 4/4. Choice (E) is 7/8 multiplied by 3/3. Thus, all those choices name the same fractional number, 7/8. Choice (A) is not equivalent to any expression for 7/8. Choice (A) is the answer.

14.   **(D)**   You must know the area of the room (length times width). Also, you must know the cost per square yard you intend to spend. Then you calculate the cost by first changing the square footage (area of room) into square yards (divide by 27 sq. ft). Then multiply the cost per yard times the number of yards needed to get the cost of carpeting the room. Thus, Choice (D) is correct.

15.   **(C)**   You should first note that there is a gap in the graph (between -3 and -1) and that -3 and -1 are excluded from the plotted data. This is due to the open circles around the two numbers. The OR condition will be needed to describe values plotted. X will have either a value below -3 OR a value above -1, but not including those numerals. Choice (A) includes values greater than -3 right on through, including -1. Choice (B) describes the interval that is the gap or unplotted part of the number line between -3 and -1. Choice (D) is wrong because it includes the points -3 and -1 with the equals part of the symbol, $\leq$ or $\geq$. Choice (C) is the correct answer. It describes what has been plotted.

16.   **(E)**   You can compare the relative size of these metric units, just as you can compare inches, feet, and miles. The largest unit listed is the kilometer (1,000 meters). It is a unit appropriate for measuring long distances traveled. The next smaller unit is the hectometer (100 meters in a hectometer). The dekameter consists of 10 meters. Thus, it is much too large also for measurement of objects like a pencil. The meter is close to our English yard. You would not normally measure a pencil with a meter stick. That leaves only the centimeter. It is one hundredth of a meter (100 cm equals a meter). It would be most suitable. A new pencil is about 18 to 19 cm long. Choice (E) is correct.

17.   **(B)**   You want perimeter (the distance around the outside of the figure). The distance is 12 cm + 4 cm + 4 cm + 2 cm + 8 cm + 6 cm, or 36 cm. You should note that the absent indentation distances are found as follows: 8 + ? = 12 for the horizontal distance. 4 + ? = 6 for the vertical distance. The correct choice is (B).

18. **(A)** You subtract the cost of the chair (P) from the total dollars (M) to get the cost of the couch. Thus, (M – P) dollars represents the cost of the couch. Choice (A) is correct.

19. **(D)** You figure the approximate amount of degrees for the graph by multiplying .32 by 360. This is about 115 degrees, or about one third of 360 degrees. Choice (A) is only 90 degrees of the circle. Choice (B) is half of the circle, or 180 degrees. Choice (C) is over 180 degrees. Choice (E) is about 70 degrees or slightly under one fifth of the circle. Choice (D) is about 115 degrees or 32% of the circle. Thus, Choice (D) is correct.

20. **(A)** You simply need to know the names and values for each place to the left of the decimal point for whole numbers and for each place to the right of the decimal point for decimals. The place value names for the whole numbers to the left of the decimal point are: ones (9), tens (0), hundreds (6), thousands (5), ten thousands (2), hundred thousands (8), millions. The decimal place value names to the right of the decimal point are tenths (.4), hundredths (.07), thousandths (.003). The correct digit is 8, Choice (A).

21. **(E)** You know that the original price is $350. You are asked what part or fraction is the reduction ($70) of the original price. Thus 70/350 is the ratio between the reduction and the whole or original price. 70/350 means 70 ÷ 350. Choice (E) is correct.

22. **(C)** You set up the problem as follows:

$$\frac{\text{one faculty}}{\text{students}} = \frac{\text{total faculty}}{\text{student body}}$$

OR

$$\frac{1}{12} = \frac{x}{1500}$$

Solving the proportion by cross multiplying:

$12x = 1,500$ (cross multiplying)

$x = 1,500 ÷ 12$ (dividing each side of equation by 12)

$x = 125$ faculty

23. **(E)** The probability of two events dependent upon each other (making 1st shot, and making 2nd shot after making first shot) is the product of the two probabilities. Thus, .48 x .60 yields .2880, or 28.8%. Choice (E) is correct.

24. **(E)** You can reason about the validity of each statement by keeping in mind that John took more strides to pace off the same distance as Jack. This must mean that his stride is slightly shorter than Jack's. Choice (A) is wrong. Jack's stride is longer than John's, since he covered the distance in fewer strides. Choice (B) is wrong. It says the same as Choice (A). Choice (C) is wrong, since this is just the difference in total number of strides across the field for the two boys. Also, it is a foolish statement physically. Choice (D) is wrong. We know nothing about the shoe sizes of either Jack or John. Choice (E) is correct.

25. **(D)** You should recognize the graphing convention in algebra that an empty circle about a number point on the number line means to exclude that number value. Thus, the interval is between 3 and 7 but excludes 3 and 7. Thus Choice (A) is wrong. This shows a difference and not a numerical interval. Choice (B) is wrong. This shows the interval between

-4 and +10. Choice (C) is wrong because the interval is greater than that. Choice (E) is wrong because X is not equal to 3 nor is X equal to 7 as this expression states an interval of 3 to 7 including 3 and 7. Choice (D) is correct.

Section 3: Literature and Fine Arts

1.   **(C)**   After studying the musical piece, you are asked to choose which statement is the best description. The music is in two flats, indicated by the key signature at the beginning of each line, so (A) is not the correct choice. The only time signature shown is at the end of the segment and follows a double bar, which indicates a change in the time. Thus, the time signature for the segment shown is not obvious (B). The bass pattern, when studied, does reveal itself to be repetitive (C). There is no rest in the bass clef (D) and the piece is not for two voices (E), thus making (C) the only correct choice.

2.   **(D)**   The first four choices given are types of staging. Choice (E) is not; therefore, it is an invalid choice. Thrust staging has the stage projecting into the audience and the audience surrounding the stage on three sides. The audience in the picture is on only two sides of the stage, which is known as central staging (D). Proscenium (B) is traditional staging in a theatre with a proscenium arch. Theatre-in-the-round has the audience completely surrounding the playing area. Choice (D) is the correct answer.

3.   **(D)**   While the sonnet "My mistress' eyes are nothing like the sun" is Shakespearean, this does not make it different from other sonnets. A majority of sonnets are written in this form, so (A) is incorrect. The poem does describe the appearance of a beloved woman; this choice is incorrect, however; because many other sonnets do the same. Beautiful women were traditional subject matter for Elizabethan sonneteers. The sonnet does follow the proper conventions necessary to label it as one, so (E) is also wrong. (D) is the correct answer because Shakespeare undermines the traditional beauty of the women who are normally written about and states that his mistress is far more beautiful than the other "goddesses," even though she is realistically ordinary.

4.   **(C)**   The last two lines of a Shakespearean sonnet generally provide an ironic twist to the rest of the poem. In this sonnet, the lines refute the argument of the rest of the poem because the speaker states that even though his mistress is ordinary he still finds her beautiful. Thus, choice (C) is the correct answer.

5.   **(A)**   Choice (A) is correct because the poem is witty in the way it takes standard sonnet conventions (a woman's eyes, lips, hair, etc.) and twists them to make a point. By doing this, Shakespeare is also satirizing standard sonnet conventions of his time (which he himself never hesitated to employ). The poem is not intense (B), sarcastic (C), brooding (D), or sentimental (E). "Sentimental" denotes "looking fondly back on," which the speaker is not doing; the woman is his mistress, not his past mistress.

6.   **(B)**   You are asked to determine which of the buildings named is pictured. Each edifice listed is built in a different style, which should be easily recognizable. Notre Dame Cathedral is French, characterized by its flying buttresses. This is a picture of the frieze of the west cella of the Parthenon, which is characterized by Doric columns (as pictured) and

the high-relief metopes of the Doric frieze. The Sistine Chapel (C), Michelangelo's master-piece, is known for its frescoes and barrel-vaulted ceilings. Versailles (D), is the palace of Louis XIV, outside of Paris, and is an example of the ornate style of baroque grandeur. One distinguishing factor is that all the choices other than the Parthenon are structures which are in much better repair, since they are more recent than the pictured ruins of the Parthenon.

7.   **(A)**   The squatting position of the figure is indicative of a low position, like that of a slave (A). Since he is wearing only a cloak thrown back over one shoulder, this, too, indicates the clothing of a commoner or a person of low status. The action, that of sharpening a knife, is a job which would be designated to a slave. The muscle structure of the figure would not really indicate social level, making (B), (C), (D) and (E) unlikely choices.

8.   **(B)**   This question tests your knowledge of the development of the English language. This passage is taken from one of Chaucer's *Cantebury Tales*, written in the late fourteenth century. This is evident from the highly "irregular" spelling of words such as "dwellynge" ("dwelling") and "povre" ("poor"). (A) is incorrect because a translation would be translated into standard, modern English. Choice (C) is wrong, because while the poem may be romantic, it is impossible to tell from this passage. Elizabethan English is completely different from Middle English, so (D) is incorrect, and (E) is wrong because it is impossible to tell from the passage whether or not the speaker is a foreigner. (B) is the correct answer.

9.   **(B)**   This question asks you to look at the print and come to some conclusions. Since each figure is holding or playing a musical instrument (double aulos, lute and harp), it can be surmised that they are musicians (A). Choice (B) states that the artwork creates the illusion of depth. Since there is not a strong sense of depth, and you are looking for the exceptional choice, this is the correct answer. The lack of a three-dimensional aspect (D) and the absence of a background against which the figures are placed, all add to the conclusion that this is an Egyptian tomb painting (C).

10.   **(D)**   The pictured statue is a portrait of Augustus that was found near Rome. The effect of this figure, with the serious expression and gesture, is not comic (A). There is nothing in the stance, expression or dress to suggest levity. Conversely, although the face is not smiling, it is also not a tragic figure (B). Although the breastplate or cuirass has scenes in low relief carved on it, the figure itself is not ornate or excessively decorated (C). Finally, the large gesture and stance of an imperator, or commander-in-chief, makes for an imposing figure (D). The carved armor, careful draping of the cloak and the rod the figure holds, all add to this impression. Thus, (D) is the correct answer.

11.   **(C)**   This question asks you to read and determine the mood created by an author in a short selection. Passage (C), taken from Thomas Wolfe's "Circuses at Dawn," uses such words and phrases as "thrilling darkness"and "rush madly" to let the reader share the narrator's strange excitement as he anticipates the circus. Therefore, (C) is the correct answer.

12.   **(A)**   A dramatic monologue is a poem in the form of an extended speech by an identifiable character. Passage (A), the beginning of Robert Browning's "My Last Duchess," is unquestionably spoken by one character to another; therefore, (A) is the correct answer.

13.   **(D)**   A metaphor is a literary device whereby an author compares two seemingly

unlike things to achieve an effect. Passage (D), taken from Henry David Thoreau's essay "Civil Disobedience" compares two seemingly unlike things—the American government and a wooden gun—to make a point; therefore, (D) is the correct answer.

14. **(D)**   This question requires that you study the mood of the people in the picture and make a connection between the instruments pictured, the actions of those pictured, and the type of music being played. Since an opera (A) is usually a formal, upper-class form of music and the picture is of a coarse tavern scene, the music would not be operatic. The individuals appear festive and seem to be enjoying taking part in the merry-making, not singing a sad, serious melody (B), or a funeral hymn (C) dirge. Therefore, the correct answer is (D). The music is a light, boisterous tune.

15. **(A)**   Le Corbusier's L'Unite d'Habitation (Union for Living) is an apartment house in Marseilles. Corbusier set out to build apartments vibrating with light. This is obvious from the many windows almost covering the side of the building. Thus, choice (A) is correct. The building is obviously not a skyscraper (B), since there are no more than eight floors. The building is structured around rectangular and linear shapes, rather than cylindrical (C). And, the staircase at left is not hidden, but in full view (D).

16. **(C)**   This question tests your knowledge of the use of the dramatic term "aside". An aside is a comment spoken directly to the audience that the other actors on stage are supposedly unable to hear. Thus, the correct answer is choice (C).

17. **(D)**   You are asked to look at the structure of a building and relate to it in terms of natural forms. Since this contemporary building stacks and masses cubes or facets from a broad base to an increasingly narrow peak, much like a mountain, the correct answer is (D). It does not have wave-like lines which would connote undulating water, nor does it display any branch-like elements projecting from a trunk as on a tree. Likewise, it does not reveal the concentric spirals of a snail or nautilus shell, while answer choice (B), a city street, offers an example of a man-made, not a natural object, and is therefore not relevant to the question.

18. **(B)**   The correct answer is (B). The first two lines tell us that the speaker has been doing some inner questioning and searching. The last two lines are almost a prayer to the sea, a prayer that asks the sea to calm the speaker and "compose (him) to the end." The line which reads, "Ye who from my childhood up have calmed me" suggests that the sea has been able to calm the speaker before; it is this same calming which the speaker now "passionately desire(s)."

19. **(D)**   The correct answer is (D). The "stream of consciousness" technique is a modern invention used by writers to mimic, and if possible, duplicate, the quick workings of the human mind. This passage from James Joyce's *Ulysses* describes Molly Bloom's thoughts of the character Hugh as she thinks of him: how he slapped her "on my bottom," and how he is an "ignoramus" that "doesn't know poetry from a cabbage." The passage lacks punctuation because (as the technique ascribes) people do not think in properly punctuated sentences. The passage is meant to display how thoughts lead to other thoughts by association.

20. **(A)**   The correct answer is (A). Alliteration is a poetic device where writers repeat consonant sounds at the beginning of successive (or almost successive) words. "Fair is foul

and foul is fair" is an example of alliteration because of the repeated "f" sound; the same is true for "fog and filthy."

21. **(A)** Prose is non-metrical language, the opposite of verse. Since this passage is not written in verse, (A) is the correct answer. Iambic pentameter is five units (or "feet") of an unstressed syllable followed by a stressed syllable, so (B) is incorrect. An elegy is a poem of lamentation for the dead, so (C) is wrong. A non sequitur is a type of reasoning pattern in which the conclusion does not follow the line of reasoning used to reach it, so (D) is incorrect.

22. **(B)** Since the selection seems to be creating a setting by describing the townspeople and weather in the "little Kansas town," choice (B) is correct. It seems highly unlikely that it is taken from the climax of a short story (C) (the point of highest tension where the elements of the plot are brought together), the dénoument (D) (the unwinding of the plot following the climax), or the conclusion (A) (the final images or actions described by an author).

23. **(B)** Answer choices (A), (C), (D) and (E) all share in some way the forms and ideals of the Western Classical tradition as it was established in the arts of Greece and Rome. This tradition emphasizes the value of the human individual and expresses its humanistic convictions, in part, through an idealized representation of the human figure. Answer choice (A), a Hellenistic marble relief of the 2nd century B.C., shows this figure style in one of its earliest contexts. Examples (D) and (E), paintings from the Renaissance and Baroque periods in Europe, directly echo the ideal figure forms found in the Greek work. Choice (C), a modern work, abstracts and stylizes the human form somewhat more severely, but remains focused on the complete, nude human figure as a humanistic ideal. Only choice (B), a 16th century African bronze head, falls outside of the long continuous stream of Western European culture.

24. **(D)** Answer choices (B) and (C) show static, isolated forms which display no motion at all. Choice (E) presents subjects arranged around a central focal point in a somewhat circular format, but the painting aspires to an effect of balanced calm and stillness and cannot be said to be at all animated. Choices (A) and (D) both exhibit vigorous movement, but the motion in (A), the Greek relief, depends on the counteracting thrust of intersecting diagonal lines and repeated V-forms. Only choice (D), the *Galatea* by the Renaissance painter Raphael, establishes a truly circular motion, in which the arched form of the cupid at the bottom of the picture leads the viewer's eye upwards to the right, through the cupids in the sky, all of whom circle around the main subject in the center of the picture.

25. **(B)** Answer choices (A), (D), and (E) all follow the Classical tradition of idealized figures presented in an illusionistic, well-modelled, three-dimensional mode. Only choices (B) and (C) begin to abstract the figure to any significant degree, although choice (C), a 20th-century sculpted image of female nude, retains the sense of a rounded, softly-modelled, corporeal mass. Choice (B), however, an African bronze head, begins to facet the facial features into a series of angular planes and lines (evident in the sharp line from cheekbone to jaw) and overemphasizes the size and shape of the eyes.

26. **(B)** This question asks you to interpret the passage and look for specific sounds hinted at in the lines. Line 1 refers to the tolling of a bell (A). Line 2 refers to the "lowing herd" or sound of cows (D). Line 3 hints at the footsteps of the plowman as he "plods his weary way"

(C); this is the same sound as a man walking (E). There is no mention of the wind, however, so (B) is the correct answer.

27. **(B)**   This question asks you to choose the best paraphrase or restatement of the quotation. The correct answer is (B). "We think our fathers fools, so wise we grow," means that as we grow older, we think our fathers are fools and *we* are wise. "Our wiser sons, no doubt, will think us so," means that our sons will do the same, and thus think of us in the same way. The other choices are misinterpretations of the lines.

28. **(B)**   This question asks that you view the picture and decide what type of artwork is pictured. This is a detail of a stained glass window at Chartres Cathedral (B). The design is two-dimensional, a characteristic which artists of stained glass preferred. Stained glass is also characterized by the fine strips of lead that hold the small pieces of glass in place. These can be seen between the glass pieces in the picture. A mosaic design would have smaller pieces of tile making up the design (D). An oil painting (A) is characterized by dramatic use of high intensities to spotlight principal figures and deeper shadow for subordinate ones, subtle modeling of figures, and softness of contours. Even in a black and white photograph, it is easy to tell that there is little blending or softness in the figures and colors portrayed. Finally, a marble sculpture would be three-dimensional and free standing. Thus, the correct answer is (B).

29. **(C)**   This first stanza sets the tone for the rest of the poem. The poet tells us that this will be a "harmonious ditty," which clues us that the poem will not have a serious tone; therefore, (A) is wrong and (C) is correct. The rhyme scheme for this stanza is a-b-c-b, familiar, and will probably be repeated throughout the poem, so (B) is also incorrect. Choices (D) and (E) feature incorrect rhyme schemes for the stanza, and are, therefore, incorrect as well.

30. **(E)**   Of the five possible answer choices, (A), (C), and (D) use predominantly a black outline on a white background, with (C) employing slight tonal (i.e., grey) qualities. Choices (B) and (E) share similar densities of pure black against a white ground. Answer choice (B), however, uses the pale white faces of the figures against the heavy black for an expressive effect; in this case, the technique serves the emotional content of the picture and avoids a purely decorative effect. Only choice (E) contrasts broad areas of pure black with a large field of pure white to establish a flowing linear rhythm and produce a sophisticated decorative result.

31. **(B)**   Choices (A), (D), and (E) employ either pure black line on a white backround or pure black line with broad areas of flat black. All avoid the use of contrasting textures almost completely, and only choices (B) and (C) develop textural effects to any noticeable degree. In choice (C), however, although a soft grey texture is used widely throughout the drawing, the predominant effect is that of black line against white, and there is no expressive human content in evidence. Choice (B), a woodblock print, uses the rough gouging to model and texture the grieving human faces, setting them off against the dense black and reinforcing the emotional content of the image.

32. **(A)**   Choices (B), (C), and (E) all merge and join the forms on the page into integrated compositions, although in different ways and with differing effects. Only choices (A) and (D)

present a number of unconnected images, drawn in fine black line on a white page. The images in choice (D), however, although they are separate and discrete, are arranged in a planned, composed manner which implies a motion to the left and suggests a narrative action of some sort. In contrast, choice (A), a page of sketches from a medieval architect's notebook, presents a random assortment of unrelated subjects and motifs which are composed in no special order and suggest no specific meaning.

33. **(A)** You are asked to decide which culture this mask represents. The mask reproduced in the picture was designed to be worn by African tribesmen as they danced by firelight to the accompaniment of drums. The non-realistic features are intended to conjure up the presence of an invisible spirit. The African tradition is noted due to the large features. The correct answer is (A). The mask is not representative of the Greek culture (B), whose sculpture is clean-lined and realistic, as is the Roman (C). The Dutch culture (D) is characterized by extremely domestic- related arts with a reality of simple truths. Thus, a mask showing elongated and distorted features would not characterize the Dutch culture. Persian art also would not be distorted in the manner of this mask.

34. **(E)** These two stanzas are taken from Robert Gray's "Ode on the Death of a Favorite Cat." There is no mention of a snake, so (A) is wrong. The passage does mention a "tortoise," but only because Gray is comparing the cat's coat with a tortoise's stripes; therefore (B) is wrong. A vase is mentioned, but only because the cat "reclined" on it; (C) is also wrong. There is no mention at all of a dog, so (D) is wrong. The word "tabby" and such characteristics as "snowy beard" (whiskers) and "velvet paws" describe a cat, so (E) is correct.

35. **(C)** This question asks you to read the excerpt from William Golding's *Lord of the Flies* and determine the literary movement to which Golding ascribes. Surrealism (A) goes beyond the real into the realm of the "super-real" and often includes the world of the unconscious or dreams. Since there is nothing to suggest that this passage is anything but a true-to-life description, this choice is incorrect. Expressionistic writers (B) present life as they feel it to be, not as it appears. Again, this passage does not incorporate this style. Romantic writing (D) presents life as the writer wishes it could be and usually describes strange lands and adventures; this "normal" beach scene contains no romantic elements, so (D) is incorrect. Gothicism (E) is a style used by novelists of the eighteenth and nineteenth centuries which relies on greater-than-life heroes, villains, and a grandiose sense of the macabre. Since the passage features none of this, (E) is wrong. The correct answer is (C), because realistic writing concerns detailed descriptions of everyday life; "fledged with palm trees," "their green feathers were a hundred feet up in the air," "scattered with decaying coconuts," etc., are all realistic descriptions of the scene.

Section 4: Science

1. **(E)** Contrary to answer (A), all of the Earth's energy does not come from plants. In fact, there would be no plants without the Sun; the Sun is necessary for the plants to make food. (A) is incorrect. Since animals (B), like plants, are dependent on the Sun to provide energy, and since the Sun provides all or nearly all of the Earth's energy, (B) could not be correct. Coal (C) is fossil fuel made from plants. All of the Earth's energy does not come from

plants or coal. In fact, there would be no energy without the Sun. Since oil may have been originally made from animals, (D) is wrong for the same reasons that answer (B) was wrong. (D) should not be chosen. (E) is the correct answer. All or nearly all of the Earth's energy comes from the Sun.

2.   **(A)**   Answer (A) is the correct answer. Energy may be converted from one form to another. For example, electrical energy may be converted to light energy in the case of an electric light bulb; (B) is not the correct answer. Since kinetic energy is energy that an object possesses because of its motion; (C) is not the right answer. Potential energy (D) is that which objects possess because of their position. (D) is not the right answer and should not be chosen. Nuclear fission (E), most scientists agree, will not be the chief source of energy for the world by the year 2000, because of the many problems involved. Some of the problems involved include how to properly dispose of the nuclear waste, as well as the safety of the process. (E) is incorrect.

3.   **(D)**   The result of a father who is RH-positive and a mother who is RH-negative may be a child with *erythroblastosis fetalis*—a disease brought on by incompatibility of the mother's blood and the child's blood; the red cells of the child may be damaged to the extent that the child is unable to obtain sufficient oxygen. German measles during the first trimester of pregnancy may cause problems with the development of the unborn child. Since (D) allows you to choose both the RH-positive father and the onset of German measles during the first trimester, (D) is the correct answer. (A) is a correct answer but (B) is also correct; (D) is the only right answer since it allows the reader to choose both. (C) is an incorrect answer since there is no dange if the father is RH-negative and the mother is RH-positive. (E) should not be selected since it includes (C)—a wrong answer—along with the correct (B).

4.   **(A)**   Parasitism (A) is the correct answer. Trichinella (wormlike parasites often spread from improperly cooked pork) may enter the body of the person and live there at a disadvantage to the individual. Since *mutualism* (B) indicates two organisms which survive at a benefit to each, (B) is not correct. Trichinosis is not of benefit to the host, which might be people. *Commercialism* (C) is not an appropriate answer since it does not relate at all to the question about trichinosis. Commercialism refers to the commercial spirit or mercantilism. (C) should not be chosen. *Benevolent* (D) is not a term relating to a situation where the host organism develops a disease like trichinosis. *Benevolent* means kind, charitable, disposed to promote the prosperity of another. (D) is not the best answer. Since *benign* (E) means mild or favorable, it does not adequately describe a situation in which the organism causes danger to the host or person. (E) should not be chosen.

5.   **(E)**   (A) Since the word *organic* means pertaining to or derived from living organisms or (in chemistry), a compound containing carbon (and in some cases oxygen), answer (A) (living and non-living compound) is inappropriate. Answer (B) is incorrect; there are more organic compounds than inorganic. Since inorganic compounds (C) can be synthesized in a laboratory, (C) is incorrect. (D) does not seem logical; dead organisms cannot synthesize a compound. (D) should not be selected. (E) is the correct answer. All organic compounds contain carbon.

6.   **(C)**   The symbol for iron is *Fe*. (A) is incorrect. Despite the fact that both *phosphorous* and the symbol *Pb* both begin with *p*, (B) is not the correct answer. The correct representation

for this common element of lead is *Pb*. The correct symbol for lead is *Pb*; (C) is the correct answer. Even though plutonium and *Pb* both begin with *p*, (D) is not the correct answer and should not be chosen. Both *potassium* and *Pb* begin with *p*, but (E) is not the right choice.

7.   **(D)**   Since a meter is 39.37 inches, or about the height of a five-year-old child, (A) is not the best choice. A liter (B) is a measure of volume; it is slightly more than a quart. It is not the best unit to use to measure a piece of chalk. A gram (C) is about the weight of a paper clip; since a gram is a measure of weight (mass) and not length, gram is not the best unit to use. A decimeter (D) is one tenth of a meter; a personal reference for a decimeter is about the distance between the end of the thumb and the end of the middle finger. This distance is a little more than 3" in an adult—about the length of a new piece of chalk. (Since a meter is about 36", one tenth of 36" is a little over 3"—about the length of a new piece of chalk.) (D) is the right answer. A kilometer (E) is 1000 meters; since a meter is a little more than 3 feet, a measure of a little more than 3000 feet is not the best measure to apply to a new piece of chalk. (E) should not be chosen.

8.   **(A)**   (E) Down's Syndrome (mongolism) is a genetic disorder. There is at present no treatment or cure for this disorder, which is characterized most often by stubby fingers, retarded physical development, "slanting" eyes, large tongue, and low mentality. Down's Syndrome results when the egg cell has a total of 24 chromosomes, rather than the normal 23. (A) is the correct answer. Syphilis (B) is a sexually transmitted venereal disease; it is not genetically transmitted. (B) is not the correct answer. Malaria (C) is a disease transmitted by the infected Anopheles mosquito; since malaria is not genetic, (C) is not the best answer. Leukemia (D) is a disease characterized by the uncontrolled production of ineffectual white blood cells; it is a type of cancer. At present there is no evidence to suggest that it is genetic in origin. (C), therefore, is not the best answer. Emphysema (E) is a condition of the lungs in which they lose their elasticity. Environmental agents and smoking—not genetics—seem to bring about this disease. (E) is not the best answer.

9.   **(D)**   You would first have to recognize that HCL is hydrochloric acid, which is an acid and not a base. Then you would have to know that litmus paper turns pink in an acid. After this reasoning, the reader is now ready to make the correct choice. (A) is false; there should be a reaction. The paper should turn red. (A) is not the correct choice. Since the litmus paper does not disintegrate but instead turns red, (B) is not the best answer. Litmus paper turns blue in a base. Since HCL is an acid, the paper turns red, not blue. (C) is an incorrect answer. The litmus paper does turn red with an acid; (D) is the correct answer. There are no oxygen bubbles rising to the top because of carbonation at the time the litmus paper is inserted. (E) is a wrong answer, therefore, and should not be chosen.

10.   **(D)**   Water has properties of a base; it also has properties of an acid, and is classified as a compound. For these reasons (A), (B) and (C) alone may not be selected. Since (A), (B) and (C) are all correct, (D) allows you to choose all three answers. Since answers (A), (B) and (C) are correct, (E) (none of the above) cannot be chosen.

11.   **(C)**   Despite the fact that summer is the season when the Earth is warmest, the Earth is not closest to the Sun. The Earth is warm because of the way that the Sun's rays are concentrated on the Earth. (A) is not the correct answer. The Earth moves in an elliptical orbit about the Sun. It moves closest to the Sun in the winter. Although it is approaching its closest

Night Day

Rotation –24hrs. Revol –

position, the Earth is not closest in the fall. (B) should not be chosen. Even though the winter season (C) is the coldest, the Earth is closest to the Sun during this time. The Sun's rays are not concentrated directly on the part of the Earth that is experiencing winter; winter is, therefore, colder. (C) is the correct answer. During the spring (D), the Earth is beginning to move away from the position in the winter when it was closest to the Sun. It is not, however, closest to the Sun during the spring season. (D) is not the right choice. The Earth is not closest to the Sun in either the spring or the summer. Answer (E), which gives both these answers, is giving the reader two wrong answers. (E) is a wrong answer and should not be chosen.

12. **(B)**   The tilt of the Earth on its axis causes the seasons because it allows the rays of the Sun to be concentrated on one area. The tilt causes seasons, not day and night, so (A) is not the correct answer. The Earth rotates on its axis once every 24 hours. It is this rotation that causes day and night, so (B) is the correct answer. The revolution of the Earth about the Sun results in our calendar year—not day and night; (C) is an incorrect answer. The Earth rotates on its axis; the Sun does not move about the Earth. The Earth revolves around the Sun. (D) is not the right choice. The Earth revolves about the Sun; the Sun does not revolve around the Earth. (E) is a wrong answer and should not be chosen.

13. **(C)**   Sunshine (A) is rich in Vitamin D. Since scurvy is caused by insufficient Vitamin C, it could not result from inadequate sunshine alone. (A) is not the correct answer. Calcium (B) is necessary for bones and teeth. Its absence does not cause scurvy. Since scurvy does result from insufficient Vitamin C, answer (C) is correct. Insufficient Vitamin B may cause pellagra, but not scurvy. (D) is not the right choice. Scurvy is the result of a diet lacking in Vitamin C, not a viral infection. (E) is a wrong answer and should not be chosen.

14. **(B)**   Both plants and animals are made of cells; (A) is not the correct answer. Plant cells do usually have a nonliving cell wall; (B) is true. The Euglena (C) is a single-celled organism that swims freely like a typical animal; it can, however, manufacture food with its green chlorophyll like a plant. This is one instance of a "non-plant" with chlorophyll. (C) is incorrect. Both plant and animal cells contain DNA. (D) is, therefore, not the right choice. Fungi (E) do not manufacture their own food. They do not contain chlorophyll. (E) is a wrong answer and should not be chosen.

15. **(C)**   (A) Some elements are found in nature, but others may be made by scientists. (A) is not the correct answer. Elements may or may not be made by scientists; the nonelements are made by scientists. (B) should not be chosen. (C) is the correct answer; some elements are found in nature; others may be made by scientists. There are 107 presently-known elements—hence 107 presently-known atoms; (D) is incorrect. Steel (carbon and iron), brass (copper and zinc), and water (hydrogen and oxygen) are compounds; (E) is a wrong answer and should not be chosen.

16. **(D)**   The correct answer for the classification scheme is (D). All the other answers are incorrect because the order of items has been switched. If you are not familiar with the entire classification order, chances are you will know that the kingdom (animalia, plantia) comes first, and that the scientific name of a living thing comes from genus and species. The first item (kingdom) and the last two items (genus, species) are two good clues. Only (D) meets these qualifications. (A), (B), (C), and (E) all give the wrong order and should not be selected.

17. **(C)** (A) Neither coal, oil, nor gas are renewable. These fuels would take years to form even if all of the needed conditions and elements are present. (A) is not the correct answer. The items in (B) are nonrenewable; (B) should not be chosen. Soil, vegetation, and animals can be renewed in a relatively short period of time. (C) is the best answer. Although the other two items in item (D) are renewable, coal (a fossil fuel) is not; (D) is not the correct choice. Oil, a fossil fuel, is not renewable. Since it is nonrenewable, the entire answer of (E) should be avoided.

18. **(D)** Gravitational force is one of the forces which operates to cause interactions of matter. Since it is not the only force, however, (A) can not be selected as the correct answer. Since electromagnetic force (B) is only one of the forces from which interactions of matter result, (B) should not be chosen. Nuclear force (C) is an important force from which interactions of matter result, but it is not the only such force. (C) is an incorrect answer. All three of the forces listed in (D)–gravitational, electromagnetic, and nuclear–are correct. (D), therefore, is the correct answer. (E)–"None of the above"–is an incorrect choice since all the forces listed may result in the interactions of matter.

19. **(E)** The correct order in the scientific method is 1) State the problem, 2) Collect the data, 3) Form the hypothesis, 4) Test the hypothesis, and 5) Communicate the findings. The only answer which has the correct order is (E). (A), (B), (C), and (D) are all incorrect.

20. **(E)** (A), (B), (C) and (D) are correct statements. Since the question asks for the incorrect answer, (A), (B), (C) and (D) should not be chosen. (E) A single valid fact that completely contradicts a theory is sufficient to overthrow the theory. (E) is the correct answer to the question, since it is incorrect.

21. **(A)** All five characteristics given are those of the mammal. (A) is, therefore, the correct answer. Since mammals belong to the phylum chordata (suggesting that they all possess a notochord at some time in their life), (B) is incorrect because it omits the notochord. All the young of mammals are fed on milk; since (C) omits this, it is an incorrect choice. The young of mammals are born alive; answer (D) omits this important fact. (D) should not be selected. (E)–none of the above–is an inappropriate choice since all the answers are correct.

22. **(D)** (A) All three choices are parts of the digestive system. The pancreas secretes pancreatic juice for digestion; both the small and large intestine are readily identified as parts of the system. Since you are looking, however, for the list containing an organ that is not a part of the system, (A) should not be chosen. Bile, which comes from the gall bladder, aids digestion. All three organs in (B) aid digestion. (B) should not be chosen. All three parts named in (C) belong to the digestive system. The spleen (D) is not a part of the digestive system. Since (D) contains an organ which is not a part of the digestive system, it should be selected as the correct answer. All three parts in (E) belong to the digestive system. The liver, for instance, secretes bile into the gall bladder. Since all three parts belong to the digestive system, (E) is a wrong answer.

23. **(D)** All the items listed EXCEPT communicating and producing food are functions of living things; many animals, for instance do not produce food, and plants do not seem to communicate. Item IV (mentioned in (D)) contains "communicating" and item V (mentioned in (D)) contains "producing food". (D) is the correct choice.

24. **(C)**   Only the gravitational pull of the moon and the rotation of the Earth cause the rhythm of the tides. (C) is correct. The other answers, (A), (B), (D) and (E), are therefore, incorrect.

25. **(E)**   (A) should not be chosen because it is a true statement, and the directions instruct the reader to select the one which is not a part of the theory. (B) is not the right answer because the statement is a true one. (C) is an incorrect choice. Molecules are believed to be in rapid and ceaseless motion. (D) is not the best answer, since the statement is a true part of the molecular theory. When a molecule of water is split, it is separated into hydrogen and oxygen–not smaller molecules of water. Since (E) is not a part of molecular theory, it should be chosen.

26. **(C)**   A housefly resistant to DDT (A) did emerge as a result of the use of the pesticide. Since the directions instruct you to find the one with which scientists would not agree, (A) should not be chosen. (B) is not the right answer since it is true and, in this particular instance, you are searching for a false answer. (C) is the correct choice. Scientists would not advocate the regular use of chemicals to try to bring about "the evolution of exciting new types of organisms." Since the statement is not one that scientists would agree with, it is the choice for this question. Since (D) is a true statement, it is not the correct choice. (E) is a true statement, and not the best answer to a question asking for an incorrect choice.

27. **(D)**   (A) is not the best answer, since it is an example of recycling. The reclaiming of nitrogen by the soil (B) is an example of recycling, and is not the correct choice. The rusting away of the cans (C) is an example of recycling, and not the correct answer. The non-biodegradable can (D) is NOT an example of recycling. (D) is the correct answer. Since (E) is an example of recycling, it is not the right answer.

28. **(D)**   The amount of heat necessary to melt ice (A) is not a relevant fact since water of 50° C is not ice. (A) should not be chosen. Changing water to gas (B) does not involve raising the temperature from 50° to 90° C. (B) is not the right answer. Since I and II in (C) mention ice and gas (two forms of water not relevant to water of the temperature 50-90°C), (C) is not the best answer. (D) is the best answer. It alone contains information appropriate only to water of the temperature 50° to 90° C. (E) is a wrong answer. It refers to a gram of ice; water of the temperature 50° to 90° is not ice.

29. **(C)**   Since (A) is a true statement, it cannot be selected. The directions tell you to find the false answer. (B) is a true statement as well, and cannot be selected. Since there are many galaxies in the universe (C), stating that the Milky Way is the galaxy is false. (D) is not the best choice, since it is a true statement. (E) is not the best choice since it, too, is a true statement.

30. **(A)**   (A) is not true; all proteins are not identical in their chemical makeup. Since you are to select the false statement, (A) is the right answer. (B) is true and may not be selected. Since (C) is a true statement, (C) should not be chosen. (D) is not the best answer, since it is true. (E) is a true statement; since a false one should be selected, (E) should not be chosen.

NTE Test of Professional Knowledge

TEST 1 – ANSWER SHEET

Section 1	Section 2	Section 3
1. Ⓐ Ⓑ Ⓒ Ⓓ Ⓔ	1. Ⓐ Ⓑ Ⓒ Ⓓ Ⓔ	1. Ⓐ Ⓑ Ⓒ Ⓓ Ⓔ
2. Ⓐ Ⓑ Ⓒ Ⓓ Ⓔ	2. Ⓐ Ⓑ Ⓒ Ⓓ Ⓔ	2. Ⓐ Ⓑ Ⓒ Ⓓ Ⓔ
3. Ⓐ Ⓑ Ⓒ Ⓓ Ⓔ	3. Ⓐ Ⓑ Ⓒ Ⓓ Ⓔ	3. Ⓐ Ⓑ Ⓒ Ⓓ Ⓔ
4. Ⓐ Ⓑ Ⓒ Ⓓ Ⓔ	4. Ⓐ Ⓑ Ⓒ Ⓓ Ⓔ	4. Ⓐ Ⓑ Ⓒ Ⓓ Ⓔ
5. Ⓐ Ⓑ Ⓒ Ⓓ Ⓔ	5. Ⓐ Ⓑ Ⓒ Ⓓ Ⓔ	5. Ⓐ Ⓑ Ⓒ Ⓓ Ⓔ
6. Ⓐ Ⓑ Ⓒ Ⓓ Ⓔ	6. Ⓐ Ⓑ Ⓒ Ⓓ Ⓔ	6. Ⓐ Ⓑ Ⓒ Ⓓ Ⓔ
7. Ⓐ Ⓑ Ⓒ Ⓓ Ⓔ	7. Ⓐ Ⓑ Ⓒ Ⓓ Ⓔ	7. Ⓐ Ⓑ Ⓒ Ⓓ Ⓔ
8. Ⓐ Ⓑ Ⓒ Ⓓ Ⓔ	8. Ⓐ Ⓑ Ⓒ Ⓓ Ⓔ	8. Ⓐ Ⓑ Ⓒ Ⓓ Ⓔ
9. Ⓐ Ⓑ Ⓒ Ⓓ Ⓔ	9. Ⓐ Ⓑ Ⓒ Ⓓ Ⓔ	9. Ⓐ Ⓑ Ⓒ Ⓓ Ⓔ
10. Ⓐ Ⓑ Ⓒ Ⓓ Ⓔ	10. Ⓐ Ⓑ Ⓒ Ⓓ Ⓔ	10. Ⓐ Ⓑ Ⓒ Ⓓ Ⓔ
11. Ⓐ Ⓑ Ⓒ Ⓓ Ⓔ	11. Ⓐ Ⓑ Ⓒ Ⓓ Ⓔ	11. Ⓐ Ⓑ Ⓒ Ⓓ Ⓔ
12. Ⓐ Ⓑ Ⓒ Ⓓ Ⓔ	12. Ⓐ Ⓑ Ⓒ Ⓓ Ⓔ	12. Ⓐ Ⓑ Ⓒ Ⓓ Ⓔ
13. Ⓐ Ⓑ Ⓒ Ⓓ Ⓔ	13. Ⓐ Ⓑ Ⓒ Ⓓ Ⓔ	13. Ⓐ Ⓑ Ⓒ Ⓓ Ⓔ
14. Ⓐ Ⓑ Ⓒ Ⓓ Ⓔ	14. Ⓐ Ⓑ Ⓒ Ⓓ Ⓔ	14. Ⓐ Ⓑ Ⓒ Ⓓ Ⓔ
15. Ⓐ Ⓑ Ⓒ Ⓓ Ⓔ	15. Ⓐ Ⓑ Ⓒ Ⓓ Ⓔ	15. Ⓐ Ⓑ Ⓒ Ⓓ Ⓔ
16. Ⓐ Ⓑ Ⓒ Ⓓ Ⓔ	16. Ⓐ Ⓑ Ⓒ Ⓓ Ⓔ	16. Ⓐ Ⓑ Ⓒ Ⓓ Ⓔ
17. Ⓐ Ⓑ Ⓒ Ⓓ Ⓔ	17. Ⓐ Ⓑ Ⓒ Ⓓ Ⓔ	17. Ⓐ Ⓑ Ⓒ Ⓓ Ⓔ
18. Ⓐ Ⓑ Ⓒ Ⓓ Ⓔ	18. Ⓐ Ⓑ Ⓒ Ⓓ Ⓔ	18. Ⓐ Ⓑ Ⓒ Ⓓ Ⓔ
19. Ⓐ Ⓑ Ⓒ Ⓓ Ⓔ	19. Ⓐ Ⓑ Ⓒ Ⓓ Ⓔ	19. Ⓐ Ⓑ Ⓒ Ⓓ Ⓔ
20. Ⓐ Ⓑ Ⓒ Ⓓ Ⓔ	20. Ⓐ Ⓑ Ⓒ Ⓓ Ⓔ	20. Ⓐ Ⓑ Ⓒ Ⓓ Ⓔ
21. Ⓐ Ⓑ Ⓒ Ⓓ Ⓔ	21. Ⓐ Ⓑ Ⓒ Ⓓ Ⓔ	21. Ⓐ Ⓑ Ⓒ Ⓓ Ⓔ
22. Ⓐ Ⓑ Ⓒ Ⓓ Ⓔ	22. Ⓐ Ⓑ Ⓒ Ⓓ Ⓔ	22. Ⓐ Ⓑ Ⓒ Ⓓ Ⓔ
23. Ⓐ Ⓑ Ⓒ Ⓓ Ⓔ	23. Ⓐ Ⓑ Ⓒ Ⓓ Ⓔ	23. Ⓐ Ⓑ Ⓒ Ⓓ Ⓔ
24. Ⓐ Ⓑ Ⓒ Ⓓ Ⓔ	24. Ⓐ Ⓑ Ⓒ Ⓓ Ⓔ	24. Ⓐ Ⓑ Ⓒ Ⓓ Ⓔ
25. Ⓐ Ⓑ Ⓒ Ⓓ Ⓔ	25. Ⓐ Ⓑ Ⓒ Ⓓ Ⓔ	25. Ⓐ Ⓑ Ⓒ Ⓓ Ⓔ
26. Ⓐ Ⓑ Ⓒ Ⓓ Ⓔ	26. Ⓐ Ⓑ Ⓒ Ⓓ Ⓔ	26. Ⓐ Ⓑ Ⓒ Ⓓ Ⓔ
27. Ⓐ Ⓑ Ⓒ Ⓓ Ⓔ	27. Ⓐ Ⓑ Ⓒ Ⓓ Ⓔ	27. Ⓐ Ⓑ Ⓒ Ⓓ Ⓔ
28. Ⓐ Ⓑ Ⓒ Ⓓ Ⓔ	28. Ⓐ Ⓑ Ⓒ Ⓓ Ⓔ	28. Ⓐ Ⓑ Ⓒ Ⓓ Ⓔ
29. Ⓐ Ⓑ Ⓒ Ⓓ Ⓔ	29. Ⓐ Ⓑ Ⓒ Ⓓ Ⓔ	29. Ⓐ Ⓑ Ⓒ Ⓓ Ⓔ
30. Ⓐ Ⓑ Ⓒ Ⓓ Ⓔ	30. Ⓐ Ⓑ Ⓒ Ⓓ Ⓔ	30. Ⓐ Ⓑ Ⓒ Ⓓ Ⓔ
31. Ⓐ Ⓑ Ⓒ Ⓓ Ⓔ	31. Ⓐ Ⓑ Ⓒ Ⓓ Ⓔ	31. Ⓐ Ⓑ Ⓒ Ⓓ Ⓔ
32. Ⓐ Ⓑ Ⓒ Ⓓ Ⓔ	32. Ⓐ Ⓑ Ⓒ Ⓓ Ⓔ	32. Ⓐ Ⓑ Ⓒ Ⓓ Ⓔ
33. Ⓐ Ⓑ Ⓒ Ⓓ Ⓔ	33. Ⓐ Ⓑ Ⓒ Ⓓ Ⓔ	33. Ⓐ Ⓑ Ⓒ Ⓓ Ⓔ
34. Ⓐ Ⓑ Ⓒ Ⓓ Ⓔ	34. Ⓐ Ⓑ Ⓒ Ⓓ Ⓔ	34. Ⓐ Ⓑ Ⓒ Ⓓ Ⓔ
35. Ⓐ Ⓑ Ⓒ Ⓓ Ⓔ	35. Ⓐ Ⓑ Ⓒ Ⓓ Ⓔ	35. Ⓐ Ⓑ Ⓒ Ⓓ Ⓔ

NTE CORE BATTERY–Test 1
TEST OF PROFESSIONAL KNOWLEDGE
Section 1

TIME: 30 Minutes
35 Questions

DIRECTIONS: Each of the following questions and incomplete statements is followed by five answer choices. Select the choice which best answers each question.

1. A well written instructional objective contains which of the following elements?
   I. A statement of an observable, measurable behavior?
   II. A criterion of acceptable performance.
   III. The condition under which the student will demonstrate the behavior.
   IV. What the teacher will do to cause the students' behavioral change.
   (A) I and II only.
   (B) I, II and III only.
   (C) I, II and IV only.
   (D) II, III, and IV only.
   (E) I, II, III, and IV.

2. A student is asked to relate the contents of a graph to her classmates. This task is on which level of Bloom's Taxonomy?
   (A) Knowledge
   (B) Comprehension
   (C) Application
   (D) Analysis
   (E) Synthesis

3. The principal of a high school may search the locker of a student under which of the following circumstances?
   (A) The student has been misbehaving during the entire previous period.
   (B) The principal has just spoken to the student body about substance abuse and wants to ensure that there are no drugs on the school grounds.
   (C) The principal has obtained a search warrant.
   (D) The principal has reason to believe that there are drugs in the locker.
   (E) The student was arrested the night before for dealing drugs and the principal wants to see if he is doing so at school as well.

4. According to court decisions, which activities dealing with religious beliefs may be conducted in the public schools?

(A) Reading a neutral school prayer each morning.

(B) Reading a Bible selection each morning relating to the importance of proper deportment and motivation.

(C) Discussion of the belief systems of various selected religions.

(D) Setting aside two minutes of silence each morning to allow students to pray silently to themselves.

(E) Alternate daily among each religion within the student body and selecting each day a prayer for recitation from that religion.

5. The main provisions of the Education for All Handicapped Children Act (P.L. 94-142) are:

I. Handicapped children must be placed in a mainstreamed environment.

II. IEPs should be developed for each identified student.

III. Handicapped students should be placed in the least restrictive environment.

IV. All evaluation procedures must be non-discriminatory.

(A) I, II, and III. (D) II, III, and IV.

(B) I, II, and IV. (E) I, II, III, and IV.

(C) I, III, and IV.

6. All of the following teaching models would be appropriate in the development of higher order thinking skills EXCEPT

(A) discussion. (D) sociodrama.

(B) expository. teacher centered (E) cooperative learning.

(C) inquiry.

7. The teacher will tend to utilize an essay test when he/she wants to

I. emphasize high-level cognitive skills.

II. allow for student creativity and analysis.

III. provide a broad sampling of student knowledge.

IV. minimize the chance of student bluffing.

(A) I and II only. (D) II and IV only.

(B) II and III only. (E) I, II, III and IV.

(C) III and IV only.

8. Generally speaking, most standardized tests

I. are appropriate in difficulty for a defined population.

II. are high in discrimination power.

III. are high in reliability index.

IV. have a good biserial correlation.

(A) I and II only. (D) II and IV only.

(B) II and III only. (E) I, II, III and IV.

(C) III and IV only.

9. Of the various organizations that represent teachers at the bargaining table, the largest of these is the

   (A) AFT.   (D) NEA.

   (B) ASCD.   (E) AEA.

   (C) NTA.

10. In teacher questioning behavior, an increase in wait time tends to lead to

    (A) fewer questions asked by the students.

    (B) a reduction in divergent thinking.

    (C) more discipline problems.

    (D) fewer discipline problems.

    (E) a decrease in student response behavior.

11. A teacher finds an interesting, copyrighted article in a journal that would be excellent to use and distribute to her classes the very next day. The teacher may use the article without written permission

    (A) under no circumstances since it is copyrighted.

    (B) for one year only since there is no time to receive written permission.

    (C) for as long as she wants, so long as she does not charge the students for the article, thus making a profit.

    (D) for as long as she wishes, so long as she gives credit to the publication and the author.

    (E) Both (C) and (D).

12. There is evidence that questions asked by teachers tend to be at the knowledge and comprehension levels.

    (A) This is appropriate in that students need to have a knowledge base in education.

    (B) This is inappropriate in that students tend to dislike the more difficult comprehension level questions.

    (C) This is appropriate in that the higher level abilities will come as a matter of course when lower level needs are attended to.

    (D) This is inappropriate in that students will perform only at the level at which they are expected to perform.

    (E) All of the above.

13. Cooperative learning groups function best when

    (A) the groups are homogeneously grouped by ability.

    (B) the groups are heterogeneously grouped by ability.

    (C) the students are grouped by sex.

    (D) the students are grouped by grades.

    (E) the students are permitted to form their own groups.

14. One of the main goals of a multicultural education program is to:

    I. assimilate all children into the American melting pot.

    II. offer children different cultural alternatives.

    III. recall traditions and events of the past that are no longer relevant to American education, but which still have meaning to the minority child.

IV. teach children about festivals and holidays such as Cinco de Mayo and Martin Luther King Day.

(A) I only.   (D) IV only.

(B) II only.   (E) I and IV only.

(C) III only.

15. Research indicates that the behavior a teacher demonstrates towards a student is shaped by:

I. the student's physical appearance.

II. gossip heard from other teachers.

III. information contained in the student's cumulative record.

IV. the student's race or ethnic background.

V. the student's social class.

(A) I, II, and III only.   (D) II and III only.

(B) I, III, IV, and V only.   (E) all of the above.

(C) I, III, and V only.

16. Teachers sometimes discourage the achievement of low achieving students by

(A) providing too little wait time when asking questions.

(B) providing excessive negative reinforcement.

(C) demanding too much from the student.

(D) (A) and (B).

(E) all of the above.

17. Research has shown that the use of "Writing Across the Curriculum" projects have

(A) improved writing skills of students, but have actually decreased content area skills since more time is devoted to writing.

(B) improved content area skills since students utilize higher level thinking skills but have had little effect on writing skills since few subject area teachers are able to teach writing.

(C) improved writing skills as well as content area skills.

(D) shown little effect on either content or writing skills since most students view writing as a chore.

(E) None of the above.

18. The employment of tracking programs in schools tends to result in the following:

I. The most academically able students progress at an accelerated rate.

II. Minority students are benefited by receiving increased opportunities to socialize with their peers.

III. Students in the lower tracks receive the remediation needed to allow them to succeed.

IV. All tracks progress at accelerated rates since the individuals in the groups are similar in ability.

(A) I only.   (D) II, and III only.

(B) I and III only.   (E) All of the above.

(C) I, III, and IV only.

Inquiry Model
Scientific
method

19. The chief benefit of the inquiry model of learning is that students
    (A) feel more positive about the school experience.
    (B) acquire concepts and theories at a more rapid rate.
    (C) improve dramatically in their reading scores.
    (D) learn to apply the scientific method.
    (E) All of the above.

20. According to Piaget's theory of cognitive development, each of the following are included as stages of development EXCEPT
    (A) sensorimotor.   (D) concrete operations.
    (B) progenerative.   (E) formal operations.
    (C) preoperational.

21. Many African-American students speak a dialect of non-standard English called "eubonics." Effective teachers of these students should
    (A) discount the relevance of this information when planning instruction because standard English is needed to advance in society.
    (B) attempt to correct students when they use eubonics and always insist on the proper English pronunciations.
    (C) understand that eubonics is a cultural form of expression which the students use in formal and informal situations.
    (D) become fluent in eubonics so that they will be prepared to communicate when the need arises.
    (E) be sympathetic with the student and allow him to complete all of his work in the non-standard format.

22. Intelligence testing has come under fire because minority and poor students as a group consistently exhibit low achievement. Explanations of their results
    I.   point to a cognitive deficit which allows them to be competent in specific skills which are not measured by intelligence tests.
    II.   suggest that they may lack the experiences which are the basis of many of the test items found on intelligence examinations.
    III. lead many experts to believe that such tests should not be administered to these students.
    IV.   indicate that these students were achieving satisfactorily until the tests became more rigorous.
    (A) I and III only.   (D) I and IV only.
    (B) II and III only.   (E) I, III, and IV only.
    (C) II, III, and IV only.

23. Landmark Supreme Court decisions in 1954 and 1955 struck down
    (A) practices of de facto segregation which were not sanctioned by many states.
    (B) practices of de facto segregation which were sanctioned by many states.
    (C) practices of de jure segregation which were not sanctioned by many states.
    (D) practices of de jure segregation which were sanctioned by many states.
    (E) practices of devoir segregation that were sanctioned by many states.

segregation by law

24. Teachers must consciously develop good habits of questioning and be able to recognize poor ones. All of the following questions are examples of poor questioning techniques, EXCEPT

   (A) Which triangles should we prove congruent and how will they help us prove AB parallel to CD?

   (B) What is the relationship between the area of a circle and the circumference of a circle?

   (C) What method shall we use to solve this problem (pause) James?

   (D) How about these two angles?

   (E) No methods exist to solve this problem, do they?

25. Humanism in education stresses the welfare and growth of the individual students. All of the following would be true of this approach to education EXCEPT

   I. Individual differences are important but the individual must be subordinate to the group.

   II. Emphasizes the clarification of values that the pupil already holds without imposing new values.

   III. Education should help to make pupils sensitive to justice and injustice, and help them behave in ways that are consistent with the teachers moral judgments.

   IV. Fosters competition for grades and increases pressure to achieve high test scores.

   V. Teachers will help the student develop concerns for the feelings and needs of others.

   (A) III only.   (D) II and V only.

   (B) I and IV only.   (E) I, III, and IV only.

   (C) III and V only.

26. A teacher exhibits an authoritative teaching style by rewarding

   (A) convergent thinking.

   (B) divergent thinking.

   (C) both convergent and divergent thinking.

   (D) controlled behavior on the part of the student.

   (E) independent thinking and learning.

27. As a means to assure variety in methods of instruction, classroom teachers might use which of the following sources?

   I. Classic philosophical concepts

   II. Current educational views

   III. Other teachers

   IV. Anecdotal articles about teaching in newspapers or magazines of all sorts

   (A) I, II, and III only.   (D) II only.

   (B) I, and II only.   (E) I, II, III, and IV.

   (C) II and III only.

28. "Given a poem by Maya Angelou, the student will read the poem aloud," illustrates a specific learning outcome that lacks the

   (A) task confronting the learner.

(B)   expected observable behavior.

(C)   criterion level of performance.

(D)   content.

(E)   conditions under which the task will be performed.

29.   Public Law 94-142 requires all of the following to participate in the multidisciplinary evaluation of them to create an I.E.P. for a student:

I.   parent or guardian.

II.   special educator.

III. administrator or teacher.

IV.   student. *Does not have to attend.*

(A)   I and II only.

(B)   I, II, and III only.

(C)   I, II, III, and IV.

(D)   II and III only.

(E)   II and IV only.

30.   Traditional educators continue to hold that the purpose of education is to

I.   train students to become problem solvers who learn from life experience.

II.   emphasize the mastery of facts and information.

III. expect students to learn all subject matter at all grade levels.

IV.   give attention to test scores and grade-level achievement.

(A)   I and II only.

(B)   II and IV only.

(C)   I, II, and III only.

(D)   II, III, and IV only.

(E)   I, II, III, and IV.

31.   Each of the following is an anticipated development in American education by the year 2000 EXCEPT the

(A)   expansion of early childhood education.

(B)   expansion of education for elderly and retired people.

(C)   continued expansion of unionization of teachers.

(D)   expansion of year-round school schedules.

(E)   less parent and student control of educational choices and directions.

32.   Cultural pluralism refers to

(A)   preservation and enhancement of different cultures in a society.

(B)   maintenance and support for the "melting pot" theory.

(C)   the identification of two distinct cultures.

(D)   the requirement of bilingual programs.

(E)   the historical process of acculturation.

33.   Public Law 94-142, the Education for All Handicapped Children Act, requires all of the following EXCEPT *Does Not Require mainstreaming*

(A)   mainstreaming.

(B)   an Individualized Education Program (I.E.P.).

(C)   placement by parental approval.

(D)   private school compliance.

(E)   free public education for handicapped learners between the ages of three and twenty-one.

34.   When compared with the society of the previous decade, American society today is likely to be composed of

(A)   more single parent households headed by the father.

(B)   more single parent households headed by the mother.

(C)   just as many single parent households headed by the father as headed by the mother.

(D)   traditional households with both the mother and the father at home.

(E)   the same proportion of types of households as the previous decade.

35.   Which of the following does NOT exert a direct legal influence on local schools?

(A)   School boards

(B)   School superintendents

(C)   Teachers' organizations

(D)   Parent-teacher organizations

(E)   Principals

Section 2

TIME: 30 Minutes
35 Questions

DIRECTIONS: Each of the following questions and incomplete statements is followed by five answer choices. Select the choice which best answers each question.

---

1. The conventional view of good classroom management deals with concepts such as
   I.   lesson planning.
   II.   evaluation of students.
   III. utilization of teaching materials.
   IV.   maintaining a controlled, low-volume atmosphere.
   (A) I and II only.   (D) IV only.
   (B) I, II, and III only.   (E) I, II, III, and IV.
   (C) II, III, and IV only.

2. The teaching strategy which is most appropriate for a subject-centered curriculum is
   (A) inquiry. Divergent thinking   (D) guided discovery. Led to a specific conclusion through a series of questions
   (B) lecture/discussion.   (E) group investigation. → open ended Not appropriate
   (C) simulation. Learner centered

3. Programmed instruction is considered to have all of the following advantages EXCEPT
   (A) there is little dependence on general academic skills or abilities. relies on reading ability
   (B) basic subject matter can be presented.
   (C) feedback can be provided throughout the lesson.
   (D) students can learn at their own rates.
   (E) it can help students understand a sequence of complex material.

4. School-based health clinics are controversial primarily because they
   (A) compete with traditional medical services.
   (B) are likely to interfere with academic study.
   (C) are costly.
   (D) often offer birth control counseling. Birth control
   (E) advocate immunizations.

5. A factor which works against the expansion of high quality early childhood programs is
   (A) strong demand for child care.
   (B) societal attitude toward the need for early childhood education.
   (C) lack of active parental involvement in planning programs.
   (D) desire of parents to keep their children at home.
   (E) lack of funding.

6. An individualized education program (I.E.P.) is a federally mandated educational plan for a
    - (A)   college-bound learner.
    - (B)   vocational-technical track learner.
    - (C)   slower learner.
    - (D)   handicapped learner.
    - (E)   gifted learner.

7. Each individualized education program (I.E.P.) must include all of the following EXCEPT
    - (A)   the child's present level of performance and functioning.
    - (B)   quarterly goals.
    - (C)   specific special education services to be provided.
    - (D)   projected dates for initiation of special services.
    - (E)   anticipated duration of special services.

8. Some of the problems associated with rigid homogeneous ability groups are that
    - I.   teachers tend to favor teaching average or above-average groups rather than low ability groups.
    - II.   students who are labelled low-ability usually perform poorly.
    - III.   the ability of a teacher to provide individualized programs is diminished.
    - IV.   unfavorable self-concept is reinforced among students placed in low-ability groups.
    - (A)   I and II only.
    - (B)   I, II, and III only.
    - (C)   I, II, III, and IV.
    - (D)   I and III only.
    - (E)   I, II, and IV only.

9. A mastery learning model attempts to provide all learners with
    - (A)   equal time for learning.
    - (B)   opportunities to meet minimum requirements.
    - (C)   equal mastery in their learning.
    - (D)   the necessary preparation for college.
    - (E)   alternative routes for remedial or reinforcement activities.

10. A nongraded school plan attempts to do all of the following EXCEPT
    - (A)   provide multiple aged learning groups.
    - (B)   provide individualized learning centers.
    - (C)   provide different time schedules for learners.
    - (D)   provide group rather than individual measures of achievement.
    - (E)   provide for horizontal articulation among subjects.

11. The word "education" has its roots in Latin. Which of the following Latin terms most accurately describes the process of education or educating?
    - (A)   "Educare;" i.e., putting in or "answering."
    - (B)   "Educere;" i.e., leading out or "questioning."
    - (C)   "Educand;" i.e., person to be educated.
    - (D)   All of the above.
    - (E)   Only (A) and (B).

12. Which of the following definitions best describes the word "pedagogy"?
    (A) The art of teaching.
    (B) The art of learning.
    (C) The science of teaching.
    (D) The science of learning.
    (E) The art and science of teaching and learning.

13. If epistemology is the "study of the logical structure of knowledge," how would you define "espistemological skepticism?"
    (A) Doubt about the structure of knowledge.
    (B) Doubt about the reality of knowledge.
    (C) Doubt about the structure and reality of knowledge.
    (D) Doubt that knowledge exists.
    (E) None of the above.

14. The term "didactics" is gaining more and more acceptance among educators. It implies the following:
    (A) Teaching style
    (B) Lecture method
    (C) Instructional scheme
    (D) All of the above.
    (E) None of the above.

15. Which of the following labels best describe John Dewey (1859-1952)?
    (A) American psychologist
    (B) American educator
    (C) American philosopher
    (D) All of the above.
    (E) None of the above.

16. There have been six major coherent philosophical orientations to teaching that have been developed in response to the questions with which all teachers must grapple. Five of these philosophical orientations are listed below with a brief description of each of these orientations. All of the following descriptions are correct EXCEPT:
    (A) Perennialism - views truth as a constant and the aim of education as ensuring that students acquire knowledge of these unchanging truths.
    (B) Progessivism - child centered, concerned with problem-solving strategies that would enable students to cope with changes.
    (C) Essentialism - students would learn appropriate methods for dealing with the significant crises that confront the world: war, depression, international terrorism, hunger, inflation and ever-accelerating technological advances.
    (D) Existentialism - focuses on the experiences of the individual. Existentialists judge the curriculum according to whether or not it contributes to the individual's quest for meaning.
    (E) Behaviorism - based upon the principle that desirable human behavior can be the product of design, rather than accident.

17. A sixth grade teacher is planning to start a social studies lesson using the inquiry method. Which of the following statements would start a good inquiry lesson?
    I.   There are fewer farms today than 50 years ago, but American farmers grow more food today than they did 50 years ago.

II. People do not work hard anymore.

III. Most students dislike history.

IV. Changes in life-style affect language usage.

(A) I only.
(D) I, II, and III only.

(B) II and III only.
(E) I, II, III, and IV.

(C) I and IV only.

18. According to Mager, instructional objectives should be stated as behavioral objectives. A teacher should specify quantitatively what a student will be able to do, rather than just what he or she should know at the end of a lesson, unit or course. Which of the following is the best example of a behavioral objective?

(A) "The student will explain the reasons for the Bill of Rights."

(B) "The student will express herself/himself in class when the subject of the Bill of Rights is raised."

(C) "The student will write a research paper on the Bill of Rights."

(D) "The student will list the ten issues covered in the Bill of Rights and will get eight of the ten issues correct."

(E) "The student will demonstrate skills for democratic living."

19. Research on students' self-esteem indicates that teachers should do all of the following EXCEPT

(A) group students according to ability, so that the lower ability student does not have to compete with the higher ability student.

(B) develop a classroom environment that encourages respectfulness, personal regard, and fairness.

(C) provide opportunities for students to participate in decision making, interaction, and self-discipline.

(D) encourage students to engage in a self-evaluation progress.

(E) provide instruction aimed at personal and social development.

20. In 1975 Congress enacted Public Law 94-142 (The Education of All Handicapped Children Act). This law specified the use of individualized education programs (IEP) to identify individual needs and capacities. By law these IEP's must specify all of the following EXCEPT

(A) the student's present educational achievement level.

(B) appropriate annual and short-range educational goals.

(C) special services to achieve or implement the goals.

(D) the extent to which the handicapped student can be placed in a regular classroom.

(E) monthly review of instructional goals, progress, and implementation plans.

yearly review

21. Ms. Lu takes every appropriate opportunity to confront her students with social problems and then help them work toward solutions. She feels strongly about the importance of having students learn about social problems, as well as discovering what they can do about them. To her, a major part of her responsibility as a teacher is to raise the consciousness level of her students in regard to the problems that confront all human beings. Ms. Lu's teaching methods are mostly aligned with which of the

following philosophies?

(A)   Reconstructionism   (D)   Essentialism

(B)   Behaviorism   (E)   Progressivism

(C)   Existentialism

22.   Simply placing students in groups and telling them to work together does not in and of itself promote greater understanding of mathematical principles and the ability to communicate one's mathematical reasoning to others. According to current research, only under certain conditions do group efforts become more productive than individual efforts. Those conditions are:

I.   Teachers must clearly structure positive interdependence within each student learning group.

II.   Students must engage in promotive (face-to-face) interaction while completing math assignments.

III.   Teachers must ensure that all students are individually accountable to complete math assignments and promote the learning of their groupmates.

IV.   Students must learn and frequently use required interpersonal and small-group skills.

V.   Teachers must be careful to group only those students who get along well together.

(A)   I, II, and III only.   (D)   I, III, IV, and V only.

(B)   I, II, III, and IV only.   (E)   I, II, III, and V only.

(C)   I, II, and IV only.

23.   Taxonomies in education serve the following purposes(s):

(A)   To formulate learner objectives

(B)   To articulate contents and methods

(C)   To design curricular priorities

(D)   To understand developmental processes

(E)   All of the above.

24.   The term "objectives" is primarily used in

(A)   Curricular development.   (D)   Formulating learning goals.

(B)   Educational psychology.   (E)   All of the above.

(C)   Educational technology.

25.   "Holistic" growth or development includes all of the following EXCEPT

(A)   mental growth or development.

(B)   psychomotoric growth or development.

(C)   organizational growth or development.

(D)   personal growth or development.

(E)   social growth or development.

26.   Cueing, modeling, and reinforcement schedules are behavioristic techniques that

(A)   aid discipline.

    (B)   enhance teaching and learning.

    (C)   encourage appropriate responses.

    (D)   Include all of the above.

    (E)   Exclude all of the above.

27. Erikson's theory of development helps educators to design what type of objectives?

    (A)   Psychosomatic   (D)   Sociocultural

    (B)   Psychosexual   (E)   Sociobiological

    (C)   Psychosocial

28. The decade of reform of teacher education was prompted by

    (A)   poor teaching and low student achievement.

    (B)   international union organizing and national unionization of teachers.

    (C)   teacher shortages and concerns about international trade.

    (D)   teacher shortages and an increase in school administrators.

    (E)   the firing of many unqualified, yet tenured teachers.

29. Merit-pay plans

    I.   are novel ideas embraced by the majority of teachers.

    II.   change the traditional salary schedule.

    III.   are resisted by teachers.

    IV.   are becoming a popular way of financing educational reform.

    (A)   I, II and IV.   (D)   I and IV.

    (B)   II and III.   (E)   I, II, III and IV.

    (C)   III and IV.

30. When a teacher enters a classroom with preconceived expectations concerning the academic achievement of the class, students in the class will have a tendency to achieve according to those expectations. This is an example of

    (A)   field independence.   (D)   field dependence.

    (B)   the pollyanna effect.   (E)   failure on demand.

    (C)   self-fulfilling prophecy.

31. Equality of educational opportunity means

    I.   giving everyone the same opportunity to receive an education in public supported colleges.

    II.   giving everyone the opportunity to receive a high-school education.

    III.   giving everyone the same opportunity for the same chance to receive an education.

    IV.   giving everyone the opportunity to go to the university of their choice.

    (A)   I and II.   (D)   I, II, and IV.

    (B)   II and III.   (E)   I, II, III, and IV.

    (C)   III only.

32. State legislation affecting teachers has the greatest impact on
    (A) certification, licensing, and training.
    (B) certification, teaching methods, and career advancement.
    (C) certification, training, and credentialing.
    (D) certification, recruitment, and training.
    (E) certification, licensing, and salary.

33. Teachers may perpetuate sex roles for their students by engaging in teaching behaviors which support societal images of males and females. These teaching behaviors
    I. can be both positive and negative.
    II. are intentional, because the teacher is preparing the student for the real world.
    III. may elevate or stifle individual self-awareness and growth.
    IV. have greatly increased in educational institutions.
    (A) I and II.   (D) III and IV.
    (B) I and III.   (E) None of the above.
    (C) II and III.

34. The school superintendent
    (A) is usually a member of the school board.
    (B) is usually an independent contractor.
    (C) is an employee of the school district.
    (D) is an *ex officio* member of the board.
    (E) is an employee of the state.

35. The federal government has
    (A) no direct control over local education.
    (B) has direct control over local education.
    (C) has no indirect means of control over local education.
    (D) indirectly controls local education through direct legislation.
    (E) administers total control over local education.

Section 3

TIME: 30 Minutes
35 Questions

DIRECTIONS: Each of the following questions and incomplete statements is followed by five answer choices. Select the choice which best answers each question.

---

1. Block grants instituted as a method of funding education during the Reagan presidency were viewed by educational liberals as

    I. equitable methods of financing public education programs.
    II. conservative attempts to dilute categorically funded programs.
    III. a method to allow states greater control over program funding.
    IV. harmful to existing programs which supported minority group children.

    (A) I and III.
    (B) II and III.
    (C) II, III and IV.
    (D) III and IV.
    (E) II and IV.

2. Sally has a problem with inappropriate behavior in class. Specifically, she seems to spend more time out or her seat than in her seat. Her teacher is interested in using behavior management principles to address Sally's behavior. Which of the following strategies should always be considered first and/or nearly always used in combination with the other approaches listed in order to modify behaviors such as Sally's out of seat behavior?

    (A) Time Out
    (B) Extinction
    (C) Punishment
    (D) Positive Reinforcement
    (E) Removal of Positive Reinforcement

3. In the United States the group responsible for education is

    (A) the Department of Education
    (B) the Department of Health and Human Services
    (C) the Committee on Education and Labor
    (D) the Committee on Labor and Public Welfare
    (E) the Department of Educational Services

4. The NEA and AFT represent

    I. teachers.
    II. principals.
    III. superintendents.
    IV. school board members.

    (A) I.
    (B) I and II.
    (C) II and IV.
    (D) III and IV.
    (E) All of the above.

145

5. In the *Lau v. Nichols et al* case,
    (A) the Supreme Court found a violation of the Fourteenth Amendment.
    (B) Title VI of the 1964 Civil Rights Act provided the basis for a remedy.
    (C) bilingual education was found to be constitutionally protected.
    (D) students who spoke non-standard English were to be taught only in their mother tongues.
    (E) the Supreme Court found a violation of students' First Amendment rights.

6. In the *Lau* case the Supreme Court ruled that
    (A) schools must implement bilingual education programs.
    (B) schools could teach in any languages in which their teachers had expertise.
    (C) schools give non-English speaking children special help in learning English.
    (D) schools implement immersion programs.
    (E) only schools that could afford it had to teach bilingual education.

7. People with more education generally
    (A) have a higher unemployment rate.   (D) tend to be unhappier.
    (B) earn more money.   (E) tend to have more marital problems.
    (C) are limited in career choices.

8. The typical American teacher
    (A) is female.
    (B) is about 50 years old.
    (C) has taught for 25 years.
    (D) does not belong to the National Education Association or similar organizations.
    (E) spends an average of six and a half hours a day at school.

9. Students generally like teachers who
    I.   have a sense of humor.
    II.   are perceived as being fair.
    III. are perceived as liking students.
    IV.   are perceived as being hard workers.
    (A) I only.   (D) I and IV only.
    (B) I and II only.   (E) I, II, III, and IV.
    (C) I, II, and III only.

10. All of the following are true about private elementary and secondary schools in the United States EXCEPT that
    (A) they are growing in enrollment.
    (B) they consist mainly of religious schools.
    (C) they pay their teachers less than do most public schools.
    (D) they tend to not have fully certified teachers.
    (E) they represent another career option for students in teacher education programs.

11. Merit pay for teachers is
    (A) generally opposed by teachers' unions.
    (B) used in a majority of school districts.
    (C) a recent development.
    (D) thought of by teachers as a morale enhancer.
    (E) not expected to be more widely implemented in the future.

12. A teacher's total compensation usually includes all of the following EXCEPT
    (A) paid vacation days.   (D) health benefits.
    (B) salary.   (E) retirement benefits.
    (C) unemployment insurance.

13. School districts are required by law to provide
    I.   retirement benefits.   III. unemployment insurance.
    II. medical insurance.   IV. provision for sick leave.
    (A) I, and II only.   (D) III and IV only.
    (B) II and IV only.   (E) I, II, III, and IV.
    (C) I, III, and IV only.

14. Which of the following is NOT a finding presented in the "A Nation At Risk" report? *HAS changed*
    (A) The quality of schools hasn't changed much since the "Sputnik" era.
    (B) Many teachers are coming from the bottom quarter of college graduates.
    (C) Teacher preparation curriculum is weighted heavily with education rather than content courses.
    (D) Many teachers are required to supplement their income by "moonlighting" with a second job.
    (E) Severe shortages exist for certain kinds of teachers.

15. The Holmes Group recommended all of the following EXCEPT
    (A) a major in education for prospective teachers.
    (B) a graduate teacher education program.
    (C) graduate study in a teaching field for secondary teachers.
    (D) a long-term, well-supervised internship.
    (E) a commitment to a multicultural society.

16. In the *Brown v. Board of Education of Topeka* decision, the U.S. Supreme Court
    (A) mandated a system of funding for public schools.
    (B) granted permission for busing as a means of integration.
    (C) rejected the notion of separate but equal schools.
    (D) created new rights for minorities.
    (E) permitted racial quotas for teacher recruitment.

17. The right to an education is assured to children in the United States
    (A) by citizenship status.
    (B) by the parents' payment of taxes in a school district.

(C)   by residence in a school district.

(D)   by documented legal alien status.

(E)   by state constitutions.

18.   Under the doctrine of in *loco parentis*, courts have upheld the rules and regulations of local boards of education, especially with regard to

(A)   teacher conduct.   (D)   student dress.

(B)   student conduct.   (E)   parents' rights.

(C)   the authority of a principal.

19.   The American Federation of Teachers (AFT) is affiliated with the

(A)   AFL-CIO.

(B)   Political Action Committee for Education.

(C)   National Education Association.

(D)   National Association of Secondary School Principals.

(E)   U.S. Department of Education.

20.   The National Education Association (NEA) refuses to merge with the American Federation of Teachers (AFT) because

(A)   the NEA has stronger political clout.

(B)   each holds very different political views.

(C)   the NEA is too large.

(D)   the AFT is affiliated with organized labor.

(E)   their organizational structures are too different.

21.   The federal mandate for a least restrictive learning environment, with regard to disabled students, is the result of

(A)   *Brown v. Board of Education of Topeka.*

(B)   the Carnegie Commission of Education.

(C)   the Holmes Group.

(D)   the Education and Improvement Act of 1981.

(E)   Public Law 94-142.

22.   Which of the following psychological principles can best be met by exhibiting notices, articles and materials reflecting student achievement in a three-dimensional display in the main lobby of the school?

(A)   Incidental learning may occur subconsciously under unpredictable circumstances.

(B)   The retention of learning is enhanced when more than one stimulus is applied.

(C)   A sense of belonging and security are of paramount importance in the learning process.

(D)   A student responds to learning experiences only when motivated.

(E)   Students have individual differences as well as group similarities.

23. Which decision of the U.S. Supreme Court declared that separate-but-equal schools are inherently unequal and required them to integrate with all deliberate speed?

    (A) *Tinker v. Des Moines*   (D) *S-1 v. Turlington*

    (B) *Goss v. Lopez*   (E) *Plyler v. Doe*

    (C) *Brown v. Topeka*

24. Which Amendment of the Constitution of the United States protects a teacher's freedom of expression?

    (A) First   (D) Tenth

    (B) Fourth   (E) Fourteenth

    (C) Fifth

25. In regard to student records, the Family Rights and Privacy Act (also known as the Buckley Amendment) requires educators to

    (A) provide all requesting parties with unrestricted access to student records.

    (B) furnish copies of student records to parents only.

    (C) furnish copies of student records to students only.

    (D) provide copies of student records to the media upon request.

    (E) maintain confidentiality of information in the records.

26. A contract to teach, signed by an individual, is a written agreement between the teacher and the

    (A) superintendent.   (D) teachers union.

    (B) local school board.   (E) school principal.

    (C) state school board.

27. Which of the following is the best example of integrated teaching practices?

    (A) After reading a story from a basal reader, students take a spelling test on words from the story.

    (B) While teaching a social studies unit on "westward expansion," the teacher reads *Little House on the Prairie* to the class.

    (C) After reading some books about American Indians, students construct a model of a tribal dwelling and share it with the class.

    (D) Each student reads a book and writes a report on it to share with the class.

    (E) In small groups, students design an ethnic dance which they perform for the class.

28. Which of the following statements about dialects is NOT true?

    (A) All people speak with some type of dialect.

    (B) Dialects contribute to reading problems.

    (C) Dialects are as rule-governed and systematic as standard English.

    (D) Low-status dialect should be eliminated from a child's speech.

    (E) Dialects are associated with race, class, ethnicity, and region.

29. Which of the following practices are appropriate means of informal assessment procedures?

    I.   Achievement tests   IV.   Literature logs
    II.   Reading logs   V.   Informal interest inventories
    III.   Writing portfolios

    (A)   I and III only.   (D)   II, III, and V only.
    (B)   I and V only.   (E)   II, IV, and V only.
    (C)   II, III, and IV only.

30. Which of the following communication behaviors are determined by cultural expectations?

    I.   Eye contact   III.   Emphasis on high grades
    II.   Silence   IV.   Leadership roles

    (A)   I and II only.   (D)   I, III, and IV only.
    (B)   III and IV only.   (E)   I, II, III, and IV.
    (C)   I, II, and IV only.

31. Which of the following situations is the best example of providing a sexually nonbiased curriculum?

    (A)   Teacher A supplements the state curriculum unit on "Men Who Settled the West" with the study of Annie Oakley and Belle Star.

    (B)   Teacher B always tells the girls in her ninth grade classroom that they can successfully compete with the boys at any level and they should strive to accomplish anything they want.

    (C)   Teacher C faithfully devotes the month of March to Women's History Month and teaches only about women during that time.

    (D)   Teacher D has instituted a new unit of study entitled "Uncommon Women" which includes the study of famous women writers, politicians, and athletes.

    (E)   Teacher E has changed science textbooks recently, and is now incorporating the contributions of women scientists throughout his lectures and supplemental readings.

32. When is it appropriate to use instructional objectives which are based upon norm referenced rather than criterion referenced, standards, for students with disabilities who are, for example, mainstreamed into a math class?

    (A)   It is appropriate to use instructional objectives which are based upon norm referenced standards when the standards are related to subject areas other than that of the class into which the student is mainstreamed.

    (B)   It is never appropriate to use instructional objectives which are based upon norm referenced standards for students with disabilities.

    (C)   It is never appropriate to use instructional objectives which are based upon criterion referenced standards for students with disabilities.

    (D)   It is appropriate to use instructional objectives which are based upon norm referenced standards for math performance only, if that is what is used for the students in the math class without disabilities.

    (E)   The determination of the appropriateness of the use of instructional objectives based upon norm referenced standards will depend upon the goals for mainstreaming the student with disabilities into the math class, as listed in the Individualized Education Plan for the student with disabilities.

33. In attempting to change a student's inappropriate behavior, all of the following would be crucial pieces of information for a teacher to have in order to attempt to change the inappropriate behavior, EXCEPT

(A) current consequences of the behavior.

(B) current antecedents to the behavior.

(C) what is reinforcing to the student.

(D) strategies attempted by other teachers in the past to change the behavior.

(E) a very specific description/definition of the inappropriate behavior.

34. The least restrictive environment of most individuals with disabilities is

(A) the regular class.

(B) the special day class in which students with similar disabilities are grouped together.

(C) the segregated school.

(D) based upon a label given to a student.

(E) dependent upon student performance on intelligence tests.

35. Which of the following is the best example of a criterion referenced behavioral objective?

(A) Given a list of second grade words, Johnny (a second grader) will correctly read 90% of the words for 3 consecutive weeks.

(B) Johnny (a second grader) will read at the second grade level as measured by the Wide Range Achievement Test.

(C) Given a list of second grade words, Johnny (a second grader) will increase his correct reading of words by one word per week for 5 consecutive weeks.

(D) Given a list of second grade words, Johnny (a second grader) will correctly read the number of words representing the class average for words read for 3 consecutive weeks.

(E) Given a list of second grade words, Johnny (a second grader) will score in the 80th percentile for words correctly read by second graders at his school for 3 consecutive weeks.

TEST OF PROFESSIONAL KNOWLEDGE

ANSWER KEY

SECTION 1

1.	(B)	10.	(D)	19.	(D)	28.	(C)
2.	(B)	11.	(B)	20.	(B)	29.	(B)
3.	(D)	12.	(D)	21.	(C)	30.	(D)
4.	(C)	13.	(B)	22.	(B)	31.	(E)
5.	(D)	14.	(B)	23.	(D)	32.	(A)
6.	(B)	15.	(E)	24.	(C)	33.	(A)
7.	(A)	16.	(D)	25.	(E)	34.	(B)
8.	(E)	17.	(C)	26.	(A)	35.	(D)
9.	(D)	18.	(A)	27.	(A)		

SECTION 2

1.	(B)	10.	(D)	19.	(A)	28.	(C)
2.	(B)	11.	(E)	20.	(E)	29.	(B)
3.	(A)	12.	(E)	21.	(A)	30.	(C)
4.	(D)	13.	(C)	22.	(B)	31.	(C)
5.	(E)	14.	(D)	23.	(E)	32.	(D)
6.	(D)	15.	(D)	24.	(E)	33.	(B)
7.	(B)	16.	(C)	25.	(C)	34.	(C)
8.	(E)	17.	(C)	26.	(D)	35.	(A)
9.	(B)	18.	(D)	27.	(C)		

SECTION 3

1.	(C)	10.	(D)	19.	(A)	28.	(D)
2.	(D)	11.	(A)	20.	(D)	29.	(C)
3.	(D)	12.	(A)	21.	(E)	30.	(E)
4.	(A)	13.	(C)	22.	(D)	31.	(E)
5.	(B)	14.	(A)	23.	(C)	32.	(E)
6.	(C)	15.	(A)	24.	(A)	33.	(D)
7.	(B)	16.	(C)	25.	(E)	34.	(A)
8.	(A)	17.	(E)	26.	(B)	35.	(C)
9.	(E)	18.	(B)	27.	(C)		

DETAILED EXPLANATIONS OF ANSWERS

NTE CORE BATTERY–Test 1

TEST OF PROFESSIONAL KNOWLEDGE
Section 1

1. **(B)** Question one is based on the design of instruction. Answers (C), (D), and (E) can be eliminated from consideration since each of those includes IV, which is based on the behavior of a teacher, rather than of a student. (A) can also be eliminated since it does not include a statement of the conditions under which the student will demonstrate the behavior. Thus, the best answer is (B), since it is expressed in terms of learner behavior, has a criterion of level of acceptable performance, and states the conditions under which the learner will exhibit the behavior.

2. **(B)** Question two is based on the design of instruction. Bloom's Taxonomy represents a hierarchy of learning tasks, each somewhat more demanding than the last. Knowledge level requires that the student present the information in the same format in which it was given him/her. Since the information is not being presented in the same format as given to the student, (A) is not a viable answer. Comprehension level involves the manipulation of some data, either translating it from one form to another or restating it in one's own words. In this situation the student must translate the material from a graphic representation to a verbal one. Hence, (B) is the best response. Application (C) requires that some rule must be selected by the student and used to solve the problem. Analysis (D) requires that some complex entity must be broken down to its constituent parts and examined to see how the parts work together to create the whole. Synthesis (E) would involve the creative meshing of elements to create a new and unique entity.

3. **(D)** Question three is based on the constitutional rights of students. In this instance, item (A) and item (E) can both be eliminated since there is no direct relationship indicated between the student's past behavior and the contents of the locker. Item (B) can similarly be eliminated since, again, this alone would not allow a school official to search the student's property without cause. A school official does not need a search warrant to search a student locker, while a police officer would, thus (C) is not an appropriate answer. (D) is clearly the best response because the school official must have some reason to suspect that the student's locker contains an illegal substance in order to search it, although the rules are not as stringent as for a police officer who must legally demonstrate due cause.

153

4. **(C)** Question four is based on the constitutional rights of students. (C) would be the best answer since it is treating the different religions in a neutral manner, and is not attempting to indoctrinate anyone to the beliefs of a particular religion, or obligating one to participate in the belief structure of a religious group. (A) would be inappropriate since a specific prayer is being either mandated or offered as a suggested format. (B) is also inappropriate in that it is suggesting that the truth is to be found within the confines of one particular religion. (D) suggests that prayer is mandated and seems to suggest that it is expected that all students either must or should pray. (E), while appearing even handed, still obligates students to participate in religious activities, while the school's role should be one neutrality.

5. **(D)** Question five is based on the constitutional rights of students. (D) is the most appropriate response because it states three of the main provisions of the law. While the law does provide for mainstreaming, it does not mandate it in all cases. In some obvious cases the placement of a handicapped child in a regular classroom would be totally inappropriate. The law merely states that the child should be placed in the least restrictive environment under which he/she can adequately function. For this reason (A), (B), (C), and (E) are all inappropriate answers.

6. **(B)** Question six is based on the implementation of instructional design and conditions that facilitate learning. (B) is the most appropriate answer in that it is the only teaching model listed which is teacher centered, rather than learner centered, and which deals with the idea of teach and test. In this method the learners are told the information and they are to remember it and reiterate it for the test. In all of the other methods listed the students are required to participate in the learning in more than a passive manner, thus, higher level thinking skills will be employed.

7. **(A)** Question seven is based on the evaluation of student achievement and instructional effectiveness. Item (A) is the correct answer because an essay test by its very nature includes the higher level thinking skills of analysis, synthesis, and evaluation, and it allows the students to be creative in their responses, an option which is generally not available in more objective testing means. Essay tests tend to limit the sampling of student knowledge, rather than broadening it, thus items (B), (C) and (E) can be eliminated, and essay tests are more open to bluffing by students who write well, yet may not know the answer to a specific question, thus eliminating items (C), (D), and (E).

8. **(E)** Question eight is based on the evaluation of student achievement and instructional effectiveness. Item (E) is the most appropriate answer in that most standardized tests are commercially prepared, and thus have been developed and measured to apply to a specific population, and thus are compared to certain "norms." There tends to be a wide dispersal in the scores, thus having a high power of discrimination between one score and another. It is designed so that if a student were to take different forms of the same test the scores would be very close to identical, thus there is a high rate of reliability, and finally, those students who have a low score will have a tendency to have any selected item incorrect, while those with a high score will exhibit a tendency to have any selected item correct.

9. **(D)** Question nine is based on the knowledge of the teaching profession and of professional teaching behaviors. Item (D) is the most appropriate response in that the National Education Association represents approximately four times as many teachers at the

bargaining table than does the next largest group, the American Federation of Teachers. The other groups listed do not represent any teachers in the collective bargaining process.

10. **(D)** Question ten is based on the evaluation of student achievement and instructional effectiveness. Item (D) is the most appropriate response in that as students are given more time to think of an appropriate response, they are more likely to come to the correct response. This tends to reinforce answering behavior, thus causing an increase in answering behavior and eliminating response (E) as a possible answer. This increases the probability of appropriate behavior on the part of the learner. Item (A) is inappropriate in that students, when given the additional time tend to ask further questions, rather than fewer. Since students have additional time to think they tend to increase their levels of divergent thinking, thus eliminating response (B).

11. **(B)** Question eleven is based on judicial policy as related to classroom practice. Response (B) is the most appropriate response. Federal law states that a teacher may use copyrighted material for instructional purposes without permission if there is insufficient time to obtain permission before intended use of the material. This would eliminate (C), (D), and (E), since the teacher would have time to obtain permission after initial use of the article. (A) would be inappropriate in that the law does provide provisions for a teacher to utilize copyrighted materials.

12. **(D)** Question twelve is based on the evaluation of student achievement and instructional effectiveness. Item (D) is the most appropriate response. Children tend to live up to the expectation that teachers and parents hold for them. If teachers expect students to think at higher levels, they must be expected to perform at the higher levels. (A) is inappropriate in that while students need a knowledge base, it is important that education not stop at that level, and that it proceed to the higher levels. (B) as well is inappropriate in that it is the overuse of knowledge and comprehension questions that lead many students to find school boring. (C) is inappropriate in that most students will not progress, by themselves, to the higher levels.

13. **(B)** Question thirteen is based on the implementation of instructional design and conditions that facilitate learning. Item (B) is the most appropriate response. When students are able to interact with one another, their levels of achievement tend to rise most significantly. The more able students both serve as role models for the less able and are also able to give academic encouragement, aid, and support when needed. When groups are homogeneously grouped, achievement tends to fall, thus eliminating responses (A), (C), and (D). Often when students are permitted to pick their own groups, they tend to group themselves homogeneously in one form or another.

14. **(B)** Question fourteen is based on the implementation of instructional design and conditions that facilitate learning. (B) is the most appropriate response. The goal of multicultural education is to teach students about their own cultures and about the cultures of others with the dual aims of mutual and self respect. Its guiding principle is that there is no one model America—different cultural traditions shape each of us. It is more than adding a few heroes and holidays to an already set curriculum, thus eliminating choices (D) and (E). There is heritage, thus eliminating choice (A). Multicultural education accepts the premise that part of who we are depends on who we were, and that the events of the past are still a part of us today, thus eliminating choice (C).

15. **(E)** Question fifteen is based on recognizing extraclassroom influences on teachers. (E) is the most appropriate response. Teachers, as all individuals, act on the biases that they possess. Teachers have been shown to react less favorably to a less physically attractive student. They have also been shown to incorporate into their attitudinal structure what they have heard "through the grapevine" from other teachers. They tend to be swayed by information contained in the students cumulative record. And finally, teachers have also been shown to react differently to students whose racial, ethnic, or social class is different from their own.

16. **(D)** Question sixteen is based on the implementation of instructional design and conditions that facilitate learning. Item (D) is the most appropriate response in that research has shown that teachers tend to provide less able students less time to formulate a response to a question than they do more able students. It has also been shown that teachers respond with more negative interactions and fewer positive interactions with less able students than they do with more able students. (C) is an inappropriate response in that evidence has been shown that teachers tend to demand less of the less able student, and that this set of lower expectations tends to further widen the gap of achievement between the two groups of students.

17. **(C)** Question seventeen is based on the implementation of instructional design and conditions that facilitate learning. Item (C) is the most appropriate response in that research has shown that writing across the curriculum has positively affected both writing ability and content area skills. Part of the reason for this has been that it tends to utilize the higher order thinking skills, mentioned in response (B), thus helping to develop a deeper understanding of the content area. Other research has shown that writing is a skill best developed through hands on practice. "Writing across the curriculum" puts together the two, yielding positive results both in the content area as well as in the area of writing itself.

18. **(A)** Question eighteen is based on the implementation of instructional design and conditions that facilitate learning. Item (A) is the most appropriate response in that the only group which has been shown to receive any benefits from tracking has been the most academically talented. Research has indicated that due to lower expectations of teachers of the lower tracked students, their rate of progress has been considerably retarded, thus eliminating the viability of all the other responses. Other research has indicated that minority students have been disproportionately placed in lower track classes, perpetuating false stereotypes about ethnic minority students and their chances at academic success.

19. **(D)** Question nineteen is based on the implementation of instructional design and conditions that facilitate learning. Item (D) is the most appropriate response in that the inquiry method of learning is the utilization of the scientific method, and thus the students learn how to learn. In this method the students collect data, formulate and test hypotheses, revise their hypotheses as necessary, and retest. As a concluding experience they form conclusions and generalizations. While students may result in feeling more positive about school when the inquiry model is utilized (A), this is a side note and not the main benefit. One of the drawbacks of this technique is that information is gained more slowly than, for example, in expository teaching (B). No correlation has been found between this method and reading scores (C) .

20. **(B)** Question twenty deals with implementing instructional design and conditions. Choice (B) is the only response that was not identified by Piaget as a developmental stage.

Choice (A) begins at birth and extends to about age two. Choice (C) begins at age two and extends to about age six. Choice (D) begins at age seven and extends to about age eleven. Choice (E) begins at age eleven and extends through adulthood.

21. **(C)** Question twenty-one is related to diagnosing student needs. Response (C) is the correct alternative because it suggests that effective teachers display cultural sensitivity when planning and delivering lessons. Additionally, teachers need to be aware of the influence of cultural expressions in learning. Alternative (A) is incorrect because it lacks recognition of cultural sensitivity. (B) is an inappropriate reply because there is not sufficient time available in the typical instructional period to address all the nuances of language use which occur during teaching. We can eliminate (D) because of the futility in trying to understand dialects of a major language. Because of the lack of consistency of dialects, African-Americans in one part of a city may use entirely different patterns of communication than AfricanAmericans in other sections of a city while still using the basics of eubonics. (E) is inappropriate because constant use of eubonic expressions will not prepare the student for success in our society.

22. **(B)** Alternative (B) is the correct response. This question is concerned with responding to educational issues and keeping abreast of knowledge in one's field. Both responses II and III reflect the research in the area of testing fairness. Alternative I reflects the position of those who feel that intelligence tests are culturally fair as they now stand. Item IV has never been shown.

23. **(D)** This question deals with recognizing legislation regarding racial justice the correct response is item (D). In 1954, with the Brown vs. Board of Education of Topeka case, and 1955 with Brown II, the court struck down the doctrine of "separate but equal." This policy was found to be in violation of the fourteenth amendment of the constitution. This policy was identified as de jure segregation. Responses (A) and (B) refer to de facto segregation, an issue which was not found to be unconstitutional by the Supreme Court. Alternative (C) is incorrect because in 1954 southern states and border states had laws supporting the notion of "separate but equal." There is no such thing as devoir segregation (E).

24. **(C)** This question is related to implementing instructional design and conditions that facilitate learning. Answer (C) is the only question using good questioning techniques. It asks a question, gives the students in the class time to formulate an answer, and then calls on one of the students for the answer. Question (A) is a multiple question and although a student may know which triangles need to be proved congruent, he may not know how congruent triangles will help prove AB parallel to CD. If the question were asked in two parts then more students would be likely to respond. Question (B) is an ambiguous question. Many different correct answers to this question could be given. Question (D) is an elliptical question, it asks for nothing specific and leaves itself open to less than serious responses. Question (E) is a leading question, which may influence the student before he or she has thought the actual question through to completion.

25. **(E)** This question is related to demonstrating knowledge of the teaching profession and of professional teaching behaviors. Humanism in education emphasizes clarification of values that the pupil holds and helping students develop concerns for the feelings and needs of others. It does not advocate subordination to the group (I), student moral judgments

consistent with teacher moral judgments (III), or in fostering competition for grades and increased pressure to achieve high test scores (IV). For these reasons the best possible answer for this question is (E).

26. **(A)** Question twenty-six is related to implementing instructional design and conditions that facilitate learning. Choice (A), rewarding convergent thinking, focuses on a teacher's tendency to view all problems as having a single solution. (B) suggests the opposite teacher view and is characteristic of a non-authoritarian teaching style. Choice (C) offers two mutually exclusive teaching styles, both authoritarian and nonauthoritarian, by rewarding convergent and divergent thinking. The final choice, (D), is tempting, but focuses only on classroom management behaviors of the authoritarian teacher and doesn't include a teacher's approach to other teaching behaviors. Choice (E) is incorrect, as an authoritarian teacher would be too controlling to be able to actively encourage independent thinking and learning on the part of the student.

27. **(A)** This question relates to knowing how to identify, obtain, and develop available resources. The correct choice is (A), since it most clearly suggests resources which research and practice indicate are most useful in preparing for instruction. Choice (B) ignores other teachers as a useful resource for planning. Choices (C) and (D) suggest that previous theory and practice are not useful in preparing for instruction. Choice (E) suggests that anecdotal reports in the media should influence how a teacher selects methods and content for instruction which is inconsistent with professional practices.

28. **(C)** This question relates to the writing of objectives or outcomes. Choice (A) can be eliminated, since the task is given- the reading of a poem. Choice (B), related to choice (A), is the observable behavior of reading a poem. The learning outcome clearly has content specified, a poem, so choice (D) can be eliminated. The conditions under which the task is to be performed are stated, "Given a poem by Maya Angelou...", so choice (E) can be eliminated. (C), the criterion level of performance, is lacking in the statement of the learning outcome, since the level of proficiency is not stated. Choice (C) is the best choice.

29. **(B)** This question relates to recognizing students' rights and governmental policy, and the implications of these for classroom practice. Public Law 94-142 (Education of All Handicapped Children Act) encourages, but does not require, that the student attend a multidisciplinary evaluation team meeting–so any answer including option IV should be eliminated. It does require that a parent or guardian, special educator, administrator or teacher be present. Choice (A) looks like a reasonable possibility, but an administrator or teacher must also be involved. Choice (D) could be selected, if one wasn't aware the parent must be involved in the development of the IEP. Likewise, choice (E) is a plausible choice, if one thought the IEP was a matter between the special education teacher and the student.

30. **(D)** Question thirty is based on implementing instruction and conditions which facilitate learning. In this question, one must consider which views of instruction are considered traditional and which are considered modern. Option I can be eliminated, since it is a fairly concise summary of John Dewey's view of teaching, and therefore considered modern. Options II and IV are traditional views, supported by traditionalists and the "back to basics" movement. A less clear option is III, the view that all students can learn all subjects at all grade levels, given enough teacher and student effort. This view is not held by modern

educational researchers who suggest differential cognitive development determines subject "readiness" at different ages for different learners. Since choice (D) includes all of the options considered traditional views of education, (D) is the best choice.

31. **(E)** Question thirty-one is based on recognizing extraclassroom influences on teachers and students, and demonstrating knowledge of the teaching profession. Choices (A) and (B) both reflect a knowledge that educational programs are expanding among age groups usually not represented in traditional educational programs. Choice (C) acknowledges the increasing influence unions are having among teachers. The "boomlet" caused by the "babyboomers" settling down to raise families is causing districts to seek alternative remedies to lack of classroom space, such as suggested by choice (D). Choice (E) is the exception, because the contrary is true: parents and students are taking an increasingly active role in the development of educational programs.

32. **(A)** Question thirty-two refers to recognizing extraclassroom influences on teachers and students. Choice (B) might seem a likely choice because of societal familiarity with the term "melting pot"; it refers, however, to the opposite of cultural pluralism, requiring different ethnic groups to subsume their own identity to the majority group. Choice (C) might be selected, since the mention of more than one culture could be associated with pluralism. Though cultural pluralism encourages the bilingual programs mentioned in choice (D), it does not require them. Choice (E) should be eliminated immediately, since the historical process of acculturation is related to the "melting pot" concept given in choice (B). Cultural pluralism refers to the preservation and enhancement of different cultures in a society, so choice (A) is the best response.

33. **(A)** Question thirty-three is related to recognizing students' constitutional rights and implications for classroom practice. Mainstreaming, choice (A), is often thought of as a requirement of PL 94-142; it is not. A least restrictive environment is required by the law, but this concept is not equivalent to mainstreaming. IEP's, choice (B), and parental approval, choice (C), are clearly required by the law. Choice (D), private school compliance may not be as widely known a requirement of the law as choices (A)–(C). Similarly, uncertainty with the exact age requirements of the law may cause one to select (E) as the exception; it is a requirement.

34. **(B)** Question thirty-four is related to recognizing extraclassroom influences on teachers and students. While choice (A) is likely to be rejected as the most likely choice, selection among choices (B)–(E) might not be as obvious. One might at first choose the correct response, (B), but question that response when given the other options which suggest either no difference between the numbers of fathers or mothers heading households, or no changes since the last decade or in the last several decades. Upon further reflection, (B) should be chosen.

35. **(D)** Question thirty-five is related to recognizing the organization, structure, and governance of the school. Choice (A) clearly is mandated by law as having an influence on local schools. School superintendents (B), acting as an agent for school board policy, have immediate legal responsibility for setting and implementing district policy as determined by the school board. The principal (E) derives similar legal responsibility from the school board. Teachers' organizations (C) have a legally determined influence on schools, for example, in

contract negotiations and inservice programs. Only parent-teacher organizations, choice (D), are without a legal basis for any influence they might have on schools, though such organizations may have profound indirect influence on local schools.

Section 2

1. **(B)** Question one is related to implementing instructional design and conditions that facilitate learning. In this question, one must have a view of classroom management which sees it as a complex analytical process. This analytical process seeks to create an environment that is conducive to teaching and learning. Though the traditional view of classroom management would hold one need merely control classroom behavior to create such an environment, a more conventional view would be less controlling of behaviors and more concerned with orchestrating learning materials and the learning environment. Choice (B) reflects such a view and is, therefore, the best choice.

2. **(B)** Question two is related to designing instruction. Inquiry, choice (A) , is best suited to develop divergent thinking. Different "right" answers are encouraged, rather than one answer drawn from the subject content. Simulation, (C), is best suited where the personal involvement of the learner is required, such as in social studies or business. Simulations are more learner-than subject-centered. Choice (D), guided discovery, is a viable option since the learner is led to a specific conclusion through a series of questions. This method is, however, more indirect than is required by a subject-centered curriculum. Group investigations, (E), can be open-ended for both content and method, and are therefore inappropriate for a subject-centered curriculum. The convergence elicited by lecture/discussion, (B), is best suited to such a curriculum and thus, the best choice.

3. **(A)** Question three is related to instructional design. Choice (A) ignores the fact that programmed instruction, even when computer-based, relies heavily on reading ability and thus, is the exception. There can be demanding effects on the poor reader. The other four choices, (B)-(E), are characteristic of programmed instruction.

4. **(D)** Question four relates to implementing conditions that facilitate learning. School-based clinics do not compete with traditional medical services, since patients at such clinics usually have no other health care, so choice (A) should be eliminated. Students visit clinics during non-class time or when sick, so choice (B) can be rejected. Cost-effectiveness is one of the hallmarks of such clinics, so (C) is rejected. (E) is eliminated since immunizations are required by law anyway, and clinics provide a convenient service for parents and students. Birth control counseling, (D), is a source of controversy in school-based clinics as in society at large, so (D) is the best choice.

5. **(E)** Question five is related to recognizing extraclassroom influences. Choice (A) is not correct since a strong demand for child care supports the need for early childhood programs. Similarly, (B)-(D) reflect types of societal support demonstrated for early childhood programs. The one factor missing from societal support of such programs is funding, either public or private. (E) is the best choice.

6. **(D)** Question six is related to recognizing students' constitutional rights and governmental policy. An IEP is an individualized educational program for a handicapped learner. Choices (A) and (E) would probably be rejected, if one is aware an IEP is related to special education. Choice (B) might be selected if one thought vocational-technical education and a competency-based curriculum involved a prescription like an IEP (C) should not be chosen, because not all slower learners are classified under the law as handicapped learners, and therefore do not require an IEP for their education.

7. **(B)** Question seven is related to recognizing students' constitutional rights and governmental policy. Under PL 94-142 (Education of All Handicapped Children Act), annual goals, not quarterly goals, are required. Teachers should be familiar with this major component of the law. The other choices offered also are required by the law, though one might not be aware that a schedule for both entry, (D), and exit, (E), are required under PL 94-142.

8. **(E)** Question eight is related to designing instruction. To choose the correct set of problems associated with ability grouping, one must be familiar with the negative association some teachers and students have for placement in low ability groups. Teachers tend to not want to teach low ability groups. Students tend to feel poorly about themselves when placed in low ability groups. Knowing this, options I, II, and IV are credible. Since the demands on the teacher for individualizing instruction would be lessened by a more homogeneous class of students, option III should be eliminated. This leaves choice (E), the choice without option III, as the best choice.

9. **(B)** Question nine is related to instructional design. (A) should be rejected as a choice, since mastery of material requires differential timeliness for different learners. (B), the correct response, might not at first appear to be the best response, since mastery learning might connote total or complete learning of material, not minimum requirements. Choice (C) is very tempting, since it uses the term "mastery"; however, students of different abilities may master more or less material within a group. Choice (D) should be rejected, because mastery learning, though helpful in college preparation, is not integral to college preparation. (E) is a characteristic of programmed learning, not mastery learning, and also should be rejected.

10. **(D)** Question ten is related to designing appropriate instruction. A nongraded school plan does provide multiple age learning groups, groups based on ability rather than age, so choice (A) is not the exception. Similarly, nongraded schools do provide individualized learning centers, (B), different time schedules for learners, (C), and horizontal articulation among subjects, (E); so these should not be chosen as the exception. Since individual ability based on individual, not group measures, are used to measure achievement and determine placement, (D), should be chosen as the exception.

11. **(E)** This question is related to demonstrating conceptual knowledge of the teaching or educating profession. This type of question requires you to have a foundational understanding of what "educating" semantically implies. In this case, answer (E) is the best response, since true educating is a process that balances "answering" (A) and "questioning" (B) on the part of the teacher and the student. In other words, teaching (i.e., educare) or questioning (i.e., educere) alone do not constitute educating. Only applied together and in balance, "educare" and "educere" contribute to the true educational process.

12. **(E)** This question is related to demonstrating conceptual knowledge of the teaching or educating profession. The word "pedagogy" is particularly common among European educators. It highlights the notion that teaching is not only an art but also a science designed to enhance teaching and learning. Therefore, answer (E) is the best response to question twelve. More than any other human service profession, pedagogy draws heavily from artistic as well as scientific aspects of teaching and learning. For example, diagnostic-prescriptive skills draw primarily from the science of psychology; communication and motivational skills, however, also have roots in the performing arts.

13. **(C)** This question is related to demonstrating conceptual·knowledge of the teaching or educating profession. Since a skeptic doubts reality and epistemology is the study of the logical structure of knowledge, answer (C) is the best choice. This particular test item is designed to assess your ability to infer deductively.

14. **(D)** This question is related to demonstrating conceptual knowledge of the teaching and educating profession. Answer (D) is the most appropriate one, since didactics or didacticism refers not only to teaching but also to instructing and lecturing.

15. **(D)** This question is related to demonstrating knowledge of the teaching profession. Since John Dewey made major contributions to all three disciplines (i.e., psychology, education, and philosophy), answer (D) is the best response.

16. **(C)** This question is related to demonstrating knowledge of the teaching profession and of professional teaching behaviors. It is important for teachers to know the different philosophical orientations of education. According to essentialist philosophy, schooling should be practical and provide children with sound instruction that prepares them to live life: schools should not try to set social policies. Therefore all of the above are correct except (C).

17. **(C)** This question is related to planning objectives, diagnosing needs, identifying resources, and designing instruction. Here, the answer choices (A)-(E) present five possible correct combinations. You must decide which of the items I-IV are appropriate statements to start an inquiry type lesson. The best answer in this case is (C). The Statements I and IV provide the students the opportunity to observe, identify and hypothesize, and research the statements. Statements II and III would be extremely difficult for students to research. They are too broad and need clarification.

18. **(D)** This question is related to planning objectives, diagnosing needs, identifying resources, and designing instruction. According to Mager instructional objectives should state not only what a student will be able to do at the end of a lesson, unit or course but also at what level of accuracy the student must perform. The only objective that meets both of these criteria is the objective in answer (D)

19. **(A)** This question is related to demonstrating knowledge of the teaching profession and of professional teaching behaviors. According to research done by Beane, all of the above answers would improve students' self-esteem, except (A). The research on self-esteem indicates that to improve students self-esteem they should be grouped for a variety of purposes, rather than ability grouping only. The correct answer would be (A).

20. **(E)** This question is related to recognizing students' constitutional rights and state, federal and judicial policy and the implications of these for classroom practice. According to Public Law 94-142, a *yearly* review of instructional goals, and implementation plans must take place. All of the other answers are specified by the law. The correct answer is (E).

21. **(A)** This question is related to demonstrating knowledge of the teaching profession and of professional teaching behaviors. It is important for teachers to know the different philosophical orientations of education. Ms. Lu's philosophy of teaching is best aligned with the reconstructionist teacher who believes that students should learn appropriate methods for dealing with the significant crises that confront the world: war, depression, international terrorism, hunger, inflation, and ever-accelerating technological advances. Therefore, the correct answer is (A).

22. **(B)** This question is related to implementing instructional design and conditions that facilitate learning. It requires you to apply your knowledge of curriculum to the adaptation of a specific instructional design. Here, the answer choices (A)-(E) present five possible correct combinations. You must decide which of the items I-V are appropriate grouping considerations. The best answer in this case is (B). (B) contains all of the choices, except V, and V is not appropriate, in that part of the reason for cooperative groups is to increase the social responsibilities of students.

23. **(E)** Question twenty-three is related to planning objectives and diagnosing needs. Educational taxonomies are designed for mental and psychomotoric development, in order to assist the educational planners in all of the activities spelled out under this test item. The answer is, therefore, (E). Teachers should use these planning tools in order to develop a sense of direction, focus, and priority.

24. **(E)** Question twenty-four is related to planning objectives and diagnosing needs. Since the term "objectives" appears throughout the educational literature, its usage is not only very specific but also quite general. The best answer for this test item is, therefore, (E) which implies that "objective(s) in education" refer(s) to any desired end.

25. **(C)** Question twenty-five is related to planning objectives and diagnosing needs. The answer here is (C), since it does not relate to "holistic" growth or development. When planning learner objectives, the developmental educator makes sure that "holistic" growth or development is a desired end since it includes developmental aspects of the whole or entire person. Wholeness or holistic growth are, therefore, synonymous and include (A), (B), (D), and (E).

26. **(D)** Question twenty-six is related to implementing instructional designs and conditions that facilitate teaching and learning. Cueing, modeling, and reinforcement schedules are effective means to bring about appropriate behavior(s) on part of the student and the teacher. All three techniques have the potential to create a classroom environment conducive to teaching and learning. The answer is, therefore, (D).

27. **(C)** Question twenty-seven is related to implementing instructional design and conditions that facilitate learning. Since Erikson's developmental theory focuses on the individual and her/his environment conditions, it can be labeled a psychosocial theory. The best answer is, therefore, (C).

28. **(C)** This question is related to educational issues. The correct alternative is (C) because initial educational reform documents cited the ability of the United States to compete economically in an international market as a major indicator in the decline of education. These reports also noted that teacher shortages would affect the delivery of quality education. Alternative (A) is incorrect because while student achievement was a concern of the reform movement, the expediency for reforms was not motivated by desires to improve teaching. The issues of unionization were not a major catalyst in preliminary reports on teacher reform, thus item (B) is incorrect. An overabundance of school administrators is a recent issue being addressed in educational reform literature. It was not seen in the first stages of the reform movement in the 1980's. Choice (E) was not an initial contributor to the reform, although there have been numerous court cases involving the issue of retaining former, non-tenured teachers who had failed to meet the minimum NTE requirements.

29. **(B)** This question is related to knowledge of the teaching profession. The correct selection is (B). Merit pay plans have been conceived as a way to adjust teacher salary schedules in a manner which rewards "good" teaching. Because it is difficult to judge good teaching many teachers feel that merit pay will be used unfairly by administrators who may, for example, reward teachers who are their favorites. Merit pay plans are new ideas spawned from the teacher reform dialogue, yet they are not embraced by the majority of teachers. Thus, response (A) is incorrect. Any item having IV as a possible answer is incorrect because merit pay is not a method of financing educational reform. It is a reform measure which must be funded.

30. **(C)** This question relates to evaluation of student achievement and instructional effectiveness. Section (C) is correct because the self-fulfilling prophecy describes how many teacher attitudes toward student achievement can be formulated. While an inappropriate method of evaluation and instructional effectiveness, the self-fulfilling prophecy has influenced teachers' decisions concerning the academic achievement of their students. Alternatives (A) and (D) relate to cognitive processing styles of humans which may impact instruction. The Pollyanna effect, (B), has little bearing on teachers' expectations of their students. Choice (E) is not correct, as the aforementioned teacher's expectations of the class may have been high, rather than low.

31. **(C)** This question deals with recognizing the spirit and implications of state and federal judicial policies. Choice (C) is the correct alternative. Since higher education is thought by many to be the most important training one can have in achieving success one might think that alternatives suggesting equality of educational opportunity relates to high school and college or university training is the appropriate response. However, the concept is very general. Equality of educational opportunity impacts all levels of schooling. Therefore, selection (C) is the most appropriate response.

32. **(D)** This question deals with keeping abreast with knowledge in one's field and requires general knowledge of the role of the state in teacher issues. Item (D) is the correct response because it is illustrative of the three most common areas of state influence on teaching. Items (A) and (E) are not the best responses because "certification" and "licensing" are equivalent terms. Item (B) is inappropriate because the state does not mandate specific teaching methodologies. Item (C) closely follows item (A) and is incorrect because there is little difference between "credentialing" and "certification."

33. **(B)** This question deals with recognizing children's developmental patterns and extraclassroom influences on students. Societal roles exert a strong influence on student self-awareness and identity formation. Stereotypic sex roles do limit self-image and do not foster a healthy self-esteem. However, positive gender images are fairly strong cultural factors, also impacting student self-image. Thus, while gender stereotyping may be harmful, researchers do not want to suggest that we eliminate all so-called female roles and all so-called male roles. Consequently item (B) is the correct response to the question. Item II is not correct because it suggests that gender-typing is an intentional act or process carried out by the teacher, when it may, in fact, be unintentional. "IV" is an inappropriate response because sex-role stereo-typing has not yet greatly diminished. There are many instances of sexist material in teaching materials, although progress is being made.

34. **(C)** This question refers to the candidate's response to knowledge about the teaching profession. Item (C) is the correct response. School superintendents are generally hired by the school boards for whom they work. Thus, they are employees of that school district. All of the other responses do not offer the factual clarity of the correct response.

35. **(A)** This item refers to knowledge about the teaching profession. The federal government has no direct control over education. Thus selection (B) would be incorrect. The federal government does have several means of indirect control over education, so alternative (C) would be incorrect. Since it has no direct control over education the federal government cannot direct legislation to specific local education districts, nor does it maintain total control (E), obviously. Thus, selection (D) is incorrect. Item (A) is the best alternative for an answer to this question.

Section 3

1. **(C)** This item deals with teacher knowledge about the profession. The correct response is (C). The Block Grant method of federal funding of public education was criticized because of the latitude of distribution of funds given to state governors. Many believed that because of the lack of guidelines for use, funds which once supported the desires of minority students would be channelled into more popular programs. Item (C) contains the elements which formed the liberal criticism of Block Grants. Item (A) is incorrect because the liberals did not view the funding method as equitable.

2. **(D)** This question relates to encouraging appropriate behavior. Answer (D), positive reinforcement, should always be the first method of choice in modifying behavior. Oftentimes by itself it will be an effective strategy for changing behavior. However, in the cases when other methods are also needed to curtail behaviors dangerous to the individual with the behavior problem, or others, positive reinforcement strategies should be used in conjunction with other methods. Each of the other choices may be used at some time, but less frequently as the strategy of choice, and never as an accompaniment to all the other behavior modifying strategies.

3. **(D)** This question deals with knowledge about the profession. The senate group responsible for education is (D).

4. **(A)** This question deals with knowledge about professional organizations for teachers. While membership in these two organizations is not restricted, they only represent teacher concerns in a variety of forums. The correct response is (A).

5. **(B)** This item requires the prospective teacher to be aware of students' constitutional rights. Response (B) is the correct answer because the court ruled that the instructional practices in the San Francisco school district were biased and constituted a violation of the Civil Rights Act.

6. **(C)** This item requires the prospective teacher to be aware of students' constitutional rights. The Lau decision did not specify any particular remedy related to classroom instruction. Thus selections (A) and (D) are incorrect. The court said that students must be given the opportunity to learn standard English. Item (C) is the correct response. Response (B) is incorrect because it implies that schools could teach students in languages which have no bearing on the direction of the Lau decision. Item (E) is incorrect because the ruling applies to all schools.

7. **(B)** Question seven is related to recognizing extraclassroom influences on the teacher and students. Since people with more education generally have higher incomes, choice (B) is an immediate strong candidate for selection. Choice (A) is in contradiction to the facts which support (B), so (A) can be eliminated. Option (C) should be eliminated, because the increased career flexibility offered by education would expand, not limit, career choices. No studies support the contention that more highly educated people tend to be unhappier than less educated people; in fact, studies suggest the contrary, so choice (D) should be eliminated. For similar reasons, choice (E) should be rejected. No data suggests that more highly educated people have a higher rate of marital problems. Choice (B), regarding increased earning ability for people with more education, should be retained as the best answer.

8. **(A)** Question eight is related to demonstrating knowledge of the teaching profession. Choice (A) is correct, since the majority of public school teachers in the United States is female. Despite media reports about the aging of the members of the teaching profession, the average age of all teachers is about 40, so choice (B) should be rejected. Again, contrary to media reports, the typical teacher has taught about 15 years, so choice (C) should be rejected. Most teachers belong to the National Education Association, thus (D) can be eliminated. And finally, since most teachers spend a little over eight hours each day at school, choice (E) should be rejected.

9. **(E)** Question nine is related to implementing instruction design and conditions that facilitate learning. Option I is generally thought of as a quality which students like in a teacher, so it is likely to be chosen. The other options, II, III, and IV, may be not as well known as qualities which a well-liked teacher possesses. It is important to note in these other three choices that students need only perceive the qualities listed. The teacher need not actually possess them. In any case, only choice (E) lists all four options, so (E) is the best answer.

10. **(D)** Question ten is related to recognizing the variance in school system policy based on the organization, structure, and governance of schools. Private school enrollment is expected to increase throughout this decade, so choice (A) is not the exception. A high

percentage of private schools is religious, so (B) should not be chosen. Recent studies found that private schools pay their teachers about half of what their public counterparts would receive. Choice (C) should, therefore, not be chosen as the false statement. Since about 85% of teachers in private schools are fully certified, and private schools are attempting to hire increasing numbers of certified teachers, choice (D) is the exception and a likely response. The discussion regarding each of the preceding choices tends to support the idea that private schools are an option for students in teacher education programs, so choice (E) should be rejected. Choice (D) is the best response.

11.   **(A)**   Question eleven is related to knowledge of the teaching profession. The National Education Association, the American Federation of Teachers, and other teachers' organizations are on record as opposing merit pay, so choice (A) appears to be a correct response. Some form of merit pay is being used in more and more school districts, but not in a majority of districts, so choice (B) should be rejected. However, since more and more districts are implementing and are expected to continue implementing some form of merit pay, choice (E) should be rejected. Choice (D) is not correct, because many teachers and administrators see merit pay as causing morale problems.

12.   **(A)**   Question twelve relates to knowledge of the teaching profession. Choice (A), paid vacation days, is offered by *very few* school districts. Most teachers are compensated only for the 170-190 days they are involved with pupils or pupil-related activities, so choice (A) should be chosen as the exception. Teachers are almost never paid for holidays or summers. Choice (B), salary, is clearly part of teacher compensation, so it should not be chosen as the exception. Though unemployment insurance, choice (C), health benefits, (D), and retirement benefits (E), are not always provided, each is more likely to be provided by an employer as part of total compensation than paid vacation days.

13.   **(C)**   Question thirteen relates to knowledge of the teaching profession. Since option II, medical benefits, is the only one not required by law, any choice which offers option II should be rejected; therefore, choices (A), (B) and (E) should be eliminated. Choice (D) is plausible, but it is missing one of the compensation provisions required by law, option I, retirement benefits. Since (D) does not include this option, choice (D) is not the best choice. Only choice (C) contains all of the required employment compensations offered as options.

14.   **(A)**   Question fourteen relates to knowledge of the teaching profession. Choice (A) concerning the quality of schools was not one of the findings presented in "A Nation at Risk." The contrary was suggested; that is, the report suggested that "a rising tide of mediocrity" characterized recent trends in education. Choice (B) might be selected, if one thought teachers came from a higher segment of the pool of college graduates. Choice (C) might be selected, if one thought one's general education or major course requirements were part of a teacher preparation program. Such content courses are not part of such programs. Many teachers, especially those with families, are required to supplement their teaching income, so choice (D) should be rejected. Lastly, as reported in "A Nation At Risk," severe shortages exist for teachers of mathematics, foreign languages, and other specialist fields, so (E) should be eliminated as the best choice.

15.   **(A)**   Question fifteen relates to knowledge of the teaching profession. Choice (A), a major in education for prospective teachers, was recommended *against* by the Holmes Group.

This was one of their more publicized and controversial recommendations. Choice (A) is the exception and is the correct choice for this question. The commission recommended both a graduate teacher education program, choice (B), and graduate work in one's teaching field, choice (C) for secondary school teachers. These two choices are not the exceptions. Regarding choice (D), the group recommended a year-long, supervised internship program previous to teacher certification, so (D) is not the exception. Though choice (E), a recommendation to a multicultural society among educators may seem a tempting choice, it was one of its recommendations. Choice (E) should not be selected as the exception.

16. **(C)** Question sixteen relates to recognizing the spirit and implication of state and federal policy. Since recent court decisions regarding equitable funding for schools have been publicized in the media, choice (A) regarding school funding might be selected. Brown vs. Board of Education of Topeka was decided in 1954, so simply on the basis of chronology, (A) should be eliminated. Though busing is a means some districts have used to meet the requirements of this Supreme Court decision, busing was not mandated by it, so choice (B) should be rejected. The issue of "reverse discrimination" also has been publicized in the media, so one might choose (D) as required by the Brown decision; it is not, so choice (D) should be rejected. Similarly, racial quotas in employment has been an issue recently, so choice (E) might be chosen as the best response; racial quotas are not part of this Court decision, so (E) should be eliminated. The concept of separate but equal schools was rejected by the 1954 Brown vs. Board of Education of Topeka Supreme Court decision, so (C) is the correct choice.

17. **(E)** Question seventeen is related to recognizing students' constitutional rights. Choices (A) and (D) seem reasonable for best response. If citizenship were required for a public school education, (A) would be a better choice than (D); however, neither U.S. citizenship or legal alien status guarantees a student the right to a public school education. Choices (B) and (C) also appear related. Payment of taxes by a parent to a district or parental residence in a district seem like reasonable assurances of a student's right to an education, but neither is a guarantee. Residence in a district merely guarantees attendance within that particular school district. Choice (E), mandate by states' constitutions, is the legal basis for an American child's education and is, therefore, the best choice.

18. **(B)** Question eighteen is related to recognizing students' rights and judicial policy. Though not all court rulings have upheld the right of school boards to regulate student conduct (e.g., *Tinker v. Des Moines Independent Community School District*), many significant rulings have upheld that right. Choice (B), related to student conduct, is the best selection. Though there is a legal basis for school boards to set rules and regulations for teacher conduct, that basis is unrelated to the doctrine of in loco parentis. Thus choice (B) should be eliminated. Similarly, the authority of the principal and parents' rights are unrelated to in loco parentis, so choices (C) and (E) should be rejected. The doctrine may seem to support a school board's right to regulate student dress, choice (D), but *Long v. Zopp* (1973) and subsequent rulings have held that if dress or grooming do not cause specific negative consequences, they may not be proscribed.

19. **(A)** Question nineteen is related to demonstrating knowledge of the teaching profession. The AFT is affiliated with the American Federation of Labor-Congress of Industrial Organizations (AFL-CIO), so choice (A) is correct. It is widely known that the AFT

and the National Education Association (NEA) have refused to join into one educational organization, so choice (C) should be eliminated. The Political Action Committee for Education (PACE) is a subgroup of NEA, so choice (B) can be rejected. As a private educational organization, the AFT cannot be affiliated with a governmental entity, the U.S. Department of Education; thus choice (E) also can be eliminated.

20. **(D)** Question twenty is related to demonstrating knowledge about the teaching profession. Choice (D) is the best selection, since the NEA has long held that affiliation with organized labor is "beneath" the professional status of teachers. Both the NEA and AFT have significant political clout, so choice (A) is not correct. Politically, both organizations tend to support Democratic candidates and positions, so (B) should not be chosen. Size is not a consideration in merging the two organizations; in fact, when joined to its affiliate, the AFL-CIO, the AFT would be a larger entity, so (C) should be rejected. Similarly, both organizations contain similar bureaucratic structures, so choice (E) should be rejected.

21. **(E)** Question twenty-one is related to recognizing students' constitutional rights and implications for classroom practice. Brown vs. Board of Education of Topeka was a U.S. Supreme Court decision which dealt with racial segregation, so choice (A) should not be chosen. The Carnegie Commission on Education and the Holmes Group issued reports which dealt with teacher education, not special education, so choices (B) and (C) should both be eliminated. The Education and Improvement Act of 1981 provided Chapter 1 and Chapter 2 funds for education, but did not mention the concept of least restrictive learning environment, so choice (D) should be eliminated. Public Law 94-142 specifically mandates the least restrictive educational environment for handicapped students, so choice (E) is the best response.

22. **(D)** The question is related to implementing instructional design and conditions that facilitate learning. It requires you to consider the psychological implications of the physical environment of the school in choosing the best answer. Answer (A) can be eliminated since the posting of student achievement materials would not spur subconscious learning, necessarily. Answer (B) can be eliminated since the display is presenting only one stimulus at a time. Answer (C) can be eliminated since sense of belonging and security are social activities involving other people, not inanimate objects. Answer (E) can be eliminated since it does not pertain directly to displays of student work. The best answer is (D) because it provides extrinsic learning, which tends to spark learning since motivation comes from the desire within the student to want to learn. The honor display is an example of an extrinsic learning tool.

23. **(C)** This question is related to recognizing students' constitutional rights and implications for classroom practice. Specifically, it relates to racial justice within the public education system. Answer (A) can be eliminated since it pertains to students' right to freedom of expression. Answer (B) can be eliminated since it pertains to students' right to procedural due process. Answer (D) can be eliminated since it pertains to the expulsion of handicapped students. Answer (E) can be eliminated since it pertains to children of alien parents. Therefore, answer (C) is the correct answer.

24. **(A)** This question is related to recognizing students' constitutional rights and implications for classroom practice. Answer (B) can be eliminated since it pertains to search

and seizure rights. Answer (C) can be eliminated since it pertains to the right against self-incrimination. Answer (D) can be eliminated since it pertains to the rights of the states. Answer (E) can be eliminated since it deals with equal protection rights. Therefore, answer (A) is the correct answer.

25. **(E)**   This question is related to recognizing students' constitutional rights and federal policy and the implications of these for classroom practice. It requires an understanding of federal law and the impact of it on educational practices in the area of student records. If you know that the Buckley Amendment addresses the confidentiality of student records, answers (A) and (D) can be eliminated fairly quickly. While answers (B) and (C) deal with who the records can be released to, it would be unreasonable to limit the released to these parties only. "Only" is the key word here. Therefore, answer (E) is the best answer since it is also the main provision of the Buckley Amendment.

26. **(B)**   This question is related to demonstrating knowledge of the teaching profession and of professional teaching behaviors. Specifically, it is related to knowing a teacher's rights. An understanding of the legal regulations regarding teacher contracts is essential in order to answer this question. Since teacher contracts cannot be signed between individuals, answers (A) and (E) can be quickly eliminated. Since the teacher does not work for the union, answer (D) can also be eliminated. While the teacher is a state employee, the contract must be signed with the board which has direct responsibility for the local education program. Therefore, answer (C) is eliminated and answer (B) is the correct response.

27. **(C)**   This question is based on design of instruction. You need to choose the best of the possible choices. In this case, you should read each answer and decide which of the given options is the most representative of an integrated curriculum. In this question, each choice is an example of some type and/or degree of integrated instruction so your task is to decide the degree to which the practice is integrated. Choice (A) uses reading materials to generate spelling lists. Choice (B) integrates literature with the teaching of social studies while the students are asked to listen to the book. Choice (C) asks the children to read several book related to American Indians, use math and art to construct a replica of a tribal dwelling, and then orally explain their project to the class. Choice (D) requires reading, writing, and speaking on the part of the students, but there is no common content on which the reading is based. Choice (E) involves the students in dance and music, but this choice does not specify any reason for or content related to the assignment. Choice (C) is the best example of integrated curriculum because it involves integrating reading, speaking, listening, math, and art with the social studies curriculum.

28. **(D)**   This question is based on cultural and community influences. It is a negatively stated question which deals with two issues: characteristics/stereotypes of dialects and classroom practices for working with children who speak low-status dialects. You are to choose the answer that is *not* true. The best way to answer this question is to read through all the choices carefully and eliminate the statements which are obviously true and then choose from among those left. Choices (C) and (E) can be eliminated quickly because linguists have shown that dialects are equally adequate and are based on the factors listed in (E). Choice (A) is a correct statement since all people speak with different degrees of dialect depending on the social context in which they are speaking. So the two choices left which could be the correct answer are (B) and (D). Choice (B) could be the correct answer, since dialects imply

language difference, not language deficit, and therefore do not always imply a problem with reading. However, many teachers do not understand characteristics of dialect and often confuse dialect miscues in oral reading with comprehension problems. In this case, the teacher's perception of the dialect can cause reading problems for the child. The best choice is (D). While a teacher may feel strongly about encouraging a standard dialect for every child, a child's home language should always be accepted. Questions such as this must be read carefully because they require you to read for the one incorrect answer, instead of the one correct answer.

29. **(C)** This question is based on evaluating student achievement. In this question, you must determine which of the examples listed are informal means of assessment. Here, the answer choices represent two or three possible combinations. You should read over all the options and eliminate those that are not informal means of assessment. Option I can be eliminated because a standardized test is classified as formal assessment and Option V can be eliminated because informal interest inventories do not offer any information which can be used for assessment. The correct answer is (C).

30. **(E)** This question is based on recognizing cultural influences and expectations. This question asks you to recognize which of the given verbal and non-verbal communication patterns are culturally based. The answers give you combinations of two or three options as well as one choice including all four options. To answer this question, you should read each option and decide which of these patterns can be attributed to cultural expectations. All of the behaviors listed in I-IV are culturally determined patterns of communication. The correct answer for this question is (E).

31. **(E)** This question is related to issues of sex equity in the curriculum. Since this question asks you to identify the "best example" of a sexually nonbiased curriculum, you should assume that there may be several correct answers to this question. To answer this question, you should read carefully through all of the answers and choose the one that is the best example of the ones that are given. Choice (A) indicates the inclusion of two women in a unit of study that is obviously devoted to men only. It is a move toward recognizing the contributions of women and could be a correct answer. Choice (B) can be eliminated because the teacher is making statements which are solely directed to girls, and it does not indicate any classroom practices to reinforce that belief. Choice (C) could be the correct answer since this teacher obviously devotes an entire month to the study of women. Choice (D) is another move toward integrating women as it emphasizes the women who are perceived as being different--"uncommon" in the fields of writing, politics, and sports. Choice (E) is another possible correct answer since teacher E. has integrated the contributions of women into both his/her lecture information and additional readings. At this point Choices (A) and (B) can be eliminated and the best choice from (C), (D), and (E) can be made. Choice (C) represents only one month of the curriculum and does not truly integrate the contributions of women throughout the entire curriculum but separates them into one unit of study. Choice (D) implies the fact that the only women who make worthy contributions to society are "uncommon women" and perpetuates a negative stereotype. Choice (E), of the examples given, is the best choice because it indicates that women are consistently represented throughout all areas of the science curriculum and that additional effort is being made to include women though the supplementary readings.

32. **(E)** Question thirty-two is related to planning instructional objectives. Answer (A) relates to objectives unrelated to the actual matter at hand, that is, goals for the student who is being mainstreamed, and can therefore be eliminated. Answers (B) and (C) can both also be eliminated because there are some situations in which mainstreaming objectives may be based upon norm referenced and or criterion referenced standards. Answer (D) could be correct. However, students may be mainstreamed for reasons other than ones related to academic performance in a regular class, which leaves answer (E). Students are mainstreamed for a variety of reasons, and it is only by referencing the Individualized Education Plan that the regular education teacher can be sure what those reasons are. Therefore, (E) is the correct answer.

33. **(D)** This question is based on implementing instructional design and conditions that facilitate learning. All of the choices provide information potentially useful to the teacher interested in modifying a student's behavior. However, answer (D) is the least important of the choices for several reasons. Clearly, appropriate behavior programs can be developed by knowing consequences, (A), antecedents, (B), reinforcers (C), as well as having a clear idea of what it is that is to be changed (E). But if any of these areas are not known, it is questionable how effective the behavior modifying program will be. A successful program can be implemented without knowing what has been attempted in the past. Additionally, unless the teacher is knowledgeable about the rigor with which specific procedures were used in the past, the information is moot as procedures are often applied inappropriately. The answer therefore is (D).

34. **(A)** This question relates to the grouping of students. The basic fact behind this question is that most individuals with disabilities have mild disabilities, such as mild learning problems or speech and language problems, which can be remediated within the regular class. The correct answer therefore is (A). Regarding the remaining choices, special day classes, (B), are for students with disabilities significant enough for them to need to be removed from the mainstream. Thus, because these disabilities are more significant, there are fewer of these students. Answer (C), the segregated school, should be reserved for only the most disturbed students who are dangerous to themselves or others. Answer (D) is incorrect because a label is not the basis for placement. Students may acquire a label as a result of their placement, but it is not, and should not be, the criteria for placement. Finally, answer (E) is incorrect because, in addition to the reasons listed above, legally, students cannot be placed in special education on the basis of intelligence test scores alone. The correct answer therefore is letter (A).

35. **(C)** This question is based on instructional objectives. A criterion referenced behavioral objective is one in which the standard for comparison is the student's own past performance. In contrast, norm referenced objectives relate to performance in reference to a standard established for a group. Answers (D) and (E) can therefore be eliminated, as they are related to comparison to a classroom or a school-wide norm. Answer (A) can also be eliminated, as there is the norm referenced standard of second graders reading second grade words. Once again, answer (B) determines student performance in reference to a national standard. Only answer (C) provides an objective for Johnny linked to his own current reading performance, in other words, that is criterion referenced. The correct answer therefore is (C).

National Teachers Examination

CORE BATTERY

Test 2

NTE Test of Communication Skills

TEST 2 – ANSWER SHEET

Section 1: Listening

1. Ⓐ Ⓑ Ⓒ Ⓓ Ⓔ
2. Ⓐ Ⓑ Ⓒ Ⓓ Ⓔ
3. Ⓐ Ⓑ Ⓒ Ⓓ Ⓔ
4. Ⓐ Ⓑ Ⓒ Ⓓ Ⓔ
5. Ⓐ Ⓑ Ⓒ Ⓓ Ⓔ
6. Ⓐ Ⓑ Ⓒ Ⓓ Ⓔ
7. Ⓐ Ⓑ Ⓒ Ⓓ Ⓔ
8. Ⓐ Ⓑ Ⓒ Ⓓ Ⓔ
9. Ⓐ Ⓑ Ⓒ Ⓓ Ⓔ
10. Ⓐ Ⓑ Ⓒ Ⓓ Ⓔ
11. Ⓐ Ⓑ Ⓒ Ⓓ Ⓔ
12. Ⓐ Ⓑ Ⓒ Ⓓ Ⓔ
13. Ⓐ Ⓑ Ⓒ Ⓓ Ⓔ
14. Ⓐ Ⓑ Ⓒ Ⓓ Ⓔ
15. Ⓐ Ⓑ Ⓒ Ⓓ Ⓔ
16. Ⓐ Ⓑ Ⓒ Ⓓ Ⓔ
17. Ⓐ Ⓑ Ⓒ Ⓓ Ⓔ
18. Ⓐ Ⓑ Ⓒ Ⓓ Ⓔ
19. Ⓐ Ⓑ Ⓒ Ⓓ Ⓔ
20. Ⓐ Ⓑ Ⓒ Ⓓ Ⓔ
21. Ⓐ Ⓑ Ⓒ Ⓓ Ⓔ
22. Ⓐ Ⓑ Ⓒ Ⓓ Ⓔ
23. Ⓐ Ⓑ Ⓒ Ⓓ Ⓔ
24. Ⓐ Ⓑ Ⓒ Ⓓ Ⓔ
25. Ⓐ Ⓑ Ⓒ Ⓓ Ⓔ
26. Ⓐ Ⓑ Ⓒ Ⓓ Ⓔ
27. Ⓐ Ⓑ Ⓒ Ⓓ Ⓔ
28. Ⓐ Ⓑ Ⓒ Ⓓ Ⓔ
29. Ⓐ Ⓑ Ⓒ Ⓓ Ⓔ
30. Ⓐ Ⓑ Ⓒ Ⓓ Ⓔ
31. Ⓐ Ⓑ Ⓒ Ⓓ Ⓔ
32. Ⓐ Ⓑ Ⓒ Ⓓ Ⓔ
33. Ⓐ Ⓑ Ⓒ Ⓓ Ⓔ
34. Ⓐ Ⓑ Ⓒ Ⓓ Ⓔ
35. Ⓐ Ⓑ Ⓒ Ⓓ Ⓔ
36. Ⓐ Ⓑ Ⓒ Ⓓ Ⓔ
37. Ⓐ Ⓑ Ⓒ Ⓓ Ⓔ
38. Ⓐ Ⓑ Ⓒ Ⓓ Ⓔ
39. Ⓐ Ⓑ Ⓒ Ⓓ Ⓔ
40. Ⓐ Ⓑ Ⓒ Ⓓ Ⓔ

Section 2: Reading

1. Ⓐ Ⓑ Ⓒ Ⓓ Ⓔ
2. Ⓐ Ⓑ Ⓒ Ⓓ Ⓔ
3. Ⓐ Ⓑ Ⓒ Ⓓ Ⓔ
4. Ⓐ Ⓑ Ⓒ Ⓓ Ⓔ
5. Ⓐ Ⓑ Ⓒ Ⓓ Ⓔ
6. Ⓐ Ⓑ Ⓒ Ⓓ Ⓔ
7. Ⓐ Ⓑ Ⓒ Ⓓ Ⓔ
8. Ⓐ Ⓑ Ⓒ Ⓓ Ⓔ
9. Ⓐ Ⓑ Ⓒ Ⓓ Ⓔ
10. Ⓐ Ⓑ Ⓒ Ⓓ Ⓔ
11. Ⓐ Ⓑ Ⓒ Ⓓ Ⓔ
12. Ⓐ Ⓑ Ⓒ Ⓓ Ⓔ
13. Ⓐ Ⓑ Ⓒ Ⓓ Ⓔ
14. Ⓐ Ⓑ Ⓒ Ⓓ Ⓔ
15. Ⓐ Ⓑ Ⓒ Ⓓ Ⓔ
16. Ⓐ Ⓑ Ⓒ Ⓓ Ⓔ
17. Ⓐ Ⓑ Ⓒ Ⓓ Ⓔ
18. Ⓐ Ⓑ Ⓒ Ⓓ Ⓔ
19. Ⓐ Ⓑ Ⓒ Ⓓ Ⓔ
20. Ⓐ Ⓑ Ⓒ Ⓓ Ⓔ
21. Ⓐ Ⓑ Ⓒ Ⓓ Ⓔ
22. Ⓐ Ⓑ Ⓒ Ⓓ Ⓔ
23. Ⓐ Ⓑ Ⓒ Ⓓ Ⓔ
24. Ⓐ Ⓑ Ⓒ Ⓓ Ⓔ
25. Ⓐ Ⓑ Ⓒ Ⓓ Ⓔ
26. Ⓐ Ⓑ Ⓒ Ⓓ Ⓔ
27. Ⓐ Ⓑ Ⓒ Ⓓ Ⓔ
28. Ⓐ Ⓑ Ⓒ Ⓓ Ⓔ
29. Ⓐ Ⓑ Ⓒ Ⓓ Ⓔ
30. Ⓐ Ⓑ Ⓒ Ⓓ Ⓔ

Section 3: Writing

1. Ⓐ Ⓑ Ⓒ Ⓓ Ⓔ
2. Ⓐ Ⓑ Ⓒ Ⓓ Ⓔ
3. Ⓐ Ⓑ Ⓒ Ⓓ Ⓔ
4. Ⓐ Ⓑ Ⓒ Ⓓ Ⓔ
5. Ⓐ Ⓑ Ⓒ Ⓓ Ⓔ
6. Ⓐ Ⓑ Ⓒ Ⓓ Ⓔ
7. Ⓐ Ⓑ Ⓒ Ⓓ Ⓔ
8. Ⓐ Ⓑ Ⓒ Ⓓ Ⓔ

9. Ⓐ Ⓑ Ⓒ Ⓓ Ⓔ
10. Ⓐ Ⓑ Ⓒ Ⓓ Ⓔ
11. Ⓐ Ⓑ Ⓒ Ⓓ Ⓔ
12. Ⓐ Ⓑ Ⓒ Ⓓ Ⓔ
13. Ⓐ Ⓑ Ⓒ Ⓓ Ⓔ
14. Ⓐ Ⓑ Ⓒ Ⓓ Ⓔ
15. Ⓐ Ⓑ Ⓒ Ⓓ Ⓔ
16. Ⓐ Ⓑ Ⓒ Ⓓ Ⓔ
17. Ⓐ Ⓑ Ⓒ Ⓓ Ⓔ
18. Ⓐ Ⓑ Ⓒ Ⓓ Ⓔ
19. Ⓐ Ⓑ Ⓒ Ⓓ Ⓔ
20. Ⓐ Ⓑ Ⓒ Ⓓ Ⓔ
21. Ⓐ Ⓑ Ⓒ Ⓓ Ⓔ
22. Ⓐ Ⓑ Ⓒ Ⓓ Ⓔ
23. Ⓐ Ⓑ Ⓒ Ⓓ Ⓔ
24. Ⓐ Ⓑ Ⓒ Ⓓ Ⓔ
25. Ⓐ Ⓑ Ⓒ Ⓓ Ⓔ
26. Ⓐ Ⓑ Ⓒ Ⓓ Ⓔ
27. Ⓐ Ⓑ Ⓒ Ⓓ Ⓔ
28. Ⓐ Ⓑ Ⓒ Ⓓ Ⓔ
29. Ⓐ Ⓑ Ⓒ Ⓓ Ⓔ
30. Ⓐ Ⓑ Ⓒ Ⓓ Ⓔ
31. Ⓐ Ⓑ Ⓒ Ⓓ Ⓔ
32. Ⓐ Ⓑ Ⓒ Ⓓ Ⓔ
33. Ⓐ Ⓑ Ⓒ Ⓓ Ⓔ
34. Ⓐ Ⓑ Ⓒ Ⓓ Ⓔ
35. Ⓐ Ⓑ Ⓒ Ⓓ Ⓔ
36. Ⓐ Ⓑ Ⓒ Ⓓ Ⓔ
37. Ⓐ Ⓑ Ⓒ Ⓓ Ⓔ
38. Ⓐ Ⓑ Ⓒ Ⓓ Ⓔ
39. Ⓐ Ⓑ Ⓒ Ⓓ Ⓔ
40. Ⓐ Ⓑ Ⓒ Ⓓ Ⓔ
41. Ⓐ Ⓑ Ⓒ Ⓓ Ⓔ
42. Ⓐ Ⓑ Ⓒ Ⓓ Ⓔ
43. Ⓐ Ⓑ Ⓒ Ⓓ Ⓔ
44. Ⓐ Ⓑ Ⓒ Ⓓ Ⓔ
45. Ⓐ Ⓑ Ⓒ Ⓓ Ⓔ

NTE CORE BATTERY–Test 2
TEST OF COMMUNICATIONS SKILLS
Section 1: Listening

TIME: 30 Minutes
40 Questions

Part A

DIRECTIONS: In this section, you will hear short statements and questions. When you hear a statement, select the answer which best restates or supports what you heard. When you hear a question, select the choice which best answers the question. The questions and statements are NOT written in your book. **They will not be repeated**.

1. (A) Mrs. Johnson would probably have difficulty relating to her peers.
    (B) Mrs. Johnson was perceived as being too arrogant.
    (C) Mrs. Johnson had no previous teaching experience.
    (D) The school board feared that Mrs. Johnson would have difficulty relating to her young students.

2. (A) 23 million Americans are functionally illiterate.
    (B) Fewer than 23 million Americans are functionally illiterate.
    (C) More than 23 million Americans are functionally illiterate.
    (D) Many Americans are functionally illiterate.

3. (A) A decision has been made.
    (B) A decision to teach is forthcoming.
    (C) A decision not to teach is inevitable.
    (D) A decision has not been made.

4. (A) They were in the dictionary.
    (B) They were in the chapters.
    (C) They were in the glossary.
    (D) They were in the index.

5. (A) Mr. Ross is an excellent teacher.
    (B) Mr. Johnson's teaching abilities are not as good as Mr. Ross' teaching abilities.
    (C) Mr. Johnson is a terrible teacher.
    (D) Mr. Johnson needs to improve his teaching abilities.

6. (A) Small rural schools   (C) Large rural schools
    (B) Small inner city schools   (D) Large inner city schools

7. (A) Too much time was spent on each item.
    (B) Too many items were on the agenda.
    (C) The meeting did not fare as well as had been planned.
    (D) Not enough time was allotted for each item.

8. (A) Teachers must love children in order to help them achieve.
    (B) Teachers must feel and show concern for children in order to help them better achieve.
    (C) Teachers must secretly empathize with students in order to help them achieve.
    (D) Teachers must be perfect role models for students in order to help them achieve.

9. (A) Most of the students in this school can't read.
    (B) Most of the students in this school are reading far below grade level.
    (C) Approximately 40% of the students in this school have difficulties in reading.
    (D) A majority of the students in this school experience reading problems.

10. (A) Laboratory materials   (C) A well-written science textbook
     (B) *National Geographic* magazine (D) An Almanac

11. (A) AFL and CIA   (C) NEA, AFT, and CIO
     (B) NEA and AFT   (D) NEA

12. (A) IRA's membership is 100,000.
     (B) IRA's membership exceeds 100,000.
     (C) IRA's membership is less than 100,000.
     (D) IRA's membership totals 50,000.

13. (A) The library has many different books.
     (B) The library contains *Ebony, Look, Essence, National Geographic*, and *Newsweek*.
     (C) The library contains an assortment of reading materials.
     (D) The library contains many different reference materials.

Part B

DIRECTIONS: In this section, you will hear short conversations between two people. After each conversation, a third person will ask you questions about what was discussed. When you hear a question, select the choice which best answers the question based on what you heard. The conversations and questions are NOT written in your test book. **They will not be repeated.**

14.
- (A) Mrs. Austin strongly encouraged paddling as a solution to the problem.
- (B) The principal, Mr. Berry, was in total agreement with Mrs. Austin's suggestion.
- (C) Mr. Berry completely misunderstood Mrs. Austin's suggestion.
- (D) Mr. Berry was willing to try anything in order to improve test scores.

15.
- (A) The principal is relying heavily on Mrs. Austin to suggest ways to improve test scores.
- (B) Mrs. Austin explicitly stated several good alternatives to paddling.
- (C) Mr. Berry misunderstood Mrs. Austin's "get tough" suggestion.
- (D) Mr. Berry does not support paddling.

16.
- (A) Johnny had no school materials.
- (B) Johnny was not interested in the subject.
- (C) Johnny left the assignment at school.
- (D) Johnny didn't understand the assignment, and his parents didn't have time to help.

17.
- (A) Two times
- (B) Three times
- (C) Four times
- (D) None

18.
- (A) Yes, Johnny is very honest.
- (B) Yes, Johnny is an honor student.
- (C) No, Johnny is a very dishonest person.
- (D) No, Johnny had failed several times to turn in his work.

19.
- (A) The teacher should recommend suspension.
- (B) The teacher should forget the incident and help Johnny with the assignment.
- (C) The teacher should arrange a conference with Johnny's parents.
- (D) The teacher should recommend that Johnny spend one hour in the Detention Hall.

20.
- (A) Mark was asleep in class.
- (B) Mark was annoying Susan.
- (C) Mark was talking aloud in class.
- (D) Mark was a good student.

21.
- (A) Susan had broken his pencil.
- (B) The class encouraged this devious act.
- (C) It's natural for children to meddle with each other.
- (D) Mark was angry because Susan had hit him.

22.
- (A) No one saw him pull Susan's hair.
- (B) He was afraid of being punished.
- (C) He is a pathological liar.
- (D) Lying is natural for all little boys.

23. (A) Student 1 was not interested in school.
     (B) Student 2 is gullible.
     (C) It cannot be determined from the conversation.
     (D) Student 1 had something important to do.

24. (A) Student 2 was beinng difficult.
     (B) Student 2 was not as gullible as Student 1 thought.
     (C) Student 2 was really interested in school.
     (D) Student 1 gave no good reason for skipping.

25. (A) Student 2 was really a sissy.
     (B) Student 1 may have felt that such a derogatory word would change
          Student 2's mind.
     (C) Student 2 had always portrayed signs of being a wimp.
     (D) Student 1 couldn't think of anything else to say.

Part C

DIRECTIONS: In this section, you will hear several short talks. After each talk,
a second voice will ask questions about the talk. When you hear a question,
select the choice which best answers the question based on what you heard.
The short talks are NOT written in your test book. **They will not be repeated.**

26. (A) No one   (C) Teachers
     (B) Schools in general   (D) Students and teachers

27. (A) Teachers should get tough.
     (B) Teachers should require regular class attendance.
     (C) Teachers should facilitate these changes by making their classes interesting
          and relevant.
     (D) Teachers should encourage completion of homework assignments.

28. (A) The speaker is angry.   (C) The speaker is indifferent.
     (B) The speaker is concerned.   (D) The speaker is nonjudgmental.

29. (A) Schools are not what they used to be.
     (B) Students need to study more.
     (C) Teachers need to demand more.
     (D) Teachers and students need to change if test scores are going to be increased.

30. (A) Crime   (C) School dropout
     (B) Teenage pregnancy   (D) Problems facing schools today

31. (A) Crime   (C) School dropout
     (B) Teenage pregnancy   (D) Drugs

32. (A) Many problems exist in schools today.
    (B) School officials must act now to alleviate social problems that impact schools.
    (C) Teenage pregnancy is the leading hindrance to educational opportunity.
    (D) Crime is the leading problem today that affects school.

33. (A) Corporal punishment should return.
    (B) Positive reinforcement and curriculum modification have failed to deter crime.
    (C) The only way to control children is to beat them.
    (D) Schools should close because children cannot be disciplined.

34. (A) The speaker is modest.
    (B) The speaker is cool, calm, and collected.
    (C) The speaker is angry.
    (D) The speaker is uncaring.

35. (A) The curriculum has been completely rewritten to accommodate the children.
    (B) The curriculum has been completely eliminated and replaced with interesting content.
    (C) The curriculum has been supplemented by other materials.
    (D) The curriculum has been adjusted to accommodate the needs of children.

36. (A) "Monsters in the classroom"
    (B) "A Plea for Corporal Punishment"
    (C) "Positive Reinforcement Doesn't Work"
    (D) "Techniques for Disciplining Children"

37. (A) Plan an appropriate time to study.
    (B) Plan an appropriate place to study.
    (C) Take notes as you study.
    (D) Develop a study schedule.

38. (A) Planning an appropriate time to study
    (B) Choosing an appropriate place to study
    (C) Developing a study schedule
    (D) Developing discipline

39. (A) Planning a time to study is important for success
    (B) Good students develop study schedules
    (C) Good study habits and discipline are necessary for success
    (D) Choosing an appropriate place to study is necessary for success

40. (A) More time to do other things (C) Good grades
    (B) Less effort and time (D) Teacher approval

Section 2: Reading

TIME: 30 Minutes
30 Questions

DIRECTIONS: Each passage is followed by questions based on its content. After reading the passage, choose the best answer to each question. Answer all questions based on what is indicated or implied in that passage.

Questions 1 through 3 are based on the following passage.

If teachers want to help their students improve reading skills, these professionals should give credence to Dr. Macey James's theory. Dr. James, an Associate Professor of Reading at Blue Ridge University, believes that literacy environments must provide children the opportunity to engage in actual application of reading skills taught. He proposes 12 rules for reading improvement:

1. Read.

2. Read in the morning.

3. Read.

4. Read in the evening.

5. Read.

6. Read at night.

7. Read novels and books.

8. Read magazines and newspapers.

9. Read comics, recipes, driving manuals, catalogs.

10. Read.

11. Read.

12. Read, Read, Read, R-E-A-D!!!

1.   According to this passage, Dr. James probably believes that
    (A)   reading can be fun.
    (B)   reading is fundamental and should be required of all children.
    (C)   practice makes perfect.
    (D)   teachers should encourage children to read instead of playing.
    (E)   teaching other subjects is not as important as teaching reading.

2.   According to this passage, Dr. James probably believes that children should read
    (A)   basically novels and books.
    (B)   materials which are related to real life experiences.
    (C)   materials which are meaningful, as opposed to materials which are humorous.

(D) A variety of materials.

(E) Materials which express accepted values and lifestyles.

3. Which one of the following statements best summarizes this passage?
   (A) Children should read extensively
   (B) Children should read all types of materials
   (C) Children should read novels and books
   (D) There are 12 rules for reading improvement
   (E) Children should extensively read all types of materials

Questions 4 through 6 are based on the following passage.

The old expression, "You can lead a horse to the water, but you can't make him drink," is true. However, if you make the horse thirsty, you won't have to make him drink. This is true of children. If teachers make their classes interesting and stimulating, children will automatically come to class, do their homework, and study.

4. If teachers expect their students to learn, teachers must

   (A) motivate their students.   (D) teach their students.

   (B) love their students.   (E) praise their students.

   (C) discipline their students.

5. Based on this passage, what assumption can you make?
   (A) School, in general, is boring
   (B) Teachers don't know how to teach
   (C) Children don't like school
   (D) Classes that are stimulating yield better results
   (E) Children don't perform well because they don't study

6. Which of the following best paraphrases the main idea of this passage?

   (A) Teacher consistency   (D) Active teaching

   (B) Direct instruction   (E) Modeling concepts

   (C) Reinforcement of content

Questions 7 through 9 are based on the following passage.

Abraham Lincoln was the 16th President of the United States, and Columbus discovered America in 1492. So what? Do children need to know these details?

7. What is the main idea of this passage?
   (A) Abraham Lincoln was the 16th President of the United States.
   (B) Columbus discovered America in 1492.
   (C) Teaching irrelevant facts is a waste.
   (D) Abraham Lincoln and Columbus were great men.
   (E) Children need to know details.

8. What audience do you think this passage is intended for?
   (A) Parents, since they are their children's first teachers.

     (B)   Elementary teachers, since they are responsible for building children's foundations.

     (C)   All teachers.

     (D)   Secondary teachers, since they are responsible for content that is taught.

     (E)   College professors, since they are responsible for smoothing out students' rough edges prior to employment.

9.   How relevant is the author's evidence that teaching irrelevant facts is a waste?

     (A)   It is very relevant and speaks directly to the idea presented.

     (B)   No evidence is explicitly given; it is implied.

     (C)   It is moderately relevant and somewhat speaks directly to the idea presented.

     (D)   The evidence presented is not relevant at all.

     (E)   The evidence presented is appropriate only if you read between the lines.

Questions 10 through 13 are based on the following passage.

It is a known fact that for the first time a generation will not outstrip its parents educationally or economically. In fact, this generation of students won't even equal their parents' efforts.

10.   What is the main idea of this passage?

     (A)   Parents are economically and educationally better off than their children.

     (B)   Parents are ahead of their children economically.

     (C)   Parents are ahead of their children educationally.

     (D)   Parents and their children are about equal educationally.

     (E)   Parents and their children are about equal economically.

11.   Which of the following is an unstated assumption made by the author?

     (A)   This generation of students is lazy.

     (B)   This generation of students refuses to study.

     (C)   Parents are more industrious than their children.

     (D)   Parents are smarter than their children.

     (E)   Parents were more interested in school than their children are.

12.   Does the author adequately support his/her argument?

     (A)   The support is very adequate.

     (B)   The support is somewhat adequate.

     (C)   Marginally, the author's argument is supported.

     (D)   The author's evidence is not appropriate at all.

     (E)   The author provides no support for his/her idea presented in the passage.

13.   Which of the following is a fact presented in the passage?

     (A)   Parents are smarter than their children.

     (B)   Parents are more industrious than their children.

     (C)   Economically, parents are better off than their children.

(D)   The author believes that parents are educationally and economically superior to their children.

(E)   Educationally, parents are better off than their children.

Questions 14 through 17 are based on the following passage.

Believe it or not, 45 to 50 percent of the students graduating from high school today do not possess adequate basic skills. On achievement tests, students in the United States rank far below students enrolled in schools of other countries. Because of this, our society is filled with over 23 million Americans who are functionally illiterate. By the year 2000, it is predicted that this number will rise to 100,000. Truly, intellectual mediocrity has invaded our society. This decline in academic excellence is due to a lack of parental involvement. Parents are not actively involved in the education of their children. They do not support the schools, and they continuously make excuses for the mistakes of their children. According to parents, it's always the school's fault, particularly the teachers. Come on parents!!! We need your support.

14.   What is the main idea of this passage?
(A)   Intellectually, American students are performing poorly.
(B)   Parents are not supportive of our schools.
(C)   Children are not as smart as they used to be.
(D)   45 -50 percent of our high school graduates lack basic skills.
(E)   Over 23 million Americans are functionally illiterate.

15.   Which of the following best summarizes this passage?
(A)   Parents are not involved in the education of their children.
(B)   Intellectually, children are not performing well.
(C)   Parents make too many excuses for their children.
(D)   Because of a lack of parental involvement, American students are not performing well academically.
(E)   Parents and children are responsible for the low academic achievement of American students.

16.   Based on the information given, does the author adequately support the main idea of the passage?
(A)   The evidence given adequately supports the main idea.
(B)   The main idea is only marginally supported.
(C)   The evidence given is very limited.
(D)   The author provides an abundance of support for the main idea.
(E)   The main idea is not supported.

17.   With reference to the reason for intellectual mediocrity among American students, evaluate the author's argument in terms of strength.
(A)   The author's argument is very strong.
(B)   The author's argument is strong but could have been stronger.
(C)   The argument is too limited.

(D)   The author's argument is too strong.

(E)   There is no argument to support the reason for intellectual mediocrity.

Question 18 is based on the following statement.

If you can read this sentence, thank a teacher!!!

18.   In summary, this sentence suggests that
   (A)   Teachers are competent.
   (B)   Teacher education programs are doing a good job of training teachers.
   (C)   Teachers are concerned.
   (D)   Teachers deserve praise for their efforts.
   (E)   Teachers deserve all of the raises they receive.

Questions 19 through 22 are based on the following passage.

Despite what many think, history classes are filled with students who have difficulty reading and understanding their history books. This is called a readability mismatch. Generally, the reading levels of the history books exceed the reading levels of the students who must utilize these books. When this mismatch occurs, students become frustrated and do not perform at levels commensurate with their listening capacity (potential).

In order to alleviate this mismatch, it is recommended that teachers (1) supplement the books with lower level materials that stress the same concepts, (2) rewrite the books, (3) use peer tutoring, (4) tape the books for those students who are experiencing difficulties, or (5) use films and filmstrips to teach different concepts.

19.   In this passage, the author states that there is a mismatch between the reading levels of students and the reading levels of the history books they use. Which statement below best supports this idea?
   (A)   The author states that students are having difficulty reading their history books.
   (B)   The author states that students are having difficulty.
   (C)   The author really provides no support for this idea.
   (D)   The author states that students become frustrated.
   (E)   The author states that students do not perform at levels commensurate with their listening capacity.

20.   With reference to the author's idea of a mismatch, which of the statements below adequately evaluates the strength of his argument?
   (A)   The argument, even though it is not supported, is very strong.
   (B)   The argument is only moderately strong.
   (C)   The argument is without substance.
   (D)   The argument is weak.
   (E)   There is no argument.

21.   Of the five suggestions offered by the author, which one is the least appropriate for teachers?

(A)   Supplement the books.   (D)   Tape the books.

(B)   Rewrite the books.   (E)   Use films and filmstrips.

(C)   Use peer tutoring.

22.   One of the author's suggestions is for teachers to tape materials in books that are too difficult. To which of the following subjects would this be <u>least</u> applicable?

(A)   Science   (D)   Geography

(B)   Economics   (E)   Health

(C)   Math

Questions 23 through 26 are based on the following passage.

The educational reforms of the 1980s were numerous. Standards were raised, students and teachers were tested and assessed as never before, curriculum revision was at an all-time high, and teacher education programs took on a new look. Sad to say, however, the reformers who have engineered these changes have failed to consider the urban/inner city child — the black child, the Hispanic child, the underachievers, the slow learners, the learning-disabled child. Rather, the reforms of the 1980s have forced schools to return to a system of tracking minority and other less abled students into remedial classes, while their counterparts are enrolled in Greek mythology, Victorian prose, romantic literature, geometry, trigonometry, and calculus. No wonder minority and other less abled students do poorly on standardized entrance examinations!

23.   In reference to the educational reforms of the 1980s, which of the following is an opinion, according to this passage?

(A)   These reforms have failed to address the needs of urban/inner city children.

(B)   Standards were raised.

(C)   Students and teachers were tested and assessed as never before.

(D)   Curriculum revision was at an all-time high.

(E)   Teacher training programs have taken on a new look.

24.   Which of the following best expresses the topic of this passage?

(A)   Curriculum revision

(B)   Increased standards

(C)   The underserved urban/inner city child

(D)   Revised teacher training programs

(E)   Increased testing of students and teachers

25.   Which of the following best expresses the author's reasons for the low performance of urban/inner city children on standardized tests?

(A)   Standards are too high.

(B)   Courses assigned are too difficult.

(C)   Students are tested too frequently.

(D)   Teacher training programs have failed.

(E)   Courses taken do not adequately prepare these children for the tests.

26. What is the author's attitude toward the educational reforms of the 1980s?
    (A) Supportive
    (D) Anger
    (B) Indifferent
    (E) Appeasing
    (C) Critical

Questions 27 through 30 are based on the following passage.

Teacher negotiation is very beneficial. It leads to an amplification of roles for teachers. This amplification empowers teachers to actively participate in the decision-making process in terms of working conditions and salary improvements.

Other benefits derived from teacher negotiation are not as tangible as the aforementioned ones, but they are equally as important. Research shows that when teachers have input into their professional lives, their self-esteem, morale, and accountability are improved.

Both the tangible and intangible benefits derived from teacher negotiation indicate that teacher negotiation is a worthwhile process.

27. What is the main idea of this passage?
    (A) Through negotiation, teachers' salaries improve.
    (B) Through negotiation, conditions for teachers improve.
    (C) Through negotiation, teachers' self-esteem improves.
    (D) Through negotiation, teachers' morale improves.
    (E) Through negotiation, teachers receive more power.

28. Is the author's argument for teacher negotiation adequately supported by details?
    (A) The argument is fully supported.
    (B) The argument is somewhat supported.
    (C) No argument is made. The passage simply presents facts.
    (D) The argument is too limited.
    (E) The argument is not supported at all.

29. Which of the following best describes the organization of the passage?
    (A) A problem is presented and several solutions given.
    (B) A major idea is chronologically summarized.
    (C) A controversial issue is presented and defended.
    (D) Several interrelated ideas are presented to support an implied idea.
    (E) A numerical list is delineated to support an idea.

30. Which of the following is supported by the author?
    (A) Only tangible benefits are important.
    (B) Only tangible benefits are worth fighting for.
    (C) The intangible benefits are more important.
    (D) Intangible benefits are equally as important as tangible benefits.
    (E) There is no difference between tangible and intangible benefits.

Section 3: Writing

TIME: 30 Minutes
45 Questions

Part A

DIRECTIONS: Each of the following sentences may contain an error in diction, usage, idiom, or grammar. Some sentences may be correct. Some sentences may contain one error. No sentence contains more than one error.

If there is an error, it will appear in one of the underlined portions labeled (A), (B), (C), or (D). If there is no error, choose the portion labeled (E). If there is an error, select the letter of the portion that must be changed in order to correct the sentence.

1. Jack Newberry, along with his classmates, is an avid reader who is liable to finish
                     A   B   C   D
100 books this year. No error.
                      E

2. Ms. Ackmon's strict classroom rules appeared to have no affect on her students'
        A   B   C   D
disruptive behavior. No error.
                      E

3. The principal demanded that his teachers turn in their lesson plans by March 1st, but
        A   B   C
the assignment had all ready been completed. No error.
                      D   E

4. The teacher evenly divided the supplies between all of her students . No error .
                A   B   C   D   E

5. Each of the four boys was reproached because they did not complete the
                             A   B   C   D
assignment. No error.
            E

6. Every girl in Ms. Johnson's class was given valuable information as to how they
   A   B   C   D
could avoid teenage pregnancy. No error.
                               E

187

7. It is <u>easier</u> to learn math <u>than making</u> <u>subjects and verbs</u> <u>agree</u> . <u>No error.</u>
      A   B   C   D   E

8. Rosie <u>really</u> wanted to enroll in a <u>geometry class</u> , but she was afraid <u>it</u> would require
       A   B   C

<u>to</u> much of her time. <u>No error.</u>
D   E

9. Teachers who <u>look</u> <u>well</u> always <u>make</u> a good impression on <u>their</u> students.
            A   B   C   D

<u>No error.</u>
E

10. <u>Most</u> of the students in the class are <u>much</u> <u>smarter</u> than <u>me.</u> <u>No error.</u>
    A   B   C   D   E

11. There <u>are</u> <u>less</u> students enrolled at <u>Ross Elementary School</u> this <u>academic year</u> .
        A   B   C   D

<u>No error.</u>
E

12. As a teacher, there is really no reason for <u>you</u> <u>becoming</u> upset because students refuse
                                             A   B

to do <u>homework</u> ; students <u>these days</u> are naturally lazy. <u>No error.</u>
       C   D   E

13. The <u>teachers'</u> aides at Ross Elementary School <u>were</u> applauded for <u>there</u> outstanding
       A   B   C

work, praise <u>they'd</u> never received before. <u>No error.</u>
           D   E

14. The <u>new teacher</u> <u>can't hardly</u> wait <u>to take on</u> her new assignment at the <u>one-room</u>
       A   B   C   D

schoolhouse on Selinsky Drive. <u>No error.</u>
                           E

15. Neither John <u>or</u> his brother <u>was</u> present for the <u>school's</u> annual play. <u>No error.</u>
     A   B   C   D   E

16. Its time for reading; put up your math books and take out the story we began
      A   B   C   D
reading yesterday. No error.
                          E

17. The students in the class, they told the teacher of their desire to read instead of
         A   B   C   D
writing. No error.
            E

18. Ms. Rose is an honorable teacher which deserves more recognition than she gets.
              A   B   C   D
No error.
   E

19. Ms. Spakes, the better teacher in the school , has been named "Teacher-of-the-year."
                     A   B   C   D
No error.
   E

20. Approaching the teacher's desk, Mark asked , " Can I pass out the math books?"
                         A   B   C   D
No error.
   E

21. "Teachers, before entering your classroom each day, remember to plan , to review,
                          A   B
and rehearse your presentation well ." No error.
      C   D   E

22. The teacher reproached her students: "You shouldn't of displayed such awful
                                                      A   B
manners in the presence of the principal . No error.
            C   D   E

23. During several days, the lead teacher at Boxie Middle School was deathly ill and
          A   B   C   D
could not report for work. No error.
                                    E

24. The <u>principal</u> , Mr. Mores, was very <u>disgruntled</u> because the <u>students</u> <u>hanged</u> the
       A   B   C   D

picutre in the wrong place. <u>No error.</u>
                               E

– cannot teach

25. <u>To teach</u> well, <u>your skills</u> must be fully developed, and you <u>must</u> have a desire to
      A   B   C

help <u>children learn</u> . <u>No error.</u>
        D   E

Part B

> **DIRECTIONS:** In each of the following sentences, some portion of the sentence is underlined. Under each sentence are five choices. The first choice has the same wording as the original. The other four choices are reworded. Select the letter of the best choice which rewrites the sentence correctly.

26. The principal unexpectedly resigned as the school year began and applied for early retirement.

    (A)   The principal unexpectedly resigned as the school year began and applied for early retirement.

    (B)   The principle unexpectedly resigned as the school year began and applied for early retirement.

    (C)   As the school year began and the principal unexpectedly resigned, he applied for early retirement.

    (D)   The principal applied for early retirement after the school year began, and he unexpectedly resigned.

    (E)   As the school year began, the principal unexpectedly resigned and applied for early retirement.

27. The new teacher is looking forward to have me in her class.

    (A)   to have me in her class.   (D)   to have had me in her class.

    (B)   to have me in class.   (E)   to having me in her class.

    (C)   to having had me in her class.

28. Having completed the task on time, the principal gave Ms. Wharton a huge raise.

    (A)   the principal gave Ms. Wharton a huge raise.

    (B)   a huge raise was given to Ms. Wharton.

    (C)   the principal gave a huge raise to Ms. Wharton.

    (D)   Ms. Wharton was given a high raise by the principal.

    (E)   Ms. Wharton's principal recommended to the board a raise.

29. The teacher who is truly dedicated <u>attends conferences regularly, belongs to professional organizations, and likes to read in order to keep abreast of what's going on.</u>

(A) attends conferences regularly, belongs to professional organizations, and likes to read in order to keep abreast of what's going on.

(B) attends conferences regularly, belongs to professional organizations, and reads in order to keep abreast of what's going on.

(C) likes to attend conferences regularly, belongs to professional organizations, and likes to read in order to keep abreast of what's going on.

(D) attends conferences regularly, has membership in professional organiza-tions, and likes to read in order to keep abreast of what's going on.

(E) attends conferences regularly, likes to belong to professional organizations, and likes to read in order to keep abreast of what's going on.

30. The boy was ill, he did not go to school today.

(A) The boy was ill, he did not go to school today.
(B) The boy was ill, he didn't go to school today.
(C) The boy was ill, he didn't attend school today.
(D) The boy was sick, he didn't attend school today.
(E) The boy was ill. He did not go to school today.

singor / phural

31. Ms. Franklin, a third-grade elementary teacher, is one of those educators <u>who is always willing to do more than expected.</u>

(A) who is always willing to do more than expected.
(B) whom are always willing to do more than expected.
(C) which are always willing to do more than expected.
(D) who are always willing to do more than expected. —*correct*
(E) which is always willing to do more than expected.

feel well

32. The most rewarding experience in teaching <u>is when the children do well.</u>

(A) is when the children do well.   (D) occurs when the children do good. *wrong ADJ*
(B) is when the children do good.   (E) occurs when the children do well. *correct*
(C) was when the children do well.

well adverb

33. Gloria is taller <u>than any girl in the class.</u>

(A) than any girl in the class.   (D) than any other girl in the class.
(B) than each girl in the class.   (E) Than most girls in the class.
(C) than all of the girls in the class.

34. <u>If the teacher would have done her job, she</u> would never have been dismissed.

(A) If the teacher would have done her job, she
(B) If the teacher would of done her job, she
(C) If the teacher would have done her job; she

(D)   If the teacher had done her job, she

(E)   If the teacher had done her job. She

35.   Two teachers taught at this school for over 30 years, and they still like it.

    (A)   taught at this school   (D)   have taught at this school

    (B)   has taught at this school   (E)   teached at this school

    (C)   are teaching at this school

Part C

> **DIRECTIONS:** Each of the passages below is followed by several questions or incomplete sentences. Under each question or sentence are five choices. Select the letter of the best choice and darken the corresponding oval.

Questions 36-40 are based on the following passage.

(1) The melt-water stream draining out along the floor of a glacier cave gives evidence of its origin. (2) It goes without saying that the origin of another kind of cave can be gotten from the pounding of sea waves at the mouth of a sea cave. (3) Solution caves, however, have always been a source of wonder to man. (4) How do these extensive, complex, and in some places beautifully decorated passageways develop?

(5) Solution caves are formed in limestone and similar rocks by the action of the water. (6) _____ (7) After a rain, water seeps into the cracks and pores of soil and rock and percolates beneath the land surface. (8) _____, some of the water reaches a zone of soil and rock where all the cracks are already filled with water. (9) The term water table refers to the upper surface of this saturated zone. (10) Calcite (calcium carbonate), the main mineral of limestone, is barely soluble in pure water. (11) Rainwater, however, absorbs some carbon dioxide as it passes through soil and decaying vegetation. (12) The water, combining chemically with the carbon dioxide, forms a weak carbonic acid solution which slowly dissolves calcite. (13) This acid slowly dissolves calcite, forms solution cavities, and excavates passageways. (14) This results in a solution cave.

(15) A second stage in cave development is when there is lowering of the water table. (16) During this stage, the solution cavities are stranded in the unsaturated zone where air can enter. (17) This leads to the deposition of calcite, which forms dripstone features, beautiful formations in strange shapes on the inside of caves.

36.   In the context of the sentences preceding and following which of the following is the best choice for Sentence 6?

    (A)   These caves can be considered part of a huge subterranean plumbing system.

    (B)   You can think of these caves as part of a huge subterranean plumbing system.

    (C)   The formation of these caves can be thought of in terms of a huge subterranean plumbing system.

    (D)   If you think of it, these caves are similar to a huge subterranean plumbing system.

    (E)   When one visualizes the formation of these caves, one could compare them to part of a huge subterranean plumbing system.

37. Which of the following is the best way to combine Sentences 13 and 14?
    (A) This acid dissolving results in solution cavities, passageways, and caves.
    (B) Solution caves are formed when this acid dissolves solution cavities and passageways.
    (C) Slowly, this acid dissolves calcite, and the resulting effects are that cavities and passageways become caves.
    (D) Excavating cavities, passageways, and caves, the acid slowly dissolves calcite.
    (E) This acid slowly dissolves calcite, excavating cavities and passageways which eventually become solution caves.

38. In relation to the passage as a whole, which of the following best describes the writer's intention in paragraph 2?
    (A) To provide an example
    (B) To propose a solution to a problem
    (C) To describe a location
    (D) To examine opposing evidence
    (E) To explain a process

39. Which of the following sentences does not contain a statement of opinion?
    (A) 3   (D) 17
    (B) 4   (E) none of the above
    (C) 7

40. Based on the preceding sentence which of the following adverbs would best begin Sentence 8?
    (A) However   (D) Moreover
    (B) Eventually   (E) Mostly
    (C) Consequently

Questions 41-45 are are based on the following passage.

(1) Dripstone features are called <u>speleotherms</u>, and they can take several beautiful forms. (2) When these structures are highlighted by lanterns or electric lights, they transform a cave into a natural wonderland. (3) Some people feel that electric lights have no place in a cave. (4) The most familiar decorative dripstone features are <u>stalactites</u> and <u>stalagmites</u>. (5) Stalactites hang downward from the ceiling and are formed as drop after drop of water slowly trickles through cracks in the cave roof. (6) Each drop of water hangs from the ceiling. (7) The drop of water loses carbon dioxide. (8) It then deposits a film of calcite. (9) Stalagmites grow upward from the floor of the cave generally as a result of water dripping from overhead stalactites. (10) An impressive column forms when a stalactite and stalagmite grow until they join. (11) A <u>curtain</u> or <u>drapery</u> begins to form in an inclined ceiling when the drops of water trickle along a slope. (12) Gradually, a thin sheet of calcite grows downward from the ceiling and _____ in graceful decorative folds like a drape.

(13) These impressive and beautiful features appear in caves in almost every state, making for easy access for tourists looking for a thrill. (14) In addition, the size and depth of many caves in the United States also impress even the most experienced tourist accustomed to many very unique sights. (15) Seven caves have more than 15 passage miles, the longest being the Flint-Mammoth Cave system in Kentucky with more than 169 miles.

(16) The deepest cave in the United States is Neff Canyon in Utah. (17) _____
_____. (18) However, Carlsbad Cav-
erns boasts the largest room, the Big Room which covers 14 acres. (19) These are sights not
to be missed by those who appreciate the handiwork of Mother Nature.

41. Which of the following sentences breaks the unity of paragraph 1 and should be
    omitted?

    (A) Sentence 1   (D) Sentence 10
    (B) Sentence 3   (E) Sentence 12
    (C) Sentence 4

42. Which of the following is the best way to combine Sentences 6, 7, and 8?

    (A) Each drop of water deposits a film of calcite as it is hanging from the ceiling
         and losing carbon dioxide.
    (B) When hanging, water drops lose carbon dioxide and create a film of calcite.
    (C) In the process of losing carbon dioxide, the drops of water hang from the ceiling
         and deposit calcite.
    (D) Hanging from the ceiling, losing carbon dioxide, and depositing calcite are the
         drops of water.
    (E) Hanging from the ceiling, each drop of water loses carbon dioxide and deposits
         a film of calcite.

43. In relation to the passage as a whole, which of the following best describes the writer's
    intention in paragraph 2?

    (A) To describe some examples
    (B) To provide a summary
    (C) To convince the reader to change an opinion
    (D) To persuade the reader to follow a course of action
    (E) To detail a chain of events

44. In the context of the sentences preceding and following which of the following is the
    best choice for Sentence 17?

    (A) Although many people are thinking that the deepest cave is Carlsbad Caverns
         in New Mexico.
    (B) Although, many people think the deepest cave is existing is Carlsbad Caverns
         in New Mexico.
    (C) As a matter of fact, many people think the deepest cave exists in New Mexico
         in Carlsbad Caverns.
    (D) However, many people think the deepest cave is Carlsbad Caverns in New
         Mexico.
    (E) In addition, many people think the deepest cave is located in New Mexico in
         Carlsbad Caverns.

45. Which of the following is the correct verb choice for Sentence 12?

    (A) hangs   (D) has hung
    (B) hung   (E) had hung
    (C) hanging

Section 4: Essay

TIME: 30 Minutes

DIRECTIONS: Plan and write an essay on the topic given below. DO NOT WRITE ON ANY OTHER TOPIC OTHER THAN THE ONE SPECIFIED. AN ESSAY ON ANY OTHER TOPIC IS UNACCEPTABLE.

What specific characteristics do you think a person must possess in order to be an effective teacher? Fully explain each characteristic and show how the absence of each will reduce effectiveness in the classroom.

TEST OF COMMUNICATION SKILLS

ANSWER KEY

SECTION 1: LISTENING

1.	(D)	11.	(B)	21.	(C)	31.	(B)
2.	(C)	12.	(C)	22.	(B)	32.	(C)
3.	(D)	13.	(B)	23.	(C)	33.	(A)
4.	(C)	14.	(C)	24.	(C)	34.	(C)
5.	(B)	15.	(B)	25.	(B)	35.	(D)
6.	(A)	16.	(D)	26.	(D)	36.	(B)
7.	(C)	17.	(A)	27.	(C)	37.	(C)
8.	(B)	18.	(D)	28.	(B)	38.	(D)
9.	(D)	19.	(B)	29.	(D)	39.	(C)
10.	(C)	20.	(B)	30.	(D)	40.	(C)

SECTION 2: READING

1.	(C)	9.	(B)	17.	(C)	25.	(E)
2.	(D)	10.	(A)	18.	(D)	26.	(C)
3.	(E)	11.	(C)	19.	(C)	27.	(B)
4.	(A)	12.	(E)	20.	(A)	28.	(B)
5.	(D)	13.	(D)	21.	(B)	29.	(C)
6.	(D)	14.	(A)	22.	(C)	30.	(D)
7.	(C)	15.	(D)	23.	(A)		
8.	(C)	16.	(A)	24.	(C)		

SECTION 3: WRITING

1.	(C)	13.	(C)	25.	(B)	37.	(E)
2.	(C)	14.	(B)	26.	(E)	38.	(E)
3.	(D)	15.	(B)	27.	(E)	39.	(C)
4.	(B)	16.	(A)	28.	(D)	40.	(B)
5.	(B)	17.	(B)	29.	(B)	41.	(B)
6.	(D)	18.	(C)	30.	(E)	42.	(E)
7.	(B)	19.	(A)	31.	(D)	43.	(D)
8.	(D)	20.	(C)	32.	(E)	44.	(D)
9.	(B)	21.	(C)	33.	(D)	45.	(A)
10.	(D)	22.	(A)	34.	(D)		
11.	(B)	23.	(A)	35.	(D)		
12.	(A)	24.	(D)	36.	(A)		

DETAILED EXPLANATIONS OF ANSWERS
NTE CORE BATTERY–Test 2

TEST OF COMMUNICATION SKILLS
Section 1: Listening

Part A

1.   **(D)**   Here you must choose the item that is best supported by the information given in the statement. It is possible that Mrs. Johnson could have been denied employment for all of the reasons given, but only one is clearly supported by the information given. There is no support for choices (A), (B), and (C). The fact, however, that Mrs. Johnson has a Ph.D. Degree in Elementary Education suggests that she, because of her advanced training and superior knowledge base, might experience difficulty relating to her students. Choice (D) is the correct answer.

2.   **(C)**   Here you must pick the choice that is best supported by the information given. The preposition "over" in this sentence means "more than." Therefore, choice (C) is correct: more than 23 million Americans are functionally illiterate. Choices (A), (B), and (D) do not answer the question.

3.   **(D)**   For this question, you must pick the choice that most clearly answers the question. It is evident that a decision has not been made. Choice (D) is the correct answer. Choice (A) is incorrect because a decision has not been made. Choices (B) and (C) are incorrect because there is no information that suggests that a decision to teach is forthcoming or a decision not to teach is inevitable. According to the question, indecisiveness exists.

4.   **(C)**   Here you are required to pick the choice that most directly answers the question, that is, the choice that locates definitions in the already-designated book. Choice (A) is incorrect because the already-designated book is not a dictionary. Choice (B)is incorrect, because chapters rarely contain a collection of definitions. Choice (D) is incorrect because definitions are never found in the index. Choice (C) is the correct answer.

5.   **(B)**   Here you must pick a choice that is supported by information given. Nothing in the statement suggests that Mr. Ross is an excellent teacher, choice (A). Nothing in the statement suggests that Mr. Johnson is a terrible teacher, choice (C). Finally, there is nothing in the statement which suggests that Mr. Johnson needs to improve his teaching abilities, choice (D) The correct answer is (B)— Mr. Johnson is not as good as Mr. Ross.

6.   **(A)**   Here you are required to pick the choice that most directly answers the question. Choices (B), (C), and (D) are incorrect because discipline problems are more likely to occur in inner city schools and in large rural schools than in small rural schools. The choice is (A)— small rural schools.

7.   **(C)**   Here you are to pick the choice that is best supported by the information given. There is no support for choices (A), (B), or (D). It is apparent that the meeting did not fare as well as had been planned. Choice (C) is the correct answer.

8.   **(B)**   Here you must pick a choice that is best supported by the information given in the statement. It is possible to love children, and secretly empathize with them, positively advance their academic well-being. It is also impossible to be a "perfect" role model to each and every student. Choices (A), (C) and (D) are all admirable goals, but only choice (B) supports the original statement.

9.   **(D)**   Here you must pick a choice that is best supported by the information given in the statement. Choice (A) is incorrect because the statement does not suggest that most of the students at the school can't read. According to the statement, most of the students have difficulties in reading. There is a difference. Choice (B) is incorrect because the statement does not suggest that most of the students are reading below grade level. It's possible to be reading on grade level, yet have difficulty in one or more areas of reading. Choice (C) is not supported by the statement because 40% is not equal to *most*. *Most* implies that a majority of the students have difficulties in reading. The choice that is clearly supported by the statement is (D).

10.   **(C)**   Here you must pick the choice that most directly answers the question, that is, the choice which identifies a book that will meet the children's needs in science. Choices (A) and (B) are inappropriate because they are not books. Choice (D) is inappropriate because the "S" encyclopedia, while it is a book, is not sufficient as a complete science book. The answer is choice (C).

11.   **(B)**   Here you must pick the choice that most directly answers the question. Choice (A) is inappropriate because AFL and CIO are not professional organizations which support teachers. These organizations, which have been combined, AFL-CIO, support labor's blue-collar workers. Choices (C) and (D) are inappropriate because the question requests the identification of two professional organizations, not one, and certainly not three. The correct answer is (B).

12.   **(C)**   Here you are to pick a choice that is best supported by the information given. The statement indicates that IRA's membership is almost 100,000. Therefore, choices (A) and (B) are incorrect. Choice (D) is also incorrect because 50,000 does not suggest a membership that is nearly 100,000. The correct answer is choice (C).

13.   **(B)**   Here you must pick a choice that is best supported by the information given. According to the statement, the school's library contains an assortment of magazines. Choice (A) is incorrect because the statement does not indicate that the library has many different books. Choice (C) is incorrect because the statement does not indicate that the library has a variety of reading materials. Choice (D) is inappropriate because the statement does not

indicate that the library contains many different reference materials. Even though choices (A) (C), and (D) are correct, they are not supported by the statement. Choice (B) is the correct answer.

Part B

14.　**(C)**　Based on the dialogue between Mrs. Austin, the lead teacher, and Mr. Berry, the principal, it is evident that Mr. Berry misunderstood Mrs. Austin's "get tough" suggestion, choice (C). It can be safely assumed that Mrs. Austin was suggesting higher academic standards, not paddling. Choices (A), (B), and (D) are not supported by the dialogue. If you listened carefully, Mrs. Austin suggested that they "get tough." No paddling, as stated in choice (A), was recommended. Therefore, choice (B) is incorrect because Mr. Berry cannot be in total agreement with a suggestion that Mrs. Austin never made. Choice (D) is incorrect because Mr. Berry was *not* willing to try anything to improve test scores—no paddling.

15.　**(B)**　Choices (A), (C), and (D) are all supported by the conversation between Mr. Berry and Mrs. Austin. It is evident that Mr. Berry is relying heavily on Mrs. Austin to suggest ways to improve test scores. It is evident that Mr. Berry misunderstood Mrs. Austin's "get tough" suggestion, and it is evident that Mr. Berry does not support paddling. It is false, however, that Mrs. Austin suggested several alternatives to paddling. She simply stated: "there's more than one way to skin a cat." She made no concrete suggestions. Choice (B) is the correct answer.

16.　**(D)**　Here you must pick the choice that is best supported by the information given. Choices (A), (B), nor (C) are supported by the information given in the conversation. The answer is choice (D). Based on the conversation, it is evident that Johnny didn't understand the assignment, and it is also evident that Johnny's parents didn't have time to help him.

17.　**(A)**　The question is a straightforward one that requires a straightforward answer. Johnny had previously failed to turn in his homework twice. This was the third time. The answer is choice (A). Choices (B), (C), and (D) are not supported.

18.　**(D)**　This question requires you to read between the lines and make an inference. The conversation does not explicitly state that Johnny was lying; but since he had failed three times to turn in his homework, it can be safely inferred that the teacher did not believe Johnny. Nothing in the conversation supports choices (A), (B) nor (C). Choice (D) is the correct selection.

19.　**(B)**　Based on the information given, you are asked to render a judgment (evaluation) and make a recommendation. Choices (A) and (D) are inappropriate because no disciplinary action should be taken until all evidence is in. By the same token, choice (C) is inappropriate because the teacher should not just turn her back, especially since Johnny has consistently failed to turn in his homework. Choice (B) is the most appropriate answer.

20.　**(B)**　Here you are to pick a choice that is supported by information given. Choices (A), (C) and (D) are in no way supported by the conversation. Choice (B) is the correct answer.

21. **(C)**   Since the answer is not explicitly given you are required to infer about a cause-effect relationship. Choices (A), (B) and (D) are rather far-out inferences to make, even though all three may be true. The most logical answer, though, is (C). It is natural for children to meddle with each other.

22. **(B)**   Here you are asked to infer because the answer is not explicitly stated. Choice (A) is incorrect because Ms. Rayburn saw Mark pull Susan's hair. Choice (C) cannot be inferred. There should be supporting evidence. Choice (D) is incorrect because lying is not a natural act, and it is not common among all little boys. It's possible that Mark lied because he was afraid of being punished, choice (B).

23. **(C)**   There is no mention in the conversation about why the first student wanted to skip school.

24. **(C)**   Choices (A), (B) and (D) are all possible answers, but none is supported by the information given (Conversation). It is evident, though, that Student 2 is really interested in school because he didn't want to miss the final examination review sessions. The correct answer is (C).

25. **(B)**   Here you must infer because the cause for Student 1's action is not given. Nothing in the conversation leads one to believe that Student 2 was really a sissy or portrayed past signs of being a wimp. Also, to say that Student 1 couldn't think of anything else to say is a far-out conclusion. Therefore, choices (A), (C), and (D) are inappropriate. Choice (B) however, does make sense: Student 1 may have felt that such derogatory remark might change Student 2's mind.

26. **(D)**   Here you are required to identify specific details. The speaker blames the students for not coming to class participating in class discussions, completing homework, and studying. The speaker also blames the teacher for not holding the attention of students. Clearly the speaker blames both the students and the teachers, choice (D).

27. **(C)**   Again, you are required to identify specific details in this short talk. Choices (A), (B), and (D) are all supported by the information given in the short talk, but the question asks for specific recommendations for the teacher. Demanding that students attend class, do homework, participate in class, and study can be encouraged by anyone, including the principal and the parents; but only the teachers can make their classes interesting and relevant—choice (C).

28. **(B)**   Here you are to identify the speaker's tone, his/her mood or emotion. The speaker is not angry, and he/she is not indifferent (doesn't care). The speaker is concerned, choice (B). The speaker is critical judgmental because he/she is concerned about the situation.

29. **(D)**   Here you are to identify the central thought or the main idea. Choice (A) is in no way supported by the talk. Choices (B) and (C) are supported, but they are merely details. They are examples of how students need to change. Choice (D) is the correct answer. Teachers and students need to change, and the speaker gives specific recommendations.

30. **(D)**   This question requires you to identify the major topic of this short talk. Choices (A), (B), and (C) are all mentioned in the talk as problems facing schools today. The main topic is (D): problems facing schools.

31. **(B)** This question requires you to identify a major detail. Crime is mentioned as one of the leading problems, and dropout is mentioned as a problem that occurs because of the leading problem of teenage pregnancy. Drugs were never mentioned by the speaker. The answer is choice (B): teenage pregnancy.

32. **(C)** This question requires you to summarize the speaker's message. Choice (A) is too general. The speaker specifically mentions problems that exist. Choice (B) is inappropriate because no mention is made of action to alleviate the problems delineated. Choice (D) contains erroneous information. The speaker stated that crime is one of the leading problems, not the leading problem, facing schools today. Therefore, choice (C) is the correct choice.

33. **(A)** This question asks you to identify an assumption, an idea a speaker must have in mind based on what he or she is saying. An assumption is generally unstated. Because the speaker, at the end of his message, asks for the paddle, it can be assumed that he supports corporal punishment. Also the speaker notes that positive reinforcement and curriculum modification have failed to deter crime. This notation, coupled with a plea for the paddle, supports the assumption, choice (A), that corporal punishment should reappear. Choice (B) cannot be an assumption because it is stated as a fact. There is no justification for choices (C) and (D).

34. **(C)** This is a straightforward question that requires identification of the speaker's tone. The word "infuriating" suggests that the speaker is angry, choice (C). Choices (A), (B), and (D) are not supported.

35. **(D)** This question requires you to connotatively define a word. To modify a curriculum is to change it, not to completely rewrite it, eliminate it, or supplement it. The correct answer is (D).

36. **(B)** Choosing an appropriate title for a short talk requires the use of several skills: identifying the main topic and main idea, summarizing major ideas, and paraphrasing a message. Your choice must embody the main idea, and it must also address the message being portrayed. You must carefully evaluate each choice enroute to choosing the one that best fits the content of the message. Choice (A) is inappropriate because "Monsters in the classroom" is not broad enough to convey the intended message. The same is true of choice (C). Choice (D) is inappropriate because the speaker does not talk about or suggest a number of "Techniques for Disciplining Children." He/she mentions a couple of techniques that have not worked, but one technique is mentioned as a possible solution—the paddle. It's clear that choice (B), "A Plea for Corporal Punishment," is the most appropriate title.

37. **(C)** This question requires an analysis to determine which study skill was not mentioned. Choices (A), (B), and (D) were all mentioned by the speaker. Taking notes is an excellent study habit, but it was not mentioned by the speaker. The correct answer is choice (C). Remember to listen carefully for small words that may change the meaning of a question. This question asks for the study habit which was *not* suggested by the speaker.

38. **(D)** This question requires good common sense and basic comprehension. A plan is no good unless it is followed. Students must have the discipline to stick to plans developed. Choices (A), (B), and (C) are all important, but choice (D), developing discipline, is the most important.

39.   **(C)**   This question requires you to identify the main idea of the talk. Choices (A), (B), and (D) are too narrow and limited to be main ideas. More is involved than planning a time, choice (A); developing study schedules, choice (B), and choosing an appropriate place, choice (D). The most appropriate choice is (C).

40.   **(C)**   This question requires an analysis (cause-effect relationship) and assumption. Good study habits and discipline do not necessarily translate into more time to do other things, less effort and time, or teacher approval. One can, however, safely assume that good study habits and discipline will yield good grades, choice (C).

Section 2: Reading

1.   **(C)**   This question requires you to identify the main idea of this reading selection. The main idea is the central thought of a passage. In this passage, Dr. James is suggesting that children should be given an opportunity to read a great deal in order for their reading skills to improve. This passage strongly suggests that "practice makes perfect" - choice (C). There is no support for choices (A), (B), (D), or (E).

2.   **(D)**   This question requires you to infer about the types of materials children should read. According to Dr. James's rules, all types of materials are suggested. Therefore, choices (A), (B), (C) and (E) are incorrect because these choices limit the materials children should read. Choice (D) is the correct answer.

3.   **(E)**   This question requires you to choose the statement that best summarizes the passage. Two important points are expressed: children should read extensively, and children should read all types of materials. Only choice (E) expresses both of these points.

4.   **(A)**   This question requires you to see the relationship between motivation and student performance. If teachers, according to the passage, expect their students to perform well, teachers must make their classes both interesting and stimulating. In other words, teachers must motivate their students, choice (A).

5.   **(D)**   In order to answer this question, you have to understand the main idea of the passage. The passage clearly states that teachers who make their classes interesting don't have to make students do their work. Therefore, it can be assumed that classes that are stimulating yield better results, choice (D). None of the other choices is supported by the information given.

6.   **(D)**   Of the possible choices, choice (D) best paraphrases the idea presented in this passage. There is a direct relationship between active teaching and interesting and stimulating classes. Active, energetic teachers usually stimulate their students to learn. Nothing in the passage supports the ideas of teacher consistency, direct instruction, reinforcement, or modeling.

7.   **(C)**   The main idea of this passage is not explicitly stated. It is implied. It is clear that the passage questions the teaching of irrelevant facts such as *Abraham Lincoln was the 16th President of the United States*, and *Columbus discovered America in 1492*. The passage is not about Abraham Lincoln or Columbus [choices (A) and (B)], nor does the passage address

the greatness of these men [choice (D)]. Choice (E) is not supported at all. The most appropriate choice is (C).

8.   **(C)**   This question requires you to pick the choice that best shows the relationship of the passage to its intended audience. All teachers should be careful not to teach irrelevant facts that will soon be forgotten, choice (C). Choices (A), (B), (D), and (E) are all inappropriate because each of these choices singles out one specific group which is responsible for properly educating children.

9.   **(B)**   This question requires you to pick the choice that best demonstrates the appropriateness of the author's evidence which supports the idea expressed. If you carefully read the passage, you noted that the author really does not present any evidence, explicitly. This eliminates choices (A), (C), (D), and (E). Since no evidence is explicitly given, the most appropriate choice is (B).

10.   **(A)**   This question requires you to identify the main idea of this passage. Choices (B) and (C) are limited because the passage indicates that parents outstrip their children both educationally and economically, choice (A). Choices (D) and (E) are inappropriate because the passage indicates that students will not even equal the educational and economic accomplishments of their parents .

11.   **(C)**   This question asks you to go beyond the facts that are presented in the passage. Choices (A) and (B) may be true, but the passage neither states nor implies anything that supports them. Also, just because this generation of students will not outstrip or even equal its parents educationally or economically, this does not support the assumptions that parents are smarter than their children, and parents were more interested in school than their children are. It can be assumed, though, that parents are generally more industrious than their children, choice (C).

12.   **(E)**   A careful rereading of the passage will reveal that the author presents an idea but no support for the idea. No empirical data is presented which clearly shows that parents are educationally and economically superior to their children. For example, in 1945, 85 percent of first-graders entering school graduated. In 1962, only 45 percent of the first-graders entering school graduated. Choice (E) is the correct answer. Choices (A), (B), (C) and (D) are not supported.

13.   **(D)**   This question requires you to determine which of the above statements is a fact. The passage contains no facts. Even though the passage begins with "It is a known fact that... no evidence is presented; therefore, choices (A), (B), (C), and (E) are incorrect. However, the author does believe that parents are educationally and economically superior to their children. This is a fact, choice (D).

14.   **(A)**   The question asks you to identify the main idea, the central thought of this passage . Choices (D) and (E) are supporting details. Neither of them can be supported and therefore cannot be the main idea. Since there is no evidence of how smart children were in the past, no comparison can be made, thus eliminating choice (C). While the passage does state that parents are not supportive of our schools, choice (B) is not the main idea of the passage. It's the main idea of the second paragraph only. Choice (A) is the correct answer.

15. **(D)**   The author makes two points in this passage: American students are not performing well academically, and a lack of parental involvement is the reason for this intellectual mediocrity. Choices (A) and (B) only express one of these two points. Choice (C) is true, according to the passage, but it only supports the reason for low academic achievement among American students—a lack of parental involvement. Choice (E) is not appropriate because the author does not hold the children responsible for the problem. The most appropriate answer is choice (D).

16. **(A)**   The author states that 45-50 percent of high school graduates lack basic skills; American students score lower on achievement tests than students in schools of other countries. He also states that over 23 million Americans are functionally illiterate. These three statements more than support the main idea of the passage—inferior academic achievement. To say that the main idea is marginally supported is not true. To say that the evidence is limited or that there is no evidence at all is also untrue. To say that there is an abundance of support is untrue, but the evidence given is adequate to support the main idea, choice (A).

17. **(C)**   Since the author blames only parents for the poor academic performance of American students, the argument has to be judged as being too limited. Certainly, there must be many reasons why American students are not performing well academically. A lack of parental involvement is only one reason—choice (C).

18. **(D)**   The word "thank" translates into praise for a group of people who are doing an excellent job. Because of their hard work, teachers should be praised for their work. Choice (D) summarizes the statement better than any other of the choices. Choice (E) may appear to be the correct answer, but since you can't give teachers raises, this is not an appropriate answer.

19. **(C)**   The author's idea in this passage is considered an opinion since no empirical data is available to support the idea. Unsupported statements are merely opinions that may be accepted or rejected. The author really provides no support for the idea expressed—choice (C).

20. **(A)**   Even though no concrete evidence is given, the author does make a strong argument that a mismatch does exist. When students have difficulty reading and understanding story books, frustration sets in, and students do not perform at levels commensurate with their listening capacity. Choice (A) is the appropriate answer. One might think that no argument exists, choice (E), but it does. "Despite what many think," sets the stage for the opposing view of the author.

21. **(B)**   This question requires an evaluation. No one, particularly teachers, has the time to rewrite books. The choice is obvious—(B). This is the *least* appropriate strategy for teachers. Be sure to read questions carefully. You may have missed the word *least*, as opposed to *most*.

22. **(C)**   Again, you are asked to make an evaluation with reference to appropriateness. It would be very difficult to tape math formulas and diagrams. Therefore, the most appropriate choice for an answer of least applicability is choice (C)—math.

23. **(A)** This question requires you to distinguish between facts and opinions. Choices (B), (C), (D) and (E) are facts that need no justification. The general population, especially inservice and preservice teachers, is aware of these striking changes. Whether the reforms mentioned in choices (B), (C), (D) and (E) have failed to meet the needs of the urban/inner city child is an opinion that cannot be proved as a fact. Everyone will agree that standards were raised, students and teachers were tested and assessed as never before, curriculum revision was at an all-time high, and teacher training programs have taken on new looks. However, not everyone will agree that the needs of the urban/inner city child are not being met—choice (A).

24. **(C)** In order to identify the topic of this passage, you must first identify the main idea—*the reforms of the 1980s have failed to meet the needs of the urban/inner city child.* Choices (A), (B), (D), and (E) are reforms that have taken place. Each is too limited in scope and support to be the main topic. Choice (C), the underserved urban/inner city child, is the main topic.

25. **(E)** This question requires you to engage in analysis. It requires you to identify the stated relationship between the low performance of urban/inner city children on standardized tests and the reasons for such low performance (cause-effect relationship). Choices (A), (B), (C), and (D) are all inappropriate due to inaccurate interpretations of ideas presented in the passage. For example, the passage stated that standards were raised, but it was never indicated that these standards were too high. The most appropriate choice is (E).

26. **(C)** Not much explanation is needed here to explain the author's attitude. His/her attitude is clearly critical because it is established that the reforms have not met the needs of the urban/inner city child. The appropriate choice is (C).

27. **(B)** This question requires an identification of the main idea of this passage. Nothing in the passage suggests that negotiation gives teachers more power, choice (E). Negotiation is a method of improving conditions (in general) for teachers. Choices (A), (C), and (D) are singularly-improved conditions that are too limited to be the main idea of this passage. The passage speaks to several improved conditions—choice (B).

28. **(B)** The author clearly supports the argument for teacher negotiation, citing research studies for justification. However, since no empirical data is given with sources identified, the argument is not considered fully supported. Therefore, choice (B) is the most appropriate answer.

29. **(C)** This question requires you to identify the organization of the passage. Choice (A) is inappropriate because no problem is presented. Choices (B) and (E) are inappropriate because no numerical or chronological lists are enumerated. Choice (D) is inappropriate because the main idea is not implied; it's obvious and stated: *Negotiation empowers teachers....* The most appropriate choice is (C). A controversial issue is presented and defended.

30. **(D)** This question requires you to identify an evaluation made by the author. If you carefully read the passage, you noted that the author views intangibles to be just as important as tangibles—choice (D). None of the other choices are supported. The question asked is very straightforward and is answered in the passage. You were not asked to provide an evaluation. You were asked to identify an evaluation made by the author.

Section 3: Writing

Part A

1.   **(C)**   The error in this sentence occurs at (C). The word "liable" suggests a legal obligation: "Mr. Watson is liable for the damage to his neighbor's fence." Since there is no legal obligation for Jack Newberry to read 100 books this year, the word "likely" is a better choice, "Jack Newberry, along with his classmates, is an avid reader who is likely to finish 100 books this year."

2.   **(C)**   The error in this sentence occurs at (C). "Affect" is a verb which means to influence. Effect is a noun which means result. It suggests a completed action.

Affect: His low grade in chemistry did not affect his overall grade-point average. The subject of this sentence is grade, the verb is "did affect".

Effect: His low grade in chemistry had little effect on his overall grade-point average. The subject of this sentence is grade. The verb is had. Effect is a noun which serves as the direct object of the verb had. As a general rule, affect is a verb; effect is a noun.

3.   **(D)**   The error in this sentence occurs at (D). "All ready" means completely ready: "The children were all ready for recess." Already means previously: "The teacher wanted the boy suspended, but the principal felt that the boy had already been punished enough." Sentence 3 does not suggest an action of being completely ready, but it does suggest that something had been previously completed.

4.   **(B)**   The error in this sentence occurs at (B). "Between" commonly applies to only two objects or persons. Among is generally used to refer to three or more objects or persons.

Between: The school is located between Lyle and Deman, the two longest streets in the city.

Among: Among the four boys in the class, Johnny is the most intelligent.

5.   **(B)**   The error in this sentence occurs at (B). The subject of this sentence is each. Each, as a rule, takes singular verbs and pronouns. In the above sentence, the singular verb was is used to agree with the singular subject "each", but the pronoun "they" is in disagreement with the singular subject each because they is plural. The sentence should read: "Each of the four boys was reproached because he did not complete the assignment."

6.   **(D)**   The error in this sentence occurs at (D). Every, as a rule, takes singular verbs and pronouns. In the above sentence, the singular verb "was" is used to agree with the singular subject every, but the pronoun they is in disagreement with the singular subject every because "they" is plural. The sentence should read: "Every girl in Ms. Johnson's class was given valuable information as to how she could avoid teenage pregnancy."

7.   **(B)**   The error in this sentence occurs at (B). A lack of parallelism exists. "To learn" should be matched by "to make" in order for parallelism to exist. The sentence should read: "It is easier to learn math than to make subjects and verbs agree."

8.   **(D)**   The error in this sentence occurs at (D). "Too" is always used to denote excessiveness: "I ate too much; it is too hot in the room; the examination was too difficult; I enrolled in too many classes this semester."

9.   **(B)**   The error in this sentence occurs at (B). Good is an adjective. "Well" is an adverb.

Good: The teacher did a good job. The adjective good describes the type of job she did.

Well: The teacher did the job well. The teacher, in other words, did well. Well modifies the verb did.

10.   **(D)**   The error in this sentence occurs at (D). Pronouns following "as" and" than" should be nominative case pronouns — I, we, they, he, she." Most of the students in the class are much smarter than I." The verb am is understood. "Most of the students in the class are much smarter than I am", not "me am".

11.   **(B)**   The error in this sentence occurs at (B). "Less" refers to singular amounts: "The enrollment this year is less than the enrollment for the previous year." Enrollment is singular and requires use of the adjective less. In referring to plural items that can be counted, one would use the adjective fewer: "There are fewer students enrolled at Ross Elementary School this academic year."

Less: I gained less weight last year. Fewer: I gained fewer pounds last year.

12.   **(A)**   The error in this sentence occurs at (A). When an "ing" verb form (becoming) is preceded by a pronoun (you), the pronoun must be possessive: "As a teacher, there is really no reason for your becoming upset because students refuse to do homework: students these days are naturally lazy."

Example 1: The teacher was proud of me completing the homework. Since completing is a verb form ending in ing, the pronoun preceding it should be possessive: "the teacher was proud of my completing the homework."

Example 2: The coach was upset at me finishing last in the track meet. Since finishing is a verb form ending in ing, the pronoun preceding it should be possessive; "the coach was upset at my" finishing last in the track meet.

13.   **(C)**   The error in this sentence occurs at (C). Be careful not to confuse "their" and "there."

There: There are six boys in the house.   Their: The boys are in their house (possessive).

Sentence number 13 should read: "The teachers' aides at Ross Elementary School were applauded for their outstanding work, praise they'd never received before."

14.   **(B)**   The error in this sentence occurs at (B). "Can't hardly" is a double negative and should not be used. The sentence should read: "The new teacher can hardly wait to take on her new assignment at the one-room schoolhouse on Selinsky Drive."

or

"The new teacher can't wait to take on her new assignment at the one-room schoolhouse on Selinsky Drive."

15. **(B)** The error in this sentence occurs at (B). Always use "or" with either: "Either John or his brother will raise the school's flag this morning." Always use nor with neither: "Neither John nor his brother was present for the school's annual play."

16. **(A)** The error in this sentence occurs at (A). "Its" is a possessive pronoun and is used to show ownership: "the table has four legs for its support." The first part of sentence number 16 needs a subject and a verb; therefore, the contraction for "it is" (it's) must be used:" It's time for reading; put up your math books and take out the story we began reading yesterday."

17. **(B)** The error in this sentence occurs at (B). This sentence contains a double subject—"students" and "they." Both are not needed: "The students in the class told the teacher of their desire to read instead of writing."

18. **(C)** The error in this sentence occurs at (C). In referring to people, always use who or that, never "which." Which is used to refer to inanimate objects.

19. **(A)** The error in this sentence occurs at (A). "Better" is used to compare two persons or two things: John is better at math than Joe. Use best when comparing more than two: "Ms. Spakes, the best teacher in the school, has been named "Teacher-of- the-Year.""

20. **(C)** The error in this sentence occurs at (C). "Can" implies that one has the ability to perform: "Mary's IQ suggests that she can make straight A's." "May" is used when one seeks permission to do something: Approaching the teacher's desk, Mark asked, "May I pass out the math books?"

21. **(C)** The error in this sentence occurs at (C). A problem with parallelism exists. The sentence should read: "Teachers, before entering your classroom each day, remember to plan, to review, and to rehearse your presentation well." Since plan and review are preceded by to, "rehearse" should be preceded by to also.

22. **(A)** The error in this sentence occurs at (A). "Shouldn't of," "wouldn't of," and "ought not" of are examples of non-standard expressions. Sentence number 22 should read: "The teacher reproached her students: "You shouldn't have displayed such awful manners in the presence of the principal.""

23. **(A)** The error in this sentence occurs at (A). "During" is used to denote a specific period of time: "Ms. Watson is on duty during the lunch hour." In sentence number 23, the word "for" should be used instead of "during": "For several days, the lead teacher at Boxie Middle School was deathly ill and could not report for work."

24. **(D)** The error in this sentence occurs at (D). "Hanged" refers to the act of putting someone to death: The student was hanged for not doing his homework. Hung refers to the act of suspending something from a given point or place: "The principal Mr. Mores. was very disgruntled because the students hung the picture in the wrong place."

25. **(B)** The error in this sentence occurs at (B). "Your skills" cannot teach. The infinitive phrase, "To teach well," must reference "you": "To teach well, you must have skills that are fully developed, and you must have a desire to help children learn."

Part B

26.　**(E)**　This sentence contains a misplaced modifier. If you carefully reread the sentence, it appears that the school year began and applied for early retirement. In all sentence structures, modifiers must be placed near the words they complement (modify). The school year did not apply for retirement; it was the principal who applied. For clarity purposes, the entire sentence must be reconstructed. Choice (A) is merely a replica of the sentence in error. Choice (B) is the same as Choice (A), except for the word principle instead of principal. The words "principle" and "principal" often confuse people. "Principal" refers to the head of a school, a leader: "The principal is the instructional leader in the school." "Principle" refers to a law, a rule, a doctrine: "The principles of freedom for teachers must be adhered to by all administrators." Choice (C) separates the actions of the principal and suggests that his application for early retirement is the main thrust of the sentence. Yes, the principal did apply for early retirement, but more importantly, he unexpectedly resigned. Choice (D) also suggests that the principal's application for early retirement is the main thrust of the sentence. The principal must resign before he can apply for retirement. Choice (E) is the correct answer. It portrays a logical sequence of events: the school year begins; the principal unexpectedly resigns; the principal then applies for early retirement. Unlike Choice (A), which suggests that the school year applied for early retirement, Choice (E) clearly states that the principal resigned and applied for early retirement.

27.　**(E)**　This is an awkward sentence. The participial phrase "to having" should be used instead of the infinitive phrase "to have." Choice (E) is the correct answer.

Examples

1. The theater teacher wants "to have" me in the school play.

2. The theater teacher is looking forward "to having" me in the school play.

Choice (A) is incorrect because it is the same as the bold sentence portion which is in error. Choice (B) is practically the same as Choice (A). The only difference between the two is that her is missing from Choice (B). Choices (C) and (D) denote actions that have already occurred, while the sentence itself suggests an action will occur in the future (is looking forward). Choice (E) is the correct answer.

28.　**(D)**　This sentence contains a dangling participle. It appears that the principal completed the task. In choices (A) and (C), again it appears that the principal completed the task. In Choice (B), it appears that the raise completed the task. Choice (E) is awkward and does not follow a logical sequence. Ms. Wharton's principal recommended a raise to the board. Choice (E) is also unclear in that it does not tell for whom the raise was recommended. Choice (D) is the correct answer.

29.　**(B)**　The sentence contains faulty parallelism. Choice (A) is the same as the bold sentence portion which is in error. Choices (C), (D) and (E) do not present the characteristics of a dedicated teacher in a parallel manner. In Choice (C), the three verb phrases that introduce the dedicated teacher's characteristics are "likes to attend, belongs to," and "likes to read." These verb phrases must be consistent: "likes to attend, likes to belong to," and "likes to read," or one might use the three simple verbs "attends," "belongs," and "reads." The same inconsistency is true of Choices (D) and (E). Choice (B) is the correct answer.

30. **(E)**   This is considered a run-on sentence. A comma cannot be used to separate two complete sentences. It's not strong enough. Choices (A), (B), (C) and (D) share the same problem. They are all run-on sentences. Choice (E) is the correct answer.

31. **(D)**   The pronoun who in this sentence refers to educators (plural), not to Ms. Franklin (singular). "Who" is plural because it refers to educators, which is plural. Therefore, the verb following "who" should be plural. Choice (A) is incorrect because it is the same as the bold sentence portion which is in error. Choice (B) is wrong because whom is incorrect. It can never be used as the subject of a clause or a sentence. Choice (C) is incorrect because which can never be used to refer to people. The same is true for choice (E). Choice (D) is the correct answer.

32. **(E)**   A faulty idiom is the error in this sentence. "Is when" should never be used. "Occurs when" is a better choice. Choices (A) and (C) are incorrect because they both include the nonstandard expression "is when." Choice (B) is incorrect because it includes the nonstandard expression "is when," and it also contains an error in word choice. The adverb well should be used instead of the adjective good. Choice (D) is incorrect because the adjective good is used instead of the adverb well. Choice (E) is the correct answer.

33. **(D)**   Gloria cannot be taller than herself. Therefore she is taller than any other girl in the class. The correct answer is (D).

34. **(D)**   "Would have done" is incorrect. The subjunctive mood (past) is needed here. The correct form is "had done." Choice (A) is incorrect because it is the same as the bold sentence portion which is in error. Choice (B) is incorrect because "would of" is nonstandard English, and it should never be used. Choice (C) is incorrect because this is a complex sentence consisting of one dependent clause and one independent clause. These two clauses are separated by a comma, not a semicolon. Choice (E) is incorrect because it is not a complete sentence which expresses a complete thought. Choice (D) is the correct answer.

35. **(D)**   Use of the past tense verb "taught" suggests that these two teachers are no longer at the school; however, the last part of the sentence unequivocally states that they are still at the school. To indicate that an action has occurred in the past and still continues requires the use of the present perfect tense — "have taught." Choice (A) is incorrect because it is a replica of the underlined sentence portion which is in error. Choice (B) is incorrect because of a verb agreement problem. Has is used with singular subjects. Have is used with plural subjects. Since "teachers" is plural, have should be used instead of has. Choice (C) is incorrect because the verb phrase "are teaching" is in the present tense. A verb or verb phrase denoting past tense is necessary in this case. Choice (E) includes an incorrect tense formation. The past tense of "teach" is "taught," not "teached." Choice (D) is the correct answer.

36. **(A)**   (A) is the best choice because it is precise and uses a voice consistent with the rest of the passage. Choice (B) and (C) both slip into the less formal "you." Choice (E) is too formal, using "one." Choice (C) is somewhat acceptable but uses the passive voice construction, "can be thought of."

37. **(E)**   Choice (E) clearly shows the pattern of events, a sequence of cause-and-effect. Choice (A) contains the incorrect construction, "This acid dissolving"; it should be, "This

acid's dissolving." Choice (B) neglects to extend clearly the process of cave formation to show that the passageways become caves. Choice (C) is somewhat acceptable, but it contains the awkward phrasing, "effects are that." Choice (D) reverses the cause with the effect, and so confuses the issues.

38.   **(E)**   The second paragraph explains the process (E) by which dripstone features are formed in a cave. This process takes place in a location—caves—but description, choice (C), is not the main intent of the paragraph. Choices (A), (B), and (D) would be more suitable to persuasion.

39.   **(C)**   Sentence 7 is the only one of the four listed that does not contain a statement of opinion. Sentence 3 (A) calls the caves a "wonder to man." Sentence 4 (B) has "beautifully decorated passageways." Sentence 17 (D) calls the dripstone features "beautiful formations." Since beauty and wonder are different for each person, these are opinions of the author and not statements of fact.

40.   **(B)**   Within the context of the sentence preceding it, this sentence requires an adverb of time. Only choice (B) fullfills that requirement. Choices (A), (C), (D), and (E) are not adverbs of time.

41.   **(B)**   Choice (B) breaks the unity of the paragraph by digressing slightly into an opinion about the presence of electric lights in a natural setting. As the main thrust of the passage is to discuss the beauty of caves in the United States, this idea is out of place. This sentence also mentions the opinions of "some people," a vague reference. The other choices contain no digressions.

42.   **(E)**   Choice (E) concisely combines ideas while effectively showing the sequence of events. Choice (A) puts the cause, "losing carbon dioxide," after the effect, "deposits a film of carbon dioxide." Choice (B) could be better worded by revising, "When hanging, water drops." Choice (C) erroneously presents hanging from the ceiling as part of the process of losing carbon dioxide. Choice (D) completely loses the cause-and-effect and presents events as an unrelated list.

43.   **(D)**   The intent of the second paragraph builds to the last sentence, in which the persuasive (D) intent becomes evident. Although the paragraph provides some examples, choice (A), those examples bolster the persuasive intent. Choice (C) could be plausible if the writer had indicated an acknowledgment of the reader's aversion to caves. Choices (B) and (E) are more appropriate for the first paragraph.

44.   **(D)**   Choice (D) makes a complete sentence that is correctly puntuated. Choice (A) is a fragment and contains the awkward "people are thinking." Choice (B) contains the poor phrase "is existing." Choices (C) and (E) could be moderately acceptable, but they have two prepositional phrases in a row beginning with "in" at the end of the sentence.

45.   **(A)**   The verb needed in this sentence must agree with the verb "grows." The only one of the five choices provided that does this is (A) "hangs."

Section 4: Essay

The following essay received scores at the highest end of the scale used in NTE essay scoring.

Essay A

When I think of what specific characteristics a person must possess in order to be an effective teacher I think of these characteristics: upstanding values, compassion, and a thorough knowledge of their subject matter.

First, a person who becomes a teacher must keep in mind that they are a role model to the children in their midst. Their private and professional life must be beyond reproach. A teacher is responsible for setting values as well as teaching values. A teacher has a big influence on a child's life; therefore, a teacher must be careful about the kinds of signals he sends out to the children in his environment. Today, it is hard to tell teachers from students because they dress alike, wear their hair alike, associate together, and act the same. A teacher should set himself apart if he is to be a positive influence on the students he comes in contact with. Once a teacher loses his credibility and/or self-respect, he is no longer effective in the classroom.

Compassion is a quality that allows a teacher to have a sense of humor, get to know students' qualities, and be supportive of students' efforts. A teacher must be able to laugh with his students. This creates a relationship between learner and teacher, and shows the students that the teacher has a human side, and tells the students that the teacher is approachable. A good teacher will get to know each of his student's learning abilities and styles. This will allow the teacher to get the most from each student. Compassion allows the teacher to empathize with the students who are having problems in school or at home by being supportive and by providing a positive direction. Students can be turned off if they perceive that a teacher does not care.

Finally, if a person is going to be an effective teacher, he must have a thorough knowledge of his discipline. This gives the teacher a sense of confidence and allows the teacher to be well organized. An effective teacher knows and likes what he teaches, and the enthusiasm will show and will become a part of the students. Without a good mastery of the subject matter, a teacher is unable to make well-informed decisions about objectives to be covered.

In conclusion, by possessing and demonstrating upstanding values, showing compassion, and exhibiting a thorough knowledge of his subject area, the right person can make a good teacher. If students are to learn, they must be influenced by persons who have all three of these characteristics.

Explanation of Essay A

This essay, even though it contains minor errors in punctuation and pronoun-antecedent agreement, is well written, as evidenced by the clarity, organization, and mature language.

The opening sentence is a complex sentence. Therefore, a comma should have been used to separate the dependent clause ("When I think of what specific characteristics a person must possess in order to be an effective teacher,") from the rest of the sentence (the independent clause). Also, in the first sentence, the pronoun *their* (plural) is used to refer to *a person* (singular). This a pronoun-antecedent disagreement. The pronoun *his* or *her* should have been used. This problem disappears later, suggesting that the writer may have been careless. Always save enough time to proof your essay. When writing hurriedly, it's very easy to make careless mistakes: their for there, a for an, no for know.

The writer adequately introduces the topic "Characteristics of an Effective Teacher" by outlining the three characteristics to be discussed. Each of the three paragraphs of the body contains a characteristic as the main idea and details to explain and/or support it. The conclusion is a summary of the essay and an explanation of why these characteristics are important. The reader should have no difficulty understanding the message the writer is conveying.

The following essay received scores in the middle of the NTE scoring scale.

Essay B

A teacher must have the following characteristics in order to be effective: dedication, knowledge of the subject matter, and versatility. A dedicated teacher is one who is always willing to go that extra mile to help a student to learn. A dedicated teacher is not one who is just looking for a paycheck every other week. This type of teacher will find the students' weaknesses and start building on those points day-by-day. A dedicated teacher is also a caring person who will help build confidence in students' ability to learn. Without this type of dedication, there will be a decrease in effective teaching because if the teacher does not show his dedication and concern for the students to learn the material, then the students will not reflect that initiative to learn.

Teachers must be knowledgeable in the subject areas that they are teaching. Teachers with more formal education, teaching experience, and hours of training are more successful in helping students achieve educational goals. Now, without this knowledge and education, you will have a reduction in the effective teaching method. Teachers who do not know the academic subject that they are teaching cannot make clear presentations or use effective teaching strategies. They cannot answer questions fully and must be very evasive in their answers.

Another characteristic that a teacher must possess is the versatility to teach slower and advanced learners in a manner that both will be able to receive and retain the given information. A teacher must be able to make the subject matter *come alive*, demanding quality work meeting personal as well as academic needs of students and adding humor to the classroom. With the absence of this versatility, a teacher will only reach a small number of students in the classroom.

All of the above characteristics are important. Teachers who do not possess them will have difficulty reaching their students, and the drop-out rate will continue to climb.

Explanation of Essay B

The writer of this essay addresses the topic well, and the essay is without major errors in mechanics of grammar. Nevertheless, the essay lacks clarity in organization and presentation of ideas. No introductory paragraph exists. This is very important because the introductory paragraph sets parameters for the remaining parts of the essay. The writer, in this case, combined the introduction and the first paragraph of the body. The introduction should have read: *A teacher must have the following characteristics in order to be effective: dedication. knowledge of subject matter, and versatility.* In earlier years, a one-sentence paragraph was not allowed. That, however, is no longer true ("A dedicated teacher...") should have been the beginning of the next paragraph.

The remaining paragraphs are well organized. Each is introduced by a characteristic (the main idea), and that characteristic is explained and supported by adequate details. However, a bit of ambiguity exists in paragraph three: *A teacher must be able to make the subject matter come alive, demanding quality work meeting personal as well as academic needs of students and adding humor to the classroom.* For clarity purposes, there should have been a comma after work and a comma after students.

Some awkward expressions exist throughout the essay, but considering the time factor (30 minutes), this essay is considered adequate.

The following essay received scores at the lowest end of the NTE scoring scale.

Essay C

If you pick up a newspaper, turn on your radio, you will hear, see, and read about the declining of education. Discipline is a problem, test scores are down, and the teacher is being slained. Society has asked the perplexing question: What makes an effective classroom teacher?

First, to become an effective classroom teacher, there has to be an internal love within self, along with external love of the art of teaching. Secondly, devotion, dedication, and discipline among self and the environment in which you are entering will demonstrate the first procedure of effectiveness in the classroom and set up the essential elements involved in teaching. Thirdly, carrying the three "P's" in your heart will produce an effective classroom teacher, being *"Proud"* of what you are, being *"Patient"* with whom you are teaching, and being *"Persistent"* in what you are teaching. Finally, living beyond the classroom, I think, is the most effective in an effective classroom teacher, staying beyond your paid time, getting emotionally involved with your students after your paid time and setting up the ability to cope with the stress of the educational process before your paid time. In order to endure effectiveness, there is long-suffering, perservance, and understanding any situation at any given moment to entitle all children to a worthwhile education of an effective classroom teacher.

Explanation of Essay C

The writer of this essay partially addresses the topic, but the essay itself is totally unacceptable. The initial paragraph, which should have outlined the characteristics to be discussed, leads one to believe that the essay will address "declining of education," "test scores," and "slained teachers." To identify problems that demand effective teachers is an acceptable way to introduce the topic, but the writer of this essay does it very poorly. Additionally, the past participle of *slay* is *slain*, not *slained.*

The writer does present the characteristics of an effective teacher, but these characteristics are all contained in one paragraph, and they are very unclear due to poor word choice, ambiguous expressions (awkward), and poor sentence structure. Three paragraphs should have been used, one for each characteristic; and each should have contained details to explain and support the characteristic.

This essay is filled with awkward expressions that suggest an inability to effectively use the language: "declining of education," "internal love within self," "external love of the art of teaching," "demonstrate the first procedure of effectiveness in the classroom," "set up the essential elements," "Finally, living beyond the classroom, I think, is the most effective in an effective classroom teacher," "staying beyond your paid time," and others.

The writer excessively uses "you" and "your"—second person. Essays should be written in the third person—he, she, they, or the noun teacher or teachers should have been used.

NTE Test of General Knowledge

TEST 2 – ANSWER SHEET

Section 1: Social Studies

1. Ⓐ Ⓑ Ⓒ Ⓓ Ⓔ
2. Ⓐ Ⓑ Ⓒ Ⓓ Ⓔ
3. Ⓐ Ⓑ Ⓒ Ⓓ Ⓔ
4. Ⓐ Ⓑ Ⓒ Ⓓ Ⓔ
5. Ⓐ Ⓑ Ⓒ Ⓓ Ⓔ
6. Ⓐ Ⓑ Ⓒ Ⓓ Ⓔ
7. Ⓐ Ⓑ Ⓒ Ⓓ Ⓔ
8. Ⓐ Ⓑ Ⓒ Ⓓ Ⓔ
9. Ⓐ Ⓑ Ⓒ Ⓓ Ⓔ
10. Ⓐ Ⓑ Ⓒ Ⓓ Ⓔ
11. Ⓐ Ⓑ Ⓒ Ⓓ Ⓔ
12. Ⓐ Ⓑ Ⓒ Ⓓ Ⓔ
13. Ⓐ Ⓑ Ⓒ Ⓓ Ⓔ
14. Ⓐ Ⓑ Ⓒ Ⓓ Ⓔ
15. Ⓐ Ⓑ Ⓒ Ⓓ Ⓔ
16. Ⓐ Ⓑ Ⓒ Ⓓ Ⓔ
17. Ⓐ Ⓑ Ⓒ Ⓓ Ⓔ
18. Ⓐ Ⓑ Ⓒ Ⓓ Ⓔ
19. Ⓐ Ⓑ Ⓒ Ⓓ Ⓔ
20. Ⓐ Ⓑ Ⓒ Ⓓ Ⓔ
21. Ⓐ Ⓑ Ⓒ Ⓓ Ⓔ
22. Ⓐ Ⓑ Ⓒ Ⓓ Ⓔ
23. Ⓐ Ⓑ Ⓒ Ⓓ Ⓔ
24. Ⓐ Ⓑ Ⓒ Ⓓ Ⓔ
25. Ⓐ Ⓑ Ⓒ Ⓓ Ⓔ
26. Ⓐ Ⓑ Ⓒ Ⓓ Ⓔ
27. Ⓐ Ⓑ Ⓒ Ⓓ Ⓔ
28. Ⓐ Ⓑ Ⓒ Ⓓ Ⓔ
29. Ⓐ Ⓑ Ⓒ Ⓓ Ⓔ
30. Ⓐ Ⓑ Ⓒ Ⓓ Ⓔ

Section 2: Math

1. Ⓐ Ⓑ Ⓒ Ⓓ Ⓔ
2. Ⓐ Ⓑ Ⓒ Ⓓ Ⓔ
3. Ⓐ Ⓑ Ⓒ Ⓓ Ⓔ
4. Ⓐ Ⓑ Ⓒ Ⓓ Ⓔ
5. Ⓐ Ⓑ Ⓒ Ⓓ Ⓔ
6. Ⓐ Ⓑ Ⓒ Ⓓ Ⓔ
7. Ⓐ Ⓑ Ⓒ Ⓓ Ⓔ
8. Ⓐ Ⓑ Ⓒ Ⓓ Ⓔ
9. Ⓐ Ⓑ Ⓒ Ⓓ Ⓔ

10. Ⓐ Ⓑ Ⓒ Ⓓ Ⓔ
11. Ⓐ Ⓑ Ⓒ Ⓓ Ⓔ
12. Ⓐ Ⓑ Ⓒ Ⓓ Ⓔ
13. Ⓐ Ⓑ Ⓒ Ⓓ Ⓔ
14. Ⓐ Ⓑ Ⓒ Ⓓ Ⓔ
15. Ⓐ Ⓑ Ⓒ Ⓓ Ⓔ
16. Ⓐ Ⓑ Ⓒ Ⓓ Ⓔ
17. Ⓐ Ⓑ Ⓒ Ⓓ Ⓔ
18. Ⓐ Ⓑ Ⓒ Ⓓ Ⓔ
19. Ⓐ Ⓑ Ⓒ Ⓓ Ⓔ
20. Ⓐ Ⓑ Ⓒ Ⓓ Ⓔ
21. Ⓐ Ⓑ Ⓒ Ⓓ Ⓔ
22. Ⓐ Ⓑ Ⓒ Ⓓ Ⓔ
23. Ⓐ Ⓑ Ⓒ Ⓓ Ⓔ
24. Ⓐ Ⓑ Ⓒ Ⓓ Ⓔ
25. Ⓐ Ⓑ Ⓒ Ⓓ Ⓔ

Section 3: Literature and Fine Arts

1. Ⓐ Ⓑ Ⓒ Ⓓ Ⓔ
2. Ⓐ Ⓑ Ⓒ Ⓓ Ⓔ
3. Ⓐ Ⓑ Ⓒ Ⓓ Ⓔ
4. Ⓐ Ⓑ Ⓒ Ⓓ Ⓔ
5. Ⓐ Ⓑ Ⓒ Ⓓ Ⓔ
6. Ⓐ Ⓑ Ⓒ Ⓓ Ⓔ
7. Ⓐ Ⓑ Ⓒ Ⓓ Ⓔ
8. Ⓐ Ⓑ Ⓒ Ⓓ Ⓔ
9. Ⓐ Ⓑ Ⓒ Ⓓ Ⓔ
10. Ⓐ Ⓑ Ⓒ Ⓓ Ⓔ
11. Ⓐ Ⓑ Ⓒ Ⓓ Ⓔ
12. Ⓐ Ⓑ Ⓒ Ⓓ Ⓔ
13. Ⓐ Ⓑ Ⓒ Ⓓ Ⓔ
14. Ⓐ Ⓑ Ⓒ Ⓓ Ⓔ
15. Ⓐ Ⓑ Ⓒ Ⓓ Ⓔ
16. Ⓐ Ⓑ Ⓒ Ⓓ Ⓔ
17. Ⓐ Ⓑ Ⓒ Ⓓ Ⓔ
18. Ⓐ Ⓑ Ⓒ Ⓓ Ⓔ
19. Ⓐ Ⓑ Ⓒ Ⓓ Ⓔ
20. Ⓐ Ⓑ Ⓒ Ⓓ Ⓔ
21. Ⓐ Ⓑ Ⓒ Ⓓ Ⓔ
22. Ⓐ Ⓑ Ⓒ Ⓓ Ⓔ
23. Ⓐ Ⓑ Ⓒ Ⓓ Ⓔ
24. Ⓐ Ⓑ Ⓒ Ⓓ Ⓔ

Section 4: Science

1. Ⓐ Ⓑ Ⓒ Ⓓ Ⓔ
2. Ⓐ Ⓑ Ⓒ Ⓓ Ⓔ
3. Ⓐ Ⓑ Ⓒ Ⓓ Ⓔ
4. Ⓐ Ⓑ Ⓒ Ⓓ Ⓔ
5. Ⓐ Ⓑ Ⓒ Ⓓ Ⓔ
6. Ⓐ Ⓑ Ⓒ Ⓓ Ⓔ
7. Ⓐ Ⓑ Ⓒ Ⓓ Ⓔ
8. Ⓐ Ⓑ Ⓒ Ⓓ Ⓔ
9. Ⓐ Ⓑ Ⓒ Ⓓ Ⓔ
10. Ⓐ Ⓑ Ⓒ Ⓓ Ⓔ
11. Ⓐ Ⓑ Ⓒ Ⓓ Ⓔ
12. Ⓐ Ⓑ Ⓒ Ⓓ Ⓔ
13. Ⓐ Ⓑ Ⓒ Ⓓ Ⓔ
14. Ⓐ Ⓑ Ⓒ Ⓓ Ⓔ
15. Ⓐ Ⓑ Ⓒ Ⓓ Ⓔ
16. Ⓐ Ⓑ Ⓒ Ⓓ Ⓔ
17. Ⓐ Ⓑ Ⓒ Ⓓ Ⓔ
18. Ⓐ Ⓑ Ⓒ Ⓓ Ⓔ
19. Ⓐ Ⓑ Ⓒ Ⓓ Ⓔ
20. Ⓐ Ⓑ Ⓒ Ⓓ Ⓔ
21. Ⓐ Ⓑ Ⓒ Ⓓ Ⓔ
22. Ⓐ Ⓑ Ⓒ Ⓓ Ⓔ
23. Ⓐ Ⓑ Ⓒ Ⓓ Ⓔ
24. Ⓐ Ⓑ Ⓒ Ⓓ Ⓔ
25. Ⓐ Ⓑ Ⓒ Ⓓ Ⓔ
26. Ⓐ Ⓑ Ⓒ Ⓓ Ⓔ
27. Ⓐ Ⓑ Ⓒ Ⓓ Ⓔ
28. Ⓐ Ⓑ Ⓒ Ⓓ Ⓔ
29. Ⓐ Ⓑ Ⓒ Ⓓ Ⓔ
30. Ⓐ Ⓑ Ⓒ Ⓓ Ⓔ

(Section 1 continued)

10. Ⓐ Ⓑ Ⓒ Ⓓ Ⓔ
11. Ⓐ Ⓑ Ⓒ Ⓓ Ⓔ
12. Ⓐ Ⓑ Ⓒ Ⓓ Ⓔ
13. Ⓐ Ⓑ Ⓒ Ⓓ Ⓔ
14. Ⓐ Ⓑ Ⓒ Ⓓ Ⓔ
15. Ⓐ Ⓑ Ⓒ Ⓓ Ⓔ
16. Ⓐ Ⓑ Ⓒ Ⓓ Ⓔ
17. Ⓐ Ⓑ Ⓒ Ⓓ Ⓔ
18. Ⓐ Ⓑ Ⓒ Ⓓ Ⓔ
19. Ⓐ Ⓑ Ⓒ Ⓓ Ⓔ
20. Ⓐ Ⓑ Ⓒ Ⓓ Ⓔ
21. Ⓐ Ⓑ Ⓒ Ⓓ Ⓔ
22. Ⓐ Ⓑ Ⓒ Ⓓ Ⓔ
23. Ⓐ Ⓑ Ⓒ Ⓓ Ⓔ
24. Ⓐ Ⓑ Ⓒ Ⓓ Ⓔ
25. Ⓐ Ⓑ Ⓒ Ⓓ Ⓔ

25. Ⓐ Ⓑ Ⓒ Ⓓ Ⓔ
26. Ⓐ Ⓑ Ⓒ Ⓓ Ⓔ
27. Ⓐ Ⓑ Ⓒ Ⓓ Ⓔ
28. Ⓐ Ⓑ Ⓒ Ⓓ Ⓔ
29. Ⓐ Ⓑ Ⓒ Ⓓ Ⓔ
30. Ⓐ Ⓑ Ⓒ Ⓓ Ⓔ
31. Ⓐ Ⓑ Ⓒ Ⓓ Ⓔ
32. Ⓐ Ⓑ Ⓒ Ⓓ Ⓔ
33. Ⓐ Ⓑ Ⓒ Ⓓ Ⓔ
34. Ⓐ Ⓑ Ⓒ Ⓓ Ⓔ
35. Ⓐ Ⓑ Ⓒ Ⓓ Ⓔ

NTE CORE BATTERY–Test 2
TEST OF GENERAL KNOWLEDGE
Section 1: Social Studies

TIME: 30 Minutes
30 Questions

DIRECTIONS: Each of the following questions and incomplete statements is followed by five answer choices. Select the choice which best answers each question.

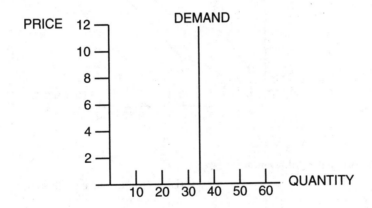

1. According to the graph above, the demand for salt is represented by a vertical line, which statement below best describes the relationship between the price and the quantity demanded?
   (A) Demand will increase as the price goes up.
   (B) Demand will decrease as the price goes down.
   (C) Demand is independent of price.
   (D) Demand and price are inversely related.
   (E) None of the above.

2. An example of a cult is —
   (A) the Roman Catholic Church.   (D) None of the above.
   (B) Buddhism   (E) All of the above.
   (C) Hinduism

3.   Which city would probably be the coolest in August?
     (A)   Chicago   (D)   Cairo
     (B)   Denver   (E)   Buenos Aires
     (C)   Paris

4.   "Free Enterprise" is associated primarily with WHAT kind of economic system?
     (A)   Authoritarianism   (D)   Socialism
     (B)   Communism   (E)   Capitalism
     (C)   Entrepreneurism

Questions 5 and 6 refer to the following graph.

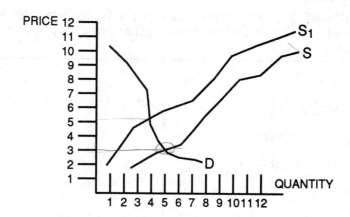

5.   The original equilibrium price is:
     (A) $3   (D)   There is no equilibrium.
     (B) $5   (E) $7.00
     (C) $1.50

6.   According to the graph, SUPPLY has
     (A)   decreased.   (D)   tripled.
     (B)   increased.   (E)   None of the above.
     (C)   not changed.

7.   Upon its adoption by Congress, the Ordinance of 1787 primarily affected which of the following regions of the United States?
     (A)   The Old Northwest   (D)   The Louisiana Purchase
     (B)   New England   (E)   The South
     (C)   The Pacific Northwest

8.   Thomas Paine was the author of which of the following?
     (A)   The Bill of Rights   (D)   Poor Richard's Almanac
     (B)   The Constitution   (E)   The Declaration of Independence
     (C)   Common Sense

9. Which of the following weaknesses in the Articles of Confederation led to the Constitutional Convention of 1787?
   (A) The executive branch had too much power.
   (B) The national treasury had too much power.
   (C) The legislative branch had too much power.
   (D) The states had too much power.
   (E) The Supreme Court had too much power.

10. Which of the following Supreme Court cases held that a police officer must inform an arrested person of their constitutional rights?
    (A) *Plessy* v. *Ferguson*   (D) *Marbury* v. *Madison*
    (B) *Brown* v. *Board of Education*   (E) *Miranda* v. *Arizona*
    (C) *Bakke* v. *Regents of California*

11. The philosophy of Manifest Destiny is best described by which of the following?
    (A) All men, regardless of color, have the right to be free
    (B) A house divided against itself cannot stand
    (C) From sea to shining sea
    (D) Women should have the right to vote
    (E) Life, liberty and the pursuit of happiness

12. The continent of Africa is bordered by which ocean?
    (A) Pacific   (D) (B) and (C).
    (B) Atlantic   (E) (A) and (B).
    (C) Indian

13. Question 13 refers to the map below

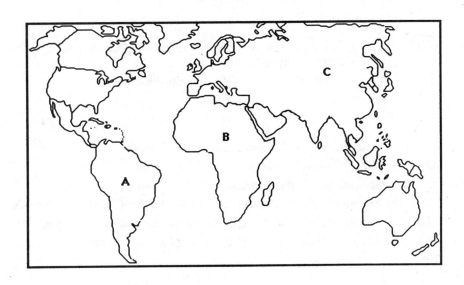

Which of the following continents are not labeled?

(A)   North America and South America

(B)   South America and Australia

(C)   Europe and Asia

(D)   Australia and North America

(E)   Asia and Africa

14.   *Directions:* Facts are statements that can be proven true or false. Opinions are statements that are considered to be beliefs or feelings that cannot be proven.

Read the *italic* portion of each of the following statements and identify the one that is an opinion.

(A)   *America is a wonderful place* in which new immigrants can enjoy the freedoms of life.

(B)   Many of the new immigrants from Italy *were from rural areas from the northern part of the country.*

(C)   From time to time, *the United States has seen some of its own citizens who supported the idea of limiting the number of immigrants* who can come to this country.

(D)   Beginning in the early 1880s, the largest tide of immigration began. During the next 20 years, *almost 9 million people* set foot on American soil for the first time.

(E)   *The political, economic, and religious conditions at home* forced immigrants to make America their new homeland.

15.   The piece of civil rights legislation listed below that was not ratified was:

(A)   Women's Suffrage (1920).

(B)   The Equal Pay Act of 1963.

(C)   The Voting Rights Act of 1965.

(D)   The Equal Rights Amendment of 1971.

(E)   *Roe* v. *Wade* (1973).

16.   The terminology that was used to describe the prevention of any further expansion of Soviet influence around the world was called:

(A)   sphere of influence.   (D)   domino theory.

(B)   containment.   (E)   thaw.

(C)   Cold War.

17.   The Three-Fifths compromise in the Constitution refers to

(A)   the ratio of female to male voters.

(B)   the Senate-House division in Congress.

(C)   the number of colonies that were allowed to ratify the Constitution initially.

(D)   the number of amendments that would be allowed in the Constitution.

(E)   a black person was considered three-fifths of a white person.

18. Direct election to the Senate began in 1913. This was so recent in our nation's history because:
    (A) the Senate was not created when the Constitution was written.
    (B) the Founding Fathers feared too much democracy.
    (C) there were not enough landowners to run for office when the Constitution was written.
    (D) Philadelphia was the capital at that time.
    (E) the House of Representatives felt unfairly unconstrained.

19. Machiavelli's "The Prince", a very popular political work written during the Renaissance, analyzed theories of governing. Machiavelli believed
    (A) government needs the trust, respect, and above all, the confidence of the people to rule effectively.
    (B) royalty is the best form of government.
    (C) treachery, deceit, and fear are acceptable ways to rule.
    (D) the Italian government is the role model for all governments.
    (E) all men are created equal.

20. United Nations Forces are stationed in several countries in the world. They are there because
    (A) the World Court ordered them there.
    (B) other nations requested them.
    (C) world law is enforceable.
    (D) the country agreed to accept them.
    (E) the United States wants them there.

21. Which of the following is NOT a constraint on tropical agriculture?
    (A) Undependability of rain
    (B) Greater prevalence of pests and diseases
    (C) High temperatures at night, promoting water loss
    (D) Poor soil fertility
    (E) Winter thaw resulting in flooding, soil and nutrient losses

22. The "White Man's Burden" was used to justify Colonialism. This was a belief that
    (A) it takes a lot of effort for white people to do things.
    (B) white men, but not white women, do most of the work.
    (C) white people have a unique mission in life to "civilize" non-whites.
    (D) non-whites usually have less responsibility than whites.
    (E) white people need to overcome adversity to succeed.

23. Which group of states best describes the Southwest?
    (A) New Mexico, Texas, Arizona   (D) New Mexico, Colorado, Oregon
    (B) Florida, New Mexico, Arizona   (E) Colorado, Arizona, Kansas
    (C) New Mexico, Arizona, Ohio

24. At which battle were bows and arrows a key weapon?
    (A) The Battle of the Bulge
    (B) The Battle of Hastings
    (C) The Battle of Waterloo
    (D) The Battle of New Orleans
    (E) The Battle of Yorktown

25. The Dred Scott decision was important because
    (A) it held that slaves were property not people.
    (B) it held that slaves could become free men .
    (C) it held that slavery was illegal.
    (D) it held that slavery was legal in California.
    (E) it required all slave owners to treat slaves fairly.

26. Young Jacques was born in Korea but adopted at an early age (3 months) by a French family in Brittany. He grew up and always thought of himself as French. This process of becoming a member of a culture is called
    (A) enculturation.
    (B) xenophobia.
    (C) maturation.
    (D) cultural diffusion.
    (E) cultural borrowing.

27. Generally, rivers run
    (A) from south to north.
    (B) from west to east.
    (C) from north to south.
    (D) out of bays.
    (E) from higher elevations to lower elevations.

28. The growing season of an area (number of frost-free days) can be affected by all of the following except
    (A) nearby location of a very large lake.
    (B) presence of a river valley.
    (C) presence of fertile soil.
    (D) latitude.
    (E) elevation.

29. The Declaration of Independence includes
    (A) the establishment of checks and balances.
    (B) the Bill of Rights.
    (C) the first laws passed by the government.
    (D) the assertion of people's inalienable rights.
    (E) a plea for a court system.

30. Indicate the correct chronological order:
    1. The Articles of Confederation
    2. The Declaration of Independence
    3. The Constitution of the United States of America
    (A) 1, 2, 3
    (B) 2, 1, 3
    (C) 3, 2, 1
    (D) 2, 3, 1
    (E) 1, 3, 2

Section 2: Mathematics

TIME: 30 Minutes
25 Questions

DIRECTIONS: Each of the following questions and incomplete statements is followed by five answer choices. Select the choice which best answers each question.

---

1. To find the rational number equivalent to 4 3/16, we
   (A)   multiply 4 and 16 and to this product add 3.
   (B)   add 4 and 3, multiply this sum by 16.
   (C)   add 4 and 3, place over 16 to get 7/16.
   (D)   multiply 4 and 3 and place over 16 to get 12/16.
   (E)   multiply 4 and 16, add 3 to this product, divide the sum by 16.

2. 5/3 is between which of the following pairs of numbers?
   (A)   0 and 1   (D)   1.3 and 1.6
   (B)   .3 and .9   (E)   1.3 and 1.7
   (C)   .3 and 1.3

3. $7/12 + 4/9 =$
   (A)   Apply the rule, invert the divisor and multiply.
   (B)   Since there is no real world experience for the division of rational numbers, this is a meaningless expression.
   (C)   Divide 7 by 9 and divide 12 by 4, multiply the two quotients.
   (D)   Multiply 4 and 7 then divide this product by the product of 12 and 9.
   (E)   We recall from basic arithmetic that (1) any number divided by one is the number and (2) any number multiplied by its multiplicative inverse is one and (3) if we multiply the two components of a quotient by the same number we do not change the value of the quotient. Using these facts the quotient becomes 63/48.

4. In the formula for area of a circle, $A = \pi r^2$, if r is increased from 2 to 3, then A is
   (A)   increased by a factor of 1.   (D)   increased by a factor of 9/4.
   (B)   increased by a factor of 5.   (E)   increased by a factor of 4/9.
   (C)   increased by a factor of 9.

5. The area of a rectangle is always
   (A)   equal to the area of two triangles.   (D) $A = S^2$
   (B)   cannot be found without dimensions.   (E)   None of the above.
   (C) $A = 1/2$ bh.

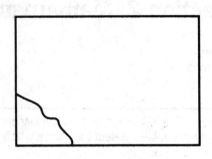

6. This is an illustration of a window with a crack in the pane of glass. Upon first viewing the illustration, a child sees a picture that looks like a rectangle, more or less ignoring the crack, or the squiggly line in it. What kind of perception is the child using?

    (A) Geometric
    (B) Euclidean
    (C) Topologic

    (D) Projective
    (E) Spatial

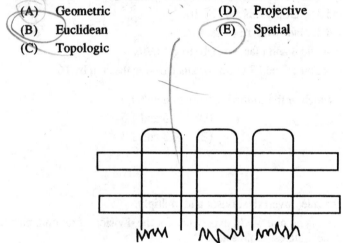

7. A child draws the picture above. S/he tells you, the teacher, that this represents the fence that is beside her/his grandpa's house. What kind of perception is the child using?

    (A) Euclidean
    (B) Projective
    (C) Topologic

    (D) Geometric
    (E) Reality

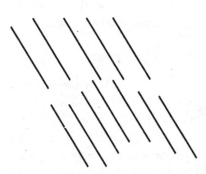

8. Jose, a 9 year old, has devised his own numeration system. It is based on one hand. How would Jose determine "how many" are in this collection of pick-up sticks?

    (A) Count as we always do; there are twelve.

    (B) Put in bundles of ten. Count the number of bundles of ten and then count the single sticks.

    (C) Put in bundles of five. Count the bundles of five and the single sticks.

    (D) It will be impossible for Jose to determine.

    (E) This cannot be determined without more information about Jose's system.

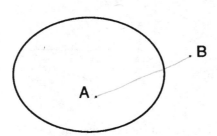

9. To draw a line from A to B requires the line to _____ the simple closed curve, because the simple closed curve separates the inside where point A is from the outside where point B is located.

    (A) connect   (D) separate

    (B) be between   (E) close

    (C) intersect

10. Marty's mother gave him $5 to buy groceries at a neighborhood store. He left at 9 a.m., walked three blocks to the store, bought a gallon of milk for $1.99 and a loaf of bread for $1.43. Marty arrived at home at 10:05 a.m. How much money did Marty spend at the store? To solve this problem the child must

    (A) add all the numbers.

    (B) add all the numbers except the first one and subtract the sum from the first number.

(C)   add the cost of the items purchased.

(D)   add the cost of the items purchased and subtract the sum from the money mother gave him.

(E)   add all the money values together.

11.   Consider the following argument: If Billy has a temperature, then he is not healthy. Billy is not healthy. Conclusion: Billy has a temperature.

(A)   This is a valid conclusion.

(B)   The valid conclusion is: Billy does not have a temperature.

(C)   There is no valid conclusion from the given premises.

(D)   The valid conclusion is: Billy is healthy.

(E)   These three statements as premises would form a valid argument.

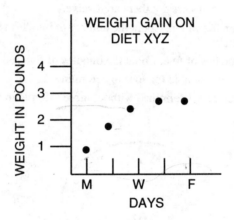

12.   Which of the following statements best represents a true conclusion from this graph?

(A)   The weight gain was constant.

(B)   One day only half a pound was gained.

(C)   The weight gain was a half pound every day but one.

(D)   There was no apparent weight gain from Thursday to Friday.

(E)   None of the above is true.

13.   The number represented by 12 $_{hexadecimal}$ is _____.

(A)   a computer related base system

(B)   a dozen, as in a dozen eggs

(C)   one group of sixteen and two units

(D)   one group of sixty and two units

(E)   None of the above.

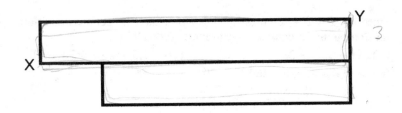

14. If Mary lives at the spot marked X and Petro lives at the spot marked Y, how many different ways may Mary walk (always on a sidewalk, illustrated by a line segment) to Petro's? Mary is not allowed to retrace her steps.

    (A) Her shortest route is either to the left or to the immediate right.

    (B) There are two ways to leave Mary's house; once that is done, there is one way from the left route and two from the right path of her home.

    (C) There are too many ways once you get past the first two from Mary's house.

    (D) There are only two ways, one to the "top" of her house, North and the other East.

    (E) The answer cannot be determined.

15. Consider the set of numbers: 1, 1/2, 1/4, 1/8, 1/16, 1/32, 1/64,... that goes on and on and on. Which of the following statements best represents the pattern observed?

    (A) There is no pattern here.

    (B) It starts at 1 and ends at 0.

    (C) Each number to the right is half the size of its predecessor.

    (D) There is no end.

    (E) It has multiples of 2.

16. Consider the argument: If you are paid Saturday, then you will pay me Monday. You do not pay me Monday. Conclusion: You are not paid on Saturday.

    (A) The conclusion is valid.

    (B) The valid conclusion is: you pay me Monday.

    (C) The valid conclusion is: you get paid Saturday.

    (D) The valid conclusion is: you do not get paid Saturday.

    (E) There is no valid conclusion for these two premises.

17. If Carlos buys the paint, then Tom will paint the barn. Tom paints the fence. Why can't one guarantee that Carlos bought the paint?

    (A) Carlos had to buy the paint, otherwise Tom wouldn't have painted the fence.

    (B) Tom may have had enough paint to paint the fence but not enough to paint the barn.

    (C) If Tom painted the fence, he painted the barn and Carlos had to buy the paint.

    (D) These two statements are not enough to guarantee anything; they are not even enough premises to form an argument.

    (E) This represents *p q* and *q* through *p*; a valid argument for Tom and hence one may guarantee that Carlos bought the paint.

18. Since A + B = B + A represents the commutative property for addition, what is an illustration for the commutative property for addition?

    (A)　6 + 4 = 7 + 3　　　　　　　　(D)　2/3 + 4/5 = 4/5 + 2/3

    (B)　11479 + 2695 = 2695 + 11794　(E)　85 - 91 = 91 - 85

    (C)　217 + 695 = 596 + 712

19. Miguel has four sets of 3 links like these . He wants to make one chain of 12 links for the least cost. It costs 25 cents to cut a link and 95 cents to weld a cut link closed. What is the minimum cost?

    (A)　Two cuts and two welds costing $2.40.

    (B)　Three cuts and two welds costing $2.65.

    (C)　Three cuts and three welds costing $3.60.

    (D)　Four cuts and three welds costing $3.85.

    (E)　Four cuts and four welds costing $4.80.

20. Sun Ping left home with some cash. At the bank she deposited half of her cash in her Christmas Club account. On the way out she gave $1 to the local drum and bugle corps solicitations. She had lunch at the Tea Rose Room giving a $1.50 tip and spending half of her remaining cash for lunch. Half of her remaining cash went for bus fare home. She arrived home with $2.25. How much cash did Sun Ping have when she left home? To solve this problem, the best method is

    (A)　trial and error.　　　　　　(D)　deductive logic.

    (B)　working backward.　　　　　(E)　modeling.

    (C)　analytical/algebraic.

21. These dots represent a pattern. What needs to be done to create the next two items in the pattern?

    (A)　A relationship needs to be determined.

    (B)　The triangle's size needs to increase for each item.

    (C)　Cannot be determined.

    (D)　The number of dots needs to increase for each item.

    (E)　A row of dots is "added" to the preceding figure and the new row has one more dot than the preceding row.

22.
11	111	1111
11	111	1111
121	12, 321	?

To find the pattern all one needs do is:

(A)   Understand basic rules of addition.

(B)   Choose 1,234,321 since it would seem to follow.

(C)   Recognize that multiplication is being used.

(D)   No pattern exists, so nothing needs to be done.

(E)   Hypothesize the relationship between the numbers above and below the lines, and verify with multiplication.

23.   Miss Tea presents a problem to her first grade class. She talks as she draws a picture on the chalkboard, "Susie sees five bluebirds on the birdbath. Miss Kitty, a white Persian neighbor's cat enters the yard. Three birds fly away." and she erases three of the birds. "How many are left?" What is Miss Tea teaching?

(A)   Short term memory   (D)   Subtraction concept

(B)   The children's listening skills   (E)   Subtraction facts

(C)   Addition concept

24.   Missy has three pairs of slacks and two shirts. She has a pair of green slacks and a pair of red slacks and a pair of blue slacks. She has a tan turtleneck and a white polo shirt. How many different outfits has Missy? What is the better technique for teaching this problem?

(A)   Multiply 3 x 2.

(B)   Using a flannel board, select 3 objects for each pair of slacks and 2 objects for the 2 blouses. Let the children imagine the various combinations.

(C)   Using objects, the teacher makes the various outfits of blouses and slacks until all are found.

(D)   Let each child have enough manipulation so each can have 3 objects (paper slacks) and 2 objects (paper blouses) and create each outfit, recording the combination to "keep count."

(E)   Make a picture on the board to represent a pair of pants and lines to represent the 3 pairs for it. Place an X at the end of each line for the turtleneck and an O for each blouse e. g., and count the X's and O's.

25.   Every child in the second grade class gets 12 tomato seeds to plant. After several weeks the teacher has each child count the number of seeds in his/her pot. The teacher asks each child to tell the class the number of seeds that germinated. They make a graph. Describe what the teacher is teaching.

(A)   Biology—growing plants.

(B)   Reality of farming—not all seeds grow.

(C)   Statistics—graphing data.

(D)   Probability—probability of germinating seeds.

(E)   Projects to take home on nutritious foods.

Section 3: Literature and Fine Arts

TIME: 30 Minutes
35 Questions

DIRECTIONS: Each of the following questions and incomplete statements is followed by five answer choices. Select the choice which best answers each question.

> Now thou art dead, no eye shall ever see,
> For shape and service, spaniel like to thee.
> This shall my love do, give thy sad death one
> Tear, that deserves of me a million.

1. The above poem is an example of a(n)

    (A) allegory.   (D) kenning.

    (B) elegy.   (E) refrain.

    (C) ballad.

2. Lines 3-4 contain an example of

    (A) enjambment.   (D) Homeric simile.

    (B) personification.   (E) epigram.

    (C) onomatopoeia.

> Study is like the heaven's glorious sun,
> That will not be deep-searched with saucy looks.
> Small have continual plodders won
> Save base authority from others' books.
> These earthly godfathers of heaven's lights,
> That give a name to every fixed star
> Have no more profit of their shining nights
> Than those who walk and wot* not what they are.
> (*know)

3. The speaker of these lines is most likely a

    (A) student.   (D) thief.

    (B) professor.   (E) villain.

    (C) clergyman.

4. The lines "Small have continual plodders won / Save base authority from others' books" mean

    (A) books are key in the acquisition of knowledge.

    (B) only one's opinions are important—not facts found in books.

    (C) study is long and tedious, but ultimately rewarding.

(D) knowledge and authority are eventually given to those who pursue them.

(E) all that is gained by study are the simple and worthless opinions of others.

5. The last four lines of the passage suggest that

(A) study is a pursuit for the old and tired.

(B) anyone, whether he be a genius or simpleton, can name things and recite facts.

(C) many geniuses are simpletons, and vice versa.

(D) study ruins intuitive wonder, such as that caused by the stars.

(E) All of the above.

6. "These earthly godfathers" are most likely

(A) professors.   (D) lovers.

(B) astronomers.   (E) poets.

(C) artists.

Georges Pompidou National Center of Art and Culture, Paris

7. Which of the following seems most true of the building pictured above?

(A) It relies on broad areas of unbroken surfaces.

(B) It uses industrial forms and materials to suggest a living organism.

(C) It is conceived and designed on a human scale.

(D)   It owes a debt to the Classical past.

(E)   It achieves an effect of poetic calm, balance, and remove.

Chartres Cathedral, France

8.   Which of the following best describes the sculpture on the building pictured above?

(A)   It tells a detailed story with a definite sequence.

(B)   It dominates the facade of the building.

(C)   It draws heavily on Classical mythology.

(D)   It is contained by the architectural forms of the doorways.

(E)   It was probably applied as an afterthought.

From the mountains on every side rivulets descended that filled all the valley with verdure and fertility, and formed a lake in the middle, inhabited by fish of every species and frequented by every fowl whom nature has taught to dip the wing in water. This lake discharged its superfluities by a stream, which entered a dark cleft of the mountain on the northern side, and fell with dreadful noise from precipice to precipice till it was heard no more.

9.   The narrative technique in this passage can be described as

(A)   painstakingly descriptive.

(B)   full of comparisons and contrasts.

(C)   vague in its descriptions of landscape.

(D)   negative in connotation.

(E)   surrealistic.

Metropolitan Museum of Art, New York

10.   In the example pictured above, the folds of the garment serve to
      (A)   define the forms of the human figure.
      (B)   counteract the vigorous motion of the figure.
      (C)   establish a sense of three-dimensional space.
      (D)   help tell the story behind the figure's movements.
      (E)   create a dynamic surface pattern which dominates the composition.

Antonio Pollaiuolo, *Hercules and Antaeus*, c. 1475. Museo Nazionale, Florence.

11. The sculpture pictured above suggests which of the following?

    (A) The rolling motion of a wheel

    (B) The balanced action of a lever

    (C) The twisting spiral of a screw

    (D) The flowing motion of liquid

    (E) The interlocking action of gears

(A)   There was a knight who was a lusty liver.
    One day as he came riding from the river
    He saw a maiden walking all forlorn
    Ahead of him, alone as she was born.
    And of that maiden, spite of all she said,
    By very force he took her maidenhead.

(B)   That time of year thou mayst in me behold
    When yellow leaves, or none, or few, do hang
    Upon those boughs which shake against the cold,
    Bare, ruined choirs where late the sweet bird sang.

(C)   My love is like to ice, and I to fire.

(D)   With how sad steps, O moon, thou climb'st the skies!
    How silently, and with how wan a face.

(E)   Hail to thee, blithe Spirit!
        Bird thou never wert—
        That from Heaven, or near it,
        Pourest thy full heart
        In profuse strains of unpremeditated art.

12.   Which passage uses the literary device of simile? *C*

13.   Which passage employs personification? *D*

14.   Which passage uses the device of apostrophe? *E*

15.   In the example shown above, which of the following contributes most to the effect
        of a photographic snapshot?
        (A)   The inclusion of the horse and the dog
        (B)   The middle-class character of the subjects
        (C)   The perspective grid behind the figures
        (D)   The off-center composition and the random cropping of the figures
        (E)   The strong dependence on outline

Abbey church of St. Michael, Hildesheim, West Germany.

16. The building pictured above depends for its effect on:
    (A) the interplay of diagonal and vertical lines.
    (B) the broad expanse of window glass.
    (C) a subtle arrangement of curving, rhythmic forms.
    (D) the viewer's point of view from ground level.
    (E) the bold massing of simple cubic forms.

Temple of Hera at Paestum, Italy.

17. Which of the following is fundamental to the design of the building pictured on the previous page?

(A) A combination of intersecting diagonal lines

(B) A simple repetition of vertical and horizontal forms

(C) A continuous expanse of unbroken wall surface

(D) A combination of columns and arches

(E) A complex interplay of many varied shapes

(A) Of man's first disobedience, and the fruit
Of that forbidden tree whose mortal taste
Brought death into the world, and all our woe,
With loss of Eden, till one great Man
Restore us, and regain the blissful seat,
Sing, Heavenly Muse…

(B) My poem's epic, and is meant to be
Divided in twelve books; each book containing,
With love, and war, a heavy gale at sea,
A list of ships, and captains, and kings reigning,
New characters; the episodes are three;
A panoramic view of Hell's in training,
After the style of Virgil and of Homer,
So that my name of Epic's no misnomer.

(C) Yet once more, O ye Laurels, and once more
Ye Myrtles brown, with Ivy never-sear,
I come to pluck your Berries harsh and crude,
And with forc'd fingers rude,
Shatter your leaves before the mellowing year.
Bitter constraint, and sad occasion dear,
Compels me to disturb your season due:
For Lycidas is dead, dead ere his prime…

(D) But at my back I always hear
Time's winged chariot hurrying near;
And yonder all before us lie
Deserts of vast eternity.
Thy beauty shall no more be found,
Nor, in thy marble vault, shall sound
My echoing song; then worms shall try
That long-preserved virginity,
And your quaint honor turn to dust,
And into ashes all my lust:
The grave's a fine and private place,
But none, I think, do there embrace.

(E)   Lo! 'tis a gala night
Within the lonesome latter years!
An angel throng, bewinged, bedight
In veils, and drowned in tears,
Sit in a theater, to see
A play of hopes and fears,
While the orchestra breathes fitfully
The music of the spheres.

18.   Which passage comes from a mock epic?

19.   Which passage employs the theme of *carpe diem*?

20.   Which passage is from a pastoral elegy?

> Careful observers may foretell the hour
> (By sure prognostics) when to dread a shower:
> While rain depends, the pensive cat gives o' er
> Her frolics, and pursues her tail no more.
> Returning home at night, you'll find the sink*
> Strike your offended sense with double stink.
> If you be wise, then go not far to dine;
> You spend more in coach hire than save in wine.
> A coming shower your shooting corns presage,
> Old aches throb, your hollow tooth will rage.
> (*sewer)

21.   Which genre of poetry does this passage exemplify?

    (A)   Epic   (D)   Ode

    (B)   Satiric   (E)   Lyric

    (C)   Parodic

22.   The phrase "(By sure prognostics)" is _____ in tone .

    (A)   sarcastic   (D)   Both (A) and (B).

    (B)   playful   (E)   Both (A) and (C).

    (C)   angry

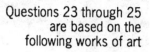

Questions 23 through 25
are based on the
following works of art

(A) National Gallery, Washington, D.C.

(C) Albright-Knox Art Gallery, Buffalo

(B) Metropolitan Museum of Art, New York

(D) Sammlung Thyssen-Bornemisza, Lugano, Italy   (E) Museum of Art, Carnegie Institute, Pittsburgh

23. Which of the examples pictured above makes the most direct contact with the viewer?

24. In which example does the pose and expression of the sitter convey aristocratic disdain?

25. Which example breaks down the forms of the subject and merges them with the background?

WHEN BRITAIN REALLY RULED THE WAVES

When Britain really ruled the waves
   (In good Queen Bess's time)—
The House of Peers made no pretense
To intellectual eminence,
   Or scholarship sublime;
Yet Britain won her proudest bays*
In good Queen Bess's glorious days!

When Wellington thrashed Bonaparte,
   As every child can tell,
The House of Peers, throughout the war,
Did nothing in particular,
   And did it very well:
Yet Britain set the world ablaze
In good King George's glorious days!

And while the House of Peers withholds
   Its legislative hand,
And noble statesman do not itch
To interfere with matters which
   They do not understand,
As bright will shine Great Britain's rays
As in good King George's glorious days!
(*honors)

26.   In this poem, the ruling body of Britain is described as

   (A)   a very successful legislative institution.

   (B)   a body which makes wise decisions.

   (C)   a body which is supported by the British.

   (D)   a group of disinterested and unintelligent noblemen.

   (E)   a group of highly talented diplomats and legislators.

27.   The tone of this poem can be described as

   (A)   lauding.   (D)   satisfied.

   (B)   parodic.   (E)   patriotic.

   (C)   satiric.

National Palace Museum, Taipei, Taiwan

28.   Which of the following seems most true of the example pictured above?
       (A)   The artist attempted a realistic depiction of three-dimensional space.
       (B)   The picture probably illustrates an episode in a narrative.
       (C)   The execution was slow, painstaking, and deliberate.
       (D)   Both the script and the leaves share a quality of quick, fluid calligraphy.
       (E)   The painting depends on a wide range of contrasting tones.

   There was a time when I went every day into a church, since a girl I was in love with knelt there in prayer for half an hour in the evening and I was able to look at her in peace.

   Once when she had not come and I was reluctantly eyeing the other supplicants I noticed a young fellow who had thrown his whole lean length along the floor. Every now and then he clutched his head as hard as he could and sighing loudly beat it in his upturned palms on the stone flags.

29.   By using the term "supplicants," the author implies that
       (A)   everyone in the church is there to celebrate a mass.
       (B)   everyone in the church is devout.
       (C)   everyone in the church is guilty of something.
       (D)   everyone in the church is a hypocrite.
       (E)   everyone in the church is damned.

(A)

(B)

(C)

(D)

(E)

30. In which example does the landscape act as a backdrop for a carefully composed figure group?

31. In which example does the location of the horizon line emphasize the figure's isolation?

32. Which example shows the greatest tendency to abstract and simplify the forms?

33. The costume key pictured above would be most appropriate for which of the following plays?

    (A) Ibsen's *A Doll's House*   (D) Aristophane's *The Birds*

    (B) Shakespeare's *Twelfth Night*   (E) Chekhov's *The Cherry Orchard*

    (C) Shaw's *Pygmalion*

Can we expect to glean information about places and times from a novel? Can anybody be so naive as to think he or she can learn anything about the past from those buxom best-sellers that are hawked around by book clubs under the heading of historical novels? But what about the masterpieces? Can we rely on Jane Austen's picture of landowning England with baronets and landscaped grounds when all she knew was a clergyman's parlor? And *Bleak House*, that **fantastic** romance within a **fantastic** London, can we call it a study of London a hundred years ago? Certainly not. And the same holds for other such novels in this series. The truth is that great novels are great fairy tales—and the novels in this series are supreme fairy tales.

34. The word "fantastic" in bold means

    (A) loaded with adventure.   (D) historical.

    (B) unreal.   (E) nonsensical.

    (C) ridiculous.

35. The author's attitude toward such writers as Jane Austen and Charles Dickens is one of

    (A) respect.   (D) disdain.

    (B) defiance.   (E) condescension.

    (C) mockery.

Section 4: Science

TIME: 30 Minutes
30 Questions

DIRECTIONS: Each of the following questions and incomplete statements is followed by five answer choices. Select the choice which best answers each question.

1. When is the Earth farthest from the Sun?
   (A) During the fall
   (B) During the winter
   (C) During the spring
   (D) During the summer
   (E) During the fall and winter

2. Which of the following metric measurements is most useful in determining the weight of a dime?
   (A) A kilometer
   (B) A liter
   (C) A hectometer
   (D) A kilogram
   (E) A gram

3. The best source of Vitamin A in one's diet is which of the following?
   (A) Milk, cheese, and dairy products
   (B) Meats, eggs, dried peas and beans
   (C) Cereals, breads, and grain products
   (D) Leafy, green and yellow vegetables
   (E) Fresh citrus fruits

4. Which is true of iodine in the body?
   (A) Iodine is poisonous and even small amounts are hazardous to the health of an individual.
   (B) Iodine has been proven to be a factor in preventing tooth decay.
   (C) Miniscule amounts of iodine are needed for building bones.
   (D) Iodine is an essential constituent of hemoglobin, the oxygen-carrying pigment in red blood cells.
   (E) Iodine is required for proper functioning of the thyroid gland.

5. All of the following are true EXCEPT which one?
   (A) Everything in the universe is in motion.
   (B) The Milky Way is one of thousands of galaxies that form the universe.
   (C) The motion of the stars about the Earth is most apparent at night when one can observe their turning about the Earth.
   (D) The solar system is a tiny speck in the vast Milky Way.
   (E) The use of instruments has been important in the study of Earth and the universe.

6. Enzymes in the digestive tract serve which function(s)?
    (A) To enable molecules to pass into the bloodstream by passing through the membranes of the small intestine.
    (B) To transform complex molecules into a form in which the cells of the body can use them for energy or for building new structures.
    (C) To cause the fusion of food molecules so that they can be absorbed by the parts of the body.
    (D) All the above.
    (E) (A) and (B) only .

7. All of the following are true of food webs and chains EXCEPT which one?
    (A) Implicit in a food chain and a food web is a natural system of checks and balances.
    (B) The shorter the food chain the greater the efficiency from the standpoint of energy flow.
    (C) An example of the shortest food chain is the people in India and China who feed primarily on plant foods.
    (D) The introduction of cattle between people and plants in a food chain reduces the efficiency.
    (E) The food chain is non-continuous; it does not require a flow of energy or a recycling of materials from consumer back to producer.

8. Which of the following statements are true of gravitational force?
    I.   The production of an electromagnet is an example of gravitational force.
    II.   The rhythm of tides is an example of the effect of gravitational force.
    III. The law of gravity states that all bodies in the universe attract each other.
    IV.   The strength of gravitational force between two bodies depends on the mass (quantity of material) in them.
    V.   The strength of gravitational force between two bodies depends on the distance between them.
    (A) All of the above.
    (B) None of the above.
    (C) I, II, III only.
    (D) II, III, IV, V only.
    (E) III, IV, V only.

9. A litmus test conducted on lime water would have which of the following results?
    (A) There is no effect on the color of the litmus paper.
    (B) The litmus paper disintegrates.
    (C) The litmus paper turns blue.
    (D) The litmus paper turns red.
    (E) The carbonation causes oxygen bubbles to rise to the top.

10. Which of the following statements about the structure of matter is a true statement?

    (A) Elements cannot be broken down into simpler substances.

    (B) Molecules built of more than one kind of atom are known as elements.

    (C) There are more than 4 million known elements used to create the more than 4 million identified compounds.

    (D) All elements are equally abundant in nature.

    (E) Compounds might be compared to the 26 letters of the alphabet; elements to the hundreds of thousands of words constructed from the alphabet.

11. Which best describes the nature of the environmental crisis?

    (A) The advance of technology has reached a level where processes and products threaten the earth's environment.

    (B) The environmental crisis is limited to highly industrialized areas.

    (C) The oceans and atmospheres purify pollutants.

    (D) All the above.

    (E) (B) and (C) only.

12. By which means do we measure a calendar year?

    (A) Tilt of the Earth on its axis.

    (B) Rotation of the Earth about the Sun.

    (C) Revolution of the Earth about the Sun.

    (D) Phases of the moon.

    (E) Revolution of the Sun about the Earth.

13. Night blindness may be the result of which of the following?

    (A) Insufficient sunshine   (D) Insufficient Vitamin A

    (B) Insufficient calcium   (E) A viral infection

    (C) Insufficient Vitamin C

14. The Sun has been burning and radiating energy into space for billions of years, according to some scientists. Which of the following refute this theory?

    (A) The Sun could burn for a *total* of 80,000 years.

    (B) A newer theory is gravitation as a source of energy; if particles fall closer together because of their mutual attraction, the energy is converted into heat.

    (C) In the case of the Sun serving like a nuclear reactor, hydrogen atoms join to form helium atoms.

    (D) All the above.

    (E) (A) and (B) only.

15. All of the following are fundamental ideas of Dalton's atomic theory EXCEPT which one?

    (A) All matter is composed of a limited number of basic particles called atoms.

    (B) Each atom of an element is identical to all others.

(C)   Atoms can be broken into simpler substances by chemical means in a laboratory.

(D)   Molecules consist of a definite combination of atoms; all molecules of one particular kind have an identical atomic construction.

(E)   New combinations of atoms to produce new molecules and new substances may be brought about by chemical changes.

16.   Antibodies produced in an animal to treat a human disease may be borrowed from blood extracted from animals and prepared for injection in which of the following?

(A)   Serum   (D)   Toxin

(B)   Antibiotic   (E)   Gene

(C)   Vaccine

17.   Below are five lists of animals. Which of the lists contains only animals belonging to the phylum ARTHROPODA?

I.   Monkeys, spiders

II.   Monkeys, great apes

III.   Bees, monkeys, great apes

IV.   Sand dollars

V.   Wasps, lobster

(A)   IV only.   (D)   I and II

(B)   II only.   (E)   V only.

(C)   III and II

18.   All of the following are means of heat transfer EXCEPT which one(s)?

I.   Condensation

II.   Conduction

III.   Radiation

IV.   Convection

V.   Transportation

(A)   III, IV, V   (D)   I and V only.

(B)   I, II, III   (E)   III and V only.

(C)   II, III, IV

19.   When a celery stalk is cut and placed in tinted water, which of the the statements below describes what one would observe in 3 or 4 hours?

(A)   One side of the celery stalk becomes tinted where the colored water rises; the other side remains unchanged where the colored water leaves the stalk.

(B)   Only the part of the celery stalk that is in the tinted water becomes tinted; the fibrous stalk of the celery, unlike more tender plants, resists the absorption of the tinted water.

(C)   The vegetable will die within 3-4 hours because of the impure liquid in which it is placed.

(D) The veins of the transportation system will carry the tinted liquid upward in the plant.

(E) The plant will release clear liquid into the container to replace the colored material being absorbed; soon the water in the container will become clear and the normally clear liquid in the plant will be replaced by tinted water.

20. The magnetism of a substance is NOT due essentially to which of the following?

(A) The magnetic properties of its atoms.

(B) The arrangement of its atoms.

(C) The position of its poles.

(D) All the above.

(E) (A) and (B) only.

21. Several theories exist on the total extinction of dinosaurs; which of the following is the WEAKEST explanation for this happening?

(A) An increase in the temperature as a result of the greenhouse effect may have affected the reproductive capability.

(B) The collision of the Earth with an asteroid may have caused a cloud of dust which blocked the sunlight for a period of months and years.

(C) Cold water spillover from the Arctic altered the world's climate, reduced the salinity of the oceans, and killed many of the marine species.

(D) Tectonic plate activity (which may also have triggered volcanic eruptions) altered the environment.

(E) The dinosaurs exterminated themselves as weaker dinosaurs were killed by stronger ones.

22. All of the following are true of the structure of the Earth EXCEPT which one?

(A) The uttermost shell of the Earth which extends for about 25 miles is the crust.

(B) The hot liquid rock in pockets within the crust is called magma.

(C) Beneath the crust is the mantle.

(D) At the center of the Earth is a metallic core.

(E) The thickest of the Earth's three parts (crust, mantle, core) is the core.

23. On the periodic table the symbol *Fe* represents which of the following?

(A) Iron   (D) Magnesium

(B) Fluorine   (E) Mercury

(C) Lead

24. Which of the following resources are renewable?

(A) Coal, oil, gas

(B) Metals, soil, coal

(C) Vegetation, animals, soil

(D) Freshwater, coal, vegetation

(E) Oil, soil, vegetation

25. All of the following are parts of the circulatory system EXCEPT which one?
    (A) Artery
    (B) Capillaries
    (C) Veins
    (D) Heart
    (E) Seminal vesicles

26. Which of the following is NOT true?
    I.   Atoms are composed of electrons, protons, and neutrons; other particles have been discovered but these are the most important.
    II.   Electrons are extremely light atomic particles possessing a quantity of electricity designated as a positive charge.
    III. The rapidly moving electron is held in its orbit by the proton in the nucleus, which has a negative charge.
    IV.   The charges of the electron and the proton are equal and opposite.

    (A) All the above.
    (B) I, II
    (C) II, III
    (D) III, IV
    (E) I, IV

27. Which of the following are equal?
    (A) One kilometer equals one mile.
    (B) One kilogram equals one pound.
    (C) One gram equals one ounce.
    (D) One milliliter equals one cubic centimeter.
    (E) One quart equals one liter.

28. Moving a coil of wire near a magnet or moving a magnet near a coil of wire
    (A) causes electrons to flow in the coil.
    (B) causes a weak link in the electric circuit.
    (C) results in atomic fusion.
    (D) is the principle of the generator.
    (E) (A) and (D) only.

29. Which of the statements below are examples of observing, predicting, and generalizing **in that order**?
    I.   Magnetized needles point in a north-south direction when suspended freely.
    II.   The magnet will probably attract this nail since it is made of iron.
    III. The magnet attracted all our objects made of iron.
    IV.   The students did not have time to compare large and small magnets.

    (A) I, II, III
    (B) I, II, IV
    (C) II, III, IV
    (D) III, II, I
    (E) III, I, II

30. All of the following conclusions reached by scientists are true EXCEPT which one?

   (A) More complex forms of life appeared before simple forms of life as is evidenced by the fact that dinosaurs preceded marsupials like the opossum.

   (B) The Earth has experienced major structural and climatic changes in its history.

   (C) Some types of life on Earth have become extinct.

   (D) Life has existed on Earth for 3 billion years.

   (E) The kinds of living things on the Earth have been different in different periods.

TEST OF GENERAL KNOWLEDGE

ANSWER KEY

SECTION 1: SOCIAL STUDIES

1.	(C)	9.	(D)	17.	(E)	25.	(A)
2.	(E)	10.	(E)	18.	(B)	26.	(A)
3.	(E)	11.	(C)	19.	(C)	27.	(E)
4.	(E)	12.	(D)	20.	(D)	28.	(C)
5.	(A)	13.	(D)	21.	(E)	29.	(D)
6.	(A)	14.	(A)	22.	(C)	30.	(B)
7.	(A)	15.	(D)	23.	(A)		
8.	(C)	16.	(B)	24.	(B)		

SECTION 2: MATHEMATICS

1.	(E)	8.	(C)	15.	(C)	22.	(E)
2.	(E)	9.	(C)	16.	(A)	23.	(D)
3.	(E)	10.	(C)	17.	(D)	24.	(D)
4.	(D)	11.	(C)	18.	(D)	25.	(C)
5.	(A)	12.	(D)	19.	(C)		
6.	(B)	13.	(C)	20.	(B)		
7.	(E)	14.	(B)	21.	(E)		

SECTION 3: LITERATURE AND FINE ARTS

1.	(B)	10.	(E)	19.	(D)	28.	(D)
2.	(A)	11.	(B)	20.	(C)	29.	(C)
3.	(A)	12.	(C)	21.	(B)	30.	(A)
4.	(E)	13.	(D)	22.	(D)	31.	(D)
5.	(D)	14.	(E)	23.	(C)	32.	(E)
6.	(B)	15.	(D)	24.	(B)	33.	(B)
7.	(B)	16.	(E)	25.	(A)	34.	(B)
8.	(D)	17.	(B)	26.	(D)	35.	(A)
9.	(C)	18.	(B)	27.	(C)		

SECTION 4: SCIENCE

1.	(D)	9.	(C)	17.	(E)	25.	(E)
2.	(E)	10.	(A)	18.	(C)	26.	(C)
3.	(D)	11.	(A)	19.	(D)	27.	(D)
4.	(E)	12.	(C)	20.	(E)	28.	(E)
5.	(C)	13.	(D)	21.	(E)	29.	(D)
6.	(E)	14.	(A)	22.	(E)	30.	(A)
7.	(E)	15.	(E)	23.	(A)		
8.	(D)	16.	(A)	24.	(C)		

DETAILED EXPLANATIONS OF ANSWERS
NTE CORE BATTERY–Test 2

TEST OF GENERAL KNOWLEDGE
Section 1: Social Studies

1. **(C)**   The graph shows an example of totally inelastic demand. In this situation, the quantity demanded does not respond to any change in price. Regardless of whether the price of the product increases or decreases, the same quantity will be demanded. Within normal or realistic price ranges, for example, the amount of table salt (a necessary commodity) demanded will not change due to a fluctuation of price. Therefore, the correct response is (C).

2. **(D)** The correct answer is (D). Although all religions conform to the conditions representative of a cult--a structured worship of a supernatural object or being, and the laws and conditions regarding that worship--the modern definition refers primarily to minority groups whose practices set them apart, in obvious ways, from socieity as a whole. The religions represented, (A) Catholicism, (B) Buddhism, and (C) Hinduism are too wide spread and integrated into societies throughout the world to be regarded as cults.

3. **(E)**   The correct answer is (E). Chicago, Paris, and Cairo are all very hot in August. Denver, despite its elevation, is still generally warm in the summer with cool nights. August in Buenos Aires is a winter month, since that city is in the southern hemisphere. The weather would be cool and often rainy.

4. **(E)**   "Socialism" is defined as an economic system where the principal means of production are owned by the state. "Communism" refers to a socialist type of economic system based on the writings of Karl Marx. "Entrepreneurism" is actually a misnomer. An entrepreneur refers to an individual who creates a business for profit. The correct answer is (E). The definitions for "Free Enterprise" and "Capitalism" are actually interchangeable: an economic system based on private ownership of property, competition, and profits.

5. **(A)**   The answer to this question requires a knowledge of procedures of graphing. "S" refers to an original supply curve, "S_1" refers to a newly established supply curve. "D" refers to a demand curve. *Therefore, to find the "original" equilibrium price, it is necessary to find the intersection of the "S" and "D" curves.* (B) is incorrect because that is the point of intersection of the "S_1" and "D" curves. (C) is incorrect because there is no intersection at that point. (D) is also incorrect because since there is an intersection, there will be an equilibrium. Therefore, the answer is (A).

6.   **(A)**   Observing the directional change from the "S" to "S₁" curves answers this question. In this case the curve has shifted to the left. The supply curve, therefore, has decreased. Thus letters (B), (C), (D) and (E) are incorrect. Letter (A) is the correct response.

7.   **(A)**   The Ordinance of 1787 was designed to bring order and federal control to the newly acquired western frontier. This included the present-day states Ohio, Indiana, Illinois, Wisconsin, Iowa, and part of Minnesota. Therefore (A) is the correct answer. (B) and (E) are incorrect geographic areas. The geographic area denoted by (C) was not yet explored or claimed by the U.S. and (D) would not become a part of the U.S. until the Jefferson administration.

8.   **(C)**   (A) and (B) are incorrect because the Bill of Rights was authored by the Constitutional Convention following the Revolutionary War. The Declaration of Independence (E) was largely authored by Thomas Jefferson. (D) was authored by Benjamin Franklin. (C) is the correct answer.

9.   **(D)**   (A) is incorrect since the central government did not have an executive branch. (B) is also incorrect since the national government did not have the power to tax and the legislative branch could not enforce what it was able to pass. There was no Supreme Court until it was established by the Constitution. (D)—too much power was vested in the states— is correct.

10.   **(E)**   (A) was a case decided in 1896 instituting separate but equal. (B) reversed *Plessy v. Ferguson.* (C) was a case concerning reverse discrimination from the 1970s. (D), *Marbury v. Madison* was the cornerstone of judicial review. (E) is the correct answer. The decision in this case ruled that an individual must, by law, be notified of his/her legal rights. It was handed down in 1965.

11.   **(C)**   Manifest Destiny deals with the belief that the United States should grow and expand from the Atlantic across the entire continent. This belief grew as the United States acquired land through various purchases and treaties during the 1800s. (A) addresses emancipation best stated by Lincoln in 1863. Lincoln also verbalized (B) referring to the national internal division of the Civil War. (D) was addressed through the term universal suffrage. (E) was taken from the Declaration of Independence. It refers to individual freedom.

12.   **(D)**   Africa is bordered by the Atlantic on the west, the Mediterranean on the north, the Indian Ocean on the east and the juncture of the Indian and Atlantic Oceans on the south. The Pacific is a minimum of 3,000 miles from Africa, so (A) and (E) must be incorrect. (B) and (C) are technically correct, as described above, but since only one answer is called for, (D) must be correct.

13.   **(D)**   This question refers to the current world map. The correct answer is (D).

14.   **(A)**   (B), (C), (D) and (E) are all types of information that can be determined through studying records, opinion polls, interviews and other data. (A), however, is opinion. The use of the word "wonderful" is subjective and is an attitude unique to individuals.

15.   **(D)**   (A), (B), (C) and (E) were bills that were legalized by the Congress during the 20th century. Answer (D), the Equal Rights Amendment of 1971, has been twice attempted

to be written into the Constitution to no avail. The last attempt was made in 1985.

16. **(B)**   The correct answer is (B). Spheres of influence were territories or nations that allied themselves with the United States or the Soviet Union. The Cold War is defined as the period between 1946 and 1989 where the United States and the Soviet Union were party to a tense relationship. The Domino Theory was President Eisenhower's term used to describe the way Southeast Asia would fall if the Soviets were able to gain control of just one nation. All the rest would fall like a row of dominoes. A thaw is described as an easing of tension.

17. **(E)**   (A) was not considered because women could not vote until the twentieth century. (B) refers to the formula for representative membership in the House and Senate. In the House, states are divided into districts based on population. In the Senate, membership is 2 Senators per state. (C), the number of colonies initially needed to ratify the Constitution, refers to the decision of all 13 colonies to ratify. (D), number of amendments, is unlimited. There is no limit to the number of amendments that can be added to the Constitution. (E) is the correct response. The concept of 3/5 refers to the decision to count each black as only 2/3 of an individual.

18. **(B)**   (A) is incorrect because both houses of Congress were created at the same time. (C) is incorrect because this concept is not a part of the philosophy of Democracy. (D) is not related to this question. (B) is correct. The Founding Fathers feared that direct election by the people would result in loss of power of the government. (E) may have been felt by some, but it was never a factor in this discussion.

19. **(C)**   Machiavelli's theory of government supported notions that less-than-honest means of governing were acceptable. Therefore (A) is incorrect. (B) is incorrect because of the fact that Machiavelli did not publicize his support of the Italian government. (B) might possibly be a correct answer as its form follows Machiavellian theory. However, (C) is the correct answer. These kinds of infamous forms of governing more closely correspond to Machiavellian concept. (E) would be antithetical to Machiavelli's beliefs.

20. **(D)**   This question tests one's knowledge of the powers of the United Nations. All answers may have some application to the questions. However, (D) is the most appropriate answer. The United Nations has the ability to station troops only when the respective country accepts them. In times of crisis, (A) may be acceptable. (B), demanding protection, may be acceptable, however, the World Court does have the power to use discretion in assigning troops. (C) is incorrect. The World Court has the power to establish law or a position but a country does not have to subscribe to the World Court's decisions. (E) is immaterial since each nation is a sovereign state.

21. **(E)**   There are a variety of factors that constrain tropical agriculture. (A) is a constraint because rainfall is inconsistent. Due to the climate and other geographic factors a great number of different pests and diseases exist. (C) is also a constraint. Due to the geographic location, higher temperatures denote a greater rate of evaporation. (D) is also a constraint. The type of vegetation serves to deplete the soil of nutrients. However, (E) is NOT a constraint due to the fact that there is no winter thaw in the tropics.

22. **(C)**   The concept of "White Mans Burden" refers to the idea that the white man has

a responsibility to help those less fortunate. (A) is incorrect. "White Man's Burden" is not the same as "a lot of effort" for whites. (B) is incorrect because "White Man's Burden" refers to a societal concept, not just male. (D) is incorrect because non-whites might not have less responsibility, just less opportunity. (E) is incorrect because this is a generalization that is not based on fact. (C) is the correct response.

23. **(A)** The Southwest refers to several states located in the southwestern U.S. (B) is incorrect because Florida is located in the southeastern U.S. (C) is incorrect because Ohio is located in the upper Midwest. (D) is incorrect because Oregon is located in the northwestern U.S. (E) is wrong because Kansas is not in the Southwest. Therefore, (A) is the correct response.

24. **(B)** The correct answer is (B). The Battle of Hastings, the key onslaught of the Norman invasion was largely decided by the accurate use of bows and arrows. The battles of Waterloo and New Orleans of the 19th century were fought with guns and the Battle of the Bulge in World War II also involved the use of tanks. The Battle of Yorktown is incorrect because it was largely a naval battle fought in the American Revolution.

25. **(A)** The Dred Scott decision declared that slaves were not considered human beings but property belonging to slave owners. (B) therefore is incorrect. (C) did not occur until the development of the Emancipation Proclamation. (D) is incorrect because California was admitted to the union as a free state. (E) is incorrect because it was neither law nor common practice. Therefore (A) is the correct response.

26. **(A)** (B) is incorrect because xenophobia refers to a fear of strangers. (C) is incorrect because it refers to a developmental process in all humans. (D) is incorrect because it refers to the process of passing cultural traits from one culture to another. (E) refers to the adaptation of cultural traits of one culture by members of another culture. The correct answer is (A).

27. **(E)** (A), (B) and (C) are incorrect because river flow is not limited to a particular direction. (D) is incorrect because rivers flow *into* bays. (E) is the correct response. Due to gravity and the change in elevation, rivers flow from higher to lower elevations.

28. **(C)** Areas located near large lakes, such as Lake Erie, benefit from the "lake effect" which keeps frosts at bay for a longer time from killing frosts. The growing seasons of areas of land that are farther and farther from the equator are adversely affected. Areas generally of higher elevation will be frostier than lowland areas. Fertile soil, however, has no effect on the length of a growing season. An area which has a very long growing season could contain either fertile or very poor soil. Therefore, (C) is the correct response.

29. **(D)** is the correct answer. The assertion of people's inalienable rights was made by Jefferson when he wrote in the Declaration of Independence that all persons possess "certain inalienable rights," among them, "Life, Liberty, and the pursuit of Happiness." The establishment of checks and balances was set up in the Constitution of the United States of America. The Bill of Rights are the first ten amendments to the Constitution concerning freedoms not to be interfered with by the government. There is no mention of a court system in the Declaration.

30. **(B)** is the correct answer. The Declaration of Independence was signed on July 4, 1776. The Articles of Confederation were adopted in 1777 and ratified by all states in 1781. The Constitution of the United States of America took its finished form in 1787 and was ratified by the states between 1787 and 1790.

Section 2: Mathematics

1. **(E)** Although (A) may appear nearly correct it does not reflect the needed denominator. (B), (C) and (D) reflect incorrect interpretation of mixed numbers. When teaching mixed numbers and equivalent fraction forms the following calculation/symbolism represents the correct mathematics—concept and skill:

$4\ 3/16 = 4 + 3/16 = 4/1\ \ 3/16 = 4/1 \times 16/16 + 3/16 = 64/16 + 3/16 = 67/16.$

2. **(E)** (A) "obviously" is incorrect as is (B) since 5/3 is greater than 1. Construct a number line.

Divide each unit into thirds

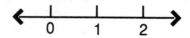

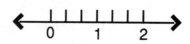

$$\frac{0}{3}\ \frac{1}{3}\ \frac{2}{3}\ \frac{3}{3}\ \frac{4}{3}\ \frac{5}{3}\ \frac{6}{3}$$

Convert to decimal equivalent

$4/3 = 1.333...\ 5/3 = 1.6666... \approx 1.67$

1.67 is greater than 1.6 so (D) is incorrect. Hence 1.333 <1.667 <1.7 so (E) is the correct response.

3. **(E)** (A) is tempting, however, it is the result of (E), and the best explanation for this operation. The complete rationale for the rule and the concepts it entails are best illustrated by an example: $8 + 2 = 4$ and $8 \times 10 + 2 \times 10 = 80 + 20 = 40$ and $8 \times 1/2 + 2 \times 1/2 = 4 + 1 = 4$. Furthermore this fact $2 \times 1/2$ represents the multiplicative inverse and the corresponding properties of (a) multiplicative identity and (b) division by (the identity element)1.

Thus $n + 1 = n$ for all n. $a \times 1/a = 1$ for all nonzero a. $a \times b + c \times b = a + c$ for all nonzero b.

Thus $7/12 + 4/7 = (7/12 \times 7/4) + (4/7 \times 7/4) = (7/12 \times 7/4) + 1 = 7/12 \times 7/4$ and hence invert the divisor and multiply.

4.   **(D)**   It may be helpful in this type of problem to let $r = 2$ and then $r = 3$, calculating Areas A for each and comparing.

$A_1 = 4\pi$ and $A_2 = 9\pi$ Area A_2 for the larger radius is 9/4 times 4π or Area A_1, the area for the smaller radius is increased by a factor of 9/4.

Do not confuse the increase of 1 unit in the radius with the increase of area—a fallacy exhibited in Choice A.

Just because 9 and 4 differ by 5, this does not imply 9π and 4π differ by 5, they differ by 5π but not by a *factor* of 5 or of 5π. Likewise the area does not increase by 9 square units nor by a factor of 9 square units so (C) like (A) and (B) is unacceptable. (E) is the multiplicative inverse of (D) and would imply the second area is 4/9 of the first or $16/9\pi$ which is equally incorrect.

5.   **(A)**   Given any rectangle, drawing one of the diagonals results in two triangles of equal area (congruent triangles). Thus every triangle has area equal to two triangles.

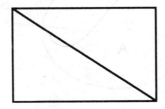

6.   **(B)**   The child is observing the four-sided figure, with opposite sides parallel and at least one (all four in fact) right angles—all concepts are Euclidean. There is no projective nor topologic concepts of equal or greater importance to the child. No projective property exists and the broken part formed by the squiggly line representing separation or discontinuity of topology is not foremost. Geometric choice (A) is not specific enough nor is spatial choice (E) which frequently has three-dimensional connotations.

7.   **(E)**   The child draws not necessarily what he sees but what he knows—the posts are all the same height and perpendicular to the ground and rails and the rails are equally spaced (parallel). The concept of projectivity which is used to represent three-dimensional space on a two-dimensional plane is lacking in this child—common until age 8, 12 or even 16 years in America.

8.   **(C)**   Base five is similar to base ten, but smaller.

Base Five		Base Ten	
Model Set	Numeral	Model Set	Numeral
	0		0
X	1	X	1
XX	2	XX	2

XXX	3	XXX	3
XXXX	4	XXXX	4
XXXXX	10	XXXXX	5
One basic bunch			
XXXXX X	11	XXXXXXXXXX	10
XXXXX XX	12	one basic bunch	
etc.		etc.	

This involves the fundamental concepts of the numeration system: digits, ciphering, zero, place value, etc.

9. **(C)** It is true a line connects point A and point B, but the line intersects or crosses the simple closed curve. Thus (A) is not correct. Similarly, the simple closed curve is between point A and point B since no line can be drawn between them without crossing the simple closed curve; however the line is not between the curve. The sentence is grammatically correct but conceptually nonsensical. Therefore (B) is not correct. A line connecting point (A) and point B crosses or *intersects* the simple closed curve; hence (C) is the correct choice.

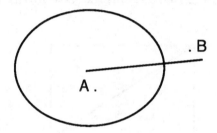

Separation is the concept illustrated by the simple closed curve; it separates the inside of the curve from the outside of the curve. The line through point A and point B does not represent a separation, therefore (D) is not correct. Although the curve is closed, the line through point A and point B does not represent a closed curve; hence (E) is not correct.

10. **(C)** To add all the numbers implies a smorgasbord—adding money, clock hours, blocks—a totally unusual approach to a very real world problem that is full of distractions, irrelevant data. Thus (A) is incorrect. (B) is no better and in fact suggests we subtract most of the clock and dollar and block figures from another dollar figure. (D) will result in the cash remaining after the purchases, not what is spent. (E) has us adding to our purchase the money used to pay for them. It defies reality. Thus only (C) satisfies the needs of this problem—adding the cost of the items purchased to find the total amount spent.

11. **(C)** The inference pattern represented by this argument is an invalid inference pattern, $p \rightarrow q$ and q therefore p. It is a commonly used, but invalid argument form. It uses an incorrect assumption that a converse statement is equivalent to the original statement. Some authors contend this invalid form is a misapplication of the negation of the consequence or misapplication of the concept of the contrapositive. It is an invalid inference pattern.

12. **(D)** (A) is incorrect because the weight gain is *not* constant, it varies from 0 to .25

to .75. (B) is incorrect because a 1/2 lb. was gained from Tuesday to Wednesday and from Wednesday to Thursday, two days. Similarly for Choice (C). (D) is correct because the weight for Thursday and Friday remained the same, hence no apparent weight gain.

13. **(C)** Hexadecimal is the base sixteen system of the computer with symbols 0, 1, 2, 3, 4, 5, 6, 7, 8, 9, A, B, C, D, E, F. This is found more and more on newer hand-held calculators. Base hexadecimal has a basic collection or bundle of ////////////////. This $12_{hexadecimal}$ is //////// ////// // or Choice (C). A dozen means base ten one bundle of ten ///////// and 2 more.

14. **(B)** (A) is incorrect because we weren't asked for the shortest route. There are two ways to go from Mary's house $\llcorner$. Once that first move is made, say North ↑, there is only one way to go, East →), and since that is direct to Petro's, there is one of the routes. If we go East on the first move, we can continue East → until we go to the intersection and then head North ↑. This is the second route. Once we go East → from Mary's house we could go South ↓, then turn East → at the intersection and eventually North ↑ at the next intersection. This is our third route. There are no more. Hence (B) is our only choice.

15. **(C)** This is a common pattern in mathematics, $(1/2)^n$ where n is 0, 1, 2, 3,... any natural number and the sequence becomes 1, 1/2, 1/4, 1/8, 1/16, 1/32, 1/64, 1/128,.... It starts at 1, but it never will be 0 since the numerator is always 1 and although the value of the fraction decreases, the value will always be positive, never zero, never negative. It never stops! (D) is true, but does not describe the pattern, merely one fact about this sequence. (E) is also incorrect, because there are no multiples (that implies whole numbers) of 2, but powers of 1/2. Multiples also connote positive exponents and to arrive at "multiples of 2" we would have to use negative exponents. Thus (C) is the best choice for representing the pattern illustrated.

16. **(A)** The inference pattern represented by this argument is a valid inference pattern, $p \rightarrow q$ and $\sim q$ therefore $\sim p$. It is often called the indirect method of proof. Some authors consider it an application of the concept of the contrapositive. It is a valid inference pattern.

17. **(D)** The second premise almost equals the consequence of the conditional premise, but it is different. This is not an illustration of the invalid inference pattern $p \rightarrow q$ and q therefore p (of problem 11). It does not represent any valid inference pattern. There is no indication that the antecedent ever is enacted; i.e., is true. At best this is a poor attempt at the misapplication of the converse as an invalid inference pattern.

18. **(D)** We are seeking an illustration of the computative pattern for addition in which we need the same numbers in a different order about the addition operation. (A) is incorrect because $4 \neq 7$ and $6 \neq 3$; equality for each set of symbols would be required for the pattern. (B) has $2695 = 2695$ but $11479 \neq 11794$. (C) illustrates a mirror image for the numerals about equality but this does not represent commutativity. (D) has the order of the number reversed but the operation symbol of addition and satisfies the property. (E) is false. Subtraction does not have the commutative property.

19. **(C)** To convince yourself, make a model of paper using tape to act as the weld. (A) is false. Although (B) appears to yield the same results, the actual statement does not indicate the cost since the last sentence omits the number of cuts and welds. (E) is false, there is a least expensive way. (D) fails; a single long chain will not result. There are several ways to arrive

at the one solution, 3 cuts and 3 welds result in a minimal cost of $3.60. 3 x .25 + 3 x .95 = 3.60 Here is one way:

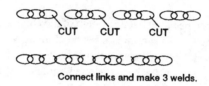

CUT   CUT   CUT

Connect links and make 3 welds.

20. **(B)** The most direct and simplest method is the working backward method. Even if modeling is done, it must be done backward or else the less efficient trial and error method must be employed. An analytic/algebraic solution is possible but for most people it is too involved. A pictorial representation of modeling might work, but is very inefficient. Deduction logic is not a logical approach.

Backward: $2.25 when she got home. Thus she spent $2.25 on her fare so she had $4.50 when she left the Tea Rose Room. Since she spent half her cash for lunch, lunch cost $4.50 and she had $9.00 after paying the tip or $10.50 before the tip (when she entered the Tea Rose Room). She gave $1 in charity, then had $11.50 when she left the bank. Since she paid half her cash to her account, she must have had $23 when she left home.

21. **(E)** If we "add" one more dot to the last row to create the 5th row for the next triangle we get

It works!

Try again add one dot, get 6 dots and make the next triangle, row 6 with 6 dots.

Again it works

(A) is too vague since it does not describe fully what needs to be done. (B) doesn't describe how to make the bigger triangle. (C) is not a solution since the problem can be determined. (D) hints, but is not explicit about what you do with the number of dots.

22. **(E)** Choice (A) is not a solution. Addition is not the implied operation. (B) shows a good guess with no indication why intuition or what intuition is being employed. It reflects a wild choice that may not really "work." (C) implies the mathematics that verifies the pattern

but does not indicate what the pattern really is. (D) is not correct since there is a pattern involved in the problem. In (E), a pattern emerges that does not rely on any mathematical operation. The pattern is hypothesized and can be verified by multiplication later on. This kind of pattern recognition is sought.

23. **(D)** Here subtraction is based on the action of separating out a subset of a set and being concerned with the remaining subset. This is the verbal problem, action/operation orientation that children naturally associate with the basic concept of subtraction (the work of Piaget). It is not primarily concerned with number facts, so (E) is not the best choice. (A), (B) and (C) are inappropriate responses for the question.

24. **(D)** Although (E), a tree or even a Cartesian product might be appropriate, the teacher active, student passive approach coupled with the unnatural (for the masses of children) conceptual approach to multiplication is not the better teaching technique. (B) and (C) again reflect a passive role for children who learn by manipulation, active roles. (D) provides for the matching (a less abstract type of Cartesian product) and an active role for the learner. It is a premultiplication activity. (A) is a meaningless fact at this stage.

25. **(C)** Although (A), (B) and (E) may be a part of the overall activity, none of them are really a part of this portion of the activity—counting the plants that are alive, and creating a graph of how many children have each specific number of living tomato plants from 0 to 12. It is not (D) since there is no mention of calculating the probability of how many living plants we have divided by the number of seeds planted; furthermore, more may have germinated than are alive after several weeks. The activity here is statistical—a graph to describe the (current condition) data.

Section 3: Literature and Fine Arts

1. **(B)** An elegy is a serious poem lamenting the death of an individual or group of individuals. Passage (B) is Robert Herrick's "Upon His Spaniel Tracy," an elegy which mourns the death of his favorite dog. Thus, passage (B) is the correct answer.

2. **(A)** Enjambment occurs when a line of poetry "runs on" to the next line, causing a slight pause in mid-sentence or thought. Line three reads, "This shall my love do, give thy sad death one." The reader is left wondering, "One what?" It is not until line four that the poet explains that he will give one "Tear." Thus, choice (A) is the correct answer.

3. **(A)** The speaker of these lines is Berowne, a reluctant student in Shakespeare's *Love's Labor's Lost.* You can discern that the lines are spoken by a student because they are a reaction *against* study and those who pursue it ("Small have continual plodders won...") It would be highly unusual for a professor to say such things, and the other three choices are, of course, possible, but not within the limited context of the passage.

4. **(E)** Restated, the lines mean, "Little (small) have those who constantly (continually) plod through their studies gained (won), except (save) for some common, throwaway knowledge (base authority) from others' books." Choice (E) comes closest to this, and is thus the correct answer.

5. **(D)** These lines suggest that the astronomers who name "every fixed star" get no more out of their studies than simpletons "that walk and wot not what they are." Choice (D) comes closest to this meaning, and is thus the correct answer.

6. **(B)** The meaning of this phrase can be found in the words which follow it: "That give a name to every fixed star." Astronomers are usually responsible for the naming of stars, so choice (B) is correct.

7. **(B)** The building pictured in the example—the contemporary "Beaubourg" art museum and cultural center in Paris—dispenses entirely with the ideas and philosophies of the classical past and with the styles and forms of traditional architecture. It is conceived instead on a huge industrial scale and, rather than projecting an atmosphere of quiet balance and poetic calm, it seeks to involve itself and its visitors in the dynamic life and culture of the modern city. Therefore, rather than concealing its structural and mechanical components behind a finished, exterior wall, the Beaubourg intentionally exposes its "anatomy", using pipes, ducts, tubes, and funnels of a modern industrial plant to reveal both its structure and its functions to the people in attendance. The visitor's ability to perceive the building's processes at work creates the sense that both building and people are part of a huge living organism.

8. **(D)** The jamb statues on the Early Gothic cathedral at Chartres, France (c. A.D. 1145-1170) draw their subject matter and thematic content not from classical mythology but from Christian ideology and belief. The figure groupings in the three main portals illustrate scenes from the Life and Passion of Christ, such as His birth, the Presentation in the Temple, and, in the center, the Second Coming. However, these scenes are not specifically arranged in a continuous narrative sequence and do not "tell a story". The sculpture itself, though it covers much of the building's facade, cannot be said to dominate, since it is strictly controlled and contained within the space allotted to it. The static, motionless figures conform closely to their architectural framework and are therefore subordinate to the structural forms of the doorways.

9. **(C)** (C) is the correct response because the author of this passage does little to give the reader a sense of what the landscape looks like in detail. Phrases such as "filled all the valley with verdure and fertility" do nothing to describe the details of the scene, such as the flora and fauna. "Fish of every species" and "every fowl whom nature has taught to dip the wing in water" are extremely vague, giving no description of what the fish and birds look like. The passage involves no comparisons or contrasts (B), and it does not have a negative connotation. Although the description is vague, it is still realistic, not surrealistic (E).

10. **(E)** In the eighteenth century Japanese woodblock print pictured in the example, the artist used the folds of the garment and its bold design to create an animated surface pattern of diagonal lines and shapes. These diagonals, far from minimizing the motion of the dancer, emphasize his athletic leaps and turns, although they give no specific information about the story behind his dance. Further, the drapery folds do not cling to the dancer's body and define the three-dimensional forms of his anatomy, as they would in a Western tradition, but, rather, obscure his body almost completely, reassert the picture surface, and deny any sense of actual, three-dimensional space.

11. **(B)** The Renaissance sculptor who created the small figure group shown in the example was intent on conveying the physical stresses and strains of two wrestlers in violent conflict. To express the ferocity of the fight he has exaggerated the tautness of the muscles and the rigid tension in the bodies; to illustrate the climactic moment at which one fighter lifts the other from the ground to break his back, he has shown the brief instant during which the raised figure is balanced against his opponent's stomach. In the viewpoint shown, there is no suggestion of either the rolling motion of a wheel or the flowing of liquid, and there is apparently none of the spiral torsion of a screw. The figures do seem to interlock somewhat like a set of gears, but the simple machine they most resemble is the lever, with the fulcrum located at the balance point between the two men's abdomens.

12. **(C)** A simile is a literary device which uses the word "like" to compare two often unlike things. "My love is like to ice, and I to fire" suggests that the speaker's love interest is cold to him, while he or she is very much in love with the other.

13. **(D)** Personification is a literary device which gives human characteristics to inanimate objects or animals. In the phrase in choice (D), the moon is given a face which has a "wan" expression, and it is given legs, with which it "climb'st the skies." Thus the moon has attained human aspects, and is therefore personified.

14. **(E)** Apostrophe is the act of addressing someone or something directly in a poem. Choice (E) begins with "Hail to thee, blithe Spirit!" which is the first line of Percy Bysshe Shelley's "To a Skylark." The poet addresses the bird directly at the very start of the poem.

15. **(D)** Edgar Degas (1834-1917), the French Impressionist artist who painted the picture shown in the example, was strongly influenced by the ability of the camera to capture a subject in a fleeting moment and in a spontaneous, seemingly unposed manner. In *Viscount Lepic and His Daughters*, 1873, the artist has constructed an off-center composition in which the main subject moves to the right and seems about to exit the picture. Both the viscount and his two young daughters are abruptly cut off at or near the waist, the dog is half-hidden behind one of the children, and the man standing to the left barely enters the picture. This random cropping of objects is reminiscent of a photographic snapshot. Further, the focal center of the picture is located in the empty plaza behind the figures. The painting therefore owes little either to Greek sculpture, which usually represented the full human figure in idealized form, or to Renaissance perspective, which carefully balanced its figures within an illusionistic space. It also shows no apparent debt to the numerous styles of children's book illustration or to the severe abstractions of much primitive art.

16. **(E)** The example shows the church of St. Michael's at Hildesheim, Germany (c. A.D. 1001-1031). It is typical of Early Romanesque architecture in its dependence on thick blank walls with little or no ornamental decoration, and in its massing of simple cubic and cylindrical forms. The effect of this building is less that of a structural framework supporting walls, roofs, and windows, than of a combination of building blocks which have been sectioned and than glued together. Except for the arched shape of the windows, with their tiny glassed areas, the building completely avoids curving forms, while the only diagonals are those of the roof lines, which are functionally necessary but not fundamental to the building's cubic character. Finally, a spectator's ground-level point of view might make this building seem larger and more dramatic, but it, too, is not essential to the architects' conception.

17. **(B)** The Greek Doric temple pictured in the example illustrates a type of architecture known as post-and-lintel (or *trabeated*) construction, in which long horizontal beams rest atop a series of vertical supports. In the Greek temple, the cylindrical columns act as supports for the large marble "beam" (or the *architrave*), which, in turn, supports the roof. The Doric temple thus achieves an appearance of Classical balance and perfection through the calculated repetition of a minimum variety of forms. The temple avoids unbroken wall surfaces, instead playing off the solids and voids of the columns and the spaces between, while the only diagonals are those of the triangular front gable (the *pediment*). The building is completely devoid of arches, which were known to the Greeks but were rarely used and gained prominence only in Roman architecture.

18. **(B)** This passage from Byron's "Don Juan" is an example of mock epic: a poem written in epic style designed to parody and satirize this literary tradition. The playful spirit of the passage ("So that my name of Epic's no misnomer") as well as its larger implications (epics are formulamatic and predictable) mark it, like Chaucer's *The Nun's Priest's Tale*, as a true mock epic.

19. **(D)** The theme of *carpe diem*, Latin for "seize the day," urges people to enjoy their present pleasures and lives, because the future is so uncertain. In Andrew Marvell's "To His Coy Mistress," the speaker is attempting to seduce his mistress by reasoning with her along these lines. He states that "time's winged chariot" is always near and that, once dead, she will no longer hear his "echoing song."

20. **(C)** A pastoral elegy is, by definition, a poem dealing with rural life which mourns the death of someone. Choice (C), taken from John Milton's "Lycidas," fits this description. It begins with the speaker plucking berries "harsh and crude" because "Lycidas is dead, dead ere his prime." The speaker is comparing the berry, whose leaves are "shattered before the mellowing year," to Lycidas, who also died "ere his prime. (Actually, the poem is about a friend of Milton's, Edward King, who was drowned in the Irish Sea.) The combination of nature and death mark "Lycidas" as a pastoral elegy.

21. **(B)** The passage, taken from Jonathan Swift's "Description of a City Shower," is satiric in that it attacks, with humor, a subject or practice which the poet finds ridiculous; in this case, it is the practice of assigning meaning to seemingly "unrelated" occurrences to foretell the weather. Swift is mocking those who feel that such things as a cat which stops chasing its tail, the sewer letting out a "double stink," or even the raging of a "hollow tooth" could, "foretell the hour... when to dread a shower."

22. **(D)** The phrase is certainly sarcastic because in this passage Swift is mocking those who feel that such things as sewers and "old aches" can foretell the weather; "By sure prognostics," then, comes to mean exactly the opposite, i.e. these "signs" foretell nothing! This phrase, like the rest of the passage, is also playful in tone, not angry as choice (C) states. Thus, choice (D), which covers both (A) and (B), is correct.

23. **(C)** Two of the examples shown, choices (D) and (E) are profile portraits, in which the sitters do not turn their gazes out of the picture space, thus eliminating any possibility of eye contact with the viewer. Two other examples, choices (A) and (B), show the subjects in nearly full face, but the sitter in choice (A) glances introspectively down to his left, while the subject in choice (B) looks toward us but, with aristocratic remove, keeps his own gaze just

out of the line of our view. Only choice (C) presents a subject in full face who looks directly at the viewer with his large, warm eyes. this sarcophagus portrait from Roman Egypt, c. A.D. 160, intent on expressing the warmth and humanity of the deceased subject, not only effected full eye contact with the viewer, but also portrayed the subject's eyes as abnormally large and deep.

24. **(B)** Neither the clothing, the sitters, the expressions, nor the styles of choices (A) and (C) convey in any specific way that the subjects are aristocrats. Choice (E) appears to be a royal person and is therefore probably an aristocrat, but the painting is highly stylized and abstracted and projects little of the sitter's personality. Only choices (B) and (D) show subjects who are clearly wealthy, well-born, and well-bred. Choice (D), however, is a profile portrait which is so formalized as to be neutral and devoid of expression. Choice (B), by contrast, presents a subject whose rich clothing, haughty posture, elegantly cocked wrists, and, especially, distant expression mark him as a wealthy young man whose circumstances make him superior to most.

25. **(A)** The two Renaissance portraits, choices (B) and (D), show the forms and features of their subjects as clearly-defined, well-modelled, and set within a basically naturalistic space. The portrait in choice (C), too, though painted in a sketchier style, models the forms of the face in a lucid, convincing, realistic manner in order to project the sitter's personality. Only choices (A) and (E) begin to abstract the figure and undermine the conventional sense of form in the search for new pictorial styles. Choice (E), however, stresses the flatness of the design and encloses all of its forms in a bold black outline. Only in choice (A), the *Boy in a Red Vest* by the French painter Paul Cézanne, is the specific subject less important than the way the artist treats it. Here, the painter breaks the outlines of the figure and disintegrates its forms, linking them with the background space in a new kind of picture construction.

26. **(D)** This poem, written by William S. Gilbert in 1882, is a satiric look at the ineffectuality of the British Parliament and its inability (in the poet's opinion) to do anything worthwhile. Phrases such as "The House of Peers made no pretense / To intellectual eminence" and "The House of Peers, throughout the war, / Did nothing in particular, / And did it very well" show the author's disdain for the noble men who inherited their Parliament seats and had no real interest in the political goings-on of England. The fact that, as the poet mentions, Britain becomes an empire in spite of the House of Peers adds to the satiric yet humorous tone of the poem.

27. **(C)** The satire in the poem is evident in the author's depiction of the success of Britain in spite of the ineffectual "House of Peers," and the satire is given a prophetic nature as the author wonders if the same success will continue, as if the Parliament will always be useless. The poem certainly does not laud (praise) the Parliament (A), and the poet is not satisfied (D), with the House's past performances. The poem is not a parody (B), and although the poet seems proud of England's successes, the poem is not patriotic in its tone (E).

28. **(D)** In the Chinese ink painting shown in the example, the artist exploited the fluid, calligraphic character of the ink-and-brush technique. In rendering the graceful bamboo leaves, he did not attempt to suggest illusionistic three-dimensional space, as a Western artist might, but let his forms lie firmly on the two-dimensional picture plane. Further, he restricted his range of tones to a dense black and one grey, and, even though written script is included in the picture, this isolated image of the bamboo plant does not relate an episode in a story.

Instead, the artist has drawn upon years of technical training and practice to create a picture in which both the script and the plant forms act as kind of spontaneous, rhythmic "writing".

29. **(C)** A supplicant is one who seeks forgiveness in a religious sense. Therefore, by labeling the parishioners as such, the author is implying that they are all guilty of various crimes against their religion, and have come to the church seeking forgiveness.

30. **(A)** Of the five answer choices, only (A) and (B) can be said to show groups of figures in a landscape; choices (D) and (E) show one or two isolated figures in a landscape setting, and choice (C) contains no landscape elements at all. Choice (B), however, though it presents a number of figures within a topographic view, carefully avoids formally composed and arranged groups and seeks instead to achieve an effect of direct, unposed observation. Only choice (A) uses a composed group as its focal point: the line of schoolboys, seemingly engaged in a moment of spontaneous play, has been painstakingly arranged to lead the viewer's eye from the darker forms at the right to the white-shirted boy at the center. The entire group is set in a broad meadow against a distant, level horizon line which lends balance and stability to the whole composition.

31. **(D)** Only choices (A), (B), and (D) include visible horizon lines: in choice (A) the horizon is integrated with the figure group, and in choice (B) the figures, though small and insignificant within the broad landscape space, are busy in normal workaday activities and do not seem especially isolated. Choice (D), however, Andrew Wyeth's *Christina's World*, 1948, places a solitary figure in a broad, empty landscape space bounded by a high, distant horizon. The helpless isolation of the stricken woman in the field is emphasized by the distance which separates her from her home high on the horizon.

32. **(E)** Only choices (D) and (E) appear to simplify their contents in any significant way. Choice (D) simplifies by eliminating unnecessary subject matter and concentrating on a few essential images, such as the figure, the field and sky, and the buildings. Its style, however, is not abstract but realistic, and is based on close observation of actual details. Choice (E), in contrast, presents actual, observed forms, but distills and refines them into basic, almost abstract shapes: the trees to the right appear as a simple dark mass, while the houses are reduced to a combination of basic planes which reflect light and color. All secondary detail and texture, as of the wood siding of the houses, is carefully, rigorously suppressed.

33. **(B)** This question asks you to look at a set of costumes for a play and to match the costumes with the appropriate play. The costumes are definitely from the Elizabethan era, and even if you do not know the other authors and titles listed, you should be able to match a Shakespearean play with these Elizabethan costumes. The correct answer is (B).

34. **(B)** The author's point here is that the so-called "historical novels" which exist in out canon of literature are, in fact, anything but "historical." "Fantastic" usually refers to something unreal, as it does here, making choice (B) the correct answer.

35. **(A)** If you selected anything but choice (A), you were too hasty in making your decision. The author is not mocking the famous *writers*, but those readers which read their works as historical treatises. The author refers to their novels as "fairy tales," but not in a condescending way; he is simply categorizing the novels as works of fiction ("supreme," in fact) which should be read as such.

Section 4: Science

1. **(D)** During the summer, the Earth is farthest from the Sun. The reason for the warmth during this period is the concentration of the Sun's rays on the Earth. (D) is the right choice. Despite the fact that winter is the season when the Earth is coldest, the Earth is not farthest from the Sun in the winter or the fall (which precedes winter). (A) is not the correct answer. The Earth moves in an elliptical orbit about the Sun. It moves closest to the Sun in the winter. It is farthest from the Sun in the summer. (B) should not be chosen. Even though the winter season is the coldest, the Earth is closest to the Sun during this time. The Sun's rays are not concentrated directly on the part of the Earth that is experiencing winter; winter is, therefore, colder. Spring is an incorrect answer; (C) should not be chosen. The Earth is not farthest from the Sun in either fall or winter. Answer (E), which gives the reader both these answers, is giving the reader two wrong answers. (E) should not be chosen.

2. **(E)** A gram is about the weight of a paper clip. It would be a good unit to use to determine the weight of a dime. (E) is the best answer to choose. A kilometer is 1000 meters (one meter is slightly longer than a yard). Using this unit would not easily result in the weight of a dime. (A) should not be chosen. A liter is slightly more than a quart. The weight of a dime could not easily be determined using this measurement. (B) is not the correct answer. Since a hectometer is equal to 100 meters, it is not the best measurement to use in determining the weight of a dime. (C) is not the correct answer. A kilogram is 1000 grams or about 2.2 pounds. It is not the best measurement to use to determine the weight of a dime, although it is possible. (D) is not the right answer and should not be chosen.

3. **(D)** Leafy, green and yellow vegetables are the best sources of Vitamin A. (D) is correct. Milk, cheese, and dairy products are excellent sources of calcium. They are not, however, the best source of Vitamin A. (A) is an incorrect answer. Meats, eggs, dried peas and beans are good sources of protein. They are not, however, the best sources of Vitamin A. (B) is an incorrect answer. Cereals, bread and grain products are necessary to a balanced diet. They are not, however, the best sources of Vitamin A. (C) is an incorrect answer. Fresh citrus fruits are rich in Vitamin C; they are not, however, the best source of Vitamin A. (E) is not correct.

4. **(E)** (E) is the best answer and should be chosen. Iodine is required for proper functioning of the thyroid gland. (A) Small amounts of iodine are necessary to good health since it is required for proper functioning of the thyroid gland. (A) should not be chosen. Fluorine, not iodine, is a factor in preventing tooth decay. Answer (B) is incorrect. Iodine is not needed for bonebuilding. It is, however, necessary for the proper functioning of the thyroid gland. (C) should not be chosen. Iron, not iodine, is an essential constituent in building the oxygen-carrying pigment of the blood. (D) is not the best answer.

5. **(C)** It is the Earth that is turning and not the stars. Answer (C), which suggests that it is the stars which turn, is a false statement and should be selected by the reader since the question states that all the statements are true EXCEPT one. The other statements (A), (B), (D), and (E) are true and should not be selected by the reader.

6. **(E)** (E) enables the reader to choose (A) and (B), both of which are correct: enzymes

enable molecules to pass into the bloodstream after the transformation of complex molecules into a simpler form. (C) is totally incorrect since it discusses fusing the molecules, not breaking down the food molecules. Answer (D) cannot be selected since it includes the correct answers (A) and (B) and the incorrect (C).

7. **(E)** The food chain is continuous—not non-continuous. Since the directions ask for the item which is not true, (E) is the correct choice. All the other answers (A), (B), (C), and (D) are true and cannot be selected as the correct choice since a false item (E) is indicated.

8. **(D)** All the statements about gravitational force are true except for I. Since (D) enables the reader to select all the items (II, III, IV, V) except I, it is the best answer to the question. It is evident that the production of an electromagnet is the result of electricity and not the result of gravitational force; I is incorrect and is not included in the list under (D)—the right answer.

9. **(C)** Since lime water is a base, the result of placing litmus paper in it is that the paper turns blue; (C) is the correct answer. Since there is an effect—the paper turns blue, (A) is not the correct answer. Since the litmus paper does not disintegrate, (B) is not the correct answer. (D) is not the correct answer since litmus paper turns blue—not red—in a base. There is no carbonation resulting from placing litmus paper in lime water; (E) is not, therefore, the correct answer.

10. **(A)** Since elements cannot be broken down into simpler substances, (A) is a true statement and the right answer. (B) is incorrect since molecules which are built of more than one kind of atom are known as compounds—not elements. There are not more than 4 million identified elements; rather there are 107 identified elements. Answer (C), then, is not to be selected. All elements are not equally abundant in nature; some are more plentiful than others. (D) should not be selected as the right answer. Elements—not compounds—might be compared to the 26 letters of the alphabet; compounds—not elements—might be compared to the words; (E) is an incorrect choice.

11. **(A)** Since the advance of technology has reached a level where (A) is correct. It is the only acceptable choice. (B) is false; the environmental crisis is not limited to highly industrialized areas but is global in nature. (B) cannot be chosen. The oceans and atmospheres do not purify pollutants as (C) suggests; rather the oceans and atmosphere distribute the life-destroying pollutants everywhere. Since answer (D) suggest that all the above are correct, it cannot be selected. Since both (B) and (C) are false, answer (E), which includes both those choices, should not be chosen by the reader.

12. **(C)** It takes *approximately* 365 days for the Earth to revolve around the Sun; by this means we measure the calendar year. (C) is the correct answer. The tilt of the Earth on its axis causes the concentration/lack of concentration of the Sun's rays on certain parts of the Earth; the result is the seasons of the year—not the calendar year. (A) should not, therefore, be chosen. As a result of the rotation of the Earth about the Sun, the Earth has day and night—not a calendar year. (B) is an incorrect response. The phases of the moon do not necessarily coincide with the calendar year; (D) is incorrect. The Sun does not revolve about the Earth; rather the Earth revolves about the Sun. (E) is an incorrect choice.

13. **(D)** Insufficient Vitamin A (found in leafy, green and yellow vegetables) may result in night blindness; (D) is the best choice. Sunshine is rich in Vitamin D; the lack of sunshine may cause disease, but not necessarily night blindness. (A) should not be chosen. Insufficient calcium may result in poor teeth and bone formation, but does not necessarily result in night blindness; (B) should not be chosen. Insufficient Vitamin C may cause scurvy but not necessarily night blindness; (C) should not be selected. A viral infection does not necessarily cause night blindness; (E) is not a good choice.

14. **(A)** If the Sun could burn for only 80,000 years, (A) refutes the above theory of the Sun's having burned for billions of years; (A) best refutes the above theory. (B) Energy converted to heat because of gravitational attraction does not necessarily refute the above theory and should not be selected. Hydrogen atoms could join to form helium atoms and result in the "burning" of the Sun; since (C) does not refute the above theory, it is not the answer to be selected. (D) encompasses all the above answers and should not be chosen. (E) includes both (A)—a correct answer—and (B)—an incorrect answer—and should not be the selected answer.

15. **(E)** All the answers are indeed part of the fundamental ideas of Dalton's atomic theory except (E). Atoms cannot be broken into anything simpler by ordinary chemical means; (E) should not be selected. The other items (A), (B), (C), and (D) are true as they are stated.

16. **(A)** A SERUM does consist of antibodies produced in an animal to treat a human disease, borrowed from blood extracted from such an animal, and prepared for injection into a human; (A) is the correct answer. An ANTIBIOTIC (B) is a substance produced by a living organ that can kill microbes or stop their growth; (B) is not the correct answer. A VACCINE (C) is a preparation of weakened or killed germs; you should not select (C). A TOXIN (D) is a poisonous substance produced by some disease-causing microorganisms; (D) is not, therefore, the correct choice. A GENE (E) is a hereditary unit located on the chromosome; (E) does not fit correctly in the sentence.

17. **(E)** Both WASPS and LOBSTERS belong to the phylum *Arthropoda* which means joint-footed; (E), which enables the reader to select both of these in V, is the correct answer. Answer (A) which includes sand dollars is an incorrect response; sand dollars belong to the Echinoderms—not the Arthropods. If you selected (B)—monkeys and great apes—you probably had the Anthropoids (human-like primates) confused with the Arthropods—joint-footed creatures; (B) should not be chosen. Only bees of the list sand dollars, monkeys, and great apes (C) are Arthropods; if you chose this answer you probably were linking the Anthropoids and Arthropods together; (C) is incorrect. Only the spiders in the list monkeys, spiders and sand dollars of answer (D) are Arthropods; (D) is an inappropriate response.

18. **(C)** CONDUCTION (a method of heat transfer in which energy is moved from molecule to molecule by collision or bombardment), CONVECTION (heat transfer when the heavier, colder air pushes the warmer, lighter air upward and a whole volume of heated material circulates), and RADIATION (heat transfer by waves) are the only three correct means of heat transfer listed; (C) contains all of these. Since TRANSPORTATION and CONDENSATION are not means of heat transfer, their inclusion in answers (A), (B), (D),

and (E) precludes the selection of these answers as the correct ones; since none of these answers includes all three means of heat transfer mentioned earlier (CONDUCTION, RADIATION, and CONVECTION), no answer but (C) is suitable.

19. **(D)** Since the veins of a plant carry water upward in the plant, (D) is the correct answer; the veins will also carry the colored water upward and result in a tinted celery stalk. (B) is incorrect; if the colored water left the stalk on one side, the stalk on the other side would also be colored. The colored water does not kill the plant within 3-4 hours; (C) is inappropriate. (E) is a false statement; there is no change in the color of the liquid in the glass. (E) is incorrect.

20. **(E)** Since the magnetism of a substance is due BOTH to the magnetic properties of its atoms AND the arrangement of its atoms, (E)—which allows the reader to select both (A) and (B) is the correct answer. Although (A) and (B) are both true, the reader who selects only one or the other has omitted part of the correct answer. The position of the poles (C) does not determine the magnetism of a substance; therefore (C) alone should not be selected. (D), which includes the incorrect answer (C), should not be selected. The only totally correct and complete answer is (E).

21. **(E)** According to Darwin's theories of survival of he fittest and natural selection, stronger dinosaurs killing weaker dinosaurs would not result in extinction but survival. (E) is incorrect and therefore the answer to be selected since the question asked for the WEAKEST explanation. The other possible answers (A), (B), (C), and (D) are theories as to why the dinosaurs are now extinct. Since, however, the reader is asked to select the WEAKEST explanation, none of these should be chosen.

22. **(E)** All the answers given are correct as they are written; the only answer which is incorrect is (E). Since the question asks for the answer which is not true ("All of the following are true of the structure of the earth EXCEPT..."), (E) is the answer the reader should select. The thickest of the Earth's three parts is the mantle, not the core; the mantle, of course, is the layer between the crust and the core, or center.

23. **(A)** On the periodic table Fe is the symbol for iron; (A) is the correct answer. The symbol for Fluorine is F; answer (B), therefore, is incorrect. The symbol for Lead is Pb; (C) should not be chosen, however. Magnesium (D) is represented by Mg; (D) is not an appropriate choice. Mercury (E) is represented on the periodic table by Hg; (E) cannot be chosen as the correct answer.

24. **(C)** Of all the items listed, the only ones which can be replenished are soil, vegetation (plants), freshwater, and animals; (C) is the correct answer because it lists three items, all of which are on the above list. Coal, oil, gas, and metals are all nonrenewable resources. Each of the other answers (A), (B), (D), and (E) contain at least one of the nonrenewable resources, and therefore should not be chosen.

25. **(E)** All parts listed are parts of the circulatory system except the seminal vesicles (E); the seminal vesicles are saclike structures in the male used to store sperm. The vesicles, then, are part of the reproductive system—not part of the circulatory system. Answers (A), (B), (C), and (D) are all correct and should not be chosen as the answers since an incorrect choice is needed.

26. **(C)**   Answer (C) is the correct choice since it includes the two false statements II and III; the directions call for the answers which are not true. Choice II is false since electrons have a negative—not a positive—charge. Answer III is false since the proton in the nucleus has a positive charge, not a negative charge as the statement reads. The rest of the choices are true. No other choices include both the false answers and include true statements. Only (C) is a satisfactory answer.

27. **(D)**   One milliliter (ml) equals one cubic centimeter (cc); (D) is the correct answer. A kilometer is less than—not equal to—one mile; (A) is incorrect. A kilogram is equal to 2.2 pounds; it is more than—not equal to—a pound and is therefore, not the correct answer. Since a gram is not equal to an ounce (one gram is approximately .03 of an ounce), (C) should not be selected. A liter is more than and not equal to a quart; (E) is not the correct answer.

28. **(E)**   When a magnet moves near a coil of wire or when a coil of wire moves near a magnet, the electrons flow and electricity can be generated (the principle of the generator). Answer (E) incorporates both of these answers and is the correct answer. Neither a weak link in the electric circuit nor atomic fusion result from such movement, so neither (B) nor (C) can be correctly chosen.

29. **(D)**   Three types of items were asked for in this question. First the reader was asked to identify an observation; item III ("The magnet attracted all our objects made of iron.") is an observation. Second, the question asked for a prediction; Item II ("The magnet will probably attract this nail since it is made of iron.") is an example of a such a prediction. Third, the question asked for a generalization. Item I ("Magnetized needles point in a north-south direction when suspended freely.") Only one answer (D) gives the answers in this order; (D) is, therefore, the correct answer. The other answers (A), (B), (C), and (E) do not include all the correct responses or do not include them in the correct order; none of them should be selected.

30. **(A)**   The question asks for the statement which is not true. (A) is not true according to most scientists; *simple* forms of life appeared, according to most theories, before complex forms of life. Dinosaurs are more simple than the opossum—a mammal; (A) is the best choice since it is the only false statement. (B), (C), (D), and (E) are all true and are not the correct choices.

NTE Test of Professional Knowledge

TEST 2 – ANSWER SHEET

Section 1	Section 2	Section 3
1. Ⓐ Ⓑ Ⓒ Ⓓ Ⓔ	1. Ⓐ Ⓑ Ⓒ Ⓓ Ⓔ	1. Ⓐ Ⓑ Ⓒ Ⓓ Ⓔ
2. Ⓐ Ⓑ Ⓒ Ⓓ Ⓔ	2. Ⓐ Ⓑ Ⓒ Ⓓ Ⓔ	2. Ⓐ Ⓑ Ⓒ Ⓓ Ⓔ
3. Ⓐ Ⓑ Ⓒ Ⓓ Ⓔ	3. Ⓐ Ⓑ Ⓒ Ⓓ Ⓔ	3. Ⓐ Ⓑ Ⓒ Ⓓ Ⓔ
4. Ⓐ Ⓑ Ⓒ Ⓓ Ⓔ	4. Ⓐ Ⓑ Ⓒ Ⓓ Ⓔ	4. Ⓐ Ⓑ Ⓒ Ⓓ Ⓔ
5. Ⓐ Ⓑ Ⓒ Ⓓ Ⓔ	5. Ⓐ Ⓑ Ⓒ Ⓓ Ⓔ	5. Ⓐ Ⓑ Ⓒ Ⓓ Ⓔ
6. Ⓐ Ⓑ Ⓒ Ⓓ Ⓔ	6. Ⓐ Ⓑ Ⓒ Ⓓ Ⓔ	6. Ⓐ Ⓑ Ⓒ Ⓓ Ⓔ
7. Ⓐ Ⓑ Ⓒ Ⓓ Ⓔ	7. Ⓐ Ⓑ Ⓒ Ⓓ Ⓔ	7. Ⓐ Ⓑ Ⓒ Ⓓ Ⓔ
8. Ⓐ Ⓑ Ⓒ Ⓓ Ⓔ	8. Ⓐ Ⓑ Ⓒ Ⓓ Ⓔ	8. Ⓐ Ⓑ Ⓒ Ⓓ Ⓔ
9. Ⓐ Ⓑ Ⓒ Ⓓ Ⓔ	9. Ⓐ Ⓑ Ⓒ Ⓓ Ⓔ	9. Ⓐ Ⓑ Ⓒ Ⓓ Ⓔ
10. Ⓐ Ⓑ Ⓒ Ⓓ Ⓔ	10. Ⓐ Ⓑ Ⓒ Ⓓ Ⓔ	10. Ⓐ Ⓑ Ⓒ Ⓓ Ⓔ
11. Ⓐ Ⓑ Ⓒ Ⓓ Ⓔ	11. Ⓐ Ⓑ Ⓒ Ⓓ Ⓔ	11. Ⓐ Ⓑ Ⓒ Ⓓ Ⓔ
12. Ⓐ Ⓑ Ⓒ Ⓓ Ⓔ	12. Ⓐ Ⓑ Ⓒ Ⓓ Ⓔ	12. Ⓐ Ⓑ Ⓒ Ⓓ Ⓔ
13. Ⓐ Ⓑ Ⓒ Ⓓ Ⓔ	13. Ⓐ Ⓑ Ⓒ Ⓓ Ⓔ	13. Ⓐ Ⓑ Ⓒ Ⓓ Ⓔ
14. Ⓐ Ⓑ Ⓒ Ⓓ Ⓔ	14. Ⓐ Ⓑ Ⓒ Ⓓ Ⓔ	14. Ⓐ Ⓑ Ⓒ Ⓓ Ⓔ
15. Ⓐ Ⓑ Ⓒ Ⓓ Ⓔ	15. Ⓐ Ⓑ Ⓒ Ⓓ Ⓔ	15. Ⓐ Ⓑ Ⓒ Ⓓ Ⓔ
16. Ⓐ Ⓑ Ⓒ Ⓓ Ⓔ	16. Ⓐ Ⓑ Ⓒ Ⓓ Ⓔ	16. Ⓐ Ⓑ Ⓒ Ⓓ Ⓔ
17. Ⓐ Ⓑ Ⓒ Ⓓ Ⓔ	17. Ⓐ Ⓑ Ⓒ Ⓓ Ⓔ	17. Ⓐ Ⓑ Ⓒ Ⓓ Ⓔ
18. Ⓐ Ⓑ Ⓒ Ⓓ Ⓔ	18. Ⓐ Ⓑ Ⓒ Ⓓ Ⓔ	18. Ⓐ Ⓑ Ⓒ Ⓓ Ⓔ
19. Ⓐ Ⓑ Ⓒ Ⓓ Ⓔ	19. Ⓐ Ⓑ Ⓒ Ⓓ Ⓔ	19. Ⓐ Ⓑ Ⓒ Ⓓ Ⓔ
20. Ⓐ Ⓑ Ⓒ Ⓓ Ⓔ	20. Ⓐ Ⓑ Ⓒ Ⓓ Ⓔ	20. Ⓐ Ⓑ Ⓒ Ⓓ Ⓔ
21. Ⓐ Ⓑ Ⓒ Ⓓ Ⓔ	21. Ⓐ Ⓑ Ⓒ Ⓓ Ⓔ	21. Ⓐ Ⓑ Ⓒ Ⓓ Ⓔ
22. Ⓐ Ⓑ Ⓒ Ⓓ Ⓔ	22. Ⓐ Ⓑ Ⓒ Ⓓ Ⓔ	22. Ⓐ Ⓑ Ⓒ Ⓓ Ⓔ
23. Ⓐ Ⓑ Ⓒ Ⓓ Ⓔ	23. Ⓐ Ⓑ Ⓒ Ⓓ Ⓔ	23. Ⓐ Ⓑ Ⓒ Ⓓ Ⓔ
24. Ⓐ Ⓑ Ⓒ Ⓓ Ⓔ	24. Ⓐ Ⓑ Ⓒ Ⓓ Ⓔ	24. Ⓐ Ⓑ Ⓒ Ⓓ Ⓔ
25. Ⓐ Ⓑ Ⓒ Ⓓ Ⓔ	25. Ⓐ Ⓑ Ⓒ Ⓓ Ⓔ	25. Ⓐ Ⓑ Ⓒ Ⓓ Ⓔ
26. Ⓐ Ⓑ Ⓒ Ⓓ Ⓔ	26. Ⓐ Ⓑ Ⓒ Ⓓ Ⓔ	26. Ⓐ Ⓑ Ⓒ Ⓓ Ⓔ
27. Ⓐ Ⓑ Ⓒ Ⓓ Ⓔ	27. Ⓐ Ⓑ Ⓒ Ⓓ Ⓔ	27. Ⓐ Ⓑ Ⓒ Ⓓ Ⓔ
28. Ⓐ Ⓑ Ⓒ Ⓓ Ⓔ	28. Ⓐ Ⓑ Ⓒ Ⓓ Ⓔ	28. Ⓐ Ⓑ Ⓒ Ⓓ Ⓔ
29. Ⓐ Ⓑ Ⓒ Ⓓ Ⓔ	29. Ⓐ Ⓑ Ⓒ Ⓓ Ⓔ	29. Ⓐ Ⓑ Ⓒ Ⓓ Ⓔ
30. Ⓐ Ⓑ Ⓒ Ⓓ Ⓔ	30. Ⓐ Ⓑ Ⓒ Ⓓ Ⓔ	30. Ⓐ Ⓑ Ⓒ Ⓓ Ⓔ
31. Ⓐ Ⓑ Ⓒ Ⓓ Ⓔ	31. Ⓐ Ⓑ Ⓒ Ⓓ Ⓔ	31. Ⓐ Ⓑ Ⓒ Ⓓ Ⓔ
32. Ⓐ Ⓑ Ⓒ Ⓓ Ⓔ	32. Ⓐ Ⓑ Ⓒ Ⓓ Ⓔ	32. Ⓐ Ⓑ Ⓒ Ⓓ Ⓔ
33. Ⓐ Ⓑ Ⓒ Ⓓ Ⓔ	33. Ⓐ Ⓑ Ⓒ Ⓓ Ⓔ	33. Ⓐ Ⓑ Ⓒ Ⓓ Ⓔ
34. Ⓐ Ⓑ Ⓒ Ⓓ Ⓔ	34. Ⓐ Ⓑ Ⓒ Ⓓ Ⓔ	34. Ⓐ Ⓑ Ⓒ Ⓓ Ⓔ
35. Ⓐ Ⓑ Ⓒ Ⓓ Ⓔ	35. Ⓐ Ⓑ Ⓒ Ⓓ Ⓔ	35. Ⓐ Ⓑ Ⓒ Ⓓ Ⓔ

NTE CORE BATTERY–Test 2
TEST OF PROFESSIONAL KNOWLEDGE
Section 1

TIME: 30 Minutes
35 Questions

DIRECTIONS: Each of the following questions and incomplete statements is followed by five answer choices. Select the choice which best answers each question.

---

1. Which of the following two arguments accurately supports the use of *cooperative learning* as an effective method of instruction?

    I.   Cooperative learning groups facilitate healthy competition between individuals in the group.

    II.   Cooperative learning groups allow academic achievers to carry or cover for academic underachievers.

    III. Cooperative learning groups make each student in the group accountable for the success of the group.

    IV.   Cooperative learning groups make it possible for students to reward other group members for achieving.

    (A)   I and II   (D)   III and IV

    (B)   II and III   (E)   II and IV

    (C)   I and III

2. A student is continually speaking out in class. The teacher does not want this behavior to continue so he verbally reprimands the student after each outburst. The student's "speaking out" behavior increases following the reprimands. Which one of the following statements best explains the effect of the teacher's behavior on the student's behavior?

    (A)   The teacher's behavior served as a positive reinforcer for the student.

    (B)   The teacher's behavior served as a negative reinforcer for the student.

    (C)   The teacher's behavior served as a presentation punishment for the student.

    (D)   The teacher's behavior served as a removal punishment for the student.

    (E)   The teacher's behavior served to extinguish the student's behavior.

3. Which one of the following statements is an example of Piaget's *conservation* ?

    (A)   A student is able to explain why the amount of water poured from a short, wide beaker into a tall, narrow beaker remains constant.

    (B)   A student can count forward from 1 to 25 and backward from 25 to 1.

    (C)   A student who used to call all small, furry animals "cats" can now distinguish between a cat and a skunk.

    (D)   A student can place 10 sticks of various lengths in order from shortest to tallest.

    (E)   A student, seeking cognitive balance, is motivated to solve a novel problem.

4.   A student scored at the 75th percentile on a measure of academic achievement. Which interpretation below best represents the student's achievement?

    (A)   The student was able to answer 75 percent of the test questions correctly.

    (B)   The student answered 75 test items correctly and 25 test items incorrectly.

    (C)   The student scored higher than 75 percent of those who took the test.

    (D)   The student achieved 75 percent of the instructional outcomes and objectives.

    (E)   The student scored higher than 25 percent of those who took the test.

5.   A student refuses to recite the pledge of allegiance at school each morning. During a conference between the teacher and the student's parents, it is uncovered that the student and his parents object to the recitation based on religious doctrine. What rights do the student and his parents have in this case?

    (A)   The student does not have the right to refuse reciting the pledge. He must do so or risk suspension from school.

    (B)   The student has the right to be exempted from reciting the pledge if doing so conflicts with his religious beliefs.

    (C)   The student has the right to refuse reciting the pledge but he must stand at attention as the other students recite it.

    (D)   The student must not be in defiance of any state statute requiring students to recite the pledge. If the state does not have a law specifically addressing the issue, then the student can refuse to recite the pledge.

    (E)   Refusing to recite the pledge is illegal and the parents of the student can be held responsible for his actions.

6.   Do teachers have the right to strike?

    (A)   Yes. It is any teacher's constitutional right to strike without fear of dismissal from his or her job.

    (B)   Yes, but only those teachers who belong to the National Education Association or the American Federation of Teachers may do so.

    (C)   No. The Supreme Courts of every state have ruled that public employees do not have the right to strike. At the same time, however, teachers cannot be discharged for striking.

    (D)   No. Public employees do not have the right to strike unless a state statute or city ordinance permits striking as a part of collective bargaining. The U.S. Supreme Court ruled that boards of education can discharge teachers who are striking illegally.

    (E)   No. Teachers cannot strike for higher pay, but they can strike for better working conditions in extreme situations.

7.   If a unit test measures an adequate sample of the instructional domain, representing appropriate outcomes and objectives, it can be said to demonstrate which type of validity evidence?

(A) Content-related (D) Predictive-related
(B) Construct-related (E) Concurrent-related
(C) Criterion-related

8. The Holmes Group Report *Tomorrow's Teachers* and the Carnegie Report *A Nation at Risk* propose major changes in
   (A) the curriculum offered at the elementary and secondary level.
   (B) minimum competency testing prior to secondary school graduation.
   (C) the way teachers are educated at colleges and universities.
   (D) the use of technology in the classroom.
   (E) science and math teachers' salaries.

9. All of the following issues have been addressed and upheld by U.S. courts as legal rights of students EXCEPT:
   (A) Students suspended from school have the right to a hearing before the school board.
   (B) Students can sue school districts if their constitutional rights have been violated.
   (C) Students may challenge a school board's decision to remove books from the school library.
   (D) Students of illegal alien parents have a right to a free public education.
   (E) Students have the right to nondisruptive expression of opinions.

10. According to attribution theory, which two students listed below are operating from an external locus of control?
    I. Student A says, "I did poorly on the test because I didn't study hard enough."
    II. Student B says, "The way the teacher explained the material didn't make sense."
    III. Student C says, "The test was too long. I didn't have time to finish."
    IV. Student D says, "I spent a lot of time reviewing but I wasn't able to grasp the material."
    (A) I and II (D) I and III
    (B) II and III (E) II and IV
    (C) III and IV

11. According to Robert Gagne, all types of learning outcomes can be categorized into which of the following taxonomies?
    (A) Awareness, knowledge, application
    (B) Theory, practice
    (C) Cognitive, affective, psychomotor
    (D) Verbal information, intellectual skills, cognitive strategies, motor skills, attitudes
    (E) The learner, the teacher, the classroom

12. Historically, school curricula have emphasized three major areas. Which one of the lists below identifies these three areas?

    (A) Scope, sequence, and integration

    (B) Psychology, philosophy, and history

    (C) Political, sociological, and environmental forces

    (D) Society, learners, and knowledge

    (E) Objectives, outcomes, and evaluations

13. Which one of the definitions listed below best defines the term *learning disability*?

    (A) The inability to focus on any one activity for a normal length of time

    (B) A visual, auditory, tactual, or kinesthetic perceptual disorder

    (C) An auditory or visual memory deficit

    (D) Difficulty in relating ideas in a logical sequence

    (E) A discrepancy between achievement and intellectual ability

14. According to cognitive psychologists, presenting new concepts to students should be done as a sequence. Which of the following responses (selected from the list of possibilities) represents the correct order for presenting new concepts?

    I.   A prototype example

    II.   A non-example

    III   A less obvious example

    IV.   The name and definition of the concept

    V.   Relevant and irrelevant attributes

    (A) I, III, II, IV, V   (D) IV, I, V, II, III

    (B) IV, V, I, III, II   (E) IV, I, II, III, V

    (C) II, IV, V, III, I

15. The objective *The student will be able to recite the Preamble to the U.S. Constitution* represents which one of Bloom's outcomes of learning for the cognitive domain?

    (A) Knowledge   (D) Analysis

    (B) Comprehension   (E) Evaluation

    (C) Application

16. Prior to 1954, many states allowed segregation in schools, citing a "separate but equal" Supreme Court ruling (*Plessy v. Ferguson,* 1896) as justification. In 1954, another Supreme Court ruling (*Brown v. the Board of Education of Topeka*) repudiated the 1896 decision. The new ruling, making public school segregation illegal, was based on which one of the following rationales?

    (A) The dual system of education cost too much money.

    (B) Schools were to maintain a racial balance similar to that of the district.

    (C) Separate but equal facilities were inherently unequal.

    (D) School busing could remedy the desegregation process.

    (E) Segregation was acceptable in theory but not in practice.

17. All of the following arguments are advantages of peer tutoring EXCEPT
    (A) tutors free the teacher to work with students having serious learning problems.
    (B) tutors and tutees develop appropriate social skills.
    (C) tutoring programs significantly improve the self-esteem of tutors and tutees.
    (D) tutors learn to care more deeply about other students' learning difficulties.
    (E) some tutees learn more from their tutors than the regular classroom teacher.

18. A teacher reinforces a student's approximations of a desired behavior until the actual behavior is demonstrated. According to behavioral theory, what type of reinforcement is this?
    (A) Extinction   (D) Shaping
    (B) The Premack principle   (E) Chaining
    (C) Generalization

19. Social learning theorist Albert Bandura would agree most strongly with which one of the following statements regarding learning?
    (A) Learning is the result of reinforcing conditions which maintain or increase behaviors conducive to it.
    (B) Learning occurs vicariously from observing others' successes and failures.
    (C) Learning occurs as students modify their existing schemas to fit new situations.
    (D) Learning is the ability to acquire, process, store, and retrieve information about the environment.
    (E) Learning is the pairing of a neutral stimulus with an unconditioned stimulus in order to produce a conditioned response.

20. John Scopes, a biology teacher from Dayton, Tennessee, challenged which of the following laws involving the rights of teachers?
    (A) A law prohibiting the teaching of evolution in public schools
    (B) The law which gave states the constitutional right to authorize corporal punishment
    (C) A law which reinstated a teacher's right to teach a variety of political views including Marxism
    (D) The law which denied teachers the right to strike
    (E) A law making teachers liable for student injuries occurring in the classroom

21. Which one of the following teaching models, derived from operant conditioning, was designed to allow students to work at their own pace?
    (A) Inquiry training   (D) Mastery learning
    (B) Direct instruction   (E) Discovery
    (C) Role playing

22. Maria Montessori would agree philosophically with which one of the following statements regarding preschool education?
    (A) Emphasis on structure and carefully planned activities may restrict a child's development.

(B)   Children who work independently in a planned environment may not adapt well to the traditional group instruction found in most public schools.

(C)   Teaching methodologies which benefit handicapped children are different from those benefiting the non-handicapped.

(D)   Educational curricula should emphasize practical skills, sensory stimulation, and academic preparation.

(E)   The development of social skills should be emphasized so children can cope in a competitive environment.

23.   Identify the two classroom activities which demonstrate the use of divergent thinking.

    I.   Students generate a variety of possible solutions to an environmental problem.

    II.   Students use an algorithm to solve word problems in mathematics involving fractions.

    III.   Students memorize specific dates regarding the war in Viet Nam.

    IV.   Students suggest hypotheses for the science experiment results.

    (A)   I and II   (D)   II and III

    (B)   I and III   (E)   II and IV

    (C)   I and IV

24.   Which one of the following measures of central tendency should be used when a set of test results includes an extremely low score?

    (A)   Arithmetic average   (D)   Most frequently reported score

    (B)   Mean   (E)   Mode

    (C)   Median

25.   Below are three different views regarding the relationship between thought (cognition) and language development. Identify each view with the individual who advocates it.

    I.   Language and cognition are parallel, thus independent, processes.

    II.   Language development is a product of cognitive development.

    III.   Initially, language and thought develop independently but, eventually, the two converge.

    (A)   I is Chomsky, II is Piaget, III is Vygotsky

    (B)   I is Skinner, II is Gesell, III is Erikson

    (C)   I is Cole, II is Wood, III is Weaver

    (D)   I is Kohlberg, II is Bandura, III is Gagne

    (E)   I is Brown, II is Lenneberg, III is McNeill

26.   Teachers who advocate mastery learning want their students' test result distributions to be

    (A)   positively skewed.   (D)   normal.

    (B)   negatively skewed.   (E)   bell-shaped.

    (C)   rectangular.

27. While a majority of individuals become teachers for altruistic reasons, they leave the profession because
    (A) they become apathetic about education in general.
    (B) they feel frustrated by the lack of cooperation received from administrators and parents.
    (C) of their poor relationships with students and colleagues.
    (D) it provides low financial rewards.
    (E) students are seldom able to live up to their expectations.

28. Student A, in her first month as a ninth grader, received a grade equivalent score of 10.2 for vocabulary, 10.6 for reading, 8.0 for spelling, and 11.0 for comprehension on the Stanford Achievement Test. From these results, student A's teacher can make which of the following conclusions?
    (A) Student A should be moved to a tenth grade English class.
    (B) Student A is poor at spelling but above average in reading, comprehension, and vocabulary.
    (C) Student A has the same raw score in vocabulary as the median student at the tenth grade, second month who took the same test.
    (D) Student A would receive the same set of scores on a similar achievement measure.
    (E) If student A retakes the same achievement test at the end of the year, she will most likely advance another grade level.

29. For the objective *Given the interest, interest rate, and time, the student will be able to compute the principal accurately*, the
    (A) condition is *be able to compute*.
    (B) criterion is *accurately*.
    (C) performance is *the student will be able to*.
    (D) standard is *given the interest, interest rate, and time*.
    (E) level of quality is *compute the principal*.

30. In 1647, Massachusetts passed the "Old Deluder Satan" Act. This law required
    (A) parents to teach their children to read the Bible.
    (B) colleges to establish teacher education programs.
    (C) communities of fifty (or more) families to hire a teacher.
    (D) children to attend school until age ten.
    (E) teachers to be licensed.

31. All of the following statements about Kounin's *withitness* are true EXCEPT:
    (A) a teacher's ability to convey that he or she is aware of classroom events is a necessary characteristic of effective management.
    (B) overlapping, movement management, maintaining group focus, and programming are characteristics of *withit* teachers.
    (C) *withit* teachers establish classroom routines early in the school year.

    (D)   successful or *withit* teachers have clearly defined expectations of students.

    (E)   the absence of *withit* characteristics guarantees ineffective management.

32.   Of the following functions, which would be considered the responsibility of the federal government toward education?

    I.   guarantee equal educational opportunities for all citizens

    II.   provide most of the financial support to local school districts

    III.   gather and interpret data on educational trends

    IV.   determine district curricula

    (A)   I and II   (D)   II and IV

    (B)   I and III   (E)   III and IV

    (C)   II and III

33.   While he hoped that teachers selected instructional materials and strategies because of students' needs and interests, Goodlad found instead that a vast majority made decisions based on their need to

    (A)   meet objectives through paper and pencil tests.

    (B)   adapt resources to their own teaching style.

    (C)   manage classroom behaviors.

    (D)   provide structure to the lesson presentation.

    (E)   cover specific content information.

34.   Those who support critical thinking as an important skill to acquire believe it

    (A)   is teachable.

    (B)   occurs naturally in an educational environment.

    (C)   is an innate quality.

    (D)   is best addressed outside of the classroom.

    (E)   takes the place of rote learning or memorization.

35.   An individualized education plan (IEP) includes all of the following pieces of information EXCEPT

    (A)   an analysis of the student's achievement level.

    (B)   a description of the services to be provided.

    (C)   a medical and psychological diagnosis.

    (D)   a list of short- and long-term goals.

    (E)   a schedule for checking the student's progress.

Section 2

TIME: 30 Minutes
35 Questions

DIRECTIONS: Each of the following questions and incomplete statements is followed by five answer choices. Select the choice which best answers each question.

1. Which two situations best demonstrate norm-referenced testing?

   I. Teacher A compares each student's essay with those written by the rest of the class.

   II. Teacher B gives a passing grade to students who can answer 12 of the 15 problems.

   III. Teacher C reports scores as standard deviations from the mean on a normal curve.

   IV. Teacher D assigns an "A" to all students who score above 92 percent correct on the exam.

   (A) I and II
   (B) I and III
   (C) II and III
   (D) II and IV
   (E) III and IV

2. Individualized or programmed instruction has been criticized for all of the following EXCEPT

   (A) it penalizes students who work rapidly.
   (B) it isolates students from each other.
   (C) the tasks tend to be familiar and monotonous.
   (D) it promotes surface-level understandings of concepts.
   (E) it focuses on extrinsic motivation.

3. Which of the following teacher statements most effectively demonstrates an I-message?

   (A) I think your behavior is immature and inappropriate for a ninth grader.
   (B) When I tell you to stop talking, I mean right now.
   (C) I will continue the lesson when all of you are quiet.
   (D) Your talking distracts me so much I can't think about my lecture.
   (E) I really like it when all of you are quiet so I can talk.

4. Advocates of specifically stated learning outcomes and performance (behavioral) objectives would be least likely to view teaching as a(n)

   (A) science.
   (B) technology.
   (C) art form.
   (D) learned skill.
   (E) profession.

5. According to Robert Mager (*Preparing Instructional Objectives*), a well written objective has three parts: 1) the expected behavior to be performed, 2) the condition(s) under which it is to be performed, and 3) the performance quality expected. Which one of the examples below best satisfies Mager's definition of an instructional objective?

    (A) Given a map of Europe, the student will know the capitals of at least 5 countries.

    (B) From memory, the student will be able to recite the first stanza of Longfellow's *Evangeline*.

    (C) With the use of references, the student will write an essay about drug abuse.

    (D) Given a list of nouns and verbs, the student will circle all of the nouns.

    (E) From a conversion chart, the student will understand how to change inches into centimeters without making any errors.

6. Below are four statements made by teachers I, II, III and IV after they unsuccessfully asked students to be quiet. Which statement or statements would be considered appropriate by those who practice Lee Canter's assertive discipline techniques?

    I.   I've asked you to stop talking, now I really mean it.

    II.   See this well-behaved student? I want the rest of you to act just like him.

    III. Students, you know the rules; because you were talking, which is not allowed when I am talking, you will be expected to be at detention after school today.

    IV.   If you don't stop talking, I'll come over to your house tonight and talk while you're on the phone with a friend.

    (A) I only.   (D) I and III

    (B) II only.   (E) II and IV

    (C) III only.

7. Which of the statements below best describes Public Law 94-142?

    (A) Bilingual instruction will be provided for those students whose primary language is something other than English.

    (B) Vocational education will be offered for students in rural areas where funds are insufficient.

    (C) All handicapped students will be mainstreamed into the regular classroom.

    (D) Extracurricular activities will include equal opportunities for males and females.

    (E) Educational experiences for all students will occur in the least restrictive environment.

8. From the descriptions below, choose the instructional technique which would most likely be advocated by behaviorist B.F. Skinner.

    (A) A discovery lesson where students are free to learn from their errors

    (B) An individualized lesson where information is presented in small, sequential steps

    (C) An expository lesson where students listen to the instructor's interpretation of the text

(D) An inductive lesson where students attempt to find a rule which applies to presented examples

(E) Any lesson presentation which uses positive reinforcement to strengthen the student's intrinsic desire to learn

9. The *Pygmalion Effect* is explained by which of the following examples?

(A) Labels given to a student through testing can influence the way a teacher thinks about him or her.

(B) A student will continually work to his or her potential regardless of teacher expectations or other classroom conditions.

(C) A teacher predicts that a student will do well in class and the prediction comes true.

(D) A student is able to accurately determine his or her potential prior to completing a task.

(E) All students are born with their potential for academic success already determined.

10. During a lecture given by Teacher A, a student begins to talk. Teacher A sternly asks the student to be quiet. As she proceeds with her lecture, she notices many students are no longer making eye contact with her. Instead they are looking down at their papers as if she had also reprimanded them. What classroom event is this scenario describing?

(A) Negative reinforcement (D) Momentum

(B) The ripple effect (E) Assertive discipline

(C) Overlapping

11. Benjamin Bloom's taxonomy of educational outcomes for the cognitive domain includes all of the following EXCEPT

(A) comprehension. (D) organization.

(B) evaluation. (E) synthesis.

(C) knowledge.

12. Which of the techniques below is least likely to be used during empathetic or active listening?

(A) Block out external noise and other distractions.

(B) Listen to verbal messages and watch for non-verbal clues.

(C) Distinguish between thinking and feeling messages.

(D) Identify with the speaker's feelings.

(E) Give advice which is appropriate to the problem.

13. A test is considered reliable if it

(A) yields consistent results over time and administrations.

(B) measures what it purports to measure.

(C) predicts future performances on a similar measure.

(D) adequately samples the instructional content.

(E) measures achievement or ability of some construct.

14. Those who believe that American schools should follow a "melting pot" perspective would

   (A) seek educational enculturation.

   (B) prefer multicultural and multilingual educational experiences.

   (C) want physically separate, yet equal, educational experiences for each race.

   (D) advocate using the metric system.

   (E) focus on cultural differences.

15. In reference to bilingual education, a "sink or swim" method of language learning is

   (A) based on the 1974 *Lau v. Nichols* decision where students who cannot speak English are provided instruction.

   (B) a relatively simple and successful approach for novice teachers to use.

   (C) unconstitutional according to the U.S. Supreme Court.

   (D) often used as the only approach available to non-English speaking students.

   (E) significantly effective, but only for those whose first language is Spanish.

16. Which of the following questions is answered by the test portion of the instructional decision-making process?

   (A) Why did my students learn what they did?

   (B) Will my students remember this information?

   (C) Can my students perform?

   (D) Is the material learned by my students important?

   (E) Is the instrument being used valid and reliable?

17. Read the following scenario and decide the level at which Jake is operating according to Kohlberg's theory of moral development.

   Jake is an average math student and so are his friends, Margaret and Bill. Before an upcoming weekly exam, Margaret and Bill steal a test copy from the teacher's desk. They ask Jake if he would like a copy too but Jake declines. The test is given and, the following day, returned to the students. Margaret and Bill performed so well they raised the curve. Jake, who had a "C" for 72 percent on the previous week's test, received a "D" for 74 percent on this one. Jake tells the teacher about Margaret and Bill stealing the test. He does so because he feels cheating violates school rules and is, therefore, wrong.

   (A) Punishment focused

   (B) Obedience oriented

   (C) Conventional

   (D) Ethical

   (E) Post conventional

18. A teacher uses a test to select gifted students for an advanced algebra class. What kind of evaluation is this?

   (A) Formative

   (B) Summative

   (C) Diagnostic

   (D) Placement

   (E) Standardized

19. According to Erikson, consciously organizing one's drives, beliefs, and abilities by making personal choices occurs during which of the following stages of development?

   (A)   Initiative vs. Guilt
   (D)   Intimacy vs. Isolation
   (B)   Industry vs. Inferiority
   (E)   Generativity vs. Stagnation
   (C)   Identity vs. Role Confusion

20. Which of the situations below is least likely to affect the validity of test results?

   (A)   A student knows the material but has difficulty reading the test items.
   (B)   The test directions for completing each section on the test are unclear.
   (C)   Many of the test items are poorly constructed.
   (D)   A student completes the test as quickly as possible.
   (E)   The test items are inappropriate for the outcomes being measured.

21. Identify the two arguments against the use of instructional objectives.

   I.   We can do a better job of teaching if we determine, in advance, what it is we expect our students to be able to do at the end of instruction.
   II.   We cannot assume that the outcomes of learning are always predictable, or always measurable.
   III.   Planning instruction by specifying and ordering prerequisite skills means that each subject must be analyzed according to the type of learning involved.
   IV.   Novel or creative performance outcomes are often appropriate and desirable.

   (A)   I and II
   (D)   II and III
   (B)   I and III
   (E)   II and IV
   (C)   I and IV

22. From the test items listed below, identify the one which best measures the objective *The student will be able to solve word problems using percent.*

   (A)   12 = __?__ of 80 (short answer)
   (B)   .02 = 20 percent (true or false)
   (C)   John correctly answered 8 of 12 questions on a test. What percent is this? (short answer)
   (D)   Sara ate 3/4 of a pie. How much is left? (short answer)
   (E)   Maria received a 90 percent on her test. Explain why this is a good score. (essay)

23. Non-directive teaching stems from which philosophy listed below?

   (A)   Idealism
   (D)   Pragmatism
   (B)   Humanism
   (E)   Epistemology
   (C)   Realism

24. An advance organizer, developed by David Ausubel, involves the use of

   (A)   an outline presented prior to instruction.
   (B)   simple examples, complex examples, and non-examples.

     (C)   extrinsic rewards to motivate students to achieve.

     (D)   statements which concurrently introduce and sum up the to-be-learned material.

     (E)   outside resources such as guest speakers, videos, and computer simulations.

25.   Which student is functioning at Piaget's concrete operational level?

     (A)   Student A understands laws of conservation and can classify and seriate.

     (B)   Student B can reason inductively.

     (C)   Student C can apply the scientific method to solve problems.

     (D)   Student D has developed concerns about social issues and personal identity.

     (E)   Student E can manipulate a number of variables at one time.

26.   Which of the definitions below best describes the term *evaluation*?

     (A)   An instrument or procedure designed to assess some sample of learned behavior

     (B)   Methods of instruction which follow general learning outcomes and specific performance objectives

     (C)   Assigning a numerical description to a sample of behaviors

     (D)   A systematic process of collecting, analyzing, and interpreting student achievement

     (E)   Test scores which are compared to a performance standard

27.   Increasing short-term memory duration and capacity would involve

     (A)   retrieval and reconstruction.

     (B)   interference and decay.

     (C)   organization and elaboration.

     (D)   rehearsal and chunking.

     (E)   productions and schemas.

28.   From the examples, choose the one which describes an *availability deficiency*.

     (A)   Student A cannot remember the word list because she does not know which one of her rehearsal strategies is appropriate for the situation.

     (B)   Student B cannot remember the list even though he uses a cumulative rehearsal strategy.

     (C)   Student C cannot remember the list because she lacks the ability to rehearse, even when prompted by the teacher.

     (D)   Student D finds a partial rehearsal strategy to be more helpful than a naming rehearsal strategy when he attempts to memorize the list.

     (E)   Student E has a variety of rehearsal strategies available to her.

29.   Which of the following terms have a relationship similar to the one between idealism and pragmatism?

     (A)   Existence and perceptions   (D)   Ontology and reality

     (B)   Knowledge and reality   (E)   Philosophy and education

     (C)   Thoughts and experiences

30. A realist would agree with which of the following statements?
    (A) Perceptions are misleading.
    (B) All knowledge is innate.
    (C) We live in a meaningless world.
    (D) Empirical observations form reality.
    (E) Reality is thought, not sensed.

31. Which of the following instructional strategies would appeal to a teacher who prefers to have students organize data, sense problems, hypothesize, and develop concepts?
    (A) Inquiry   (D) Direct instruction
    (B) Classroom meeting   (E) Role playing
    (C) Mastery learning

32. From the following group, choose one who would be least likely to approve of a student-centered curriculum.
    (A) A humanist   (D) A reconstructionist
    (B) An essentialist   (E) An existentialist
    (C) A progressivist

33. Knowing that the next number is 10 in the series 2, 4, 6, 8… represents what type of reasoning?
    (A) Conclusive   (D) Aesthetic
    (B) Deductive   (E) Inclusive
    (C) Inductive

34. Based on an idealistic philosophy, the purpose of education is to _____ the great ideas of the _____.
    (A) criticize—past   (D) focus on—future
    (B) explain—present   (E) verify—philosophers
    (C) preserve—culture

35. Reliability and validity refer to the
    (A) interpretation of the test results and not the test itself.
    (B) quality of the test items constructed.
    (C) outcomes and objectives being measured by the test.
    (D) trait (e.g., intelligence) being measured by the test.
    (E) appropriateness of the test for the students being tested.

Section 3

TIME: 30 Minutes
35 Questions

DIRECTIONS: Each of the followiing questions and incomplete statements is followed by five answer choices. Select the choice which best answers each question.

---

1. Teacher A suspects that one of her students is being neglected and abused. His arms are bruised, his appearance is disheveled, and his attitude is lethargic. Which of the following responses describes the most appropriate action for the teacher to take?

    (A)   Teacher A should continue to watch for signs of abuse over the next few weeks. If she notes a reoccurrence, she should tell the principal.

    (B)   Teacher A needs to confront the student's parents about her suspicions.

    (C)   Teacher A should counsel the student about his appearance and attitude.

    (D)   Teacher A must report her suspicions to the principal or counselor so that they can contact a social service agency.

    (E)   Teacher A does not have the right to interfere in students' family matters.

2. Which one of the following terms is synonymous with *engaged time*?

    (A)   Independent practice

    (B)   Fixed interval schedule

    (C)   Allocated time

    (D)   Time on task

    (E)   Variable ratio schedule

3. A principal at a high school conducts a search of a student's locker for drugs after the student is caught smoking marijuana on school grounds. Is the principal violating the student's Fourth Amendment rights to be secure against unreasonable searches and seizures?

    (A)   Yes. The Fourth Amendment protects all citizens against unreasonable searches.

    (B)   Yes. The principal must obtain a search warrant prior to locker inspection.

    (C)   Yes. The principal needs to call a law enforcement agency in order to conduct a locker search.

    (D)   No. The principal has the right to search lockers if doing so is related to the circumstances which initiated the search in the first place.

    (E)   No. Persons under the age of eighteen are not protected by the Fourth Amendment.

4. Which of the following strategies is/are appropriate for modifying instruction to fit individual needs?

    I.   Identify individual performance objectives for each student

II. Vary activities and materials to meet the needs of fast and slow learners

III. Adapt the reading level so it matches the student's ability

(A) II only. (D) II and III

(B) I and II (E) I, II, and III

(C) I and III

5. Identify the planning activity below which best describes *task analysis*.

(A) Teacher A describes what it is his students will be doing when they demonstrate accomplishment of a learning skill.

(B) Teacher B identifies learning in terms of general and specific goals to be met by his students.

(C) Teacher C creates interesting learning activities to demonstrate specific content terms she wants her students to know.

(D) Teacher D identifies the knowledge she wants her students to acquire, then organizes it into a hierarchy of skills and subskills.

(E) Teacher E describes each of the learning activities as cognitive, affective, or psychomotor.

6. What is one major problem with grading students on effort and improvement?

(A) It penalizes the best students because they improve the least.

(B) It is too objective for use in the average classroom.

(C) It signals to the poorer students that attempt is more important than accuracy.

(D) It increases hostility between poor students, average students, and good students.

(E) It requires teachers to use a dual marking system.

7. According to Robert Gagne, "Educational programs have the important ultimate purpose of teaching students to

(A) define concepts."

(B) memorize critical facts."

(C) solve problems."

(D) identify relationships."

(E) generalize beyond the information presented."

8. What type of heuristic (problem solving strategy) is being used by Student A in the following scenario?

Student A has to read a three hundred fifty page novel for her literature class. Because she has only one week to complete the novel, she feels overwhelmed by the task. She decides to break the assignment into seven sections of fifty pages each and reads one section per day. This, to her, is manageable.

(A) Analogical thinking (D) Algorithm

(B) Means-ends analysis (E) Imagery

(C) Functional fixedness

9. Which one of the following statements best describes an *open-ended question*?
   (A) Teacher A asks convergent questions.
   (B) Teacher B expects his students to complete the sentence *The Civil War ended on* _____.
   (C) Teacher C wants his students to ask questions during class discussions.
   (D) Teacher D questions her students, waits for a response, then provides feedback.
   (E) Teacher E tells her students to respond to the questions as they see fit. No answer will be judged as right or wrong.

10. Teacher A gives her students 10 minutes to study 25 unfamiliar spelling words, then she tests them. What is most wrong with Teacher A's approach?
   (A) Teacher A doesn't provide sufficient motivation for the students to learn the list.
   (B) Teacher A is extending the students' short-term memory capacity beyond its limits.
   (C) Teacher A doesn't provide adequate examples of the spelling words prior to the testing.
   (D) The task is simple rote, rather than meaningful, learning.
   (E) Teacher A does not use an advance organizer.

11. According to information processing theorists, the mind is analogous to a
   (A) computer.   (D) radio.
   (B) camera.   (E) video recorder.
   (C) television.

12. Kohlberg's theory of moral development has been criticized for being
   (A) too theoretical.
   (B) based on a small sample of subjects.
   (C) more appropriate for male moral development than female.
   (D) based on the development of his own children.
   (E) impossible to replicate.

13. Who would be (would have been) most likely to make the following statement?

   The focus of education should be on the child; where he or she is free to nurture innate abilities through contact with the environment.

   (A) John Locke   (D) Jean Jacques Rousseau
   (B) Mortimer Adler   (E) William C. Bagley
   (C) Robert Hutchins

14. A school district increases its educational requirements. All students must now have a "C" average in their academic coursework in order to graduate from high school. According to many leading educators, what is the major concern regarding the district's decision?
   (A) The district may see an increase in the drop-out rate.

(B)   Standardized test scores may decrease.

(C)   There will be an increase in non-academic subject enrollment.

(D)   Teachers will be forced to work harder.

(E)   There will be pressure from the community to lower the standards.

15.   Teacher A uses behavior modification to manage his students' behaviors. For example, he gives tokens which can be traded for "free time" to students who are quiet during a guided practice session in math. Teacher B does not believe that behavior modification is an effective method of classroom management. Which of the following statements might be made by Teacher B to argue against behavior modification?

(A)   It promotes extrinsic, rather than intrinsic, motivation.

(B)   It only works to reduce minor behavior disruptions.

(C)   It increases the amount of time students have to complete their assignments.

(D)   It uses rewards and punishments systematically.

(E)   It reduces self-esteem.

16.   Lesson planning can best be described as

(A)   stating performance outcomes and objectives.

(B)   reviewing necessary prerequisite skills.

(C)   organizing content and materials.

(D)   creating effective questions.

(E)   a sequence of educational events.

17.   John Dewey is noted for

I.   advocating progressive education.

II.   incorporating democratic practices into the educational process.

III.   formulating a theory of cognitive development.

IV.   initiating the kindergarten movement.

(A)   I and II   (D)   II and IV

(B)   I and III   (E)   III and IV

(C)   II and III

18.   What conclusions have been reached about learning styles research?

I.   There are too many inconsistencies in the research to make generalizations possible.

II.   Teachers should be sensitive to the idea that students do not all learn in the same way.

III.   There is enough evidence to support comprehensive curricular changes focusing on individual learning styles.

(A)   I only.   (D)   I and II

(B)   II only.   (E)   II and III

(C)   III only.

19. *Wait time* refers to

   (A) the time allowed for non-teaching activities.

   (B) the length of time a teacher waits for a student to respond to a question.

   (C) a "counting to ten" technique before over-reacting to a disruptive student.

   (D) the time a student has his or her hand in the air prior to a teacher response.

   (E) the interval between when an assignment is given and when it is received.

20. Students who have AIDS are legally classified as (a) _____ and are admitted to school (b) _____.

   (A) (a) homebound; (b) if other students are not present.

   (B) (a) handicapped; (b) when they are medically approved.

   (C) (a) a health risk; (b) under no circumstances.

   (D) (a) quarantined; (b) after 40 days of negative blood tests.

   (E) (a) normal; (b) unconditionally.

21. Which of the following activities is grounds for dismissal of tenured public school teachers?

   (A) Teaching evolution in science class

   (B) Refusing to volunteer for extracurricular activities

   (C) Challenging an administrative decision

   (D) Incompetency

   (E) Exercising academic freedom

22. A step-like pattern illustrates what would happen following which type of reinforcement schedule designed to increase hand-raising behaviors?

   (A) A teacher reinforces students every time they raise their hands.

   (B) A teacher reinforces students' hand raising after varied intervals of time.

   (C) A teacher randomly reinforces some students' hand-raising behavior, but not others.

   (D) A teacher reinforces students after every 5 episodes of hand-raising.

   (E) A teacher does nothing to encourage or prevent hand-raising behaviors.

23. Student A repeatedly interrupts her teacher's social studies lesson by asking irrelevant questions. When the teacher asks her why she is interrupting, the student replies, "Your lesson is boring!" According to Gordon (*Teacher Effectiveness Training*), who owns this "deviant student" problem?

   (A) The student   (D) The class

   (B) The teacher   (E) It is shared by the teacher and the class

   (C) It is shared by the teacher and student

24. All of the following test items are appropriate for Bloom's synthesis level of the cognitive domain EXCEPT:

   (A) You are to write an original composition which is analogous to the story read in class.

   (B) From your knowledge about areas of circles and volumes of cubes, find the volume of the cylinder.

(C)   Summarize the main points of the chapter on the water cycle.

(D)   Create a story about Tom Sawyer living in the 1990s.

(E)   Design a paper airplane using your knowledge of aerodynamics.

25.   Which of the following examples involving high school students is least like *tracking*?

(A)   Students are grouped according to their educational and vocational plans.

(B)   All students are required to complete the same academic requirements for graduation.

(C)   Students are allowed to choose two electives during their junior and senior years.

(D)   All students who receive at least a "B" in their freshman algebra course are able to take advanced algebra.

(E)   Students in one literature class receive instruction at a faster pace than students in a different section of the same class.

26.   Which one of the following correlation coefficients is strongest?

(A)   -.50   (D)   +.39

(B)   -.25   (E)   +.76

(C)   +.099

27.   Classical conditioning is to (a)_____ as operant conditioning is to (b)_____.

(A)   (a) rats; (b) dogs

(B)   (a) psychology; (b) physiology

(C)   (a) Pavlov; (b) Skinner

(D)   (a) continuous reinforcement; (b) intermittent reinforcement

(E)   (a) conditioned stimulus; (b) conditioned response

28.   The SQ3R (or PQ4R) method refers to which of the following?

(A)   Intellectual ability   (D)   Procedural knowledge

(B)   Problem solving   (E)   Computer programming

(C)   Effective reading skills

29.   Student A is considered by her teacher to be of normal intelligence. During the year, the teacher finds out that Student A scored between 105 and 109 on the Stanford-Binet Intelligence Scale. From these results, the teacher should do which of the following?

(A)   Request further testing in order to uncover possible learning disabilities.

(B)   Continue to believe that Student A is of normal intelligence.

(C)   Enroll Student A in a gifted program.

(D)   Discount the results as unreliable.

(E)   Correlate the test results with other measures of intelligence.

30.   Because the United States Constitution does not specifically mention education, the Tenth Amendment has been interpreted to mean that educational functions and responsibilities are reserved for

(A)   individual citizens.   (D)   institutions of higher education.

(B)   business.   (E)   local school teachers.

(C)   states.

31.   Because of the Soviet Union's Sputnik, the U.S. educational curricula focus of the late 1950s shifted to

      (A)   foreign language learning.   (D)   communications.

      (B)   science and mathematics.   (E)   humanism and global understanding.

      (C)   national defense.

32.   Which of the following arguments best supports the *middle school* concept?

      (A)   Middle schools have overwhelming support of parents.

      (B)   There is less financial stress than with the traditional elementary, junior high, and high school arrangement.

      (C)   Middle schools help to alleviate overcrowding at the secondary level.

      (D)   Middle schools provide a smooth transition from childhood to adolescence.

      (E)   It promotes a healthy climate for youth.

33.   All of the following issues would be supported by teacher organizations (for example, the National Education Association or the American Federation of Teachers) EXCEPT:

      (A)   collective bargaining.   (D)   increased teachers' salaries.

      (B)   tenure.   (E)   teacher empowerment.

      (C)   alternative licensing.

34.   The Educational Consolidation and Improvement Act (Chapter 1) was designed to

      (A)   promote desegregation.

      (B)   enhance multicultural programs.

      (C)   assist the disadvantaged.

      (D)   initiate Head Start.

      (E)   incorporate small districts into larger ones.

35.   Student A's parents wish to see her personal school records. Can they?

      (A)   No. School records are the private property of the school district.

      (B)   Yes. They can see the records with written permission from school officials.

      (C)   Yes. They can see the records but only if they agree to meet with someone who is qualified to interpret the test data.

      (D)   Yes. If they have a specific reason for wanting to see the records, they may do so.

      (E)   Yes. They can see the records, unconditionally.

TEST OF PROFESSIONAL KNOWLEDGE

ANSWER KEY

SECTION 1

1.	(D)	10.	(B)	19.	(B)	28.	(C)
2.	(A)	11.	(D)	20.	(A)	29.	(B)
3.	(A)	12.	(D)	21.	(D)	30.	(C)
4.	(C)	13.	(E)	22.	(D)	31.	(E)
5.	(B)	14.	(B)	23.	(C)	32.	(B)
6.	(D)	15.	(A)	24.	(C)	33.	(E)
7.	(A)	16.	(C)	25.	(A)	34.	(A)
8.	(C)	17.	(C)	26.	(B)	35.	(C)
9.	(B)	18.	(D)	27.	(D)		

SECTION 2

1.	(B)	10.	(B)	19.	(C)	28.	(C)
2.	(A)	11.	(D)	20.	(D)	29.	(C)
3.	(D)	12.	(E)	21.	(E)	30.	(D)
4.	(C)	13.	(A)	22.	(C)	31.	(A)
5.	(D)	14.	(A)	23.	(B)	32.	(B)
6.	(C)	15.	(D)	24.	(D)	33.	(C)
7.	(E)	16.	(C)	25.	(A)	34.	(C)
8.	(B)	17.	(C)	26.	(D)	35.	(A)
9.	(A)	18.	(D)	27.	(D)		

SECTION 3

1.	(D)	10.	(B)	19.	(B)	28.	(C)
2.	(D)	11.	(A)	20.	(B)	29.	(B)
3.	(D)	12.	(C)	21.	(D)	30.	(C)
4.	(E)	13.	(D)	22.	(D)	31.	(B)
5.	(D)	14.	(A)	23.	(B)	32.	(D)
6.	(A)	15.	(A)	24.	(C)	33.	(C)
7.	(C)	16.	(E)	25.	(B)	34.	(C)
8.	(B)	17.	(A)	26.	(E)	35.	(E)
9.	(E)	18.	(D)	27.	(C)		

DETAILED EXPLANATIONS OF ANSWERS
NTE CORE BATTERY–Test 2

TEST OF PROFESSIONAL KNOWLEDGE
Section 1

1.   **(D)**   The correct response is (D), III and IV. The question asks for examples of arguments which support cooperative learning as an effective method of instruction. Statement I does not support cooperative learning and, in fact, argues against it. Cooperation between group members, not competition, is essential for successful learning groups. Statement II supports one of the "pitfalls" of cooperative learning; that is, if cooperative learning groups are not properly facilitated, an academic achiever might attempt to carry or cover for an academic underachiever's learning experience. This is counterproductive to cooperative learning where the success of each individual benefits the group. Statement III is a supportive argument, thus, a correct response. Each member of the cooperative learning group must do his or her part (i.e., learn) so that the group can be successful. Statement IV is a supportive argument and a second correct response. Cooperative learning groups give students a reason to support and reward each other for achieving because each individual's success is also dependent upon the success of other group members.

2.   **(A)**   The correct response is (A), the teacher's behavior served as a positive reinforcer for the student. This question is on decision-making, encouraging appropriate behavior, and managing the classroom. The question asks for the best explanation for the scenario demonstrating Skinner's principles of reinforcement. Because any stimulus which increases a behavior (as is the case with the student's outbursts) is a reinforcer, only responses (A) and (B) can be considered possibilities. Any stimulus which is added (the reprimand) and increases the targeted behavior (the outburst) is a positive reinforcer. The definition fits the situation described so choice (A) is correct. Any aversive stimulus which is removed (needed for negative reinforcement but not the case here) and increases the targeted behavior (the outbursts) is a negative reinforcer. Thus, choice (B) is incorrect. A presentation punishment decreases a behavior by adding an aversive stimulus. While it seems that an aversive stimulus was added (a verbal reprimand by the teacher), the behavior did not decrease, so choice (C) is incorrect. A removal punishment decreases a behavior by removing an aversive stimulus. Again, the teacher's reprimand did not decrease the student's behavior. Thus, choice (D) is incorrect. Extinction occurs when no stimulus is added or removed and the behavior stops (neither case is true for this scenario), so choice (E) is incorrect.

3.   **(A)**   The correct response is (A), a student is able to explain why the amount of water poured from a short, wide beaker into a tall, narrow beaker remains constant. This question is on extraclassroom influences on students (development). The question asks about Piaget's

concept of conservation; the idea that certain properties (e.g., amount) remain the same even when other properties change (e.g., height, width), so response (A) is correct. This is an example of conservation. The student is able to explain why the amount of water remains the same even though the height and width of the beaker changes. Response (B) is incorrect because it is an example of reversibility; the ability to think backwards through a cognitive operation. Response (C) is incorrect as this is an example of accommodation; altering a cognitive structure in order to take in new information. Response (D) is incorrect since this is an example of seriation; the ability to arrange items sequentially (in this case, from shortest to tallest). Choice (E) is incorrect because instead of demonstrating conservation, it is an example of equilibration.

4.   **(C)**   The correct response is (C), the student scored higher than 75 percent of those who took the test. This question is on evaluating student performance (interpreting data). The question asks for a distinction between a norm-referenced measurement (percentile) and a criterion-referenced measurement (percent). Seventy-five percent, a criterion-referenced measure, shows the percent of items answered correctly and not the individual's standing among all the test takers (which is what the question asks). Thus choice (A) is incorrect. The question being asked does not indicate the number of test items on the measure of academic achievement, therefore, it would be impossible to know the number of accurate or inaccurate responses given by the student. Thus, choice (B) is incorrect. Choice (C) is correct because a percentile is a norm-referenced measure which indicates an individual's score in relationship to all other scores. The individual scored higher than 75 percent of those who took the test. The question does not indicate how many or which outcomes and objectives (if any) were measured, so choice (D) is incorrect. While the response is a norm- referenced measure using percentile and, technically, the student did do better than at least 25 percent of those taking the test, but the question asks for the best interpretation of the test results. Response (C) is a more accurate representation of the results than response (E).

5.   **(B)**   The correct response is (B), the student has the right to be exempted from reciting the pledge. This question is on students' constitutional rights. The question asks about students' and parents' rights regarding the recitation of the pledge of allegiance. According to a West Virginia court ruling (*West Virginia State Board of Education v. Barnette*, 1943), no one can force citizens to confess their faith to the country. Choice (A) is incorrect because the response contradicts the court's ruling that citizens cannot be made to confess their faith to the country. Schools cannot legally enforce a suspension ruling in this case, so choice (B) is correct. According to the West Virginia court ruling, students and parents can object to the recitation of the pledge based on religious beliefs. Choice (C) is incorrect, because as with response (A), the school cannot require that a student stand at attention while refusing to recite the pledge. A federal appeals court decided that students could refuse to recite the pledge, even in defiance of a state law instructing them to do so. Thus, choice (D) is incorrect. Choice (E) is incorrect because refusing to recite the pledge is not illegal.

6.   **(D)**   The correct response is (D). Teachers do not have the right to strike except when state statutes specifically permit it. This question is on teacher ethics (teachers' rights and responsibilities). This question asks if teachers have the right to strike. Responses (A), (B) and (E) can be eliminated because it is illegal for teachers to strike except when state statutes permit it. The Supreme Court of Connecticut (*Norwalk Teachers' Association v. the Board of Education*, 1951) and the Supreme Court of New Hampshire (*City of Manchester v.*

Manchester Teachers' Guild, 1957) ruled that teachers, as public employees, do not have the right to strike. The Supreme Court of Minnesota (*Board of Education of City of Minneapolis v. Public School Employee Union*, 1951) ruled that public employees do have the right to strike unless a state statute, ordinance, or rule makes it illegal. Minnesota quickly passed an antistrike law. Seven states have statutes permitting strikes. Thus, response (C) is incorrect. while more than twenty have statutes prohibiting them. The U.S. Supreme Court ruled that boards of education can discharge illegally striking teachers.

7.   **(A)**   The correct response is (A), content-related. This question is on evaluating student performance (developing and using assessment instruments). The question asks for the type of validity evidence which measures outcomes and objectives, Response (A) is correct because content validity evidence compares the test tasks to the instructional domain. Response (B) is incorrect since construct-related evidence demonstrates how well a test measures some characteristic or quality such as intelligence. Response (C) is incorrect because criterion-related evidence demonstrates how well a test can predict future performances or how well a test estimates performance on some other measure. Response (D) is similar to response (C). It focuses on prediction of future performance. Response (E) is also similar to response (C). Concurrent validity evidence is an estimate of how well a test can predict performance on some similar measure.

8.   **(C)**   The correct response is (C), the way teachers are educated. This question is on teacher ethics (demonstrating knowledge of the teaching profession). Response (A) is incorrect because The Holmes Group and Carnegie Report do not address curricular changes. Response (B) is incorrect for the same reason as (A). The groups do not address minimum competency testing. Response (C) is correct since both reports focus on teacher education reform. While response (D) is mentioned in the Carnegie Report, it is done so in such a way as to use technology as an incentive to attract bright, talented teachers and not as the basis for reform, so response (D) is incorrect. Response (E) is incorrect because while both reports suggest that teachers should be paid well for their expertise, neither targets science and math teachers as sole recipients of salary increases.

9.   **(B)**   The correct response is (B), all have been upheld except school districts being sued. This question is on students' constitutional rights. Response (A) is incorrect because the *Goss v. Lopez* (1975) decision stated that students could not be suspended without a hearing. Response (B) is correct since during the *Wood v. Strickland* (1975) case, the court ruled that students could sue individual school board members, but not school districts. Response (C) is incorrect because in 1982, the U.S. Supreme Court ruled that students could challenge the removal of books from the school library under certain circumstances (*Board of Education, Inland Trees Union Free School District No. 26 v. Pico*). Response (D) is incorrect due to the fact that the *Plyler v. Doe* (1982) decision gave children of illegal aliens the right to a free public education. Response (E) is incorrect because the U.S. Supreme Court ruled "in absence of a specific showing of constitutionally valid reasons to regulate their speech, students are entitled to freedom of expression."

10.   **(B)**   The correct response is (B), II and III. This question is on extraclassroom influences on students. The question asks for an identification of the students who are operating from an external locus of control. According to attribution theory, these individuals explain their behavior in relationship to outside people and forces. Response (A) is incorrect because only Student B is explaining his/her actions as controlled by outside forces. Student

A is saying that he/she is responsible for the grade received; an internal locus of control. Response (B) is correct because Student B and Student C are attributing their grade to external forces (the teacher and the length of the test). Response (C) is incorrect because Student D is taking responsibility for the grade received but not Student C. Responses (D) and (E) are incorrect because they include Students A and D who are functioning from an internal locus of control.

11. **(D)**   The correct response is (D), verbal information, intellectual skills, cognitive strategies, motor skills, attitudes. This question is on planning (writing objectives and gathering relevant information). The question asks for Gagne's taxonomy of learning outcomes. He proposes that there are a variety of learned capabilities: 1) verbal information which includes knowledge of facts; 2) intellectual skills which include knowledge of concepts and rules; 3) cognitive strategies which are capabilities governing learning and remembering; 4) motor skills or physical capabilities; and 5) attitudes which are positive or negative reactions to persons, things, or situations. Response (A) is incorrect. While awareness, knowledge, and application can be seen as a taxonomy of sorts, it is not Gagne's categorization for learning outcomes. Response (B), theory and practice, is not a taxonomy and is not addressed by Gagne as a way to organize types of knowledge. Response (C) is incorrect because it addresses Bloom's taxonomy or domain of learning, not Gagne's. Response (D) is correct as addressed above. Response (E) is incorrect. The three terms, the learner, the teacher, and the classroom, do not make up a taxonomy. They do not describe types of learning outcomes either (the classroom, for example, is not a type of knowledge).

12. **(D)**   The correct response is (D), society, learners, and knowledge. This question is on planning (gathering relevant information and identifying resources). The question asks for the major sources of curricular decisions. According to Saylor, Alexander, and Lewis (*Curriculum Planning*), there have been three major influences. One hundred years ago, the emphasis was on knowledge. By the turn of the century, there was an increasing emphasis on the learner, in part because of G. Stanley Hall and John Dewey. During the depression, there was an emphasis on preparing individuals to live in society. The '30s and '40s reemphasized the role of the learner. During the '50s and '60s, there was a return to a knowledge emphasis. The '70s and '80s focused on society. Now, in the '90s, we are seeing a shift toward knowledge; specifically science and math. Response (D) is the only one which appropriately answers the question.

13. **(E)**   The correct response is (E), a discrepancy between achievement and intellectual ability. This question is on extraclassroom influences on children (development). The question asks for the best definition of the term *learning disability*. While responses (A), (B), (C), and (D) are possible characteristics of a learning disabled student, response (E) involves one characteristic which appears to be consistently agreed upon by experts.

14. **(B)**   The correct response is (B), IV, V, I, III, II. The question is on methods of instruction and selecting instructional strategies. The question asks about the correct sequence for presenting new concepts to students. The correct order is: 1) name the concept and give its definition, 2) describe relevant attributes of the concepts (i.e., describe its properties), 3) give prototypical examples of the concept, 4) give less obvious examples, and, finally, 5) give non-examples to prevent overgeneralization. Response (B) demonstrates the appropriate order.

15. **(A)** The correct response is (A), knowledge. This question is on planning (writing instructional objectives). The question asks for an identification of Bloom's outcome of learning which matches the performance stated in the objective. Response (A) is correct. The knowledge category of the cognitive domain is defined as remembering previously learned material. Reciting the Preamble would be remembering previously learned material, so response (A) is correct. Comprehension requires the learner to grasp the meaning of the material. Simple recitation does not require comprehension. Thus, response (B) is incorrect. Response (C) is incorrect because application is the ability to transfer the knowledge learned to novel situations. This is not called for in the objective. Response (D) is incorrect because analysis requires the breaking down and examination of parts of learned materials in order to understand the structure. Evaluating learned materials involves making judgments about the value of the material learned. The objective does not require the learner to make judgments, so response (E) is incorrect.

16. **(C)** The correct response is (C), separate but equal facilities were inherently unequal. This question is on students' constitutional rights. The question asks for the justification behind the Supreme Court ruling against segregated schools. On May 17, 1954, the Court ruled that a separate but equal doctrine had no place in education. The Court stated: *Does segregation of children in public schools solely on the basis of race, even though the physical facilities and other tangible factors may be equal, deprive the children of the minority group of equal educational opportunities? We believe that it does.* Response (A) is incorrect because money was not a factor in the ruling. Response (B) is incorrect because the Court further ruled: *The Constitutional command to desegregate schools does not mean that every school in every community must always reflect the racial composition of the school system as a whole.* Response (C) is correct because it reflects the statement made by the Supreme Court at the time of the decision. Response D is incorrect. Busing was not an issue in 1954, although it was eventually used as a means to comply with the ruling. Response (E) is incorrect because segregation was not accepted by the Supreme Court, in theory or practice.

17. **(C)** The correct response is (C), tutoring programs do not significantly improve self-esteem. This question is on methods of instruction. According to Good and Brophy (*Looking in Classrooms*), advantages of peer tutoring include: 1) tutors free the teacher to work with students having serious learning problems, so response (A) is incorrect. 2) tutors and tutees develop interpersonal skills so response (B) is not the exception. 3) tutors learn to care more deeply about the learning of others, so response (D) is incorrect and 4) some tutees learn more from a tutor than the teacher, so response (E) is incorrect. Response (C) is correct because it was found through a review of research literature (Cohen, Kulik, and Kulik, 1982; *American Educational Research Journal*) that tutoring programs were insignificant in improving tutors' or tutees' self-esteem.

18. **(D)** The correct response is (D), shaping. This question is on decision-making (encouraging appropriate behavior). The question asks for the term which fits the definition of using small steps combined with reinforcing feedback to help students learn appropriate behaviors. Response (A) is incorrect because extinction is eliminating a behavior by removing reinforcers. This does not fit the situation described. Response (B) is incorrect because the Premack principle refers to the use of a desired activity to help reinforce less desired activities. Again, this does not fit the situation. Response (C) is incorrect since generalization is a "spreading" of responses from the conditioned one to similar unconditioned ones. Response (D) is correct because shaping is a procedure where close approximations of

a behavior are reinforced. Response (E) is incorrect since chaining is linking two or more learned behaviors together.

19. **(B)** The correct response is (B), learning occurs vicariously. This question is on extraclassroom influences on students (development). Response (A), which describes operant conditioning rather than social learning, is incorrect. Response (B) is correct because Bandura, while he accepts many principles of behavioral learning theory, argues that vicariously experiencing the consequences for appropriate and inappropriate behaviors is directly linked to learning—something largely ignored by behaviorists. Response (C) is incorrect since it is describing Piaget's notion of learning through the process of accommodation. Response (D) is incorrect because it is addressing learning from an information-processing view. Response (E) is incorrect because it describes classical conditioning rather than Bandura's social learning theory.

20. **(A)** The correct response is (A), a law prohibiting the teaching of evolution. This question is on teacher ethics (knowing teachers' rights and responsibilities). The question asks about John Scopes' role in challenging a law involving teachers' rights. The law he challenged was passed in Tennessee in 1925. It banned the teaching of evolutionary theory in the classroom. The famous Scopes Monkey Trial resulted. Scopes lost the case and was charged with teaching evolution in his classes but the trial did bring national attention to the issue regarding a teacher's right to teach conflicting points of view. Eventually, the Supreme Court ruled that the ban on teaching evolution violated teachers' and students' rights and allowed for certain religious views to determine the curriculum. This was found to be a violation of the First Amendment (separation of church and state).

21. **(D)** The correct response is (D), mastery learning. This question is on methods of instruction. The question asks for the teaching model which is designed in such a way that students work at their own pace. Response (A) is incorrect because inquiry training is designed to teach students a process for investigating and explaining phenomena (e.g., scientific method). Response (B) is incorrect because direct instruction, while behaviorally oriented, is designed to transform learning tasks into subtasks which are taught separately. Response (C) is incorrect since role playing is designed to help students explore human relations through group interaction. Response (D) is correct because mastery learning is designed as individually paced instruction. Response (E) is incorrect since discovery learning is designed so that students develop hypotheses from available data.

22. **(D)** The correct response is (D), the curriculum should emphasize practical skills, sensory stimulation, and academic preparation. This question is on methods of instruction as well as on extraclassroom influences on students (development). The question asks for the basic philosophical belief held by Montessori regarding preschool education. Montessori focused on structured programs and carefully chosen teaching methodologies. Response (A) is incorrect because the statement, then, is an argument against Montessori's beliefs. Response (B) is also an argument against Montessori education. Response (C) is incorrect because Montessori began her educational career as a physician working with handicapped children. She believed her success with these children could be generalized to non-handicapped children. Response (D) is correct since the Montessori curriculum included three types of experiences; practical, sensory, and academic preparation. Response (E) is incorrect. A major criticism regarding Montessori is her emphasis on self-pacing and independence at the expense of socialization.

23. **(C)**   The correct response is (C), I and IV. This question is on methods of instruction. The question asks for examples of divergent thinking; a type of thought process where several creative or unusual solutions are given to any one problem. Responses I and IV [response (C)] demonstrate divergent thinking. Students are asked to consider a variety of possible solutions to a problem. Choices II and III [included in responses (A), (B), (D), and (E)] are examples of convergent thinking; a type of thought process which results in a single, conventional solution.

24. **(C)**   The correct response is (C), the median. This question is on evaluating student performance (interpret data). The question asks for the measure of central tendency which is best when test results include an extreme score. Response (A) is incorrect because the arithmetic average, which is the same as Response (B), the mean, takes into account the value of each score, so an extremely high or low score will influence it. Response (C) is correct because the median, or counting average, is the mid-score, so extremely high or low scores will not affect its value. Responses (D) and (E) represent the most popular score, the mode. It is the least reliable measure and, therefore, inappropriate for computing the average score.

25. **(A)**   The correct response is (A), Chomsky, Piaget, and Vygotsky. The question is on extraclassroom influences on students (development). The question asks for the theorists who advocate three theories of language and cognitive development. The first point of view, that language and cognition are independent, parallel processes, is advocated by Noam Chomsky. The second point of view, that language development is a direct result of cognitive development, is held by Jean Piaget. The third point of view, that language and cognition initially develop separately but later converge, is held by Lev Vygotsky. Thus, Response (A) is correct.

26. **(B)**   The correct response is (B), negatively skewed. This question is on evaluating student performances. Response (A) is incorrect because a positively skewed distribution would mean that many more students received low test scores than high test scores. Teaching for mastery test results should be the opposite—where most scores pile up at the high end of the distribution—as with a negatively skewed curve [response (B)]. Response (C) is incorrect because a rectangular distribution would not demonstrate mastery. Response (D) and (E) are the same. Both are incorrect because, with a normal or bell-shaped distribution, a majority of scores fall in the middle. This does not represent mastery of the material.

27. **(D)**   The correct response is (D), it provides low financial rewards. This question is on teacher ethics (demonstrate knowledge of the teaching profession). The question asks why teachers leave the profession. Surveys of exiting teachers show that teachers most often leave for financial reasons. Response (D) addresses this. The other responses. (A), (B), (C) and (E) may be true for individual cases, but none is the major reason for leaving the profession.

28. **(C)**   The correct response is (C), student A has the same raw score as the median student who is in the tenth grade at the second month. This question is on evaluating student performance (interpreting test data). The question asks for an interpretation of test data from a standardized test. Response (A) is incorrect because the test results are not to be interpreted as an indication of where the student should be placed. Response (B) is incorrect since test results are not to be interpreted as "what should be." A norm is simply an average score made by the student taking the test. Fifty percent of the students will be above this, fifty percent will be below. Response (C) is correct because the test data are to be interpreted as raw scores in

which fifty percent of those taking the test fall below and fifty percent fall above. Response (D) is incorrect since it cannot be assumed that scores on different measures are comparable. Response (E) is incorrect because a teacher cannot expect all students to gain a full grade equivalent each year.

29. **(B)** The correct response is (B), the criterion is *accurately*. This question is on planning and writing instructional objectives. According to Robert Mager, an objective has three characteristics: the performance (what the student is able to do), the condition or conditions (the circumstance under which the performance is to occur), and the criterion (quality expected for the performance). Response (A) is incorrect because the condition would be *given the interest, interest rate, and time*. Response (B) is correct since the criterion or expected level of performance is *accurately*. Response (C) is incorrect because the performance is *be able to compute*. Response (D) is incorrect because the standard is the same as the criterion. Response (E) is incorrect because the level of quality is the same as the criterion.

30. **(C)** The correct response is (C), communities of fifty (or more) families to hire a teacher. This question is on teacher ethics (demonstrate knowledge of the teaching profession). The question asks for the purpose of the "Old Deluder Satan" Act of 1647. This act required every town of fifty or more families to hire a reading and writing teacher. The act was designed to outwit Satan because the Puritans believed ignorance led to sin. Response (C) addresses this issue best.

31. **(E)** The correct response is (E), the absence of *withitness* guarantees ineffective management. This question is on decision making. The question asks for the statement which is false regarding Kounin's *withitness*. All response statements (A), (B), (C) and (D) describe *withitness* accurately except (E) which suggests it is a necessary prerequisite to effective management. While it can be said that *withit* teachers are effective managers, it cannot, at the same time, be said the non-*withit* teachers are ineffective.

32. **(B)** The correct response is (B), I and III. This question is on students' constitutional rights (local/state/federal policies and laws). The federal government's role in education has traditionally been to ensure equal educational opportunities for all students and to gather accurate and reliable information about education and make it available to the American people. Financial support has increased during the past decades, but the main financial support for schools remains at the state or local level. This is also true for curricular decisions. Response (B) correctly states this.

33. **(E)** The correct response is (E), cover specific content. This question is on planning. The question asks about Goodlad's findings when he researched teacher decision-making processes regarding instruction. Goodlad (*Behind the Classroom Door*) observed 150 classrooms in 67 schools and found very little evidence for teacher planning which went beyond "the coverage of topics selected largely from courses of study and textbooks" (p. 78). Response (E) addresses this.

34. **(A)** The correct response is (A), is teachable. This question is on methods of instruction. The question asks about the beliefs of those who advocate critical thinking as an important educational skill. Response (A) is correct because these teachers believe that critical thinking is teachable, therefore, they incorporate activities into their lessons which

promote this type of thinking. Response (B) is incorrect since critical thinking does not necessarily occur naturally or innately (as response (C) suggests). Response (D) is incorrect because these teachers would not agree that critical thinking is best addressed outside of the classroom. Instead, it is to be incorporated into a variety of settings. Response (E) is incorrect because critical thinking is not to take the place of role learning but, rather, parallel it.

35. **(C)** The correct response is (C), a medical and psychological diagnosis. This question is on extraclassroom influences (school policies). The question asks about the type of information found on an individualized education plan. All of the information included in the response choices (A), (B), (D) and (E) is to be included except a medical or psychological diagnosis of the learning problem. These are not always necessary when identifying a student's needs.

Section 2

1. **(B)** The correct response to question 1 is (B), situations I and III demonstrate norm-referenced testing. This question is regarding the evaluation of student performance. The question asks about norm-referenced testing; a procedure where an individual's performance is described in terms of its relative position in a group. Teacher A and Teacher C are using norm-referenced testing because they are comparing an individual score or grade with that of the group. Teacher B and Teacher D are using criterion-referenced testing which compares an individual's performance against some standard (e.g., number or percent of items correct).

2. **(A)** The correct response to question 2 is (A), individualized instruction does not penalize students who work rapidly. This question is on selecting appropriate methods of instruction. The question asks about advantages and disadvantages of programmed or individualized instruction. Response (A) is correct because programmed instruction allows for students to work at their own rate, whether slowly or rapidly, it does not penalize fast workers. This is not a criticism of programmed instruction, rather, it is a strength. Responses (B), (C), (D), and (E) are incorrect because programmed instruction has been criticized for isolating students (they work independently), for using familiar and monotonous tasks (often a short paragraph is read and a few questions are answered, then the procedure is repeated), for promoting surface-level understanding of concepts (the focus is most often on rote learning), and for focusing on extrinsic motivators (the learner is allowed to continue only when questions are answered correctly) .

3. **(D)** The correct response to question 3 is (D), explaining how someone's behavior is affecting you is an *I-message*. This question is on decision-making (encouraging appropriate behavior and communicating expectations). The question is about *I-messages* which are clear, non-threatening statements describing how you are affected by someone's behavior. It is considered an approach which allows individuals to choose, for themselves, whether or not they will change inappropriate behaviors. Response (A) is not an *I-message*. It is clearly threatening and it focuses on the inappropriate behavior rather than how the behavior is affecting the individual making the statement. Response (B) is also threatening, focusing on what the speaker wants and not how he or she feels. Response (C), again, does not tell how the speaker feels about the inappropriate behavior. Response (D) is correct

because the speaker tells those who are misbehaving how the behavior affects him or her; it is distracting. The last response (E), while stated more positively, only says how the speaker would feel if the behavior exhibited were different.

4.   **(C)**   The correct response to question 4 is (C), advocates of specific objectives and outcomes are least likely to view teaching as an art form. This question is on planning. How one views the role of a teacher may determine whether or not specific objectives and outcomes will be part of the planning repertoire. Individuals who heartily advocate the use of specific objectives and outcomes (e.g., Mager) view teaching as a science or technology. Having a "plan of action" which states where you are going is the only way you will get there. Knowing how to write specific objectives (a learned skill) allows you to map your course. Because of the above statements, responses (A), (B), and (D) are incorrect. Response (C), an art form, is correct because it focuses on teaching as a creative and spontaneous endeavor. Individuals who see teaching as an art form feel that planning specific outcomes might inhibit creative learning (sticking to the plan is sometimes viewed as more important by science and technology people than spontaneous teaching and learning). Response (E) is incorrect because regarding teaching as a profession is unrelated to the above arguments. One can see teaching as a science or technology and a profession and one can see teaching as an art form and a profession.

5.   **(D)**   The correct response to question 5 is (D), given a list of nouns and verbs, the student will circle all of the nouns. This question is on planning. Instructional objectives, according to Mager, include an observable/measurable performance, a condition, and a criterion. Response (A) is incorrect because it is not an objective. To "know" the capitals of at least 5 countries is not a measurable performance. Response (B) is incorrect, although it is an acceptable objective. The question, however, asks for the response which best satisfies the definition. Response (B) has a performance (recite) and a condition (from memory) but it does not state any criteria about how well the student is to perform (e.g., Is the student to recite without errors?). Response (C) is similar to Response (B). The statement includes a performance (write) and a condition (with references) but no criteria about how well the student is to perform. Response (D) is correct because it includes a performance (circle), a condition (given a list), and a criterion (all). Response (E) is incorrect because "understanding" is not measurable.

6.   **(C)**   The correct response to question 6 is (C), III only. This question is on decision-making (communicating expectations and managing the classroom). Assertive discipline is a classroom management approach which focuses on the teacher's right to teach and the students' right to learn. With this approach, rules are explicitly stated as are the consequences which occur when the rules are not followed. Response (A) is incorrect because the statement does not include a follow-through on the consequences. "Now I really mean it" is a vague, meaningless statement. Response (B) is incorrect since a statement which makes an example of a well-behaved student is not a technique used with assertive discipline. Again, it does not focus on the inappropriate behavior nor the consequences for it. Response (C) is correct because the statement includes both the inappropriate behavior and its consequence; a technique advocated by Canter. Response (D) is incorrect because of Statement I which is not correct. Response (E) is incorrect because both statements II and IV are incorrect.

7.   **(E)**   The correct response to question 7 is (E), educational experiences for all students

will occur in the least restrictive environment. The question is on students' constitutional rights. PL 94-142 is the Education for All Handicapped Children Act which was passed in 1975. It supports the student's right to be placed in the regular classroom, if appropriate, and if not, be given special assistance elsewhere at public expense. Response (A) is incorrect because it deals with bilingual education and not handicapped children. Response (B), about vocational education, is incorrect because it does not deal with the handicapped. While Response (C) is about handicapped children, PL 94-142 does not require all students to be mainstreamed, only those for whom the situation is appropriate. Response (D) is about extracurricular activities and not handicapped children. Response (E) is correct because it suggests that handicapped children be placed in the least restrictive environment, which may or may not include mainstreaming.

8. **(B)** The correct response to question 8 is (B), an individualized lesson where information is presented in small, sequential steps. The question is on methods of instruction (selecting instructional strategies). B.F. Skinner advocated the use of individualized or programmed instruction and is, in fact, the primary person behind "teaching machines." Response (A) is inappropriate from Skinner's perspective because it allows students to make errors. This may create strong associations between the concept and the error, a harmful practice from a behavioral perspective. Response (B) is correct because Skinner advocated individualized instruction where each student completes his or her work assignments (learn) in small, sequential steps. This allows for frequent rewards (the correct answer is rewarded) and the immediate correction of errors. Response (C) has all of the students working at the same pace, along with the teacher, so it is incorrect. Skinner preferred that students work individually, at their own pace. Response (D) is incorrect because it involves an inductive lesson where students form hypotheses about a concept. As with Response (A), students are allowed to make errors, therefore, allowing for incorrect associations which have to be relearned correctly at a later time. Response (E) is incorrect because Skinner would not focus on a student's intrinsic motivation to learn. Instead, he would advocate external rewards to structure behavior.

9. **(A)** The correct response to question 9 is (A), labels can be self-fulfilling. This question is on decision-making (encouraging appropriate behavior). It is well documented in the educational and psychological literature (originally by Rosenthal and Jacob) that teachers' expectations can be influenced by their prior knowledge of the student. In education, this is sometimes due to labels from standardized or diagnostic tests. Response (A) is correct because it demonstrates the Pygmalion or self-fulfilling prophecy effect. Response (B) is incorrect because it makes the opposite statement. Response (C), while it is sometimes true, is incorrect because it does not describe the Pygmalion Effect as well as Response (A). Response (D) may also be true, however, it does not describe the concept asked for in the question. Response (E) is a theory about the origins of our potential and not about a self-fulfilling prophecy.

10. **(B)** The correct response to question 10 is (B), the ripple effect. This question is on decision-making (managing the classroom). Kounin's ripple effect is defined as "how a teacher's method of handling the misbehavior of one child influences other children who are audiences to the event but not themselves targets" (*Discipline and Group Management in the Classroom*, p. 2). The scenario describes a teacher who reprimands a student, then she observes the other students' reaction to the reprimand. This is similar to Kounin's definition of the ripple effect, therefore, Response (B) is correct. Response (A) is incorrect or at least

impossible to determine. The scenario does not include an explanation about whether or not the targeted behavior (the student's talking) decreased; a necessary ingredient for negative reinforcement. Response (C) is incorrect. Overlapping refers to a teacher's ability to attend to and supervise several classroom activities simultaneously. The scenario is more specific about the students' behavior following a teacher's reprimand than it is about the teacher's ability to keep track of classroom events. Response (D) is incorrect. Momentum, although described by Kounin, actually refers to a teacher's ability to keep the classroom environment moving; that is, students are on task. The scenario does not address the teacher's ability to manage movement. Response (E) is incorrect. Lee Canter describes assertive discipline in terms of rights; the teacher's right to teach and the student's right to learn. In order to respect everyone's rights the teacher addresses students in a clear, firm, and unhostile manner. From the scenario, it is impossible to determine the type of rapport the teacher has with her students.

11. **(D)**   The correct response to question 11 is (D), organization. This question is on planning and writing instructional objectives. Bloom's taxonomy of educational outcomes for the cognitive domain includes the following: knowledge, comprehension, application, analysis, synthesis, and evaluation, so responses (A), (B), (C) and (E) are not exceptions. Organization [response (D)] is not included in the taxonomy.

12. **(E)**   The correct response to question 12 is (E), give advice. This question is on decision-making, communicating expectations, and encouraging appropriate behavior. Response (A) (block out external noise and other distractions) is an important part of active listening as is response (B) (listen to verbal and watch for non-verbal messages), response (C) (distinguish between thinking and feeling messages), and response (D) (identify with the speaker's feelings). The only response incongruent with active listening is (E) (give advice which is appropriate to the problem) .

13. **(A)**   The correct response to question 13 is (A), it yields consistent results over time and administrations. This question is on evaluating student performance. The definition of reliability, according to Gronlund, is "how consistent test scores or other evaluation results are from one measurement to another" (*Measurement and Evaluation in Teaching,* 6th edition, page 77). Response (A) speaks to the consistency of test results over time and administrations, so it is consistent with the definition provided above. Responses (B), (C), (D), and (E) are all describing characteristics of validity.

14. **(A)**   The correct response to question 14 is (A), seek educational enculturation. This question is on extraclassroom influences (community influences and policies which affect the teacher). Response (A), seek educational enculturation, means to adapt to the prevailing culture which, in this case, would be "American." Cultural differences, from a "melting pot" perspective would be lost or blended into something representing "Americanism." Educational enculturation means the same thing, that various cultural differences would be blended into one new culture. Response (B) refers to more of a "tossed salad" perspective where all cultures are mixed together in society without losing their individual flavors, identities, or customs. Response (C) focuses on cultural separateness rather than cultural mixing. Response (D), using the metric system, would go against enculturation in America where a standard weight system is used. Response (D) focuses on cultural differences which is not a "melting pot" perspective.

15. **(D)**   The correct response to question 15 is (D), often used as the only approach

available to non-English speaking students. This question is on students' constitutional rights. Prior to the *Lau v. Nicholas* decision in 1974 (where the U.S. Supreme Court ruled that schools must take steps to assist students who find learning difficult or impossible because they do not speak English), a "sink or swim" approach was often used as the sole method of language learning. This meant that students learned the English language informally, on their own. They were thrown into an English-speaking classroom and if they learned the language, they survived. Response (A) refers to the federal law which attempted to deal with the "sink or swim" method, and not the method itself. Response (B) is incorrect because the teacher had a relatively small role in teaching language where a "sink or swim" method was used. Response (C) is false, the Supreme Court did not find the method unconstitutional. Response (D) is correct as explained above. Response (E) is false because no relationship has been found between the effectiveness of the "sink or swim" method and the primary language spoken by the student learning English.

16. **(C)** The correct response to question 16 is (C), "Can my students perform?" This question is on evaluating student performance. The purpose of a test is to determine whether or not students are able to perform the stated objectives and outcomes. Response (A) is incorrect because a test will not tell a teacher why a student learned one thing and not another. Response (B) is incorrect because a test cannot tell a teacher whether or not something will be remembered. It only reveals what the student knew when he or she was taking the test. Response (C) is correct because a good test will demonstrate which of the learning outcomes and objectives can be performed by students. Response (D) is incorrect because a test, if it is not well thought out, can measure trivial and irrelevant information just as it can measure important knowledge. Response (E) is incorrect since a test is never judged as valid or reliable. The terms validity and reliability refer to the results of the test and not the test itself.

17. **(C)** The correct response to question 17 is (C), conventional. This question is on extraclassroom influences on children (development). Kohlberg's theory of moral development has six stages and three levels. Each level (preconventional, conventional, or postconventional) demonstrates a way in which individuals deal with moral decisions. Responses (A) and (B) are incorrect because the punishment-obedience orientation stages of Kohlberg's theory occur at the preconventional level where moral judgments are based on avoiding punishment rather than a sense of right and wrong according to authority and law. Response (C) is correct because at the conventional level of Kohlberg's theory, individuals view morality as following laws and respecting authority in order to maintain social order. This description fits Jake who told the teacher in order to uphold the school rule against cheating. Responses (D) and (E) come from Kohlberg's final level where right and wrong are a matter of individual conscience involving abstract concepts of justice, equality, and humanity. Jake is not operating at the postconventional level.

18. **(D)** The correct response to question 18 is (D), placement. This question is on evaluating student performance. A placement evaluation is concerned with a student's entry level ability. Instead of placement, Response (A) refers to a formative evaluation which is used to monitor learning progress during instruction. Response (B) refers to a summative evaluation which is used to evaluate students' progress at the end of a course or unit of instruction. Again, it is not appropriate for the situation described in the question. Response (C), a diagnostic evaluation, is used to uncover learning difficulties and prescribe corrective instruction. Response (D) is correct because a placement evaluation focuses on a student's aptitude (knowledge and skills needed) in order to determine whether or not he or she would

be successful in some pre-specified placement or class. Response (E), standardized, is not a type of evaluation.

19. **(C)** The correct response to question 19 is (C), identity vs. role confusion. This question is on extraclassroom influences on students (development). According to Erikson, adolescence is a time to consciously think about one's identity, beliefs, and personal drives. He calls this stage of development "identity vs. role confusion." Adolescents are to "discover" who they are in order to prepare themselves for the future. Response (C) is correct because it addresses this period of adolescence. Responses (A), (B), (D), and (E) involve the tasks Erikson believes will be accomplished at other stages of life.

20. **(D)** The correct response to question 20 is (D), a student completes the test as quickly as possible. This question is on evaluating student performance. Valid test results are possible when a test measures what it purports to measure. For example, a valid test could measure knowledge of some class subject. Response (A) would affect the validity of the test results. A poor reader may possess the knowledge which is to be measured by the test but can't report it because of his or her reading ability. Response (B) would also affect validity. Again, a student may possess the appropriate knowledge but fail to report it on the test because he or she does not understand what to do. Response (C) will affect test validity for the same reason as Responses (A) and (B). Poorly constructed items might not measure the knowledge which is intended to be measure. Response (D) is correct because if a student hurries through a test, it will probably not affect his or her knowledge of the subject, therefore, the test will be an accurate representation of the knowledge possessed by the student at the time of the test. Response (E) is incorrect because if test items do not match the intended outcomes, the test results will not be valid.

21. **(E)** The correct response to question 21 is (E), II and IV. The question is on planning (writing instructional objectives). Those who advocate the use of instructional objectives argue that they assist teachers in the decision-making process by concretely demonstrating a course of action for instruction and analyzing the prerequisite skills. Response I is an argument for instruction objectives. Writing objectives is a method of planning ahead of time what will have been learned by the end of instruction, so response (A) is not an exception. Response II is an argument against instructional objectives. It is not possible to know in advance what learning will occur and the learning which does occur cannot always be measured by a specific instructional objective. Thus, it is part of the correct response (E). Response III is an argument for instructional objectives. By analyzing the tasks to be completed by students, it is possible to teach prerequisite skills first, so it is not an exception. Response IV is an argument against instructional objectives. This statement refers to the idea that instructional objectives inhibit creativity or novel types of learning because everything is planned ahead of time, so it is the second part of response (E).

22. **(C)** The correct response to question 22 is (C), the short answer item. This question is on evaluating student performance by developing appropriate assessment instruments. The objective *The student will be able to solve word problems using percent* requires the student to calculate percent problems which are stated in word problem form. Response (A) is not a word problem although the student must calculate percent. Response (B) is not a word problem either. Response (C) is a word problem and it asks the student to calculate percent. Response (D) is a word problem but the response may be given as a fraction and not a percent. Response (E) is a word problem but the student is not asked to calculate. Instead he or she

must evaluate whether or not a score of 90 percent is good.

23. **(B)** The correct response to question 23 is (B), humanism. This question is on methods of instruction. Non-directive teaching is based on a counseling model developed by humanist Carl Rogers. In non-directive teaching, the role of the teacher is to facilitate and guide students' intellectual development and to share ideas with them through honest communication. Response (A) focuses on an idealistic perspective where the teacher's role is to pass on knowledge to students. This approach would require the teacher to be at the center of the learning process so he or she would need to take a direct and active role. Response (B) is correct because humanism advocates a non-directive approach. Response (C), realism, as with idealism, would require the teacher to take a direct and active role in the learning process. Response (D), pragmatism, is a student centered approach to learning where problem solving and discovery are emphasized. This approach, however, expects the teacher to take an active role in teaching students to survive in the world. Response (E), epistemology, refers to the study or science of knowledge and is not a teaching model.

24. **(D)** The correct response to question 24 is (D), statements which concurrently introduce and sum up material. This question is on methods of instruction. David Ausubel describes his concept of an advance organizer as an initial statement or framework for the to-be-learned, whether prose or tutorial. Response (A), an outline, is incomplete. An advance organizer may be in outline form, prior to prose learning, for example, but it does more than this. An advance organizer introduces and sums up the material at an abstract level to provide the student with structure for learning. Response (B) does not fit the definition of an advance organizer at all. Neither does response (C) or response (E).

25. **(A)** The correct response to question 25 is (A), the student understands laws of conservation and can classify and seriate. This question is on extraclassroom influences on students (development). Response (A) is correct. Piaget describes the concrete operational stage of his theory of development as a time when children can conserve (certain properties remain constant regardless of changes in other properties), classify (grouping objects into categories), and seriate (arrange objects in sequence). Responses (B), (C), (D), and (E) are all describing Piaget's notion of formal operations.

26. **(D)** The correct response to question 26 is (D), a systematic process. This question is on evaluating student performance. Response (A) describes a test rather than evaluation. Response (B) is referring to teaching methods and response (C) to measurement. Response (D) is correct because evaluation is a systematic process which includes testing and measurement. Response (E) is incorrect because it describes criterion-referenced testing.

27. **(D)** The correct response is (D), rehearsal and chunking. This question is on extraclassroom influences on students (development). According to information processing theorists, short-term memory duration and capacity can be increased through the processes of rehearsal and chunking. Response (A), retrieval and reconstruction, involves processes which move information which is stored in long-term memory to short-term memory but do not increase the capacity or duration of short-term memory. Response (B), interference and decay, inhibits the capacity and duration of short-term memory, not increase its capacity. Response (C), organization and elaboration, is a process for getting information from short-term memory into long-term memory. Response (D) is correct because rehearsal (repeating the information over and over) increases the duration of short-term memory and chunking

(combining bits of information into some single unit) and increases the capacity of short-term memory (or at least increases the amount of information which can be held there). Response (E) refers to how procedural knowledge (productions) and declarative knowledge (schemas) are stored in long-term memory

28. **(C)** The correct response to question 28 is (C), student C lacks the ability to rehearse. This question is on extraclassroom influences on students (development). An availability deficiency is defined as the inability to use various cognitive strategies. Only response (C) addresses the inability to rehearse. Students A, B, and D have some ability to actively rehearse, whether on demand or if told to do so. Student E is not deficient.

29. **(C)** The correct response to question 29 is (C), thoughts and experiences. This question is on selecting methods of instruction. Idealism deals with thoughts and ideas as the basis of reality while pragmatism deals with experiences. Response (A) is most likely to be describing existentialism and realism. Response (B) is incorrect because knowledge and reality are terms used by a variety of philosophical perspectives, not just idealism and pragmatism. Response (C) is correct because idealism deals with thoughts while pragmatism deals with experiences. Response (D) and response (E) do not describe the two terms.

30. **(D)** The correct response to question 30 is (D), empirical observations form reality. This is basic to realism. Response (A) argues against realism, therefore, it is incorrect. Response (B), again, argues against realism which would suggest that no knowledge is innate. Instead, all knowledge is learned. Response (C) is an existential statement. Response (D) is correct; a realist would believe that empirical observations form reality. Response (E), like (A) and (B), is an argument against realism rather than an argument for it.

31. **(A)** The correct response to question 31 is (A), inquiry. This question is on methods of instruction. Response (A) is correct because inquiry is an instructional method which deals with organizing data, sensing problems, hypothesizing, and developing concepts. The approach is deductive rather than inductive. The other responses (B), (C), (D) and (E) do not fit the method described in the question.

32. **(B)** The correct response to question 32 is (B), an essentialist. This question is on methods of instruction (selecting instructional strategies). An essentialist curriculum focuses on a subject-centered curriculum; the "three R's" at the elementary level or the academic disciplines of English, science, math, history, and foreign language at the secondary level. Responses (A), (C), (D), and (E) advocate a student-centered curriculum.

33. **(C)** The correct response to question 33 is (C), inductive reasoning. This question is on extraclassroom influences on students and methods of instruction. Response (A) is incorrect. Condusive is not a type of reasoning. Response (B) is incorrect because deductive reasoning involves the formulation of examples from a known rule or principle. This is not the case here. Response (C) is correct because inductive reasoning involves making hypotheses based on examples or instances to form a conclusion. This type of reasoning is called for in the question stem. Responses (D) and (E) are not types of reasoning.

34. **(C)** The correct response is (C), preserve the great ideas of the culture. This question is on methods of instruction. Response (A) is incorrect because idealists would not focus on

the criticism of great ideas. Response (B) is incorrect because the focus is on great ideas of the past and their relationship to the present, and not the explanation of present ideas. Response (C) is correct since idealists focus on ideas, especially those which explain humanity in terms of thoughts rather than perceptions. Response (D) is incorrect because idealism is not necessarily focused on the future. Response (E) is incorrect because it is not possible to prove philosophical ideas in an empirical sense.

35.   **(A)**   The correct response is (A), interpretation of the test results and not the test itself. This question is on evaluating student performance. Reliability and validity refer to the interpretation of test results; how accurately one can say the results represent the knowledge intended to be measured in a consistent manner. Response (A) addresses this. Response (B) is incorrect. While the quality of the test item is important and it contributes to the accuracy of the test interpretation (i.e., validity and reliability), it does not, in itself, assure that test results will be valid and/or reliable. For example, a multiple-choice item may be well written, following all of the rules of proper test construction, but not measure what it intends to measure in a consistent manner. Response (C) is incorrect. Reliability and validity do not refer to the outcomes being measured, however, the more closely the test represents the intended outcomes and instruction, the more likely it is that the test results will be valid. Response (D) is incorrect. The trait being measured by the test addresses construct validity but it does not guarantee reliability. For example, personality inventories measure a variety of traits, but they are not extremely reliable. Response (E) is incorrect. Validity and reliability only refer to the test results; how confidently you can say that the test measures what it purports to measure over time and administrations. The appropriateness of the test for the student who is taking it can influence test results, however it is not, in itself, reliability and validity.

Section 3

1.   **(D)**   The correct response is (D), the teacher should report her suspicions to authorities. This question is on teacher ethics (teacher rights and responsibilities). Response (A) is incorrect because in some states, failure to immediately report suspected child abuse is a misdemeanor. Response (B) is incorrect because the teacher should not report her suspicions to the parents. Response (C) is incorrect because the teacher is not trained to counsel the student about abuse and neglect. Response (D) is correct for the reason stated above. Response (E) is incorrect because teachers are required to report abuse in most states. Failure to do so is sometimes illegal.

2.   **(D)**   The correct response is (D), time on task. This question is on classroom management (encourage appropriate behavior). The question asks for a definition of engaged time; the amount of time a student actually spends doing his or her assigned work. It is synonymous with time on task, therefore, response (D) is correct. Response (A) is incorrect because independent practice refers to the independent rehearsal of new knowledge. Response (B), a technique where reinforcement is allocated over a constant time interval, is incorrect. Response (C) is incorrect because allocated time refers to the amount of time set aside by the teacher for student learning. Allocated time does not automatically guarantee engaged time. Response (E) is incorrect because variable ratio schedules reinforce students after an unpredictable number of appropriate behavior responses.

3. **(D)**   The correct response is (D), the principal has not violated the student's rights if he or she has reasonable cause for conducting the search. This question is on students' constitutional rights. Response (D) is based on the a Supreme Court ruling (*New Jersey v. T.L.O.*) which set a standard for school searches. The Court decided a search could be conducted if it was related in scope and circumstance to the interference which prompted the search in the first place. In addition, it has been argued that school lockers are school property and may be searched by officials if reasonable cause exists. Response (D) addresses this.

4. **(E)**   The correct response is (E) I, II, and III. This question is on methods of instruction. The question is about individualized instruction; each student following a plan designed to meet his or her own needs, interests, and abilities. According to Woolfolk (*Educational Psychology, 1990*), all of the following events may be tailored to individualized instruction: 1) the pace of learning, 2) the instructional objectives, 3) the activity or materials, 4) the reading level, 5) the method by which students demonstrate what they have learned. Response (E) (all of the strategies) addresses this.

5. **(D)**   The correct response is (D), breaking tasks into skills and subskills. This question is on planning. The question asks for a definition of task analysis. Response (A) is incorrect because Teacher A is writing specific performance objectives. Response (B) is incorrect because Teacher B is also writing objectives. Response (C) is incorrect because Teacher C is using creativity to design interesting lessons but she is not necessarily using a task analysis approach. Response (D) is correct because Teacher D breaks learning tasks into the basic skills and subskills needed to complete the learning task. This fits the definition of *task analysis*. Response (E) is incorrect because Teacher E is using Bloom's taxonomy to identify domains of learning.

6. **(A)**   The correct response is (A), it penalizes the best students. This question is on evaluating student performances. The question asks for a major problem associated with evaluating students on effort and improvement. One problem with this type of evaluation is that the best students, who are often working at maximum potential, improve the least. They are penalized because they were initially competent, so response (A) is correct. Response (B) is incorrect because grading on improvement or effort is often subjective, not objective. While this type of grading may signal to the poorer student that effort takes precedence over accuracy, this is not always viewed negatively or as a problem. Sometimes students need to know that their efforts are important, even if accuracy does not follow, so response (C) is incorrect. Response (D) is incorrect because research does not support the idea that increased hostility between students occurs because of high grades received for effort. Response (E) is incorrect because a dual marking system is not viewed as the problem. It is viewed, by many educators, to be the solution. One grade is given for achievement and one grade is given for effort, attitude, or improvement.

7. **(C)**   The correct response is (C), to solve problems. This question is on planning. The question asks for the completion of a quote by Gagne. By problem solving, Gagne means formulating new answers and creating solutions. Response (C) is correct.

8. **(B)**   The correct response is (B), means-ends analysis. This question is on methods of instruction. Response (A) is incorrect because an analogical strategy requires the problem solver to use the structure of one problem solution as a guide for the new problem. Response

(B) is correct because a means-ends analysis is a heuristic where the final goal (in this case, to read 350 pages) is divided into subgoals (7 sections of 50 pages). Response (C) is incorrect because functional fixedness is not a heuristic. Instead, it is the failure to solve a problem because the solution requires novel thinking. Response (D) is incorrect because an algorithm is not a heuristic. An algorithm is a step-by-step prescription for problem solving guaranteed to succeed. A heuristic will often lead to a solution, but not always. Response (E) is not a heuristic, therefore, it is incorrect.

9. **(E)** The correct response is (E), students' responses are not judged as right or wrong. The question is on evaluating student performance. Response (A) is incorrect because convergent thinking requires one specific answer. *Open-ended questions* allow students to respond in any manner they choose because no answer is right or wrong. Response (B) is incorrect because there is only one correct response to the question about the Civil War. Response (C) is incorrect since Teacher C may ask single-response questions as well as open-ended ones. Response (D) is incorrect because it does not describe *open-ended questions*. Response (E) is correct because the response fits the definition described above.

10. **(B)** The correct response is (B), the teacher is extending short-term memory capacity beyond its capacity. This question is on methods of instruction. The question is asking why the teacher's method of instruction and testing is unacceptable. Response (A) is incorrect since the statement about her teaching is not specific enough to determine whether or not the students are motivated. Response (B) is correct because according to cognitive theorists, short-term memory capacity is about 7 items or units of information. This is much less memory capacity than that called for in the assignment. Additionally, there is little time for students to rehearse or organize the words in order to "transfer" them to long-term memory. Response (C) is incorrect because as with response (A), there is not enough information to determine whether or not the teacher gives adequate examples. Response (D) is incorrect because while the task involves rote learning—this in itself is not bad—which is a necessary part of spelling lessons. Response (E) is incorrect since an advance organizer is not always a necessary component of effective teaching.

11. **(A)** The correct response is (A), a computer. This question is on extraclassroom influences on students (development). Information processing theorists study computer functions in order to better understand such things as language development, problem solving, reasoning, or other workings of the mind.

12. **(C)** The correct response is (C), it is more appropriate for males than females. This question is on extraclassroom influences on students (development). Response (A) is incorrect because Kohlberg's theory is theoretical, as it should be. Response (B) is incorrect since Kohlberg used an adequate number of subjects. Response (C) is correct because Carol Gilligan's research, for example, demonstrates that females do not develop morally in the same way as males do. Response (D) is incorrect since it is describing a criticism of Piaget, not Kohlberg. Response (E) is incorrect because Kohlberg's theory has generated a great deal of research.

13. **(D)** The correct response is (D), Rousseau. This question is on teacher ethics; demonstrating knowledge of the profession. The question asks for the person who advocates a child-centered curriculum focusing on naturalistic contact with the environment. Response

(A) is incorrect because Locke, an empiricist philosopher, would not agree with the notion that abilities are innate. In fact, he is credited with proposing the "blank slate" or "tabula rasa" theory. Response (B) is incorrect as is Response (C) because both men view subject matter as the essential component of education, not the child. Response (D) is correct since Rousseau advocated a child-centered curriculum. Response (E) is incorrect because Bagley, like Adler and Hutchins, emphasized subject matter as the focus of education. He believed the individual was present to learn essential facts.

14. **(A)** The correct response is (A), there might be an increase in the drop-out rate. The question is on extraclassroom influences. The question asks about an adverse effect of increasing academic standards. Response (A) is correct because many educators believe the trend to increase standards may, at the same time, increase the drop-out rate. Those students who were border-line between passing and failing will, after the increased standards are in effect, be failing, thus, increasing the temptation to drop out. Response (B) is incorrect since increased standards would most likely have a positive (if any) effect on standardized test scores. Response (C) is incorrect because schools have graduation requirements which include a blend of academic and non-academic subjects. Increasing standards does not mean a decrease in academic course requirements. Response (D) is incorrect since there is no indication that teachers will have to work harder. Response (E) is incorrect because opinion polls show that communities favor the increased academic standards.

15. **(A)** The correct response is (A), behavior modification promotes extrinsic motivation. This question is on decision-making. Response (A) is correct because it is an argument against the use of behavior modification. Response (B) is incorrect because the statement is false. Behavior modification has worked effectively for serious misbehaviors. Response (C) is incorrect because increasing engaged time may be an argument for the use of behavior modification rather than an argument against it. Response (D) is incorrect because while it is true that behavior modification uses rewards and punishers in a systematic way, it can be said that all management strategies use some sort of rewards, but possibly, less systematically. Response (E) is incorrect since behavior modification does not decrease self-esteem.

16. **(E)** The correct response is (E); a sequence of educational events. This question is on planning. The question asks for the best description of lesson planning. Most educators agree that lesson planning is a sequence of events leading to effective teaching. Responses (A), (B), (C), and (D) are all components of the sequence but none is, in itself, lesson planning.

17. **(A)** The correct response is (A), I and II. The question is on teacher ethics and demonstrating knowledge of the teaching profession. The question is asking about John Dewey's contributions to education. He is noted for his progressive educational ideas where schools are learning laboratories. Additionally, he advocated the incorporation of democratic principles into the curriculum where learners are free to test their own beliefs and values. Response (A) (I and II) speaks to Dewey's accomplishments. Piaget formulated a theory of cognitive development (III). Froebel created the kindergarten (IV).

18. **(D)** The correct response is (D), I and II. This question is on extraclassroom influences on students. Learning styles research is popular, however, it is often misinterpreted. Problems with research methodologies, inappropriate testing instruments, and contradictory findings from study to study have led researchers to conclude that the inconsistencies prevent broad generalizations about how students prefer to take in sensory

information (Response I is correct). Because the data are inconclusive, researchers suggest that teachers focus on being sensitive to individual differences by presenting materials in a variety of ways (Response II is correct) rather than developing new curricula for each type of cognitive style (Response III is incorrect).

19. **(B)** The correct response is (B), the length of time a teacher waits for a response to a question. This question is on methods of instruction. The question asks for an example of *wait time*. Response (B) is the only one which fits the definition; *wait time* is the length of time a teacher waits for a student to respond to a question before giving up or asking another student.

20. **(B)** The correct response is (B), (a) handicapped; (b) when they are medically approved. This question is on student constitutional rights. Response (B) accurately describes the current education position on AIDS. The other responses, (A), (C), (D) and (E) are false.

21. **(D)** The correct response is (D), incompetency. This question is on teacher ethics. While the school must follow due-process procedures, tenured teachers may be dismissed for incompetence, so response (D) is correct. Response (A) is incorrect because teachers cannot be dismissed for teaching controversial issues. Response (B) is incorrect since refusing to volunteer for additional assignments is not grounds for dismissal. Response (C) is incorrect because teachers have the right to challenge administrative decisions. Response (E) is incorrect since academic freedom refers to a teacher's right to teach courses suited to his or her area of competence.

22. **(D)** The correct response is (D), reinforcing students after every 5th hand raising episode. This question is on methods of instruction. Response (A) (which is incorrect) demonstrates continuous reinforcement. This action would create a steadily increasing line which eventually tapers off. Response (B) describes a variable ratio schedule. As with all varied schedules, a steadily increasing line graphically represents what will happen with this type of reinforcement. Response (C) is similar to response (B) except that the number of times the behavior goes by (rather than length of time) without reinforcement varies. Response (D) is correct. Students will increase their hand raising behavior just prior to being reinforced, then the behavior will level off until it is once again close to reinforcement time. Response (E) describes extinction which is shown as a decreasing line.

23. **(B)** The correct response is (B), the teacher. This question is on decision making. According to T. Gordon, author of *TET: Teacher Effectiveness Training*, teacher-owned problems are those where the student's behavior interferes with the teacher's need to teach (Response (B) addresses this). Student-owned problems are not caused by the teacher, so response (A) is incorrect. Teacher and student shared problems occur when the teacher and the student interfere with each other's needs. Thus, response (C) is incorrect. Responses (D) and (E) are not problem types according to Gordon.

24. **(C)** The correct response is (C), summarize the main points. This question is on planning. Bloom's synthesis level involves bringing bits of information from a variety of sources together to form a new whole. Response (A) is at the synthesis level. The student is to take information from a story and rewrite it. Response (B) is at the synthesis level. The student uses old knowledge about geometry to derive a new formula. Response (C) is not

at the synthesis level, therefore, it is the correct choice. Summarizing demonstrates comprehension of the material but not a blending of knowledge. Response (D) and response (E) are at the synthesis level because both require the use of old knowledge to create new learning experiences.

25. **(B)**   The correct response is (B), all students are required to complete the same academic requirements. This question is on methods of instruction. *Tracking* refers to separating students into different curricular paths. For example, college bound students are advised to take advanced science and math courses while vocationally bound students are not. Response (B), depicting homogeneous grouping of students, is least like *tracking*.

26. **(E)**   The correct response is (E), +.76. This question is on evaluating student performance. The question asks for the interpretation of correlational data. Correlation coefficients vary from -1.00 to +1.00. The stronger the relationship between two variables, the closer the measurement is to -1.00 or +1.00. Zero represents no correlation between two variables or measures. +.76 is closest to +1.00, therefore, it is the strongest. Response (A) (-.50) is next strongest, followed by Response (D) (+.39), Response (B) (-.25), and Response (C) (+.099).

27. **(C)**   The correct response is (C), (a) Pavlov; (b) Skinner. This question is on extraclassroom influences on students. The question is an analogy focusing on the relationship between classical and operant conditioning. Response (A) is incorrect because the first classical conditioning experiments used dogs while much of the operant conditioning research used rats; the opposite of Response (A). Response (B) is incorrect because both types of behavior conditions are psychological, however, Pavlov (classical conditioning) was a physiologist. Response (C) is correct since Pavlov is the "father" of classical conditioning while Skinner advanced the theory of operant conditioning. Response (D) is incorrect because both terms refer to operant conditioning. Response (E) is incorrect since the relationship between the two terms does not fit the stem.

28. **(C)**   The correct response is (C), reading skills. This question is on methods of instruction. The question asks for a description of the SQ3R (or PQ4R) method. It is a study skill technique for reading new material. SQ3R is an acronym for *survey, question, read, recite, and review*. PQ4R, a variation of the SQ3R is an acronym for *question, read, reflect, recite, review*. Response (C) addresses this.

29. **(B)**   The correct response is (B), continue to believe that Student A is of normal intelligence. This question is on evaluating student performance. Response (A) is incorrect because IQ tests are not necessarily designed to uncover learning disabilities. The Stanford-Binet has a mean of 100 and a standard deviation of 16. Student A falls within the normal range. Thus, response (B) is correct. Response (C) is incorrect since Student A's score would not suggest she is of the gifted caliber. Response (D) is incorrect because the Stanford-Binet is supported by reliable norms. Response (E) is incorrect since the teacher has no need to test Student A again. The results of the test were consistent with the teacher's beliefs.

30. **(C)**   The correct response is (C), states. The question is on teacher ethics. The question asks who is responsible for educating citizens of the United States. Response (C) is correct.

31. **(B)** The correct response is (B), science and mathematics. This question is on methods of instruction. The question is asking about the curricular shift of the late 1950s. After the Soviet Union launched Sputnik, the U.S. government and citizens became concerned about lagging behind in areas critical to national defense. One way to catch up would be to emphasize science and math in the school curriculum. Response (B) refers to the science and math emphasis. Response (A) is incorrect because Sputnik did not lead to an increase in foreign language requirements in schools. Response (C) is incorrect because while a concern for national defense prompted the shift, the focus of the curriculum (which the question addresses) was changed to science and math, not defense. Response (D) and response (E) are incorrect because communication was not the focus, nor was humanism and global education.

32. **(D)** The correct response is (D), middle schools provide a smooth transition between childhood and adolescence. The question is on extraclassroom influences. Response (A) is incorrect because while middle schools have become more and more popular over the past few years, support for them is not overwhelming. Response (B) is incorrect because there is little difference, financially, between middle schools and traditional schools. The same number of students are being served regardless of the grade arrangement. Response (C) is incorrect because middle schools do not change population figures at the secondary level. Response (D) is correct since the argument behind middle schools is that they parallel what we know about students' developmental processes. Response (E) is incorrect because junior high schools are just as likely to provide a healthy climate as middle schools.

33. **(C)** The correct response is (C), alternative licensing. This question is on teacher ethics (professional organizations). The question asks about teacher organizations and what they do and do not support. Response (A) is incorrect since collective bargaining is an important tool for promoting salary increases and better working conditions, thus, it is supported by teacher organizations. Response (B) is incorrect because tenure protects teachers from unfair dismissals so it is supported by teacher organizations. Response (C) is correct because alternative licensing refers to allowing individuals who have not completed a teacher training program to teach, most often because they have some expertise in their field. Teacher organizations take the position that teachers need special training in order to fully understand how to teach. Response (D) is incorrect since teacher organizations would not be against higher salaries. Response (E) is incorrect because teacher empowerment is an important issue, regarded highly by teacher organizations.

34. **(C)** The correct response is (C), assist the disadvantaged. This question is on students' rights and responsibilities. The question is asking for the purpose of the Educational Consolidation and Improvement Act (Chapter 1). The act was designed to enhance educational opportunities for the disadvantaged. Response (C) correctly identifies this.

35. **(E)** The correct response is (E), they have the right to review the records unconditionally. The question is on students' rights and responsibilities. The question asks if parents have the right to see their child's school records. All parents have access to their child's personal file, regardless of the reason for wanting to see it. Response (E) addresses this.

National Teachers Examination

CORE BATTERY

Test 3

NTE Test of Communication Skills

TEST 3 – ANSWER SHEET

Section 1: Listening

1. Ⓐ Ⓑ Ⓒ Ⓓ Ⓔ
2. Ⓐ Ⓑ Ⓒ Ⓓ Ⓔ
3. Ⓐ Ⓑ Ⓒ Ⓓ Ⓔ
4. Ⓐ Ⓑ Ⓒ Ⓓ Ⓔ
5. Ⓐ Ⓑ Ⓒ Ⓓ Ⓔ
6. Ⓐ Ⓑ Ⓒ Ⓓ Ⓔ
7. Ⓐ Ⓑ Ⓒ Ⓓ Ⓔ
8. Ⓐ Ⓑ Ⓒ Ⓓ Ⓔ
9. Ⓐ Ⓑ Ⓒ Ⓓ Ⓔ
10. Ⓐ Ⓑ Ⓒ Ⓓ Ⓔ
11. Ⓐ Ⓑ Ⓒ Ⓓ Ⓔ
12. Ⓐ Ⓑ Ⓒ Ⓓ Ⓔ
13. Ⓐ Ⓑ Ⓒ Ⓓ Ⓔ
14. Ⓐ Ⓑ Ⓒ Ⓓ Ⓔ
15. Ⓐ Ⓑ Ⓒ Ⓓ Ⓔ
16. Ⓐ Ⓑ Ⓒ Ⓓ Ⓔ
17. Ⓐ Ⓑ Ⓒ Ⓓ Ⓔ
18. Ⓐ Ⓑ Ⓒ Ⓓ Ⓔ
19. Ⓐ Ⓑ Ⓒ Ⓓ Ⓔ
20. Ⓐ Ⓑ Ⓒ Ⓓ Ⓔ
21. Ⓐ Ⓑ Ⓒ Ⓓ Ⓔ
22. Ⓐ Ⓑ Ⓒ Ⓓ Ⓔ
23. Ⓐ Ⓑ Ⓒ Ⓓ Ⓔ
24. Ⓐ Ⓑ Ⓒ Ⓓ Ⓔ
25. Ⓐ Ⓑ Ⓒ Ⓓ Ⓔ
26. Ⓐ Ⓑ Ⓒ Ⓓ Ⓔ
27. Ⓐ Ⓑ Ⓒ Ⓓ Ⓔ
28. Ⓐ Ⓑ Ⓒ Ⓓ Ⓔ
29. Ⓐ Ⓑ Ⓒ Ⓓ Ⓔ
30. Ⓐ Ⓑ Ⓒ Ⓓ Ⓔ
31. Ⓐ Ⓑ Ⓒ Ⓓ Ⓔ
32. Ⓐ Ⓑ Ⓒ Ⓓ Ⓔ
33. Ⓐ Ⓑ Ⓒ Ⓓ Ⓔ
34. Ⓐ Ⓑ Ⓒ Ⓓ Ⓔ
35. Ⓐ Ⓑ Ⓒ Ⓓ Ⓔ
36. Ⓐ Ⓑ Ⓒ Ⓓ Ⓔ
37. Ⓐ Ⓑ Ⓒ Ⓓ Ⓔ
38. Ⓐ Ⓑ Ⓒ Ⓓ Ⓔ
39. Ⓐ Ⓑ Ⓒ Ⓓ Ⓔ
40. Ⓐ Ⓑ Ⓒ Ⓓ Ⓔ

Section 2: Reading

1. Ⓐ Ⓑ Ⓒ Ⓓ Ⓔ
2. Ⓐ Ⓑ Ⓒ Ⓓ Ⓔ
3. Ⓐ Ⓑ Ⓒ Ⓓ Ⓔ
4. Ⓐ Ⓑ Ⓒ Ⓓ Ⓔ
5. Ⓐ Ⓑ Ⓒ Ⓓ Ⓔ
6. Ⓐ Ⓑ Ⓒ Ⓓ Ⓔ
7. Ⓐ Ⓑ Ⓒ Ⓓ Ⓔ
8. Ⓐ Ⓑ Ⓒ Ⓓ Ⓔ
9. Ⓐ Ⓑ Ⓒ Ⓓ Ⓔ
10. Ⓐ Ⓑ Ⓒ Ⓓ Ⓔ
11. Ⓐ Ⓑ Ⓒ Ⓓ Ⓔ
12. Ⓐ Ⓑ Ⓒ Ⓓ Ⓔ
13. Ⓐ Ⓑ Ⓒ Ⓓ Ⓔ
14. Ⓐ Ⓑ Ⓒ Ⓓ Ⓔ
15. Ⓐ Ⓑ Ⓒ Ⓓ Ⓔ
16. Ⓐ Ⓑ Ⓒ Ⓓ Ⓔ
17. Ⓐ Ⓑ Ⓒ Ⓓ Ⓔ
18. Ⓐ Ⓑ Ⓒ Ⓓ Ⓔ
19. Ⓐ Ⓑ Ⓒ Ⓓ Ⓔ
20. Ⓐ Ⓑ Ⓒ Ⓓ Ⓔ
21. Ⓐ Ⓑ Ⓒ Ⓓ Ⓔ
22. Ⓐ Ⓑ Ⓒ Ⓓ Ⓔ
23. Ⓐ Ⓑ Ⓒ Ⓓ Ⓔ
24. Ⓐ Ⓑ Ⓒ Ⓓ Ⓔ
25. Ⓐ Ⓑ Ⓒ Ⓓ Ⓔ
26. Ⓐ Ⓑ Ⓒ Ⓓ Ⓔ
27. Ⓐ Ⓑ Ⓒ Ⓓ Ⓔ
28. Ⓐ Ⓑ Ⓒ Ⓓ Ⓔ
29. Ⓐ Ⓑ Ⓒ Ⓓ Ⓔ
30. Ⓐ Ⓑ Ⓒ Ⓓ Ⓔ

Section 3: Writing

1. Ⓐ Ⓑ Ⓒ Ⓓ Ⓔ
2. Ⓐ Ⓑ Ⓒ Ⓓ Ⓔ
3. Ⓐ Ⓑ Ⓒ Ⓓ Ⓔ
4. Ⓐ Ⓑ Ⓒ Ⓓ Ⓔ
5. Ⓐ Ⓑ Ⓒ Ⓓ Ⓔ
6. Ⓐ Ⓑ Ⓒ Ⓓ Ⓔ
7. Ⓐ Ⓑ Ⓒ Ⓓ Ⓔ
8. Ⓐ Ⓑ Ⓒ Ⓓ Ⓔ

9. Ⓐ Ⓑ Ⓒ Ⓓ Ⓔ
10. Ⓐ Ⓑ Ⓒ Ⓓ Ⓔ
11. Ⓐ Ⓑ Ⓒ Ⓓ Ⓔ
12. Ⓐ Ⓑ Ⓒ Ⓓ Ⓔ
13. Ⓐ Ⓑ Ⓒ Ⓓ Ⓔ
14. Ⓐ Ⓑ Ⓒ Ⓓ Ⓔ
15. Ⓐ Ⓑ Ⓒ Ⓓ Ⓔ
16. Ⓐ Ⓑ Ⓒ Ⓓ Ⓔ
17. Ⓐ Ⓑ Ⓒ Ⓓ Ⓔ
18. Ⓐ Ⓑ Ⓒ Ⓓ Ⓔ
19. Ⓐ Ⓑ Ⓒ Ⓓ Ⓔ
20. Ⓐ Ⓑ Ⓒ Ⓓ Ⓔ
21. Ⓐ Ⓑ Ⓒ Ⓓ Ⓔ
22. Ⓐ Ⓑ Ⓒ Ⓓ Ⓔ
23. Ⓐ Ⓑ Ⓒ Ⓓ Ⓔ
24. Ⓐ Ⓑ Ⓒ Ⓓ Ⓔ
25. Ⓐ Ⓑ Ⓒ Ⓓ Ⓔ
26. Ⓐ Ⓑ Ⓒ Ⓓ Ⓔ
27. Ⓐ Ⓑ Ⓒ Ⓓ Ⓔ
28. Ⓐ Ⓑ Ⓒ Ⓓ Ⓔ
29. Ⓐ Ⓑ Ⓒ Ⓓ Ⓔ
30. Ⓐ Ⓑ Ⓒ Ⓓ Ⓔ
31. Ⓐ Ⓑ Ⓒ Ⓓ Ⓔ
32. Ⓐ Ⓑ Ⓒ Ⓓ Ⓔ
33. Ⓐ Ⓑ Ⓒ Ⓓ Ⓔ
34. Ⓐ Ⓑ Ⓒ Ⓓ Ⓔ
35. Ⓐ Ⓑ Ⓒ Ⓓ Ⓔ
36. Ⓐ Ⓑ Ⓒ Ⓓ Ⓔ
37. Ⓐ Ⓑ Ⓒ Ⓓ Ⓔ
38. Ⓐ Ⓑ Ⓒ Ⓓ Ⓔ
39. Ⓐ Ⓑ Ⓒ Ⓓ Ⓔ
40. Ⓐ Ⓑ Ⓒ Ⓓ Ⓔ
41. Ⓐ Ⓑ Ⓒ Ⓓ Ⓔ
42. Ⓐ Ⓑ Ⓒ Ⓓ Ⓔ
43. Ⓐ Ⓑ Ⓒ Ⓓ Ⓔ
44. Ⓐ Ⓑ Ⓒ Ⓓ Ⓔ
45. Ⓐ Ⓑ Ⓒ Ⓓ Ⓔ

NTE CORE BATTERY–Test 3
TEST OF COMMUNICATIONS SKILLS
Section 1: Listening

Part A

TIME: 30 Minutes
40 Questions

> **DIRECTIONS:** In this section, you will hear short statements and questions. When you hear a statement, select the answer which best restates or supports what you heard. When you hear a question, select the choice which best answers the question. The questions and statements are NOT written in your test book. **They will not be repeated**.

1. (A)   The assignment is on pages 23-24.
    (B)   There are 23 problems to do.
    (C)   Only the even-numbered problems on pages 23-24 were assigned.
    (D)   All the problems on pages 23-26 were assigned.

2. (A)   Many foods served on school lunch programs are high in fat.
    (B)   School lunch menus need revision.
    (C)   School lunches are terrible.
    (D)   Spoiled food is unknowingly served as part of the school lunch program.

3. (A)   You must always wait to see the dentist.
    (B)   Many dentists are very busy.
    (C)   More people should become dentists so patients would not have to wait so long for an appointment.
    (D)   It can be an upsetting experience to wait to see the dentist.

4. (A)   Air traffic controllers work long hours.
    (B)   Air traffic controllers deserve higher pay and more appreciation.
    (C)   Air traffic controllers have stressful jobs.
    (D)   Air traffic controllers will strike for more money.

5. (A)   Dinner will be served immediately.
    (B)   Not everyone at the speaker's table has been seated.
    (C)   The kitchen is still preparing the food.
    (D)   Not all the guests have arrived in the dining room.

6.   (A)   My children are in school that week.
      (B)   We are making reservations now.
      (C)   We will visit my aunt in Maine and then travel to Vermont.
      (D)   My vacation is not until August.

7.   (A)   My lawn mower needs a new blade.
      (B)   The mower works great.
      (C)   The neighbor's son mows my grass.
      (D)   The mower is five years old.

8.   (A)   Car insurance is overpriced.
      (B)   Your son is showing a lot of responsibility to buy his own insurance.
      (C)   Teenage boys should not learn to drive unless they have good grades and a sense of responsibility.
      (D)   Teenagers should be required to take a driving course every year.

9.   (A)   Crime rates are increasing in South American tourist cities.
      (B)   Crime rates are decreasing in South American tourist cities.
      (C)   More police are patrolling South American tourist cities.
      (D)   Tourists ignore the rising crime rates in South American cities.

10.   (A)   Americans like to read about rich foreigners.
      (B)   American newspapers often print stories about the rich and famous.
      (C)   Americans are interested in the lives of famous people.
      (D)   Americans considered famous people snobbish and boring.

11.   (A)   Stock market investors should not plan on short-term profits.
      (B)   Stock market investors should plan on short-term profits.
      (C)   Only foolish people invest in the stock market.
      (D)   The stock market has suffered several declines recently.

12.   (A)   In the history book on pages 77-89
      (B)   We are studying Russia.
      (C)   In school.
      (D)   It is due next Monday.

13.   (A)   Chicken is on the menu.
      (B)   Tuna casserole has been served for the last three nights.
      (C)   I hate tuna casserole.
      (D)   Tuna casserole will be served for dinner.

14.   (A)   It started to rain as soon as the laundry was on the clothesline.
      (B)   After the laundry was on the line it looked as though it might rain.
      (C)   The laundry will never dry in this weather.
      (D)   I need a new electric clothes dryer.

15. (A) The library was closed yesterday.
     (B) No, I haven't, but I'm looking forward to using the new
          system.
     (C) The research department gets all the perks.
     (D) The system is so expensive, library fines are expected to increase.

16. (A) The Air Force requires a college degree for all officers.
     (B) The Air Force offers many opportunities for training and will enable many to
          attend college.
     (C) The Air Force requires a four-year commitment for all new enlistees.
     (D) My brother does not agree with his son's decision to join the Air Force.

17. (A) Gardens should be planted in April to avoid late frost.
     (B) Gardens require a lot of work in March and April.
     (C) Gardens can be planted in March if the weather is warm.
     (D) My uncle plants his garden in February.

18. (A) Mardi Gras is a safe, family-oriented celebration.
     (B) Mardi Gras is great fun but can be dangerous for tourists unfamiliar with the
          city.
     (C) No one should drive to New Orleans for Mardi Gras because it is safer to take
          the bus.
     (D) New Orleans is a dangerous town to visit any time of the year.

19. (A) The speaker is gaining weight.
     (B) The speaker is on a diet.
     (C) The speaker is learning to cook.
     (D) The speaker is hosting many parties.

20. (A) No, I don't like to climb mountains.
     (B) Yes, the Grand Canyon is a beautiful sight.
     (C) My sister went to California last year.
     (D) I like to ski in Colorado.

Part B

DIRECTIONS: In this section, you will hear short conversations between two
people. After each conversation, a third person will ask you questions about
what was discussed. When you hear a question, select the choice which best
answers the question based on what you heard. The conversations and
questions are NOT written in your test book. **They will not be repeated.**

21. (A) His wife had a baby.   (C) His father is ill.
     (B) His daughter had surgery.   (D) His wife had surgery.

22.   (A)   Jennifer told him.   (C)   Allen told him.
     (B)   Janice told him.   (D)   He figured it out on his own.

23.   (A)   Boston is famous for fine restaurants.
     (B)   Allen's wife enjoys eating lobster.
     (C)   Allen enjoys eating lobster and will be jealous of Jennifer.
     (D)   Joe wants Jennifer to enjoy the trip and Boston is famous for lobster.

24.   (A)   To visit Allen and his wife
     (B)   To eat lobster
     (C)   To attend a sales meeting
     (D)   To tour historic places in the city

25.   (A)   Monday at 4:00   (C)   Monday at 5:00
     (B)   Wednesday at 4:00   (D)   Tuesday at 4:00

26.   (A)   None in particular   (C)   Center
     (B)   Linebacker   (D)   Quarterback

27.   (A)   At the end of the first day of practice
     (B)   After two weeks of practice
     (C)   When fall practice begins
     (D)   After he learns what positions the players prefer

28.   (A)   No, he is still telling players when to attend practice.
     (B)   No, he does not have an assistant coach.
     (C)   Yes, he has a schedule of events planned for each day of practice.
     (D)   Yes, the coach has all the fall game dates planned.

Part C

> **DIRECTIONS:** In this section, you will hear several short talks. After each talk, a second voice will ask questions about the talk. When you hear a question, select the choice which best answers the question based on what you heard. The short talks are NOT written in your test book. **They will not be repeated.**

29.   (A)   Twenty dollars a day
     (B) $2.25 an hour
     (C)   Minimum wage
     (D)   It depended on how many hours were worked.

30.   (A)   Student assistant in the computer center
     (B)   Student assistant in the library
     (C)   Student assistant in the cafeteria
     (D)   A clerk in the bookstore

31. (A) Student workers are paid low salaries.
    (B) All students need a job.
    (C) Everyone's first job is memorable.
    (D) Everyone should work in a library at some time.

32. (A) About 100 years old   (C) About 300 years old
    (B) About 200 years old   (D) About 500 years old

33. (A) The U. S. Civil War   (C) The fire of 1912
    (B) Hurricane Hugo   (D) The earthquake of 1886

34. (A) To protect against hurricanes
    (B) To permit large windows facing the harbor
    (C) To allow space for large parties
    (D) To protect against the summer heat and humidity

35. (A) To warn of quack headache cures
    (B) To comfort headache sufferers
    (C) To discuss the causes and treatments of severe headaches
    (D) To explain that only older adults have migraine headaches

36. (A) Headaches are more common than colds.
    (B) Headaches do not bother many people.
    (C) All headaches are caused by stress.
    (D) Migraines can be cured.

37. (A) A cattle herd   (C) Black sand beaches
    (B) Jungle forests   (D) A dormant volcano

38. (A) To discuss the contrasts of the features of Hawaii
    (B) To explain why Hawaii was made a state
    (C) To explain why one beach has black sand
    (D) To explain why the volcano on the Big Island is dormant

39. (A) The height can be measured both above and below sea level.
    (B) The height measured above sea level makes it the tallest mountains in the world.
    (C) The speaker compares this mountain's height to other dormant volcanoes.
    (D) The volcano is not considered a true mountain.

40. (A) An active volcano   (C) Wind surfing
    (B) A cattle herd   (D) Rainfall

Section 2: Reading

TIME: 30 Minutes
30 Questions

DIRECTIONS: Each passage is followed by questions based on its content. After reading the passage, choose the best answer to each question. Answer all questions based on what is indicated or implied in that passage.

Questions 1 through 5 are based on the following passage.

The issue of adult literacy has finally received recognition as a major social problem. Unfortunately, the issue is usually presented in the media as a "woman's interest issue." Numerous governor's wives and even Barbara Bush have publicly expressed concern about literacy. As well-meaning as the politicians' wives may be, it is more important that the politicians themselves recognize the seriousness of the problem and support increased funding for literacy programs.

Literacy education programs need to be directed at two different groups of people with very different needs. The first group is composed of people who have very limited reading and writing skills. These people are complete illiterates. A second group is composed of people who can read and write but whose skills are not sufficient to meet their needs. This second group is called functionally illiterate. Successful literacy programs must meet the needs of both groups.

Instructors in literacy programs have three main responsibilities. First, the educational needs of the illiterates and functional illiterates must be met. Second, the instructors must approach the participants in the program with empathy, not sympathy. Third, all participants must experience success in the program and must perceive their efforts as worthwhile.

1. What is the difference between illiteracy and functional illiteracy?
    (A) There is no difference.
    (B) A functional illiterate is enrolled in a literacy education program but an illiterate is not.
    (C) An illiterate cannot read or write, a functional illiterate can read and write but not at a very high skill level.
    (D) There are more illiterates than functional illiterates in the United States today.
    (E) Both (B) and (D).

2. What does "woman's interest issue" mean in the passage?
    (A) The issue is only interesting to women.
    (B) Many politicians' wives have expressed concern over the issue.
    (C) Women illiterates outnumber male illiterates.
    (D) Politicians interested in illiteracy often have their wives give speeches on the topic.
    (E) More women need literacy education programs than men.

3.　What is the purpose of the passage?

(A)　To discuss the characteristics of successful literacy programs.

(B)　To discuss the manner in which literacy programs are viewed by the media.

(C)　To discuss some of the reasons for increased attention to literacy as a social issue.

(D)　All of the above.

(E)　None of the above.

4.　According to the passage, which of the following is NOT a characteristic of successful literacy programs?

(A)　Participants should receive free transportation.

(B)　Participants should experience success in the program.

(C)　Instructors must have empathy, not sympathy.

(D)　Programs must meet the educational needs of illiterates.

(E)　Programs must meet the educational needs of functional illiterates.

5.　What is the author's opinion of the funding for literacy programs?

(A)　Too much

(B)　Too little

(C)　About right

(D)　Too much for illiterates and not enough for functional illiterates

(E)　Directors of literacy programs should be volunteers

Questions 6 through 10 are based on the following passage.

The price of cleaning up the environment after oil spills is on the increase. After the massive Alaskan spill that created miles of sludge-covered beach, numerous smaller spills have occurred along the Gulf Coast and off the coast of California. Tides and prevailing winds carried much of this oil to shore in a matter of days. Workers tried to contain the oil with weighted, barrel-shaped plastic tubes stretched along the sand near the water. They hoped to minimize the damage. Generally, the barriers were successful, but there remained many miles of oil-covered sand. Cleanup crews shoveled the oil-covered sand into plastic bags for removal.

Coastal states are responding to the problem in several ways. California is considering the formation of a department of oceans to oversee protection programs and future cleanups. Some states have suggested training the National Guard in cleanup procedures. Other states are calling for the creation of an oil spill trust fund large enough to cover the costs of a major spill. Still other states are demanding federal action and funding. Regardless of the specific programs that may be enacted by the various states or the federal government, continued offshore drilling and the shipping of oil in huge tankers creates a constant threat to the nation's shoreline.

6.　According to the passage, where have oil spills occurred?

(A)　U. S. Gulf Coast

(B)　Alaskan coast

(C)　California coast

(D)　(A) and (B) only.

(E)　(A), (B) and (C).

7. What was the purpose of the barrel-shaped plastic tubes?
   (A) To keep sightseers away from the oil
   (B) To keep oil-soaked animals off the beach
   (C) To force the oil to soak into the sand
   (D) To keep the oil from spreading on the beach
   (E) None of the above.

8. Which of the following solutions is NOT discussed in the passage?
   (A) Create an oil cleanup trust fund
   (B) Increase federal funding for cleanups
   (C) Reduce oil production
   (D) Use the National Guard for cleanups
   (E) Create a department of oceans

9. According to the passage, which of the following is the largest oil spill?
   (A) Alaskan coastal spill   (D) Spill off the U. S. Gulf Coast
   (B) Spill off the California coast   (E) Spill in the Red Sea
   (C) North Sea oil spill

10. What is the author's opinion of the hazards created by oil spills?
    (A) Oil spills must be expected if the present methods of production and shipment continue.
    (B) Oil spills are the result of untrained crews.
    (C) Oil spills would not be a problem if the government was better prepared to cleanup.
    (D) Oil spills are the responsibility of foreign oil producers.
    (E) Oil spills are the result of the consumers demand for oil.

Questions 11 through 13 are based on the following passage.

Children, young adults, middle-aged and retirees all experience some types of stress. Excessive stress, or the inability to cope with normal levels of stress, can lead to high blood pressure, heart disease, mental disorders, infections and prolonged or aggravated minor illnesses. Although few people can actually eliminate all stress from their lives, the lack of stress can be just as bad as too much stress. Extremely low levels of stress can cause boredom and depression and can contribute to mental illness. Many adults develop strategies for coping with stress. Some of the common strategies, which may include diet and exercise, focus on goal setting, establishing deadlines and developing contingency plans. Often, adults learn to recognize their own signs of excessive stress. Common symptoms include headaches, stomach upsets, personality changes and chronic tiredness.

11. Boredom, depression, and symptoms of mental illness are the possible result of what condition?
    (A) High stress levels   (D) Insomnia
    (B) Low stress levels   (E) Heart disease
    (C) Inability to cope with stress

12. Which of the following are suggested by the passage?
     (A)   Adults can seldom eliminate all stress from daily life.
     (B)   Most adults can learn coping strategies for excessive stress.
     (C)   A certain amount of stress is desirable.
     (D)   Some people learn to recognize symptoms of excessive stress.
     (E)   All of the above.

13. Which of the following is NOT suggested as a method for coping with stress?
     (A)   Diet   (D)   Establishing deadlines
     (B)   Exercise   (E)   Sleep
     (C)   Goal setting

Questions 14 through 16 are based on the following passage.

   Reducing the amount of fat in the foods we eat is the goal of an ever increasing number of people. Many restaurants are responding to the demand for low fat foods by adding "Light" or "Good For You" entrees to their menus. These entrees are usually traditional foods prepared without added fat. Cooking methods that require little or no fat include steaming, poaching, broiling and searing. Stir-fried vegetables and chicken dishes are especially popular with diet conscious people. Almost all fried foods should be avoided when eating out, and it is best to avoid foods in cream sauces or gravies. Although salads are very healthful foods, the value of the salad can be ruined by the addition of thick, creamy salad dressings. Desserts based on fresh fruit are usually a better choice than desserts thick with cream, butter or sugar. If you are concerned about the content or preparation of any food on a restaurant menu, it is best to ask lots of questions about ingredients and methods of preparation in order to make intelligent choices.

14. What is the purpose of the author in this passage?
     (A)   To warn people of the dangers of fat in the diet.
     (B)   To suggest ways to avoid excessive fat when eating out.
     (C)   To discourage eating in restaurants.
     (D)   To encourage the use of broiling, searing and steaming to cook food.
     (E)   Both (A) and (D).

15. Which of the following should be avoided by diet conscious diners?
     (A)   Salads   (D)   Fresh fruit desserts
     (B)   Creamy sauces or gravies   (E)   All of the above.
     (C)   Stir-fried vegetables and chicken

16. According to the passage, what does "Light" or "Good For You" mean on a restaurant menu?
     (A)   These foods are not deep-fat fried.
     (B)   These foods have reduced salt.
     (C)   These foods are especially good.
     (D)   These foods are served in smaller portions.
     (E)   These foods are prepared without added fat.

Questions 17 through 20 are based on the following passage.

The pituitary is a very small gland about the size of a marble. Located at the base of the brain, the pituitary produces many different hormones which are released into the blood. Hormones produced by the pituitary control the growth of bones and the function of the kidneys. The pituitary also controls the thyroid, a gland located in the throat, which is essential in regulating metabolism. The parathyroids, four tiny glands at the back of the thyroid, control the amount of calcium and phosphate in the blood. The parathyroids are also controlled by the pituitary. The adrenal glands, also controlled by the pituitary, are located on top of the kidneys. The adrenals have many functions, including controlling the amount of sodium and potassium in the body and producing hormones used in the metabolism of food. Another important function of the adrenal glands is the production of a hormone to help people cope with stress.

17. According to the passage which of the following is NOT controlled by the pituitary?
    (A) Growth of bones
    (B) Adrenal glands
    (C) Parathyroids
    (D) Blood circulation
    (E) Metabolism

18. What do the parathyroids control?
    (A) Metabolism
    (B) Calcium and phosphate in the blood
    (C) Sodium and potassium in the blood
    (D) The kidneys
    (E) The thyroid

19. Where are the adrenals located?
    (A) Near the pituitary
    (B) At the back of the thyroid
    (C) Near the liver
    (D) Next to the parathyroids
    (E) On top of the kidneys

20. If a child is not growing at a normal rate, what glands discussed in the passage might be responsible?
    (A) Adrenals
    (B) Kidneys
    (C) Pituitary
    (D) Parathyroids
    (E) Both (C) and (D).

Questions 21 through 25 are based on the following passage.

It is estimated that over six million Americans suffer from diabetes. This disease, which often runs in families, is the result of insufficient amounts of insulin made by the body to meet its needs. Insulin is produced by the pancreas and is used by the body to take glucose from the blood for use as fuel. A deficiency results in high blood levels and low tissue levels of glucose.

There are two types of diabetes. The first type appears early in life and is the result of abnormal cells in the pancreas so that little or no insulin is made. This is juvenile diabetes. The standard treatment for juvenile diabetes is insulin replacement therapy. The second type of diabetes occurs later in life, usually during a person's fifties or sixties. In this type of diabetes the pancreatic beta cells are normal and produce normal amounts of insulin.

However, for some unexplained reason the tissues in the body have become resistant to the action of insulin. This second type of diabetes is more common in obese people than lean people.

Diet is very important in the treatment of both forms of diabetes. High levels of fat in the blood, which interfere with the absorption of insulin, are often associated with diabetes. A person who has either form of diabetes should reduce the total amount of fat to 20-25 percent of the total calories consumed and increase the amount of carbohydrates to approximately 40 percent. Simple sugars should be kept to 10-15 percent of all calories, and protein should not exceed 24 percent.

21. According to the passage, which of the following is true?
   (A) Only adult diabetics need to be concerned with diet.
   (B) Only juvenile diabetics need to be concerned with diet.
   (C) All diabetics need to be concerned with diet.
   (D) All diabetics need to count calories very carefully.
   (E) None of the above.

22. Diabetes is the result of what condition?
   (A) Abnormal beta cells in the pancreas which do not produce appropriate amounts of insulin.
   (B) Body tissues have become resistant to the action of insulin.
   (C) Obesity
   (D) Age, heredity and obesity
   (E) Both (A) and (B).

23. According to the passage, which of the following is NOT true?
   (A) Adult onset diabetes is more common in lean people than obese people.
   (B) Approximately six million Americans have diabetes.
   (C) Diabetics should consume no more than 15 percent of all calories in the form of simple sugar.
   (D) Juvenile diabetes is usually treated with insulin replacement therapy.
   (E) The tendency to diabetes often runs in families.

24. Which of the following is NOT common about adult onset diabetes?
   (A) Obesity
   (B) Diabetes in other family members
   (C) Usually begins when a person is 50-60 years old
   (D) Normal pancreatic beta cells
   (E) Decreased blood levels of insulin

25. What is the author's purpose in this passage?
   (A) To warn people of the dangers of too much fat in the diet.
   (B) To warn people of the side effect of obesity.
   (C) To inform the reader of the two types of diabetes.
   (D) To suggest an appropriate diet for avoiding diabetes.
   (E) To discuss the hereditary nature of diabetes.

Questions 26 through 28 are based on the following passage.

"Victorian literature" is the term used to refer to the literature written during the the the reign of England's Queen Victoria from 1837-1901. It is also used to refer to the presence of Victorian attitudes in literature. The "Victorian attitude" can be described as pride in the growing power and influence of England, optimism fostered by new scientific discoveries, the high moral standards held by the royal court and the Puritan ideals of the middle class. All of these factors combined to form a spirit of moral earnestness and self-satisfaction that was criticized both during and after Queen Victoria as hypocritical, false, complacent and narrow-minded. Even at the heart of the Victorian period a large part of literature either protested against Victorian attitudes or did not exhibit such traits.

Literature written during the Victorian period is complex and reflects both romantically and realistically the changes in contemporary thought and living conditions. The rise of the middle class and the publication of the first magazines are both reflected in Victorian literature. Problems related to industrialization and crowded urban areas are also discussed in detail.

26.   What statement best describes Victorian literature?

    (A)   Victorian literature reflected the high standards of the royal court.

    (B)   Victorian literature reflected the optimism of scientific discoveries.

    (C)   Victorian literature was hypocritical.

    (D)   Victorian literature was complex, many-sided and reflected many different points of view.

    (E)   None of the above.

27.   Which of the following can be inferred from this passage?

    (A)   "Victorian" refers to a narrow set of values rigidly adhered to.

    (B)   The term "Victorian" is applied rather loosely to describe all literature written during the reign of Queen Victoria regardless of whether the attitudes are "Victorian" in nature.

    (C)   Victorian literature is very optimistic because of the absence of prolonged or serious war from 1837-1901.

    (D)   Queen Victoria insisted that literature and art produced during her reign would be called "Victorian."

    (E)   Victorian literature is anti-royalty.

28.   Which of the following best describes the author's attitude in the passage?

    (A)   The author feels that Victorian literature is difficult to categorize because of its many facets.

    (B)   The author feels that all Victorian literature is old-fashioned.

    (C)   The author believes that all Victorian literature is hypocritical.

    (D)   The author feels that Victorian writers were uneducated about serious social problems.

    (E)   The author believes Victorian literature is easy to understand.

Questions 29 and 30 are based on the following passage.

Computers are appearing in almost every school in the United States. Some schools have one computer in each classroom. Other schools group all the computers in one room to form a computer lab used by different classes throughout the day. The first microcomputer was used in a classroom for instructional purposes in 1980. Today, teachers are using computers in a variety of ways to teach many subjects in the regular curriculum. Even first grade students are learning the keyboard so they can use computer assisted instruction. Computers have brought modern technology into classrooms that only a few years ago contained nothing but books and pencils.

29. What is the author's attitude toward the use of computers in schools?
    (A) Skeptical
    (B) Unfavorable
    (C) Reluctant acceptance
    (D) Very supportive
    (E) Cautious

30. According to the passage, which of the following is true?
    (A) Computers will not be used in many schools.
    (B) Computers have been used in classrooms for 30 years.
    (C) Computers will probably be used in schools for many years in the future.
    (D) Teachers are reluctant to accept computers in schools and classrooms.
    (E) Teachers save computers for use by high school students.

Section 3: Writing

TIME: 30 Minutes
45 Questions

Part A

> **DIRECTIONS:** Each of the following sentences may contain an error In diction, usage, idiom, or grammar. Some sentences may be correct. Some sentences may contain one error. No sentence contains more than one error.
>
> If there is an error, it will appear in one of the underlined portions labeled (A), (B), (C), or (D). If there is no error, choose the portion labeled (E). If there is an error, select the letter of the portion that must be changed in order to correct the sentence.

1. Children <u>do not always</u> understand <u>that</u> giving is <u>as joyous as</u> <u>to receive</u>. <u>No error.</u>
          A   B   C   D   E

2. <u>In the recent</u> political campaign, charisma and money <u>have been demonstrated</u> to
   A   B   C
have been <u>a deciding factor</u> in the outcome. <u>No error.</u>
           D   E

3. The <u>best</u> school in the country <u>is</u> located, believe it or not, in the <u>capitol</u> city of
     A   B   C
<u>Birmingham</u>, Alabama. <u>No error.</u>
    D   E

4. Emily and Louise <u>spent</u> three hours <u>discussing</u> which of the <u>two brands</u> of makeup
                 A   B   C
<u>was best</u>. <u>No error.</u>
   D   E

5. Taxpayers, <u>who</u> keep no records are at a loss <u>if audited</u> by the Internal Revenue
          A B   C   D
Service. <u>No error.</u>
      E

6. The employee <u>was</u> concerned because <u>he felt</u> that <u>he</u> had two <u>weeks</u> pay coming to
              A   B   C   D
him. <u>No error.</u>
     E

7. Janelle was determined in her mind to improve her grades before spring break.
                  A   B   C   D

No error.
  E

8. Johnny informed the teacher's aide that he was frustrated because one of the other
         A   B   C

children had busted his balloon. No error.
        D   E

9. Patrick Henry was firm in his statement, "Give me liberty or give me death. "
              A   B C   D

No error.
  E

10. The oldest remains of Homo sapiens has been traced to Africa by archaeologists.
       A   B   C   D

No error.
  E

11. They explored many roads and found the north west route to be the best. No error.
       A   B   C   D   E

12. The amount of students at Pulley Elementary School has increased tremendously
      A   B   C

in the last five years. No error.
       D   E

13. In the army there are many generals, but how many commander-in chiefs are there?
         A   B   C   D

No error.
  E

14. When one does not try , you cannot savor the taste of success. No error.
      A   B   C D   E

15. The principle is a very mean person who paddles the children every time they make
     A   B   C

mistakes, even minor mistakes. No error.
           D   E

16. For some people it is not easy to quit smoking once you are hooked. No error.
     A   B   C   D   E

17. While attending Yale University, George Mason, who is now teaching at Briargate

Elementary, completed courses in math, social studies, biology, and english. No error.
                           A   B   C   D   E

18. Instruction at Smiley High School is all together different from instruction at the
                                 A   B

nation's most promising school, James Thomas High. No error.
  C   D   E

19. The interest was deducted annually each year by the bank through its computer
              A   B   C   D

system. No error.
       E

20. Members of the Student counsel should serve as models for the other students to
                       A   B

emulate—always exemplifying the highest of morals, dedication, and intelligence. No error.
  C   D   E

21. While I waited in line for my car to be washed, the attendant totaled my bill. No error.
        A   B   C   D   E

22. Winning has become the only concern of the new basketball coach hired by the
   A   B   C   D

school board. No error.
          E

23. The teacher, upset because 80% of her students had failed their English test, walked
                       A   B

in, the principal's office and screamed at the top of her voice. No error.
 C   D   E

24. The treaty of Versailles, while ending World War I, contained the seeds for World
                     A   B   C   D

War II. No error.
       E

25. Neither the principal or the teachers will be present at the meeting of the National
       A   B

Education Association, an organization whose members are very dedicated to
                                     C   D

education. No error.
        E

Part B

> **DIRECTIONS:** In each of the following sentences, some portion of the sentence is underlined. Under each sentence are five choices. The first choice has the same wording as the original. The other four choices are reworded. Select the letter of the best choice which rewrites the sentence correctly.

26.   The elevator stuck that had the board member who could have cast a vote that would

have changed school attendance districts.

    (A)   The elevator stuck that had the board member who

    (B)   The board member stuck on the elevator

    (C)   The elevator stuck holding a board member that

    (D)   The elevator stuck with the board member who

    (E)   The stuck elevator had a board member whom

27.   Chestnut wood, which has holes that were made by worms which is sometimes used

as expensive paneling, comes from trees killed in a blight that spread across the country.

    (A)   Chestnut wood, which has holes that were made by worms which is sometimes used as expensive paneling,

    (B)   Chestnut paneling, which is expensive, has holes that were made by worms

    (C)   Expensive chestnut paneling which has holes that were made by worms

    (D)   Expensive chestnut paneling, which has wormholes,

    (E)   Expensive chestnut, with holes that were made by worms, is sometimes used as paneling,

28.   A large number of parking spaces are always needed for eight o'clock classes by

commuting students.

    (A)   A large number of parking spaces are always needed for eight o'clock classes by commuting students.

    (B)   The eight o'clock classes require commuting students to park early.

    (C)   Commuting students with eight o'clock classes always need a large number of parking spaces.

    (D)   A large number of parking spaces for commuting students are needed for eight o'clock classes.

    (E)   Many parking spaces for eight o'clock classes are always required by commuting students.

29.   Janet watched the sailboats in the lake <u>roller skating along the shore.</u>

    (A)   Janet watched the sailboats in the lake roller skating along the shore.

    (B)   Janet watched the sailboats roller skating along the shore in the lake.

    (C)   Along the shore Janet roller skated and watched the sailboats in the lake.

    (D)   While roller skating along the shore, Janet watched the sailboats in the lake.

    (E)   Janet watched, as she roller skated along the shore, the sailboats in the lake.

30.   <u>The diet program will reduce the consumption of salt and fat which will benefit</u>

    <u>everyone.</u>

    (A)   The diet program will reduce the consumption of salt and fat which will benefit everyone.

    (B)   To reduce the consumption of salt and fat everyone will benefit from this diet program.

    (C)   The diet program will reduce the consumption of salt and fat.

    (D)   The diet program, which will benefit everyone, will reduce the consumption of salt and fat.

    (E)   The diet program will reduce the consumption of salt and fat which is good for everyone.

31.   <u>The monkey paced up and down in his cage ignoring the crowds of children watching</u>

    <u>Jack.</u>

    (A)   The monkey paced up and down in his cage ignoring the crowds of children watching Jack.

    (B)   The monkey ignored the crowd of children watching Jack as he paced up and down in his cage.

    (C)   Ignoring the crowd of children, the monkey paced up and down in his cage as he watched Jack.

    (D)   Ignoring the crowd of children, the monkey watched Jack as he paced up and down in his cage.

    (E)   Watching Jack ignore the crowd of children, the monkey paced up and down in his cage.

32. With forty pages to read the book was absorbing.

    (A) With forty pages to read the book was absorbing.
    (B) The book was absorbing with forty pages to read.
    (C) With forty pages to read, Meg found the book absorbing.
    (D) Absorbing to read, the book had forty pages more.
    (E) With forty pages to read, the book was absorbing.

33. A thorough vacuuming is a necessary part of housecleaning and you should also dust

    the bookshelves.

    (A) A thorough vacuuming is a necessary part of housecleaning and you should
         also dust the bookshelves.
    (B) A thorough vacuuming and to dust the bookshelves are necessary for
         housecleaning.
    (C) Housecleaning demands dusting bookshelves and to vacuum thoroughly.
    (D) Dusting the bookshelves and vacuuming thoroughly are necessary parts of
         housecleaning.
    (E) You should dust bookshelves and vacuum for housecleaning.

34. By calling the Bureau of Tourism is the best way to learn more about camping in

    Colorado.

    (A) By calling the Bureau of Tourism is the best way to learn more about camping
         in Colorado.
    (B) Learning more about camping in Colorado by calling the Bureau of Tourism.
    (C) The Bureau of Tourism can be called so you can learn more about camping in
         Colorado.
    (D) Calling the Bureau of Tourism is the best way of learning more about to camp
         in Colorado.
    (E) The best way to learn more about camping in Colorado is to call the Bureau
         of Tourism.

35. The defeat at Gettysburg was what brought the beginning of the end for the
    Confederacy.

    (A) was what brought the beginning of the end
    (B) was bringing the beginning of the end
    (C) began the starting of the end
    (D) was the beginning of the end
    (E) started the beginning of the end

Part C

> **DIRECTIONS:** Each of the passages below is followed by several questions or incomplete sentences. Under each question or sentence are five choices. Select the letter of the best choice and darken the corresponding oval.

Questions 36-40 are based on the following passage.

(1) Using Indians to track down and fight other Indians was not a new idea during the conflict between the Whites and the Indians during the mid-1800 Indian Wars during the conquest of the Apaches. (2) The English and the French from early colonial times had exploited traditional intertribal rivalries to their own advantage.

(3) What was a novel idea of the U.S. Army during its war against the Apaches was using an Indian against members of his own tribe. (4) Gen. George Crook believed that the best work would be done by an Indian who had only just been fighting him. (5) Crook had learned that such a scout _____ the fighting habits, the hiding places, and the personalities of the Indians being pursued. (6) This method worked well for Crook and by the end of his career he had used about 500 Apache scouts.

(7) Crook demanded trust from all his troops and, in turn, he gave them his trust. (8) He paid his scouts well and on time, a very important factor. (9) Most importantly, Crook treated all the personnel under his command with dignity and respect. (10) These were good qualities. (11) These qualities no doubt earned Crook the admiration and loyalty of his Indian soldiers. (12) Though, the man himself won their respect. (13) Crook was like few West Point trained officers, _____ he understood his enemy well. (14) He learned to fight the Indians on their terms, to use the land and terrain to his advantage, and to abandon the textbook examples. (15) _____ .

(16) Crook's faith in his scouts never wavered. (17) Moreover, they gave him no grounds for worry. (18) In the annals of the Indian Wars, the story of Crook and his scouts is unique.

36. Which of the following is the best completion of Sentence 5?
     (A) would know alot about
     (B) would know a lot about
     (C) would know
     (D) would have a great deal of useful knowledge concerning
     (E) would have knowledge of

37. Which of the following is the best way to combine sentences 10, 11, and 12?
     (A) Admiring and loyal because of Crook's good qualities, the Indian soldiers gave him their respect.
     (B) Although earning the loyalty and admiration of the Indian soldiers, Crook won their respect.
     (C) Crook won the Indian soldier's respect, admiration, and loyalty because of his good qualities.
     (D) Although these good qualities no doubt earned Crook the admiration and loyalty of his Indian soldiers, the man himself won their respect.
     (E) Although the man himself earned respect, these good qualities earned Crook the Indian soldier's admiration and loyalty.

38. In relation to the passage as a whole, which of the following best describes the writer's intention in paragraph 4?
    (A) To narrate an important event
    (B) To describe the best features of the subject
    (C) To persuade readers to take a certain course of action
    (D) To provide a conclusion
    (E) To provide a summary of the passage

39. Which of the following would be the best choice for Sentence 15?
    (A) He got on a trail, with his Apache scouts to guide him, he followed his quarry relentlessly.
    (B) He got on a trail, and his Apache scouts guiding him, he followed his quarry relentlessly.
    (C) He would get on a trail, and with his Apache scouts to guide him, he followed his quarry relentlessly.
    (D) He got on a trail and he followed his quarry relentlessly, with his Apache scouts to guide him.
    (E) He would get on a trail, and with his Apache scouts to guide him, would follow his quarry relentlessly.

40. Which of the following prepositions would be most appropriate for Sentence 13?
    (A) before   (D) plus
    (B) but   (E) till
    (C) for

Questions 41-45 are based on the following passage.

Dear Senator Simon,

(1) I am writing in support of your bill that, if passed, will be instrumental in getting legislation which will put a warning label on violent television programs. (2) Violence needs to be de-glamorized. (3) _____ .

(4) Unfortunately, violence sells. (5) One of the main reasons is because violent shows are easily translated and marketed to other countries. (6) Network executives have actually requested their script writers to include more violence in certain shows with a steady audience, as well as to create new violent shows for the late evening slot just before the news.

(7) The National Institute of Health did a study. (8) In this study children viewed violent scenes. (9) After this, children are more prone to violent acts. (10) Maybe parents will pay more attention to their children's viewing if this labeling system is enacted. (11) Maybe commercial sponsors will hesitate to sponsor programs that are labeled violent, so these programs will diminish in number and children will have fewer such programs to view.

(12) Yes, I think people need to be aware of violent events happening around the world and within our own country. (13) We need to know what is happening in the Balkans, Somalia, South Africa, as well in Los Angeles riots and the bombings in New York, are just to name two examples.

(14) However, these are real events, not glamorizations.

(15) Please keep up your campaign to get rid of excessive violence!

41.   In the context of the sentences preceding and following which of the following is the best choice for Sentence 3?

    (A)   One should agree with me that excessive violence should be detested and deplored.

    (B)   I detest and deplore excessive violence.

    (C)   You can see that I think wanton violence should be detested and deplored.

    (D)   Detesting and deploring wanton violence and other such excesses is how I feel.

    (E)   Excessive violence should be detested and deplored.

42.   In relation to the passage as a whole, which of the following best describes the writer's intention in paragraph 2?

    (A)   To present background information

    (B)   To contradict popular opinion

    (C)   To provide supporting evidence

    (D)   To outline a specific category

    (E)   To rouse the emotions of the reader

43.   Why might the punctuation at the end of Sentence 15 not be appropriate for the content of the passage above?

    (A)   An author should never end a passage with an exclamation point.

    (B)   Because the author is condemning violence, she should end the letter on a passive note and not a forceful one.

    (C)   Sentence 15 is actually a question and should end with a question mark.

    (D)   Exclamation points are useless and almost never used in formal writing.

    (E)   Punctuation is not needed for ending a formal letter.

44.   Which of the following is the best way to combine Sentences 7, 8, and 9?

    (A)   After doing a study, the children viewing violent scenes at the National Institute of Health were more prone to violent acts.

    (B)   Children viewing violent scenes at the National Institute of Health were more prone to violent acts.

    (C)   After viewing violent scenes, children at the National Institute of Health were more prone to doing violent acts themselves.

    (D)   The National Institute of Health did a study proving that after viewing violent scenes, children are more prone to violent acts.

    (E)   The National Institute of Health did a study proving that children viewing violent scenes are more prone to violent acts.

45.   Which of the following would be the best revision of the underlined portion of Sentence 13?

We need to know what is happening in the Balkans, Somalia, South Africa, <u>as well in Los Angeles riots and the bombings in New York, are just to name two examples</u>.

    (A)   as well as in Los Angeles riots, and the bombings in New York just to name two examples.

    (B)   as well as, to name two examples, the Los Angeles riots and the bombings in New York.

    (C)   as well as riots in Los Angeles and the bombings in New York.

    (D)   as well as events such as the riots in Los Angeles and the bombings in New York.

    (E)   Best as it is.

Section 4: Essay

TIME: 30 Minutes

DIRECTIONS: Plan and write an essay on the topic given below. DO NOT WRITE ON ANY OTHER TOPIC OTHER THAN THE ONE SPECIFIED. AN ESSAY ON ANY OTHER TOPIC IS UNACCEPTABLE.

Explain your philosophy of homework.

TEST OF COMMUNICATION SKILLS

ANSWER KEY

SECTION 1: LISTENING

1.	(C)	11.	(A)	21.	(D)	31.	(C)
2.	(A)	12.	(A)	22.	(A)	32.	(C)
3.	(D)	13.	(D)	23.	(D)	33.	(B)
4.	(B)	14.	(B)	24.	(C)	34.	(D)
5.	(B)	15.	(B)	25.	(A)	35.	(C)
6.	(C)	16.	(B)	26.	(D)	36.	(A)
7.	(D)	17.	(C)	27.	(B)	37.	(D)
8.	(B)	18.	(B)	28.	(C)	38.	(A)
9.	(A)	19.	(A)	29.	(C)	39.	(A)
10.	(C)	20.	(B)	30.	(B)	40.	(D)

SECTION 2: READING

1.	(C)	9.	(A)	17.	(D)	25.	(C)
2.	(B)	10.	(A)	18.	(B)	26.	(D)
3.	(D)	11.	(B)	19.	(E)	27.	(B)
4.	(A)	12.	(E)	20.	(C)	28.	(A)
5.	(B)	13.	(E)	21.	(C)	29.	(D)
6.	(E)	14.	(B)	22.	(E)	30.	(C)
7.	(D)	15.	(B)	23.	(A)		
8.	(C)	16.	(E)	24.	(E)		

SECTION 3: WRITING

USAGE

1.	(D)	13.	(C)	25.	(B)	37.	(D)
2.	(D)	14.	(D)	26.	(B)	38.	(D)
3.	(C)	15.	(A)	27.	(D)	39.	(E)
4.	(D)	16.	(D)	28	(C)	40.	(C)
5.	(A)	17.	(D)	29.	(D)	41.	(B)
6.	(D)	18.	(A)	30.	(D)	42.	(A)
7.	(B)	19.	(B)	31.	(C)	43.	(B)
8.	(D)	20.	(A)	32.	(C)	44.	(D)
9.	(E)	21.	(E)	33.	(D)	45.	(D)
10.	(C)	22.	(E)	34.	(E)		
11.	(C)	23.	(C)	35.	(D)		
12.	(A)	24.	(E)	36.	(C)		

DETAILED EXPLANATIONS OF ANSWERS
NTE CORE BATTERY–Test 3

TEST OF COMMUNICATION SKILLS
Section 1: Listening

Part A

1.   **(C)**   Response (C) is correct because it states the assignment in different words. Answer (A) is incorrect because it does not specify which problems to do. Answer (B) is incorrect because we do not know how many problems were assigned. Answer (D) is incorrect because the page numbers are different from the original statement.

2.   **(A)**   Response (A) is correct because it condenses the speaker's statement but maintains the main idea. Response (B) is incorrect because the speaker does not establish that menus need revision, only that many foods with high fat content are served. Responses (C) and (D) are incorrect because these are value judgments and interpretations not made by the speaker.

3.   **(D)**   The best response is (D). Response (A) is too broad a conclusion based on the speaker's statement. Responses (B) and (C) are logical, but neither can be concluded from the speaker's statement.

4.   **(B)**   Response (B) is correct because the speaker's main idea is restated. Responses (A) and (C) are probably true statements, but neither is related to the speaker's statement. Response (D) introduces a new idea, so it is incorrect.

5.   **(B)**   The correct response is (B) because the speaker states that not all guests at the speaker's table have been seated. Response (A) is incorrect because the speaker states that dinner will be served after all guests are seated. Response (C) is incorrect because the speaker has not mentioned the kitchen or food preparation. Response (D) may be true, but the speaker does not indicate that not all guests have arrived.

6.   **(C)**   Response (C) is correct because it answers "where." Each of the other responses may be true, but only (C) answers with a place name.

7.   **(D)**   Response (D) is correct. The question asks "how old," and only (D) provides an answer related to age. Response (A) is irrelevant to the question of "how old." Response (B) may be true, but you were not asked if the mower worked well. Response (C) is not related to the age of your mower.

8. **(B)** The correct response is (B) because it is the response that is most directly related to the speaker's statement. Car insurance may be overpriced, but that is not the issue here, so response (A) is incorrect. Responses (C) and (D) both introduce topics which the speaker did not mention. Therefore, responses (C) and (D) are incorrect.

9. **(A)** The correct response is (A) because it restates the speaker's comment. Response (B) is incorrect because crime is not decreasing. Response (C) may be true, but the speaker does not mention police patrols. Response (D) is incorrect because it is the opposite of what the speaker states.

10. **(C)** Response (C) is correct because it restates the speaker's main idea. Response (A) may be true, but the speaker does not mention foreigners. Response (B) is probably true also, but it introduces "rich" which the speaker does not include. Response (D) is incompatible with the speaker's comments, and so response (D) is incorrect.

11. **(A)** Response (A) is correct. The speaker specifically states that stock investors should not plan on short-term profits. Response (B) is incorrect because it is the opposite of what the speaker states. Response (C) is incorrect because the speaker does not discuss "foolish people." Response (D) may be true, but it is incorrect because it does not respond to the statement.

12. **(A)** The best response is (A) because it names the book and page numbers. Answer (B) may be true, but it does not answer the question of "where" the assignment can be found. Answer (C) may be true, but it is not specific enough. Answer (D) is incorrect because it answers "when" not "where."

13. **(D)** The correct response is (D) because it restates the speaker's comments. Answer (A) is incorrect because chicken is not mentioned. Answer (B) is incorrect because the speaker does not provide any information about what was served for the last three nights. Answer (C) may be true, but it is irrelevant.

14. **(B)** The correct response is (B) because the gathering rain clouds the speaker mentions indicate that it might rain. Answer (A) is incorrect because the speaker does not state that rain began. Answer (C) may be true, but the speaker does not state this. Answer (D) may also be true, but it introduces a new idea not included in the speaker's statement.

15. **(B)** Response (B) is correct because it directly responds to the question concerning the computerized card catalog. Response (A) may be true, but it does not answer the question. Response (C) is irrelevant information. Response (D) is related to the new card catalog, but it is incorrect because it does not answer the question.

16. **(B)** The correct response is (B) because it restates the speaker's main idea in other words. Response (A) is not directly related to the speaker's statement, so this is an incorrect answer. Response (C) may be true for many who enlist in the Air Force, but the speaker is not discussing length of commitment, so this is an incorrect answer. Response (D) may also be true, but the speaker has not mentioned how his brother feels about the decision.

17. **(C)** The correct response is (C) because it summarizes the speaker's statement. Response (A) is incorrect because the speaker states that late frost is rare in March, not April. Response (B) is true, but the speaker does not discuss the work involved in gardening. Response (D) may also be true, but the speaker does not mention his or anyone's uncle.

18. **(B)** Answer (B) is correct because it responds to the statement that Mardi Gras is a fun celebration that can be dangerous. Answer (A) is incorrect because it is the opposite of what the speaker says. Answer (C) is incorrect because the speaker does not suggest how to arrive in New Orleans. Answer (D) is incorrect because the speaker does not discuss New Orleans at any other time of year.

19. **(A)** Answer (A) is correct. This is the only logical response to the speaker's statement. Answer (B) is incorrect because the speaker does not state or imply that he is on a diet. Answer (C) is incorrect because the speaker says he loves to cook, not that he is learning how to cook. Answer (D) is incorrect because the speaker never mentions parties.

20. **(B)** The correct answer is (B) because this statement responds directly to the question. Answer (A) is incorrect because the speaker did not ask about climbing mountains. Answers (C) and (D) are incorrect because the Grand Canyon is not in California or Colorado.

Part B

21. **(D)** Answer (D) is correct. This is a content question. Allen is not attending the meeting because his wife had emergency gall bladder surgery.

22. **(A)** This is another content question. Jennifer tells Joe that Allen is not attending the meeting so answer (A) is correct.

23. **(D)** Answer (D) is correct because Boston is famous for lobster and Joe tells Jennifer to enjoy the trip. Answer (A) may be true but this information is not included in the dialogue. Answers (B) and (C) may be true, but both are irrelevant to the conversation.

24. **(C)** The correct answer is (C) because Jennifer specifically states she will attend a sales meeting in Boston. Answer (A) is incorrect because Allen and his wife are not in Boston, so Jennifer cannot visit them there. Answer (B) is incorrect because the purpose of the trip is not to eat lobster. Answer (D) is incorrect because it is not the reason Jennifer will travel to Boston.

25. **(A)** This is a listening and memory question. The correct answer is (A) because the coach specifically says practice begins Monday at 4:00.

26. **(D)** The correct answer is (D) because the player asks the coach if he has a chance to make quarterback. The other positions are not mentioned.

27. **(B)** The correct answer is (B) because the coach states that tryouts will begin on the third day of practice, but that he will not make any decisions for two weeks.

28. **(C)**   The correct answer is (C). The coach appears organized because he explains the plans for each day of practice to the player. Answer (A) is incorrect because it does not answer the question of whether the coach is organized. Answer (B) is incorrect because the question does not ask if the coach has an assistant. Answer (D) is incorrect because the fall game schedule does not answer the question.

29. **(C)**   The correct answer is (C). The speaker states that she was paid minimum wage.

30. **(B)**   The correct answer is (B). This is a content question that requires careful listening. Answers (C) and (D) can be eliminated because the speaker does not mention the cafeteria or the bookstore. Answer (A) names the speaker's second job.

31. **(C)**   Answer (C) is correct. The speaker states the main point at the beginning of the talk. Answer (A) may be a true statement but this is not the speaker's main idea. Answer (B) presents a point of view not discussed by the speaker. Answer (C) is a generalization the speaker does not make.

32. **(C)**   Answer (C) is correct. The city is 330 years old. This information is stated by the speaker.

33. **(B)**   Answer (B) is correct. Hurricane Hugo was the most recent disaster of those listed.

34. **(D)**   Answer (D) is correct. Thick walls and high ceilings insulated the inhabitants from summer heat and humidity. The passage does not mention large windows or parties, so answers (B) and (C) are incorrect. Answer (A) is incorrect because high ceilings and thick walls were not built to protect against hurricanes.

35. **(C)**   The correct answer is (C). The speaker's purpose is to explain the causes and possible treatments for headaches. Answer (A) is incorrect because the speaker never mentions quack cures. Answer (B) is incorrect because the author is not offering sympathy to headache sufferers. Answer (D) is incorrect because the speaker states that both adults and children have migraine headaches.

36. **(A)**   Answer (A) is correct. The speaker specifically states that headaches are more common than colds. Answer (B) is incorrect because the speaker says headaches affect millions of people. Answer (C) is incorrect because the speaker states that stress is only one cause of headaches. Answer (D) is incorrect because the speaker states that there is no cure for migraines.

37. **(D)**   The correct answer is (D). The Big Island is dominated by a dormant volcano. Answer (A) is incorrect because although there is a large cattle herd on the island, it is not a physical feature. Answer (B) is incorrect because jungle forests are not mentioned by the speaker. Only one black sand beach is mentioned, so that particular physical feature cannot dominate the island.

38. **(A)**   Answer (A) is correct because the speaker concludes by stating that Hawaii is a land of contrasts. Answer (B) is incorrect because the speaker does not discuss any of the

reasons why Hawaii became a state. Answer (C) is incorrect because the speaker mentions the black sand but does not explain why it is black. Answer (D) is incorrect because the reasons why volcanoes become dormant are not explained.

39. **(A)** Answer (A) is correct. The volcano is the tallest mountain if the height is measured from its base below sea level and combined with the height above sea level. Answer (B) is incorrect because the speaker specifically explains measuring the height from the volcano base below sea level. Answer (C) is incorrect because other dormant volcanoes are not discussed. Answer (D) is not correct because the speaker does not distinguish between volcanoes and mountains.

40. **(D)** Answer (D) is correct. This is a content question. The speaker specifically states that Hilo is famous for 140 inches of rainfall each year.

Section 2: Reading

1. **(C)** Answer (C) is correct because this is the definition of illiterate and functional illiterate stated in paragraph two. Answer (A) cannot be correct because the passage clearly distinguishes a difference between illiterates and functional illiterates. Answer (B) is not correct because the definition stated is not related to participation in a program. The relative number of illiterates and functional illiterates is not discussed, so answer (D) is incorrect. Since answers (B) and (D) are incorrect, answer (E) is also wrong.

2. **(B)** Answer (B) is correct because the passage begins by stating that many politicians' wives have expressed interest in literacy. Answer (A) is incorrect because the author of the passage does not suggest that only women are interested. Answer (C) is incorrect because the passage does not discuss the number of male or female illiterates. Answer (D) is incorrect because there is no discussion in the passage of politicians' wives giving speeches. Answer (E) may be correct but there is no information in the passage to indicate that.

3. **(D)** This passage has several purposes. First, the author presents some complaints concerning the way literacy issues are presented in the media. The author also discusses the attention given literacy issues by politicians' wives. Third, the author discusses many aspects of successful literacy programs. Therefore, answer (D), which includes all of these purposes, is correct.

4. **(A)** This question must be answered using the process of elimination. You are asked to select a statement that names a possible program component which is not characteristic of successful literacy programs. Answer (A) is correct because answers (B), (C), (D) and (E) are specifically mentioned in the passage.

5. **(B)** Answer (B) is correct because the author specifically states that politicians should support increased funding for literacy programs. Answers (A) and (C) are incorrect because the author states that funding should be increased. There is no discussion of funding for different programs so answer (D) is incorrect. Answer (E) is incorrect because the use of volunteers is not discussed.

6.　**(E)**　Answer (E) is correct because the passage specifically mentions the California coast, the Alaskan coast, and the U. S. Gulf Coast as sites of oil spills.

7.　**(D)**　Answer (D) is correct because workers were trying to keep the oil in the water and away from the beach. Answer (A) is incorrect because sightseers are not discussed in the passage. The problem of oil-soaked animals is not mentioned in the passage so answer (B) is incorrect. Answer (C) is incorrect because the cleanup crews wanted to remove the oil, not let it soak into the sand.

8.　**(C)**　Answer (C) is correct. This question must be answered using the process of elimination. Cleanup trust funds, increased federal spending, using the National Guard, and creating a department of oceans are all discussed in the passage. Therefore, answers (A), (B), (D) and (E) are incorrect. Only answer (C) names a solution not mentioned in the passage.

9.　**(A)**　Answer (A) is correct. The passage describes the Alaskan spill as "massive." The spill off the coast of California and the spill off the U. S. Gulf Coast are described as "smaller." Therefore, answers (B) and (D) are incorrect. Spills in the Red Sea and the North Sea are not discussed in the passage, so answers (C) and (E) are incorrect.

10.　**(A)**　Answer (A) is correct. The last sentence of the passage specifically states that spills are a constant threat if offshore drilling and the shipment of oil in tankers continues. Answer (B) is incorrect because the passage does not discuss crews or training programs. While the passage does imply that the government should be better prepared to clean up, the author does not state that oil spills would cease to be a problem if the government was better prepared. Therefore, answer (C) is incorrect. Answer (D) is incorrect because foreign oil producers are not mentioned. Answer (E) is incorrect because consumers' demand for oil is not discussed in the passage.

11.　**(B)**　Answer (B) is correct. These symptoms are listed in the fourth sentence as the possible results of low stress levels, so answers (A) and (C) are incorrect. Neither insomnia nor heart disease is discussed in relationship to low stress, so answers (D) and (E) are incorrect.

12.　**(E)**　Answer (E) is correct. The passage states that few people can eliminate stress and that people can learn coping strategies so answers (A) and (B) are correct. Although the passage does not state that stress is desirable, the author does state that the lack of stress is harmful, so logically a certain amount of stress must be beneficial. Therefore, answer (C) is correct. Answer (D) is also correct because the passage discusses possible symptoms and states that people can learn to recognize them.

13.　**(E)**　Answer (E) is correct because sleep is not mentioned as a technique for coping with stress. This question requires the use of elimination to determine the correct answer. Diet, exercise, goal setting and establishing deadlines are all included in the sixth sentence as strategies for eliminating stress.

14.　**(B)**　Answer (B) is correct because the passage suggests several ways to reduce the total fat in what we eat. Answer (A) is incorrect because the author of the passage does not try to convince readers that too much fat in the diet is bad. The author is assuming that this is the goal of many people, as stated in the first sentence. Answer (C) is incorrect because the author states that you can reduce fat in your diet and still eat in restaurants. Answer (D) is incorrect because although these cooking methods are recommended, that is not the main purpose of the passage. Answer (E) is incorrect because (A) and (D) are also incorrect.

15. **(B)** Answer (B) is correct. The suggestion to avoid creamy sauces and gravies is in the seventh sentence. Answer (A) is incorrect because the author states that salads are healthful. Answer (C) is incorrect because stir-frying is listed as a preferred cooking method. Answer (D) is incorrect because the author suggests fresh fruit desserts. Answer (E) is incorrect because answers (A), (C) and (D) are incorrect.

16. **(E)** Answer (E) is correct. The author states this information in the third sentence. Answer (A) is probably a true statement, but the meaning is too narrow. It does not specify what cooking method is used, only that the food is not deep-fat fried.

17. **(D)** This question requires you to use the process of elimination. The passage specifically mentions the growth of bones, the adrenal glands, parathyroids and metabolism as being controlled by the pituitary. Blood circulation is not mentioned so answer (D) is correct.

18. **(B)** Answer (B) is correct because the fifth sentence specifically states that the parathyroids control the amount of calcium and phosphate in the blood. Answer (A) is incorrect because the thyroid and adrenals control metabolism. Answer (C) is incorrect because the adrenals control sodium and potassium. Answer (D) is incorrect because the pituitary controls the kidneys. Answer (E) is incorrect because the pituitary controls the thyroid.

19. **(E)** The correct answer is (E); the adrenal glands are located on top of the kidneys. Answer (A) is incorrect because the passage does not discuss anything that is located near the pituitary. Answer (B) is incorrect because the parathyroids are located at the back of the thyroids. Answer (C) is incorrect because the liver is not mentioned in the passage. Answer (D) is incorrect because the thyroid is next to the parathyroids.

20. **(C)** Answer (C) is correct because the pituitary controls the growth of bones. Answer (A) is incorrect because the adrenals control responses to stress and metabolism. Answer (B) is incorrect because the kidneys function to clean the body of waste products. Answer (D) is incorrect because the parathyroids control the amount of calcium and phosphate in the blood. Answer (E) is incorrect because although answer (C) is correct answer (D) is not.

21. **(C)** Answer (C) is correct because the passage specifically states that a person with "either form of diabetes should reduce the total amount of fat...." Answers (A) and (B) are incorrect because both adult and juvenile diabetics need to be concerned about diet. Answer (D) is incorrect because the passage does not discuss the counting of calories, only that the percentage of various foods should be monitored.

22. **(E)** This question asks for the cause of diabetes. Answer (A) is the cause of juvenile diabetes. Answer (B) is the cause of adult onset diabetes. Answer (C) is only associated with diabetes but is not the cause. Answer (D) lists three factors which are related to diabetes, but these factors are not the cause. Therefore, answer (E) is correct.

23. **(A)** This question asks you to determine which statement is false. Answer (A) is correct because adult onset diabetes is more common in obese people than lean people. Answer (B) is incorrect because it is true that approximately six million Americans have diabetes. Answer (C) is a true statement because diabetics should limit the amount of sugar in the diet to 10-15 percent. (C) is, therefore, incorrect. Answer (D) is incorrect because insulin therapy is the standard treatment for juvenile diabetes. Answer (E) is incorrect because diabetes does run in families.

24. **(E)** Answer (E) is correct. The question asks which statement is not associated with adult onset diabetes. Answer (A) is incorrect, because obesity is common among adult diabetics. Answer (B) is incorrect because all forms of diabetes tend to run in families. Answer (C) is incorrect because 50-60 years is a common time for the onset of diabetes. Answer (D) is incorrect because it is common that adult onset diabetes is characterized by normal pancreatic beta cells. Answer (E) is correct because blood insulin levels increase in diabetes, not decrease.

25. **(C)** This question asks you to judge the author's overall purpose. Answer (C) is correct because the author has prepared an informative passage concerning the two types of diabetes. Answer (A) is incorrect because although the author mentions the dangers of too much fat in the diet, that is not the major purpose for writing. Answer (B) is incorrect because the author is not suggesting that diabetes is a side effect of obesity. Instead, the author explains that diabetes is common among obese adults, but there is no cause and effect relationship. Answer (D) is incorrect because changes in the diet cannot prevent diabetes, although diet is important in managing diabetes. Although the author discusses the hereditary nature of diabetes, this is not the primary purpose of the passage. Therefore, answer (E) is incorrect.

26. **(D)** Answer (D) is correct. The question asks you to select the statement that *best* describes Victorian literature. Answer (A) states that values of the royal court are reflected in the literature. Although this is a true statement, it does not describe *all* Victorian literature. Answer (B) is partly correct also because some Victorian literature does reflect optimism from science. Answer (C) is partly correct because the passage states that some Victorian literature was hypocritical. Answer (D) is the best answer, because according to the passage, Victorian literature is "complex and reflects both romantically and realistically the changes in contemporary thought and conditions of living." Answer (E) is not correct because answer (D) is correct.

27. **(B)** This question asks you to infer. This means that some evidence for the statement you select should be present in the passage, but you should not expect to find the answer specifically stated. Answer (B) is correct because the passage discusses the various points of view taken by Victorian literature. Obviously, literature of the period represents many perspectives, so the term "Victorian" is applied loosely to all literature from this period, not just literature that represents a specific point of view. Answer (A) is incorrect because not all Victorian literature represents a narrow set of values. Answer (C) is incorrect because some Victorian literature is optimistic in tone, but not all literature of this period is optimistic. Answer (D) is incorrect because the passage does not discuss the Queen's opinions on anything. Answer (E) is incorrect because there is no evidence in the passage that literature of this period was anti-royalty.

28.   **(A)**   The correct answer is (A). The author states that Victorian literature is complex and has many points of view, so it is logical that it would be difficult to categorize. Answer (B) is incorrect because the author never discusses Victorian literature as being out-of-date or old-fashioned. Answer (C) is incorrect because although some Victorian literature is hypocritical, there is no evidence that the author believes all Victorian literature is hypocritical. Answer (D) is incorrect because the author never discusses the education of writers of the period. Answer (E) is incorrect because the author never even implies that Victorian literature is easy to understand.

29.   **(D)**   The correct answer is (D). The last sentence indicates that the author is admiring and supportive of the efforts to use computers in schools. Answer (A) is incorrect because the author gives no indication of skepticism toward computers. Answer (B) is incorrect because the author's attitude is supportive and favorable. Answer (C) is incorrect because the author expresses no reluctance toward computers. Answer (E) is incorrect because the author is not cautious in his support of computers in the schools.

30.   **(C)**   Answer (C) is correct because the author implies that computers are in schools to stay. Answer (A) is incorrect because the author states computers are used in many schools. Answer (B) is incorrect because computers have been in classrooms since 1980 which is only 10 years, not 30 years. Answers (D) and (E) are incorrect because the author does not discuss the teachers' reactions or their use of computers.

Section 3: Writing

Part A

1.   **(D)**   The error occurs at (D). "To receive" is not in parallel form with "giving." The correct form would be "Children do not always understand that giving is as joyous as receiving."

2.   **(D)**   The error in this sentence occurs at (D). Two elements are mentioned as deciding factors. The singular construction, "a deciding factor," should be the plural, "deciding factors," to make this a logical and coherent statement.

3.   **(C)**   The error in this sentence occurs at (C). *Capitol* refers to a building in which a legislature meets. Example: The Senate meets each week in the Capitol. *Capital* refers to a city which is the seat of government of a state or country. Example: Birmingham is the capital of Alabama.

4.   **(D)**   The error occurs at (D). If only two brands are being compared, the correct form is "better" not "best." The corrected sentence should be "Emily and Louise spent three hours discussing which of the two brands of makeup was better."

5.   **(A)**   The error occurs at (A). The comma is not needed since this is a restrictive (necessary) clause.

6.   **(D)**   The error occurs at (D). The apostrophe is needed here to indicate the possessive case; thus, the correct answer is "weeks'."

7.   **(B)**   The error occurs at (B). It is redundant to say "in her mind" after "determined." The phrase "in her mind" should be eliminated from the sentence. The correct sentence would be "Janet was determined to improve her grades."

8.   **(D)**   The error in this sentence occurs at (D). There is no such word as *busted. Busted* is grossly nonstandard and should be substituted with the word *burst.*

9.   **(E)**   There are no errors in this sentence. The correct choice is (E).

10.   **(C)**   The error occurs at (C). The plural subject "remains" requires a plural form of the conjugated verb. The correct form is " been traced."

11.   **(C)**   The error occurs at (C). Compound points of the compass are always written as one word. The answer is northwest.

12.   **(A)**   The error in this sentence occurs at (A). *Amount* refers to singular words. *Number* refers to plural words. Since the reference is to students, which is plural, *number* should be used instead of *amount.*

13.   **(C)**   The error occurs at (C). When a compound is hyphenated or composed of two words, the sign of the plural is added to the most important element. The correct form is commanders-in-chief.

14.   **(D)**   The error occurs at (D). The pronoun, "you," in the second person refers to "one" in the second person. This is awkward. The correct answer is another "one" here.

15.   **(A)**   The error in the sentence occurs at (A). A *principle* is a rule, a law, a regulation. Example: Schools have several principles that children must follow. Here, reference is made to a person, the *principal* of a school, the leader. When in doubt, think of the princi*pal* as your *pal.*

16.   **(D)**   The error occurs at (D). In this sentence, "you" is a pronoun which refers to "people." This is an illogical pronoun reference. The correct form would be "For most people it is not easy to quit smoking once they are hooked."

17.   **(D)**   The error in this sentence occurs at (D). Languages, such as English, Spanish, and German, should always be capitalized.

18.   **(A)**   The error in this sentence occurs at (A). *All together* suggests everyone in one group or place. Example: The school's team members are all together now. *Altogether* means entirely. Example: Instruction at Smiley High School is altogether different from...

19.   **(B)**   The error occurs at (B). The phrase "annually each year" is redundant. The correct answer is either "annually" or "each year."

20. **(A)** The error in this sentence occurs at (A). *Counsel* refers to advice. *Council* refers to a group assembled for conferences or legislation.

21. **(E)** There is no error in this sentence. The verb tense is correct, and the sentence is correctly punctuated.

22. **(E)** There is no error in this sentence. The verb tense is correct and the sentence is correctly punctuated.

23. **(C)** The error in this sentence occurs at (C). *In* means "within." Example: While standing in the hall (within a given area), the teacher ate her lunch. *Into* means "from the outside to the inside." Example: The teacher walked (from the outside) into the office (to the inside).

24. **(E)** This sentence contains no grammatical, logical, structural, or idiomatic errors. The answer is (E).

25. **(B)** The error in this sentence occurs at (B). The word *or* can never be used with *neither*. The combination is neither/nor or either/or.

Part B

26. **(B)** The problem with this sentence is wordiness and faulty subordination. The sentence is about the board member, not the elevator, so the board member should begin the sentence. Answer (B) is correct because it eliminates an unnecessary "that" clause and an unnecessary "who" clause. It also moves the idea of the board member to the beginning of the sentence. Answer (D) also uses the unnecessary "who." Answer (C) is incorrect because "that" should refer to things, not people, as it does in this construction. Answer (E) is incorrect because "whom" should not be used in this construction. Answer (A) is identical to the original.

27. **(D)** The problem with this sentence is excessive wordiness caused by overlapping subordinate clauses and phrases. Answer (D) is correct because the main idea of the sentence is clearly stated without unnecessary subordination. Answer (A) is identical to the original. Answer (B) is an improvement, but it is still wordy, and it does not logically connect with the remainder of the sentence. Answers (C) and (E) are unnecessarily wordy.

28. **(C)** The problem with this sentence is that the passive voice has been used. The active voice is always preferred in written English. In this sentence, the students need the parking spaces. Answer (C) is correct because the meaning of the sentence has not been changed but the emphasis is now correctly placed on the students. Answer (B) is incorrect because the meaning has been changed. Answers (D) and (E) do not improve the original sentence. Answer (A) is identical to the original.

29. **(D)** The problem with this sentence is misplaced modifiers. In the original sentence, "roller skating along the shore" seems to modify the sailboats in the lake. Answer (D) is correct. Answers (B), (C) and (E) all have problems related to misplaced modifiers. Answer (A) is identical to the original.

30. **(D)** The problem with this sentence is a misplaced dependent clause. "Which will benefit everyone" modifies "diet program" not "fat." Answer (D) is correct because the dependent clause is correctly placed. Answers (B) and (E) contain misplaced modifiers. Answer (C) changes the meaning of the original sentence. Answer (A) is the same as the original.

31. **(C)** The problem with this sentence is that it lacks logical arrangement of modifying phrases. Logically, the monkey is pacing, the monkey is ignoring the crowd, and the monkey is watching Jack. Answer (C) is correct, because the modifiers are correctly placed. Answers (B), (D) and (E) all have different, but illogically placed modifiers. Answer (A) is the same as the original.

32. **(C)** The problem with this sentence is that the prepositional phrase "with forty pages to read" cannot logically modify any word in the sentence. Additional information is needed, specifically, "Who had forty pages to read?" Answer (C) is correct because the original sentence requires additional information to make a logical sentence. Answer (B) changes the placement of the prepositional phrase, but both answers lack a word that the phrase can logically modify. Answer (D) is an illogical statement. Answer (E) repeats the original sentence. Answer (A) is the same as the original.

33. **(D)** The problem with this sentence is the confusing shift from the objective discussion of housecleaning to the use of the pronoun "you." The sentence needs to be revised to achieve consistency. Answer (D) is correct. Answer (B) is awkward because "vacuuming" and "to dust" are not in parallel form. Answer (C) is awkward because "dusting" and "to vacuum" are not in parallel form. Answer (E) alters the meaning of the original. Answer (A) is identical to the original.

34. **(E)** The problem with this sentence is that it lacks a subject. The phrase "by calling the Bureau of Tourism" is an adverb. Answer (E) is correct because it has a clearly defined subject. Answer (B) is incorrect because it also lacks a clear subject. Answer (C) is incorrect because it shifts to "you" in the middle of the sentence. Answer (D) is incorrect because "calling" and "to cap" are not in parallel form. Answer (A) is identical to the original.

35. **(D)** This sentence lacks unity of construction. The phrase "what brought the beginning of the end" is awkward, wordy and confusing. Answer (D) is correct because it retains the main idea and states it clearly. Answers (B), (C) and (E) are wordy and awkward. Answer (A) is identical to the original.

36. **(C)** Choice (C) is the best reduction of the wordy original. Choice (A) uses "alot" and choice (B) uses "a lot," both of which are not formal usage to mean "much." Choice (D) is almost wordier than the original. Choice (E) is a bit stiff for the tone of the article.

37. **(D)** Choice (D) presents the ideas correctly and concisely. Choices (A) and (C) use the awkward phrase "because of." Choice (B) sounds as if the first part of the sentence is unrelated to the last part. Choice (E) repeats the verb "earned" twice.

38. **(D)** Paragraph 4 is a conclusion (D), winding up the main idea, the good relationship between Crook and Indian soldiers. Choice (A) is not correct as there is no specific incident given. Choice (B) could be a second choice, but the best features of the subject are more fully

discussed earlier in the paper. Choice (C) has no bearing on this essay. Choice (E) could be a choice if there were a recounting of the main points, but the major ideas of the last paragraph are the faith Crook and the Apaches had in one another and the uniqueness of their relationship.

39. **(E)** The past progressive tense is best, as it expresses Crook's use of the scouts as a common occurrence, not as a single event, which may be implied by the past tense in the original. (A) eliminates "and" which further confuses the sentence and does not help the verb problem. (B) makes it sound even more like a singular occurrence. (C) changes only the first verb to the progressive. (D) is not incorrect, but does not clarify the sentence any, and lets the verb tense stand.

40. **(C)** The preposition needed for this sentence needs to be synonomous with "because." Only (C) "for" is appropriate within the context of the sentence. (A) and (E) both require a time factor which does not appear in the sentence. (B) "but" implies that other officers "knew the enemy well." "Plus" (D) would work in the sentence, but is not as appropriate as (C).

41. **(B)** Choice (B) keeps the first person voice and states the main point using parallel structure and concise language. Choices (A), (C), and (D) are still excessively wordy; in addition, choice (A) changes the voice to "one." Choice (E), while somewhat more concise, uses passive voice; since this letter is a call to action, passive voice weakens the argument and intent of the letter.

42. **(A)** Paragraph 2 provides background information, choice (A), for the reason there is so much violence on television. Choice (B) is incorrect as the argument in paragraph 2 is not a contradiction to anything. Choice (C) would be correct if the paragraph contained support for the main argument. While the paragraph does give some specifics, choice (D), the evidence cannot be considered as categorizing anything. Choice (E) incorrectly implies that the paragraph is written in an emotionally charged manner.

43 **(B)** Although the exclamation point at the end of line 15 is not incorrect, it ends a letter condemning violence on television on a forceful note. All aspects of a letter or essay should convey the message to the intended audience. If it condemns violence, it should not be forceful. (A), (D), and (F) are not true. (C) may be correct, but there is no evidence of it in the letter.

44. **(D)** Choice (D) is the most concise combination, one which clearly shows time sequence and cause-and-effect. Choice (A), because it has a misplaced modifier, implies that the children conducted the study. Choices (B) and (E) imply that the children were prone to violence only while they were viewing the violent acts, a slight distortion of the correct finding. Choice (C) subtly suggests that only the children at the Institute were affected by this condition, with the implication that other children are not. This failure to indicate an extension of the findings subtly distorts the original meaning.

45. **(D)** (D) would be the best revision; the phrase "are just to name two examples," besides being grammatically incorrect, is unnecessary, and the structure of (D) sets up the parallel best. (B) is the next best, but "to name two examples" is awkward and unnecessary. (A) and (C) are not specific about any particular riots (these would at least need the article "the" as in (B) and (D)).

Section 4: Essay

The following essay received scores at the highest end of the scale used in NTE essay scoring.

Essay A

Homework assignments can be an important part of the instructional program, or they can be meaningless, busy-work activities. Quality, meaningful homework assignments have several characteristics. First, they are appropriate for the age and grade level of the student. No more than 20 minutes of homework should be assigned to students in grades 1 to 4. As a student matures, longer and more complex homework assignments are appropriate. For students in grades 5 to 8 assignments that require 30 or 40 minutes to complete are appropriate. High school students are able to concentrate for longer periods of time, consequently, longer homework assignments are appropriate for them.

Second, homework assignments should be directly related to classwork. Homework quickly becomes busy-work if the teacher simply hands out another worksheet to complete. However, homework becomes a valuable learning experience if the assignment is designed to provide an additional opportunity for students to practice a new concept introduced in class.

Third, students should be able to the complete the assignment independently. An exception to this characteristic of quality homework is that teachers may occasionally ask students to complete a project or poster as homework. Students may need to consult reference books, parents, or friends in order to complete some projects. This can also be a valuable learning experience.

A fourth characteristic of quality homework assignments is that the teacher must evaluate the homework in some manner. The teacher may want to grade the assignment, have the students put answers on the chalkboard, display the papers on the bulletin board, or discuss answers as a form of evaluation. The key issue is that the teacher must acknowledge the work the student has done and give credit and recognition for a completed assignment .

The fifth characteristic of quality homework is that the teacher needs to inform parents early in the school year that homework will be assigned regularly. Parents need to be supportive of the educational plan.

Too often, teachers assign meaningless, repetitious, drill and practice activities for homework that are not specifically related to classwork. Students quickly identify these assignments as busy-work and may become resentful of future homework assignments.

Carefully planned homework assignments not only reinforce classwork, but also teach responsibility and independent work habits. Each school needs to develop a clearly defined homework policy that recognizes the necessity of making homework assignments meaningful, appropriate to the student's age and grade level, directly related to classwork, and evaluated by the teacher upon completion.

Explanation of Essay A

This essay is well planned and organized. The main idea is clearly stated in the first sentence. The author lists five characteristics of quality homework assignments and explains each. The last paragraph summarizes the writer's main points. Nevertheless, there are some problems with the essay. Several sentences in the essay are long and seem to ramble. The author does not clearly explain how parents can "be supportive of the educational plan" in relationship to homework. There are a few errors in punctuation, but the writer has demonstrated the ability to focus on a specific topic and write an organized essay with a definite introduction, body and conclusion.

The following essay received scores in the middle of the NTE scoring scale.

Essay B

All students need homework—it is an important part of the educational process. The school day is to short to allow teachers to provide time to complete all the activities students need to do. Some of these assignments must be taken home for completion.

There are to major problems with homework assignments. The first is that teachers often assign too much work to completed at home. Homework assignments should not require any more than thirty minutes to compete. If the assignment will require more time, then it should be split into two parts. The second problem is that teachers often make an assignment at the end of class. This does not give students a change to begin the assignment during class so they can ask questions if they need to. It also does not give teachers a chance to see if students have started the assignment correctly.

Homework is important! All teachers should assign homework regularly! Students need to become accustom to working on their own! Parents expect homework! It keeps students busy after school and helps develop self-responsibility!

Explanation of Essay B

The length of the essay is satisfactory for a thirty minute time period. However, the essay does not have a clearly stated main idea. Many topics are discussed (students need homework, the school day is too short, problems with homework) but the writer's position on these topics is never fully explained. The last paragraph introduces three new ideas (homework should be assigned regularly, parents expect homework, and homework develops responsibility). None of these topics is completely discussed. The essay lacks a definite introduction and conclusion. There are several spelling and punctuation errors. A word has been omitted ("be") in the second sentence of the second paragraph. The exclamation point is overused in the last paragraph.

The following essay received scores at the lowest end of the NTE scoring scale.

Essay C

Students need homework, but generally teachers give too much. Assignments are usually too long and don't allow any time for students to participate in outside activities. School need to develop a system so that students would not have homework in more than one subject every day. That way students could concentrate on one subject and not have to worry about remembering assignments in other areas.

Teachers needs to plan homework assignments that are easy to grade. Everyone know that teachers have to many papers to grade already. Homework assignments should be short and easy to grade.

Teachers should also remember to look at the football and basketball game schedules to avoid giving homework on game nights. Not fair to team members and cheerleaders to have homework on game nights. Besides, teachers can always give class time to do homework.

Explanation of Essay C

This writer has focused on the problems related to homework. The issues raised are important (assignments should not be too long, be easy to grade, and not interfere with team sports). However, the writer discusses these issues from only one point of view—that of the students. He fails to consider or even acknowledge the goals of teachers in assigning homework. The essay seems to take the opinion that "teachers don't understand." If this is true, the writer does not explain why he has this opinion. Additionally, there are numerous spelling and punctuation errors. One sentence is an incomplete thought. There are several errors in subject-verb agreement.

NTE Test of General Knowledge

TEST 3 – ANSWER SHEET

Section 1: Social Studies

1. Ⓐ Ⓑ Ⓒ Ⓓ Ⓔ
2. Ⓐ Ⓑ Ⓒ Ⓓ Ⓔ
3. Ⓐ Ⓑ Ⓒ Ⓓ Ⓔ
4. Ⓐ Ⓑ Ⓒ Ⓓ Ⓔ
5. Ⓐ Ⓑ Ⓒ Ⓓ Ⓔ
6. Ⓐ Ⓑ Ⓒ Ⓓ Ⓔ
7. Ⓐ Ⓑ Ⓒ Ⓓ Ⓔ
8. Ⓐ Ⓑ Ⓒ Ⓓ Ⓔ
9. Ⓐ Ⓑ Ⓒ Ⓓ Ⓔ
10. Ⓐ Ⓑ Ⓒ Ⓓ Ⓔ
11. Ⓐ Ⓑ Ⓒ Ⓓ Ⓔ
12. Ⓐ Ⓑ Ⓒ Ⓓ Ⓔ
13. Ⓐ Ⓑ Ⓒ Ⓓ Ⓔ
14. Ⓐ Ⓑ Ⓒ Ⓓ Ⓔ
15. Ⓐ Ⓑ Ⓒ Ⓓ Ⓔ
16. Ⓐ Ⓑ Ⓒ Ⓓ Ⓔ
17. Ⓐ Ⓑ Ⓒ Ⓓ Ⓔ
18. Ⓐ Ⓑ Ⓒ Ⓓ Ⓔ
19. Ⓐ Ⓑ Ⓒ Ⓓ Ⓔ
20. Ⓐ Ⓑ Ⓒ Ⓓ Ⓔ
21. Ⓐ Ⓑ Ⓒ Ⓓ Ⓔ
22. Ⓐ Ⓑ Ⓒ Ⓓ Ⓔ
23. Ⓐ Ⓑ Ⓒ Ⓓ Ⓔ
24. Ⓐ Ⓑ Ⓒ Ⓓ Ⓔ
25. Ⓐ Ⓑ Ⓒ Ⓓ Ⓔ
26. Ⓐ Ⓑ Ⓒ Ⓓ Ⓔ
27. Ⓐ Ⓑ Ⓒ Ⓓ Ⓔ
28. Ⓐ Ⓑ Ⓒ Ⓓ Ⓔ
29. Ⓐ Ⓑ Ⓒ Ⓓ Ⓔ
30. Ⓐ Ⓑ Ⓒ Ⓓ Ⓔ

Section 2: Math

1. Ⓐ Ⓑ Ⓒ Ⓓ Ⓔ
2. Ⓐ Ⓑ Ⓒ Ⓓ Ⓔ
3. Ⓐ Ⓑ Ⓒ Ⓓ Ⓔ
4. Ⓐ Ⓑ Ⓒ Ⓓ Ⓔ
5. Ⓐ Ⓑ Ⓒ Ⓓ Ⓔ
6. Ⓐ Ⓑ Ⓒ Ⓓ Ⓔ
7. Ⓐ Ⓑ Ⓒ Ⓓ Ⓔ
8. Ⓐ Ⓑ Ⓒ Ⓓ Ⓔ
9. Ⓐ Ⓑ Ⓒ Ⓓ Ⓔ

10. Ⓐ Ⓑ Ⓒ Ⓓ Ⓔ
11. Ⓐ Ⓑ Ⓒ Ⓓ Ⓔ
12. Ⓐ Ⓑ Ⓒ Ⓓ Ⓔ
13. Ⓐ Ⓑ Ⓒ Ⓓ Ⓔ
14. Ⓐ Ⓑ Ⓒ Ⓓ Ⓔ
15. Ⓐ Ⓑ Ⓒ Ⓓ Ⓔ
16. Ⓐ Ⓑ Ⓒ Ⓓ Ⓔ
17. Ⓐ Ⓑ Ⓒ Ⓓ Ⓔ
18. Ⓐ Ⓑ Ⓒ Ⓓ Ⓔ
19. Ⓐ Ⓑ Ⓒ Ⓓ Ⓔ
20. Ⓐ Ⓑ Ⓒ Ⓓ Ⓔ
21. Ⓐ Ⓑ Ⓒ Ⓓ Ⓔ
22. Ⓐ Ⓑ Ⓒ Ⓓ Ⓔ
23. Ⓐ Ⓑ Ⓒ Ⓓ Ⓔ
24. Ⓐ Ⓑ Ⓒ Ⓓ Ⓔ
25. Ⓐ Ⓑ Ⓒ Ⓓ Ⓔ

Section 3: Literature and Fine Arts

1. Ⓐ Ⓑ Ⓒ Ⓓ Ⓔ
2. Ⓐ Ⓑ Ⓒ Ⓓ Ⓔ
3. Ⓐ Ⓑ Ⓒ Ⓓ Ⓔ
4. Ⓐ Ⓑ Ⓒ Ⓓ Ⓔ
5. Ⓐ Ⓑ Ⓒ Ⓓ Ⓔ
6. Ⓐ Ⓑ Ⓒ Ⓓ Ⓔ
7. Ⓐ Ⓑ Ⓒ Ⓓ Ⓔ
8. Ⓐ Ⓑ Ⓒ Ⓓ Ⓔ
9. Ⓐ Ⓑ Ⓒ Ⓓ Ⓔ
10. Ⓐ Ⓑ Ⓒ Ⓓ Ⓔ
11. Ⓐ Ⓑ Ⓒ Ⓓ Ⓔ
12. Ⓐ Ⓑ Ⓒ Ⓓ Ⓔ
13. Ⓐ Ⓑ Ⓒ Ⓓ Ⓔ
14. Ⓐ Ⓑ Ⓒ Ⓓ Ⓔ
15. Ⓐ Ⓑ Ⓒ Ⓓ Ⓔ
16. Ⓐ Ⓑ Ⓒ Ⓓ Ⓔ
17. Ⓐ Ⓑ Ⓒ Ⓓ Ⓔ
18. Ⓐ Ⓑ Ⓒ Ⓓ Ⓔ
19. Ⓐ Ⓑ Ⓒ Ⓓ Ⓔ
20. Ⓐ Ⓑ Ⓒ Ⓓ Ⓔ
21. Ⓐ Ⓑ Ⓒ Ⓓ Ⓔ
22. Ⓐ Ⓑ Ⓒ Ⓓ Ⓔ
23. Ⓐ Ⓑ Ⓒ Ⓓ Ⓔ
24. Ⓐ Ⓑ Ⓒ Ⓓ Ⓔ

Section 4: Science

1. Ⓐ Ⓑ Ⓒ Ⓓ Ⓔ
2. Ⓐ Ⓑ Ⓒ Ⓓ Ⓔ
3. Ⓐ Ⓑ Ⓒ Ⓓ Ⓔ
4. Ⓐ Ⓑ Ⓒ Ⓓ Ⓔ
5. Ⓐ Ⓑ Ⓒ Ⓓ Ⓔ
6. Ⓐ Ⓑ Ⓒ Ⓓ Ⓔ
7. Ⓐ Ⓑ Ⓒ Ⓓ Ⓔ
8. Ⓐ Ⓑ Ⓒ Ⓓ Ⓔ
9. Ⓐ Ⓑ Ⓒ Ⓓ Ⓔ
10. Ⓐ Ⓑ Ⓒ Ⓓ Ⓔ
11. Ⓐ Ⓑ Ⓒ Ⓓ Ⓔ
12. Ⓐ Ⓑ Ⓒ Ⓓ Ⓔ
13. Ⓐ Ⓑ Ⓒ Ⓓ Ⓔ
14. Ⓐ Ⓑ Ⓒ Ⓓ Ⓔ
15. Ⓐ Ⓑ Ⓒ Ⓓ Ⓔ
16. Ⓐ Ⓑ Ⓒ Ⓓ Ⓔ
17. Ⓐ Ⓑ Ⓒ Ⓓ Ⓔ
18. Ⓐ Ⓑ Ⓒ Ⓓ Ⓔ
19. Ⓐ Ⓑ Ⓒ Ⓓ Ⓔ
20. Ⓐ Ⓑ Ⓒ Ⓓ Ⓔ
21. Ⓐ Ⓑ Ⓒ Ⓓ Ⓔ
22. Ⓐ Ⓑ Ⓒ Ⓓ Ⓔ
23. Ⓐ Ⓑ Ⓒ Ⓓ Ⓔ
24. Ⓐ Ⓑ Ⓒ Ⓓ Ⓔ
25. Ⓐ Ⓑ Ⓒ Ⓓ Ⓔ
26. Ⓐ Ⓑ Ⓒ Ⓓ Ⓔ
27. Ⓐ Ⓑ Ⓒ Ⓓ Ⓔ
28. Ⓐ Ⓑ Ⓒ Ⓓ Ⓔ
29. Ⓐ Ⓑ Ⓒ Ⓓ Ⓔ
30. Ⓐ Ⓑ Ⓒ Ⓓ Ⓔ

(Section 1 continued)

10. Ⓐ Ⓑ Ⓒ Ⓓ Ⓔ
11. Ⓐ Ⓑ Ⓒ Ⓓ Ⓔ
12. Ⓐ Ⓑ Ⓒ Ⓓ Ⓔ
13. Ⓐ Ⓑ Ⓒ Ⓓ Ⓔ
14. Ⓐ Ⓑ Ⓒ Ⓓ Ⓔ
15. Ⓐ Ⓑ Ⓒ Ⓓ Ⓔ
16. Ⓐ Ⓑ Ⓒ Ⓓ Ⓔ
17. Ⓐ Ⓑ Ⓒ Ⓓ Ⓔ
18. Ⓐ Ⓑ Ⓒ Ⓓ Ⓔ
19. Ⓐ Ⓑ Ⓒ Ⓓ Ⓔ
20. Ⓐ Ⓑ Ⓒ Ⓓ Ⓔ
21. Ⓐ Ⓑ Ⓒ Ⓓ Ⓔ
22. Ⓐ Ⓑ Ⓒ Ⓓ Ⓔ
23. Ⓐ Ⓑ Ⓒ Ⓓ Ⓔ
24. Ⓐ Ⓑ Ⓒ Ⓓ Ⓔ
25. Ⓐ Ⓑ Ⓒ Ⓓ Ⓔ

25. Ⓐ Ⓑ Ⓒ Ⓓ Ⓔ
26. Ⓐ Ⓑ Ⓒ Ⓓ Ⓔ
27. Ⓐ Ⓑ Ⓒ Ⓓ Ⓔ
28. Ⓐ Ⓑ Ⓒ Ⓓ Ⓔ
29. Ⓐ Ⓑ Ⓒ Ⓓ Ⓔ
30. Ⓐ Ⓑ Ⓒ Ⓓ Ⓔ
31. Ⓐ Ⓑ Ⓒ Ⓓ Ⓔ
32. Ⓐ Ⓑ Ⓒ Ⓓ Ⓔ
33. Ⓐ Ⓑ Ⓒ Ⓓ Ⓔ
34. Ⓐ Ⓑ Ⓒ Ⓓ Ⓔ
35. Ⓐ Ⓑ Ⓒ Ⓓ Ⓔ

NTE CORE BATTERY–Test 3
TEST OF GENERAL KNOWLEDGE
Section 1: Social Studies

TIME: 30 minutes
30 questions

DIRECTIONS: Each of the following questions and incomplete statements is followed by five answer choices. Select the choice which best answers each question.

---

1. Which one of the following was published earliest?
   - (A) Harriet Beecher Stowe's *Uncle Tom's Cabin*
   - (B) Mark Twain's *The Adventures of Huckleberry Finn*
   - (C) Ralph Waldo Emerson's *Nature*
   - (D) Ernest Hemingway's *The Sun Also Rises*
   - (E) Alfred T. Mahan's *The Influence of Sea Power Upon History, 1660-1783*

2. In the *Plessy v. Ferguson* case, the Supreme Court decided that
   - (A) separate but equal facilities are constitutional.
   - (B) due process of law applies only to the federal government.
   - (C) government efforts to regulate business are permissible.
   - (D) workers cannot be forbidden to join labor unions.
   - (E) laws passed by Congress may be called unconstitutional.

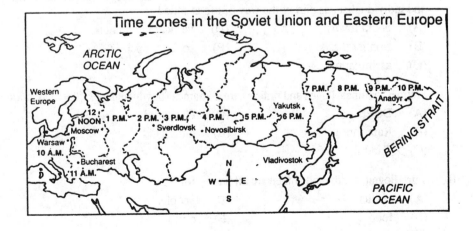

3. According to the map on the previous page, how many time zones occur in the USSR?
   (A) 12   (D) 11
   (B) 9   (E) 13
   (C) 10

4. Which of the following is the correct chronological order for the events in history listed below?
   I.   Puritans arrive in New England
   II.   Protestant Reformation begins
   III. Columbus sets sail across the Atlantic
   IV.   Magna Carta is signed in England
   (A) IV, III, II, I   (D) III, II, I, IV
   (B) IV, III, I, II   (E) II, III, I, IV
   (C) III, IV, II, I

5. The intellectual movement which encouraged the use of reason and science and anticipated human progress was called the
   (A) American System.   (D) age of belief.
   (B) mercantilism.   (E) Romantic era.
   (C) Enlightenment

6. During the American Civil War, the Battle of Gettysburg was fought in
   (A) Virginia.   (D) South Carolina.
   (B) Maryland.   (E) Pennsylvania.
   (C) Georgia.

7. The Bill of Rights (the first ten Amendments to the U.S. Constitution) deal with
   (A) limits on individual rights.   (D) basic rights and liberties.
   (B) federalism.   (E) judicial review.
   (C) expanded government.

8. The idea that the advance of American settlement in the west promoted democracy and individualism as part of the way of life is called
   (A) boom towns.   (D) vertical integration.
   (B) frontier thesis.   (E) social gospel.
   (C) assimilation.

9. Steppes, pampas, llanos and prairies are all names for which geographical location?
   (A) Desert   (D) Chaparral
   (B) Rain forest   (E) Grassland
   (C) Tundra

10. Yurt, hogan, soddy and chikee are all names for
    (A) shelter.   (D) people.
    (B) food.   (E) cities.
    (C) drink.

11. A grand jury as distinguished from a petit jury
    (A) differs only in having more members.
    (B) deals with more important cases.
    (C) gives out more severe punishment.
    (D) determines guilt or innocence in individual cases.
    (E) determines whether the evidence against various accused persons is sufficient to justify indicting them.

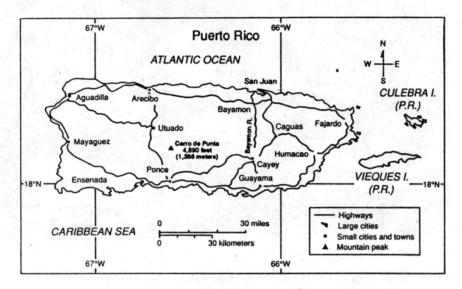

12. According to the map above, to get from Ponce to Arecibo, one would have to travel in which direction?
    (A) Southeast   (D) West
    (B) South   (E) North
    (C) East

13. Which of the following religions is polytheistic?
    (A) Judaism   (D) Islam
    (B) Zoroastrianism   (E) None of the above.
    (C) Christianity

14. The sudden violent overthrow of an existing government by a small group is referred to as
    (A) diplomacy.   (D) veto.
    (B) cold war.   (E) coup d' état.
    (C) sanction.

15. Judaism
    (A) holds that there is a single all-powerful God.
    (B) is a prophetic religion.

(C)   looks for the coming of the Messiah.

(D)   follows the Torah, the first five books of the Bible.

(E)   All of the above.

16.   From the cartoon above, what conclusion can be logically drawn?

(A)   Free trade is alive and well.

(B)   The ship will make it to port despite the icebergs.

(C)   Don't trade with other nations.

(D)   Trade between nations is not always barrier free.

(E)   Comparative advantages overcomes all difficulties.

17.   Which of the following groups did not play a role in the settlement of the English colonies in America?

(A)   Roman Catholics   (D)   Quakers

(B)   Puritans   (E)   All of the above.

(C)   Mormons

18.   The Morrill Act of 1862

(A)   abolished segregation in state supported colleges.

(B)   established the land grant system of universities.

(C)   provided for state control of education.

(D)   had no lasting effect on American education.

(E)   Only (C) and (D).

19. The effect of the 1921 Immigration Quota Act was to
    (A) sharply reduce immigration from the south and east of Europe.
    (B) greatly increase immigration from the south and east of Europe.
    (C) greatly reduce immigration from the countries of northern Europe.
    (D) reduce Mexican immigration.
    (E) reduce Chinese and Japanese immigration.

20. Aside from the native Americans who were already inhabitants, the first settlers of the southwestern part of what became the United States were
    (A) cowboys from Texas and Kansas.
    (B) French missionaries.
    (C) Spaniards and Mexicans.
    (D) gold rush miners from the east.
    (E) New England farmers.

21. In a free enterprise economy, production and consumption are allocated mainly through
    (A) trade associations.   (D) taxes and subsidies.
    (B) price changes in the markets. (E) the central banking system.
    (C) central planning.

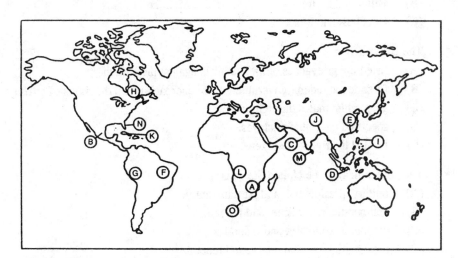

22. On the map above, which letter represents the Philippines?
    (A) K   (D) M
    (B) D   (E) O
    (C) I

WONDER HOW LONG THE HONEYMOON WILL LAST?

23. In the cartoon above, who are the bride and groom?

   (A)   Goering and Trotsky   (D)   Hitler and Mussolini
   (B)   Hitler and Stalin   (E)   Marx and Engels
   (C)   Goebbels and Marx

24. The Bill of Rights
   (A)   listed the grievances of the colonists against the British.
   (B)   forbade the federal government from encroaching on the rights of citizens.
   (C)   gave white males the right to vote.
   (D)   specified the rights of slaves.
   (E)   limited the rights of citizens.

25. The government of the United States is
   (A)   unitary, presidential, and parliamentary.
   (B)   democratic, republican, and federal.
   (C)   democratic, unitary, and federal.
   (D)   presidential, parliamentary, and federal.
   (E)   (A) and (C) only.

26. The amount of a product that people are willing to sell at a given price and time is the
   (A)   market supply.   (D)   equilibrium price.
   (B)   supply curve.   (E)   market demand.
   (C)   demand curve.

27. The principal legal forms of business organization are
   (A)   single proprietorship, partnership, corporation.
   (B)   single proprietorship, partnership, charter.

(C) corporation, charter, stock company.

(D) closed shop, open shop, union shop.

(E) None of the above.

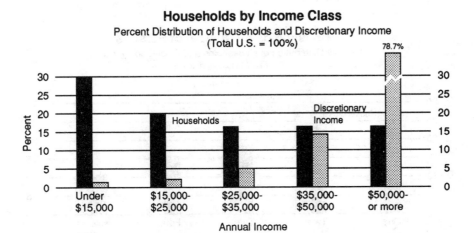

Households by Income Class

Percent Distribution of Households and Discretionary Income
(Total U.S. = 100%)

28. According to the graph "Households by Income Class" above, which one of the following statements is true?

(A) About 50% of households had under $15,000

(B) Almost 75% of households had at least $50,000 or more

(C) About 78% of households had $50,000 or more

(D) About 20% of households had between $15,000 and $25,000 annual income

(E) None of the above.

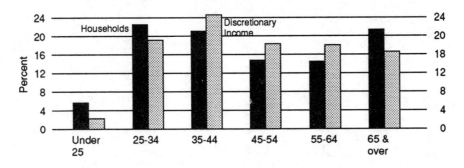

Age of Household Head

Percent Distribution of Households and Discretionary Income
(Total U.S. = 100%)

29. According to the graph, "Age of Household Head," which one of the following statements is true?

(A) Middle age households tend to have greater discretionary income

(B)   The youngest have the most discretionary income

(C)   The oldest have the most discretionary income

(D)   The older one gets, one has the least discretionary income

(E)   None of the above.

Households by Number of Persons

Percent Distribution of Households and Discretionary Income
(Total U.S. = 100%)

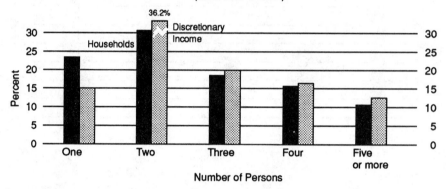

Number of Persons

30.   According to the graph, "Households by Number of Persons" which one of the following is true?

(A)   The larger the number of persons, the greater the percent of discretionary income available

(B)   The smaller the size of the household, the greater the amount of discretionary income available

(C)   Two-person households have the least discretionary income

(D)   One-person households are wealthier than larger households

(E)   None of the above.

Section 2: Mathematics

TIME: 30 Minutes
25 Questions

DIRECTIONS: Each of the following questions and incomplete statements is followed by five answer choices. Select the choice which best answers each question.

---

1. Select the, correct order from smallest to largest for the set of decimal values below:

    (A) .591, .300, .29, .190, .1   (D) .1, .190, .29, .300, .591

    (B) .1, .29, .190, .300, .591   (E) .300, .29, .190, .591, .1

    (C) .1, .29, .190, .591, .300

2. If wallpaper that is in 50 centimeter by 3 meter pieces is used to paper a wall, 8 pieces are needed. If you buy wallpaper in 25 centimeter by 1-l/2 meter pieces, how many pieces will be needed to do the same wall?

    (A) 4   (D) 32

    (B) 8   (E) 56

    (C) 16

3. **A is 3 less than 5 times B**

    Which of the following is NOT an acceptable way to express the relationship above?

    (A) $A + 3 = 5B$ (D) $B = 5A + 15$

    (B) $A = 5B - 3$ (E) $A + 1 = 5B - 2$

    (C) $B = \dfrac{A + 3}{5}$

4. To find the area of the shaded portion of the hexagon below you need the values of which of the following?

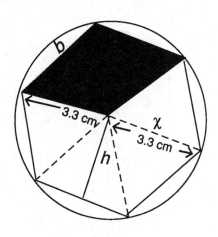

The hexagon is inscribed within a circle. b is the side of the shaded area. h is the height of one of the triangles forming the hexagon. x is the same length as the other half of the circle diameter.

(A)   3.3 only.
(B)   h only.
(C)   Both 3.3 and b.

(D)   Either 3.3 or b.
(E)   Either x or 3.3.

5.   Which step or steps do you take to construct a math sentence which describes this graph?

(A)   Note that the range is between -8 and -3.
(B)   Note that -8 is excluded and -3 included in the range.
(C)   Note that -8 is included and -3 excluded in the range.
(D)   (A) and (B).
(E)   (A) and (C).

6.   The chart gives data about the length of cargo ships docked at a port. Which of the figures below best represents the data of the table?

CARGO SHIPS

| Ship A | 300 ft. | Ship C | 450 ft. |
| Ship B | 150 ft. | Ship D | 600 ft. |

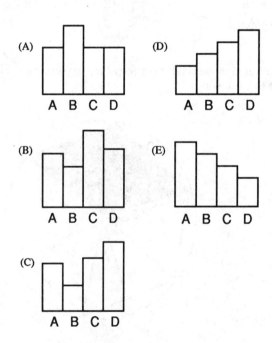

7. Round .666666 to the nearest thousandth.

    (A)   .66667   (D)   .7

    (B)   .6667   (E)   .700

    (C)   .667

8. A homeowner wants to lay a concrete driveway. The concrete area will be 10 feet wide, 50 feet long, and 6 inches deep. Concrete costs $50 a cubic yard. Estimate the approximate cost of the driveway.

    (A) $40   (D) $900

    (B) $400   (E) $9,000

    (C) $450

9.

X	Y
0	-1
1	3
2	7
4	15
8	31

Which one of the equations below expresses the relationship between X and Y in the data table above?

    (A) $Y = X - 1$ (D) $Y = 2X + 1$

    (B) $Y = X + 3$ (E) $Y = 4X - 1$

    (C) $Y = 3X - 1$

10. What is the perimeter (in centimeters) of the top rectangle in the figure below:

(Drawn to scale)

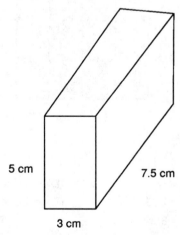

5 cm

7.5 cm

3 cm

    (A)   56.25   (D)   21

    (B)   10.5   (E)   22.5

    (C)   37.5

11. Sally, a ten-year-old girl, is very choosey about her likes and dislikes. She follows one rule without exception for her likes. What is it?

Sally Likes	**Sally Dislikes**
Bill	Bob
Annie	Jane
vanilla	chocolate
cookies	cake
Missouri	Iowa
Betty	Andria
Mississippi	Idaho
Tennessee	Florida

(A) Sally likes desserts. (D) Sally likes states and names.

(B) Sally likes states. (E) Sally likes the letters A, B, C, M, T and V.

(C) Sally likes words with double letters in them.

12. In the drawing, the large square is 1 unit on a side. Write a fractional equation which depicts the problem and the answer for the shaded area.

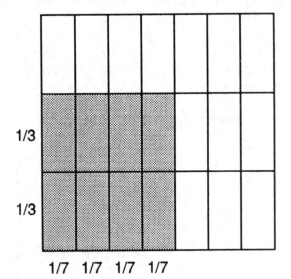

1/7 1/7 1/7 1/7

(A) 1/3 x 1/2 = 1/6 (D) 1/3 x 3/7 = 3/21

(B) 2/3 x 1/7 = 2/21 (E) 2/3 x 3/7 = 6/21

(C) 2/3 x 4/7 = 8/21

13. A number rounded to the nearest hundredth is 2.16. Which number can NOT be the original number?

(A)   2.160   (D)   2.159
(B)   2.167   (E)   2.164
(C)   2.162

14. If the student is forgetting he borrowed from the previous place value, which incorrect answer will he record for the problem below?

$$4372$$
$$-2858$$

(A)   2526   (D)   2524
(B)   1514   (E)   7230
(C)   524

15. Points A, B, C and D are on the same line. If AD = 7 and CB = 3, which number line represents the ratio between AD and CB?

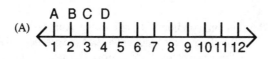

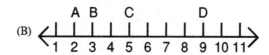

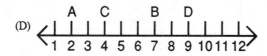

16. Which of the figures below have the same area? (figures not drawn to scale)

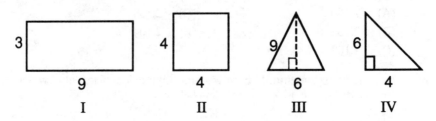

I   II   III   IV

(A) II, III and IV   (D) I, II and IV
(B) II and IV only   (E) I and III only
(C) I, II, and III

17.

1.	432	2.	*1* 74	3.	*4* 385	4.	*00* 563
	+265		+43		+667		+545
	697		18		9116		118

Examine the elementary student's work above. Analyze what the error pattern is that the student is exhibiting. If the student worked the problem 618 + 782, what incorrect answer would the student give (assuming the use of the error pattern exhibited above)?

32
618
+782

(A) 176   (D) 1112
(B) 1400   (E) 13910
(C) 164

18. Which of the figures below have the same volume? (figures not drawn to scale)

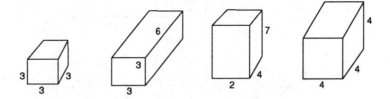

(A) II, III and IV   (D) II, and IV
(B) II and III   (E) None of them are equal in volume.
(C) I, II, and III

19.   Which number line shows all the solutions to $3 < W + 7$?

(A)

$\xleftarrow{\quad\;\;\;\bullet\;|\;\;|\;\;|\;\;|\;\;|\;}\rightarrow$ W
-4

(B)

$\xleftarrow{\quad\;\;\;\circ\;|\;\;|\;\;|\;\;|\;\;|\;}\rightarrow$ W
-4

(C)

$\xleftarrow{\quad|\;\;|\;\;\bullet\!\!\!\!=\!\!=\!\!=\!\!=\!\!=\!}\rightarrow$ W
-4

(D)

$\xleftarrow{\quad|\;\;|\;\;\circ\!\!\!\!=\!\!=\!\!=\!\!=\!\!=\!}\rightarrow$ W
-4

(E)   None of the above.

20.   Estimate and select the largest answer.

(A) $.005 + .009 =$ $\qquad$ (D) $.009 - .005 =$
(B) $.005 \times .009 =$ $\qquad$ (E) $.009 + .005 =$
(C) $.005 + .009 =$

21.   A ladder is leaning against a wall. How long is the ladder?

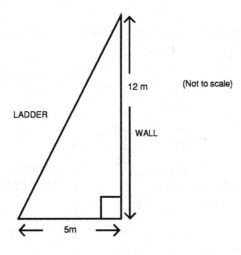

12 m $\qquad$ (Not to scale)

LADDER

WALL

5m

(A)   12 meters $\qquad$ (D)   7 meters
(B)   13 meters $\qquad$ (E)   20 meters
(C)   17 meters

22. What is the mode of these values?

     3.5, 6, 8, 6, 5, 5.5

     (A) 6   (D) 8
     (B) 5.5   (E) 3.5
     (C) 5

23. Study the water level reading in milliliters on the calibrated cylinder below. How much water is needed to have 100 ml?

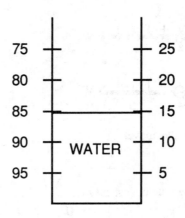

     (A) 85 ml   (D) Cannot be determined
     (B) 15 ml   (E) 75 ml
     (C) 80 ml

24. Study the characteristics listed below for Sue. What rule describes her likes?

     Sue Likes   **Sue Dislikes**
     cucumbers   celery
     pumpkins   potatoes
     peaches   spinach
     tomatoes   carrots
     apples   limas

     (A) She dislikes starchy foods.   (D) She likes fruit.
     (B) She likes red-colored food.   (E) She likes food from vines.
     (C) She dislikes stringy, chewy food.

25. FLOWCHART

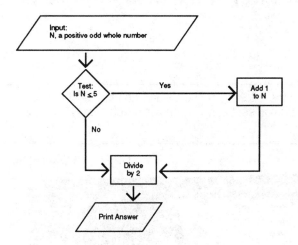

From the steps in the flowchart above, if the input is 5, the answer printed is:

(A)   3

(B)   2

(C)   1

(D)   4.5

(E)   2.5

Section 3: Literature and Fine Arts

TIME: 30 Minutes
35 Questions

DIRECTIONS: Each of the following questions and incomplete statements is followed by five answer choices. Select the choice which best answers each question.

1. Who is the cental focus in the picture above and why?

   (A) The two men lower right, because they are separate and thus draw attention

   (B) The guard at the top of the stairs, because he is the person at the highest elevation

   (C) The man to the left of the flag, because he rises above the crowd

   (D) The man on the middle of the stairs in the long, belted robe, because he is the focus of the other players

   (E) There is no central focus in the picture.

2.   Which of the figures pictured above would be most appropriate for a medieval cycle play?

(A)   1   (D)   4

(B)   2   (E)   5

(C)   3

Questions 3 through 5 are based on the following passage.

It was the best of times, it was the worst of times, it was the age of wisdom, it was the age of foolishness, it was the epoch of belief, it was the epoch of incredulity, it was the season of Light, it was the season of Darkness, it was the spring of hope, it was the winter of despair, we had everything before us, we had nothing before us, we were all going direct to Heaven, we were all going direct the other way—in short, the period was so far like the present period, that some of its noisiest authorities insisted on its being received, for good or for evil, in the superlative degree of comparison only.

There were a king with a large jaw, and a queen with a plain face, on the throne of England; there were a king with a large jaw, and a queen with a fair face, on the throne of France. In both countries it was clearer than crystal to the lords of the State preserves of loaves and fishes, that things in general were settled for ever.

3.   The vast comparisons in the above passage indicate that the speaker is describing

(A)   a placid historical time period.

(B)   a time of extreme political upheaval.

(C)   a public event.

(D)   a time when anything was possible.

(E)   the attitudes of people at war.

4.   The last sentence of the passage

(A)   mocks the self-assuredness of the governments of England and France.

(B)   comments on the horrible poverty of the two nations.

(C)   most likely foreshadows an upcoming famine or drought.

(D)   attacks the two governments for neglecting the poor, hungry masses.

(E)   alludes to the Bible to hint at the magnitude of the upcoming events.

5. The phrase, "some of its noisiest authorities insisted on its being received, for good or for evil, in the superlative degree of comparison only"
    (A) mocks the arrogance of the governments.
    (B) mocks the arrogance of the people.
    (C) compares the attitude of the people to the attitude of the governments.
    (D) Both (A) and (B).
    (E) Both (B) and (C).

Pylon Temple of Horus, Edfu

6. In the example pictured above, which of the following contributes most to an effect of stability and changeless grandeur?
    (A) The strong horizontal thrust of the architecture
    (B) The wealth of elaborate ornamental detail
    (C) The vast open courtyard with its surrounding columns
    (D) The simplified geometry of the massive forms and the sloping diagonal walls
    (E) The enormous relief carvings of the pharaohs and the gods

Galleria Borghese, Rome

7.   Which of the following seems most true of the sculpture pictured above?
      (A)   The statue is conceived as a decorative work without a narrative function.
      (B)   The figure seems to be static, passive, and introverted.
      (C)   The figure is depicted as though frozen in a moment of action.
      (D)   The figure's garments indicate that he is a soldier or warrior.
      (E)   The twisting pose of the figure contradicts the expression of the face.

Merry days were these at Thornfield Hall; and busy days too: how different from the
first three months of stillness, monotony and solitude I had passed beneath its roof!
All sad feelings seemed now driven from the house... there was life everywhere,
movement all day long.

8.   In the above passage, what is the significance of the three consecutive periods?
      (A)   They indicate a lapse in thought on the author's part.
      (B)   They indicate that the speaker is unable or unwilling to finish his/her sentence.
      (C)   They indicate that part of the quote has been omitted.
      (D)   They indicate that part of the original manuscript has been lost.
      (E)   They eliminate the need for further punctuation in the sentence.

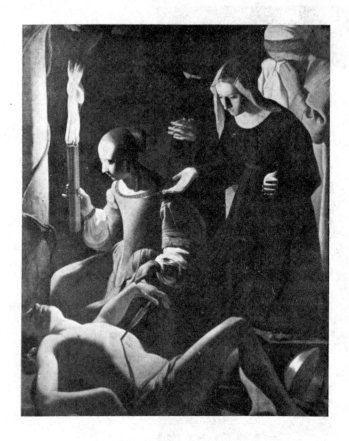

Gemäldegalerie, Staatliche Museen, Berlin-Dahlem

9.   In this painting, light is used to do all of the following EXCEPT
     (A)   model and define the forms.
     (B)   create an atmosphere of stillness and calm.
     (C)   convey a sense of intimacy.
     (D)   establish a recession into space.
     (E)   heighten the drama and poignancy of the scene.

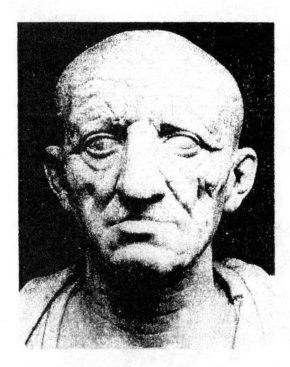

Palazzo Torlonia, Rome

10. Which of the following best describes the example pictured above?
   (A) The subject appears to be poetic, dreamy, and aristocratic.
   (B) The sculptor was not concerned with descriptive detail.
   (C) The hard material counteracts the effect desired by the sculptor.
   (D) The sculptor shows a tendency to idealize and generalize his subject.
   (E) The subject appears to be hard-bitten, pragmatic, and realistic.

   (A) Once upon a time and a very good time it was there was a moocow coming
        down along the road and this moocow that was coming down along the met a
        nicens little boy named baby tuckoo...
   (B) And thus have these naked Nantucketers, these sea hermits, issuing from their
        ant-hill in the sea, overrun and conquered the watery world like so many
        Alexanders...
   (C) A large rose tree stood near the entrance of the garden: the roses growing on
        it were white, but there were three gardeners at it, busily painting them red.
        Alice thought this a very curious thing, and she went nearer to watch them, and,
        just as she came up to them, she heard one of them say "Look out now, Five!"
   (D) Emma was not required, by any subsequent discovery to retract her ill opinion
        of Mrs. Elton. Her observation had been pretty correct. Such as Mrs. Elton
        appeared to her on the second interview, such she appeared whenever they met
        again—self-important, presuming, familiar, ignorant, and ill-bred. She had a
        little beauty and a little accomplishment, but so little judgement that she
        thought herself coming with superior knowledge of the world, to enliven and
        improve a country neighborhood...

(E)   TRUE!—nervous—very, very dreadfully nervous had I been and am; but why *will* you say that I am mad? The disease had sharpened my senses—not destroyed—not dulled them. Above all was in the sense of hearing acute. I heard all things in heaven and in the earth. I heard many things in hell.

11.   Which passage makes use of allusion?

12.   Which passage employs a discreet voice to imitate the speech of a character?

13.   Which passage is most likely taken from a 19th century novel of manners?

The Art Institute of Chicago

14.   Which of the following best characterizes the artist's approach in this picture?
   (A) Spontaneous and impulsive   (D) Passionate and romantic
   (B) Emotionally tormented   (E) Personal and revealing
   (C) Detached and systematic

Arch of Constantine, Rome

15.   In the example pictured above, the four slender columns at the front of the arch do all of the following EXCEPT

   (A)   lead the eye from ground level to the upper story.

   (B)   establish a horizontal rhythm across the facade of the arch.

   (C)   provide vital structural support for the upper story of the arch.

   (D)   help to divide the elaborate facade into regular units.

   (E)   add a purely decorative element to the combination of Classical architectural features.

(The veranda of the Voynitzevs' country house. It looks out onto a sunlit garden, with the tall trees of the forest beyond, bisected by a grassy walk.

   The whoosh of a rocket taking off. The lights come up to reveal YAKOV in the garden with a large box of assorted fireworks in his arms. Beside him stands DR. TRILETZKY, a match in his hand. They are gazing up into the sky—DR. TRILETZKY with delight, YAKOV with apprehension. There is a smell of sulfur in the air. The rocket bursts, off.)

16.   The above passage is most likely taken from

   (A)   a Victorian novel.

   (B)   the stage directions of a play.

   (C)   the critical notes to a literary work.

   (D)   the rough draft of a literary work.

   (E)   an epistolary novel.

Trans World Airlines Terminal, John F. Kennedy International Airport

17. Which of the following is an important feature of the building pictured above?

   (A) A dependence on rectilinear lines and angles

   (B) An emphasis on the structural framework of the building

   (C) An interplay of large and small geometric shapes

   (D) The use of curvilinear forms to suggest organic growth or motion

   (E) An orderly, Classically-inspired floor plan

   (A) My life closed twice before its close;
         It yet remains to see
         If immortality unveil
         A third event to me,

   (B) Hark, hark!
         Bow-wow,
         The watch-dogs bark!
         Bow-wow.
         Hark, hark! I hear
         The strain of strutting chanticleer
         Cry, "Cock-a-doodle-doo!"

   (C) A narrow fellow in the grass
         Occasionally rides;
         You may have met him. Did you not,
         His notice sudden is:
         The grass divides as with a comb,
         A spotted shaft is seen,
         And then it closes at your feet
         And opens further on.

(D)   Gather ye rosebuds while ye may,
      Old Time is still a-flying;
      And this same flower that smiles today
      Tomorrow will be dying.

(E)   Round the cape of a sudden came the sea,
      And the sun looked over the mountain's rim.
      And straight was a path of gold for him,
      And the need of a world of men for me.

18.   Which passage espouses the philosophy of *carpe diem*?

19.   Which passage employs the technique of onomatopoeia?

20.   Which passage employs the technique of alliteration?

21.   It pleased God that I was still spared, and very hearty and sound in health, but very impatient of being pent up within doors without air, as I had been for fourteen days or thereabouts, and I could not restrain myself, but I would go to carry a letter for my brother to the post-house.

The above is most likely an excerpt from which of the following?

(A)   Poem   (D)   Myth
(B)   Play   (E)   Song
(C)   Journal

22.   As he walked through the office, Raskolnikov noticed that many people were looking at him. Among them he saw the two porters from *the* house whom he has invited that night to the police-station. They stood there waiting. But he was no sooner on the stairs than he heard the voice of Porfiry Petrovitch behind him. Turning round, he saw the latter running after him, out of breath.

The above paragraph is most probably an excerpt from which of the following?

(A)   British spy novel   (D)   An existentialist short story
(B)   19th century Russian novel   (E)   A 19th century Victorian novel
(C)   A modern romance

(A)   Kozan-ji., Japan

(B)   British Museum, London

(C)   Louvre, Paris

(D)   Louvre, Paris

(E)   Lot, France

23.   Which example is intent on a naturalistic rendering of an animal's anatomy?

24.   Which example uses animals as a metaphor for human behavior?

25.   In which example are animals seen in a magic or ritual context?

> No longer mourn for me when I am dead
> Then you shall hear the surly sullen bell
> Give warning to the world that I am fled
> From this vile world, with vilest worms to dwell.

26.   The meaning of "with vilest worms to dwell" in the above lines is
    (A)   to be dead and buried.   (D)   to run from the problems of the world.
    (B)   to have descended to hell.   (E)   to live underground.
    (C)   to ring the death toll for a deceased person.

27. In his "Speech in the Virginia Convention," Patrick Henry says, "Suffer not yourselves to be betrayed with a kiss." Which of the following best describes this quote?

    (A) An example of personification   (D) Hyperbole

    (B) A mixed metaphor   (E) A Biblical allusion

    (C) A Shakespearean illusion

The National Gallery, London

28. The example pictured above most likely presents which of the following?

    (A) A passage from Classical epic

    (B) A scene from Wagnerian opera

    (C) An 18th century satire on human foibles

    (D) An episode from Shakespearean drama

    (E) An incident from the French Revolution

29. Which of the following lines is an example of iambic pentameter?

              ∪ /   ∪ /   ∪ /   ∪ /

    (A) Her deck / once red / with he/roes' blood/

              / ∪   / ∪ / ∪ /   ∪

    (B) Here goes / the try / I've al/ways known/

              / ∪ / ∪ ∪ /   ∪ ∪

    (C) She loves the / way I hold / her hand/

              / / ∪ / / ∪   / /

    (D) Al though I / knew the road / led home/

            ∪ / ∪ /   / ∪ /   /

    (E) As I lay / wait ing / for the / morn

(A) The Parthenon, Acropolis, Athens, Greece

(B) Lakeshore Drive Apartments, Chicago, Illinois

(C) Nave of Amiens Cathedral

(D) Royal Pavilion, Brighton, England

(E) San Carlo alla Quatro Fontane, Rome

30. Which example characterizes a culture which values logic and order?

31. In which example are architectural forms and materials used for a whimsical effect?

32. Which example best characterizes a culture which values technological precision and efficiency?

33. In the building pictured above, the cantilevered horizontal forms do all of the following EXCEPT

    (A)   echo the natural waterfall's rock ledge.

    (B)   emphasize the structural framework of the building.

    (C)   deny the mass and weight of the materials.

    (D)   integrate the building with the natural setting.

    (E)   rely on industrial construction materials.

> O God, do you hear it, this persecution,
> These my sufferings from this hateful
> Woman, this monster, murderess of children?
> Still what I can do that I will do:
> I will lament and cry upon heaven,
> Calling the gods to bear me witness
> How you have killed my boys to prevent me from
> Touching their bodies or giving them burial.
> I wish I never begot them to see them
> Afterward slaughtered by you.

34. These lines are spoken by

    (A)   the murderer.   (D)   a bystander.

    (B)   the father of the dead children.   (E)   a judge.

    (C)   one of the gods.

35. It can be inferred from this passage that

    (A)   the woman had a right to kill her children.

    (B)   the man deserved to lose his children.

    (C)   the rites and ceremonies of burial are extremely important.

    (D)   the gods decreed the death of the children.

    (E)   the woman will get away with the murders.

Section 4: Science

TIME: 30 Minutes
30 Questions

DIRECTIONS: Each of the following questions and incomplete statements is followed by five answer choices. Select the choice which best answers each question.

1. What causes the seasons?
    (A) Tilt of the Earth on its axis.
    (B) Rotation of the Sun about the Earth.
    (C) Rotation of the Earth about the Sun.
    (D) The distance of the Earth from the Sun.
    (E) The revolution of the Sun about the Earth.

2. Which metric measurement would be most useful in measuring the thickness of a piece of paper?
    (A) Kilometer   (D) Meter
    (B) Millimeter   (E) Hectometer
    (C) Centimeter

3. Which of the following is true of the Sun?
    (A) The Sun is a star.
    (B) The Sun is the center of a huge system of heavenly bodies which include planets (the Earth being one), asteroids, satellites, comets, and meteoroids.
    (C) The Sun shines by virtue of its own nuclear reactions.
    (D) All of the above.
    (E) None of the above.

4. Which of the following statements about vitamins is true?
    (A) They are essential as fuels.
    (B) They are used directly as growth materials.
    (C) They act as regulators of chemical activity and growth in the body.
    (D) The best place to obtain vitamins is from vitamin tablets, rather than from foods.
    (E) Taking vitamins which contain many times the minimum daily requirement is safe and can help to bring about health and physical fitness.

5. Which of the following is NOT true of cholesterol?
    (A) Egg white is low in cholesterol.
    (B) Skim milk is low in cholesterol.
    (C) Red meats, especially those marbleized with fat, are high in cholesterol.
    (D) Chicken, even without the skin, is high in cholesterol.
    (E) Fish is low in cholesterol.

6.   The weather instrument designed by scientists to measure moisture in the air is which of the following?
     (A)   Hygrometer   (D)   Thermometer
     (B)   Anemometer   (E)   Altimeter
     (C)   Barometer

7.   Which of the following resources are nonrenewable?
     (A)   Coal, oil, gas   (D)   Freshwater, coal, vegetation
     (B)   Metals, soil, coal   (E)   Oil, soil, vegetation
     (C)   Vegetation, animals, soil.

8.   Which of the following are usual functions of the digestive system?
     I.   Transportation   IV.   Reproduction
     II.   Assimilation   V.   Response to environmental stimuli
     III.   Excretion

     (A)   All of the above.   (D)   IV and V only.
     (B)   None of the above.   (E)   I, II and III
     (C)   I, IV, V

9.   Which of the following statements about matter is false?
     (A)   Matter exhibits three states: atoms, molecules, cells.
     (B)   Atoms contain nuclei and are composed of smaller particles.
     (C)   A wide variety of substances results from atoms which combine in various ways.
     (D)   All matter is composed of atoms.
     (E)   Atoms are divisible and they may also be combined.

10. Sulfur contains 16 electrons; this means that it contains _____ protons and that its atomic number is _____ .
     (A)   16, 16
     (B)   16, 32
     (C)   8, 24
     (D)   32, 48
     (E)   an indefinite number, undetermined from information given.

11. Which items are harmful to the environment?
     I.   Acid rain   IV.   Greenhouse effect
     II.   Pollutants   V.   Water table.
     III.   Ozone hole

     (A)   None of the above.   (D)   II, III, IV, V
     (B)   All the above.   (E)   I, II, III, V
     (C)   I, II, III, IV

12. Which of the following is/are NOT true of an electromagnet?
    (A) When electricity flows through a wire, the wire becomes a magnet.
    (B) An electromagnet is a permanent magnet.
    (C) The strength of an electromagnet is limited and cannot be increased easily.
    (D) (B) and (C) only.
    (E) (A), (B), and (C).

13. What causes the phases of the moon?
    (A) A shadow is thrown on the moon by the Earth.
    (B) A shadow is thrown on the moon by the Sun.
    (C) At times the Earth is not in a position to see the moon which is always lit by the Sun.
    (D) The rays of the moon do not always have time to reach the Earth; therefore at times the Earth sees only part of the moon.
    (E) The moon is turning and shows a different part of its surface to the earth at each phase.

14. Which of the following temperatures marks the boiling point of water?
    (A) 98.6° F.   (D) 100° Kelvin
    (B) 212° C.   (E) 0° C.
    (C) 100° C.

15. Listed below are five animals. Identify the phylum in which each belongs by choosing from the phylums below the sequence which matches the sequence of the animals.

    earthworm oysters bees starfish fish
    (A) Annelida, Molluska, Arthropoda, Echinodermata, Vertebrata
    (B) Mulluska, Annelida, Arthropoda, Vertebrata, Echinodermata
    (C) Arthropoda, Molluska, Annelida, Echinodermata, Vertebrata
    (D) Echinodermata, Annelida, Molluska, Echinodermata, Vertebrata
    (E) Annelida, Molluska, Echinodermata, Vertebrata, Arthropoda

16. Which of the following is not a reproductive part of a flower?
    (A) Stigma   (D) Antler
    (B) Stamen   (E) Sperm
    (C) Pistil

17. All of the following are parts of the respiratory system of humans EXCEPT which one?
    (A) Trachea   (D) Bronchial tubes
    (B) Spleen   (E) Lungs
    (C) Diaphragm

18. Enzymes in the digestive tract serve
    (A) to enable molecules to enter into the bloodstream by helping them pass through the membranes of the small intestine.

(B)   to transform complex molecules into a form in which the cells of the body can use them.

(C)   Both of the above.

(D)   Enzymes are essential since they cause molecules to fuse and to be utilized effectively by all parts of the body.

(E)   None of the above.

19.   Even the most complex machines of today contain some simple machines. Which of the following statements about simple machines is NOT true?

(A)   Some machines produce a gain in force, a gain in speed, or a change in direction of force.

(B)   A gain in force is at the expense of speed; a gain in speed is at the expense of force.

(C)   Friction (the rubbing together of two substances) is not an asset to the work of machines.

(D)   Wheels, rollers, and ball bearings may be used to substitute rolling for sliding to reduce friction.

(E)   The work put into a machine equals the work put out if one disregards friction.

20.   All of the following terms pertain to water and/or the water cycle except which one?

(A)   Condensation   (D)   Precipitation
(B)   Pollination   (E)   Transpiration
(C)   Evaporation

21.   The best source of protein in one's diet is which of the following?

(A)   Dried beans   (D)   Honey
(B)   Fruits   (E)   White potatoes
(C)   Leafy vegetables

22.   Which of the following is NOT true?

(A)   Comets generally have elongated, elliptical orbits.
(B)   Comets may circle the Sun in any direction.
(C)   Despite their size, comets are mostly "empty space."
(D)   Comets glow by their own light.
(E)   It is believed comets are the most primitive objects in the solar system.

23.   Which of the following statements is/are true?

I.   A cupful of water and a potful of water at 100° C have molecules with the same degree of activity.

II.   A potful of water has a greater number of active molecules than does a cupful of water.

III.   It takes more burning of gas to produce a potful of boiling water than a cupful.

IV.   The unit used in measuring the quantity of heat is the calorie.

V.   A calorie is the amount of heat necessary to raise 1 gram of pure water one degree Celsius.

(A)   All of the above.   (D)   I, III, IV only.

(B)   None of the above.   (E)   III, IV, V only.

(C)   I, II, III only.

24.   All of the following are true EXCEPT which one?

(A)   Solids usually expand when they are heated and contract when they are cooled.

(B)   Water is a unique liquid in that at certain temperatures it reverses the rule that liquids contract when cooled; from 39° F to 32° F (its usual freezing point) water expands slightly instead of contracting.

(C)   When water freezes into solid crystals of ice, the spaces between the molecules become larger.

(D)   Gases contract when heated and expand when cooled.

(E)   A liquid may be described as a substance which takes the shape of its container but has a size of its own.

25.   Which of the following is NOT a characteristic of the reptiles?

(A)   Their young are developed from land eggs.

(B)   Their bodies are covered by scales or bony plates.

(C)   They are air-breathing throughout life.

(D)   Reptiles have a variable body temperature.

(E)   Their young are gill-breathing throughout life.

26.   Which of the following measures could help prevent and cure the problems of pollution?

(A)   Heat from electrical power plants should be discharged into adjacent waters to rid the environment of the heat more quickly.

(B)   Sewage should be dumped into the salty waters of the ocean for purification rather than dumped into freshwater.

(C)   Waste tars and oils must be dumped into ocean waters rather than into freshwater or the soil to prevent pollution.

(D)   Industrial waste must be treated to remove toxic chemicals, phosphates, and other pollutants.

(E)   Recycling must be discontinued; the recyclable items should never be manufactured in the first place.

27.   Listed below are four parts of a plant. Their functions are listed below.

Leaf Stem Root Flower

I.   Transporter and supporter.   IV.   Food producer.

II.   Anchor and absorber.   V.   Seed disperser and communication.

III. Seed producer.

Match the function with the part by selecting the answer below which gives the function in the same order as the part with which it corresponds.

(A)   V, IV, III, II   (D)   III, II, I, IV

(B)   IV, I, II, III   (E)   I, II, III, IV

(C)   IV, II, I, II

28. Which of the following is not true about changes in plants and animals?
    (A) Changes (modifications) in plants and animals may occur very rapidly.
    (B) Physical changes in the earth have brought about changes in plant and animal forms.
    (C) Many plants and animals once living on earth have disappeared.
    (D) Intelligence is a factor in changes.
    (E) Natural selection plays a part in changes in plants and animals.

29. Scientists divide the history of the earth into eras. Which of the following answers arranges these eras into their proper sequence from oldest to most recent?
    (A) Cenozoic, mesozoic, paleozoic, precambrian.
    (B) Precambrian, paleozoic, mesozoic, cenozoic.
    (C) Mesozoic, cenozoic, paleozoic, precambrian.
    (D) Paleozoic, precambrian, cenozoic, mesozoic.
    (E) Precambrian, cenozoic, paleozoic, mesozoic.

30. A scientist wished to investigate the effect of temperature and consumption of "Z" on the size of the plants in his laboratory.

EXPERIMENT	SIZE AT MATURATION	"Z" GIVEN IN MG.	TEMPERATURE OF TERRARIUM
1	20.0"	1	68°
2	21.0"	2	70°
3	20.0"	1	69°
4	21.0"	3	71°
5	22.0"	3	72°

What is the effect of "Z" on size?
    (A) A small amount increases size regardless of temperature.
    (B) The amount of "Z" increases size but the increase in size is affected by temperature.
    (C) Cooler temperatures cause "Z" to be more effective; warmer temperatures cause "Z" to be less effective.
    (D) Maturation is slowed when "Z" is added to the diet.
    (E) Maturation is slowed when the temperature is raised.

TEST OF GENERAL KNOWLEDGE

ANSWER KEY

SECTION 1: SOCIAL STUDIES

1.	(C)	9.	(E)	17.	(C)	25.	(B)
2.	(A)	10.	(A)	18.	(B)	26.	(A)
3.	(D)	11.	(E)	19.	(A)	27.	(A)
4.	(A)	12.	(E)	20.	(C)	28.	(D)
5.	(C)	13.	(E)	21.	(B)	29.	(A)
6.	(E)	14.	(E)	22.	(C)	30.	(E)
7.	(D)	15.	(E)	23.	(B)		
8.	(B)	16.	(D)	24.	(B)		

SECTION 2: MATHEMATICS

1.	(D)	8.	(C)	15.	(D)	22.	(A)
2.	(D)	9.	(E)	16.	(E)	23.	(A)
3.	(D)	10.	(D)	17.	(D)	24.	(D)
4.	(B)	11.	(C)	18.	(E)	25.	(A)
5.	(D)	12.	(C)	19.	(D)		
6.	(C)	13.	(B)	20.	(E)		
7.	(C)	14.	(D)	21.	(B)		

SECTION 3: LITERATURE AND FINE ARTS

1.	(D)	10.	(E)	19.	(B)	28.	(C)
2.	(B)	11.	(B)	20.	(C)	29.	(A)
3.	(D)	12.	(A)	21.	(C)	30.	(A)
4.	(A)	13.	(D)	22.	(B)	31.	(D)
5.	(A)	14.	(C)	23.	(D)	32.	(B)
6.	(D)	15.	(C)	24.	(A)	33.	(B)
7.	(C)	16.	(B)	25.	(E)	34.	(B)
8.	(C)	17.	(D)	26.	(A)	35.	(C)
9.	(D)	18.	(D)	27.	(E)		

SECTION 4: SCIENCE

1.	(A)	9.	(A)	17.	(B)	25.	(E)
2.	(B)	10.	(A)	18.	(C)	26.	(D)
3.	(D)	11.	(C)	19.	(C)	27.	(B)
4.	(C)	12.	(D)	20.	(B)	28.	(A)
5.	(D)	13.	(C)	21.	(A)	29.	(B)
6.	(A)	14.	(C)	22.	(D)	30.	(B)
7.	(A)	15.	(A)	23.	(A)		
8.	(E)	16.	(D)	24.	(D)		

DETAILED EXPLANATIONS OF ANSWERS
NTE CORE BATTERY–Test 3

TEST OF GENERAL KNOWLEDGE
Section 1: Social Studies

1.   **(C)**   The question asks you to place the works by American authors in chronological order. Choice (D), about WWI, was printed in 1926. Two late 19th century works are choices (B) and (E). Choice (A) was published shortly before the Civil War (1852). The correct choice (C) was published during the transcendental era, 1836.

2.   **(A)**   The correct response (A), occurred in 1896, when the Supreme Court gave constitutional backing to segregation, ruling that separate but equal facilities on a Louisiana railroad coach did not deprive the Negro of equal protection under the 14th Amendment. This ruling was overturned in 1954, in *Brown v. Board of Education of Topeka*, which held that segregation in the elementary schools of Topeka violated the 14th Amendment.

3.   **(D)**   One should count the time zones excluding the Eastern European time zones. The correct answer is (D), 11 time zones.

4.   **(A)**   Columbus's voyages began in the 15th century. The Protestant Reformation occurred in the 16th century. The Puritans came to America in the 17th century. The Magna Carta was signed in 1215. Therefore, the best choice is (A).

5.   **(C)**   Choice (A), as conceived by Henry Clay, referred to the nationalist policy of uniting the three economic sections of the United States in the time following the War of 1812. Choice (B) is an economic theory whose principal doctrine was the belief that the wealth of nations was based on the possession of gold. Choices (D) and (E) were views tied to tradition and emotion, respectively. Choice (C) is the best possible answer.

6.   **(E)**   The question tests the geographical knowledge of the respondent. Choices (A), (B), (C) and (D) are all in the South where many Civil War battles were fought. Nevertheless, they are incorrect. Item (E) Pennsylvania is correct. This battle was known as the turning point of the war, marking the defeat of Lee's attempt to invade Pennsylvania and reach Washington.

7.   **(D)**   Contrary to choice (A), the Bill of Rights is about the expansion of individual rights, such as freedom of speech and religion. Choice (B) is not the major topic of the first ten Amendments. Since the Bill of Rights clearly spelled out a limited role for government, item (C) is wrong. The Bill of Rights had nothing to say about judicial review; this power of

the Supreme Court was assumed by it in the case of *Marbury v. Madison*, 1908. Thus, the correct response is (D).

8.   **(B)**   Choice (A) was a result of people moving west and quickly setting up communities. Choice (C) refers to the process of becoming like the majority. Item (D) is a monopolistic practice of corporations in the later 19th century. Choice (E) stressed the social responsibility of the church. The correct answer is choice (B), the idea proposed by the historian, Frederick Jackson Turner, who wrote *The Frontier in American History.*

9.   **(E)**   Choices (A), (B), (C) and (D) are incorrect. The correct choice is item (E). Steppes, pampas, llanos, and prairies are all regional terms for grassland.

10.   **(A)**   Choices (B), (C), (D) and (E) are wrong. The proper response is item (A). All of the words are regional terms for shelter.

11.   **(E)**   This question tests respondent's knowledge of the law. Responses (A), (B), (C), and (D) are incorrect. The best answer is (E). In most states accused persons cannot be put on trial for a crime unless they are first indicted by a grand jury. A grand jury, usually composed of from twelve to twenty-three members, examines the evidence against accused persons. If the grand jury finds that the evidence justifies putting the accused on trial, it indicts him or her.

12.   **(E)**   Using the compass rose for direction, one would select the north direction, making (E) the best response.

13.   **(E)**   Since choices (A), (B), (C) and (D) are all monotheistic—believe in one God— the correct choice is item (E). A polytheistic religion worships many gods; the gods worshipped by the Greeks are an example of polytheistic religion.

14.   **(E)**   Diplomacy is the means by which states try to resolve the disagreements. The cold war is an armed peace based on a balance of power. A sanction is a method of exerting pressure on a recalcitrant state, such as a trade limitation. A veto is the power to prevent the initiation of a policy or action. The correct response is choice (E). A coup d'état is a violent overthrow of an existing government by a small group. Coup d'états occur in unstable governments.

15.   **(E)**   Judaism is a monotheistic faith. Its sacred texts include writings of the Prophets. It believes that the Messiah is still to come. It adheres to the Torah. Therefore, the best answer is choice (E).

16.   **(D)**   The best possible answer to this question is item (D), since the other responses are partially or totally incorrect.

17.   **(C)**   Choices (A), (B) and (D) all played a role in the early settlements of the English colonies in America. Thus, they are incorrect choices as is item (E). The correct response is item (C), because Mormonism was founded at Fayette, New York, in 1830, by Joseph Smith. *The Book of Mormon* was published in 1830 and it described the establishment of an American colony from the Tower of Babel.

18. **(B)** The Morrill Act granted each Union state 30,000 acres for each Senator and Representative in Congress in order to endow an agricultural college. This led to the founding of 69 land grant colleges, making (B) the correct response.

19. **(A)** Until 1921 no general limitation of immigration was attempted by Congress. In that year (and again in 1924 and 1929) Congress enacted the first general restrictive legislation in its history. The act of 1921 set the quotas at 3 percent of the 1910 census, and thereby reduced the quotas from eastern and southern Europe. Thus, item (A) is correct.

20. **(C)** Cowboys (A) were relatively latecomers to the southwest. The French explored and settled in the northern part of the continent. Gold seekers came in the mid-19th century. Farmers from New England were not early settlers in the southwest. The correct answer is (C), Spainards and Mexicans.

21. **(B)** Choices (A), (C), (D), and (E) are incorrect. The right choice is (B), because in a private enterprise economy individuals have significant freedom to own and operate productive enterprises, to produce economic goods, and to develop specialized institutions like banks and insurance companies to meet their needs. Thus, price changes generally tend to indicate what is produced and consumed.

22. **(C)** The letter K represents Cuba. Letter D stands for Java. Letter M stands for Sri Lanka. Letter O refers to the Cape of Good Hope. The correct answer is (C) because letter I represents the Philippine Islands.

23. **(B)** On August 23, 1939, Germany and the Soviet Union signed a nonaggression pact, which meant that the two nations could partition Eastern Europe, each without fear of becoming involved in a second war front with the other. The leaders of the countries at this time were Hitler and Stalin, which makes (B) the correct answer. In mid-1941, Germany invaded Russia, in violation of their treaty.

24. **(B)** A list of grievances is contained in the Declaration of Independence. Choices (C) and (D) are incorrect because the Bill of Rights does not talk about voting rights or slaves. Rather than limiting the rights of citizens, the Bill of Rights extends rights. The correct answer is (B), since the document clearly states that Congress may not make laws abridging citizens' rights and liberties.

25. **(B)** Choices (A), (C), (D) and (E) are wrong. Item (B) is correct, since the people rule by electing their representatives and the powers of the government are divided on national, state and local levels.

26. **(A)** Answers (B), (C), (D) and (E) are incorrect. The best response is (A), which represents the combined willingness of individuals or firms to supply specific resources (such as labor) or products (such as wheat or cars) at specific prices.

27. **(A)** The correct answer is (A). A single or sole proprietorship is one that is owned and managed by one person. The partnership is a business that is owned by two or more individuals. The corporation (or joint stock company as it is sometimes called) is owned by stockholders, each owning one or more shares of stock. Choices (B) and (C) are partially correct. Choices (D) and (E) are totally wrong.

28. **(D)** Choice (A) is wrong because about 30% of households had under $15,000. Choices (B) and (C) are incorrect, since slightly more than 15% fell into this category. The correct choice is item (D), making item (E) incorrect. This question asks the respondent to read the graph carefully.

29. **(A)** Graph reading and interpretation is the primary focus of this question. Choice (B) is obviously wrong, since the youngest have the least income. Items (C), (D) and (E) are incorrect.

30. **(E)** Since choices (A), (B), (C) and (D) are incorrect, the right answer is (E). (A) is incorrect because the statement is not applicable to all household sizes, such as one-person, for example. (B) may seem correct, but the amount of discretionary income fluctuates up and down according to household size. (C) is completely false. Two-person households have the most discretionary income: 36.2%. (D) is false also. One-person households have less discretionary income than two-, three-, and four-person households.

Section 2: Mathematics

1. **(D)** You may wish to rewrite the decimals so that all have 3 place values: tenths, hundredths and thousandths. Note that .100 is less than .300 and .300 is less than .500. Now you only need to insert the .190 between .100 and .300 and the .290 between .190 and .300. .1 < .3 < .5. The correct Choice is (D). If the order of smallest to largest in decimals is still confusing you, try to think of .1 or .10 or .100 as all the same value and recall that .1 is closest to zero. Thus it would be less than .3 or .30 or .300 since .3 is a little farther from zero and closer to one (1.000) which makes .3 greater than .1.

2. **(D)** You will need twice as much paper length wise ($1\frac{1}{2} + 1\frac{1}{2} = 3$ meters), and twice as much paper widthwise (25 + 25 = 50). Thus all together you need 2 x 2 or 4 times as much paper to cover the same area. So 8 pieces x 4 = 32. Choice (D) is correct.

3. **(D)** You should first write out the expression in the box. (A + 3 = 5B) The numerical equation must be true. Choice (A) is the expression for the words in the box. Thus that eliminates Choice (A) Then you must know how to manipulate terms from one side or the other side to the opposite side of the equation and yet maintain the equality. After checking each of the answers you find that (D) is not an equality for (A). Choice (B) is the resulting expression after simply subtracting 3 from each side of the equation. Choice (C) is the result of dividing each side of the equation by 5 or multiplying each side by 1/5. Choice (E) is the result of adding a negative 2 to each side of the equation. Choice (D) is the best answer.

4. **(B)** You may view the hexagon as consisting of 6 triangles. Two triangles are shaded. The area of a triangle is base times its height. The base is known (b) (or 3.3). It is the same as the radius in this case since we have an inscribed hexagon. Thus only the height is needed in addition to the base. Choice (A) is wrong since you need more than one dimension to calculate area. Choice (C) is wrong since you need the base (3.3) and the height to calculate the area of a triangle. b is the side and not the height. Choices (D) and (E) are like choice (A) (insufficient data to figure area). The best answer is (B). An alternate approach, far more

complex, is to view the shaded area as 1/6th less than 1/2 the area of a hexagon. This method requires knowledge of the formula for the area of a hexagon (or n-polygon). Do you remember that?

5.　**(D)**　You should note that the range is between -8 and -3 and that -8 is excluded while -3 is included (black dot) in the range. Thus Choice (D) is correct.

6.　**(C)**　You should study the table on cargo ships first. Then you should observe the various relationships between the lengths of the ships. For example, ship A is half the length of ship D. Ship B is half the length of ship A or one-fourth the length of ship D. Ship C is 3 times the length of ship B. Finally, you should note that the graphic representation must be in correct order to match the data table. That is, ship A in the table must match with A in the graphs. Choice (A) shows ship B twice the length of the other ships and all of those ships the same length. This does not match any relationships in the table. Choice (B) shows ships A and D as the same length. This is in conflict with the data table. Choice (D) shows ship A as the shortest ship while in the table ship B is the shortest. Choice (E) shows ship A as the longest ship and ship D as the shortest. This is in opposite relationship to the table. Thus Choice (C) is the correct answer. Ships A, B, C, D are represented in correct order and in proper ratios as expressed in the table.

7.　**(C)**　You increase the digit to the left of a decimal place value by one if the digit inspected is 5 or more. For example, .26 rounds off to .3 in the tenths place, or .267 rounds off to .27 in the hundredths place. The correct Choice is (C) .667 (rounded to the nearest thousandth).

8.　**(C)**　You can use 1/2 foot for depth. Thus 1/2 x 10 x 50 gives 250 cubic foot. A cubic yard is 3 x 3 x 3, or 27 cubic feet. Thus 250 divided by 27 is about 9 to 9 1/2 cubic yards of concrete needed. Ten cubic yards would cost $500. So the cost is between $450 and $475. Choice (C) is best.

9.　**(E)**　You must determine the correct equation by substitution of all values of X (one at a time) into the equation and find the resultant value of Y after the simple mental calculations. Some equations will appear to fit one pair of values for an X value and Y value, but that equation does not necessarily hold true for all the values of X and Y in the data table. The best answer is (E)

10.　**(D)**　You should avoid confusing perimeter (P = 2L + 2W) of a rectangle with area (A = LW) of a rectangle. You must transfer the correct dimensions given to the upper rectangle. Also you must add the correct lengths and widths. (3 and 7.5, not 5). The best and only answer is (D)

(3 + 7.5 + 3 + 7.5)　　　or　　　$[p = 2\,(3) + 2\,(7.5)]$
$$p = 6 + 15$$
$$p = 21$$

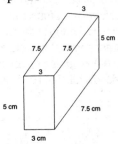

11. **(C)** You must use a planned comparison search between the two lists to help you discover the general rule. The like list has a randomness to it (names, food, states). But likewise the dislikes list has a wide variety to it. The major clue to discovering the rule is to note the pairing of one like and one dislike throughout the list. (e.g. Bill - Bob, cookies - cake, Missouri- Iowa, etc.) Study of the pairs for differences leads to the rule: Sally likes words with double letters. Other choices all have contrary items on the opposite list to invalidate the suggested rule. The correct answer is (C).

12. **(C)** You note that the shaded area is 2/3 by 4/7. You then have a multiplication or area problem of 2/3 x 4/7 or 8/21. Another way to find the area is to note these 21 rectangles and 8 of them are shaded (8/21). The correct answer is (C).

13. **(B)** You look at the digit in the place to the right of the hundredths place (3rd digit over from decimal). If this number is 0 to 4, you drop it and do not round up or do not increase the digit in the hundredths place value. Thus in (A), 2.160, the zero is dropped to give 2.16. In (B), 2.162, the two is dropped to give 2.16. In (E), 2.164, the four is dropped to give 2.16. This leaves choices (B) and (D). If the digit is 5 or greater than 5, then you increase the digit to its left by one. In (D) 2.159, the nine changes the number to 2.16. (B), 2.167, becomes 2.17. Thus choice (B) is the answer. 2.167 can not be rounded to 2.16. It rounds to 2.17.

14. **(D)** All the other answers exhibit erroneous thought patterns about the subtraction operation. Choice (A) shows subtracting the smaller digit from the larger digits without regard to the problem's subtrahend . (2358) Choice (B) is the correct answer and does not exhibit any error patterns. Choice (C) shows subtracting each place value as a separate problem. Choice (D) shows borrowing from a place value but then forgetting to reduce that place value before next subtraction. Choice (E) shows addition rather than subtraction. Thus Choice (D) is correct for showing the error stated.

15. **(D)** The best answer is (D). It is a direct representation of the ratio expressed, namely, 7 to 3. All of the other choices are different ratios than that cited. These ratios need to be checked out to be certain that there is only one representation of the ratio. If there were a 3 to 7 ratio pictured, (D) also would be incorrect since the order of comparison is critical in ratio expressions.

16. **(E)** You should not make visual comparisons of the figures since they are not drawn to scale. Instead calculate mentally the area of each figure and compare results to pick out equal areas. Figure I is a rectangle (A =L x W). Thus 9 x 3 = 27 square inches is the area. Figure II is a square (A = S^2). Thus area is 4 x 4 or 16 square inches. Figure III is an isosceles triangle (A = $\frac{1}{2}$b x h). Thus area is $\frac{1}{2}$ x 6 x 9 or 27 square inches. Figure IV is a right angle triangle (A = $\frac{1}{2}$b x h). Thus area is $\frac{1}{2}$ x 4 x 6 or 12 square inches. Choice (E) is correct.

17. **(D)** You should identify the pattern as performing addition left to right with recording of the first numeral (tens place) and carrying the second numeral (ones place). Choice (B) is the answer for the problem using proper right to left (ones, tens, hundreds) addition. Choice (A) exhibits a switch from the addition to the subtraction operation. Also the smaller numeral is subtracted from the larger numeral without regard to whether the numeral is part of the same addend or not. Choice (C) exhibits a switch from addition to subtraction and also the inversion of the problem addends. Choice (E) is adding left to right and not carrying

either—a double error in thinking. Answer (D) exhibits the reversal of the algorithm steps. The tens place is recorded and the ones place carried. Thus the answer results in 1112. Choice (D) is the erroneous answer, and thus the correct choice.

18. **(E)** You should heed the warning that the figures are not drawn to scale. Thus estimating their volumes visually could be misleading as to the correct choice.

Figure I volume: $3 \times 3 \times 3 = 27$ in^3 Figure II volume: $3 \times 3 \times 6 = 54$ in^3

Figure III volume: $2 \times 4 \times 7 = 56$ in^3 Figure IV volume: $4 \times 4 \times 4 = 64$ in^3

Comparison of results reveals that none of the figures have the same volume. Choice (E) is correct.

19. **(D)** You must first simplify the expression so that W is by itself on one side of the relational symbol (<). Add a (-7) to each side of the expression. -7 + 3 < W + 7 -7. This yields -4 < W. Now inspect the graphs for a solution. W is greater than -4. Choice (D) is correct.

20. **(E)** You can estimate these answers by moving the decimal point to the right thereby making the arithmetic operation easier.

(A) has a value of .55 (.5 + .9) or ($5 \times 10^{-3} + 9 \times 10^{-3}$) or $5 \div 9$

(B) has a value of .000045 ($5 \times 9 \times 10^{-6}$)

(C) has a value of .014

(D) has a value of .004

(E) has a value of 1.8 ($9 \times 10^{-3} \div 5 \times 10^{-3}$) or $9 \div 5$

Thus Choice (E) is correct.

21. **(B)** You use the Pythagorean theorem to solve this problem. The wall forms a right angle with the ground. The ladder is the long side of the right triangle (called the hypotenuse). The theorem states the sum of the squares of the two sides equals the square of the hypotenuse. (Ladder (hypotenuse squared) = A^2 + BG^2). Substituting the values, you should have C2 = A^2 + B^2 or L^2 = 5^2 + 12^2
L^2 = 25 + 144
L^2 = 169
L = $\sqrt{169}$ = 13 The correct choice is (B).

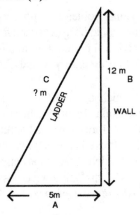

22. **(A)** You know that mode in a data set represents the number of measurement that appears with the greatest frequency. Only 6 appears more than once in the data set. Thus 6 is the mode. Choice (A) is correct.

23. **(A)** You should note that the scale on the right reads from the bottom of the cylinder upwards. The scale on the left reads from the top of the cylinder downwards. The right-hand scale measures directly the contents of the fluid in the cylinder (namely 15ml). The left-hand scale can be used to tell how much remains to be filled since the scale readings pair up to total 100ml (80 + 20, 85 + 15, 90 + 10, etc.) Choice (A) is the only correct answer since you want to know how much additional water is needed. (100 - 15 = 85).

24. **(D)** You should automatically discard choices (A) and (C) since these statements relate to dislikes. The question asks for a general statement regarding her likes. However study of the dislikes list may help you in the search for similarities among items in the likes list. Choice (B) is incorrect since not all the foods on the likes list are red. Choice (E) is wrong because apples grow on trees, not vines. One exception is enough to discard the rule since it must apply to all items on the list. Thus by elimination the correct answer is (D). She likes fruits. Note how the dislikes list supports the rule in inverse manner. There are no fruits on it.

25. **(A)** You use the value 5 and conduct the test: Is 5 less than or equal to 5? 5 is equal to 5. Thus your test answer is yes. So you add 1 to 5 giving you 6. Then 6 divided by 2 is 3. So 3 is printed. Choice (A) is correct.

Section 3: Literature and Fine Arts

1. **(D)** This question tests your ability to determine the central focus in a staged dramatic production and to explain why there is such a focus. The central attraction in this picture is the man at the center of the stairs (D). Almost all eyes are turned to him, as well as the bodies of the other characters. The men in the right foreground (A) have their backs to the audience and are directing their attention to the central character. Since this character is in a full front position, he will draw more attention than those in profile or full back, which are weaker positions. Choice (D) is correct.

2. **(B)** Figure 1 is an Elizabethan nobleman, appropriate for a play set in the 1600s. Figure 2 is a medieval old man and would be appropriate for a medieval cycle play. This is the style appropriate during the medieval period. Figure 3 is a Royalist trooper. Figure 4 is a Chinese Mandarin. Figure 5 is a late 19th century "Dandy." Choice (B) is the correct answer.

3. **(D)** The above passage, which opens Charles Dickens's *A Tale of Two Cities*, contains numerous and vast comparisons. By making these comparisons and descriptions of the time period ("we had everything before us, we had nothing before us, we were all going direct to Heaven, we were all going direct the other way," etc.), Dickens is illustrating how during this period (just before the French Revolution) anything was possible: "wisdom", "foolishness", "Light", or "Darkness". This "anything is possible" tone also foreshadows the French Revolution, which the Aristocracy never expected. Dickens will, later in the novel,

describe extreme political upheaval, but does not here, so (B) is wrong. (A) is wrong because "placid" implies settled and calm; if "anything is possible," then the times are the exact opposite. There is no mention of a public event or the attitudes of people at war, so (C) and (E) are also incorrect.

4.   **(A)**   The Bible tells of how Christ was able to feed hundreds of hungry people with only 7 loaves of bread and fish until all were satiated. By jokingly suggesting that the two governments contain the positions "lords of the state preserves of loaves and fishes," Dickens mocks their self-assuredness and unflinching certainty that the "preserves" will never be depleted and that "things in general [are] settled for ever." The phrase "clearer than crystal" helps, through its sarcasm, to give this attack more sting. All of the other choices are not alluded to or discussed in the passage, and are thus incorrect.

5.   **(A)**   The "superlative degree" refers to the utmost degree of something being compared (the *hottest* day, the *fastest* runner, the *most beautiful* object, etc.). The phrase indicates that some of the time periods "noisiest authorities" (a sarcastic euphemism for members of the governments) wanted time to be remembered as the "most" or "best" of something—regardless of whether it was "the most evil or "the most productive". All that mattered to these "authorities" was to be at the top of every comparison, regardless of its implications. Thus, (A) is correct. The people are not mentioned here, so (B) and (C) are both incorrect, as are (D) and (E).

6.   **(D)**   The Egyptian Temple of Horus, c. 212 B.C., pictured in the example displays elements typical of the monumental architecture which developed during Egypt's Old Kingdom period (c. 2600-2100 B.C.) and continued until Egypt became a province of the Roman Empire (c. 31 B.C.). This architecture achieved an effect of imposing grandeur and durability through the use of simple, solid geometric forms, constructed on an overwhelming scale and laid out with exacting symmetry. The Temple of Horus avoids any emphasis on horizontal lines, and relies instead on the sloping outer walls to visually "pull" the massive building to the ground and make it seem immovable and eternal. Additionally, although the temple carries minor ornamental detail, displays huge reliefs of figures, and is set within a large open courtyard, all of these elements are secondary to the massive character of the building itself.

7.   **(C)**   Gianlorenzo Bernini's *David* of 1623 is a perfect example of the Baroque sculptor's wish to express movement and action and to capture a fleeting moment of time. Here, the figure's twisting posture and intense facial expression create a dynamic, not a static, character, as David begins the violent twisting motion with which he will hurl the stone from his sling. His gaze is directed outward at an unseen adversary, implying interaction with another character and denying any purely ornamental conception behind this work. The figure's meager garments, far from identifying him as a warrior, emphasize both his physical vulnerability and his idealized, heroic beauty.

8.   **(C)**   This question asks you to demonstrate knowledge and awareness of a widely used symbol, the ellipsis. Within a sentence, three periods with a space after each period indicate that material has been purposefully omitted while quoting from the original. Thus, choice (C) is the correct answer.

9. **(D)** In *The Lamentation Over St. Sebastien* of 1630, the French Baroque painter Georges de la Tour used the candle held by the kneeling woman as the single light source for his picture. de la Tour specialized in this type of intimate night scene, in which the light gently but dramatically illuminates the human figures. The simplified, almost abstract forms of the figures bathed in this quiet light create a sense of Classical calm which, in this case, heightens the poignancy of the episode. All of the figures, however, occupy a shallow space toward the front of the picture plane, almost "falling" into the viewer's space. Therefore, de la Tour's light, though it models and defines the forms in space, does not create a convincing recession into depth.

10. **(E)** This marble portrait bust of the 1st century B.C. is typical of a style which flourished during the late Roman Republic, and which aimed for a literal, super-realistic depiction of a certain type of individual. The sculptor here avoided any tendency to idealize his subject, and pursued instead an expressive, realistic depiction, in which each particular feature of his subject's face and expression was painstakingly recorded. The choice of hard, chiselled marble, rather than modelled clay or incised relief, helped to accentuate the craggy details of his subject's face. The sitter here represents not the jaded, effete aristocracy of the later Roman Empire, but rather the simple, unsophisticated citizen-farmer of the earlier Republic, whose labor and determination helped to build the Roman state.

11. **(B)** This passage from Melville's *Moby Dick* contains an allusion in the phrase, "like so many Alexanders." Melville is illustrating the strength and power of whalers ("naked Nantucketers") by alluding and comparing them to Alexander the Great, the famous conqueror who died in 323 B.C.

12. **(A)** This passage, which opens James Joyce's *A Portrait of the Artist as a Young Man* is written in "baby talk" ("moocow," "nicens," "baby tukoo") to convey to readers the age, speech and mental set of the narrator. While choice (E) does imitate the speech of a character, the voice used is not nearly as discreet as choice (A).

13. **(D)** Nineteenth century novels of manners employed such themes as the importance (or unimportance) of "good breeding," the elation (and suffocation) caused by society, and the interaction of individuals within the confines of a closed country community (to name just a few). This passage, taken from Jane Austen's *Emma*, mentions "opinions" of other characters, the importance of "beauty" and "accomplishment" (note how Emma sees them as almost saving graces for Mrs. Elton), and the "improvement" of a "country neighborhood."

14. **(C)** In the example, *Sunday Afternoon on the Island of La Grand Jatte*, 1884-86, the French Post-Impressionist painter Georges Seurat developed a systematic, intellectual art in which color values were carefully calculated, composition was rigidly structured, and an overall effect of static, well-ordered design replaced the vibrant spontaneity of the earlier Impressionists' work. In *La Grand Jatte* the motionless vertical forms of the human figures are carefully positioned and repeated, and are deftly coordinated with both the diagonal shadows on the ground and with the distant horizon line. The approach overall is detached and scientific, and avoids both spontaneous emotional impulse and any poetic, personal content.

15. **(C)** The arch pictured in the example is characteristic of much later Roman imperial

architecture, in which elaborate combinations of Classical architectural elements were employed in a purely non-structural manner. Although the four columns at the front of the arch appear to lend support to the heavy upper story, they are in fact merely applied to the facade of the arch and serve no functional purpose. They do, however, create a strong vertical thrust which leads the viewer's eye to the sculpted figures above, while simultaneously setting off and accenting the three small arches which serve as the monument's basic structural units.

16. **(B)**   You can tell that this passage is taken from the stage directions of a play because of the visual and auditory descriptions you are given. Also, you are told that "lights come up" and a "rocket bursts, off," here meaning "offstage." (B) is the correct answer.

17. **(D)**   The architect of the building illustrated was intent on avoiding traditional building forms in the search for a new, expressive use of space. The design pictured, therefore, carefully avoids all reminders of the symmetrical, balanced floor plans of Classical and Renaissance architecture. It also dispenses with a conventional structural framework and with the geometric forms and angles of traditional buildings. Instead, it exploits fully the potential of a new material—in this case, poured concrete—to create dynamic, curving forms whose arcs and spirals echo both the shape of growing organisms and the motion of wind and water.

18. **(D)**   The theme of *carpe diem*, Latin for "seize the day," urges people to enjoy their present pleasures and lives, because the future is so uncertain. Passage (D), taken from Robert Herrick's, "To the Virgins to Make Much of Time," urges its readers to act now ("Gather ye rosebuds while ye may") because time will never stop and all things must come to an end ("… Tomorrow will be dying").

19. **(B)**   Onomatopoeia refers to the formation of words imitating the sound of the object or action expressed, such as "Buzz," "clang," "boom," and "meow." Passage (B) contains two examples of onomatopoeia: "Bow-wow," to imitate the barking of a dog, and "Cock-a-doodle-doo" to imitate the sound of the rooster.

20. **(C)**   Alliteration refers to the repetition of consonant sounds at the beginning of successive (or nearly successive) words in a line (or lines) of poetry. Passage (C) contains the line, "A spotted shaft is seen," which alliterates the "s" sound for poetic effect. Thus, choice (C) is correct.

21. **(C)**   You are asked to decide the literary form of the quote. Since it seems to have no poetic form, the first choice is easily negated, as is choice (E), for songs are similar in form to poems. Although a long speech in a play could be similar to this, there is no dialogue, which would normally indicate a play (B). A journal, or diary, is written in first person, as the excerpt is. Also, it puts forth everyday events and feelings, the purpose we normally associate with a journal. A myth (D) is a traditional story, usually connected with the religion of people, and attempts to account for something in nature. This quote gives no indication of mythological allusions. The correct answer is (C).

22. **(B)**   This question asks you to judge, from the paragraph given, the type of literature from which the excerpt was taken. The only choice for which any support is given is choice

(B), because the names given are Russian. The other choices can be ruled out, because there is not anything in the paragraph to support them as choices. We see no evidence of British terminology or dialect (A), nor are there specific elements of a modern romance (C). Likewise, there is not enough information to determine whether or not this is a short story with existentialist qualities (D). Therefore, you must choose the answer you *can* support, which is choice (B).

23. **(D)** Answer choices (A), (B), and (E) each contain images of animals which are based to some degree on naturalistic observation. In each case, however, the animals are presented either as black-and-white line drawings or as schematic, two-dimensional renderings, with no attempt to model the forms of the animals; and in each case, the imagery functions in either a narrative or magical context and does not intend to explore anatomy. Answer choice (C) presents a basically realistic, well-modelled animal, based on naturalistic observation and with close attention to detail, but the addition of the wings adds a fantastic touch and the animal as a whole is elegantly designed and positioned to act as the functional handle of a jar. Only answer choice (D) explores the expressive forms of the animal's musculature, here conveying a sense of untamed emotion and animal energy through the tensed, swelling muscles of the crouched jaguar.

24. **(A)** Answer choices (B) and (E) each present somewhat schematic representations of animals, the first in order to document the character and activities of an Egyptian noble, and the second to fulfill a magical, ritual function. The animal in answer choice (C) exists solely as a decorative detail on a purely functional object. Answer choice (D) shows animal behavior which might be called analogous to human behavior—i.e., the violence of the strong over the weak—but the image itself does not intend to comment directly on human life. Only answer choice (A) uses animal imagery to directly caricature human behavior. In this case, the Japanese scroll employs monkeys, frogs, hares, and foxes to mimic Buddhist religious practices.

25. **(E)** Answer choice (E) presents animal images with a high degree of naturalism in a sophisticated, abstract, almost "modern" style. The artist, however, despite his naturalism, was not concerned with perspective or with conventional pictorial space, and concentrated solely on the overlapping images of the animals, which have no narrative function. He has included a print of his own hands, possibly to indicate his magical control over the animals through these images of them. These paintings were executed on the walls of a cave in what appears to be a sacred precinct, and seem to function as magical images to ensure success in the hunt.

26. **(A)** The first line from Shakespeare's Sonnet #71 indicates that the narrator does not wish to be mourned after his death. This helped to determine the meaning of the final lines. Fleeing from this world to dwell with vilest worms can mean nothing other than being dead and buried underground, where worms feed off decaying bodies (A). There is no reference to hell, although the image of being underground could be thus misconstrued (B). The death knell, "the surly sullen bell," is used to tell the world of a death. This has no relation to the meaning of the last line. Finally, there is no indication that the narrator wishes to leave the world or is running from his problems. The thought is expressed futuristically—"when I am dead"—not longingly.

27. **(E)**   This quote from Patrick Henry's speech is a reference to Judas Iscariot who betrayed Jesus with a kiss, giving him up to the soldiers to be crucified. This is a Biblical allusion from Luke 22: 47-48 (E). Since there is no personification in the line, nor is there a metaphorical comparison, (A) and (B) are incorrect. Choice (C) is incorrect because an "illusion" is a false idea or conceptiont. Choice (D), gross exaggeration, is also an incorrect choice, since there is no overstatement in the quote.

28. **(C)**   The example pictured, by the English painter William Hogarth, satirizes 18th-century English life in a comic way. In telling the story of the human characters illustrated in the work, the picture uses a wealth of carefully chosen detail which the viewer is to "read" in a novelistic manner. The period details, therefore (as of dress, architecture, furnishings, etc.), and the attitudes and actions of the figures (the exasperated look, for instance, of the servant on the left) tell us that this is a human comedy set in the 18th century. Of the other answer choices, (A). (B), and (D) would be both historically anachronistic and weightier in subject matter. Answer choice (E) would fall roughly within the correct period, but it, too, would likely present a more dramatic content.

29. **(A)**   Choice (A) is the only correct scanned line. It contains five iambic feet and is an example of iambic pentameter. The other examples have incorrectly marked accents and feet.

30. **(A)**   Answer choices (C), (D), and (E) illustrate buildings which employ arching, curving, cylindrical, and circular forms, often in elaborate, complex combinations, and suggest the play of emotion, fantasy, or romance, but do no seem founded on any general cultural need for logic and order. Choice (B) shows a modern building whose design certainly proceeds from logical precepts, but, of the principles offered in the answer choices, technological precision seems to best characterize this example. Example (A), however, the famous 5th century B.C. Parthenon in Athens, presents a building whose design reflects perfectly the logical philosophies which defined Classical Greek culture. The Parthenon's architects were careful to construct a building of simple, refined forms, methodically repeated according to calculated ratios of size and space. The result is an effect of perfect balance and order which would be undermined by altering any one of the building's essential components.

31. **(D)**   Choices (A) and (B) illustrate structures whose severe, regularized forms seem to deny the possibility of humor and whimsy. Choice (C), a Gothic cathedral interior, uses soaring arches and strong vertical thrust to express spirituality and religious fervor, while choice (E), an Italian Baroque church exterior, conveys a sense of intellectual, nervous agitation through a contrast of convex and concave curves and the use of an overabundance of ornamental detail. Only choice (D), a 19th century English pleasure pavilion, combines a fanciful assortment of playful, whimsical shapes—as in the "Islamic" domes and minarets—to create an effect of exotic fantasy and underscore its function as a place of recreation.

32. **(B)**   Alone among the five answer choices, example (B) pares its structural forms to an absolute minimum, stressing the industrial materials—the steel of its framework and its extensive window glass—to achieve an effect of absolute structural logic and clarity. This "International Style" architecture typifies the skyscraper buildings in large cities throughout the industrial world and reflects the high cultural value placed on industrial and commercial efficiency in the modern urbanized society.

33. **(B)** In the example, the 1939 "Falling Water" house by the American architect Frank Lloyd Wright, the horizontal forms which project dramatically over the small waterfall do not emphasize the building's structural framework but, rather, deny the presence of a structural support altogether and seem almost to defy gravity. All of the other observations offered in the answer choices are valid. Consistent with Wright's conception of an "organic" architecture, the cantilevered forms echo the horizontal axis of the waterfall's rock shelf, and, even though they are rigidly cubic in form, help to merge the house with its setting. This bold construction was only possible to the architect through the use of such modern, industrial-strength building materials as poured, pre-stressed concrete, whose great strength and flexibility made possible the long projecting forms supported at one end only.

34. **(B)** This passage comes from the Greek play *Medea*, by Euripides. Medea, a woman who is being cast aside so her husband, Jason, can marry a princess, kills their two sons in retaliation. This passage shows Jason lamenting over the boys' deaths and invoking the gods to punish his ex-wife.

35. **(C)** In the passage Jason mourns that Medea killed the boys "to prevent me/Touching their bodies or giving them burial." In Greek society, the dead were honored by elaborate burial rites and ceremonies. To be buried without ceremony was considered to be dishonorable to the dead, especially when they were related to great warriors, such as Jason.

Section 4: Science

1. **(A)** It is the tilt of the Earth on its axis that determines the seasons. The tilt determines the concentration of the Sun's rays, which in turn determine the season. The Sun does not rotate about the Earth; instead the Earth rotates on its axis and revolves around the Sun. (B), therefore, is incorrect. As explained in answer (B), the Earth does not rotate about the Sun; rather the Earth rotates on its axis. (C) is incorrect and should not be selected. It is not the distance of the Earth from the Sun that determines the seasons. In fact, in the northern hemisphere the Earth is closer to the Sun in winter. (D) must, therefore, be an incorrect answer and cannot be chosen. Since the Sun does not revolve about the Earth (rather the Earth revolves about the Sun), answer (E) is incorrect.

2. **(B)** A millimeter is about the thickness of a piece of paper; it is the correct answer. A kilometer is 1000 meters; since a meter is 39.37 inches, a kilometer is 39,370 inches—certainly an inconvenient measure for the everyday person. (A) should not be chosen. A centimeter is one hundredth of a meter. Since it is about the size of a little finger turned sideways, a centimeter may not be the best measure for the average person to employ. (C) should not be selected. A meter, as stated earlier, is 39.37 inches; it (D) is not the best choice for measuring a the thickness of a piece of paper. (E) is not an appropriate choice since a hectometer would equal 100 meters or 3,937 inches.

3. **(D)** Since all of the first three statements about the sun (A), (B), and (C) are true, answer (D), which allows you to select "all the above" is the best choice. Even though (A), (B), and (C) are true statements, none could be selected singularly since it would preclude acknowledging the accuracy of the other statements. (E) is a false answer since it states that none of the first three answers are true.

4.   **(C)**   Vitamins do act as regulators of chemical activity and growth in the body; (C) is true. It is carbohydrates (not vitamins) that serve as fuels; (A) is incorrect. It is proteins (not vitamins) that are used directly as growth materials; (B) is incorrect. Since the best place to obtain vitamins, most nutritionists and physicians agree, is from the foods we eat (not from tablets), (D) is not a suitable choice. Physicians warn against megadoses of vitamins; (E) is incorrect.

5.   **(D)**   (D) is the answer to be selected since chicken is not a high source of cholesterol, especially if the skin is removed. If you did not select this answer, you may not have observed the word NOT in the question. Since answers (A), (B), (C), and (E) are all true statements, they should not be selected.

6.   **(A)**   Since a hygrometer does indeed measure moisture in the air, (A) should be selected. An anemometer (B) measures wind speed and is not to be chosen. A barometer (C) measures air pressure; (C) therefore cannot be chosen correctly. A thermometer measures temperature; it, too, is the incorrect choice. An altimeter (E) measures height; it cannot be selected as the correct choice.

7.   **(A)**   Many of the items listed in the answers to 7 are nonrenewable: coal, oil, gas, and metals. The other items (soil, vegetation, animals, and freshwater) are renewable. Only answer (A), however, contains all items which are nonrenewable and can be selected. (B), (C), (D), and (E) do not include only items which can be selected as nonrenewable and cannot be chosen as the correct answer.

8.   **(E)**   The digestive system carries food from the mouth to the esophagus, to the stomach, and to the intestines; the organs are set up to allow the absorption of food though their walls and to allow the food to be sent to all parts of the body. Transportation (I) is one duty of the digestive system. The digestive system assimilates (digests, absorbs) food so II is also a feature of the digestive system. The last function of the digestive system is excretion. Only one answer (E) enables the reader to select I, II, and III. All of the answers (A) are not appropriate. Reproduction (IV) is a function of the reproductive system, not the digestive system. Answers (A), (C), and (D), which include (IV) cannot be selected. The nervous system is primarily responsible for the individual's response to environmental stimuli. Answers (A), (C), and (D) which include (V) cannot be chosen. Since answers (I), (II), and (III) are correct, "None of the above" (B) cannot be chosen.

9.   **(A)**   Matter exhibits the three states of solids, liquids, and gases. (A) says that matter exhibits the states of atoms, molecules, and cells; (A) is incorrect and therefore the correct answer for 9—which asks for the false answer. The rest of the answers (B), (C), (D), and (E) are not appropriate since they are true statements and number 9 calls for the false statement.

10.   **(A)**   Since the number of electrons is the same as the number of protons in an atom and since the atomic number equals the number of electrons and also equals the number of protons, (A) is the correct answer. (A) states that the atomic number of sulphur is 16 and the number of protons and the atomic number is also 16; this is correct. The answers (B), (C), and (D) contain multiples of 8 but do not include the correct choices and should not be selected. Answer (E) which states that "an indefinite number, undetermined from information given" is incorrect and should not be chosen; the answer can be determined since the number of electrons is given.

11.   **(C)**   Acid rain, pollutants, ozone hole, and the greenhouse effect are harmful to the environment; answer (C) includes all these items and is, therefore, the correct answer. Answer (A) cannot be selected since it includes "None of the above." Answer (B) cannot be selected since (B) states "All the above" is the correct answer. The water table is necessary to our environment; answers (D) and (E) which include this item are incorrect. Answer (D) also omits (I), so it should be avoided. Answer (E), in addition to including (V), excludes (IV), and should not be chosen.

12.   **(D)**   An electromagnet is not a permanent magnet; it ceases to be a magnet when the electricity ceases to flow through the wire. The strength of an electromagnet can be increased when the number of coils in the wire are increased. Since (D) allows the writer to choose (B)—which states that an electromagnet is permanent—and (C)—which states that the strength of a magnet is limited, (D) should be chosen; (D) includes both incorrect answers. (A) is a true statement and should not be chosen as the correct answer. (E) includes (A) and should not be selected.

13.   **(C)**   Since the moon is always lit by the Sun, the reason the moon is not entirely seen by the Earth is because of the Earth's position while revolving around the Sun. (C), therefore, is the correct answer. (A)—describing a shadow thrown on the moon by the Earth—is not the correct answer since it describes an eclipse. The Sun does not cast a shadow on the moon; it lights the moon. (B)—which describes the casting of a shadow by the Sun instead of the casting of light by the Sun—is incorrect. (D), which states that the rays of the moon do not always reach the Earth and gives that as the reason for phases of the moon is incorrect; the moon has no light of its own. Since the moon only shows the Earth one of its sides, (E) is not an appropriate choice.

14.   **(C)**   The boiling point of water is generally regarded as 100° C or 212° F. Only answer (C) gives this correct information. Answer (A) gives the normal body temperature; (B) is followed by a *C* instead of a *F*. The other answers are incorrect

15.   **(A)**   The first sequence is the correct one. *Annelida* refers to segmented worms, like the earthworms. *Molluska* has hard-shelled animals, like the oysters. *Arthropoda* has six legged insects, like the bees. *Echinodermata* has spiny-skinned animals, like the starfish. *Vertebrata* have backbones; fish fit into that category. The sequence of the other phyla prevent the other answers—(B), (C), (D), (E)—from being correct.

16.   **(D)**   If you considered *antler* to be the correct answer you may have read the word as *anther* (the pollen-bearing part of the flower) rather than *antler* (a branching horn). The other answers are reproductive parts of a flower. A stigma (A) is the top of the style which is equipped with hairs and a sticky secretion to hold pollen grains. A stamen (B) is the part involved in pollen-making. A pistil (C) consists of three parts—ovary, style, stigma. A sperm (E) is the male reproductive nucleus.

17.   **(B)**   All the parts listed—except the spleen (B)—are part of the respiratory system. The trachea is another name for the windpipe. The diaphragm is a muscle below the lungs which allows the chest cavity to become larger or smaller. The bronchial tubes are tubes leading into the lungs. The lungs, of course, are the saclike respiratory organs. The spleen, on the other hand, is the organ near the stomach or intestine of most vertebrates; it is

concerned with the final destruction of blood cells, the storage of blood and the production of lymphocytes.

18. **(C)** Enzymes serve two main functions—both of which are stated in (A) and (B). Answer (C) allows you to choose both the correct answers. Answers (A) only or (B) only would be incomplete. Answer (D) suggests fusion of food molecules rather than the breaking down of food molecules. Answer (D) should not be chosen. Answer (E) does not allow the reader to choose any of the answers given; (E) is clearly the wrong answer and it should not be chosen.

19. **(C)** All of the statements about machines are true except (C); (C) is, therefore, the correct answer. Friction can be an asset in certain cases—contrary to what (C) would have the reader to believe. For instance, friction (the rubbing together of two substances) can prevent slipping in the work of machines. Since all the answers are true except (C), (C) should be selected.

20. **(B)** All of the terms except *pollination* relate to the water cycle. *Pollination* is the transfer of pollen for the purposes of pollination; it has to do with the reproduction of plants and not the water cycle. (B), therefore, is the correct answer. Condensation (A) refers to the reducing from one form to another—usually denser—form, as steam to water. Evaporation (C) is the act of passing off into vapor. Precipitation (D) is a deposit on the earth of rain, hail, snow, sleet, or mist. Transpiration (E) is the act of exhaling vapor through the skin or surface of green tissues in plants.

21. **(A)** Dried beans are an excellent source of protein; the others are not good sources of protein, though they contain other nutrients. Fruits (B) are not rich in protein; yellow fruits contain Vitamin A and citrus fruits contain Vitamin C. Leafy vegetables (C) contain Vitamin A, not protein. Honey (D) and white potatoes (E) are sources of carbohydrates—not protein. Dried beans (A), then, is the best answer.

22. **(D)** Since comets glow from reflected light, not their own light, (D) is a false answer and the answer sought. When comets are close to the sun, they shine by fluorescence when the gases are set aglow by ultraviolet radiation from the sun. The rest of the answers—(A), (B), (C), and (E)—are true answers but are not to be selected since the directions ask for the answer which is NOT true. (D) is the only appropriate answer.

23. **(A)** Since all the statements are true, (A) is the best—and only answer. The other items (B), (C), (D), and (E) omit important true statements.

24. **(D)** All the statements about liquids, expansion and contraction are true—except for (D). Gases actually expand when heated and contract when cooled—the opposite of what the statement reads. Answer (D) should be selected since the incorrect answer is sought.

25. **(E)** Since reptiles are not gill-breathing throughout life, (E) is NOT a characteristic of reptiles and, consequently, is the answer to be chosen. The rest of the answers—(A), (B), (C), and (D)—are true and not to be selected.

26. **(D)** The only way to prevent and/or cure the problems of pollution is to treat

industrial waste before it is discharged into the environment; (D) is the correct answer. Discharging heat into adjacent waters (A) will kill the plant and animal life there; (A) is not acceptable for preventing and curing the problems of pollution. Dumping sewage, tars, and oils into salty water or ocean waters (B) and (C) does not eliminate the problem of pollution. This process simply SPREADS the problem. Recycling (E) helps with the problem; it should not be discontinued as answer (E) suggests. The best answer is (D).

27. **(B)** Leaves produce food (IV). Stems transport and support a plant (I). The roots anchor the plant in the soil and absorb water and minerals for the plant (II). The flower produces seeds (III). (B) gives the functions in that order so (B) should be selected as the correct answer.

28. **(A)** Changes (modifications) in plants and animals usually occur very slowly over a period of time. Since answer (A) suggests that these changes occur rapidly, it is a false answer. Since the answer which is NOT true is sought, (A) should be selected. The rest of the answers—(B), (C), (D) and (E)—are true and should not be selected.

29. **(B)** Answer (B) gives the correct order of the eras. The rest of the answers—(A), (C), (D), and (E)—do not sequence the eras correctly and none of them should be selected.

30. **(B)** According to the chart, "Z" apparently increases size, but a warmer temperature seems to cause a greater increase in size; a cooler temperature seems to cause less of an increase in size. (A) is not true because after 1 mg. of "Z" at 68° size at maturation is 20"; at 69° size at maturation is 20.5". Based on the answer explanation just given, it seems that cooler temperatures cause "Z" to be less effective—not more effective—as (C) suggests; (C) is incorrect. The time of maturation is not discussed in the chart given; the size at maturation seems to be increased as a result of adding "Z" to the diet. (D) is not an acceptable answer. When the temperature is raised slightly, the size at maturation seems to be increased; no time span for reaching maturation is given in the chart, however. (E) is not an acceptable choice.

NTE Test of Professional Knowledge

TEST 3 – ANSWER SHEET

Section 1

1. Ⓐ Ⓑ Ⓒ Ⓓ Ⓔ
2. Ⓐ Ⓑ Ⓒ Ⓓ Ⓔ
3. Ⓐ Ⓑ Ⓒ Ⓓ Ⓔ
4. Ⓐ Ⓑ Ⓒ Ⓓ Ⓔ
5. Ⓐ Ⓑ Ⓒ Ⓓ Ⓔ
6. Ⓐ Ⓑ Ⓒ Ⓓ Ⓔ
7. Ⓐ Ⓑ Ⓒ Ⓓ Ⓔ
8. Ⓐ Ⓑ Ⓒ Ⓓ Ⓔ
9. Ⓐ Ⓑ Ⓒ Ⓓ Ⓔ
10. Ⓐ Ⓑ Ⓒ Ⓓ Ⓔ
11. Ⓐ Ⓑ Ⓒ Ⓓ Ⓔ
12. Ⓐ Ⓑ Ⓒ Ⓓ Ⓔ
13. Ⓐ Ⓑ Ⓒ Ⓓ Ⓔ
14. Ⓐ Ⓑ Ⓒ Ⓓ Ⓔ
15. Ⓐ Ⓑ Ⓒ Ⓓ Ⓔ
16. Ⓐ Ⓑ Ⓒ Ⓓ Ⓔ
17. Ⓐ Ⓑ Ⓒ Ⓓ Ⓔ
18. Ⓐ Ⓑ Ⓒ Ⓓ Ⓔ
19. Ⓐ Ⓑ Ⓒ Ⓓ Ⓔ
20. Ⓐ Ⓑ Ⓒ Ⓓ Ⓔ
21. Ⓐ Ⓑ Ⓒ Ⓓ Ⓔ
22. Ⓐ Ⓑ Ⓒ Ⓓ Ⓔ
23. Ⓐ Ⓑ Ⓒ Ⓓ Ⓔ
24. Ⓐ Ⓑ Ⓒ Ⓓ Ⓔ
25. Ⓐ Ⓑ Ⓒ Ⓓ Ⓔ
26. Ⓐ Ⓑ Ⓒ Ⓓ Ⓔ
27. Ⓐ Ⓑ Ⓒ Ⓓ Ⓔ
28. Ⓐ Ⓑ Ⓒ Ⓓ Ⓔ
29. Ⓐ Ⓑ Ⓒ Ⓓ Ⓔ
30. Ⓐ Ⓑ Ⓒ Ⓓ Ⓔ
31. Ⓐ Ⓑ Ⓒ Ⓓ Ⓔ
32. Ⓐ Ⓑ Ⓒ Ⓓ Ⓔ
33. Ⓐ Ⓑ Ⓒ Ⓓ Ⓔ
34. Ⓐ Ⓑ Ⓒ Ⓓ Ⓔ
35. Ⓐ Ⓑ Ⓒ Ⓓ Ⓔ

Section 2

1. Ⓐ Ⓑ Ⓒ Ⓓ Ⓔ
2. Ⓐ Ⓑ Ⓒ Ⓓ Ⓔ
3. Ⓐ Ⓑ Ⓒ Ⓓ Ⓔ
4. Ⓐ Ⓑ Ⓒ Ⓓ Ⓔ
5. Ⓐ Ⓑ Ⓒ Ⓓ Ⓔ
6. Ⓐ Ⓑ Ⓒ Ⓓ Ⓔ
7. Ⓐ Ⓑ Ⓒ Ⓓ Ⓔ
8. Ⓐ Ⓑ Ⓒ Ⓓ Ⓔ
9. Ⓐ Ⓑ Ⓒ Ⓓ Ⓔ
10. Ⓐ Ⓑ Ⓒ Ⓓ Ⓔ
11. Ⓐ Ⓑ Ⓒ Ⓓ Ⓔ
12. Ⓐ Ⓑ Ⓒ Ⓓ Ⓔ
13. Ⓐ Ⓑ Ⓒ Ⓓ Ⓔ
14. Ⓐ Ⓑ Ⓒ Ⓓ Ⓔ
15. Ⓐ Ⓑ Ⓒ Ⓓ Ⓔ
16. Ⓐ Ⓑ Ⓒ Ⓓ Ⓔ
17. Ⓐ Ⓑ Ⓒ Ⓓ Ⓔ
18. Ⓐ Ⓑ Ⓒ Ⓓ Ⓔ
19. Ⓐ Ⓑ Ⓒ Ⓓ Ⓔ
20. Ⓐ Ⓑ Ⓒ Ⓓ Ⓔ
21. Ⓐ Ⓑ Ⓒ Ⓓ Ⓔ
22. Ⓐ Ⓑ Ⓒ Ⓓ Ⓔ
23. Ⓐ Ⓑ Ⓒ Ⓓ Ⓔ
24. Ⓐ Ⓑ Ⓒ Ⓓ Ⓔ
25. Ⓐ Ⓑ Ⓒ Ⓓ Ⓔ
26. Ⓐ Ⓑ Ⓒ Ⓓ Ⓔ
27. Ⓐ Ⓑ Ⓒ Ⓓ Ⓔ
28. Ⓐ Ⓑ Ⓒ Ⓓ Ⓔ
29. Ⓐ Ⓑ Ⓒ Ⓓ Ⓔ
30. Ⓐ Ⓑ Ⓒ Ⓓ Ⓔ
31. Ⓐ Ⓑ Ⓒ Ⓓ Ⓔ
32. Ⓐ Ⓑ Ⓒ Ⓓ Ⓔ
33. Ⓐ Ⓑ Ⓒ Ⓓ Ⓔ
34. Ⓐ Ⓑ Ⓒ Ⓓ Ⓔ
35. Ⓐ Ⓑ Ⓒ Ⓓ Ⓔ

Section 3

1. Ⓐ Ⓑ Ⓒ Ⓓ Ⓔ
2. Ⓐ Ⓑ Ⓒ Ⓓ Ⓔ
3. Ⓐ Ⓑ Ⓒ Ⓓ Ⓔ
4. Ⓐ Ⓑ Ⓒ Ⓓ Ⓔ
5. Ⓐ Ⓑ Ⓒ Ⓓ Ⓔ
6. Ⓐ Ⓑ Ⓒ Ⓓ Ⓔ
7. Ⓐ Ⓑ Ⓒ Ⓓ Ⓔ
8. Ⓐ Ⓑ Ⓒ Ⓓ Ⓔ
9. Ⓐ Ⓑ Ⓒ Ⓓ Ⓔ
10. Ⓐ Ⓑ Ⓒ Ⓓ Ⓔ
11. Ⓐ Ⓑ Ⓒ Ⓓ Ⓔ
12. Ⓐ Ⓑ Ⓒ Ⓓ Ⓔ
13. Ⓐ Ⓑ Ⓒ Ⓓ Ⓔ
14. Ⓐ Ⓑ Ⓒ Ⓓ Ⓔ
15. Ⓐ Ⓑ Ⓒ Ⓓ Ⓔ
16. Ⓐ Ⓑ Ⓒ Ⓓ Ⓔ
17. Ⓐ Ⓑ Ⓒ Ⓓ Ⓔ
18. Ⓐ Ⓑ Ⓒ Ⓓ Ⓔ
19. Ⓐ Ⓑ Ⓒ Ⓓ Ⓔ
20. Ⓐ Ⓑ Ⓒ Ⓓ Ⓔ
21. Ⓐ Ⓑ Ⓒ Ⓓ Ⓔ
22. Ⓐ Ⓑ Ⓒ Ⓓ Ⓔ
23. Ⓐ Ⓑ Ⓒ Ⓓ Ⓔ
24. Ⓐ Ⓑ Ⓒ Ⓓ Ⓔ
25. Ⓐ Ⓑ Ⓒ Ⓓ Ⓔ
26. Ⓐ Ⓑ Ⓒ Ⓓ Ⓔ
27. Ⓐ Ⓑ Ⓒ Ⓓ Ⓔ
28. Ⓐ Ⓑ Ⓒ Ⓓ Ⓔ
29. Ⓐ Ⓑ Ⓒ Ⓓ Ⓔ
30. Ⓐ Ⓑ Ⓒ Ⓓ Ⓔ
31. Ⓐ Ⓑ Ⓒ Ⓓ Ⓔ
32. Ⓐ Ⓑ Ⓒ Ⓓ Ⓔ
33. Ⓐ Ⓑ Ⓒ Ⓓ Ⓔ
34. Ⓐ Ⓑ Ⓒ Ⓓ Ⓔ
35. Ⓐ Ⓑ Ⓒ Ⓓ Ⓔ

NTE CORE BATTERY–Test 3
TEST OF PROFESSIONAL KNOWLEDGE
Section 1

TIME: 30 Minutes
35 Questions

DIRECTIONS: Each of the following questions and incomplete statements is followed by five answer choices. Select the choice which best answers each question.

---

1. Given illustrations, discussion, and explanations, the students will label the parts of a flower by placing the appropriate name next to each identified part on the bulletin board. This objective is missing

   (A) the minimum level of acceptance (performance level).

   (B) the conditions.

   (C) the learning that should take place.

   (D) the behavior.

   (E) nothing is missing.

2. Mr. Towery made a test to evaluate his pupils' abilities to perform basic mathematical tasks. He had given the test to five sections of 8th grade students and it yielded similar results. It is now apparent that the test measures reading abilities better than mathematical abilities. His test does not have good

   (A) reliability.   (D) problems.

   (B) validity.   (E) reliability nor validity.

   (C) consistency.

3. The legal authority to enter into contract for services with a teacher most often resides with the

   I. school principal.   III. local school board.

   II. school superintendent.   IV. president of the local teachers' union.

   (A) I and II.   (D) III only.

   (B) II and III.   (E) III and IV.

   (C) II only.

4. The Supreme Court has ruled on significant educational issues. Of the following court cases, identify the pair in which the former established the principle of separate but equal and the latter reversed that decision.

    (A) *Brown v. The Board of Education of Topeka; Plessy v. Ferguson.*

    (B) *Tinker v. Des Moines Independent School District; Plessy v. Ferguson.*

    (C) *Plessy v. Ferguson; Brown v. Board of Education of Topeka.*

    (D) *Goss v. Lopez; Tinker v. Des Moines Independent School District.*

    (E) *Plessy v. Ferguson; Goss v. Lopez.*

5. In the legislated chain of command for U.S. school districts, which of the following represents this relationship?

    (A) Federal government, state government, local school superintendent, local school board.

    (B) State Board of Education, local school district, local school superintendent, local school board.

    (C) State Board of Education, local school district, local school board, local school superintendent.

    (D) Department of Education, local school district, individual school.

    (E) None of the above.

6. Title IX of the Educational Amendments to the Civil Rights Act of 1972 ensured that

    (A) school science and math programs would be supported with more financial assistance.

    (B) special programs for children of low-income families would be implemented.

    (C) all handicapped children would receive an appropriate education.

    (D) no educational programs receiving federal financial assistance could discriminate on the basis of sex.

    (E) a range of early childhood education programs for economically and culturally disadvantaged children would be available.

7. *De jure* segregation refers to:

    (A) segregation that has come about illegally.

    (B) segregation as a result of sex.

    (C) segregation that is a result of laws, government actions, or school policies.

    (D) segregation that is a result of housing patterns of whites and blacks.

    (E) desegregation.

8. One skill that teachers must develop is managing inappropriate behavior to encourage the elimination of conduct problems. Examples of appropriate managing techniques include

    (A) explaining the importance of avoiding situations that tempt the student to misbehave.

    (B) reminding students of consequences of a targeted inappropriate behavior.

(C)   staying near the student when a potential problem arises.

(D)   All of the above.

(E)   None of the above.

9.   If one were to observe a classroom in which the teacher advocated a policy of student initiative, free expression, individualized instruction, and value clarification, the philosophical foundation upon which the teacher built would most likely be identified as

(A)   existentialism.

(B)   perennialism.

(C)   essentialism.

(D)   behaviorism.

(E)   progressivism.

10.   The *Tinker v. Des Moines School District* case decision included the fact that

(A)   students are free to express their views at any time.

(B)   students are not free to express their views at school.

(C)   students are free to express their views on the school campus before the school day begins or after it ends, but not during class time.

(D)   students are free to express their views except when this expression disrupts class work, causes disorder, or invades the right of others.

(E)   None of the above.

11.   In most states the major source of local funds to meet the budgetary costs of the school systems is the

(A)   sales tax.

(B)   local income tax.

(C)   federal income tax.

(D)   local property tax.

(E)   excise tax on motor fuel.

12.   Federal legislation which required equal educational opportunity for all handicapped students in the public schools is explained in

(A)   the Elementary and Secondary Education Act of 1965.

(B)   the National Defense Education Act of 1958.

(C)   the Buckley Amendment.

(D)   Public Law 94-142.

(E)   Public Law 99-457.

13.   Teachers should treat all students with respect regardless of the way they behave or their achievement level. Appropriate teacher behaviors include accepting the students, but not necessarily the students' behaviors. Which of the following describes the student in judgmental terms instead of appropriately describing the behavior?

(A)   "You're late again."

(B)   "You don't have any manners."

(C)   "You didn't hand in your work four times in the past two weeks."

(D)   "You are not contributing to the group by making suggestions."

(E)   (A) and (B) are both inappropriate.

14. How did the passage of the Morrill Act of 1862 represent the changing aims of higher education in America?
    (A) It represented an extension of public support and control, and strengthened the concept of a state university system.
    (B) Areas of inquiry including law and science were elevated in importance.
    (C) A college education was now available for the rich.
    (D) It foreshadowed the eventual end of the private university movement.
    (E) It represented an extension of colleges established under religious auspices.

15. Which of the following was the author of the first book dealing with a description of black Americans in urban American and became the first leader of the NAACP?
    (A) W. E. B. Dubois   (D) Catharine Beecher
    (B) Booker T. Washington   (E) Mary Bethune
    (C) Harriet Beecher Stowe

16. Which of the following is generally considered the best first step before using a filmstrip in the classroom?
    (A) Use the material to reinforce previous learning.
    (B) Preview the material to determine the contents.
    (C) Provide good viewing standards for classroom behavior.
    (D) Provide readiness for viewing by establishing purposes and questions.
    (E) Arrange seats so that all students can see the screen.

17. The computer with its virtually instantaneous response to student input is becoming more widely used as an aid to instruction. A teacher using a computer to help with recording student progress and selecting instructional materials is an example of
    (A) Computer Assisted Instruction.
    (B) Computer Managed Instruction.
    (C) Computer Instructional Development.
    (D) Computer Based Training.
    (E) Computer Generated Graphics.

18. Which of the following is generally considered the most desirable first step in developing curriculum?
    (A) Establish and define educational objectives
    (B) Begin necessary research
    (C) Propose alternative objectives
    (D) Identify all learning constraints
    (E) Select an appropriate textbook series

19. One of the most effective ways of managing your class by ATTENTION is
    (A) reprimand those students who are misbehaving.
    (B) ignore inappropriate behavior.
    (C) be observant in catching students *being good*.
    (D) keep students doing paper and pencil work.
    (E) allow students free control of the classroom.

20. Effective ways of using praise in behavior control include which of the following?

    I.   Using students' names.
    II.   Consistently praising the same way.
    III. Praising all of the time.
    IV.   Using descriptive words when reinforcing appropriate behavior.

    (A) I and II.   (D) III and IV.
    (B) I and III.   (E) I and IV.
    (C) II and III.

21. After grading her tests, Mrs. Wallace groups the scores before assigning a letter grade. When the most frequent scores on the test fall evenly into two categories, then the distribution is said to be

    (A) bimodal.   (D) dual.
    (B) normal.   (E) multimodal.
    (C) modal.

22. Even though teachers are aware of Bloom's taxonomy of objectives, test questions do not follow this model. Students instead are generally expected to answer questions that stress

    (A) comprehension, the lowest level of the taxonomy.
    (B) synthesis, the highest level of the taxonomy.
    (C) knowledge, the highest level of the taxonomy.
    (D) comprehension, the next to lowest level of the taxonomy.
    (E) knowledge, the lowest level of the taxonomy.

23. Mrs. Rodriguez uses the discovery approach in her science class by

    (A) urging students to read about how the small pox vaccine was discovered.
    (B) asking students to propose solutions to their lab assignments.
    (C) acquainting students with famous discoveries in the field of science.
    (D) teaching students to complete their lab assignments by following set procedures.
    (E) having students prepare an oral report on a famous discovery.

24. A school whose goals are based on Robert Gagne's conclusions of learned capabilities will ultimately aim to

    (A) improve student attitude.
    (B) provide students with knowledge of fact.
    (C) provide students with general information.
    (D) equip students with problem solving skills.
    (E) improve student motor skills.

25. Which of the following statements would be a goal but not an objective?

    (A) Students will become active and informed citizens.
    (B) Students will explain the applications and value of the Bill of Rights.

(C) Students will describe the legislative process in formulating and enacting a bill into law.

(D) Students will identify constitutional amendments which guarantee individual rights and freedoms.

(E) Students will explain each of the amendments to the Constitution.

26. One of the advantages of using specific instructional objectives is that of
   (A) making learning easier.
   (B) clarity in communicating teacher expectations of student performance.
   (C) motivating students to work harder.
   (D) improved teacher control of student conduct.
   (E) monitoring student behavior.

27. When doing advanced planning to teach a specific skill of some complexity, the teacher should
   (A) consult a scope and sequence chart.
   (B) construct a behavior-content matrix.
   (C) do a task analysis.
   (D) formulate a general curriculum objective.
   (E) explicitly follow the teacher's guide.

28. When a child expresses bitter hatred for a classmate, the teacher will more likely be able to lessen the hatred if he/she
   (A) punishes the child.
   (B) forces the child to be nice to the classmate.
   (C) explains calmly that such feelings will do no good.
   (D) expresses empathy.
   (E) criticizes the child.

29. Aptitude tests attempt to predict
   (A) a person's general knowledge.
   (B) probable success in a certain field.
   (C) the degree of achievement already attained by a person.
   (D) the level of efficiency of an individual.
   (E) a person's intelligence quotient.

30. A teacher is observed to dismiss his/her class whenever the students become rowdy or undisciplined. During the semester, student behavior becomes progressively worse. Which of the following is the best evaluation of this situation?
   (A) The teacher is reinforcing the behavior of the students.
   (B) The teacher is too demanding and rigorous with the students.
   (C) The teacher's action is appropriate punishment for the behavior of the students.
   (D) The students' behavior indicates that they have not been given enough interesting work.
   (E) The teacher is punishing the behavior of the students.

31. A teacher notices that a student's behavior is becoming disruptive and moves over to stand near the student. The teacher is demonstrating
    (A) the Premack principle.   (D) proximity control.
    (B) assertive discipline.   (E) defining limits.
    (C) time out.

32. Abraham Maslow has proposed a hierarchy of needs. From LOWEST to HIGHEST in order these are
    (A) physiological, comfort, love and belonging, esteem, self-actualization, knowing and understanding, aesthetic.
    (B) physiological, safety, love and belonging, esteem, knowing and understanding, aesthetic, self-actualization.
    (C) physiological, safety, love and belonging, esteem, self-actualization, knowing and understanding, aesthetic.
    (D) physiological, safety, esteem, self-actualization, aesthetic.
    (E) None of the above.

33. Which of the following is the most constructive way of motivating students?
    (A) Testing frequently.
    (B) Telling students they may need the information in the future.
    (C) Showing students how the material to be learned will help them satisfy personal goals.
    (D) Rewarding correct responses only.
    (E) Using the traditional methods of instruction.

34. Our most accurate statement concerning the role of heredity and environment in determining I.Q. is that
    (A) it all depends on heredity.
    (B) environment is the greatest contributor.
    (C) heredity and environment are both involved.
    (D) neither heredity nor environment are contributors.
    (E) researchers have not studied the impact of heredity and environment in determining I.Q.

35. William's teacher makes note of the fact that William is at the preoperational stage of cognitive development and is capable of conservation. This means that William can
    (A) consider more than one characteristic of an object at one time.
    (B) mentally reverse actions.
    (C) solve problems by generalizing.
    (D) deal with abstractions.
    (E) realize something is the same even though it looks different.

Section 2

TIME: 30 Minutes
35 Questions

DIRECTIONS: Each of the following questions and incomplete statements is followed by five answer choices. Select the choice which best answers each question.

---

1. A sixth-grade student obtained the following derived scores on a nationally standardized achievement test battery

AREA	GRADE EQUIVALENT
Reading	8.3
Arithmetic	5.2
Language	7.6

    On the basis of these scores, one can say that the student is
    (A) below his class average in arithmetic.
    (B) above his class average in reading.
    (C) above the grade norm in language.
    (D) superior to the class in general, but needs remedial work in arithmetic.
    (E) below the grade norm in language.

2. A group of students took the same test of professional aptitude on two separate occasions. Both times they all obtained scores which placed them in the same relative position; however, later study showed that their scores correlated zero with success in their professions. It can be concluded that the test was
    (A) reliable and valid. (D) neither reliable nor valid.
    (B) reliable, but not valid. (E) either reliable or valid.
    (C) valid, but not reliable.

3. If you needed to study many characteristics of many children at different ages in the BRIEFEST time, you would employ the
    (A) cross-sectional method. (D) scientific method.
    (B) longitudinal method. (E) none of the above.
    (C) observational method.

4. If a teacher wants a principle to be transferred by students to real life situations, the teacher should
    (A) recite the correct rules to the students and have them commit these rules to memory.
    (B) let the students discover how the principle will apply by themselves on a sink-or-swim basis.
    (C) have the students memorize the appropriate concepts and generalizations.

(D) present a series of problems in such a way that the students are led to formulate the principle themselves.

(E) have the students memorize the principle and related facts.

5. More than ever, teachers must accustom themselves to working with students who come from homes in which there is only one parent. At a time when almost half of all marriages end in divorce, teachers should be aware of the stress which many students will experience, and attempt to give even greater assistance. This can be accomplished by a teacher who

I. is not personally offended when a student may act aggressively.

II. helps students maintain their self-esteem.

III. is available during the school day to listen to students' concerns.

(A) I and II.　　　　　　　　(D) III only.

(B) I and III.　　　　　　　　(E) I, II, and III.

(C) II and III.

6. Mr. Thompson has a few students who are occasionally disruptive in class. He has made a point of praising their positive behaviors. After the students have been working quietly for a few minutes, he will say, "Good, Mike and Patty, I'm glad to see you completing your English assignment. Keep up the good work!" This technique is likely to be effective because for these two students it

(A) reinforces the disruptive behavior.

(B) occurs too infrequently.

(C) specifies the behavior reinforced.

(D) is directed toward the entire group.

(E) this technique is not likely to be effective.

7. If a class in government was asked, "Why is Geneva, Switzerland selected most often as the location for summits and various meetings among foreign nations?" the teacher's objective upon which the question is based would have to be categorized at which level of Bloom's Taxonomy in the cognitive domain?

(A) Knowledge　　　　　　(D) Analysis

(B) Comprehension　　　　(E) Synthesis

(C) Application

8. Jessica is very bright and very energetic in class. She pays close attention and always knows the correct answer. Her only problem is that she rarely completes homework assignments. Her teacher should

(A) enforce the established consequences for incomplete work.

(B) ignore and extinguish the problem behavior.

(C) relax the rules so that Jessica can complete the assignments.

(D) place Jessica on a system of token reinforcement.

(E) have Jessica tested for placement in the special education program.

9. Ms. Roach's class members did extremely well on their unit test on World War II. She assigned the grade of "A" to each student. Ms. Roach is probably using

(A)   unit-referenced grading.   (D)   the normal curve.

(B)   criterion-referenced grading.   (E)   a bimodal curve.

(C)   norm-referenced grading.

10.   Desegregation was greatly accelerated during the mid-sixties to mid-seventies by several Supreme Court decisions. Which of the following case decisions supported busing of students, revision of attendance zones, or other actions to remove state-imposed segregation, as long as the desegregation plans were workable and feasible?

(A)   *Swann v. Charlotte-Mecklenberg*

(B)   *Green v. County School Board of New Kent County*

(C)   *Bradley v. Milliken*

(D)   *Brown v. Board of Education of Topeka*

(E)   None of the above.

11.   The American public demands a great deal from its schools and it is the curriculum that is the focal point of these demands. As a result the curriculum is continuously changed

I.   as student populations change.

II.   as the goals and objectives of the schools are revised.

III . as interest groups are activated.

IV.   as society changes.

(A)   I and II only.   (D)   II, III, and IV.

(B)   II and III only.   (E)   I, II, III, and IV.

(C)   II and IV only.

12.   The subject-centered curriculum focuses on cognitive aspects of learning, the student-centered curriculum emphasizes students' interests and needs—the affective aspects of learning. One of the chief advocates of the student-centered curriculum attempted to establish a curriculum that balances subject matter with students interests and needs. He also encouraged learners to experiment, to learn by solving problems, and to learn through experience. This person was

(A)   Jean Jacques Rousseau.   (D)   Friedrich Froebel.

(B)   John Dewey.   (E)   None of the above.

(C)   Johann Pestalozzi.

13.   The movement to reform elementary and secondary education has involved state government and school district initiatives to improve the quality and effectiveness of instruction. While some reform movements have not been very successful, progress is being made in some areas. In addition, some of the reform efforts launched within the past few years deal specifically with increasing the power of teachers and their role in decision-making, which is

(A)   deprofessionalization.   (D)   alternative certification.

(B)   occupational prestige.   (E)   merit pay.

(C)   teacher empowerment.

14. For the Greeks, *acculturation* was more important than formal schooling. Through acculturation Greek youth became citizens of the society. Today's educators believe that children must be *acculturated* to provide for the transmission of the culture. *Acculturation*, therefore, is

    (A) learning the concepts, values, and behavior patterns of individuals sharing a common culture through immersion and participation in the total culture.

    (B) being prepared to function first as young people and then as adults.

    (C) the rules of behavior of the society.

    (D) the continually changing patterns of learned behavior transmitted among the members of a society.

    (E) None of the above.

15. The increase in working mothers has been associated with the phenomenon of children who return to empty homes after school to sit by the television or to roam the streets. National data indicate that there may be as many as 6 million of these children between the ages of six and thirteen. These children are commonly referred to as

    (A) step-children.   (D) latch-key children.

    (B) single-parent children.   (E) extended family children.

    (C) nuclear children.

16. Educators have a major responsibility for reporting evidence that students in their classes may have been abused. The number of children reported as victims of abuse and neglect continues to increase. More than half of the reported cases involve neglect of such needs as food, clothing, or medical treatment, about one-seventh involve sexual mistreatment, and approximately 25 percent involve physical violence. Research has shown that a relatively high proportion of the victims are

    (A) low-income children.

    (B) middle-income children.

    (C) high-income children.

    (D) from any income level, there are no general trends.

    (E) from middle or high-income families.

17. Comenius, Rousseau, Pestalozzi, and Spencer challenged the older view of child depravity and passive learning that had long dominated schooling. These naturalistic educators held that the child was innately good; they believed that the stages of human growth and development provided clues for the development of educational method. These educators came to be called *naturalistic* because they believed

    (A) that a strong teacher who used authoritarian teaching methods provided the best natural education for children.

    (B) that children learn by working with and by examining the objects in their immediate natural environment.

    (C) that passive learning was the natural way for children to learn.

    (D) that there should be one set of schools for the common people and a second set of schools for the upper class.

    (E) that children were naturally evil at birth.

18. Primary or elementary institutions that offered a basic curriculum of reading, writing, arithmetic, and religion and were used to make the lower classes literate were

(A) Latin grammar schools.   (D) vernacular schools.

(B) academies.   (E) normal schools.

(C) common schools.

19. When teachers ask questions in the classroom, increasing the length of wait time will usually result in more

I.   accurate answers.

II.   creative answers.

III. student confusion about what the teacher wants.

IV.   improvement in test scores.

(A) I and IV.   (D) I, II, and I V.

(B) III only.   (E) I, II, III and IV.

(C) I and II.

20. When Mrs. Burns decided to evaluate and improve her classroom management, she probably examined

(A) classroom rules.   (D) All of the above.

(B) monitoring procedures.   (E) None of the above.

(C) motivation.

21. Plans to accomplish desegregation typically involve altering attendance areas, establishing magnet schools, busing students, pairing schools, using a cluster plan, and/or allowing controlled choice. Magnet schools attract students from various parts of the school system through the use of

(A) full-range athletic programs.

(B) specialized instructional programs.

(C) restructured boundaries.

(D) age assignments.

(E) All of the above.

22. One of the major issues in providing education for gifted and talented students is the selection of effective approaches to curriculum and instruction. The instructional approach recommended for gifted education includes emphasizing

(A) accelerated study.

(B) enrichment provided through independent study and investigative skills.

(C) understanding and appreciation of systems of knowledge.

(D) All of the above.

(E) None of the above.

23. Some aspects of multicultural education emphasize providing appropriate education for children whose cultural and/or language patterns prohibit them from learning in a traditional school. However, the broader aspects of multicultural education include

I.   ensuring positive interracial attitudes.

II.   enabling all students to function in a multicultural society.

III.. adapting instruction to learning styles of groups of students.

IV. emphasizing separatism in a way that is divisive.

(A) I and II.   (D) I, II, III, and IV.

(B) I, II and III.   (E) II, III, and IV.

(C) I, II and IV.

24. Situations in which students of different racial groups attend schools together to ensure equal and effective educational opportunity for students of all backgrounds is referred to as

(A) integration.   (D) *de jure* segregation.

(B) desegregation.   (E) *de facto* segregation.

(C) segregation.

25. Teachers with middle-class backgrounds may experience particular difficulties in understanding and motivating disadvantaged pupils because

(A) differences in dialect and language background make it difficult to communicate effectively.

(B) teachers may reject students who have different cultural patterns.

(C) they may be influenced by certain educational theorists who have raised questions concerning the learning potential of these students.

(D) All of the above.

(E) None of the above.

26. Tammy has a C-minus average. She is likely to respond to the grades she earns during the current semester by thinking that her

(A) success is due to ability and her failure is due to not studying.

(B) success is due to good luck and her failure is due to bad luck.

(C) success is due to good luck and her failure is due to lack of ability.

(D) success is due to persistence and her failure is due to lack of ability.

(E) success is due to ability and her failure is due to bad luck.

27. People who have a common ancestry and generally share language, religion, and other cultural patterns are members of the same

(A) race.   (D) ethnicity.

(B) ethnic group.   (E) All of the above.

(C) socioeconomic group.

28. The Supreme Court set up a two-pronged standard to be met for constitutionally sanctioned searches: (1) whether the search is justified at its inception, and (2) whether the search, when actually conducted, is reasonably related in scope to the circumstances which justified the interference in the first place. This two-pronged standard was established as the U.S. Supreme Court found for school authorities in

(A) *New Jersey v. T.L.O.*   (D) *Wood v. Strickland.*

(B) *Ingraham v. Wright.*   (E) None of the above.

(C) *Bethel School District No. 403 v. Fraser.*

29. John Locke believed that at birth the human mind is a blank slate, a *tabula rasa*, empty of ideas. Because of this and his writings, he is often acclaimed as a pioneer of empiricism. According to empiricism, human knowledge is

(A) acquired through the scientific method.

(B) acquired only by means of the senses.

(C) learned through the teachings of an authoritative teacher.

(D) the transmission of cultural heritage from one generation to the next.

(E) acquired through rote memorization.

30. One of Rousseau's major contributions to educational practices of today was the idea that

(A) all humans possessed inalienable rights of life, liberty, and property.

(B) the teaching of Latin should be stressed.

(C) the corruptive weaknesses of a child could only be corrected by a strong, authoritarian teacher.

(D) educators should base the curriculum on the child's interests and needs.

(E) None of these were Rousseau's ideas.

31. Many of the educational reforms associated with the progressive movement that stress the use of environmental objects, the use of concrete objects, and the cultivation of sensory experiences were based on the theories of

(A) Montessori.   (D) Robert Hutchins.

(B) George Counts.   (E) None of the above.

(C) Johann Pestalozzi.

32. Jean Piaget's cognitive theory has important educational implications including that human growth and development occur in sequential stages and that there should be activities appropriate to each cognitive stage. In the Piagetian school environment, which of the following things should occur?

I. Teachers should encourage children to explore and experiment.

II. Instruction should be individualized so that children can learn in accordance with their own readiness.

III. Children should be provided with concrete materials to touch, manipulate, and use.

IV. Teachers should concentrate on teaching skills correctly, in the precise order and in isolation.

(A) I, II, and IV.   (D) I, II, III, and IV.

(B) I, II, and III.   (E) I and II only.

(C) I, III, and IV.

33. If one were to observe in a classroom in which the teacher focused on the child as the learner rather than on the subject, activities and experiences rather than verbal and literary skills were stressed, and cooperative learning activities were stressed, the philosophical (or theoretical) foundation upon which the teacher based instruction would most likely be identified as

(A)   essentialism.   (D)   realism.

(B)   progressivism.   (E)   existentialism.

(C)   behaviorism.

34.   Classroom management consists of three major components—leadership, classroom atmosphere, and discipline. When power, domination, pressure and criticism are employed by the teacher, this is the

(A)   democratic leadership approach.

(B)   laisse-faire leadership approach.

(C)   authoritarian leadership approach.

(D)   classroom atmosphere approach.

(E)   None of the above.

35.   The fact that the impact of correcting misbehavior in one student is often felt by the others in the class is an example of

(A)   criticism.   (D)   the ripple effect.

(B)   rewards.   (E)   peer pressure.

(C)   setting limits.

Section 3

TIME: 30 Minutes
35 Questions

DIRECTIONS: Each of the following questions and incomplete statements is followed by five answer choices. Select the choice which best answers each question.

---

1. Mrs. Jones asked her class, "Why do you suppose we entered World War I?" Her question is an example of

    (A)   a convergent question.   (D)   a factual question.

    (B)   an alternate-response question.   (E)   a probing question.

    (C)   a divergent question.

2. Sara has great difficulty in mathematics and never works to improve these skills. Poor motivation would probably result from her lack of

    (A)   knowledge of results.

    (B)   success.

    (C)   interest.

    (D)   activities related to the goal of improving each math skill.

    (E)   use of concrete examples.

3. Parents tend to influence their adolescent sons and daughters in decisions that relate to

    (A)   dress.   (D)   All of the above.

    (B)   friends.   (E)   None of the above.

    (C)   choice of a college major.

4. A teacher was trying to positively reinforce students for completing assignments. The students were told that they could read their library books when their class assignments were completed. This would probably not positively reinforce the behavior for all students because:

    (A)   this does not use token reinforcers.

    (B)   what is a positive reinforcer for one student may not be a positive reinforcer for another student.

    (C)   this is an example of negative reinforcement.

    (D)   none of the students were motivated by being able to read their library books.

    (E)   none of the students completed the class assignment.

5. A sixth grade teacher wants to know how the students feel about the poetry unit. The evaluation instrument that would be most effective for this situation would be a(n):

    (A)   questionnaire.   (D)   check list.

    (B)   achievement test.   (E)   standardized test.

    (C)   teacher-made test.

6. Mrs. Lambert used pre-tests, observations of student work, homework, and questioning during instruction in her geometry class to promote learning and to gain an understanding of what skills and concepts the students still needed to reinforce and practice. This is an example of

    (A) how grades should be determined.

    (B) formative evaluation.

    (C) summative evaluation.

    (D) a poor teaching strategy.

    (E) None of the above.

7. In order for any lesson to be successful, it must be well structured. The structure of the lesson should include various techniques that will keep the students interested and motivated. One technique that should NOT be employed is

    (A) making the content relevant to the learners.

    (B) actively involving students in the lesson.

    (C) keeping your goals and objectives a secret.

    (D) being enthusiastic about the material being taught.

    (E) using a cognitive set to motivate the students.

8. The instructional strategy is described as how the teacher will present the lesson content or present the information. To choose the most effective strategy, the teacher must choose from a wide variety of methods and learning experiences. Variables that affect the selection of the appropriate instructional strategy include

    (A) content and objectives of the lesson, learner characteristics, and the learning environment.

    (B) content and objectives of the lesson, teacher characteristics, and learner characteristics.

    (C) content and objectives of the lesson, teacher characteristics, and the learning environment.

    (D) content and objectives of the lesson, teacher characteristics, learner characteristics, and the learning environment.

    (E) content and objectives of the lesson and the learner characteristics.

9. Students in the classroom will vary greatly in academic abilities. Teachers must modify instruction to fit the individual needs and interests of the students. Teachers with mainstreamed or special students must give differentiated assignments. Techniques that teachers may use to accomplish this goal include all of the following EXCEPT

    (A) varying time limits.

    (B) providing the special students with continuous one-to-one instruction, as opposed to small group instruction.

    (C) varying the level of complexity.

    (D) varying the amount of work assigned.

    (E) All of the above.

10. Mr. Watkins is observed using harsh reprimands with his students. Mrs. Wilson, the school principal, points out that criticizing students publicly, angrily, or loudly can
    (A) make students more aggressive and anxious.
    (B) increase students' undesirable behavior.
    (C) decrease students' interest in learning.
    (D) All of the above.
    (E) (A) and (C) only.

11. Developmentally delayed elementary school students tend to
    (A) have short attention spans.   (D) All of the above.
    (B) lack necessary social skills.   (E) (A) and (C) only.
    (C) be easily frustrated.

12. Billy's teacher suspects that he is developmentally delayed. The teacher's suspicions may be valid if
    (A) he behaved more maturely for awhile and then regressed to an earlier form of immature behavior.
    (B) he appears to be more independent than his same-age peers.
    (C) he behaves immaturely in all situations.
    (D) his immaturity is caused by certain environmental factors.
    (E) he has lost interest in playing with the other children.

13. Ms. Reed gives the students in her classroom a token each time they complete a math activity in the weekly unit. At the end of the week the tokens may be redeemed for special free time activities. This is an example of
    (A) extrinsic motivation.   (D) retention.
    (B) intrinsic motivation.   (E) None of the above.
    (C) transfer of learning.

14. Martin is a high achiever and typically makes all A's in school. However, he sometimes makes lower grades. Martin attributes his successes and failures (lower grades) in school to
    (A) his abilities and prejudices on the part of teachers.
    (B) his own abilities and lack of efforts on certain occasions.
    (C) knowing how to study and taking the wrong courses.
    (D) good luck and lack of abilities.
    (E) persistence and lack of abilities.

15. The fact that students should know what the expected behavior is and be aware of the negative or positive consequences which result from the behavior is a basic premise of
    (A) the psychoanalytic approach to classroom discipline.
    (B) the assertive discipline model.
    (C) the behavior modification classroom management approach.
    (D) the Kounin model based on the ripple effect.
    (E) the Glasser model of reality therapy.

16. The stages of cognitive development for children have been delineated primarily from the work of Jean Piaget. According to these stages of development, children who develop the ability to reason logically and abstractly, can test hypotheses, and reflect on their own thinking are in the stage of

(A)   sensorimotor skills.
(B)   concrete operations.
(C)   formal operations.
(D)   preoperational skills.
(E)   None of the above.

17. When John learns to spell a new word, he says the word to himself and spells it out loud to remember the spelling. This is an example of

(A)   auditory learning.
(B)   visual learning.
(C)   tactual learning.
(D)   kinesthetic learning.
(E)   mixed modality learning.

18. Public Law 94-142 requires that students with handicaps be placed in the *least restrictive environment* is defined as

(A)   having the child participate in regular educational programming to the fullest extent possible.
(B)   being individually determined.
(C)   enabling the child to make academic progress.
(D)   All of the above.
(E)   (B) and (C) only.

19. Some educators believe that high numbers of minority students are placed in special education classes to alleviate teachers' problems in dealing with culturally different children. In 1970 in *Diana v. Board of Education*, the claim of improperly classifying Mexican-American children based on IQ tests was examined. The court ruled that

I.   all children whose primary language is not English must be tested in both languages.
II.   tests cannot be solely based on vocabulary or other experienced based items.
III. districts that have a large percentage of Mexican-American students in special education classes must prove that this large percentage is a result of valid classification methods.
IV.   black students could not be placed in classes for the educable mentally retarded on the basis of IQ tests as they are currently administered.

(A)   I and II.
(B)   I and III.
(C)   I, II and III .
(D)   I, II, III and IV.
(E)   I, III and IV.

20. The Education for All Handicapped Children Act, Public Law 94-142, required, among other things, that individualized Education Programs (IEPs) should include both long-range and short-range goals and be developed for each student. There should be only one IEP per child which should be developed by

   (A) an administrator, the child's teacher(s), the parent(s) or surrogate, the child (when appropriate), and other(s).

   (B) an administrator, the child's teacher(s), the parent(s) or surrogate, and the child (when appropriate).

   (C) an administrator, the child's teacher(s), the parent(s) or surrogate, and other(s).

   (D) an administrator, the child's teacher(s), and the parent(s) or surrogate.

   (E) the child's teacher(s) and the parent(s) or surrogate.

21. The educator who believed that the purpose of education is to organize education in terms of children's patterns of growth or development and that the teachers role is to assist children in the learning process through individualizing instruction so that children can learn in accordance with their own readiness was

   (A) Herbart.   (D) Hutchins.

   (B) Piaget.   (E) None of the above.

   (C) Counts.

22. Grouping students with similar achievement levels or abilities in the same classroom is referred to as

   (A) homogeneous grouping.   (D) curriculum alignment.

   (B) heterogeneous grouping.   (E) subject-centered curriculum.

   (C) child-centered curriculum.

23. Accountability is stressed in the school system that hired Ms. Huggins. She is expected to

   (A) keep accurate records of the activities used in class and the amount of time spent teaching each subject.

   (B) list specific goals for student achievement and show evidence that her students have reached these goals.

   (C) provide proof that the best students in the class are the ones who receive the best grades.

   (D) provide IEPs for each student in the class.

   (E) keep accurate records of how much time the students spend "on task" each day.

24. Frederick believes that he can't play basketball because he is clumsy and uncoordinated. He is likely to do all of the following EXCEPT

   (A) keep trying to play basketball to improve his skills.

   (B) feel anxious or fearful when asked to participate in a game of basketball.

   (C) avoid playing basketball completely.

   (D) take his frustration out on his friends when he really wants them to help him play basketball with greater ease.

   (E) (A) and (B) only.

25. Bart, an 11-year-old, lies to a teacher who punishes the students in class rather severely for disobeying classroom rules. However, Bart is as honest as most of the children his age with his other teachers. This is more likely a situational problem than a personality problem because

    (A) this behavior is a constant part of Bart's personality.

    (B) Bart appears to be fearful of all his teachers.

    (C) Bart's behavior of being untruthful is only apparent in one particular situation.

    (D) Bart is withdrawn and frightened in all of his classes.

    (E) Bart is resentful in all of his classes.

26. Marie is an eight-year-old who has behaved poorly in school since kindergarten. She is slow to do what is expected of her and only does so under pressure. She argues and fights with other students in the classes, seldom shares, or waits her turn. Her parents report that she nags them until she gets what she wants or is punished and she often takes her sister's toys without permission. Marie appears to have conduct problems because

    I.   she is unwilling to accept the authority of others.

    II. she seldom interacts with other children.

    III. she refuses to respect the property of others.

    IV. she does not wait until others finish what they are doing.

    V.   she seldom speaks to anyone about anything.

(A)	I and III.	(D)	I, II, III, and IV.
(B)	I, II and III.	(E)	I, III, IV, and V.
(C)	I, III and IV.		

27. Les, a 13-year-old, regularly comes to class without his homework, claiming that he left it at home, lost it, or the dog ate it. The use of consequences to modify this behavior

(A)	would definitely be appropriate.	(D)	would definitely be inappropriate.
(B)	might be appropriate.	(E)	is questionable.
(C)	might be inappropriate.		

28. Ophelia often wanders around the classroom when she should be completing an individual assignment for reinforcement and/or practice. The techniques that would be most appropriate to use to handle this behavior problem would be

I.	giving verbal reinforcement.	III.	using peers as models.
II.	rewarding improvement.	IV.	planned ignoring.

(A)	I and II.	(D)	I, II and III.
(B)	I and III.	(E)	I, II, III and IV.
(C)	I, III and IV.		

29. Educators have found that there are motivational differences among children at different developmental levels. Middle school students
    (A) require immediate reinforcement and gratification.
    (B) are able to work for symbolic rewards that can be exchanged for tangible rewards at some point in the future.
    (C) are able to work toward long-term goals without short-term rewards.
    (D) are not able to evaluate their behavior objectively.
    (E) (B) and (C) only.

30. Brian made 98, 90, 86, 100, 50, 75 and 98 on seven English tests. The mode for these scores is
    (A) 85.29
    (B) 90
    (C) 98
    (D) 75
    (E) 50

31. Mr. Horton wants to encourage as many of his students as possible to do their best in class. He will probably have more success if he uses
    (A) competitive reward structures.
    (B) cooperative reward structures.
    (C) cognitive approaches to motivation.
    (D) the attribution theory approach to motivation.
    (E) Both (A) and (B).

32. The purpose of the lesson introduction, set induction, or the establishment of a cognitive set is to
    I. get the interest of the students.
    II. have the students open their textbooks.
    III. establish a conceptual framework for the information to follow.
    IV. motivate the students to learn the following information.

    (A) I and III.
    (B) I and IV.
    (C) I, II and IV.
    (D) I, III and IV.
    (E) I, II, III and IV.

33. To be an effective teacher, one must also be an effective communicator. Being an effective listener is part of being an effective communicator. All of the following are poor listening habits EXCEPT
    (A) hunting for negative evidence related to the message.
    (B) listening only for the facts in a message.
    (C) criticizing the delivery of the message.
    (D) faking attention.
    (E) avoiding difficult listening.

34.   Asking good questions is an art that can be mastered with practice. All of the following are important steps to follow as one refines the art of questioning EXCEPT

(A)   ask questions that match the lesson objective.

(B)   ask questions to help students modify their responses.

(C)   reinforce student answers sparingly.

(D)   designate the respondent before asking the question.

(E)   avoid too many questions with one-word answers.

35.   During the 1970s, policies were developed to meet specific targets for admission of minority students to higher education programs. This approach was overturned in a case that is commonly referred to as a reverse discrimination case. This Supreme Court Case in 1978 was

(A)   *Washington v. Davis.*

(B)   *School Board of Nassau County v. Arline.*

(C)   *Regents of the University of California v. Alan Bakke.*

(D)   *Wolman v. Walter.*

(E)   None of the above.

TEST OF PROFESSIONAL KNOWLEDGE

ANSWER KEY

SECTION 1

1.	(A)	10.	(D)	19.	(C)	28.	(D)
2.	(B)	11.	(D)	20.	(E)	29.	(B)
3.	(D)	12.	(D)	21.	(A)	30.	(A)
4.	(C)	13.	(B)	22.	(E)	31.	(D)
5.	(C)	14.	(A)	23.	(B)	32.	(B)
6.	(D)	15.	(A)	24.	(D)	33.	(C)
7.	(C)	16.	(B)	25.	(A)	34.	(C)
8.	(D)	17.	(B)	26.	(B)	35.	(E)
9.	(A)	18.	(A)	27.	(C)		

SECTION 2

1.	(C)	10.	(A)	19.	(C)	28.	(A)
2.	(B)	11.	(E)	20.	(D)	29.	(B)
3.	(A)	12.	(B)	21.	(B)	30.	(D)
4.	(D)	13.	(C)	22.	(D)	31.	(C)
5.	(E)	14.	(A)	23.	(B)	32.	(B)
6.	(C)	15.	(D)	24.	(A)	33.	(B)
7.	(C)	16.	(A)	25.	(D)	34.	(C)
8.	(A)	17.	(B)	26.	(C)	35.	(D)
9.	(B)	18.	(D)	27.	(B)		

SECTION 3

1.	(C)	10.	(D)	19.	(C)	28.	(D)
2.	(B)	11.	(D)	20.	(A)	29.	(B)
3.	(C)	12.	(C)	21.	(B)	30.	(C)
4.	(B)	13.	(A)	22.	(A)	31.	(B)
5.	(A)	14.	(B)	23.	(B)	32.	(D)
6.	(B)	15.	(B)	24.	(A)	33.	(A)
7.	(C)	16.	(C)	25.	(C)	34.	(D)
8.	(D)	17.	(A)	26.	(C)	35.	(C)
9.	(B)	18.	(D)	27.	(A)		

DETAILED EXPLANATIONS OF ANSWERS
NTE CORE BATTERY–Test 3
TEST OF PROFESSIONAL KNOWLEDGE
Section 1

1. **(A)** This question concerns planning directions. For this question you should be sure that all the necessary components of an objective are included, such as performance level, conditions, the learning involved, and the behavior to demonstrate the learning. The conditions of the objective are "given illustrations, discussion, and explanations'; (B) is not the correct answer. The learning is "the parts of the flower"; (C) is not the correct answer. The behavior is "by placing, the appropriate name next to each identified part on the bulletin board;" (D) is not the correct answer. Since the performance level is missing, (E) is not the correct answer. It should be noted that some educators assume that the performance level is 100 percent when it is not included in the objective. However, to avoid misinterpretation, the performance level should be included.

2. **(B)** This question concerns evaluation of achievement. To identify the correct answer this question, you must be familiar with the definitions of test reliability and test validity. A test is said to be reliable when various groups of students receive similar results on the same or similar test(s). A test is said to be valid when it measures what it is intended to measure. Consistency and problems are distractors that have been added. Since this test does not measure what the teacher intended to measure, the correct answer is (B) The test appears to be reliable because all five sections of students achieved similar results on the test, therefore (A) and (E) are not correct answers.

3. **(D)** This question is related to the knowledge of the teaching profession and of professional teaching behaviors. You need an understanding of the organization of schools to be able to answer this question correctly. You must consider the authority of the school principal, the school superintendent, and the local school board. You should recognize immediately that the president of the local teachers' union has no authority to enter into contract with a teacher for services; (E) is not correct. The correct answer to this question is (D). The local school board is the only body with this legal authority. You may interview with a principal that may recommend to the superintendent that you be hired, the superintendent may interview or simply act on the principal's recommendation, but the final authority rests with the school board. For these reasons, (A) (B) and (C) are all incorrect.

4. **(C)** This question relates to state, federal, and judicial policy. You must be familiar with each of these cases to make the correct decision. The *Tinker v. Des Moines* case upheld

student rights to freedom of speech, whether spoken or symbolic. *Goss v. Lopez* was the United States Supreme Court decision that declared that students were entitled to due process in disciplinary actions. If you know the precedents in these cases, you can eliminate (B), (C) and (E) *Plessy v. Ferguson* established the principle of separate but equal, and *Brown v. The Board of Education of Topeka* reversed that decision. Therefore, (C) is the correct answer and (A) is incorrect.

5.   **(C)**   This question relates to knowledge of the teaching profession. To be fully knowledgeable about the teaching profession, you must understand the legislated chain of command. The federal government assigns the responsibility of education to the states through the Fourteenth Amendment. Therefore, (A) is eliminated. After the State Board of Education comes the local school district, the local school board, and the local school superintendent. Since the superintendent is listed before the school board in (B), this is not the correct answer. Item (D) includes the individual school and does not include the local school board and local superintendent, it is not correct. Item (E) is not correct because "one of the above," (C) is the correct answer. Answer (C) is the only one in this order and the only acceptable answer.

6.   **(D)**   This question concerns federal policy. The National Defense Education Act of 1958 appropriated federal funds to improve science and math curricula, therefore, (A) is incorrect. The Elementary and Secondary Act of 1965 encouraged development and implementation of special programs for children of low-income families; (B) is not correct. Public Law 94-142 established a national policy so that all handicapped children would receive an appropriate education choice; (C) is incorrect. The correct answer is (D) because Title IX of the Educational Amendments to the Civil Rights Act ensured that no educational programs receiving federal financial assistance could discriminate on the basis of sex. The early childhood educational programs for economically and culturally disadvantaged children known as Operation Head Start, were the result of Johnson's "Great Society;" choice (E) is not correct.

7.   **(C)**   This question concerns recognizing students' rights and state, federal, and judicial policy. *De jure* segregation is segregation resulting from laws, government actions, or school policies specifically designed to bring about separation; the correct choice is (C). This segregation is not explicitly illegal; therefore, choice (A) is not correct. The laws are legal until they are overturned. Segregation in general relates to discrimination by race; choice (B) is not correct. Segregation that is a result of housing patterns is *de facto* segregation; choice (D) is not correct. Desegregation relates to racial groups attending the same school; choice (E) is not the correct answer.

8.   **(D)**   Question number 8 relates to classroom management skills. Examples of appropriate managing techniques include explaining the importance of avoiding situations that tempt the student to misbehave [choice (A)]. This could even be extended by helping the student complete a list of situations that should be avoided. Reminding students of consequences of a targeted inappropriate behavior is another appropriate managing technique; choice (B), especially when the student is about to commit an identified inappropriate behavior. Proximity control, staying near the student when a potential problem arises; choice (C), is also an effective managing technique. For these reasons choice (D), all of the above, is the only correct answer.

9. **(A)** This question deals with preparing lessons and facilitating learning. When you teach, you will deal with many concerns relating to the day-to-day problems of classroom management and preparing lessons. How you choose to deal with these problems will reveal your educational philosophy. Understanding the basic philosophical ideas of others can help you develop your own personal philosophy. Existentialism is a way of examining life in a very personal manner. Existentialists believe that education is a process of developing consciousness about freedom to choose and the responsibility for choice. Student initiative, free expression, individualized instruction, and value clarification would be evident in a teacher's classroom when his/her basic philosophy was existentialism. Perennialism draws heavily on the principles of realism. Perennialists prefer a subject-based curriculum. Mastering subject matter is regarded as essential training of the intellect; choice (B) is not correct. Essentialism emphasizes the authority of the teacher and the value of the subject-based curriculum; choice (C) is not the correct answer. Behaviorists deal only with what is observable and common to all humans. They do not consider a person's problems and achievements in learning; choice (D) is not correct. Progressivists stress the view that all learning should center on the child's needs and interests and believe that the aim of education should be to meet the needs of the growing child; choice (E) is not correct.

10. **(D)** This question deals with recognizing students' constitutional rights. The *Tinker v. Des Moines School District* law case involved a group of students planning to wear black armbands to school as a silent symbolic protest against the Viet Nam War. Some students wore the armbands in violation of a school policy and were suspended. Their parents filed suit and as the Supreme Court ruled in favor of the plaintiffs, the scope of students rights were outlined. The fact that students are free to express their views except when this expression disrupts class work, causes disorder, or invades the rights of others was the basic decision. Therefore, (D) is the correct choice and choices (A), (B), (C), and (E) are incorrect.

11. **(D)** This question relates to recognizing extra-classroom influences on education. The property tax is the main source of revenues for local school districts, accounting for over 90 percent of local revenues. It is, in fact, the most important tax supporting education. Therefore, choice (D) is the correct answer and (A), (C) and (E) are incorrect.

12. **(D)** This question concerns federal policy. The Elementary and Secondary Act of 1965 primarily encouraged development and implementation of special programs for children of low-income families; choice (A) is not correct. The National Defense Education Act of 1958 primarily appropriated federal funds to improve science and math curricula, choice (B) is incorrect. The Buckley Amendment, also called the Family Educational Rights and Privacy Act, gives parents access to their children's school records until the child becomes eighteen years of age. From this point on, only the student has access to the records. Access to student records by third parties was eliminated by the Buckley Amendment; choice (C) is not correct. Public Law 94-142, the Education for All Handicapped Children Act, is the federal legislation that required equal educational opportunities for all handicapped students in public schools; choice (D) is the correct answer. Public Law 99-457, the Amendment to the Education for All Handicapped Children Act, lowered the ages of children covered by the act and involves family plans; choice (E) is not correct.

13. **(B)** Question number 13 relates to classroom management and appropriate teacher behaviors. When teachers disapprove or reject a specific behavior, they must be careful not to disapprove of or reject the student(s) that acted inappropriately. "You're late again";

choice (A), "You didn't hand in your work four times in the past two weeks"; choice (C), and "You are not contributing to the group by making suggestions"; choice (D) are all appropriate statements that describe student behavior in nonjudgmental ways. "You don't have any manners"; choice (B), describes the student in judgmental ways, lt does not address a particular problem. Therefore, the correct answer is (B) and (A), (C), (D) and (E) are not correct.

14.　**(A)**　This question deals with knowledge of the teaching profession, especially the history of education. The Morrill Act of 1862 granted public land to each state based on the number of senators and representatives in Congress. The Morrill Act represented an extension of public support and control, and strengthened the concept of a state university system. Since the income from the grant was to be used to support at least one state college for agriculture and mechanical instruction, the effect was to bring higher education within reach of the masses. For these reasons, choice (A) is the correct answer. The areas of law and science were not elevated in importance; choice (B) is not correct. The Morrill Act brought higher education within the reach of the masses. A college education was already available for rich which makes choice (C) incorrect. This did not "begin the end" of the private university system because we still have private universities today; choice (D) is incorrect. This act strengthened the concept of a state university system; it did not extend religious colleges and choice (E) is not correct.

15.　**(A)**　This question relates to development of American education. W. E. B. Du Bois wrote *The Philadelphia Negro: A Social Study.* which was the pioneer work on urban blacks in America and became the first leader of the NAACP; choice (A) is correct. Booker T. Washington was named to head the Tuskegee Institute and stressed basic academic, agricultural, and occupational skills; choice (B) is incorrect. Harriet Beecher Stowe wrote *Uncle Tom's Cabin* and was Catharine Beecher's sister; choice (C) is not correct. Catharine Beecher argued that educated women were well suited to educate children; choice (D) is not correct. Mary Bethune worked within the political system to attempt to win equal opportunity for blacks and was an advocate for women's and human rights; choice (E) is not correct.

16.　**(B)**　This question relates to planning and designing instruction. There are five basic steps to presenting media effectively. They are as follows: prepare yourself, prepare the room, prepare the students, present the medium to the best advantage, and provide summary activities. Using the material to reinforce previous learning is a reason for using media in the classroom. The reason for presenting the medium would be explained as you prepare the students and would be executed as you present the medium to the best advantage; choice (A) is incorrect. Previewing the material to determine the contents is part of preparing yourself and, of the steps presented, should be completed first which makes choice (B) correct. Providing good viewing standards for classroom behavior should be introduced as you prepare the students and reinforced as you present the medium to the best advantage; choice (C) is not correct. Providing readiness for viewing by establishing purposes and questions is part of preparing the students; choice (D) is not the correct answer. Arranging seating is part of preparing the room; choice (E) is not correct.

17.　**(B)**　This question relates to knowledge of the teaching profession. Computer Assisted Instruction is when the students use the computer for direct instruction, drill and practice, and the like; choice (A) is not correct. Computer Managed Instruction is when the teacher uses the computer to help with recording student progress and selecting additional computer lessons; choice (B) is the correct answer. Computer Instructional Development is not an exact name for a computer use, but the computer is used to develop instructional materials; choice (C) is incorrect. Computer Based Training is when the computer is used to train students to master a specific skill; choice (D) is not correct. Computer Generated Graphics are pictures that are created and/or manipulated by using the computer; choice (E) is not the correct answer.

18. **(A)** This question relates to designing instruction. The first step that should be completed in developing a curriculum is to establish and define educational objectives; choice (A) is correct. Research may be needed to decide upon the best ways to meet the objectives, but cannot be completed until the objectives are developed. Proposing alternative objectives cannot be completed until the original objectives are completed and it is determined that these objectives need to be modified. The learning constraints that prohibit or deter achievement cannot be identified until the objectives are formulated. An appropriate textbook series cannot be selected until the educational objectives are developed. For these reasons, choices (B), (C) (D) and (E) are not correct.

19. **(C)** This question refers to encouraging appropriate behavior and discouraging inappropriate behavior. To control or manage your class by attention involves drawing attention to the appropriate behaviors that occur in the classroom. To do this, you must "catch" students behaving appropriately and use positive reinforcers, therefore, the correct answer is choice (C). Reprimanding students who are misbehaving, ignoring appropriate behavior, keeping students doing pencil and paper work, and allowing students free control of the classroom do not draw attention to appropriate behaviors. Therefore, choices (A), (B), (D) and (E) are not correct. Furthermore, keeping students doing paper and pencil work will lead to boredom and frustration among the students and will possibly increase inappropriate behaviors. Allowing students free control of the classroom will lead to unruliness, confusion, and complete disorganization of any classroom organization and should never be allowed.

20. **(E)** This question deals with knowing how to encourage appropriate behavior and how to extinguish inappropriate behavior. Using students' names and descriptive words when reinforcing appropriate behavior add to the effectiveness of the reinforcement because the students know the exact behavior that is being applauded. If you consistently praise in the same way, using the same words, and if you praise them too often, your words of praise will become redundant and lose their effectiveness. Therefore, the correct choice would include I and IV and the correct answer would be choice (E). All other combinations are not correct and choices(A), (B), (C) and (D) are not appropriate.

21. **(A)** This question relates to evaluating student achievement. The mode, a measure of central tendency, reflects the value of the most frequently occurring observation. When a distribution of scores has two more prevalent or frequent scores, even though they are not exactly the same, the distribution is said to be bimodal, choice (A) is the correct answer. There is not a term that refers to modes as "normal." However, a normal curve is a theoretical curve noted for its bell shape; choice (B) is not correct. If a distribution has only one peak or one value that occurs most frequently, the value is described as the mode. The "al" is only added to "mode" when describing bimodal or multimodal distributions; choice (C) is incorrect. When a distribution has two peaks, it is not described as dual. The correct term is bimodal; choice (D) is not correct. Distributions that have more than two peaks are described as multimodal; choice (E) is not correct.

22. **(E)** This question deals with designing appropriate instructional activities, planning objectives, diagnosing needs, identifying resources, and designing instruction. Even though the cognitive domain taxonomy has been taught for over 25 years in preservice and inservice training, it is estimated that over 90 percent of all test questions that students answer deal with little more than information. In other words, most of the test questions students are expected to answer stress the knowledge level of the taxonomy which is the lowest level, choice (E). Choice (C) is incorrect since knowledge is listed as the highest level. The levels of the taxonomy from lowest to highest are knowledge, comprehension, application, analysis, synthesis, and evaluation; choices (A), (B) and (D) are also incorrect for these reasons.

23. **(B)** This question deals with designing appropriate instructional activities, and with knowing how to present information clearly, ask appropriate questions, guide discussions, and the like. Although many of the ideas of Jerome Bruner influenced the emergence of open education, the basic technique he recommended was the discovery approach. The techniques he suggested for utilizing the discovery approach included stimulating guessing, calling attention to contrast, and encouraging participation. Bruner and Piaget both argued that conceptions that students discover on their own are more meaningful than those taught to them. Of the choices presented, asking the students to propose solutions to their lab assignments is the only description of a discovery learning activity; choice (B) is the correct answer. All of the other choices, (A), (C), (D), and (E) are incorrect because they involve providing information to the students not having students discover concepts on their own.

24. **(D)** This question deals with planning and designing instruction. Robert Gagne was intrigued by questions concerning the basic purposes of education. Gagne concluded that attitudes, motor skills, verbal information, intellectual skills, and cognitive strategies are the five basic types of learned capabilities. He stressed the importance of equipping pupils with the skills necessary to apply what they learn in the classroom to the real world. He further emphasized the fact that the ability to solve problems is dependent on mastery of skills and information. Therefore, the ultimate goal of a school that adhered to Gagne's research would be to equip students with problem solving skills, choice (D). Other goals of the school would probably include improving student attitudes, providing knowledge and information, and improving motor skills, but none of these would be the ultimate goal; choices (A), (B), (C) and (E) are not correct.

25. **(A)** This question relates to planning objectives and goals. Goals are extremely broad statements used to describe purposes of a unit, a course, or a school. Since educational goals are extremely broad, they may take weeks, months, or even years to complete. Objectives, on the other hand, are narrower in scope and describe the intended learning of a specific lesson or unit. Of the statements listed, only choice (A) is broad enough to be considered a goal; choice (A) is correct. While the other statements are lacking some recommended parts of a behavioral objective, they are fairly specific and describe intended learning. Therefore, choices (B), (C), (D) and (E) are incorrect.

26. **(B)** This question relates to planning objectives, specifically to why teachers should write objectives. Reasons for writing objectives include the fact that objectives direct the teaching and learning for each lesson. Writing objectives also aids in evaluating your lesson and communicating with students to let them know what is expected of them. Therefore, the correct answer is choice (B). Writing objectives may help the teacher organize the lesson, but

does not make learning easier, motivate students to work harder, improve teacher control of student conduct, nor aid in monitoring student behavior. For these reasons, choices (A), (C), (D) and (E) are not correct.

27. **(C)** This question relates to designing instruction. Task analysis is a process or method of breaking down the learning into the steps that are necessary to enable you to reach your terminal objective. In other words, it lists all of the subskills necessary for learning the more complex skill. When a teacher is doing the advanced planning to teach a specific skill, the teacher should do a task analysis; choice (C) is the correct answer. A scope and sequence chart will not break the complex skills into detailed subskills, but will give input into sequencing the information; choice (A) is incorrect. Constructing a behavior-content matrix may help classroom management, but will not help simplify a complex lesson; choice (B) is not correct. Formulating a general curriculum objective should have been completed much earlier in the planning process; choice (D) is incorrect. When teaching any lesson, it is acceptable to consult with the teacher's guide. However, teaching should involve a great deal more than following the teacher's guide. Teachers should remember that this textbook supplement is a guide, not something written in concrete. Sometimes teachers' guides provide unacceptable teaching suggestions and methodologies, therefore, choice (E) is not correct and teachers should rarely, if ever, explicitly follow the teacher's guide.

28. **(D)** This question relates knowing how to encourage appropriate behavior. If a teacher punishes a child, forces a child to be nice to a classmate, explains that feelings of hatred will do no good, or criticizes the child for his feelings when this child expresses bitter hatred for a classmate, the child will only become more resentful of the classmate. The child will feel that the classmate has caused him/her to be in trouble with the teacher. Choices (A), (B), (C) and (E) are incorrect responses. The only possible choice is (D), express empathy This will help the child feel that his/her feelings are normal and will not further alienate the child.

29. **(B)** This question refers to evaluating student achievement and instructional effectiveness. Aptitude tests measure the ability to learn new tasks. They do not measure a person's general knowledge, the degree of achievement already attained by a person, the level of efficiency of an individual, nor the person's IQ. Therefore choices (A), (C), (D) and (E) are not correct. Aptitude tests attempt to predict a person's probable success in a certain field, choice (B) is correct.

30. **(A)** This question relates to knowing how to encourage appropriate behavior and extinguish inappropriate behavior. Dismissing a class when the students become undisciplined is a way of reinforcing the behavior. This is evident due to the fact that student behavior worsened; choice (A) is the correct answer. There is no evidence that the teacher is too demanding. In fact, the teacher appears to lack control of the classroom; choice (B) is not correct. As mentioned earlier, dismissing the class is a reinforcer of the behavior, not a punishment and choice (C) is not correct. There is no way to determine what type of activities have been presented based on the facts presented; choice (D) is not correct. The teacher is not punishing the students, they are being rewarded and choice (E) is not correct.

31. **(D)** This question relates to encouraging appropriate behavior and extinguishing inappropriate behavior. Having students list their favorite activities on a card and then telling

them that they can participate in one of these activities *after* they have completed the assignment is using the Premack principle; choice (A) is not correct. When assertive discipline is practiced, the teacher clearly communicates to the students the requirements of the class and responds to students in ways that maximize student compliance; choice (B) is not correct. Time out is a behavior modification technique used when a child misbehaves and is taken from the group to sit alone for five minutes; choice (C) is not correct. Placing yourself (the teacher) close to the misbehaving student is proximity control; choice (D) is correct. Limits are defined when a teacher establishes class rules and makes sure they are understood. When these limits are tested, the teacher must demonstrate that these **are** limits; choice (E) is not correct.

32. **(B)** This question relates to children's development patterns. Maslow proposed a hierarchy of needs with deficiency needs on the bottom and growth needs in the upper portion. From lowest to highest, these needs are: survival (physiological), safety, belonging and love, self-esteem, intellectual achievement (understanding), aesthetic appreciation, self-actualization. This is the only correct order of these needs. Therefore choice (B) is the correct answer, and choices (A), (C), (D) and (E) are incorrect.

33. **(C)** This question deals with motivation implementing instructional design and conditions that facilitate learning. Testing frequently may cause some students to feel overly anxious and, in fact, have the opposite effect than the intended motivation. Choice (A) is not correct. Most students will not believe the teacher when he/she tells them that they will need this information in the future. Furthermore, students are more interested in meeting immediate needs than long-range needs; choice (B) is not correct. Of the techniques listed, showing the students how the material to be learned will help them satisfy personal goals is the most constructive way of motivating students. When teachers use this technique, they relate learning to their students' real world. The teachers realize that what the students perceive their world to be is quite different from the view of adults. Students are also interested in meeting personal goals; the correct choice is (C). Correct responses should be rewarded, but this will not be motivational to all students. Because girls want to please others, this technique may work for some of them, but this is not the most constructive way listed; choice (D) is not correct. When teachers use the traditional methods of instruction every day, students will become bored and "turned off" to learning. Furthermore, a teacher cannot meet the needs of all students, teach through students' learning styles, or motivate students without using a variety of methodologies and strategies in the classroom; choice (E) is not correct.

34. **(C)** This question relates to children's developmental patterns. During the past century, there have been heated debates about whether intelligence is determined primarily by heredity or environment. Even though the debate continues, a number of social scientists point out that both heredity and environment contribute to differences in IQ. Therefore, choice (C) is correct since it states that heredity and environment are both involved, and choices (A), (B), (C) and (E) are not correct because intelligence has been studied and heredity and environment are both contributors.

35. **(E)** This question relates to children's developmental patterns. According to Piaget's stages of cognitive development, a child in the preoperational stage gradually acquires the ability to conserve. Conservation refers to the idea that certain properties remain the same even though they may look different. Therefore, if a student can conserve, he/she will realize

that something is the same even though it looks different; choice (E) is the correct answer. When students can consider more than one characteristic of an object at one time, this is referred to as decentralization and choice (A) is not correct. Mentally reversing actions is the operation of reversibility; choice (B) is not correct. Solving problems by generalizing from concrete experiences is a characteristic of a child at the concrete operational stage and dealing with abstractions is a characteristic of students at the formal operational stage; choices (C) and (D) are not correct.

Section 2

1.   **(C)**   This question relates to evaluating student achievement and instructional effectiveness and using evaluation data to refine instruction. Grade norms, age norms, percentile norms, and standard score norms are the most common types of test norms. Norm scores do not necessarily represent especially good or desirable performance, but, rather, the normal or typical performance. Grade norms are widely used with standardized achievement tests, especially at the elementary school level. Grade equivalents indicate the average performance of students at various grade levels. Based on the scores presented in this question, the sixth grade student is above the standardized group norm in reading and language and is below the standardized group norm in arithmetic. No information is given to provide an understanding of the class average. The grade norms were derived from the performance of students in national standardization groups. Therefore, choices (A), (B) and (D) are incorrect. Choice (E) is also incorrect since the grade norm would be 6.0-6.9 depending on when the test was administered and the student's grade equivalent in language is 7.6, above the grade norm which makes choice (C) the correct answer.

2.   **(B)**   This question relates to evaluating student achievement, instructional effectiveness, and using evaluation data. A test is said to be valid if it measures what it was intended to measure. A test is said to be reliable when there is consistency of evaluation results. Since the scores on the professional aptitude test were consistent, one can conclude that the test was reliable. Since the scores on the aptitude tests did not correlate with success in professions, the test did not measure what it was designed to measure and is not valid. Therefore, one can conclude that the test was reliable, but not valid. The correct choice is (B) and choices (A), (C), (D) and (E) are not correct.

3.   **(A)**   This question relates to dealing with evaluation. In a cross-sectional survey, information is collected from a sample drawn from a predetermined population. The longitudinal method collects data at different points in time in order to study changes; choice (B) is not correct. While there are several observational methods, the fact that each is time consuming is a disadvantage to all of the methods; choice (C) is not correct. All of the choices presented relate to collection of data which is only one step in the scientific method; choice (D) is not correct. Of the methods presented, the cross-sectional method can be completed in the briefest amount of time and choice (A) is correct. Since one of the answers is correct, choice (E) cannot be correct.

4.   **(D)**   This question refers to facilitating learning. Piaget and Bruner believed that concepts and principles that students discover on their own are more meaningful than when

these same ideas are presented to them. When students are continually presented information by the teacher, they often become too dependent on others. Memorizing facts, concepts, rules, principles or generalizations is not an effective method of learning since this does not lead to long-term retention. Most facts that are memorized for a test are quickly forgotten. Of the choices presented, choices (A), (C), and (E) incorporate memorization as method of retention and are not correct. Choice (B) is also incorrect because a teacher should direct learning by asking leading questions, providing background information, and giving students opportunities to make discoveries, not leave the students to "sink or swim." Choice (D) is correct because the teacher should present a series of problems in such a way that the students are led to formulate the principle themselves.

5.   **(E)**   This question involves recognizing the extraclassroom influences on teachers and students. Shifting societal patterns do influence students and, in turn, the classroom. When nearly half of all marriages end in divorce, it is logical for a teacher to expect to have children of single-parent and blended families in the classroom. These children will experience stress that children from nuclear families may not experience. Teachers must be sensitive to the needs of these children. They can do this by not being personally offended when a student acts aggressively, by helping students maintain their self-esteem, and by being available to listen to the concerns of these students. The only choice that includes all three of these alternatives is (E). Therefore, choices (A), (B), (C), and (D) are not correct because at least one technique is omitted in each.

6.   **(C)**   This question relates to knowing how to encourage appropriate behavior. To use praise as a positive reinforcer, teachers should call the student(s) by name, wait until the appropriate behavior has occurred, and use specific statements to describe the appropriate behavior. Of the choices presented, (C) is the only one that includes one of the guidelines for using praise as a positive reinforcer. Choices (A), (B), and (D) state techniques the teacher should not employ when using praise. Choice (E) is also incorrect since one of the above, choice (C), is correct.

7.   **(C)**   This question on Bloom's Cognitive Taxonomy relates to implementing instructional design and conditions that facilitate learning. The taxonomy for the cognitive domain was prepared by Benjamin Bloom. It consists of six hierarchically ordered levels including knowledge, comprehension, application, analysis, synthesis, and evaluation. The question presented requires students to use previously acquired knowledge and comprehension and to demonstrate this knowledge by applying what they have learned to formulate the reasons why Geneva is used for summits. This describes a question at the application level, therefore, choice (C) is correct. Knowledge is mainly naming, defining, and the like, comprehension is understanding and putting things in one's own words, analysis involves discriminating, differentiating, and the like, and synthesizing is creating, designing, or modifying. Therefore, choices (A), (B), (D) and (E) are not correct.

8.   **(A)**   This question involves knowing how to extinguish inappropriate behavior. Of the choices available, choice (A) is the most correct. The teacher must enforce the established consequences for incomplete work. If this is not done, Jessica will continue to ignore the homework assignments which is inappropriate behavior for school. Ignoring this problem will not extinguish the behavior, it will probably reinforce the behavior. Choice (B) is not correct. Relaxing the rules so that Jessica has more time to complete the assignments will not

encourage her to complete the work when it is originally assigned; choice (C) is not correct. Choice (D) could be an appropriate way to deal with the problem if Jessica does finish some assignments. However, the most immediate action would be to enforce the consequences. Choice (E) is totally inappropriate since Jessica "always knows the correct answer."

9.   **(B)**   This question relates to evaluating student achievement. Based on the information presented, one can determine that the teacher is assigning grades based on comparisons of the students' work to standards for mastery of the unit. This describes criterion-referenced grading choice (B). Even though the test is described as a unit test, there is no such term as unit-referenced grading; choice (A) is not correct. Norm-referenced grading, in this case, would involve comparing each student's performance with that of the classmates; choice (C) is not correct. The normal curve is a way of describing the distribution of the scores. Since each student received an "A" a bell-shaped curve, or normal curve, would not result from the distribution of scores. A distribution of scores with two obvious peaks would have a bimodal curve. The distribution of scores in this case would not result in this type of curve. For these reasons, choices (D) and (E) are not correct.

10.   **(A)**   This question relates to state, federal, and judicial policy. To be able to answer this question, one must be familiar with the four court cases that are named. The *Swann v. Charlotte-Mecklenberg* decision in 1971 did support busing students, revision of attendance zones, or other actions to remove state-imposed segregation as long as the desegregation plans were workable and feasible, choice (A) is correct. The *Green v. County School Board of New Kent County* decision in 1968 required segregated districts to devise a desegregation plan that was realistic. The *Bradley v. Milliken* decision in 1974 basically stated that the autonomy of school districts should not be violated for desegregation purposes. *Brown v. Board of Education* in 1954 outlawed separate but equal. For all of these reasons, choices (B), (C), (D) and (E) are not correct.

11.   **(E)**   This question concerns recognizing extraclassroom influences on teachers and students including community expectations. The curricula in schools today change very rapidly. Curriculum in the past changed very slowly because society was slow to change. Today the society changes very rapidly and the curriculum must change rapidly to keep up with the changes in society. As the student populations change, as the goals of the schools are revised to meet the needs of the changing society, as interest groups are activated and as society in general changes, the curriculum must also change. The only choice that includes all four of these is (E). Because one or more are omitted from the others, they are all incorrect.

12.   **(B)**   This question relates to knowledge of the teaching profession. Jean Jacques Rousseau encouraged childhood self-expression. His philosophy is the basis for the student-centered curriculum at its *extreme*. Therefore, choice (A) is not the most correct answer. John Dewey attempted to create a curriculum that balanced the subject matter and the students' needs and interests. He noted problems with either extreme (either the student-centered or subject-centered curriculum). He also encouraged learning through experience and problem solving. Choice (B) is the correct answer. Johann Pestalozzi was also a naturalistic educator who influenced the student-centered curriculum by stressing human emotions and kindness in teaching young children, but choice (C) is not the most correct answer. Froebel stressed a permissive atmosphere and the use of games, stories, and songs in the kindergarten. This choice, (D) is not the most correct. Since choice (B) is correct, choice (E), none of the above, is not correct.

13. **(C)** This question involves knowledge of the teaching profession. Deprofessionalization involves administrative policies which require teachers to simplify instruction to ensure student mastery of skills; choice (A) is not correct. Occupational prestige refers to the respect the profession has in society; choice (B) is not correct. Teacher empowerment; choice (C) is the correct answer since it does involve increasing the power of teachers and their role in decision making. Alternative certification is obtaining teacher certification without completing traditional teacher education programs; choice (D) is not correct. Choice (E) is also incorrect since merit pay is a reward of salary increase based on performance.

14. **(A)** This question relates to knowledge of the teaching profession. To answer this question correctly, you must look for the most complete definition of acculturation. The complete definition of acculturation is learning the concepts, values, and behavior patterns of individuals sharing a common culture through immersion and participation in the total culture, which is choice (A). Choices (B), (C) and (D) are not definitions of acculturation and are not correct. Choice (E) is incorrect since "one of the above" choices is correct.

15. **(D)** This question relates to extraclassroom influences on teachers and students. Children from blended families (step-children), single-parent families, traditional or nuclear families, or extended families could return home in the afternoon to an empty house and the television. However, the correct term for these children is "latch-key children," choice (D). As more and more mothers work, more children will become latch-key children. These children may be responsible for fixing their own meals, cleaning the house, and/or taking care of siblings. They also often do not have encouragement to study or to complete assignments.

16. **(A)** This question deals with recognizing extraclassroom influences on teachers and students. Abused children can certainly come from families of any socioeconomic level. However, research has shown that a relatively high proportion of child abuse victims do come from low-income families, choice (A). Knowing this, you can eliminate all of the other choices.

17. **(B)** This question relates to knowledge of the teaching profession. It requires you to recognize the best definition of a naturalistic educator. If you are aware of the definition and basic beliefs of the child depravity theory, you can quickly eliminate choices (A) and (E). If you are familiar with the history of education and are aware that child depravity and passive learning dominated the early history of education as did dual-track systems of schools, you can eliminate choices (C) and (D). This will leave choice (B), which is what naturalistic educators believe; that children learn by working with and by examining objects in their natural environment.

18. **(D)** This question deals with knowledge of the teaching profession. You can rapidly eliminate choices (A) and (B), Latin grammar schools and academies, if you are aware that these were secondary institutions. The common school was an elementary institution. However, it was open to children of all classes and it is not the best choice (C). Normal schools were two-year institutions which were, in essence, the first teacher education institutions and is not the correct choice (E). This leaves choice (D) the vernacular schools, which is the correct answer, since these schools were primarily or elementary institutions with a basic curriculum for children of the lower classes.

19. **(C)**   The question relates to implementing instructional design and conditions that facilitate learning. To answer this question correctly, you must first be familiar with the concept of wait time. This is generally considered to be the amount of time between when the question is asked and when a student is designated to answer the question. When this wait time is increased to about five seconds, this will increase the length of student responses, the amount of questions from students, the confidence of the students, the number of accurate answers, and the number of creative answers. Accurate answers and creative answers, choice (C), compose the correct answer to this question. Wait time does not increase student confusion nor is it proved to increase test scores. Therefore, any choices that include these alternatives, (A), (B), (D) and (E) are incorrect.

20. **(D)**   This question relates to classroom management, which is part of implementing instructional design and conditions that facilitate learning. To answer this question, you must first have an understanding of classroom management. Some people think, incorrectly, that classroom management only involves discipline, but it also involves leadership and classroom atmosphere. Classroom rules, monitoring procedures and motivation, then, should all be considered when a teacher wishes to improve classroom management, choice (D).

21. **(B)**   This question relates to recognizing students' constitutional rights and state, federal, and judicial policy. The definition and purpose of magnet schools must be understood to answer this question correctly. A magnet school is a type of alternative school designed to draw students from other schools through specialized programs, personnel, and curricula. Based on this information, choice (B) is the only possible correct answer and choices (A), (C), (D) and (E) are not correct.

22. **(D)**   This question relates to planning objectives, diagnosing needs, identifying resources, and designing instruction. It also involves knowledge of the teaching profession. Scholars in the field of gifted and talented education have either emphasized acceleration through the regular curriculum or enrichment that provides for greater depth. Today, however, a combination approach is recommended which includes accelerated study, enrichment, and understanding of systems of knowledge. For these reasons, the correct choice is (D) and (A), (B), (C) and (E) are not correct.

23. **(B)**   This question on multicultural education relates to planning objectives, diagnosing needs, identifying resources, and designing instruction. However, it also deals with knowledge of the teaching profession. To answer this question correctly, you must understand multicultural education. With this understanding, you should be able to quickly eliminate option IV. Emphasizing separation in a way that is divisive is in direct opposition to the purpose of multicultural education. All choices that include this option can be eliminated, (C), (D) and (E). The aims of multicultural education include ensuring positive interracial and intergroup attitudes and contacts, enabling all students to function in a multicultural society, and adapting instruction to meet the learning styles of different groups of students. All three of these options should be included in the correct answer, choice (B). Choice (A) is not correct because it does not include all three correct options.

24. **(A)**   This question relates to knowledge of the teaching profession. Three basic definitions are required for answering this question correctly. Segregation can be defined as separation of minority and nonminority groups. Therefore, Choices (C), (D) and (E) can be

eliminated. Desegregation of schools refers to enrollment patterns in which students of different racial groups attend the same schools and integration refers to situations in which students of different racial groups attend schools together to ensure equal and effective educational opportunity for students of all backgrounds. Therefore, choice (A) is the most correct answer and choice (B) is not.

25. **(D)**   This question involves recognizing extraclassroom influences on teachers and students. Teachers with middle-class backgrounds may have trouble understanding and motivating disadvantaged or lower-class students because of poor attitudes of the teachers concerning students of different cultural patterns and their learning potential. Another reason for these difficulties is poor communication due to differences in backgrounds and dialects. Therefore, the only correct choice is (D), and (A), (B), (C) and (E) are not correct.

26. **(C)**   This question deals with motivation which relates to recognizing extraclassroom influences on students and children's developmental patterns. It also relates to diagnosing needs and classroom management or atmosphere. If students have a long history of academic ineptitude, they tend to attribute their success to good luck or other factors beyond their control and attribute their failures to lack of abilities. They also feel that attempting to improve their grades would be a waste of time since they lack the necessary abilities to do better. Based on this information, it should be evident that choice (C) is correct and choices (A), (B), (D) and (E) can be eliminated.

27. **(B)**   This question relates to extraclassroom influences on teachers and students. The differences between race, ethnic group, socioeconomic group, and ethnicity must be known to answer this question correctly. You should be able to eliminate socioeconomic group, choice (C), quite easily. This will also lead to the elimination of choice (E), all of the above. The three remaining choices include race which generally refers to groups of people with common ancestry and physical characteristics, ethnic groups which refer to groups of people with common ancestry and who generally share common languages, religions, and other cultural patterns, and ethnicity which refers to shared culture and background. Therefore, choice (B) is correct, and choices (A) and (C) are not correct.

28. **(A)**   This question relates to recognizing students' constitutional rights and state, federal, and judicial policy and the implications of these for classroom practice. A knowledge of the precedents of each case is needed to answer the question correctly. With this knowledge, you will know that choice (A), *New Jersey v. T.L.O.*, is correct. *Ingraham v. Wright* allowed corporal punishment where allowed by the state; choice (B) is not correct. *Bethel School District No. 403 v. Fraser* ruled that schools do not have to permit offensive speech, choice (C) is not correct. *Wood v. Strickland* ruled that ignorance of due process is not an excuse for not following due process, choice (D) is not correct. Since choice (A) is correct, choice (E) is not correct.

29. **(B)**   This question involves knowledge of the teaching profession. The definition of empiricism must be understood to answer this question correctly. Empiricism is defined as human knowledge acquired through the senses. The only possible correct answer is choice (B), and choices (A), (C), (D) and (E) are not correct.

30. **(D)** This question relates to knowledge of the teaching profession. Rousseau influenced the progressive movement that emphasized basing the curriculum on the child's interests and needs rather than the subject-centered approach. Based on this information, the only possible correct answer is (D) and (A), (B), (C) and (E) are not correct.

31. **(C)** This question is based on knowledge of the teaching profession. To answer this question correctly, you must have an understanding of the progressive movement and the theoretical beliefs of each person listed. Montessori emphasized a specially prepared learning environment in which children would work repeating actions and is not the correct choice, (A). Counts advocated natural work on problems of social importance and was, in fact, a progressive educator, but this is not the best choice, (B). Pestalozzi did stress the environment, use of concrete objects, and the cultivation of sensory experiences. This is the best choice, (C). Hutchins was concerned with cultivating a person's rational powers and was a leading voice for educational reform. This is not the correct choice (D), and (E) can also be eliminated at this point.

32. **(B)** This question on children's developmental patterns concerns recognizing extraclassroom influences on teachers and students. You must be familiar with Piaget's stages of cognitive development and the underlying philosophies to answer this question correctly. When reviewing the available options, you should be able to quickly eliminate option IV since this would follow the Montessori school of thought. Therefore, choices (A), (C) and (D) can be eliminated. Of the other two choices, (B) is the only one that lists all three correct options and is correct. Choice (E) does not list all of the correct options.

33. **(B)** This question relates to designing instruction, facilitating learning, and knowledge of the teaching profession. Essentialists emphasize the authority of the teacher and the value of the subject matter curriculum. Behaviorists base their philosophy on operant conditioning and believe the teacher should arrange conditions so that learning can occur. Realists stress humanistic and scientific disciplines in a subject-matter curriculum. Existentialists seek to create an awareness in each student that he/she is responsible for his/her own education. Therefore, choices, (A), (C), (D) and (E) are all incorrect. Progressivists do focus on the learner, activities, and experiences and choice (B) is correct.

34. **(C)** This question concerns conditions that facilitate learning. The leadership style of the teacher is what is directly addressed in this question. A democratic approach shares responsibility. A laisse-faire approach advocates permissiveness. The authoritarian approach advocates teacher power, domination, and criticism. Choice (C) is correct and choices (A) and (B) are not. Since this addresses leadership and not atmosphere, choice (D) is easily eliminated. Once choice (C) had been determined, choice (E) is also eliminated.

35. **(D)** This question relates to extinguishing appropriate behavior. This question is based on the Kounin model which stresses the ripple effect and group management. Kounin found that when teachers correct misbehavior in one student, it often influences the behavior of nearby students, which is the ripple effect, choice (D). You should be able to eliminate choices (A), (B) and (C) quite easily. Knowing the definition of peer pressure, pressure exerted by one's peers to behave in a certain way, can enable you to also eliminate choice (E).

Section 3

1. **(C)** This question concerns implementing instructional design and conditions that facilitate learning. To answer this question correctly, you must be familiar with the types of questions listed. Convergent question allow for one expected correct answer. An alternate-response question requires a yes/no or true/false answer. A divergent question allows for several correct responses and encourages broad answers. A factual question will simply test the student's memory and a probing question will force the student to think more clearly about an initial response. After examining the question presented, it should be evident that it is a broad question with several correct responses, choice (C). Therefore, choices (A), (B), (D) and (E) are not correct.

2. **(B)** This question is related to implementing instructional design and conditions that facilitate learning. Since there is not enough information provided to know how Sarah is taught, choices (D) and (E) can be eliminated. Sarah probably knows how she is doing in math and choice (A) can be eliminated. This leaves success, choice (B) and interest, choice (C). Sarah may have had an initial interest in math until she started having difficulty. Since she had a pattern of failure or ineptitude, she does not have any success to increase her interest or motivation and the best choice is (C).

3. **(C)** This question concerns extraclassroom influences on teachers and students. Knowledge of how adolescents are influenced is necessary to answer this question. Since peers tend to influence factors that contribute to current status such as friends and dress and parent tend to influence their adolescents in ways that will impact their futures, choice (C) is correct and choices (A), (B), (D) and (E) can be eliminated.

4. **(B)** This question is based on encouraging appropriate behavior. It is important to remember that what is positively reinforcing for one student may be negatively reinforcing for another. Therefore, the only possible correct answer is (B). While the teacher does not use token reinforcers in this situation, this is not why the reinforcement does not work, choice (A). The teacher did not intend to use negative reinforcement which eliminated choice (C). Some of the students were probably motivated by the reinforcers to complete the assignment, which eliminates (D) and (E).

5. **(A)** This question relates to evaluating student achievement and instructional effectiveness. A student questionnaire requires students to examine statements regarding attitudes, opinions, and feelings; choice (A) is correct. An achievement test measures how much a student has learned in a given area, choice (B), and is not correct. A teacher-made test is usually limited to content, not opinions or feelings and is not the best choice, (C). A check list is a list of criteria for evaluating student performance, which is not the correct choice, (D). Standardized tests are commercially developed and sample behaviors under uniform procedures; choice (E) is not correct.

6. **(B)** This question relates to evaluating student achievement and instructional effectiveness. To answer this question correctly, an understanding of formative and summative evaluation techniques is needed. Formative evaluation is used to promote learning, may take place before and during instruction, and includes, among other things, observations of

student work. Formative evaluation should not be used to determine grades. With this information, choice (B) can be determined to be the correct answer and choices (A), (D) and (E) can be eliminated. Summative evaluation is used to determine student learning and student grades after instruction has taken place and is also not the correct choice (C).

7. **(C)** This question relates to designing instruction and conditions that facilitate learning. For a lesson to be successful and well structured, the teacher should use a cognitive set to motivate the student, share goals and objectives, make the content relevant, actively involve the students, and be enthusiastic about the material. Therefore, choice (C) is what should not be done and is the correct answer; choices (A), (B), (D) and (E) are incorrect.

8. **(D)** This question relates to planning objectives, diagnosing needs, identifying resources, and designing instruction. To prepare the most effective lesson possible, the teacher must consider the content and objectives of the intended lesson, his/her teacher characteristics, the learning style characteristics of the students, and the learning environment or classroom, choice (D). All other choices omit an important ingredient and are not correct, (A), (B), (C) and (E).

9. **(B)** This question involves implementing instructional design and conditions that facilitate learning. To accommodate the needs of different students including special students, teachers should vary the time limits required to complete an assignment, vary the level of complexity of assignments, and vary the amount of work assigned. One should note that increasing the amount of work is not the same as increasing the complexity or difficulty of the assignment. Therefore, the correct choice, which should not be included, is (B) since special students often learn more in small group instruction than with one-to-one instruction. Choices (A), (C), (D) and (E) are not correct.

10. **(D)** This question involves knowing how to encourage appropriate behavior and discourage inappropriate behavior. Research does indicate that harsh reprimands, which include criticizing students publicly, angrily, or loudly can make students more aggressive and anxious, actually increase the students' undesirable behaviors, and decrease the students' interest in learning. Therefore, choice (D) is correct and choices (A), (B), (C) and (E) are not correct.

11. **(D)** This question involves knowledge of children's development patterns. Characteristics of developmentally delayed elementary school students include short attention spans, lack of necessary social skills, and becoming frustrated quite easily. Teachers should be cautioned to remember lack of social skills as one of these characteristics. For these reasons, choice (D) is correct and choices (A), (B), (C) and (E) are not correct.

12. **(C)** This question relates to children's developmental patterns. To determine if a student's behavior problem is caused by a developmental lag, the teacher should consider whether the immature behavior is apparent in all or most situations or whether it appears only at certain times under certain situations If the immature behavior occurs in most situations, choice (C), the student is probably developmentally delayed. If the child occasionally regresses, appears to be independent, has lost interest in playing with certain children or has immature behaviors in only certain environments, choices (A), (B), (D) and (E), other causes should be examined.

13. **(A)** This question involves knowing how to encourage appropriate behavior. Intrinsic motivation occurs when students are able to maintain interest and involvement in learning. Extrinsic motivation refers to situations in which the student participates to achieve some results such as tokens or grades. Transfer of learning is sometimes referred to as learning from one situation to another. Retention is described as the ability to remember information over time. Based on these explanations, choice (A) is correct and choices, (B), (C), (D) and (E) are not correct.

14. **(B)** This question deals with children's developmental patterns. Attribution theorists have concluded that high achievers will often assume that they can do better if they try harder. Therefore, they will most often attribute success to their own abilities and failure to lack of effort, choice (B). Choices (A), (C), (D) and (E) are not correct.

15. **(B)** This question relates to implementing instructional design and conditions that facilitate learning. A knowledge of classroom management approaches is necessary to answer this question correctly. Knowing that the assertive discipline model holds that specific rules must be established in the classroom with clear and appropriate consequences for positive or negative behavior will enable you to choose the correct answer, choice (B). The psychoanalytic approach, choice (A) involves uncovering the person's past to determine the cause of misbehavior. The behavior modification approach, choice (C), is based on operant conditioning. The ripple effect, choice (D), involves influencing the behavior of other students by correcting the misbehavior of one student. The Glasser model, choice (E), is the act of guiding the student toward reality.

16. **(C)** The content of this question relates to children's developmental patterns. Future teachers should be familiar with the stages of cognitive development by Piaget. Therefore, choice (C), formal operations, can easily be identified as the stage in which children develop the ability to reason logically and abstractly, and test hypotheses, and reflect their own thinking. Choices (A), (B), (D) and (E) are obviously not correct.

17. **(A)** This question relates to implementing design and conditions that facilitate learning. There are primarily three modalities of learning. The student who learns best by auditory repetition as stated in the question is an auditory learner, choice (A). The visual learner, choice (B), learns best by seeing the information. The tactual/kinesthetic learner, choices (C) and (D), learns best through hands-on manipulation and physical involvement. A student with mixed modalities will incorporate parts of each technique, choice (E). Therefore, choice (A) is the correct answer.

18. **(D)** This question involves knowledge of the teaching profession. The least restrictive environment is often defined only partially, choices (A), (B, (C) and (E). However, the complete definition does include having the child participate in regular educational programming to the fullest extent possible, being individually determined, and enabling the child to make academic progress, choice (D).

19. **(C)** This question relates to recognizing students' constitutional rights and state, federal, and judicial policy and the implications for these in classroom practice. If you read the question thoroughly, you will notice that this case involved Mexican-American children. Therefore, choices (D) and (E) which include a ruling concerning black students can be easily

eliminated. In the case under consideration, the court did rule that bilingual children must be tested in both languages, tests cannot solely be based on vocabulary, and districts must be able to prove why a large population of a certain group of students is in special education classes. The only correct choice is (C), choices (A) and (B) omit one ruling.

20. **(A)** This question relates to federal policy and knowledge of the teaching profession. When an IEP is developed for a student, it is possible that as many as five groups, choice (A), will be included. There must be someone in authority present who can make a commitment on the part of the school, which is usually an administrator. The child's teacher(s) and parent(s) or surrogate must also be present. When deemed appropriate, the child is also included as are any other(s) the parents wish to have present for the writing of the IEP. All of the other choices (B), (C), (D) and (E) omit at least one group of people.

21. **(B)** This question involves knowledge of the teaching profession. Any teacher should be able to easily identify Piaget, choice (B), as the one who believed that the purpose of education is to organize education in term of children's patterns of growth or development and that the teacher's role is to assist children in the learning process by individualizing instruction so that children can learn in accordance with their own readiness. This will automatically eliminate choices (A), (C), (D) and (E).

22. **(A)** This question involves knowledge of the teaching profession. Since a grouping technique is being discussed, choices (C), (D) and (E) can be easily eliminated. This leaves, choice (B), heterogeneous grouping, which is when students of varying ability levels are grouped together for instruction and choice (A), homogeneous grouping and the correct choice, which is grouping students by ability for subject instruction.

23. **(B)** This question is based on content knowledge of the teaching profession. A working definition of accountability is needed to answer this question correctly. Accountability is often explained as a policy requiring teachers to set specific goals for student accomplishment and then provide evidence that these goals have been met. Choice (B) most clearly reflects this and choices (A), (C), (D) and (E) should be eliminated.

24. **(A)** The content of this question reflects understanding children's developmental patterns. Often students with poor self-concepts or low-self-esteem develop emotional problems that may also create behavior or learning problems. Students who believe they are incompetent will feel anxious about the situation choices (A) and (E), avoid the situation completely choice (C), or take their frustrations out on others choice (D). They will not keep trying to improve the incompetence, choice (A).

25. **(C)** The content of this question relates to implementing instructional design and conditions that facilitate learning. When a problem appears suddenly or only in a certain situation that is triggered by a particular event or circumstance, the problem is said to be a situational problem and not a personality problem The only choice that support that Bart's problem is situational is (C). The other choices, (A), (B), (D) and (E) would all lead to the conclusion that this is a personality problem.

26. **(C)** This question is related to implementing instructional design and conditions that facilitate learning. The fact that Marie seldom interacts with children, option II, can be

quickly eliminated since she is observed arguing with other children. For the same reason and the observation that Marie often nags, the fact that Marie seldom speaks to anyone, option V, can also be eliminated. This process will eliminate choices (B), (D) and (E), which will leave choices (A) and (C). Choice (A) does not include all of the valid options Therefore, choice (C) is correct.

27. **(A)**   This question relates to implementing instructional design and conditions that facilitate learning. If a student demonstrates the behaviors described in this question, the teacher must use consequences to modify the inappropriate behavior. If this is not done, the inappropriate behavior will continue. Therefore, choice (A) is correct and choices (B), (C), (D) and (E) are not correct.

28. **(D)**   This question relates to implementing instructional design and conditions that facilitate learning. The only technique listed that would not be appropriate in this situation is planned ignoring. In this case, ignoring the inappropriate behavior would only prolong its occurrence. Choices (C) and (E) can be eliminated since they include this option. The other three techniques would all be appropriate which makes (D) the correct choice and (A) and (B) incorrect choices.

29. **(B)**   This question deals with children's developmental patterns. Requiring immediate reinforcement is a characteristic of children in the primary grades; choice (A) is not correct. Being able to work for symbolic rewards that can be exchanged for tangibles in the future is a characteristic of middle school children; choice (B) is correct. Working toward long-term goals is a characteristic of high school students; choices (C) and (E) are not correct. Choice (D) is also incorrect since it describes a characteristic of primary school students.

30. **(C)**   This question involves using evaluation data, To be able to answer this question correctly, an understanding of the mode is necessary. Very simply stated, the mode reflects the value of the most frequently occurring score. The only value that appears more than once is 98; therefore, choice (C) is correct and choices (A), (B), (D) and (E) are not correct.

31. **(B)**   This question relates to implementing instructional design and conditions that facilitate learning. Competitive reward structures tend to discourage eagerness to try and cooperative reward structures often promote motivation. Therefore, choice (B) is correct. Once this has been determined, the other choices (A), (C), (D) and (E) can be eliminated.

32. **(D)**   This question involves implementing instructional design and conditions that facilitate learning, There are several reasons to begin each lesson with a cognitive set. These include getting the interest of the students, establishing a conceptual framework for the information to follow, and motivating the student to learn the following information, choice (D). Having students open the textbooks to a certain page may, in fact, prepare the students for learning, but is not motivating nor interesting. The students probably see the textbook as boring. For all of these reasons, choices (A), (B), (C) and (E) are not correct.

33. **(A)**   This question relates to implementing instructional design and conditions that facilitate learning. All of the habits listed are poor listening habits except hunting for negative evidence related to the message, choice (A). A listener should not take what is heard at face

value, but should look for evidence that will dispute the message. Listening only for the facts in the message, criticizing the delivery of the message, faking attention and avoiding difficult listening, choices (B), (C), (D), and (E) are all poor listening habits or pitfalls that should be avoided.

34. **(D)**　The art of asking questions, the content of this question, is part of implementing instructional design and conditions that facilitate learning. The only choice listed that should not be followed when asking questions is (D), designating the respondent before asking the question. If a teacher employs this technique, the other students will quit listening when one particular student is named. The other choices, (A), (B), (C) and (E), should be followed.

35. **(C)**　This question involves recognizing students' constitutional rights and state, federal, and judicial policy and the implications for these. The *Regents of the University of California v. Alan Bakke* was the 1978 Supreme Court case which overturned holding a specific number of slots for admission to a program for certain minority groups. Therefore, choice (C) is correct and choices (A), (B), (D) and (E) are not correct.

National Teachers Examination

CORE
BATTERY

Test 4

NTE Test of Communication Skills

TEST 4 – ANSWER SHEET

Section 1: Listening

1. Ⓐ Ⓑ Ⓒ Ⓓ Ⓔ
2. Ⓐ Ⓑ Ⓒ Ⓓ Ⓔ
3. Ⓐ Ⓑ Ⓒ Ⓓ Ⓔ
4. Ⓐ Ⓑ Ⓒ Ⓓ Ⓔ
5. Ⓐ Ⓑ Ⓒ Ⓓ Ⓔ
6. Ⓐ Ⓑ Ⓒ Ⓓ Ⓔ
7. Ⓐ Ⓑ Ⓒ Ⓓ Ⓔ
8. Ⓐ Ⓑ Ⓒ Ⓓ Ⓔ
9. Ⓐ Ⓑ Ⓒ Ⓓ Ⓔ
10. Ⓐ Ⓑ Ⓒ Ⓓ Ⓔ
11. Ⓐ Ⓑ Ⓒ Ⓓ Ⓔ
12. Ⓐ Ⓑ Ⓒ Ⓓ Ⓔ
13. Ⓐ Ⓑ Ⓒ Ⓓ Ⓔ
14. Ⓐ Ⓑ Ⓒ Ⓓ Ⓔ
15. Ⓐ Ⓑ Ⓒ Ⓓ Ⓔ
16. Ⓐ Ⓑ Ⓒ Ⓓ Ⓔ
17. Ⓐ Ⓑ Ⓒ Ⓓ Ⓔ
18. Ⓐ Ⓑ Ⓒ Ⓓ Ⓔ
19. Ⓐ Ⓑ Ⓒ Ⓓ Ⓔ
20. Ⓐ Ⓑ Ⓒ Ⓓ Ⓔ
21. Ⓐ Ⓑ Ⓒ Ⓓ Ⓔ
22. Ⓐ Ⓑ Ⓒ Ⓓ Ⓔ
23. Ⓐ Ⓑ Ⓒ Ⓓ Ⓔ
24. Ⓐ Ⓑ Ⓒ Ⓓ Ⓔ
25. Ⓐ Ⓑ Ⓒ Ⓓ Ⓔ
26. Ⓐ Ⓑ Ⓒ Ⓓ Ⓔ
27. Ⓐ Ⓑ Ⓒ Ⓓ Ⓔ
28. Ⓐ Ⓑ Ⓒ Ⓓ Ⓔ
29. Ⓐ Ⓑ Ⓒ Ⓓ Ⓔ
30. Ⓐ Ⓑ Ⓒ Ⓓ Ⓔ
31. Ⓐ Ⓑ Ⓒ Ⓓ Ⓔ
32. Ⓐ Ⓑ Ⓒ Ⓓ Ⓔ
33. Ⓐ Ⓑ Ⓒ Ⓓ Ⓔ
34. Ⓐ Ⓑ Ⓒ Ⓓ Ⓔ
35. Ⓐ Ⓑ Ⓒ Ⓓ Ⓔ
36. Ⓐ Ⓑ Ⓒ Ⓓ Ⓔ
37. Ⓐ Ⓑ Ⓒ Ⓓ Ⓔ
38. Ⓐ Ⓑ Ⓒ Ⓓ Ⓔ
39. Ⓐ Ⓑ Ⓒ Ⓓ Ⓔ
40. Ⓐ Ⓑ Ⓒ Ⓓ Ⓔ

Section 2: Reading

1. Ⓐ Ⓑ Ⓒ Ⓓ Ⓔ
2. Ⓐ Ⓑ Ⓒ Ⓓ Ⓔ
3. Ⓐ Ⓑ Ⓒ Ⓓ Ⓔ
4. Ⓐ Ⓑ Ⓒ Ⓓ Ⓔ
5. Ⓐ Ⓑ Ⓒ Ⓓ Ⓔ
6. Ⓐ Ⓑ Ⓒ Ⓓ Ⓔ
7. Ⓐ Ⓑ Ⓒ Ⓓ Ⓔ
8. Ⓐ Ⓑ Ⓒ Ⓓ Ⓔ
9. Ⓐ Ⓑ Ⓒ Ⓓ Ⓔ
10. Ⓐ Ⓑ Ⓒ Ⓓ Ⓔ
11. Ⓐ Ⓑ Ⓒ Ⓓ Ⓔ
12. Ⓐ Ⓑ Ⓒ Ⓓ Ⓔ
13. Ⓐ Ⓑ Ⓒ Ⓓ Ⓔ
14. Ⓐ Ⓑ Ⓒ Ⓓ Ⓔ
15. Ⓐ Ⓑ Ⓒ Ⓓ Ⓔ
16. Ⓐ Ⓑ Ⓒ Ⓓ Ⓔ
17. Ⓐ Ⓑ Ⓒ Ⓓ Ⓔ
18. Ⓐ Ⓑ Ⓒ Ⓓ Ⓔ
19. Ⓐ Ⓑ Ⓒ Ⓓ Ⓔ
20. Ⓐ Ⓑ Ⓒ Ⓓ Ⓔ
21. Ⓐ Ⓑ Ⓒ Ⓓ Ⓔ
22. Ⓐ Ⓑ Ⓒ Ⓓ Ⓔ
23. Ⓐ Ⓑ Ⓒ Ⓓ Ⓔ
24. Ⓐ Ⓑ Ⓒ Ⓓ Ⓔ
25. Ⓐ Ⓑ Ⓒ Ⓓ Ⓔ
26. Ⓐ Ⓑ Ⓒ Ⓓ Ⓔ
27. Ⓐ Ⓑ Ⓒ Ⓓ Ⓔ
28. Ⓐ Ⓑ Ⓒ Ⓓ Ⓔ
29. Ⓐ Ⓑ Ⓒ Ⓓ Ⓔ
30. Ⓐ Ⓑ Ⓒ Ⓓ Ⓔ

Section 3: Writing

1. Ⓐ Ⓑ Ⓒ Ⓓ Ⓔ
2. Ⓐ Ⓑ Ⓒ Ⓓ Ⓔ
3. Ⓐ Ⓑ Ⓒ Ⓓ Ⓔ
4. Ⓐ Ⓑ Ⓒ Ⓓ Ⓔ
5. Ⓐ Ⓑ Ⓒ Ⓓ Ⓔ
6. Ⓐ Ⓑ Ⓒ Ⓓ Ⓔ
7. Ⓐ Ⓑ Ⓒ Ⓓ Ⓔ
8. Ⓐ Ⓑ Ⓒ Ⓓ Ⓔ

9. Ⓐ Ⓑ Ⓒ Ⓓ Ⓔ
10. Ⓐ Ⓑ Ⓒ Ⓓ Ⓔ
11. Ⓐ Ⓑ Ⓒ Ⓓ Ⓔ
12. Ⓐ Ⓑ Ⓒ Ⓓ Ⓔ
13. Ⓐ Ⓑ Ⓒ Ⓓ Ⓔ
14. Ⓐ Ⓑ Ⓒ Ⓓ Ⓔ
15. Ⓐ Ⓑ Ⓒ Ⓓ Ⓔ
16. Ⓐ Ⓑ Ⓒ Ⓓ Ⓔ
17. Ⓐ Ⓑ Ⓒ Ⓓ Ⓔ
18. Ⓐ Ⓑ Ⓒ Ⓓ Ⓔ
19. Ⓐ Ⓑ Ⓒ Ⓓ Ⓔ
20. Ⓐ Ⓑ Ⓒ Ⓓ Ⓔ
21. Ⓐ Ⓑ Ⓒ Ⓓ Ⓔ
22. Ⓐ Ⓑ Ⓒ Ⓓ Ⓔ
23. Ⓐ Ⓑ Ⓒ Ⓓ Ⓔ
24. Ⓐ Ⓑ Ⓒ Ⓓ Ⓔ
25. Ⓐ Ⓑ Ⓒ Ⓓ Ⓔ
26. Ⓐ Ⓑ Ⓒ Ⓓ Ⓔ
27. Ⓐ Ⓑ Ⓒ Ⓓ Ⓔ
28. Ⓐ Ⓑ Ⓒ Ⓓ Ⓔ
29. Ⓐ Ⓑ Ⓒ Ⓓ Ⓔ
30. Ⓐ Ⓑ Ⓒ Ⓓ Ⓔ
31. Ⓐ Ⓑ Ⓒ Ⓓ Ⓔ
32. Ⓐ Ⓑ Ⓒ Ⓓ Ⓔ
33. Ⓐ Ⓑ Ⓒ Ⓓ Ⓔ
34. Ⓐ Ⓑ Ⓒ Ⓓ Ⓔ
35. Ⓐ Ⓑ Ⓒ Ⓓ Ⓔ
36. Ⓐ Ⓑ Ⓒ Ⓓ Ⓔ
37. Ⓐ Ⓑ Ⓒ Ⓓ Ⓔ
38. Ⓐ Ⓑ Ⓒ Ⓓ Ⓔ
39. Ⓐ Ⓑ Ⓒ Ⓓ Ⓔ
40. Ⓐ Ⓑ Ⓒ Ⓓ Ⓔ
41. Ⓐ Ⓑ Ⓒ Ⓓ Ⓔ
42. Ⓐ Ⓑ Ⓒ Ⓓ Ⓔ
43. Ⓐ Ⓑ Ⓒ Ⓓ Ⓔ
44. Ⓐ Ⓑ Ⓒ Ⓓ Ⓔ
45. Ⓐ Ⓑ Ⓒ Ⓓ Ⓔ

NTE CORE BATTERY–Test 4
TEST OF COMMUNICATION SKILLS
Section 1: Listening

TIME: 30 Minutes
40 Questions

Part A

> **DIRECTIONS**: In this section, you will read short statements and questions (these will be played for you on tape during the actual exam). When you read a statement, select the answer which best restates or supports what you read. When you read a question, select the choice which best answers the question. The questions and statements will NOT be written in your book during the actual exam, and they will not be repeated.

1. *You will hear:* Teachers are born, not made!
   You will read:
   (A) "A" students make good teachers.
   (B) Ivy League colleges produce the best teachers.
   (C) Teaching is a skill that comes naturally.
   (D) Intelligence and experience are key predictors of success as a teacher.

2. *You will hear:* Girls read better than boys, but boys are better in math.
   You will read:
   (A) Girls are smarter than boys.
   (B) Boys are smarter than girls.
   (C) Girls are better readers than boys.
   (D) Girls are better in math than boys.

3. *You will hear:* Mrs. Randall attends professional meetings almost every year.
   You will read:
   (A) Mrs. Randall never misses her professional meetings.
   (B) Mrs. Randall loves to attend professional meetings.
   (C) Mrs. Randall attends professional meetings every year.
   (D) Mrs. Randall occasionally misses professional meetings, although she attends regularly.

4. *You will hear:* What time of the year is the Junior-Senior Prom?
   You will read:
   (A) The Junior-Senior Prom is in the spring.
   (B) The Junior-Senior Prom is in October.

(C)   The Junior-Senior Prom starts at 9 p.m.

(D)   The Junior-Senior Prom is in May.

5.   *You will hear:* Mrs. Jones loves teaching math; basic math, that is
        You will read:
        (A)   Mrs. Jones loves teaching math—any math.
        (B)   Mrs. Jones loves teaching basic math.
        (C)   Mrs. Jones loves teaching algebra.
        (D)   Basically, Mrs. Jones loves teaching geometry.

6.   *You will hear:* Even though Edward made all A's his senior year, he did not get a
        college scholarship.
        You will read:
        (A)   Edward did not apply for a scholarship.
        (B)   Edward did not go to college.
        (C)   Edward's previous grades may not have been as good as his senior year grades.
        (D)   Edward joined the United States Army.

7.   *You will hear:* What percentage of the seniors at Ball High fail to graduate each year?
        You will read:
        (A)   90 percent graduate   (C)   85 percent graduate
        (B)   10 percent fail   (D)   Approximately 14 people

8.   *You will hear:* The school year ended without all of the history chapters being
        covered.
        You will read:
        (A)   Too much time was spent on each chapter.
        (B)   Too many chapters were in the book.
        (C)   The instructor's planning for, or adherence to, the yearly calendar was not
                properly carried out.
        (D)   Not enough time was allowed for each chapter.

9.   *You will hear:* What are those students doing in the Biology Lab?
        You will read:
        (A)   They are probably having lunch.
        (B)   They are having a Biology Club meeting.
        (C)   They are discussing plans for the football rally.
        (D)   They are conducting experiments.

10.   *You will hear:* You must do your homework at this very moment; it's now or never!
        You will read:
        (A)   Students who do not complete their homework now will not graduate.
        (B)   Students who do not complete their homework now will not be given a chance
                to do it later.
        (C)   Students who do not complete their homework now will be suspended.

    (D)   Students who do not complete their homework now will fail the course.

11.   **You will hear:** Which is the best textbook for Math 101?
        You will read:
    (A)   Stigon's mathematics workbook
    (B)   Osborne's series of mathematics worksheets for practice
    (C)   Mathematics manipulatives
    (D)   Piston's *Mathematics for Everyday Living*

12.   **You will hear:** Nearly 3,000 students are enrolled at Anderson Elementary School.
        You will read:
    (A)   3,000 students are enrolled at Anderson Elementary School.
    (B)   2,900 students are enrolled at Anderson Elementary School.
    (C)   3,100 students are enrolled at Anderson Elementary School.
    (D)   Approximately 3,200 students are enrolled at Anderson Elementary School.

13.   **You will hear:** Mrs. Robinson, what topic are you teaching this week?
        You will read:
    (A)   Math 101   (C)   History 316
    (B)   Biology 243   (D)   The circulatory system

Part B

> **DIRECTIONS:** In this section, you will hear short conversations between two people. After each conversation, a third person will ask you questions about what was discussed. When you hear a question, select the choice which best answers the question based on what you heard. The conversations and questions are NOT written in your test book. They will not be repeated.

Questions 14 through 17 are based on the following conversation.

You will hear:

Principal: Mrs. Raymond, you have such a conglomeration of books in this room! You have so many books that it actually looks messy in here.

Teacher: Mr. Jackson, I have a variety of books because reading teachers should have different types of literature for their children to read.

Principal: The reading teacher before you never had this many books.

Teacher: Different strokes fro different folks, Mr. Jackson. Times have changed.

14. ***You will hear:*** Based on the first part of the conversation you just heard, what does the word conglomeration mean?
    You will read:
    (A) Assortment of books
    (C) Lots of books
    (B) Stack of books
    (D) Too many books

15. ***You will hear:*** Why was Mr. Jackson surprised at the variety of books in Mrs. Raymond's room?
    You will read:
    (A) Books are very expensive, and teachers generally cannot afford to purchase many books.
    (B) The teacher before Mrs. Raymond didn't have a variety of books in her room.
    (C) Children generally don't like to read, and there is no need for teachers to have lots of books.
    (D) A basal reader series was available to Mrs. Raymond, a there was no need for her to have that many extra books.

16. ***You will hear:*** What did Mrs. Raymond mean by the statement, "Different strokes for different folks?"
    You will read:
    (A) Even though people are different, they are alike in many ways.
    (B) Even though people are different, they are still folks.
    (C) People must be stroked differently because they have different ways.
    (D) People are different, and therefore they do things differently.

17. ***You will hear:*** What did Mrs. Raymond mean by the statement, "Times have changed?"
    You will read:
    (A) Children are not the same.
    (B) Schools have changed.
    (C) Teachers have changed.
    (D) Methods of teaching reading have changed.

Questions 18 through 21 are based on the following conversation.

You will hear:

Teacher:	Mr. Jackson, Rodney should be suspended. Beyond a shadow of doubt, I know that he, without permission, took money from my desk.
Principal:	Mrs. Raymond calm down. Why are you getting upset?
Teacher:	Because Rodney took money that was not his. That is against the school's policy, and it is also against the policy of my class.
Principal:	To be honest, Mrs. Raymond, you are wasting my time. This is an inner city school, and stealing is to be expected. There are more pressing problems with which we should be concerned.

18. *You will hear:* What was Mr. Jackson's reaction when Mrs. Raymond informed him that Rodney had stolen the money?

    You will read:

    (A) Mr. Jackson was surprised.

    (B) Mr. Jackson was visibly upset.

    (C) Mr. Jackson was angry.

    (D) Mr. Jackson was cool, calm, and collected.

19. *You will hear:* It is apparent that Mr. Jackson did not support Mrs. Raymond's wish that Rodney should be suspended. Why?

    You will read:

    (A) Mr. Jackson thought suspension was too harsh.

    (B) Rodney's parents requested that he be allowed to remain in school.

    (C) Rodney had committed an offense that, according to Mr. Jackson, is commonplace in inner city schools.

    (D) Stealing is really not that bad.

20. *You will hear:* Based on the conversation, which statement is true?

    You will read:

    (A) Rodney had permission to take the money from Mrs. Raymond's desk.

    (B) Mrs. Raymond was very upset, yet very calm.

    (C) Mr. Jackson was calm, yet very upset.

    (D) Rodney had violated the policies of both the school and his class.

21. *You will hear:* Based on the conversation, which statement is false?

    You will read:

    (A) Mr. Jackson was very concerned about what Rodney had done.

    (B) Mrs. Raymond was very upset about what Rodney had done.

    (C) Rodney took the money without permission, according to Mrs. Raymond.

    (D) Rodney's action is atypical of children in inner city schools.

Questions 22 through 25 are based on the following conversation.

Student 1: Have you memorized all 50 of the states in alphabetical order?

Student 2: No, and I'm not going to memorize them I think it's useless to have students memorize information that's not important.

Student 1: You're going to get an F, and your parents will be very angry.

Student 2: Let them be angry! The time has come for us students to stand up and demand that we be taught to think instead of to memorize.

22. *You will hear:* According to the conversation between Student 1 and Student 2, what was the class assignment?

    You will read:

    (A) Spell the 50 states.

    (B) Memorize the 50 states.

    (C) Memorize the 50 states in alphabetical order.

    (D) Classify the states according to region.

23. **You will hear:** Why did Student 2 refuse to do the assignment?

    You will read:

    (A)   He had other homework to do.

    (B)   He had to work after school.

    (C)   He didn't understand the assignment.

    (D)   He thought the assignment was useless

24. **You will hear:** According to Student 1, what would happen to Student 2 if he didn't memorize the 50 states in alphabetical order?

    You will read:

    (A)   He would get an F, and his parents would be angry.

    (B)   He would receive a scolding from the teacher.

    (C)   He would be suspended for 6 days.

    (D)   He would be scolded by the principal.

25. **You will hear:** Why did Student 2 think the memorization exercise was useless?

    You will read:

    (A)   Student 2 thought students should be taught to classify.

    (B)   Student 2 thought students should be taught to spell.

    (C)   Student 2 thought students should be taught to write.

    (D)   Student 2 thought students should be taught to think.

Part C

> **DIRECTIONS:** In this section, you will hear several short talks. After each talk, a second voice will ask questions about the talk. When you hear a question, select the choice which best answers the question based on what you heard. The short talks are NOT written in your test book. They will not be repeated.

Questions 26 through 29 are based on the following short talk.

It is a known fact that urban schools are not adequately meeting the needs of the children they serve. I am sick and tired of people talking about the problem, it's time to solve it. Teachers and principals who do not have the capability or the sensitivity necessary for working with urban/inner city children should be reassigned. The problem at hand threatens the entire economy of this nation, and it's time to act.

26. **You will hear:** Who, according to the speaker, is responsible for the problem associated with urban schools?

    You will read:

    (A)   Teachers   (C)   Teachers and Principals

    (B)   Principals   (D)   Parents

27. **You will hear:** What is the tone of the speaker?
    You will read:
    (A) The speaker appears angry. (C) The speaker appears indifferent.
    (B) The speaker appears surprised. (D) The speaker appears excited.

28. **You will hear:** What is the main topic of the short talk?
    You will read:
    (A) "Incapable and Insensitive Teachers and Principals"
    (B) "Meeting the Needs of Urban Students"
    (C) "Crime in the Schools"
    (D) "Urban Schools"

29. **You will hear:** According to the short talk, what specific needs of urban children are not being met?
    You will read:
    (A) Their health needs are not being met.
    (B) Their academic needs are not being met.
    (C) The speaker does not address specific needs.
    (D) Their emotional needs are not being met.

Questions 31 through 32 are based on the following short talk.

The teacher education programs at most colleges are filled with education courses that are designed to prepare persons to teach, but to teach what? Colleges and universities must begin immediately to revamp their programs to include more content (English, math, history, etc.). Teachers can't teach what they don't know, and simply staying one chapter ahead of the students is not sufficient.

30. **You will hear:** Based on this short talk, what position does the speaker take?
    You will read:
    (A) No education courses should be taught.
    (B) Too many education courses are included in the curriculum.
    (C) Not enough content courses are included in the curriculum.
    (D) Not enough education courses are included in the curriculum.

31. **You will hear:** Which one of the following implications is supported by the short talk?
    You will read:
    (A) The number of education programs should be reduced.
    (B) Education majors should master a content field.
    (C) Education courses have no value.
    (D) Education courses should be eliminated completely.

32. **You will hear:** What is the possible occupation of the person making this short talk?
    You will read:
    (A) Legislator   (C) College Professor of education
    (B) Politician   (D) Lobbyist for teachers

Questions 33 through 36 are based on the following short talk.

Some people believe that the curriculum for grades K-3 should consist of nothing but reading, writing, and arithmetic. I agree. Asking primary children to master science and social studies is a bit much. These children need to master the basics first. Then the other disciplines can be added. The reason many children don't learn to read, write, and do arithmetic is that they are overloaded with other "junk" that really adds little to the real purpose of education: survival.

33. *You will hear:* Which of the following is the best title for this short talk?
    You will read:
    (A) "Garbage in the Curriculum"   (C)   "The Elementary Curriculum"
    (B) "Too Much Too Soon"   (D)   "Curriculum Revision"

34. *You will hear:* What primary subjects are proposed by the speaker?
    You will read:
    (A) All subjects
    (B) Science and social studies
    (C) Reading, writing, and arithmetic
    (D) Only subjects that address thinking skills

35. *You will hear:* Why does the speaker think that the primary curriculum should be limited to reading, writing, and arithmetic?
    You will read:
    (A) The other subjects are boring.
    (B) The other subjects are too difficult for primary children.
    (C) Primary children need to master the basics first.
    (D) The other subjects are really "junk."

36. *You will hear:* Which one of the following implications is made by the speaker?
    You will read:
    (A) Reading, writing, and mathematics are important for grades K-3 only.
    (B) Social studies and science should not be taught.
    (C) Primary grade children should not be overloaded at the possible expense of missing basic skills.
    (D) Survival in this country depends on knowledge gained from a variety of subjects.

Questions 37 through 40 are based on the following short talk.

Crime, teenage pregnancy, and drug abuse are problems that have heavily impacted the public schools. In addition to these problems, the one that has probably impacted the schools the most is low academic achievement. In general, students do not read and write as well as they did years ago. Additionally, the thinking skills of students today will not surpass nor equal the thinking skills of children ten years ago. In order to solve the problem of low academic achievement, teachers must raise their expectations and demand that students achieve.

37. ***You will hear:*** What is the main topic of this short talk?
    You will read:
    (A)   Crime and teenage pregnancy   (C)   Low academic achievement
    (B)   Drug abuse   (D)   Problems that impact schools

38. ***You will hear:*** Which problem does the speaker identify as having the most impact on schools?
    You will read:
    (A)   Crime   (C)   Drug abuse
    (B)   Teenage pregnancy   (D)   Low academic achievement

39. ***You will hear:*** What specific problem(s) is/are identified by the speaker?
    You will read:
    (A)   Students do not read as well as they did years ago.
    (B)   Students do not write as well as they did years ago.
    (C)   Students do not read, write, and think as well as they did years ago.
    (D)   Students do not know as much history as they did years ago.

40. ***You will hear:*** Based on the short talk, what conclusion can be drawn?
    You will read:
    (A)   Students today are lazy.
    (B)   Current social problems have had a dramatic effect on the education level of today's children.
    (C)   Students today are not interested in school.
    (D)   Students today have too many other things to occupy their minds.

Section 2: Reading

TIME: 30 Minutes
30 Questions

> **DIRECTIONS:** Each passage is followed by questions based on its content. After reading the passage, choose the best answer to each question. Answer all questions based on what is indicated or implied in that passage.

Questions 1 through 4 are based on the following passage.

Inservice training for teachers, as it is presently handled, is a waste of time. Often times, the topics of discussion do not meet the needs of the teachers who mandatorily participate. This generally happens because the teachers being inserviced have no input.

Research shows that sixty percent of the elementary school teachers across the United States view inservices as useless. Eighty percent of the high school teachers surveyed indicated that inservices fail to address their needs. Even seventy-four percent of college professors surveyed indicated that inservices at their level are of no value.

1. What is the main idea of this passage?
    (A) Inservice training for teachers is a waste of time.
    (B) Inservice training for teachers is not necessary.
    (C) Elementary teachers view inservice training as useless.
    (D) High school teachers view inservice training as invaluable.
    (E) Research studies support the inadequacy of teacher inservices.

2. What is the central thought of the second paragraph?
    (A) Teachers across the United States were surveyed to determine the effectiveness training for teachers.
    (B) Elementary teachers do not support inservices as presently structured.
    (C) High school teachers do not support present inservice training.
    (D) College professors do not support current inservice practices.
    (E) Research studies support the inadequacy of teacher inservices.

3. Based on the passage, what assumption can you make regarding teachers and inservice training?
    (A) Teachers, in general, think inservices are unimportant.
    (B) Teachers, in general, are not surveyed to determine their inservice needs.
    (C) Teachers, in general, think inservices are too long.
    (D) Teachers, in general, think inservices are boring.
    (E) Teachers, in general, view inservices as whipping sticks.

4. Which of the following statements is an opinion?
   (A) Elementary school teachers, in general, think that inservices are a waste of time.
   (B) High school teachers, in general, snub inservices.
   (C) College professors, in general, question the value of inservices.
   (D) Inservice training, in general, is not important.
   (E) Teachers are forced to participate in inservices.

Questions 5 and 6 are based on the following statement.

Inquire of a principal the name of his most eminent teacher, and he will take you to the quietest room in the school.

5. Which of the following best paraphrases this passage?
   (A) Principals are very eager to respond to inquiries.
   (B) Principals know their teachers very well.
   (C) Principals are eager to show off their good teachers.
   (D) Principals like teachers who can discipline children
   (E) Principals equate teacher competence with the ability to discipline children.

6. Which of the following is of **least** importance to the principal described in the passage?
   (A) A clean room   (D) Supportive teachers
   (B) An immaculate school   (E) Effective instruction
   (C) Well-dressed teachers

Questions 7 through 10 are based on the following passage.

Based on recent research studies conducted by specialists at Rollins Graduate University, in order for teachers to provide effective instruction, they must continuously engage in diagnosis. According to the research findings, (1) students of teachers who follow prescribed diagnostic procedures perform better academically than students of teachers who do not follow prescribed diagnostic procedures; (2) teachers who engage in diagnosis have a better knowledge of their students' strengths and are able to use these strengths to positively impact learning; (3) teachers who engage in diagnosis have a better knowledge of their students' weaknesses and are able to use this knowledge to meet the needs of their students; and (4) teachers who engage in diagnosis are better able to plan instruction because they are endowed with a thorough knowledge of their students' assets and liabilities.

7. Which of the following best describes the organization of the passage?
   (A) A series of events that are chronologically listed
   (B) An unimportant issue that is presented and defended by a list of ideas
   (C) A summary of key ideas about a designated subject
   (D) A step-by-step demonstration of the solution to a problem
   (E) A listing of related arguments that support an initial concern

8.   What is the author's purpose in writing this passage?
      (A)   To report research findings
      (B)   To demonstrate research skills
      (C)   To inform parents about research findings concerning diagnosis
      (D)   To inform teachers and other school personnel about the importance of
            research
      (E)   To help teachers improve instruction

9.   What is the main idea of this passage?
      (A)   Students perform better when teachers engage in diagnosis.
      (B)   Teachers who engage in diagnosis have a better knowledge of their students'
            strengths.
      (C)   In order for teachers to provide effective instruction, they must continuously
            engage in diagnosis.
      (D)   Teachers who engage in diagnosis have a better knowledge of their students'
            weaknesses.
      (E)   Teachers should engage in research.

10.   How much intitial faith should be placed in the author's argument, based on the
      amount of support he/she provides?
      (A)   None—the author's argument was based on a non-representative sample.
      (B)   A small amount, because the author knows a bit more than the reader.
      (C)   A great deal, because the author seems totally convinced.
      (D)   A moderate amount, until more is learned about the subject and the reader can
            determine whether the cited study is valid, reliable, etc.
      (E)   The author's argument should be accepted unconditionally because it is based
            on research findings from a university.

Questions 11 through 13 are based on the following passage.

The person who goes through life, willing to accept nothing but compliments is a loser
of those things which make people great.

11.   Based on this passage, it can be inferred that the things which make people great are
      (A)   compliments.   (D)   negativism.
      (B)   constructive criticisms.   (E)   suggestions.
      (C)   pleas for change.

12.   Which of the following occupations would the message conveyed by this passage
      least affect?
      (A)   Teaching   (D)   Farming
      (B)   Medicine   (E)   Assembly line work
      (C)   Engineering

13.   How might the message conveyed by this passage apply to teaching?
      (A)   Teachers are encouraged to make mistakes so they might become great.
      (B)   Teachers are encouraged to avoid mistakes.

(C)   Teachers are encouraged to strive for praise.

(D)   Teachers are encouraged to instill the idea of perfection in their students.

(E)   Teachers are encouraged to instill in their students the idea that everyone should acknowledge his shortcomings.

Questions 14 through 18 are based on the following passage.

There's no room on the football field for "dumb jocks." Athletes who cannot consistently maintain a 2.0 grade-point average should not be permitted to participate in any sports. Athletes must realize that the purpose of school is to produce scholars, not professional ball players. If, by chance, an athlete is able to acquire a place in the professional ranks of sports, good! But the primary objective of school is the manufacturing and nurturing of productive citizens who can make worthwhile contributions to society. It is irritating to observe star quarterbacks who can't read, to observe star running backs who can't write, to observe star fullbacks who can't speak, and to observe outstanding pitchers who can't add, subtract, or multiply.

14.   What is the tone of the author of this passage?

(A)   The author is indifferent, because he doesn't care whether athletes learn or not.

(B)   The author is dismayed.

(C)   The author is surprised that athletes can play sports with less than a 2.0 grade-point average.

(D)   The author is ashamed that athletes can't maintain a 2.0 grade-point average.

(E)   The author displays no certain mood or attitude.

15.   What is the main idea of this passage?

(A)   Athletes who cannot make the grades should not be allowed to participate in any sports.

(B)   The purpose of school is not to produce professional athletes.

(C)   Some athletes can't read.

(D)   Some athletes do not possess the required basic skills.

(E)   The purpose of school is to manufacture productive citizens.

16.   According to the author of this passage, which of the following is a fact?

(A)   Star quarterbacks can't read.

(B)   Star running backs can't write.

(C)   Star fullbacks can't speak.

(D)   (A), (B), and (C).

(E)   The purpose of school is to manufacture and nurture productive citizens.

17.   Which of the following is the best title for this selection?

(A)   "Dumb Jocks"   (D)   "Grade Requirements for Athletes"

(B)   "Athletes Lack Basic Skills"   (E)   "Producing Productive Citizens"

(C)   "Producing Professional Athletes"

18. To what other school organization(s) might the message conveyed in this passage apply?

    (A) The band
    (B) The cheerleading squad
    (C) The science club
    (D) Both (A) and (C).
    (E) Both (A) and (B).

Questions 19 through 22 are based on the following passage.

At Onion High School, we administered a timed reading test to 144 seniors. Twenty minutes were allowed for the Vocabulary Section, and 30 minutes were allowed for the Comprehension Section. The results were appalling! The average grade-equivalency for vocabulary was 5.5, and the average grade equivalency for comprehension was 4.3. In an effort to determine why the results were so low, we analyzed the answer sheets. We found that of the 100 vocabulary items on the test, the students completed an average of only 45 items, but an average of 32 of these attempts were correct. On the Comprehension Section, the students attempted an average of 17 of 36 items, but they correctly answered an average of 14 items. It was quickly discovered that the students were not completing enough items to score well on the test.

During the next week, the students were given another form of the same test. They were told to use all of the time they needed. The results were amazing. The average vocabulary score rose 5 grade levels, and the average comprehension score rose 7 grade levels.

19. What is the main idea of this passage?

    (A) When given another chance, reading scores improved.
    (B) The reading scores of seniors at Onion High School were appalling.
    (C) Students at Onion High School scored lower in reading comprehension than they did in vocabulary.
    (D) Timed reading tests test speed instead of reading skill.
    (E) Reading tests are very important.

20. Which of the following is the best title for this passage?

    (A) "High School Seniors Fail Reading Test"
    (B) "Improving Reading Scores"
    (C) "Students Score Higher in Vocabulary"
    (D) "The Importance of Reading Tests"
    (E) "Slow and Careful Readers Penalized by Timed Reading Tests"

21. For whom is the conveyed message in this passage intended?

    (A) Teachers
    (B) Parents
    (C) Counselors
    (D) Both (A) and (B).
    (E) (A), (B), and (C).

22. Is the implied argument that timed reading tests test speed instead of reading skill adequately supported?

    (A) No. The evidence is shallow.
    (B) No. The population size is too small.

(C)   The implied argument is adequately supported.

(D)   The implied argument is not adequately supported because only one level of students was tested.

(E)   The implied argument is only moderately supported.

Questions 23 through 26 are based on the following passage.

I had heard that school is boring, and I wanted to see for myself. So, having secured permission from the principal, I visited Mr. Rollins' political science class at 8 a.m. in the morning. Sure enough, the children were yawning, desperately attempting to stay awake. It was the most boring class I have ever attended. The lecture method was used to inform students about the political process of electing candidates. Near the end of the class, several of the students no longer yawned; they slept. Would you believe that when the class was over, four students had to be awakened so they could attend their next classes?

At the time that I visited this class, the city's mayoral election was taking place. How interesting it would have been to have students actively involved in an election process as part of the classroom activities! The following activities could have been staged:

1. Creation of different parties—Democrats, Republicans, and Independents.

2. Election of party representation through the primary process.

3. Election of a mayor through the process of a general election.

4. Demonstration of how to register to vote and how to actually use a voting machine.

5. Planning of and student participation in debating and speech making.

Students are not the only ones asleep. Teachers need to wake up and realize that they are boring students to death.

23.   What is the main idea of this passage?
   (A)   Political science is boring.
   (B)   Students are sleeping in class.
   (C)   Teachers are boring.
   (D)   School is boring.
   (E)   More student participation is needed in school.

24.   Which of the following expresses the tone of the author?
   (A)   Encouraged at what he witnessed
   (B)   Indifferent about what he witnessed
   (C)   Angry at what he witnessed
   (D)   Shocked at what he witnessed
   (E)   Saddened by what he witnessed

25.   Does the author present sufficient evidence to support the argument that school is boring?
   (A)   Since the author visited only one class, more evidence is needed.
   (B)   The author sufficiently supports the argument.

    (C)   The author provides overwhelming support for the argument.

    (D)   The author provides no support for the argument.

    (E)   The author's support for the argument is too circumstantial.

26.   Which of the following is **not** a fact presented in the passage?

    (A)   Children were sleeping in class.

    (B)   The lecture method of delivery was used by the teacher.

    (C)   It was a political science class.

    (D)   There were 40 students in the class.

    (E)   A mayoral election was taking place at the time.

Questions 27 through 30 are based on the following passage.

Now is the time for teachers to stand up as advocates against competency testing. It's embarrassing to think that persons who have completed four-year teacher preparation programs must be tested to determine whether they are competent enough to teach.

On the other hand, colleges and universities must the embarrassed also to think that legislators have no confidence in teacher preparation programs that have been approved by the various state education agencies. In many cases, these programs have also been approved by regional and national accrediting agencies which have strict requirements that mandate continuous curriculum revision to meet the needs of changing school environments.

Teachers, along with other school officials, must help legislators understand that teaching requires many, many qualities that cannot be adequately tested. A teacher's love for children, dedication to the field of education, patience for those children who are slow, versatility in the classroom, and ability to make learning enjoyable cannot be tested. It's time for teachers to stand up and be counted.

27.   Which of the following is the best title for this passage?

    (A)   "Colleges and Universities Embarrassed by Competency Testing"

    (B)   "Teachers Annoyed by Competency Testing"

    (C)   "Teaching Involves More than Content Delivery"

    (D)   "Teachers as Advocates Against Competency Testing"

    (E)   "Standing Tall"

28.   Which of the following best supports the notion that teachers need to speak out against competency testing?

    (A)   Paragraph 1   (D)   Paragraphs 1 and 3

    (B)   Paragraph 2   (E)   Paragraphs 2 and 3

    (C)   Paragraph 3

29.   In addition to teachers, who else, according to the passage, should be embarrassed by competency testing for teachers?

    (A)   Parents   (D)   Professional organizations

    (B)   Students   (E)   Colleges and universities

    (C)   Principals

30. According to this passage, what is the major weakness of competency testing?
    (A) Teaching requires many qualities that cannot be adequately measured by tests.
    (B) Competency tests are designed to assess skills that are irrelevant.
    (C) Competency tests prove embarrassing.
    (D) Competency tests have outlived their need.
    (E) The tests are too long.

Section 3: Writing

Time: 30 Minutes
45 Questions

Part A

> **DIRECTIONS**: Each of the following sentences may contain an error in diction, usage, idiom, or grammar. Some sentences may be correct. Some sentences may contain one error. No sentence contains more than one error.
>
> If there is an error, it will appear in one of the underlined portions labeled (A), (B), (C) or (D). If there is no error, choose the portion labeled (E). If there is an error, select the letter of the portion that must be changed in order to correct the sentence.

1. Ms. Randall, a fifth-grade teacher at Burt Elementary School, is a excellent mathematician
              A   B

   who deserves lots of praise. No error.
    C   D   E

2. The top student in the history class refused to except the "Scholar Award" because
                                                A   B   C

   he had cheated on the final examination. No error.
        D   E

3. It's the union's consensus of opinion that the principal should be dismissed for reasons
    A   B   C   D

   that suggest immoral behavior. No error.
                E

4. Being that Ms. Westbrook has been tardy for six consecutive days, the principal
          A   B

   has suggested that she appear before the faculty's disciplinary committee. No error.
        C   D   E

5. In addition to teaching mathematics at Rogers High School , Ms. Westbrook enjoys
        A   B   C

   singing, dancing, and daily walks. No error.
                D   E

6. I $\underset{\text{A}}{\underline{\text{no}}}$ why Ms. Price is $\underset{\text{B}}{\underline{\text{such}}}$ a good $\underset{\text{C}}{\underline{\text{teacher}}}$: she is $\underset{\text{D}}{\underline{\text{well-trained}}}$ and works very hard to motivate her students. $\underset{\text{E}}{\underline{\text{No error.}}}$

7. At the $\underset{\text{A}}{\underline{\text{school's}}}$ annual party, the janitor, to everybody's surprise, ate $\underset{\text{B}}{\underline{\text{less}}}$ pieces of cake because he's attempting to $\underset{\text{C}}{\underline{\text{lose}}}$ $\underset{\text{D}}{\underline{\text{weight}}}$. $\underset{\text{E}}{\underline{\text{No error.}}}$

8. $\underset{\text{A}}{\underline{\text{While attending}}}$ Harvard University, Juan took $\underset{\text{B}}{\underline{\text{English,}}}$ $\underset{\text{C}}{\underline{\text{math,}}}$ Spanish, science, $\underset{\text{D}}{\underline{\text{etc.}}}$ $\underset{\text{E}}{\underline{\text{No error.}}}$

9. At the $\underset{\text{A}}{\underline{\text{beginning}}}$ of the school year, all of Ms. Johnson's students $\underset{\text{B}}{\underline{\text{were enthused}}}$ because they $\underset{\text{C}}{\underline{\text{knew}}}$ that $\underset{\text{D}}{\underline{\text{their}}}$ teacher was a caring person. $\underset{\text{E}}{\underline{\text{No error.}}}$

10. Teachers are constantly reminded that information about students is $\underset{\text{A}}{\underline{\text{confidential;}}}$ each $\underset{\text{B}}{\underline{\text{student's}}}$ name, Social Security number, and $\underset{\text{C}}{\underline{\text{where he lives}}}$ $\underset{\text{D}}{\underline{\text{are}}}$ the only information that can be given. $\underset{\text{E}}{\underline{\text{No error.}}}$

11. Ms. Ratcliff is $\underset{\text{A}}{\underline{\text{probably}}}$ the $\underset{\text{B}}{\underline{\text{nicest}}}$ teacher at Flu Elementary School, but she has a problem in two $\underset{\text{C}}{\underline{\text{areas —}}}$ discipline and $\underset{\text{D}}{\underline{\text{how to teach effectively.}}}$ $\underset{\text{E}}{\underline{\text{No error.}}}$

12. Given that two teacher applicants share $\underset{\text{A}}{\underline{\text{equal credentials,}}}$ the superintendent $\underset{\text{B}}{\underline{\text{will generally hire}}}$ the one who uses the $\underset{\text{C}}{\underline{\text{best}}}$ $\underset{\text{D}}{\underline{\text{English.}}}$ $\underset{\text{E}}{\underline{\text{No error.}}}$

13. Between 1970 and 1980, the amount of disgruntled teachers who went on strike,
        A   B   C

rose tremendously, a reality that shocked all concerned. No error.
       D   E

14. Every teacher, without question, thinks that they are the best teacher in the world, a
                                                A   B

very general belief that is too difficult to prove. No error.
         C   D   E

15. Despite the fact that the principal has warned students about hall walking, they
          A   B

continue, knowing the consequences, to ignore the principal request. No error.
         C   D   E

16. The teacher did everything that she was supposed to do; she didn't want to loose
                   A   B   C   D

her job. No error.
        E

17. The children at Westberry Elementary School possess such good manners that Ms.
                                            A   B

Twiggs would rather stop teaching then change schools. No error.
                   C   D   E

18. The reason Ms. Flix no longer teaches is because children are too unmannerly, and they
                       A   B   C

don't perform well academically. No error.
      D   E

19. To teach or not too teach is a grave dilemma for me. No error.
       A   B   C   D   E

20. Wrote one little boy: "My teacher works hard every day; since we're not the
            A   B

best children in the world, I'm sure that by the end of the day, she is so tired." No error.
       C   D   E

21. After an unusally tedious day at school, the teacher went home and soaks in a tub of
                 A   B   C   D

hot water. No error.
        E

22. The school where Mr. James' children attend is located too far from the main
             A   B   C   D

section of town. No error.
           E

23. After the school bell sounded, the children will rush to catch the bus which is usually
            A   B   C

parked on the north side of the school. No error.
        D   E

24. Irregardless of what the principal says, the teachers and students at McReynolds Middle
       A   B

School do as they please, "come hell or high water." No error.
     C   D   E

25. The principal is retiring this year because, according to the teachers, he has enough
        A   B   C

capitol to last the rest of his life. No error.
 D   E

Part B

> **DIRECTIONS:** In each of the following sentences, some portion of the sentence is underlined. Under each sentence are five choices. The first choice has the same wording as the original. The other four choices are reworded. Select the letter of the best choice which rewrites the sentence correctly.

26.   Teaching in almost all kinds of schools.

    (A)   Teaching in almost all kinds of schools.
    (B)   Teaching in all kinds of schools.
    (C)   Teaching may require work in almost all kinds of schools.
    (D)   Teaching requiring work in almost all kinds of schools.
    (E)   Teaching requiring work in all kinds of schools.

27. Of all the occupations I have heard about, <u>the one I would like to be is a teacher.</u>

   (A)   the one I would like to be is a teacher.
   (B)   the one I would like to be is teaching.
   (C)   the one that interests me the most is a teacher.
   (D)   the one that interests me the most is teaching.
   (E)   the one that I like to be most is teaching.

28. Ms. Johnson is the best teacher in the school, <u>the prettiest lady in town.</u>

   (A)   Ms. Johnson is the best teacher in the school, the prettiest lady in town.
   (B)   Ms. Johnson is the best teacher in the school.
   (C)   Ms. Johnson's the best teacher in the school.
   (D)   Ms. Johnson is the prettiest lady in town.
   (E)   Ms. Johnson is the best teacher in the school, and she is the prettiest lady in town.

29. Unable to control his class, <u>the principal fired the math teacher.</u>

   (A)   the principal fired the math teacher.
   (B)   the principal fired the Math teacher.
   (C)   the math teacher was fired by the principle.
   (D)   the math teacher was fired by the principal.
   (E)   the Math teacher was fired by the principal.

30. Ms. Prater, <u>the name of the teacher</u> next door, is pregnant and will be unable to complete the school year.

   (A)   the name of the teacher   (D)   the teacher's name
   (B)   the teacher   (E)   the teachers' name
   (C)   the name of the Teacher

31. Every student should <u>try and do his best</u> to achieve.

   (A)   try and do his best   (D)   try to do his best
   (B)   try and do well   (E)   try and do his most
   (C)   make an effort and do his best

32. The principal hit at the thief <u>running through the schoolyard with a bat.</u>

   (A)   The principal hit at the thief running through the schoolyard with a bat.
   (B)   The principal hit at the thief who was running through the schoolyard with a bat.
   (C)   The principal hit at the thief which was running through the schoolyard with a bat.

(D)   With a bat, the principal hit at the thief running through the schoolyard.

(E)   With a bat, the principal hit at the thief whom was running through the schoolyard.

33.   The graduating senior is considering the question as to whether he should go to college.

(A)   considering the question as to whether

(B)   considering the question whether

(C)   considering whether or not

(D)   considering the question if

(E)   considering the question of whether or not

34.   If one does all of his work, you should get an A.

(A)   If one does all of his work, you should get an A.

(B)   If you do all of your work, you should get an A.

(C)   If the student does all of his work, you should get an A.

(D)   If one do all of his work, you should get an A.

(E)   Should one do all of his work, you should get an A.

35.   The principal knocked on the teacher's door, and then in he comes, outraged at what

he had heard.

(A)   The principal knocked on the teacher's door, and then in he comes, outraged at what he had heard.

(B)   The principal knocked on the teacher's door, and then in he come, outraged at what he had heard.

(C)   The principle knocked on the teacher's door, and then in he came, outraged at what he had heard.

(D)   The principal knocked on the teacher's door, and then in he came, outraged at what he had heard.

(E)   The principal knocked on the teacher's door, and than in he came, outraged at what he had heard.

Part C

DIRECTIONS: Each of the passages below is followed by several questions or incomplete sentences. Under each question or sentence are five choices. Select the letter of the best choice and darken the corresponding oval.

Questions 36-40 are based on the following passage.

(1) Actually, the term "Native Americans" is incorrect. (2) Indians migrated to this continent from other areas, just earlier then Europeans did. (3) The ancestors of the Anasazi Indians of the four-state area of Colorado, New Mexico, Utah, and Arizona-probably crossed from Asia into Alaska. (4) About 25,000 years ago while the continental land bridge still existed. (5) This land bridge arched across the Bering Strait in the last Ice Age. (6) About A.D. 500 the ancestors of the Anasazi moved onto the Mesa Verde a high plateau in the desert

country of Colorado. (7) The Wetherills, five brothers who ranched the area, is generally given credit for the first exploration of the ruins in the 1870s and 1880s. (8) There were some 50,000 Anasazi thriving in the four-corners area by the 1200s. (9) _____
_____, the Anasazi had established wide-spread communities and built thousands of sophisticated structures-cliff dwellings, pueblos, and kivas. (10) They even engaged in trade with other Indians.

36. Which of the following best corrects the grammatical error in Sentence 7?

   (A) The Wetherills, a group of five brothers who ranched in the area, is generally given credit for the first exploration of the ruins in the 1870s and 1880s.

   (B) The Wetherills, five brothers who ranched in the area, are generally given credit for the first exploration of the ruins in the 1870s and 1880s.

   (C) The Wetherills are generally given credit for the first exploration of the ruins in the 1870s and 1880s, five brothers who ranched in the area.

   (D) The Wetherills, generally given credit for the first exploration of the area, is five brothers who ranched in the area.

   (E) Best as it is.

37. Which of the following sentences would best fit between Sentences 9 and 10?

   (A) Artifacts recovered from the area suggest that the Anasazi were artistic, religious, agricultural, classless, and peaceful.

   (B) By 12,000 to 10,000 B.C., some Indians had established their unique cultures in the southwest.

   (C) The Navaho called their ancestors the Anasazi, the Ancient Ones.

   (D) I think it is unfortunate that such a unique and innovative culture should have disappeared from the country.

   (E) Before Columbus reached the New World, the Anasazi had virtually disappeared.

38. Which of the following is an incomplete sentence?

   (A) 4   (D) 7

   (B) 5   (E) 10

   (C) 6

39. Which of the following best completes Sentence 9?

   (A) At their zenith which was from A.D. 700 to 1300

   (B) At their zenith B.C. 700 to 1300

   (C) At their zenith, from A.D. 700 to 1300,

   (D) At their zenith, being A.D. 700 to 1300,

   (E) At their zenith, of A.D. 700 to 1300,

40. In Sentence 1, the author has placed the phrase "Native Americans" in quotation marks in order to

   (A) imply that Native Americans are not really native.

   (B) show that the phrase is new.

   (C) increase awareness of the plight of the Native American.

   (D) separate Native Americans from American Indians.

   (E) question the spelling of both words.

Questions 41-45 are based on the following passage.

(1) A growing number of businesses are providing day care facilities for the children of their employees. (2) Some companies charge a standard fee, but most provide the day care free or at a nominal cost. (3) These care programs provide services that _____

_____ .

(4) If they should help with day care at all is what many companies are trying to decide. (5) In the event parents need to work overtime, centers are even open on weekends, and some companies _____ special initiative in building company loyalty of each employee by making arrangements for special field trips to zoos and museums. (6) Is this kind of care really necessary? (7) Should businesses really be in the business of day care.

(8) Experts in the field cite many advantages for this system. (9) Therefore, loyalty to the company is built, so morale climbs. (10) Studies show that when a company helps its employees blend parent and worker roles, absenteeism and tardiness drop. (11) In addition, workers feel the company has taken more of a personal interest in them. (12) Most companies also provide various health care programs for their employees. (13) Turnover becomes a much less significant factor for managers. (14) Human resource managers also estimate that every $1 spent on these programs returns $2 or more in increased productivity.

41. Which of the following best completes Sentence 3?
   (A) continue, through the early teens, of the children.
   (B) continue through the children and their early teens.
   (C) continue through the children's early teens.
   (D) continue on through the early teens of the children.
   (E) Best as it is.

42. Which of the following would be a better way to structure Sentence 4?
   (A) What many companies are trying to decide is if they should help with day care at all.
   (B) Unsure if they should help with day care at all, many companies are trying to decide.
   (C) Many companies, unsure if they should help with day care at all, are trying to decide.
   (D) Many companies are trying to decide if they should help with day care at all.
   (E) Many companies are trying to help with day care at all.

43. Which of the following would be an acceptable choice in Sentence 5?
   (A) show   (D) A and B.
   (B) have been showing   (E) A, B, and C.
   (C) have shown

44. Which of the following sentences is irrelevant in the second paragraph and should be eliminated?
   (A) 8   (D) 14
   (B) 10   (E) None of these.
   (C) 12

45. Which of the following best improves the sequence of ideas in the second paragraph?
   (A) Reverse Sentences 8 and 9   (D) Place Sentence 9 after 11
   (B) Place Sentence 13 before 9   (E) Delete Sentence 8
   (C) Delete Sentence 11

Section 4: Essay

TIME: 30 Minutes

DIRECTIONS: Plan and write an essay on the topic given below. DO NOT WRITE ON ANY OTHER TOPIC OTHER THAN THE ONE SPECIFIED. AN ESSAY ON ANY OTHER TOPIC IS UNACCEPTABLE.

As a beginning teacher, you will encounter the awesome problem of declining academic achievement among American youth. Knowing that this problem exists, what steps will you take to ensure that your students' academic performance reflects their potential? Explain each step and provide justification for the procedures you will employ.

TEST OF COMMUNICATION SKILLS

ANSWER KEY

SECTION 1: LISTENING

1.	(C)	11.	(D)	21.	(D)	31.	(A)
2.	(C)	12.	(B)	22.	(C)	32.	(C)
3.	(D)	13.	(D)	23.	(D)	33.	(B)
4.	(A)	14.	(A)	24.	(A)	34.	(C)
5.	(B)	15.	(B)	25.	(D)	35.	(C)
6.	(C)	16.	(D)	26.	(C)	36.	(C)
7.	(B)	17.	(D)	27.	(A)	37.	(D)
8.	(C)	18.	(D)	28.	(B)	38.	(D)
9.	(D)	19.	(C)	29.	(C)	39.	(C)
10.	(B)	20.	(D)	30.	(C)	40.	(B)

SECTION 2: READING

1.	(A)	9.	(C)	17.	(D)	25.	(A)
2.	(E)	10.	(D)	18.	(E)	26.	(D)
3.	(B)	11.	(B)	19.	(D)	27.	(D)
4.	(D)	12.	(E)	20.	(E)	28.	(E)
5.	(E)	13.	(E)	21.	(E)	29.	(E)
6.	(E)	14.	(B)	22.	(C)	30.	(A)
7.	(E)	15.	(A)	23.	(D)		
8.	(E)	16.	(E)	24.	(E)		

SECTION 3: WRITING

1.	(B)	13.	(B)	25.	(D)	37.	(A)
2.	(A)	14.	(A)	26.	(C)	38.	(A)
3.	(C)	15.	(D)	27.	(D)	39.	(C)
4.	(A)	16.	(D)	28.	(E)	40.	(A)
5.	(D)	17.	(D)	29.	(D)	41.	(C)
6.	(A)	18.	(B)	30.	(B)	42.	(D)
7.	(B)	19.	(C)	31.	(D)	43.	(E)
8.	(D)	20.	(D)	32.	(D)	44.	(C)
9.	(B)	21.	(C)	33.	(E)	45.	(D)
10.	(C)	22.	(A)	34.	(B)		
11.	(D)	23.	(B)	35.	(D)		
12.	(C)	24.	(A)	36.	(B)		

DETAILED EXPLANATIONS OF ANSWERS
NTE CORE BATTERY–Test 4

TEST OF COMMUNICATION SKILLS
Section 1: Listening

Part A

1. **(C)** Here you must choose the item that is best supported by the information given in the statement. It is possible that "A" students do make good teachers, choice (A). It is also possible that Ivy League colleges produce good teachers, choice (B); and there is no doubt that intelligence and experience are key predictors of success as a teacher, choice (D). Neither one of these choices, however, is supported by the statement, "Teachers are born, not made!" The correct answer is (C). If teachers are born and not made, then teaching is a skill that comes naturally.

2. **(C)** You are to choose the item which is best supported by the information given. According to the statement, girls read better, but boys are better in math. Choices (A), (B) and (D) are not supported. The correct answer is (C). According to the statement, girls are better readers than boys.

3. **(D)** Here you are required to pick the choice that is supported by the information given in the statement. Since Mrs. Randall attends professional meetings *almost* every year, it can be safely assumed that she misses occasionally. The correct answer is choice (D). The statement *does not*, if you listened carefully, support choices (A), (B) or (C).

4. **(A)** Here you are required to pick the choice that most directly answers the question. The question does not ask for a specific month or time of day for the Junior-Senior Prom. Therefore, choices (B), (C) and (D) are incorrect. The question solicits the time of the year that the Junior-Senior Prom is held. The correct answer is choice (A).

5. **(B)** Your must pick the choice which is supported by the information given in the statement. The statement does not suggest that Mrs. Jones loves teaching any math, choice (A); algebra, choice (C); or geometry, choice (D). The statement explicitly states that Mrs. Jones loves teaching basic math. The correct answer is choice (B).

6. **(C)** You are to pick the choice that is supported by the information given in the statement. None of the choices are supported by the statement, but since grade-point average

is generally one of the criteria used in awarding scholarships, it can be inferred that Edward's previous grades were not as good as the grades he made in senior year. The correct answer is choice (C). Choices (A), (B) and (D) are not supported, not even by inference.

7. **(B)** Here you are required to pick the choice that most directly answers the question. Choice (D) can immediately be eliminated because the question asks for a percentage, not a number. Since the question asks for the percentage of seniors who fail to graduate, choices (A) and (C) appear grossly inaccurate. The correct answer is choice (B). If you missed this item you must make an effort to listen carefully in the future. The question asks for the percentage of seniors who fail to graduate, not the percentage who graduate.

8. **(C)** Here you are to pick the choice that is best supported by the information given. There is no support for choices (A), (B), or (D). It is apparent that the teacher either improperly planned for the school year, or did not properly implement the calendar plan.

9. **(D)** Here you are to pick the choice that most directly answers the question. It is unlikely that students would be having lunch in the Biology Lab, choice (A). Because of the equipment in a Biology Lab, it is highly unlikely that students would be permitted to hold meetings in the lab, choices (B) and (C). The correct answer is choice (D). The students are probably conducting experiments.

10. **(B)** Here you must pick the choice that is supported by the information given. The expression "now or never" does not suggest that students who do not complete their homework now will not graduate, choice (A); will be suspended, choice (C); or will fail the course, choice (D). "Now or never" simply means that students who do not complete their homework now will not be given an opportunity to complete it later, choice (B).

11. **(D)** You are required to pick the choice that most directly answers the question. The question asks for the name of a textbook. Choices (A), (B) and (C) are not textbooks. The correct answer is choice (D). It is obvious that *Mathematics for Everyday Living* is a textbook because it is italicized.

12. **(B)** You are to pick the choice that is best supported by the information given. "Nearly 3,000 students" is fewer than 3,000. Therefore, choices (A), (C) and (D) are incorrect. The correct answer is choice (B).

13. **(D)** You are to pick the choice that directly answers the question. The question establishes a time frame of one week. This suggests that Mrs. Robinson certainly could not teach full Math 101 (A), Biology 243 (B), or History 316 (C) classes in just one week. Mrs. Robinson, however, could teach the topic of the circulatory system in one week. The answer is choice (D).

Part B

14. **(A)** You are to pick the choice which is supported by the conversation you just heard. Mrs. Raymond indicated that as a reading teacher, she should have a variety of books in her class because children should be exposed to different types of literature. Based on Mrs.

Raymond's response to Mr. Jackson's use of the word conglomeration, it is rather obvious that choice (A) is the correct answer. Choices (B), (C) and (D) are not synonymous with **variety.**

15. **(B)** You are to pick the choice that is supported by the conversation. The conversation clearly reveals that Mr. Jackson was surprised at the variety of books that Mrs. Raymond had in her room because the previous teacher did not have such an assortment of books. Therefore, the correct answer is (B).

16. **(D)** You are to pick the choice which is supported by the conversation. Read choices (A), (B) and (C) and you will note that none of these statements is supported by the conversation. Choice (D) is the correct answer. "Different strokes for different folks" means that people do things differently.

17. **(D)** You are to pick the choice that is supported by the conversation. It is clear that the conversation implies that methods of teaching reading have changed. As opposed to using one reader for the entire year, teachers now use a variety of literature—unlike the previous reading teacher. Choices (A), (B) and (C) may all be correct, but they are not supported directly, nor are they implied.

18. **(D)** You are to pick the choice that is supported by the conversation. According to the conversation, Mr. Jackson could not understand why Mrs. Raymond was upset, because stealing is common in inner city schools. Therefore, choice (D) is the correct answer. Mr. Jackson was cool, calm, and collected. Choices (A), (B) and (C) are not supported.

19. **(C)** You are to pick the choice which is supported by the conversation. According to the conversation between Mr. Jackson and Mrs. Raymond, Mr. Jackson doesn't feel that stealing is that bad, since it is commonplace in inner city schools, choice (C). Therefore, he probably did not support Mrs. Raymond. Choices (A), (B) and (D) are not supported. Choice (A) is a possible answer, but since Mr. Jackson didn't apparently see anything wrong with stealing—at this particular school—he probably would not support any disciplinary action.

20. **(D)** You are to pick the choice which is supported by the conversation. Choices (A), (B) and (C) and not supported by the conversation. Choice (D) is the correct answer. Mrs. Raymond stated that both the school's policy and the class' policy had been violated.

21. **(D)** You are to pick the choice which is supported by the conversation. Nothing in the conversation supports the statement that stealing is atypical of children in inner city schools. In fact, according to Mr. Jackson's statement, it is quite typical. Therefore, choice (D) is the correct answer.

22. **(C)** You are to pick the choice that is supported by the information given in the conversation. If you listened carefully, the assignment was to memorize the 50 states in alphabetical order, choice (C). The students were not asked to spell the states, choice (A). Choices (B) and (D) also are not supported by information given in the conversation.

23. **(D)** You are to pick the choice that is supported by the information given in the conversation. It is very obvious that choice D is the correct answer. Choices (A), (B) and (C) are not supported by the information given.

24. **(A)**   You are to pick the choice that is supported by the information given in the conversation. Student 1 informed Student 2 that if he did not memorize the 50 states in alphabetical order, he would receive an F and his parents would be angry, choice (A). The other choices are not supported by information given in the conversation.

25. **(D)**   You are to pick the choice which is supported by the information given in the conversation between Student 1 and Student 2. Clearly, choices (A), (B) and (C) are neither supported nor implied by the information given. The correct answer is choice (D). Student 2 thought students should be taught to think.

Part C

26. **(C)**   You are to pick the choice that is supported by the short talk. While the speaker does not explicitly blame teachers and principals for the urban school problem, he/she implies that they are to blame by stating that those teachers and principals who do not have the capability or the sensitivity necessary for working with urban/inner city children should be reassigned. The correct answer is (C). Choice (A) is not the answer because it addresses only teachers. Choice (B) is not the answer because it addresses only principals. Choice (D) is never mentioned in the short talk.

27. **(A)**   You are to pick the choice which is supported by the information given in the short talk. The speaker says that he/she is sick and tired of people talking about the problem. This suggests that the speaker is angry, choice (A) The other choices, if you listened carefully, are not supported.

28. **(B)**   You are to pick the choice that is supported by the information given in the talk. The talk is about the unmet needs of urban students, choice (B). Choice (A) is mentioned as a possible reason for the needs of urban students not being met. Choice (C), "Crime in the Schools," is never mentioned. Choice (D) is too broad to be the main topic. This talk speaks specifically to the unmet needs of urban students. It does not address urban schools in general.

29. **(C)**   Since the speaker does not mention "health needs," "academic needs," or "emotional needs," (A), (B) and (D) can be eliminated. The correct answer is (C) because the speaker does not address any specific needs.

30. **(C)**   You are to pick the choice that is supported by the short talk. It is very clear that the speaker is suggesting that education majors need more content, choice (C). Choices (A), (B) and (D) are not supported.

31. **(A)**   You are to pick the choice that is supported by the short talk. The speaker implies that the number of education courses should be reduced, choice (A), but none of the other choices are supported. The short talk does not suggest that education majors should master a content field, choice (B); it does not suggest that education courses have no value, choice (C); and the speaker definitely does not suggest that education courses should be eliminated, choice (D).

32. **(C)**   You are to pick the choice that is supported by the short talk or implied by the information in the short talk. Of the four choices, the person most likely to be concerned about

the content of the education program would be the college professor, choice (C). The other persons would be more concerned about teachers' rights and responsibilities.

33. **(B)** You are to pick the choice that is supported by the short talk. The speaker clearly states that the curriculum requires too much too soon of primary children, choice (B). The speaker implies that there is garbage in the curriculum, but this is not the main topic. Choice (C), "The Elementary Curriculum," is too broad to be the title of this short talk. Choice (D), "Curriculum Revision," is not addressed. The speaker does not address revision of the curriculum. It is requested that certain subjects be withheld until later.

34. **(C)** You are to pick the choice that is supported by the short talk. Clearly, the speaker states that reading, writing and arithmetic should be taught in the primary grades, K-3 (C). Choices (A) and (D) are not supported at all. Choice (B) has some support, but the speaker thinks these subjects should be taught at a later time—after grade three.

35. **(C)** You are to pick the choice that is supported by the short talk. Choice (D) is a likely correct answer, but this statement by the speaker is secondary to the need for primary children to master the basic skills first, choice (C). The other choices are not supported.

36. **(C)** You are to pick the choice that is supported by the short talk. Choices (A), (B) and (D) are not supported. The speaker does, however, imply that primary grade children should not be overloaded at the expense of missing basic skills, choice (C). Even though the speaker labels social studies and science as "junk," he/she does not suggest that the subjects should not be taught.

37. **(D)** You are to pick the choice that is supported by the short talk. Choices (A), (B) and (C) are too limited because the talk mentions all of them as problems that confront the schools. The correct answer is choice (D), problems that impact the schools.

38. **(D)** You are to pick the choice that is supported by the short talk. The speaker clearly identifies low academic achievement as the problem that has probably impacted the schools the most, choice (D). The speaker indicates that crime, teenage pregnancy, and drug abuse have heavily impacted the schools, but low academic achievement is listed as having the most impact.

39. **(C)** You are to pick the choice that is supported by the short talk. The speaker clearly states that students do not read, write, and think as well as they did years ago, choice (C). Choices (A) and (B) are correct, but they are too limited. Choice (D) is never mentioned.

40. **(B)** You are to pick the choice that is supported by the short talk. Based on the information given only choice (B) can be the correct answer. Choices (A), (C) and (D) may be true, but they are not supported.

Section 2: Reading

1.   **(A)**   This question requires you to identify the main idea. You may be led to choose (E) as the main idea because research studies do support the idea that in-services are inadequate, but the research studies specifically support the main idea, choice (A)—*In-service training for teachers is a waste of time*. The research studies evidence this notion. Choice (B) is not supported at all. You cannot assume that in-services are not necessary just because teachers view them as a waste of time. Choices (C) and (D) are too specific to be main ideas. They serve as support for the main idea.

2.   **(E)**   If you searched the second paragraph for the main idea, you didn't find it because here the main idea is unstated. It is implied. You may have thought that choice (A) is the main idea, but this choice speaks to training of teachers in general. The paragraph and the entire passage speak specifically to in-service training, training that occurs while teachers are in-service (teaching). Choices (B), (C) and (D) are too specific to be the main idea. They are supporting details for choice (E) the implied main idea.

3.   **(B)**   This question requires you to make an assumption about teachers and in-service training. Assumptions are unstated, yet enough information is given to support them. Choices (A), (C), (D) and (E) are all inappropriate assumptions because nothing in the passage supports them. Because the author states that present in-services do not address the needs of teachers, it can be safely assumed that teachers are not surveyed to determine their in-service needs—choice(B).

4.   **(D)**   Choices (A), (B), (C) and (E) are all facts. The passage states that teachers are forced to participate (mandatorily)—choice (E). Research supports choices (A), (B) and (C). However, choice (D) has no support at all. The passage does not state that in-services, in general, are unimportant. The passage views in-services, in their present state, as being worthless. Choice (D) is the opinion.

5.   **(E)**   A good paraphrase sufficiently summarizes what is said or written. The main point expressed in this passage is that principals think teachers who can keep children quiet are good teachers. Choices (A), (B), (C), and (D) do not adequately address the main point. Choice (E) is the appropriate answer— *Principals equate competence with the ability to discipline children.*

6.   **(E)**   This question requires an evaluation based on your interpretation of the passage. It is apparent that this principal is concerned about things which are important but things which do not directly translate into effective teaching. He/she is satisfied as long as the building is clean, the children are quiet, and the teachers do not disagree. Effective instruction is his/her least concern— choice (E)

7.   **(E)**   This question asks you to analyze the way in which the author organizes the passage. Choice (A) is not correct because the listing of findings from the research is not chronological. Choice (B) is incorrect because the issue is important, and the passage consists of a listing of findings, not of ideas. The list of findings are statements based on research data. Choices (C) and (D) are incorrect because no general summary or step-by-step demonstration

takes place. Choice (E) explains the organization: A list of related arguments about research findings support an initial concern about the effectiveness of diagnosis.

8.   **(E)**   This question requires you to identify the author's purpose for writing it. The author does not tell you why he/she is writing this passage; but he/she does state that for teachers to be effective in the classroom, they must engage in continuous diagnosis. Therefore, it can be assumed that the author wants to help teachers improve instruction—choice (E). Choices (A) and (B) may be true, but they have no support. Choice (C) is not appropriate because there is no need to inform parents about the diagnosis since they will not be directly involved in diagnosis. Choice (D) may be true, but it is a logical choice. The correct answer is (E).

9.   **(C)**   This question requires you to identify the main idea of the passage. Choices (A), (B) and (D) are supporting details for the main idea—choice (C)—In order for teachers to provide effective instruction, they must continuously engage in diagnosis. Main ideas are usually supported by details. Choices (A), (B), and (D) have no support. Choice (E) is incorrect because there is no suggestion that teachers involve themselves in research activities. The focal point is on the results of research, not an established need to perform research.

10.   **(D)**   The best response to this question is choice (D). The author supported his argument with a research study conducted by "specialists," but did not, at all, delve into the procedures, sample population, or evaluation methods used by the researchers. Nothing is known about the reliability or validity of the study, the expertise of the researchers, the principles upon which the study was based, or the motivation of the people performing the inquiry. More information is needed before an educated evaluation of this argument can be reached. Choice (A) is inappropriate because researchers, not the author, conducted the study. Also, not enough is known about the sample to determine whether or not it is, indeed, represetative. Choices (B), (C) and (E) are inappropriate because they directly conflict with the reasoning behind the correct answer, (D).

11.   **(B)**   The answer here is fairly straightforward. It can be inferred that the things which make people great are constructive criticisms—choice (B). Choices (C) and (E) may be adequate, but they are not explicit enough to convey the need for one to accept constructive criticisms. The negativism makes choice (D) inappropriate. Choice (A) is incorrect because the author explicitly states that the person who only accepts compliments cannot grow.

12.   **(E)**   This question requires you to choose the occupation to which this passage would *least* apply. The question requires you to apply information interpreted. You must choose the occupation which offers the least opportunity for error. That would be choice (E)—the assembly line worker, who does the same thing over and over on a daily basis, has less chance of making a mistake. That's not true of teachers, doctors, engineers, and lawyers because of the variety of situations and people they encounter.

13.   **(E)**   The question requires you to identify how the message conveyed in this passage applies to teaching. Choices (A) and (B) are inappropriate because the author does not encourage or discourage mistakes. Choices (C) and (D) are inappropriate because people

who seek praise and practice perfection generally find it difficult to accept constructive criticisms. Teachers can apply the message conveyed in this passage by instilling in their students the idea that everyone should acknowledge his shortcomings—choice (E).

14. **(B)** This question requires you to identify the tone of the author of this passage. Choice (E) is incorrect because the author does display an explicit mood, "irritating." If the situation is irritating, then it can be assumed that the author is dismayed—choice (B). Choice (A) is incorrect because the author is not indifferent. The author actually takes a stand. The adjectives "surprised" and "ashamed" that are used in choices (C) and (D) do not necessarily translate into dismay. Therefore, these two choices are inappropriate.

15. **(A)** The main idea of this passage is choice (A)—*Athletes who cannot make the grades should not be allowed to participate*. Choices (B), (C), (D) and (E) are supporting details that are too limited to serve as main ideas. There is no support for either of these as the main idea, and main idea must be supported.

16. **(E)** According to the author, it is irritating to observe star quarterbacks who can't read. The author is not saying that star quarterbacks, in general, can't read. This is an example of the problem at hand. The same is true of the other statements: star running backs who can't write; star fullbacks who can't speak; and outstanding pitchers who can't add, subtract, or multiply. These are merely examples of the problem detailed by the author. The main idea is (E)—*The purpose of school is to manufacture and nurture productive citizens*.

17. **(D)** Choices (A), (B), (C) and (E) are all supporting details for the main idea. The central idea or thought of this passage is not about dumb jocks, lack of basic skills among athletes, producing professional athletes, or producing productive citizens. The main idea is choice (D)—*Grade Requirements for Athletes*.

18. **(E)** The message of grade requirements for participation should also apply to the band and the cheerleading squad. Both of these organizations require large amounts of time for participation. Persons with low grades should use their time to study. The correct answer for this question is choice (E). Belonging to the science club does not usually require lots of time, and a person aligned with such a club just might improve his/her grades and/or interest in science.

19. **(D)** The main idea in this passage is implied, not directly stated. If you carefully read the passage, though, you had no problem selecting the best choice for the main idea. Choice (A) is true; choice (B) is true; choice (C) is true; and choice (E) is also true, even though this statement is not made in the passage. However, none of these is the main idea. The central thought centers around students performing tremendously better when given all of the time they need. A second testing demonstrated that timed reading tests test speed instead of reading skill—choice (D).

20. **(E)** The answer here is obvious: If you are a slow reader, you will be penalized on timed reading tests—choice (E). The object of this passage is to show that students do better when given ample time. This passage is not intended to show how poorly students performed, and it certainly does not address the importance of reading tests.

21. **(E)** Since parents, teachers, and counselors will have access to students' scores, they all need to understand that timed reading tests favor fast readers. This prevents the pressure usually applied when children do not perform well. The correct answer is (E).

22. **(C)** It is very clear that the author adequately supports the argument that timed reading tests test speed instead of reading skill—choice (C). Even though only seniors took the test and only 144 students took the test, the difference in scores from pre-test to post-test was so large that the time element had to make a difference. No, the evidence is not shallow.

23. **(D)** This question requires you to identify the main idea of the passage. Choices (A), (B), (C), and (E) do not have enough support to serve as main ideas. They are supporting ideas for choice (D), the main idea. The opening sentence of this passage speaks of school, in general, as being boring.

24. **(E)** Certainly, the author is not encouraged by what was seen —choice (A). At the end of the passage, several recommendations were made, suggesting that the author was discouraged. Choice (B) is inappropriate because the author is not indifferent. Indifference suggests that one is accepting of a situation, no matter what the outcome might be. The author is not angry—choice (C) and the author is really not shocked—choice (D) because it was rumored that school is boring. The author appears saddened—choice (E).

25. **(A)** The author's evidence is not circumstantial because a visit was actually made to the class. Choice (D) is incorrect because the author does provide some support, but that support cannot be considered overwheliming—choice (C), or even sufficient— choice (B). Clearly, more evidence is needed—choice (A).

26. **(D)** This question requires you to identify a major detail in the passage. Choices (A), (B), C) and (E) are all details presented by the author, but the number of students in the class was never mentioned—choice (D).

27. **(D)** This question requires you to identify the best title for the passage. This passage involves two things: (1) teachers as advocates and (2) competency testing. In the opening sentence, the author pleads for teachers to stand up as advocates against competency testing and tells why they should do so. Clearly, the best title is choice (D). Choice (A) is not the best title because the passage does not encourage colleges and universities to be advocates against competency testing. The passage only mentions the embarrassment they must feel. Choice (B) is too limited because the passage does not deal with teachers' attitudes. Choice (C) is a correct statement that's supported, but this choice serves only to support the main idea. Choice (E) is much too broad.

28. **(E)** It is clear that paragraph 3 provides the best support. Explained in this paragraph are many qualities which cannot be tested. This is sufficient evidence that competency testing does not insure excellent teachers—choice (C). Choosing the correct answer for item #28 requires an evaluation of evidence presented.

29. **(E)** This question requires you to identify a detail in the passage. Choices (A), (B) and (D) are never mentioned in the passage. The correct choice is (E).

30. **(A)** This question requires an analysis of competence tests in terms of their weaknesses. Choices (B), (D) and (E) are inappropriate because they are not supported by the passage. Also, neither is an implied weakness. Choice (C) is mentioned in the passage, but embarrassment is a human quality, not a quality of competency tests. The most appropriate answer is choice (A)—*Teaching requires many qualities that cannot be adequately measured by tests.*

Section 3: Writing

Part A

1. **(B)** The error in this sentence occurs at (B). The article **a** precedes words that begin with consonant sounds: "Ms. Randall is a good teacher." The article **an** precedes words that begin with vowel sounds: "Ms. Randall, **a** fifth-grade teacher at Burt Elementary School is an excellent mathematician who deserves lots of praise."

2. **(A)** The error in this sentence occurs at (A). Except means excluding: "All students attended the science fair except Mary." "Accept" means to take or receive: "The top student in the history class refused to accept the "Scholar Award" because he had cheated on the final examination."

3. **(C)** The error in this sentence occurs at (C). Since consensus means a general opinion, the phrase "consensus of opinion" is wordiness. The word consensus, by virtue of its definition, can stand alone: "It's the union's consensus that the principal should be dismissed for reasons that suggest immoral behavior."

4. **(A)** The error in this sentence occurs at (A). "Being that" is bad diction. The sentence should read: "Since Ms. Johnson has been tardy for six consecutive days, the principal has suggested that she appear before the faculty's disciplinary committee."

5. **(D)** The error in this sentence occurs at (D). This sentence contains faulty parallelism. Ms. Westbrook enjoys singing, dancing, and walking, not singing, dancing, and daily walks.

6. **(A)** The error in this sentence occurs at (A). "No" suggests disagreement or refusal: "No! I will not help you with your homework." "Know" suggests knowledge of or consciousness: "I know why Ms. Price is such a good teacher: She is well-trained and works very hard to motivate her students."

7. **(B)** The error in this sentence occurs at (B). Less refers to amount: "The janitor ate less cake." Fewer refers to number: "At the school's annual party, the janitor to everybody's surprise, ate fewer pieces of cake because he's attempting to lose weight."

8. **(D)** The error in this sentence occurs at (D). Etc., which means "and others," should not be used in formal writing. The sentence should read: "While attending Harvard University Juan took English, math, Spanish, science, and other general courses."

9. **(B)** The error in this sentence occurs at (B). Enthused should never be used in formal writing. The sentence should read: "At the beginning of the school year all of Ms. Johnson's students were enthusiastic because they knew that their teacher was a caring person."

10. **(C)** The error in this sentence occurs at (C). A portion of this sentence, "where he lives," is not parallel to name and social security number. The sentence should read: "Teachers are constantly reminded that information about students is confidential; each student's name, social security number, and address are the only information that can be given."

11. **(D)** The error in this sentence occurs at (D). Again, a lack of parallelism exists. The end of the sentence should read:

".....two areas—how to discipline and how to teach effectively." or
".....two areas—discipline and effective teaching."

12. **(C)** The error in this sentence occurs at (C). This sentence contains faulty comparison. When comparing two persons as two things, "better" is the correct word to use: "Given that two teacher applicants share equal credentials, the superintendent will generally hire the one who uses the better English." When more than two persons or two things are being compared, "best" is the appropriate word to use: "Of all the children in the class Mary is the best math student."

13. **(B)** The error in this sentence occurs at (B). Amount refers to quantity in mass. Number refers to persons and objects that can be counted: "The teachers brought a large amount of paper and a large number of pencils."

14. **(A)** The error in this sentence occurs at (A). "Every" is singular, denoting each one, each teacher. Therefore the antecedent for "every" should be "she"; not "they": "Every teacher without question, thinks she is the best teacher in the world; a very general belief that is too difficult to prove."

15. **(D)** The error in this sentence occurs at (D). The request for no "hall walking" was made by the principal (possessive). The sentence should read: "Despite the fact that the principal has warned students about hall walking, they continue, knowing the consequences of ignoring the principal's request."

16. **(D)** The error in this sentence occurs at (D). Loose means not tight. The teacher did not want to lose her job.

17. **(D)** The error in this sentence occurs at (D). Then means "at that time" or "next in sequence." "I went to James Elementary, then I stopped by the administration building." "Than" is used to show comparisons: "The children at Westberry Elementary School possess such good manners that Ms. Twiggs would rather stop teaching than change schools."

18. **(B)** The error in this sentence occurs at (B). The word "reason" suggests a cause or a purpose. Therefore, it is not necessary to use "because": "The reason Ms. Flix no longer teaches is that children are too bad, and they don't perform well academically."

or

"Ms. Flix no longer teaches because children are too unmannerly, and they don't perform well academically."

In neither of the examples are the words reason and because used together. They share the same meaning.

19. **(C)** The error in this sentence occurs at (C). "Too" is used to show excessiveness (too hot, too cold, too slow). Since no element of excessiveness is apparent in this sentence, to should be used: "To teach or not to teach is a dilemma for me."

20. **(D)** The error in this sentence occurs at (D). So means therefore: "I was tired so I didn't go to school today." A better word here would be very: "Wrote one little boy: "My teacher works hard every day; since we're not the best children in the world, I'm sure that by the end of the day she is very tired."

21. **(C)** The error in this sentence occurs at (C). Since the verb went is in the past tense, the verb "soaks" must also be in the past tense: "After an unusually tedious day at school, the teacher went home and soaked in a tub of hot water."

22. **(A)** The error in this sentence occurs at (A). The "where" is an unnecessary addition to the sentence and can be deleted: "The school Mr. James' children attend is located too far from the main section of town."

23. **(B)** The error in this sentence occurs at (B). A parallelism problem exists because "sounded" is in the past tense and will rush is in the future tense. The sentence should read: "After the school bell sounded, the children rushed to catch the bus which is usually parked on the north side of the school."

24. **(A)** The error in this sentence occurs at (A). There is no such word as irregardless. Regardless is sufficient.

25. **(D)** The error in this sentence occurs at (D). Capitol refers to a statehouse where legislators meet: "The teachers stood on the steps of the capitol and demanded a raise." Capital refers to the cities that are capitals of states, and it also refers to assets (money, property): "The teachers stood on the steps of the capitol and demanded more capital."

Part B

26. **(C)** Sentence 26 is not complete. It is a fragment. A complete sentence contains a subject and a verb, and it expresses a complete thought, Choices (A), (B), (D) and (E) are all incorrect because they do not contain verbs, and they do not express complete thoughts. Choice (C) is the correct answer. In addition to expressing a complete thought, the sentence contains a subject "teaching" and a verb "may require."

27. **(D)** This sentence is unclear because a teacher is not an occupation. A teacher is a person who performs the occupation of teaching. Choices (A) and (C) are incorrect because a teacher is not an occupation. Choices (B) and (E) are incorrect because one cannot be an occupation. It's impossible for a person to be teaching. That person, however, may be a teacher. Choice (D) is the correct answer.

28. **(E)** Sentence 28 is a simple sentence which contains two ideas—the best teacher and the prettiest lady. It is best to write two simple sentences, one idea in each; or one might choose to develop one compound sentence containing both ideas. Choice (A) is incorrect because both ideas are expressed in one simple sentence. This should not be done. Choices (B) and (D) are incorrect because each expresses only one idea. Choice (C) is incorrect because the sentence contains no verb. The apostrophes attached to Ms. Johnson makes that noun possessive. It is not a contraction for Ms. Johnson is, as many people tend to believe. Choice (E) is the correct answer.

29. **(D)** Sentence 29 suggests, according to its structure, that the principal was unable to control the class. This sentence contains a misplaced modifier. In all sentence structures, modifiers must be placed near the words they complement. Choice (A) is incorrect because it is merely a replica of the underlined sentence portion which is in error. Choice (B) is incorrect for two reasons: It suggests, according to structure, that the principal could not control the class. Also, math should not be capitalized because it is a common noun. Only proper nouns should be capitalized. Choice (C) is incorrect because the word principle refers to a rule, to a law, to a doctrine—not to the leader of a school (principal). Choice (E) is incorrect because "Math Teacher" does not specify a specific teacher by name and should not be capitalized. Choice (D) is the correct answer.

30. **(B)** The appositive, "the name of the teacher next door" suggests that the word name is pregnant and will be unable to complete the school year. "The name of" is not necessary in order for the appositive to make sense. Choice (A) is incorrect. It is a replica of the underlined sentence portion which is in error. Choice (C) is incorrect because teacher is a common noun and should not be capitalized. Choice (D) is incorrect because the expression, "the teacher's name," is not necessary since the name is given. Choice (E) is incorrect for two reasons: The expression, "the teachers' name" is not necessary since the name is given. Also, teachers' is plural possessive. Ms. Prater is singular, one person. Choice (B) is the correct answer.

31. **(D)** It is impossible for one to "try to do his best" and at the same time "do his best." The expression "try and" suggests and impossibility. The sentence should read: "Every student should try to do his best to achieve." The correct answer is (D).

32. **(D)** According to the structure of this sentence, the thief was running through the schoolyard with a bat. Instead, the principal had the bat. This is a case of a misplaced modifier. The modifier should be placed near the word it complements. Choice (A) is incorrect because it is a replica of the sentence in error. Choice (B) is incorrect because it contains a misplaced modifier—the thief has the bat instead of the principal. Choice (C) is incorrect because it contains the same misplaced modifier as Choice (B). Also, which cannot be used to refer to a person. Choice (E) is incorrect because the verb phrase "was running" needs a subject. Whom can never be used as a subject. Who is the appropriate pronoun to use. Choice (D) is the correct answer.

33. **(E)** This sentence contains excessive wordiness. The graduating senior is not considering the question. He is considering whether he should go to college. Choices (A), (B), (C) and (D) are all examples of unnecessary wordiness or incorrect grammar. Choice (E) is the correct answer.

34. **(B)** This sentence contains a shift in person—from "one" to "you." The person must remain constant: If "I" do my work, "I" will graduate. Choices (A), (C) and (E) are all incorrect because they contain shifts in person. Choice (D) is incorrect for two reasons: shift in person and subject verb disagreement. "Do" is used with plural subjects. Does is reserved for singular subjects. Choice (B) is the correct answer.

35. **(D)** This sentence contains a shift in tense (time). The time shifts from past tense (knocked) to the present tense (comes). Choice (A) is incorrect because it is a replica of the sentence in error—shift in time. Choice (B) is incorrect for two reasons: shift in time and subject-verb disagreement. "Come" is used with plural subjects. "Comes" is used with singular subjects. Since he is singular, the singular verb "comes" should have been used, even though it is in the wrong tense. Choice (C) is incorrect because of word choice. "Principle" is a rule, law, or doctrine. In this sentence, reference is made to the leader of a school. "Principal" is the correct word choice. Choice (E) is wrong because of word choice. Then should have been used instead of than. Than references a comparison. No comparison is being made in this sentence. Choice (D) is the correct answer.

36. **(B)** "The Wetherills" is plural, and the verb must agree. Choice (B) correctly changes "is" to "are"; the rest of the sentence is fine. (A) adds the singular "a group" which may make the verb "is" seem right, though it still modifies "The Wetherills" and must agree accordingly. (C) corrects the verb problem, but misplaces the clause "five brothers who ranched in the area" at the end of the sentence where it is unclear. (D) fails to correct the verb disagreement and places the clause at the end of the sentence, which alters the sense.

37. **(A)** Choice (A) best continues the topic of Sentence 9, which concerns the cultural achievements of the Anasazi, and provides a nice transition toward the final sentence. (B) concerns an entirely different historical epoch, and is clearly irrelevant. (C) may fit somewhere in this essay, but not between Sentences 9 and 10, where this new fact would seem obtrusive. (D) introduces the personal voice of the author which is contrary to the expository tone in the passage thus far, and which would not fit between the factual content of Sentences 9 and 10. (E) would be a good topic sentence for a new paragraph, but would not be good here.

38. **(A)** Sentence 4 is a dependent prepositional clause and would be best added onto Sentence 3.

39. **(C)** The years of the Anasazi's zenith are best set off by commas and turned into a prepositional phrase, and of the two choices which do this, (C) uses "from," which is more appropriate than (D) "being." Without the punctuation, choice (A) is awkward; if the phrase were set off by commas, it would be acceptable, though (C) is more concise. (B) is just wrong; from the context of the passage it is clear that the Anasazi thrived in the years A.D and not B.C.

40. **(A)** Quotation marks are occasionally used for an ironic effect. In the passage the author places "Native Americans" in quotation marks because they are not truly native (A). They migrated to North America across a land bridge from Asia. (B), (C), and (D) may all be true, but they are not appropriate given the context of the passage. (E) is simply wrong.

41. **(C)** "Children's early teens" is much neater and clearer than "the early teens of the children." (A) introduces unnecessary punctuation. (B) is nonsensical ("continue through the children"). (D) adds "on" which does nothing but further convolute the original sentence.

42. **(D)** (D) makes a clear and simple sentence out of the clumsy original. The structures of (A), (B), and (C) duplicate the confusions of the original.

43. **(E)** "Showing" in the original sentence is clearly wrong, and any of these three forms would be acceptable.

44. **(C)** Sentence 12 introduces a new issue in the middle of the paragraph and would best be eliminated.

45. **(D)** The idea in Sentence 9 about company morale and employee loyalty would be best placed in support of the ideas in Sentence 11, that the workers feel that the company has taken interest in them. "Therefore" sets up a logical relation which is not present between Sentences 8 and 9.

Section 4: Essay

The following essay received scores at the highest end of the scale used in NTE essay scoring.

Essay A

In order to ensure that my students' academic performance reflects their potential, I will take the following steps: thorough diagnosis, active teaching, and constant monitoring of students' work.

On a daily basis, I will engage in thorough diagnosis to determine if my students are benefiting from instruction. For those students who are not benefiting from instruction, I will make immediate adjustments to meet their needs. These adjustments may mean modification in terms of teaching strategies, materials being used, lesson plans, the amount of work required, or even the learning environment. Teachers must understand that diagnosis provides a blueprint for instruction. Without diagnosis, students' needs cannot be adequately determined and ultimately met.

On a daily basis, I will engage in active teaching. I will not rely on excessive seat work, involving students in workbook sessions that are boring and uninteresting. Instead, I will actively teach required concepts, test to see if these concepts have been mastered, and reteach, if necessary. Children are sent to school to be taught, not to be bored to death with useless workbook activities that provide time for teachers to grade their papers and complete other activities. If teachers actively teach, children will learn.

On a daily basis, I will monitor my students' work to make sure that they stay on task. Research indicates that when teachers constantly monitor the work of their students, test scores improve. Teachers must regularly check students' work to make sure that assignments are completed and are completed correctly.

I believe that by engaging in daily diagnosis, actively teaching, and constantly monitoring classroom work, my students will do well academically and will adequately perform on any required standardized tests. I observed these steps in operation during my student teaching. They actually work!

Explanation of Essay A

The writer addresses the topic very well, meeting all of the conditions specified in the topic. The writer, in paragraph one, outlines the steps that he will take to ensure that his students' academic performance reflects their potential. In paragraph two, the writer addresses the first step, provides an explanation and the required justification. In paragraph three, the writer addresses the second step, provides an explanation and the required justification; and paragraph four contains the fourth step, an explanation, and the required justification. The final paragraph is a summary of the entire essay.

It is apparent that this essay is well organized and is free of grammatical errors, including spelling. Ideas are presented logically, and any audience would be able to follow and understand such a presentation. Even though the writer is a bit wordy, this verbosity does not detract from the meaning of the essay.

Please note that each paragraph has a main idea (one of the three steps mentioned), and the main idea in each paragraph is supported by an explanation and justification. Too many ideas in a paragraph may confuse the reader. If the paragraph is about *hats*, only hats can be discussed in that paragraph. If you want to talk about *shoes*, you must develop another paragraph that addresses nothing but the topic of shoes.

The following essay received scores in the middle of the NTE scoring scale.

Essay B

I feel first I must let children know that education is not a game. I will start with a firm foundation that is a mixture of work and patience. By this, I mean children need to know school is serious business, and the purpose of education is to learn and become economically stable. I will also let them know what my role as a teacher is: to promote learning and understanding. I would let each child know that he is teachable, and he can learn. Implementing confidence in children first is very important. Children must first know they are capable individuals with the ability to do anything. Once this foundation is established I can begin teaching.

First, in order to ensure that my students perform academically, I must know something about each child. It is important to know what kind of background experiences each child has and what kind of living arrangments exist. By doing this, I will know how to approach each child and apply the principles associated with meeting individual needs. This is very important if children are going to improve academically.

Next, I need to find out where each child is academically and work from that point forward. This means that I must diagnose first to see what each student knows already. Without this information, I will not know what to teach.

Finally, I must make my teaching sessions interesting. I would use many angles to bring the lesson across to students.

So, I would learn several ways to get the information over to students. The same approach does not work for all students. This variety helps when students begin to get bored. We must make allowence for diversaty in students.

I understand that teaching is not a easy task, but those who decide to dedicate themselfs to this profession should use all resources available.

Explanation of Essay B

This essay meets the conditions of the topic: steps to be used to ensure academic performance equal to students' potentials, explanation of each step, and justification for each step. However, problems exist with the initial and final paragraphs. Too many ideas are presented in the first paragraph. The writer talks about building a firm foundation that has a mixture of work and patience. One would think that the remaining part of the paragraph will address a firm foundation of work and patience. Instead, the writer talks about the role of the teacher and implementing confidence in children. Too many ideas are presented in paragraph one. This paragraph should serve as an introduction to the entire essay, presenting the topic to be discussed.

The final paragraph should summarize the essay. In this case, a different concept is discussed—dedication. In the summary, the writer should have briefly mentioned the suggested steps as ways to ensure that students perform academically, along with a one-sentence summary of the effects of these recommendations.

The final two paragraphs contain misspelled words (allowence, diversaty, and themselfs), but considering the 30-minute time limit, these may be overlooked, given the possibility that the time factor may have forced these spelling errors.

Poor word choice and limited vocabulary are evident throughout the essay, but these do not cause a degree of vagueness that misleads the reader.

The following essay received scores at the lowest end of the NTE scoring scale.

Essay C

To ensure that my students academic performance reflects their potential, I would: First and foremost, start where the students are. All of the students will not be similar in their capability levels, therefore, detecting where the student is is vital. To implement this I would diagnose their strength levels by administering relatively simple tests and tasks. Afterwards, I would devise a chart that distinguished the students strengths and weaknesses. This will allow me to monitor the students progress. Then, I would ensure that the students have ample opportunity to think. Based upon what level the student is at, I would utilize group and individual assignments and projects for each individual.

Explanation of Essay C

In addition to problems with sentence structure, word choice, punctuation, and general use of the English language, the writer has failed to meet the conditions outlined in the topic. In reality, the writer mentions only one step and does not do a good job of explaining and justifying it. More than one step should have been recommended—at least three.

This essay lacks depth, fullness, and organization. It is definitely evident that the writer is not skilled at presentation of ideas in any form. This is a one-paragraph essay that fails to meet the standards of formal writing.

NTE Test of General Knowledge

TEST 4 – ANSWER SHEET

Section 1: Social Studies

1. Ⓐ Ⓑ Ⓒ Ⓓ Ⓔ
2. Ⓐ Ⓑ Ⓒ Ⓓ Ⓔ
3. Ⓐ Ⓑ Ⓒ Ⓓ Ⓔ
4. Ⓐ Ⓑ Ⓒ Ⓓ Ⓔ
5. Ⓐ Ⓑ Ⓒ Ⓓ Ⓔ
6. Ⓐ Ⓑ Ⓒ Ⓓ Ⓔ
7. Ⓐ Ⓑ Ⓒ Ⓓ Ⓔ
8. Ⓐ Ⓑ Ⓒ Ⓓ Ⓔ
9. Ⓐ Ⓑ Ⓒ Ⓓ Ⓔ
10. Ⓐ Ⓑ Ⓒ Ⓓ Ⓔ
11. Ⓐ Ⓑ Ⓒ Ⓓ Ⓔ
12. Ⓐ Ⓑ Ⓒ Ⓓ Ⓔ
13. Ⓐ Ⓑ Ⓒ Ⓓ Ⓔ
14. Ⓐ Ⓑ Ⓒ Ⓓ Ⓔ
15. Ⓐ Ⓑ Ⓒ Ⓓ Ⓔ
16. Ⓐ Ⓑ Ⓒ Ⓓ Ⓔ
17. Ⓐ Ⓑ Ⓒ Ⓓ Ⓔ
18. Ⓐ Ⓑ Ⓒ Ⓓ Ⓔ
19. Ⓐ Ⓑ Ⓒ Ⓓ Ⓔ
20. Ⓐ Ⓑ Ⓒ Ⓓ Ⓔ
21. Ⓐ Ⓑ Ⓒ Ⓓ Ⓔ
22. Ⓐ Ⓑ Ⓒ Ⓓ Ⓔ
23. Ⓐ Ⓑ Ⓒ Ⓓ Ⓔ
24. Ⓐ Ⓑ Ⓒ Ⓓ Ⓔ
25. Ⓐ Ⓑ Ⓒ Ⓓ Ⓔ
26. Ⓐ Ⓑ Ⓒ Ⓓ Ⓔ
27. Ⓐ Ⓑ Ⓒ Ⓓ Ⓔ
28. Ⓐ Ⓑ Ⓒ Ⓓ Ⓔ
29. Ⓐ Ⓑ Ⓒ Ⓓ Ⓔ
30. Ⓐ Ⓑ Ⓒ Ⓓ Ⓔ

Section 2: Math

1. Ⓐ Ⓑ Ⓒ Ⓓ Ⓔ
2. Ⓐ Ⓑ Ⓒ Ⓓ Ⓔ
3. Ⓐ Ⓑ Ⓒ Ⓓ Ⓔ
4. Ⓐ Ⓑ Ⓒ Ⓓ Ⓔ
5. Ⓐ Ⓑ Ⓒ Ⓓ Ⓔ
6. Ⓐ Ⓑ Ⓒ Ⓓ Ⓔ
7. Ⓐ Ⓑ Ⓒ Ⓓ Ⓔ
8. Ⓐ Ⓑ Ⓒ Ⓓ Ⓔ
9. Ⓐ Ⓑ Ⓒ Ⓓ Ⓔ

10. Ⓐ Ⓑ Ⓒ Ⓓ Ⓔ
11. Ⓐ Ⓑ Ⓒ Ⓓ Ⓔ
12. Ⓐ Ⓑ Ⓒ Ⓓ Ⓔ
13. Ⓐ Ⓑ Ⓒ Ⓓ Ⓔ
14. Ⓐ Ⓑ Ⓒ Ⓓ Ⓔ
15. Ⓐ Ⓑ Ⓒ Ⓓ Ⓔ
16. Ⓐ Ⓑ Ⓒ Ⓓ Ⓔ
17. Ⓐ Ⓑ Ⓒ Ⓓ Ⓔ
18. Ⓐ Ⓑ Ⓒ Ⓓ Ⓔ
19. Ⓐ Ⓑ Ⓒ Ⓓ Ⓔ
20. Ⓐ Ⓑ Ⓒ Ⓓ Ⓔ
21. Ⓐ Ⓑ Ⓒ Ⓓ Ⓔ
22. Ⓐ Ⓑ Ⓒ Ⓓ Ⓔ
23. Ⓐ Ⓑ Ⓒ Ⓓ Ⓔ
24. Ⓐ Ⓑ Ⓒ Ⓓ Ⓔ
25. Ⓐ Ⓑ Ⓒ Ⓓ Ⓔ

Section 3: Literature and Fine Arts

1. Ⓐ Ⓑ Ⓒ Ⓓ Ⓔ
2. Ⓐ Ⓑ Ⓒ Ⓓ Ⓔ
3. Ⓐ Ⓑ Ⓒ Ⓓ Ⓔ
4. Ⓐ Ⓑ Ⓒ Ⓓ Ⓔ
5. Ⓐ Ⓑ Ⓒ Ⓓ Ⓔ
6. Ⓐ Ⓑ Ⓒ Ⓓ Ⓔ
7. Ⓐ Ⓑ Ⓒ Ⓓ Ⓔ
8. Ⓐ Ⓑ Ⓒ Ⓓ Ⓔ
9. Ⓐ Ⓑ Ⓒ Ⓓ Ⓔ
10. Ⓐ Ⓑ Ⓒ Ⓓ Ⓔ
11. Ⓐ Ⓑ Ⓒ Ⓓ Ⓔ
12. Ⓐ Ⓑ Ⓒ Ⓓ Ⓔ
13. Ⓐ Ⓑ Ⓒ Ⓓ Ⓔ
14. Ⓐ Ⓑ Ⓒ Ⓓ Ⓔ
15. Ⓐ Ⓑ Ⓒ Ⓓ Ⓔ
16. Ⓐ Ⓑ Ⓒ Ⓓ Ⓔ
17. Ⓐ Ⓑ Ⓒ Ⓓ Ⓔ
18. Ⓐ Ⓑ Ⓒ Ⓓ Ⓔ
19. Ⓐ Ⓑ Ⓒ Ⓓ Ⓔ
20. Ⓐ Ⓑ Ⓒ Ⓓ Ⓔ
21. Ⓐ Ⓑ Ⓒ Ⓓ Ⓔ
22. Ⓐ Ⓑ Ⓒ Ⓓ Ⓔ
23. Ⓐ Ⓑ Ⓒ Ⓓ Ⓔ
24. Ⓐ Ⓑ Ⓒ Ⓓ Ⓔ
25. Ⓐ Ⓑ Ⓒ Ⓓ Ⓔ
26. Ⓐ Ⓑ Ⓒ Ⓓ Ⓔ
27. Ⓐ Ⓑ Ⓒ Ⓓ Ⓔ
28. Ⓐ Ⓑ Ⓒ Ⓓ Ⓔ
29. Ⓐ Ⓑ Ⓒ Ⓓ Ⓔ
30. Ⓐ Ⓑ Ⓒ Ⓓ Ⓔ
31. Ⓐ Ⓑ Ⓒ Ⓓ Ⓔ
32. Ⓐ Ⓑ Ⓒ Ⓓ Ⓔ
33. Ⓐ Ⓑ Ⓒ Ⓓ Ⓔ
34. Ⓐ Ⓑ Ⓒ Ⓓ Ⓔ
35. Ⓐ Ⓑ Ⓒ Ⓓ Ⓔ

Section 4: Science

1. Ⓐ Ⓑ Ⓒ Ⓓ Ⓔ
2. Ⓐ Ⓑ Ⓒ Ⓓ Ⓔ
3. Ⓐ Ⓑ Ⓒ Ⓓ Ⓔ
4. Ⓐ Ⓑ Ⓒ Ⓓ Ⓔ
5. Ⓐ Ⓑ Ⓒ Ⓓ Ⓔ
6. Ⓐ Ⓑ Ⓒ Ⓓ Ⓔ
7. Ⓐ Ⓑ Ⓒ Ⓓ Ⓔ
8. Ⓐ Ⓑ Ⓒ Ⓓ Ⓔ
9. Ⓐ Ⓑ Ⓒ Ⓓ Ⓔ
10. Ⓐ Ⓑ Ⓒ Ⓓ Ⓔ
11. Ⓐ Ⓑ Ⓒ Ⓓ Ⓔ
12. Ⓐ Ⓑ Ⓒ Ⓓ Ⓔ
13. Ⓐ Ⓑ Ⓒ Ⓓ Ⓔ
14. Ⓐ Ⓑ Ⓒ Ⓓ Ⓔ
15. Ⓐ Ⓑ Ⓒ Ⓓ Ⓔ
16. Ⓐ Ⓑ Ⓒ Ⓓ Ⓔ
17. Ⓐ Ⓑ Ⓒ Ⓓ Ⓔ
18. Ⓐ Ⓑ Ⓒ Ⓓ Ⓔ
19. Ⓐ Ⓑ Ⓒ Ⓓ Ⓔ
20. Ⓐ Ⓑ Ⓒ Ⓓ Ⓔ
21. Ⓐ Ⓑ Ⓒ Ⓓ Ⓔ
22. Ⓐ Ⓑ Ⓒ Ⓓ Ⓔ
23. Ⓐ Ⓑ Ⓒ Ⓓ Ⓔ
24. Ⓐ Ⓑ Ⓒ Ⓓ Ⓔ
25. Ⓐ Ⓑ Ⓒ Ⓓ Ⓔ
26. Ⓐ Ⓑ Ⓒ Ⓓ Ⓔ
27. Ⓐ Ⓑ Ⓒ Ⓓ Ⓔ
28. Ⓐ Ⓑ Ⓒ Ⓓ Ⓔ
29. Ⓐ Ⓑ Ⓒ Ⓓ Ⓔ
30. Ⓐ Ⓑ Ⓒ Ⓓ Ⓔ

NTE CORE BATTERY–Test 4
TEST OF GENERAL KNOWLEDGE
Section 1: Social Studies

TIME: 30 Minutes
30 Questions

DIRECTIONS: Each of the following questions and incomplete statements is followed by five answer choices. Select the choice which best answers each question.

---

1. Which of the following does **not** fall within the authority of most state governors?
   - (A) Name a person to fill the unexpired term of one of the state's U.S. Senators
   - (B) Call out the national guard to quell civil unrest
   - (C) Veto laws passed by the legislature
   - (D) Pardon a prisoner or reduce the sentence
   - (E) Make foreign policy

2. In American government, "Checks and Balances" were developed to
   - (A) regulate the amount of control each branch of government would have.
   - (B) make each branch of government independent from one another.
   - (C) give the president control.
   - (D) give the Supreme Court control.
   - (E) give Congress control.

3. Indicate the correct chronological order of the Presidents.
   - (A) Abraham Lincoln, Woodrow Wilson, Theodore Roosevelt, Franklin D. Roosevelt
   - (B) Abraham Lincoln, Theodore Roosevelt, Woodrow Wilson, Franklin D. Roosevelt
   - (C) Abraham Lincoln, Franklin D. Roosevelt, Woodrow Wilson, Theodore Roosevelt
   - (D) Abraham Lincoln, Woodrow Wilson, Franklin D. Roosevelt, Theodore Roosevelt
   - (E) Abraham Lincoln, Theodore Roosevelt, Franklin D. Roosevelt, Woodrow Wilson

4. The practice of viewing other societies and cultures in terms of one's own cultural standards best describes
   - (A) Ethnocentrism.
   - (B) Institutionalization.
   - (C) Social Placement.
   - (D) Social Control.
   - (E) Bigotry.

5. The capacity of a person or social unit to exercise authority or influence on others, regardless of active resistance best describes

    (A) Wealth.   (D) Status.
    (B) Prestige.   (E) Class.
    (C) Power.

6. The Populists and Progressives are examples of political parties that developed

    (A) as third party organizations outside the Democrat and Republican parties.
    (B) to enlist support for the Democratic and Republican parties.
    (C) to protest the current political parties.
    (D) originally as women's organization.
    (E) Both (A) and (C).

7. Which of the following states was not part of the original 13 colonies?

    (A) Delaware   (D) Maryland
    (B) Virginia   (E) Georgia
    (C) Vermont

8. Which of the following was **not** a cause of the American Revolution?

    (A) Alien and Sedition Acts   (D) Writs of Assistance
    (B) Quebec Act   (E) None of these.
    (C) Stamp Act

9. Directions: RELEVANT information will help us solve a problem or aid us in answering a question. IRRELEVANT information does not aid us in solving a problem or in answering a question. You are trying to answer the question "WHAT DO RECENT TRENDS IN TERRORIST ACTIVITY TELL US ABOUT THE TWO MAIN TYPES OF TERRORISM—LOCAL AND INTERNATIONAL?" To answer the question, you skim through a book containing different kinds of statistical information. Below are a list of the titles of the tables, graphs, and charts. Read each title and select the one that is irrelevant to the above question.

    (A) "Terrorist Acts Involving Citizens or Territories or More Than One Nation (1985)"
    (B) "International Terrorism Around the World (1984)"
    (C) "U.S. Casualties (Wounded and Killed) of International Terrorism (1984)"
    (D) "Local Terrorism Activities During the 1896 Haymarket Square Riot"
    (E) "Types of Terrorist Acts and Their Location (1986)"

10. Directions: Read each of the following statements and select the one that NEITHER supports nor opposes the idea of assimilating immigrants into the United States.

    (A) By being a haven for those being politically and religiously oppressed, the U.S. became rich in a variety of thoughts, ideas, and philosophies.
    (B) If these immigrants are going to live in the U.S. they must learn our language. We don't have the time or the money to make signs that are written in more than one language.
    (C) Between 1868 and 1882, more than 200,000 Chinese came to the U.S.

(D)   Immigrants take jobs away from native Americans, causing higher unemployment. The foreigners come here looking for work. Each job they get is one less job for an American to fill.

(E)   Immigrants should be permitted to settle in their own ethnic groups. In this way, they will be able to enjoy the security of being with their own people. In due time, they will begin to slowly adopt the American way of life.

11.   Read the following statements and determine the one that supports the idea of government sponsored child care.

(A)   "Most parents choose not to send their children to licensed child care facilities."

(B)   "Experts predict that a two-year freeze in social spending could save $860 billion by 2015—a significant start on reducing the debt."

(C)   "Government-licensed child care centers would provide my kids a secure atmosphere and valuable early learning experiences."

(D)   "This is just another expensive government program that the taxpayers can't afford."

(E)   "Only a miniscule percentage of parents take their kids to licensed child care centers. This doesn't justify this kind of action."

12.   Medicare and Medicaid were two programs that were part of a government financed health system introduced during the administration of

(A)   Lyndon Johnson (1963-1969)

(B)   Richard Nixon (1969-1974)

(C)   Gerald Ford (1974-1977)

(D)   Jimmy Carter (1977-1981)

(E)   Ronald Reagan (1981-1989)

13.   The Arab oil embargo of 1973 had a great impact on life in the United States. One of the root causes of this embargo was

(A)   The cheap prices that OPEC (the Organization of Petroleum Exporting Countries) was charging for a barrel of oil.

(B)   Jimmy Carter's energy policies.

(C)   The United States' support of Israel in the Middle East.

(D)   The 1980 oil glut.

(E)   The lack of construction of nuclear power plants.

14.   The writings of John Locke and Montesquieu, European philosophers who believed in democracy, influenced our structure of government. They advocated

(A)   parliamentary democracy.

(B)   a system of checks and balances.

(C)   strong local governments, followed by weak state and national governments.

(D)   direct election to the Supreme Court.

(E)   a benevolent dictatorship.

15. Women got the right to vote
    (A) with the Emancipation Proclamation.
    (B) with the Bill of Rights.
    (C) after WWI.
    (D) after WWII.
    (E) with the Treaty of Guadaloupe Hidalgo.

16. Tension between two different economies also contributed to the Civil War. The agrarian South was in conflict with the _____ North.
    (A) industrial   (D) slave-owning
    (B) farming   (E) isolationist
    (C) seafaring

17. Which of the following is correctly matched with the following map of Southeast Asia?

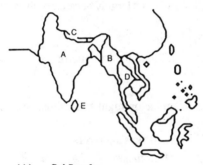

    (A) Sri Lanka   (D) India
    (B) Burma   (E) Nepal
    (C) Thailand

18. Where is Central America located on the following map?

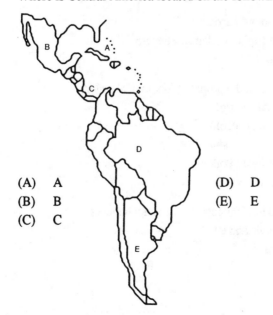

    (A) A   (D) D
    (B) B   (E) E
    (C) C

19. Capitalism describes the American economic system. It got its name because
    (A) it was first described by Alfred Benson Capital.
    (B) it was first used in Washington, D.C.
    (C) it is a different type of communism.
    (D) money, also called capital, is invested for personal profit.
    (E) it emanates from various state capitals.

20. Countries with very little rainfall have a problem growing food. They usually have to
    (A) use salt water from the closest ocean to grow crops.
    (B) change to a more centralized economy.
    (C) plant fruit orchards instead of crops.
    (D) graze animals because they use less water than crops.
    (E) install irrigation systems to grow crops.

21. The Church of England broke with the Catholic Church largely because of the actions of which ruler?
    (A) Elizabeth II   (D) Mary I
    (B) Louis the XIV   (E) William the Conqueror
    (C) Henry the VIII

22. Generally regions near the equator are hot. What factor might cause those regions to be noticeably cooler than expected?
    (A) Dense population   (D) Swift flowing rivers
    (B) Higher elevation   (E) All of these.
    (C) A lack of trees

23. What event in 1957 began the Space Race?
    (A) The launching of Sputnik by the Soviet Union.
    (B) The Berlin Air Lift
    (C) The breaking of the sound barrier
    (D) The successful space flight of Alan B. Shepard
    (E) The launch of Skylab

24. Which of these presidents are in the proper chronological order?
    (A) Lincoln, Jefferson, Wilson, Polk
    (B) Jefferson, Wilson, Polk, Lincoln
    (C) Jefferson, Polk, Lincoln, Wilson
    (D) Jefferson, Lincoln, Wilson, Polk
    (E) Polk, Jefferson, Lincoln, Wilson

25. The world's fair in Chicago in 1893 commemorated what event?
    (A) The expedition of Lewis and Clark
    (B) The end of World War I

(C) The opening of the transcontinental railroad

(D) The birth of William Penn

(E) Columbus' arrival into North America

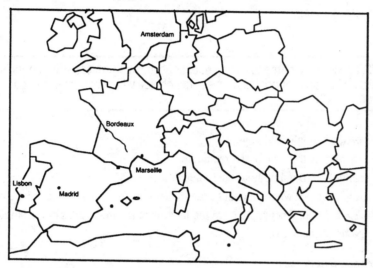

26. Which of the cities on the map above would be most unlikely to be a port city?

    (A) Bordeaux   (D) Marseille

    (B) Amsterdam   (E) Madrid

    (C) Lisbon

27. Which of the following are cultural universals?

    (A) Food   (D) (A) and (B) only.

    (B) Language   (E) (A) and (C) only.

    (C) Chairs

28. In 1898 the United States acquired all but the following by war

    (A) Cuba   (D) The Philippines

    (B) Guam   (E) Sumatra

    (C) Puerto Rico

29. During some severe winters the amount of heating oil will occasionally be insufficient to meet short-term needs. Prices may rise dramatically in the short term. This could be seen as an example of

    (A) A classic supply-demand curve   (D) All of the above.

    (B) Cost benefit analysis   (E) (A) and (C).

    (C) Price gouging

30. Which of the following items would **not** be considered a natural resource?

    (A) Petroleum   (D) Gasoline

    (B) Wildlife   (E) Water

    (C) Timber

Section 2: Mathematics

TIME: 30 Minutes
25 Questions

DIRECTIONS: Each of the following questions and incomplete statements is followed by five answer choices. Select the choice which best answers each question.

---

1.   The area of a triangle is always
    (A)   equal to half the area of a rectangle.
    (B)   cannot be found without the dimensions.
    (C) $A = a + b + c$ where a, b and c are the lengths of the three sides of a triangle.
    (D) $A = 1/2$ abc, where a, b, c are the lengths of the three sides of a triangle.
    (E)   None of the above.

2.   A scalene triangle has
    (A)   three equal sides.   (D)   a right angle.
    (B)   two equal sides.   (E)   three sides unequal in length.
    (C)   an obtuse angle in it.

3.   In the formula for the volume of a cube,s units on a side is $V = s^3 = sss$. If the length of the sides is doubled, what happens to the volume?
    (A)   Volume is doubled
    (B)   Volume is tripled
    (C)   Volume is quadrupled (increased by a factor of 4)
    (D)   Volume is increased by a factor of 8
    (E)   Volume is decreased

4.   Consider the following argument:
My coat is in the hall or in the bedroom.
My coat is not in the bedroom.
Therefore my coat is in the hall.
    (A)   The argument is invalid.
    (B)   The argument is valid.
    (C)   A valid argument is not available.
    (D)   The valid conclusion is my coat is not in the hall.
    (E)   The valid conclusion is my coat is not in the bedroom.

5.   Consider the following argument:
If I work, then I make money.
I do not work.
Therefore I do not make money.

  (A) The argument is invalid.

  (B) The argument is valid.

  (C) A valid argument is not available.

  (D) The valid conclusion is I make money.

  (E) The valid conclusion is I have money invested.

6. Consider the following argument:

  If a felony was involved, then the extradition papers were signed.

  The extradition papers were not signed.

  Therefore a felony was not involved.

  (A) The argument is invalid.

  (B) The argument is valid.

  (C) A valid argument is not available.

  (D) The valid conclusion is a felony was involved.

  (E) The valid conclusion is the extradition papers were signed.

7. Consider the following argument:

  If Barry saw the sunset, then it was snowing.

  Barry saw the sunset.

  Therefore it was snowing.

  (A) The argument is invalid.

  (B) The argument is valid.

  (C) A valid argument is not possible.

  (D) The valid conclusion is it was not snowing.

  (E) The valid conclusion is Barry did not see the sunset.

8. Mrs. Garcia was looking at her windows. One in her living room resembled the picture below. She said to her son Pedro, "All I can see is that pane of glass." What kind of perception is Mrs. Garcia using?

  (A) Geometric   (D) Topologic

  (B) Euclidean   (E) Spatial

  (C) Projective

9. Aaron lived on one side of the river and Samuel on the other. The river is wide, very wide. Aaron knows that the river _____ Samuel and himself.

(A) connects   (D) is between

(B) is inside   (E) is following

(C) is outside

10. Why is 1/2 called a unit fraction?

    (A) People frequently use the expressions half a unit, meaning half an inch or half cup, thus it is a unit fraction.

    (B) The number two is in the denominator.

    (C) It is between 0 and 1, the basic unit.

    (D) Unit fractions have one in the numerator.

    (E) It is less than one, the unit.

11. How would you find a fraction between 7/10 and 9/16?

    (A) Pick a fraction whose numerator is between the numerators of the given fraction and a denominator between the given denominator.

    (B) Add the two fractions, divide the sum by 2, this gives an average and ensures a fraction between (these) two fractions.

    (C) Draw a number line, find 7/10 and 9/16 on the number line. Identify a point and hence a number between them.

    (D) This can't always be done, some fractions have no numbers between them.

    (E) Write out all the fractions between 7/10 and 9/16 and choose the middle fraction.

12. 3/4 x 7/5 =

    (A) First find a common denominator. Convert the fractions to ones having the common denominator. Multiply the new numerators and place this product over the common denominator.

    (B) First find a common denominator. Multiply the numerators together and place over the common denominator.

    (C) Multiply the two numerators to get the new numerator. Multiply the two denominators to get the new denominator. This new fraction is the desired product.

    (D) Cross multiply to get 3 x 5 and 4 x 7 so the new fraction is 15/28.

    (E) Multiply the numerators to get a new numerator; the denominator of the desired product is the common denominator.

13. In the formula $p = 2 (l \times w)$ where l is the length of a rectangle and w is the width, if each dimension is tripled, what happens to the perimeter?

    (A) It is tripled   (D) It is increased by a factor of 12

    (B) It is doubled   (E) It is unchanged

    (C) It is increased by a factor of 6

14. Consider the set of numbers, 1, 1/2, 1/3, 1/4, 1/5, 1/6, ... It goes on and on and on. Which of the following statements best describes the observed pattern?

    (A) There is no pattern here.

    (B) Except for the first number, all the rest are fractions.

    (C) The denominators are the counting numbers.

(D)   Each number is smaller than the number on its left, except for 1.

(E)   The set of numbers start at 1 and end at 0.

15.   A + (B + C) = (A + B) + C represents the associative property for addition. Which of the following is an example of this pattern?

(A)   15 + 7 = (8 + 7) + 7 = (9 + 8) + 8

(B)   24 = 20 + 4 = (2 x 10) + 4

(C)   5 + (7 + 9) = (5 + 7) + 9

(D)   5 + (7 + 9) = 5 + 16

(E)   5 + (7 + 9) = (7 + 9) + 5

16.   Given the following illustrations of mathematical properties, which of the following is not an illustration of a **true** mathematical property?

(A)   9 + 0 = 9 = 0 + 9   (D)   4 x (3 + 2) = (4 x 3) + (4 x 2)

(B)   7 + 11 = 11 + 7   (E)   7/8 x (9/5 x 2/11) = (7/8 x 9/5) x 2/11

(C)   1/2 - 2/3 = 2/3 - 1/2

17.   José set his analog alarm clock for 8 o'clock. He was very tired, having risen at 4 o'clock that morning; so he went to bed right after supper, a little after seven o'clock. For how many hours did José sleep?

(A)   Less than one hour

(B)   More than one hour but less than twelve

(C)   More than twelve hours

(D)   More than twelve hours and less than thirteen

(E)   Eight hours

18.   These numbers represent a pattern. Please list the next two numbers in this pattern: 1, 1, 2, 3, 5, 8, 13, 21, 34, … To do so the student must

(A)   add 10 to 34 and 11 to the sum.

(B)   repeat 34 and add 2 to it, the pattern repeats.

(C)   add the two preceding numbers to arrive at the next.

(D)   add 21 to 34 and 21 to that sum.

(E)   There is no pattern here.

19.   Ingrid wanted to escape from the prison camp. She knew she would need $100 for airfare once she evaded the three guards. Like some guards, the three that were on night duty could be bribed, if the price was right. She figured she could satisfy their greed if she offered each half of whatever money she had with her when she met each. She sent a coded message to her accomplice for money to escape. What problem solving technique did she use to determine the amount of money she needed?

(A)   Analytic/algebraic   (D)   Draw a picture, diagram

(B)   Working backwards   (E)   Solve a similar problem that is simpler.

(C)   Trial and error

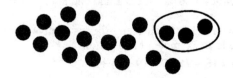

20.   The text has a picture on page 57 similar to the one shown above. It is a picture of 18
       marbles with three of them encircled. On page 57 to the right of this picture is a set
       of exercises for the fourth graders to solve. Here are a few.

       12. $16 \div 4 =$

       13. $18 \div 3 =$

       14. $25 \div 5 =$

       What relationship, if any, exists between the picture and the exercises?

       (A)   There is no relationship.

       (B)   Pictures are added to children's books to make them more attractive.

       (C)   Fourth graders used to like marbles. This must be an old book.

       (D)   Since six groups of three makes 18, this picture reminds children of their
              multiplication facts.

       (E)   Since the picture shows a set and one subset, it is a hint to the solution of
              exercise 13.

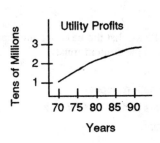

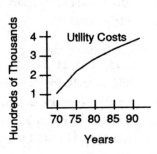

21.   The two graphs pictured above were presented to a citizen's utility board. Which of
       the following statements best explains the information contained in the graphs?

       (A)   Costs have risen over the profit margin.

       (B)   Because of the scales, costs are nearly equal to profit.

       (C)   Profits are soaring while costs are nearly constant.

       (D)   Both costs and profits are increasing.

       (E)   Costs appear to be leveling off over the past decade after years of rapid rise,
              while profits have been decreasing.

22.   Which graph below best represents the given data?

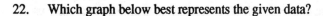

The number of children	2	5	11	2	1
The number of inches in heights	47	48	52	53	57

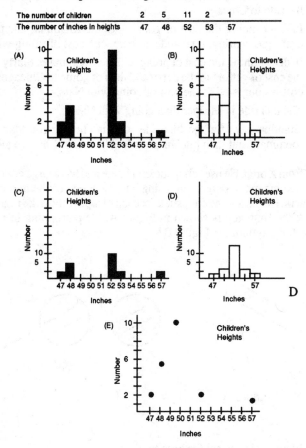

23.   Artemus loves olives. She ate five big stuffed olives from the antipasto tray before lunch. She had six more during lunch with one stalk of celery; after lunch she ate seven more. How many olives did she eat? To solve the problem

(A)   it makes a difference if we add them in the order she ate them or if we add them in reverse order.

(B)   add all the numbers mentioned in the problem.

(C)   convert the number names to numerals and then add.

(D)   add the three numbers together.

(E)   remember that she ate olives and celery in this problem. Add only the numbers associated with the three times she ate olives.

24.   Marty wants to go to Florida for New Year's. Grandpa said he will pay her fare from Chicago to Florida, but she has to get to Chicago. Marty is short on cash. To go from school with her roommate to within seven miles of the bus depot to Chicago will cost her $7 in gas cost sharing and $7.50 for a taxi to the depot. If Marty goes with Nate, he'll take her all the way to Chicago for $25. Since the bus fare is $20, Marty decides to save money and go with her roommate and then hitchhike to the depot. Is Marty saving money? To solve this problem you must:

(A) Determine the cost of going with her roommate and compare with the cost of the ride to Chicago.

(B) In determining the cost of going with the roommate include all associated costs, gas sharing, taxi, and compare with cost of riding with Nate.

(C) In determining the cost of going with her roommate, Marty needs to consider the cost of getting to the depot and then of going to Chicago by bus. This total cost is compared to the cost of going with Nate.

(D) The bus ride is cheaper than going with Nate.

(E) Grandpa pays for the bus ride so it is cheaper for Marty to go with her roommate and then hitchhike, so let Nate go to Chicago alone.

25. Yuk is from Korea. He uses chopsticks at home and has a large collection. He decides to practice his math assignment using base two, one of the numeration systems of computers. He places one chopstick for each of the symbols, he regroups after joining the sets, the first step is shown in Figure A, the regrouping in Figure B. What is incorrect, if anything, in Figure B?

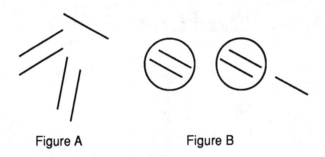

Figure A   Figure B

(A) Figure B is correct for base two.

(B) There are only five chopsticks, regrouping is not necessary.

(C) The solution is 101, nothing is incorrect in Figure B.

(D) Figure B is not totally regrouped, it needs to group the two sets of two into one bundle of groups of two.

(E) The solution is 21, nothing is incorrect in Figure B.

Section 3: Literature and Fine Arts

TIME: 30 Minutes
35 Questions

DIRECTIONS: Each of the following questions and incomplete statements is followed by five answer choices. Select the choice which best answers each question.

1. The costumes pictured above would be most appropriate for which of the following?

    (A)   Ancient Greek drama   (D)   A passion play

    (B)   A Medieval cycle play   (E)   A Shakespearean play

    (C)   A mid-nineteenth century play

2.   The setting pictured above is an example of which of the following?

(A)   Expressionism   (D)   Realism

(B)   Symbolism   (E)   None of the above.

(C)   Impressionism

It is very seldom that mere ordinary people like John and myself secure ancestral halls for the summer.

A colonial mansion, a hereditary estate, I would say a haunted house and reach the height of romantic felicity—but that would be asking too much of fate!

Still I will proudly declare that there is something queer about it.

Else, why should it be let so cheaply? And why have stood so long untenanted?

John laughs at me, of course, but one expects that.

John is practical in the extreme. He has no patience with faith, an intense horror of superstition, and he scoffs openly at any talk of things not to be felt and seen and put down in figures.

John is a physician, and *perhaps* (I would not say it to a living soul, of course, but this is dead paper and a great relief to my mind)—*perhaps* that is one reason I do not get well faster.

You see, he does not believe I am sick! And what can one do?

If a physician of high standing, and one's own husband, assures friends and relatives that there is really nothing the matter with one but temporary nervous depression—a slight hysterical tendency—what is one to do?

My brother is also a physician, and also of high standing, and he says the same thing.

So I take phosphates or phosphites—whichever it is—and tonics, and air and exercise, and journeys, and am absolutely forbidden to "work" until I am well again.

Personally, I disagree with their ideas.

3. John is characterized by the speaker as
   (A) arrogant.
   (B) trustworthy.
   (C) cunning.
   (D) realistic.
   (E) possessive.

4. The speaker views writing as
   (A) annoying.
   (B) therapeutic.
   (C) laborious.
   (D) painful.
   (E) whimsical.

5. We can infer from the passage that the speaker
   (A) is insane.
   (B) is of solid mental health.
   (C) has no real occupation.
   (D) strongly dislikes her husband.
   (E) is planning to murder her husband.

6. The architect of the building pictured above probably relied primarily on which of the following?
   (A) Internal steel cables
   (B) Prestressed concrete
   (C) Oak timber framing
   (D) Stone masonry and mortar
   (E) Sheet glass

Flying Hores Poised on One Leg on a Swallow, Wuwei

7. The pose of the horse in the sculpture pictured above serves to express

    (A) physical aging and decay.   (D) military prowess.

    (B) massiveness and stability.   (E) moral fortitude.

    (C) lightness and motion.

It was Phaethon who drove them to Fiesole that memorable day, a youth all irresponsibility and fire, recklessly urging his master's horses up the stony hill. Mr. Beebe recognized him at once. Neither the Ages of Faith nor the Age of Doubt had touched him; he was Phaethon in Tuscany driving a cab. And it was Persephone whom he asked leave to pick up on the way, saying that she was his sister—Persephone, tall and slender and pale, returning with the Spring to her mother's cottage, and still shading her eyes from the unaccustomed light. To her Mr. Eager objected, saying that here was the thin edge of the wedge, and one must guard against imposition. But the ladies interceded, and when it had been made clear that it was a very great favour, the goddess was allowed to mount beside the god.

8. Which of the following helps characterize Phaethon and Persephone as a "god" and "goddess?"

    I.   Their names   III.   Her eyes

    II.   His occupation   IV.   Her build

    (A) I only.   (D) II, III, and IV only.

    (B) I and II only.   (E) I, II, III, and IV.

    (C) I, II, and III only.

9. Which of the following best describes the example pictured above?
   (A) Monumental architecture dominates the scene.
   (B) The scene is viewed from the window of a passing train.
   (C) Human drama is the artist's main concern.
   (D) The composition has a dramatic central focus.
   (E) The scene is viewed as though from a second-story window.

David Smith, Cube XVIII, 1964

10. Which of the following is probably true of the sculpture pictured on the previous page?
    (A) The artist modelled it with his hands.
    (B) The artist poured it into a mold.
    (C) The artist shaped his materials with a blowtorch and welding tools.
    (D) The artist shaped natural materials with a chisel.
    (E) The artist used industrial forms as he found them.

(A)

> **Where the Bee Sucks, There Suck I**
>
> Where the bee sucks, there suck I:
> In a cowslip's bell I lie;
> There I couch when owls do cry.
> On the bat's back I do fly
> After summer merrily.
> Merrily, merrily shall I live now
> Under the blossom that hangs on the bough.
>
> William Shakespeare

(B)   George had turned at the sound of her arrival. For a moment he contemplated her, as one who had fallen out of heaven. He saw radiant joy in her face, he saw the flowers beat against her dress in blue waves. The bushes above them closed. He stepped quickly forward and kissed her.

From *A Room with a View*

(C)

> Life, how and what is it? As here I lie
> In this state chamber, dying by degrees,
> Hours and long hours in the dead night, I ask
> "Do I live, am I dead?" Peace, peace seems all.
> Saint Praxed's ever was the church for peace;
> And so, about this tomb of mine.
>
> From *St. Praxed's*

(D)   Generous tears filled Gabriel's eyes. He had never felt like that himself towards any woman but he knew that such a feeling must be love.
The tears gathered more thickly in his eyes and in the partial darkness
he imagined he saw the form of a young man standing under a dripping
tree. Other forms were near. His soul had approached that region where
dwell the vast hosts of the dead. He was conscious of, but could not
apprehend their wayward and flickering existence. His own identity was
fading out into a grey impalpable world: the solid world itself which
these dead had one time reared and lived in was dissolving and dwindling.

From *The Dubliners*

(E)
                    There was a time when meadow, grove, and stream
                        The earth, and every common sight,
                            To me did seem
                        Apparelled in celestial light,
                    The glory and the freshness of a dream.
                    It is not now as it hath been of yore;
                            Turn wheresoe'er I may,
                            By night or day
                    The things which I have seen I now can see no more.

From an Ode by William Wordsworth

11.   Which speaker considers himself a part of nature?

12.   Which passage is most likely taken from a dramatic monologue?

13.   Which speaker has just experienced a personal revelation?

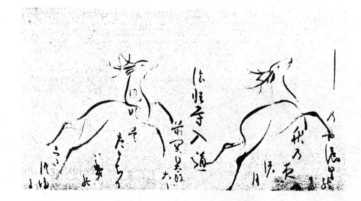

Tawaraya Sotatsu and Hon-Ami Roetsu, *Deer and Calligraphy*

14.   Which of the following is the most important artistic device in the example shown
       above?

    (A)   Line   (D)   Volume

    (B)   Tone   (E)   Hue

    (C)   Color

Banqueting House at Whitehall, Inigo Jones, London, 1619.

15.   Which of the following **does not** contribute to order and regularity in the example pictured above?

   (A)   The repeated second-story window design

   (B)   A facade which lacks deep recesses and voids

   (C)   The use of columns at the center and corners of the building

   (D)   A subtle use of the arch

   (E)   The balustrade running across the roof line

Jacques Louis David, *Oath of the Horatii*, 1784.

16.   In the painting illustrated on the previous page, all of the following are important compositional devices EXCEPT

(A)   the perspective grid of the checkerboard floor.

(B)   the strong highlighting of the foreground figures.

(C)   the arcade of arches in the background.

(D)   the vigorous movement of the main figure group.

(E)   the intersecting lines of the arms and the swords.

17.   The building pictured above was produced in which of the following countries?

(A)   Japan   (D)   Greece

(B)   Indonesia   (E)   Nigeria

(C)   Easter Island

(A)   For shade to shade will come too drowsily,
        And drown the wakeful anguish of the soul.

(B)   Rocks, caves, lakes, fens, bogs, dens, and shades of death.

(C)   'Twas brillig, and the slithy toves
        Did gyre and gimble in the wabe

(D)   Because I could not stop for Death—
        He kindly stopped for me—

(E)   … yet from these flames
        No light, but rather darkness visible

18. Which passage contains an oxymoron?

19. Which passage uses assonance?

20. Which passage is written in iambic pentameter?

Come, now, there may as well be an end of this! Every time I meet your eyes squarely I detect the question just slipping out of them. If you had spoken it, or even boldly looked it; if you had shown in your motions the least sign of a fussy or fidgety concern on my account; if this were not the evening of my birthday and you the only friend who remembered it; if confession were not good for the soul, though harder than sin to some people, of whom I am one,—well, if all reasons were not at this instant converged into a focus, and burning me rather violently in that region where the seat of emotion is supposed to lie, I should keep my trouble to myself.

Bayaro Taylor, Beauty and the Beast, Tales from Home (1872)

21. The speaker of the above passage feels
    (A) guilty.
    (B) anxious.
    (C) ashamed.
    (D) sorrowful.
    (E) relieved.

22. The speaker feels that confession is
    (A) unnecessary.
    (B) nonsensical.
    (C) healthy.
    (D) impossible.
    (E) comical.

(A) Subjects Bringing Gifts to the King (detail) from the stairway to the royal audience hall, Persepolis c. 500 B.C. Limestone

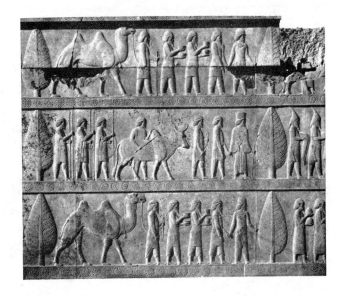

(B) King Smenkhkare and Meritaten Tel-el-Amanra, c. 1360 B.C.

(C) The Warrior Vase, Mycenae, c. 1200 B.C.

541

(D) Psalm 150, from the Utrecht Psaltar c. 830

(E) Sarcophagus, Caere (Cerveteri), c. 520 B.C.

23.   Which example seeks to give a schematic representation of a ceremonial event?

24.   In which example is the human figure most stylized and repeated in order to fit its container?

25.   In which example do the figures show the greatest tendency toward rhythmic calligraphy?

The Sick Rose

O Rose, thou art sick.
The invisible worm
That flies in the night
In the howling storm

Has found out thy bed
Of crimson joy,
And his dárk sécret love
Does thy life destroy.

William Blake

26. The imagery in this poem is mainly
    (A) religious.
    (B) sexual.
    (C) animal.
    (D) light.
    (E) darkness.

27. The word "life" in line 8 means
    (A) passion.
    (B) spirit.
    (C) love.
    (D) beauty.
    (E) memory.

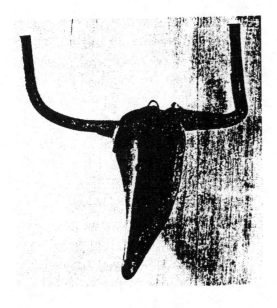

Pablo Picasso, Bull's Head, 1943.

28. In combining found objects to make the sculpture shown on the previous page, the artist sought to create

   (A)   a contrast of line and tone.

   (B)   a religious symbol.

   (C)   a visual analogy to a living creature.

   (D)   a metaphor for human experience.

   (E)   a functional device.

Nothing else was said; a new danger was being carried towards them by the river. Some wooden machinery had just given way on one of the wharves, and huge fragments were being floated along. The sun was rising now, and the wide area of watery desolation was spread out in dreadful clearness around them—in dreadful clearness floated onwards the hurrying, threatening masses. A large company in a boat that was working its way along under the Tofton houses, observed their danger, and shouted, "Get out of the current!"

But that could not be done at once, and Tom, looking before him, saw Death rushing on them. Huge fragments, clinging together in fatal fellowship, made one wide mass across the stream.

"It is coming, Maggie!" Tom said, in a deep hoarse voice, loosing the oars, and clasping her.

From *The Mill On The Floss*

29. The above passage contains which of the following conflicts?

   1.   Man vs. Man   4.   Man vs. Nature

   2.   Man vs. Society   5.   Man vs. Self

   3.   Man vs. God

   (A)   3 only.   (D)   1, 2, and 3 only.

   (B)   4 only.   (E)   1, 2, 4, and 5 only.

   (C)   1 and 2 only.

(A)

Questions 30 through 33
are based on the
following works of art

(B)

(C)

(D)

(E)

30. In which example do carefully-rendered decorative details on the figure's costume help to visually relate the main subject to the background?

31. In which example is an off-center subject cropped to produce the effect of a casual photograph?

32. In which example does the subject's off-center position lead the viewer's eye out of the picture?

Taj Mahal, Agra, India, 1632-1654

33. In the example pictured above, which of the following contributes LEAST to the weightless appearance of the building?

   (A) The repetition of the graceful domed forms

   (B) The four tall, slender towers

   (C) The choice of white marble as a building material

   (D) The reflecting pool in the foreground

   (E) The symmetrical arrangement of the structures

Morning clatters with the first L train down Allen Street. Daylight rattles through the windows, shaking the old brick houses, splatters the girders of the L structure with bright confetti.

The cats are leaving the garbage cans, the chinches are going back into the walls, leaving sweaty limbs, leaving the grimetender necks of little children asleep. Men and women stir under blankets and bedquilts on mattresses in the corners of rooms, clots of kids begin to untangle to scream and kick.

At the corner of Riverton the old man with the hempen beard who sleeps where nobody knows is putting out his picklestand. Tubs of gherkins, pimentos, melonrind, piccalilli give out twining vines and cold tendrils of dank pepperyfragrance that grow like a marshgarden out of the musky bedsmells and the rancid clangor of the cobbled awakening street.

The old man with the hempen beard who sleeps where nobody knows sits in the midst of it like Jonah under his gourd.

34. The language of this passage is reminiscent of

   (A) The Bible.   (D) a literature textbook.

   (B) Shakespeare.   (E) a rough draft.

   (C) stage directions.

35. The man's namelessness lends him an air of

   (A) anxiety.   (D) heroism.

   (B) insignificance.   (E) humor.

   (C) fear.

Section 4: Science

TIME: 30 Minutes
30 Questions

DIRECTIONS: Each of the following questions and incomplete statements is followed by five answer choices. Select the choice which best answers each question.

---

1. Which of the following does **not** have potential energy?

    I.   A moving automobiie   IV. Gunpowder

    II. Expanding gas   V.   Stretched rubber band

    III. Water at the top of a dam

    (A) I and II only.   (D) III only.

    (B) III and II only.   (E) V only.

    (C) III, IV, and V.

2. The law of conservation of matter and energy states

    (A) that matter and energy cannot be destroyed.

    (B) that either matter or energy can be changed into other forms of matter or energy.

    (C) that energy can be changed from one form to another.

    (D) All of the above.

    (E) None of the above.

3. Which of the following is true of Einstein's deduction(s) on the relationship between energy and mass?

    (A) $e=mc^2$

    (B) The total amount of matter and energy in the universe always stays the same.

    (C) Matter cannot be changed into energy nor energy into matter.

    (D) All the above.

    (E) (A) and (B) only.

4. The result of a deficiency of calcium in the body is that

    (A) the body converts carbon into calcium if the situation becomes critical.

    (B) the vertebrate body "robs" calcium from the skeleton.

    (C) the body fails to replace, atom for atom, the normal withdrawal.

    (D) All the above.

    (E) None of the above.

5. Sound energy is a type of which of the following?

    (A) Mechanical energy   (D) Nuclear energy
    (B) Electrical energy   (E) Heat energy
    (C) Wave energy

6. All of the following statements about plants are true EXCEPT which one?

    (A) The plant kingdom is divided into 2 major phyla called the tracheophytes and the bryophytes.
    (B) The plant kingdom is divided into two broad groups: plants that produce seeds and plants that do not produce seeds.
    (C) Plants are living things that can make their own food.
    (D) Chlorosynthesis is the process by which plants utilize light energy to create their own food.
    (E) Gymnosperms are a class of woody plants which bear their seeds in a cone.

7. Which of the metric terms is most appropriate for measuring the height of a doorknob from the floor?

    (A) Meter   (D) Decimeter
    (B) Liter   (E) Kilometer
    (C) Gram

8. Which of the following is true of the roots of plants?

    (A) Roots generally can do little to hold plants in the ground since most soils are so shallow.
    (B) In a diffuse root system, there is a primary root that grows until it is the largest root in the root system.
    (C) In a taproot system the primary taproot grows until it is the major root in the system.
    (D) Only plants with a diffuse root system store food in the roots since the taproots live for such a short time.
    (E) Roots help with absorption of water and minerals, support of the plant, and storage of food, but they cannot help with reproduction.

9. Which of the following is the symbol on the periodic table for hydrogen?

    (A) H   (D) Hi
    (B) Hy   (E) Hn
    (C) He

10. Which of the following is **not** a mammal?

    (A) A bat   (D) An elephant
    (B) A whale   (E) A shark
    (C) A gibbon

11. Which of the following best describes people in general?
    (A) Herbivorous
    (B) Carnivorous
    (C) Omnivorous
    (D) Migratory
    (E) Hibernating

12. To help blood to clot, physicians may use which vitamin in surgical operations?
    (A) Vitamin A
    (B) Vitamin B
    (C) Vitamin C
    (D) Vitamin D
    (E) Vitamin K

13. The two long, pointed teeth near the front of the human mouth are properly called which of the following?
    (A) Central incisors
    (B) Canines
    (C) Premolars
    (D) Molars
    (E) Lateral incisors

14. Which of the following statements about protozoans is **false**?
    (A) Protozoans are tiny, simple, one-celled animals.
    (B) They are made up of single cells.
    (C) The amoeba is the simplest protozoan.
    (D) A slipper-shaped protozoan is the euglena.
    (E) Protozoans are very tiny, simple, one-celled protists.

15. Which of the following is **not** a means used for controlling harmful insects?
    (A) Destroy the environment in which the insects live.
    (B) Establish quarantine laws to prevent the importing of insects into a country.
    (C) Use chemicals to control harmful insects.
    (D) Import or make use of local natural enemies.
    (E) Use nuclear fusion to destroy colonies.

16. Energy is best defined as which of the following?
    (A) Ability to do work
    (B) Ability to move other matter
    (C) Ability to produce a chemical change
    (D) All the above.
    (E) None of the above.

17. What kind of energy includes light rays and radio waves?
    (A) Mechanical energy
    (B) Heat energy
    (C) Electrical energy
    (D) Radiant energy
    (E) Nuclear energy

18. Which of the following is the number of permanent teeth normally in the mouth of an adult human?

    (A) 24   (D) 20
    (B) 28   (E) 32
    (C) 36

19. Which of the following is true of chemical energy?

    I.   Chemical energy is really a form of potential energy.
    II.   Chemical energy is really a form of kinetic energy.
    III. Chemical energy is released when a chemical reaction takes place and new substances are formed.
    IV.   New substances are formed from the action between the electrons in the outermost shells or the energy levels in atoms of the different substances.
    V.   Chemical energy comes from the nucleus of the atom when the atom splits in two.

    (A) I, II, III   (D) I, III, IV
    (B) II, III, IV   (E) I, II, V
    (C) III, IV, V

20. Which of the following statements about the bee order is **false**?

    (A) In a bee colony there are three kinds of bees: queen, drones, and workers.
    (B) The queen is the egg-laying bee.
    (C) The drone is the largest bee in the colony.
    (D) Fertilized eggs develop into non-egg-laying females or workers.
    (E) Unfertilized eggs develop into males, which are the drones.

21. Which of the following statements about stems is **not** true?

    (A) Herbaceous stems are usually soft and green and have no woody tissue in them.
    (B) Woody stems are stiff and grow longer and thicker than herbaceous stems.
    (C) Removal of bark in a circular section all the way around a tree is called girdling and will result in a thicker bark and a healthier plant or tree.
    (D) The cambium is the thin tissue between the bark and wood which forms new wood and a growth ring.
    (E) The formation of layers in a woody stem makes it possible to estimate the age of a tree if one counts the number of annual rings.

22. Identify the statement below which is true of the splitting of the atom or nuclear fission.

    (A) Scientists can combine lighter atoms to form heavier atoms.
    (B) An example is a hydrogen bomb.
    (C) Vast amounts of energy are given off because matter from the lighter atoms is changed into energy when atoms are joined.
    (D) Energy is obtained by getting the nucleus of the atoms to break up or split in two.
    (E) The energy process is identical to that which occurs in the sun.

23. Which of the following is true of heat energy?
    I.   Heat energy is the energy produced by moving molecules.
    II.   The faster the molecules move, the more kinetic energy the substance has.
    III. The faster the molecules move, the hotter a substance becomes.
    IV.   To produce the faster speed, molecules use heat so the substance is cooler.
    V.   The slower the molecules move, the more heat is produced in a substance since molecules are not using heat.
    (A)   I, II, III.   (D)   IV and V.
    (B)   I and II.   (E)   V only.
    (C)   II and III.

24. Which of the following is **not** a stage in complete metamorphosis?
    (A)   Egg   (D)   Adult
    (B)   Larva   (E)   Nymph
    (C)   Pupa

25. Which is closest to normal body temperature?
    (A)   100° C.   (D)   212° F.
    (B)   32° F.   (E)   37° C.
    (C)   50° C.

26. When two glass tumblers are stuck, one inside the other, they can be loosened best by
    (A)   allowing them both to cool in a cool, dry place.
    (B)   by pouring hot water on the outside tumbler after filling the inside tumbler with equally hot water.
    (C)   by pouring hot water on the outside tumbler after filling the inside tumbler with cold water.
    (D)   by pouring cold water on the outside tumbler after filling the inside tumbler with cold water.
    (E)   by pouring cold water on the outside tumbler after filling the inside tumbler with hot water.

27. All of the following statements about the refrigerator found in most American homes are true EXCEPT which of the following?
    (A)   Inside the pipe in the refrigerator is a gas called Freon.
    (B)   A compressor changes the gas into a liquid.
    (C)   The Freon travels under pressure to the freezer; here the pressure is taken away.
    (D)   When the pressure is taken away, the Freon becomes a gas again; as it evaporates it takes heat with it.
    (E)   The Freon is then in gas form and is discharged into the air surrounding the refrigerator.

28. All of the following are true of plants EXCEPT which one?
     (A) Seed plants may be divided into angiosperms and gymnosperms.
     (B) The seeds of angiosperms are enclosed in a protective coat called a fruit.
     (C) Gymnosperms are also called conifers because they produce woody cones.
     (D) The cone is the "fruit" of the conifers and is made up of scales.
     (E) Most conifers have leaves which drop off during the fall season; they are said to be deciduous.

29. All of the following statements about cells are true EXCEPT which one?
     (A) Cells are structural units of all living things.
     (B) Cells are filled with a living material called protoplasm.
     (C) A group of the same kind of cells working together is called a tissue.
     (D) Vacuoles carry out all the activities that living things do in order to live.
     (E) The activities that living things do (respirate, circulate, digest, excrete, grow) are called life processes.

30. Which of the following statements about magnets is **false**?
     (A) Magnets are materials that will attract items made of iron, steel, cobalt, and nickel.
     (B) Natural magnets found in the ground are called lodestones.
     (C) Magnetized atoms group together in domains, or large clusters, which line up with north-seeking poles at one end and south-seeking poles at the other.
     (D) The older theory which said that magnetism was due to molecules behaving as tiny magnets with all the north-seeking poles facing in one direction and the south-seeking poles facing in the other is not currently held as true by most scientists.
     (E) The earth does not behave as a huge magnet because it is not a magnet.

TEST OF GENERAL KNOWLEDGE

ANSWER KEY

SECTION 1: SOCIAL STUDIES

1.	(E)	9.	(D)	17.	(B)	25.	(E)
2.	(A)	10.	(C)	18.	(C)	26.	(E)
3.	(B)	11.	(C)	19.	(D)	27.	(D)
4.	(A)	12.	(A)	20.	(E)	28.	(E)
5.	(C)	13.	(C)	21.	(C)	29.	(E)
6.	(E)	14.	(B)	22.	(B)	30.	(D)
7.	(C)	15.	(C)	23.	(A)		
8.	(A)	16.	(A)	24.	(C)		

SECTION 2: MATHEMATICS

1.	(A)	8.	(D)	15.	(C)	22.	(A)
2.	(E)	9.	(D)	16.	(C)	23.	(E)
3.	(D)	10.	(D)	17.	(A)	24.	(C)
4.	(B)	11.	(B)	18.	(C)	25.	(D)
5.	(A)	12.	(C)	19.	(B)		
6.	(B)	13.	(A)	20.	(E)		
7.	(B)	14.	(C)	21.	(D)		

SECTION 3: LITERATURE AND FINE ARTS

1.	(E)	10.	(C)	19.	(B)	28.	(C)
2.	(D)	11.	(A)	20.	(A)	29.	(B)
3.	(D)	12.	(C)	21.	(B)	30.	(B)
4.	(B)	13.	(D)	22.	(C)	31.	(C)
5.	(C)	14.	(A)	23.	(A)	32.	(D)
6.	(D)	15.	(D)	24.	(C)	33.	(E)
7.	(C)	16.	(D)	25.	(D)	34.	(C)
8.	(B)	17.	(A)	26.	(B)	35.	(B)
9.	(E)	18.	(E)	27.	(D)		

SECTION 4: SCIENCE

1.	(A)	9.	(A)	17.	(D)	25.	(E)
2.	(D)	10.	(E)	18.	(E)	26.	(C)
3.	(E)	11.	(C)	19.	(D)	27.	(E)
4.	(C)	12.	(E)	20.	(C)	28.	(E)
5.	(C)	13.	(B)	21.	(C)	29.	(D)
6.	(D)	14.	(D)	22.	(D)	30.	(E)
7.	(A)	15.	(E)	23.	(A)		
8.	(C)	16.	(D)	24.	(E)		

DETAILED EXPLANATIONS OF ANSWERS
NTE CORE BATTERY–Test 4

TEST OF GENERAL KNOWLEDGE
Section 1: Social Studies

1.   **(E)**   Part of the power of the governor is the ability to name people to fill empty seats in the Senate for that state (A). As head of a state's executive branch, the governor can use the national guard in times of civil unrest, natural disasters, or for any emergency situation identified by the governor (B). As part of the checks and balances of one branch of government on another, the governor has the authority to veto laws passed by the legislature (C). Also, as a check on the judicial branch, the governor may pardon or reduce the sentence of a prisoner (D). The area of trade agreements, however, is within the jurisdiction of the federal government (more specifically, the Congress and the President) because the implications of such treaties go far beyond individual state boundaries. Therefore, the correct response is choice (E).

2.   **(A)**   Because of the interdependence as explained above, (B) is not correct. Branches of the Federal government do not achieve independence from each other due to checks and balances. Answers (C), (D) and (E) are also not correct because they deal with only one branch, and checks and balances involves the manner in which the branches interrelate. Answer (A) is correct, because checks and balances control and regulate the power and actions of the three branches of the Federal government.

3.   **(B)**   (B) is the correct answer. Abraham Lincoln was in office between 1860 and 1864. Theodore Roosevelt was in office between 1901 and 1904. Woodrow Wilson was in office between 1912 and 1916. Franklin D. Roosevelt was in office between 1932 and 1944.

4.   **(A)**   This is the definition of ethnocentrism (A). (B) Institutionalization is the patterning of social interaction in ways that reduce the possibility for tension, conflict, and deviance. (C) Social Placement is the allocation of positions in a society. (D) Social Control are processes which attempt to maintain conformity to existing norms; maintenance of the status quo. (E) Bigotry is the practice of intolerance of any creed, belief or race.

5.   **(C)**   Wealth describes goods and material possessions which have social value. Prestige is defined as the amount of esteem and deference an individual receives from others. Power is the ability to attain individual goals or socially determine the lives of others. Status is the position or rank of an individual in relation to others; based on prestige or social honor. Class is a term to denote rankings based upon one's relationship to economic forces. Therefore, (C) is the correct answer.

6. **(E)**   The Populists of the late 1800's and the Progressives of the early 1900's arose due to dismay with the current Democratic and Republican political platforms. Therefore (B) is incorrect. These two groups organized themselves and campaigned outside of the structure of the Democratic and Republican parties. Therefore, the answer to the question is (E).

7. **(C)**   The answer is (C). The original colonies included Delaware (A), Virginia (B), Maryland (D) and Georgia (E), which were then part of the original thirteen states. Vermont was originally owned by Massachusetts, but claimed independence later and subsequently joined the United States as the 14th state in 1791.

8. **(A)**   The answer is (A). The Quebec Act (B) occurred in 1774; and because it seemed to give greater advantage to French Canadians, it aroused the ire of the American colonists. The Stamp Act (C) of 1765 was seen as unfair taxation by the colonists. The Writs of Assistance (D) in 1766 made unfair demands on the colonists. Thus, all were causes of the Revolution. The Alien and Sedition Acts occurred in 1798 during the administration of John Adams, almost twenty years after the Revolution began.

9. **(D)**   Answer (D) fits this question—1896 should not be considered a recent trend.

10. **(C)**   The correct answer is (C). The statement, "Between 1868 and 1882, more than 200,000 Chinese came to the U.S.," neither supports nor opposes the idea of assimilating immigrants into the United States. To demonstrate this, compare selection (A) with the question. Selection (A) provides a positive consequence of immigration (a variety of thoughts, ideas, and philosophies). Selection (C) gives no reason, for or against, the immigration of the Chinese between 1868 and 1882.

11. **(C)**   Answer (A) does *not* support child care; rather, it provides a reason against child care. Answer (B) provides an economic reason against government-sponsored child care. Answer (D) reflects the opinion that the Federal government should not be involved in expensive programs at the taxpayers' expense and that child care would be one of these programs. Answer (E) is a reason against government-sponsored child care and only a small percentage of people would be using it. Answer (C) is correct because the response supports child care as a viable program for children.

12. **(A)**   Answer (A) is correct. As a part of LBJ's Great Society programs, health care programs financed by Federal and state governments were instituted during his terms in office. (B) is not correct as Nixon's administration did not initially enact these programs. (C) is not correct as Ford's administration did not initially enact these programs. (D) is not correct as Carter's administration did not enact these programs. (E) is not correct as the Reagan administration attempted to decrease many social programs.

13. **(C)**   Answers (B) and (D) occurred after 1973. Answer (E), nuclear power plant construction, was still in its infancy at this time. Three Mile Island was still six years away. Nuclear power was not as intimidating in 1973 as it would become in the 1980s. Answer (A), cheap prices for a barrel of oil, is the reverse of what actually happened. Oil prices saw a steady increase that particular year. Therefore, (C) is the correct response.

14.   **(B)**   The correct answer is (B). The key to answering this question is in the question itself. The question asks about "our structure of government." The United States does not have a parliament, but has a representative democracy. Those who govern the nation acquire their position through competition and elections. Therefore, (A) is incorrect. (C) is wrong because the national government takes precedence over the state and local governments. The local governments must work within the legal, economic, and other various frameworks set forth by the state and national governments. Of the three levels of government, the local government is the weakest and most dependent. (D) is incorrect because Supreme Court judges are not elected to the Supreme Court but are appointed by the President of the United States when a vacancy in the Supreme Court occurs and when the Senate approves the nomination. Finally, (E) is incorrect because a dictatorship, however benevolent, implies a lack of democracy.

15.   **(C)**   Letter (C) is the correct answer. Women got the right to vote with the passage of the 19th Amendment in 1920. World War I ended in 1918. Choice (A) is not correct as the Emancipation Proclamation enacted by President Lincoln in 1863 during the American Civil War, freed black slaves in the militarily occupied South. The Bill of Rights, answer (B), or the first 10 Amendments to the Constitution, were approved in 1789 and did *not* give women the right to vote. Choice (D) is not correct as World War 11 was over in I 945 and the 19th Amendment was passed in 1920. (E) ended the Mexican-American War in 1848, it had nothing to do with women's suffrage.

16.   **(A)**   (A) is the correct answer. The North's economy was more diversified than the South's. The North possessed a greater manufacturing capacity than did the South. The South, with its economy being dominated by its reliance on agriculture, (cotton, tobacco, etc.) was not nearly as well industrially equipped to sustain a war with the far more industrially diversified Northern states. (B) is not correct because, while the North did have farming, farming would not have caused a conflict with the agrarian-based economy of the Southern states. (C) is not correct because the North did not rely on international trade via the seas for its economic livelihood. (D) is not correct, as in the vast majority of Northern states slavery was either illegal or economically impractical. Isolationist sympathies (E) had nothing to do with disagreements with the South.

17.   **(B)**   (B) is correct. Burma's distinctive location and elongated shape makes it noticeably different from the other available countries. (A) is not correct as Sri Lanka is an island nation south of India. (C) is not correct as Thailand is to be found in a more eastern location than Burma. (D) is not correct as India, being west of Burma, is far larger than Burma. (E) is not correct as Nepal, being on India's northern border and part of China's southern border, is a smaller country than Burma.

18.   **(C)**   The correct answer is (C). (A) marks the Bahamas, (B) is Mexico, (D) is Brazil, and (E) is Argentina.

19.   **(D)**   The correct answer is (D). Capitalism may be defined as the private ownership of land, the means of production, and exchange. Money, as (D) states, is invested for personal profit. This is the basis of the American economic system. Therefore, (D) is the correct answer. (C) is incorrect. Capitalism is not a different type of communism. According to Karl Marx, who conceptualized the historical development of communism, the conflicts arising

out of capitalism would ultimately lead to communism. But, capitalism is not a form of communism. Alfred Benson Capital may have conceptualized capitalism, but, that fact alone does not substantiate the reason why "Capitalism describes the American economic system." (A) is incorrect. Similarly, the fact that Washington, D.C. is the place of origin, also does not substantiate capitalism as describing the American economic system. (B) is incorrect. For the same reason (E) is incorrect.

20. **(E)** The correct answer is (E). (A) is incorrect because salt water cannot be used for irrigation. It changes the pH balance in the soil, making the soil incapable of sustaining plant life. (B) might occur, but not necessarily in response to lack of rainfall. (C) is incorrect because fruit orchards typically require much more water, and the source of water must be both predictable and readily available. Crops are less affected from a few days without water than are animals. Grazing animals require much more water.

21. **(C)** The correct answer is (C). Henry's dissatisfaction with the Pope's edicts regarding, among other things, divorce, was responsible for his differences with the Catholic Church. Louis was a French king and therefore had no contact with the Church of England. Mary was a devout Catholic and Elizabeth is the reigning Queen of England, nearly 500 years after Henry's break. William was a Catholic who led the Norman invasion of England in 1066.

22. **(B)** The correct answer is (B). A lack of trees (C) may *increase* the temperature. Though swift rivers would be cool, they would be unlikely to lower the region's temperature significantly. Dense population (A) would not affect regional temperature.

23. **(A)** The correct answer is (A). The Berlin Air Lift had nothing to do with space. Supersonic flight (C) was only coincidental to space flight. Shepard's flight was a result of the space race. As of 1990, Skylab is still a proposed mission, so (E) is incorrect.

24. **(C)** (C) is the correct answer. Jefferson was the third president (1801-1809) and Lincoln was the sixteenth (1861-1865), so (A) is incorrect. Wilson served 1913-1921, taking the country through World War I, and Polk served from 1845-49 during the Mexican American War. Thus, both (B), (D) and (E) are out of order.

25. **(E)** (E) is the correct answer as Columbus had first arrived on the North American continent in 1493, 400 years earlier. The end of World War I was after 1893. Penn's birth had no connection to Chicago. Despite Lewis and Clark exploring new territory in 1803, it was west of the Mississippi River and neither the date nor the place would be a logical cause for celebration of this event. The railroad was completed in Utah in 1869, so a celebration in Chicago 24 years later is far-fetched.

26. **(E)** The correct answer is (E). Madrid is neither on the ocean, nor does it lie on a river with ocean connections. Amsterdam (B), Lisbon (C), and Marseille (D) are on the sea, and Bordeaux has ocean port connections because of the Garonne River.

27. **(D)** Cultural universals refer to those objects or ideas that all cultures possess. Food and language (oral, written, or both) are found in every culture. Some cultures have chairs,

but many sit on rocks, squat, or build other objects for support while sitting. Thus chairs (C) are *not* universals, so (E) is also wrong. The only possible answer is (D), since it includes both (A) and (B).

28. **(E)** The correct answer is (E), a Dutch colony now part of Indonesia. The others were all acquired, at least for a time, by the U.S. and as a result of the Spanish American War. Cuba was freed within ten years by the United States, the Philippines became independent in 1946. Both Guam and Puerto Rico are American Commonwealths.

29. **(E)** The correct answer is (E). Cost benefit analysis is merely a way to observe phenomena. (A) would describe the events in the question, but since some sellers often raise prices unreasonably (C) is also correct.

30. **(D)** A natural resource is anything of value that is provided by nature. Thus, wildlife, timber, water and petroleum fit the definition of a natural resource. Gasoline (D) is a product that results from the refining of petroleum.

Section 2: Mathematics

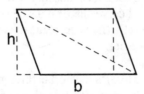

1. **(A)** Given any triangle, a rectangle may be formed that is equal in area to two triangles. This is why the area of a triangle is given by A = 1/2 bh. This parallelogram can be made into two triangles. Formulas do not need dimensions. Thus (B) is incorrect. (C) represents perimeter not area. (D) is an incorrect recall of the area formula and is nonsense here.

2. **(E)** (A) defines an equilateral triangle. (B) defines an isosceles triangle. (C) Some scalene triangles have obtuse angles but many more do not, they have only acute angles or acute angles and one right angle. This is an incomplete choice, hence inappropriate. (D) is inappropriate but is sometimes correct similar reasoning as in (C).

3. **(D)** For problems of this type it helps to substitute dimensions for the letters, follow the directions and compare the original volume and the volume of the changed figure. Original cube is 1 unit on a side, volume is 1 cubic unit. Changed cube is 2 units on a side, volume is 2 x 2 x 2 = 8 cubic units. Volume is increased by a factor of 8 when each dimension is doubled.

4. **(B)** The inference pattern represented by this argument is a valid argument form (called disjunctive syllogism) $p \vee q$ and $\sim q$ therefore p. It is a common form used in daily conversation; i.e., if one part of an or statement does not occur, the other part does.

5.   **(A)**   The inference pattern represented by this argument is an invalid inference pattern, p → q and ~ p therefore ~ q. It is a commonly used, but invalid argument form. It uses an incorrect assumption that an inverse statement is equivalent to the original statement. Some authors consider this a misapplication due to incorrect or incomplete understanding of the contrapositive. It is an invalid inference pattern; no conclusion will result from the two premises.

6.   **(B)**   The inference pattern represented by this argument is valid, p → q and ~ q, therefore ~ p. It is an example of the indirect method of proof. Some authors consider it the application of the contrapositive. It is valid and the conclusion follows from the two premises.

7.   **(B)**   This is a valid inference pattern, p → q and p therefore q. It is the most frequently used direct method of proof. The conclusion follows from the two premises.

8.   **(D)**   The concept of separation or discontinuous (not a continuous, solid pane of glass) is a topologic spatial concept. When it supersedes the mention or recognition of the geometric (rectangular) shape, we conclude the topologic concepts dominate or even supersede the Euclidean concept of shape. Separation is more elemental than shape (Piaget).

9.   **(D)**   The river is between Aaron and Samuel, since Aaron must cross (intersect) the river to reach Samuel. The river does not connect the two, a bridge would do that, so (A) is not a choice. There is no closed curves here so inside (interior) and outside (exterior) is inappropriate, thus so is (B) and (C). (E) refers to the river as a geographic entity and we are concerned with geometric properties.

10.   **(D)**   Part of (A) may be a true statement, but this is not the reason fractions with a one in the numerator are called unit fractions. By definition a unit fraction is a number of the form 1/2, 1/3, 1/4, …, 1/a, … and so on, where the denominators are non-zero natural numbers and the numerator is always 1. Although it is true that the unit fractions are between 0 and 1, this is not the reason why fractions of the form 1/a are called unit fractions; furthermore there are numerous fractions between 0 and 1 that *are not* unit fractions (consider 2/3, 3/5, 3/4, 7/9, 11/16), so it is a true statement but not the correct choice for the question. (E) and (B) are not appropriate solutions to the problem.

11.   **(B)**   (A) may or may not work. It cannot be substantiated by proof. One counter example will suffice, try 8/11. To be true 9/16 < 8/11 < 7/10 however 8/11 is greater than 9/16 *and* also greater than 7/10, not less than, as betweenness dictates. (C) is a good idea, but how do you identify the value of that point? It is not an adequate explanation. Although (D) is true, 1/2 and 2/4 are two fractions with no number between them, the subtlety of rationale number and fraction is probably not well known at this stage. (E) may or may not work, but this is time consuming and it would be difficult to find a middle point or find a value which would represent a fraction between the two. (B) is still the "rule" for finding a number between two numbers.

12.   **(C)**   Please do not find common denominators when multiplying fractions, it is unnecessary. The rule for multiplication is (C), given in symbols a/b x c/d = ac/bd.

13. **(A)** In a problem like this substitute numbers for the letters and compare, p = 2 (l + w) if l = 3 inches, w = 1 inch p = 2 (3 + 1) = 2 x 4 = 8. Then triple the dimension l = 9, w = 3 p = 2 (9 + 3) = 2 x 12 = 24. 24 is three times eight, so the perimeter is tripled when each dimension is tripled.

14. **(C)** There are many interesting facts about this sequence, l/n, where n = 1, 2, 3, ...(B) and (D) are true but do not reflect the pattern. (A) and (E) are not true; the sequence never ends and it is never 0.

15. **(C)** (A) is not an equality, nor a pattern. (B) is true, but is unrelated to the associative property for addition. (D) is true, but does not illustrate the associative property for addition. (E) The commutative property for addition is illustrated here, not the regrouping of numbers, as the associative property requires. This represents A + B = B + A where A is 5 and B is (7 + 9). (C) has A = 5, B = 7 and C = 9. Property A + (B + C) = (A + B) + C. Illustrate 5 + (7 + 9) = (5 + 7) + 9, choice (C).

16. **(C)** (A) represents an instance of the additive identity element, 0. Zero added to any number does not change the value of the numbers nor does adding a number to zero change the value of the number. (B) represents the commutative property for addition. (C) is a false statement. There is no commutative property for subtraction. (D) represents the distributive property; i.e., multiplicative distribution over addition. (E) represents the associative property for multiplication.

17. **(A)** José set his analogue alarm clock at 8 o'clock, but there is no indication whether it is a.m. or p.m. which is often, but not always, indicated on digital clocks. Thus by going to bed a little after 7 o'clock p.m., he was aroused by his alarm clock at 8 o'clock p.m., less than one hour later.

18. **(C)** This is the Fibonacci sequence, that is, we add 1 and 1 to get 2; 1 and 2 to have the sum 3 for the fourth term; 2 and 3 sum to 5; 3 and 5 are 8; 5 and 8 are 13; 8 + 13 = 21; 13 + 21 = 34; 21 + 34 = 55; 34 + 55 = 89, etc. This is an iterative formulation. You add the two preceding terms to arrive at the next: symbolizing $f_1 + f_2 = f_3$; $f_2 + f_3 = f_4$.

19. **(B)** Working backwards is the most efficient method for most people, but there are other ways, such as trial and error or algebraic equations. Working backward: She needs $100 at the end and there are three guards. Guard 3, Guard 2, Guard 1 Fare = $100. Guard 3 gets half of her amount and she has the other half for her fare so Guard 3 gets $100. This means she has $200 when she leaves Guard 2 who gets a $200 bribe. Prior to reaching Guard 2, Ingrid has $400. This means she gave Guard 1 $400 so she must have started with $800. As a check: Start with $800 and share half with Guard 1, which leaves Ingrid with $400. Next, Ingrid now has $400 and shares half with Guard 2, which leaves her with $200. Finally, Ingrid has $200 and shares half with Guard 3, which leaves her with $100. Thus, Ingrid has $100 for her fare.

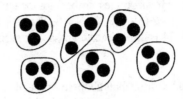

20. **(E)** The definition of division is the separation of subsets of equal size from a set— a special case of subtraction, subset of a set (complement of a set). So the picture enables one to separate out sets of three from the 18 and there are six sets of three so the physical/pictorial problem illustrates Exercise 13.

21. **(D)** Both graphs illustrate an increase. Utility profits, while not strong, are increasing consistently. Costs have also increased, yet not above the profit margin (note that profit is measured in tens of millions, and costs in hundreds of thousands).

22. **(A)** (B), (C), (D) and (E) distort the pictures by not having equal intervals for the numbers in either the horizontal scale (B), the vertical scale (C) or both (D) or they carelessly plot points incorrectly (E). The words of caution in 21 are appropriate here. Read the labels, notice the scales and whether or not the scales are representing equal spaces for the measures.

23. **(E)** When solving word problems make sure you understand what you are to find, the number of olives Artemus ate. Ignore the irrelevant data, the stalk of celery she ate. Change the words for numbers to numerals, especially for the relevant facts—5 olives, 6 more olives, 7 more olives. $5 + 6 + 7 = 18$ olives. (A) is true but to what does *them* refer, celery *and* olives? It is unclear and hence not an appropriate method for solving problems. (B) is even worse for distractors—if we did this we'd add the number of stalks of celery to the number of olives and we don't want to do that. (C) Again, what do we add? It fails to specify we add the number of olives eaten. (D) Which three of the four numbers are we to add? It does not address the problem.

24. **(C)** The cost of going to Chicago: With Nate - $25 With roommate - $7 for shared cost of gas + taxi $7.50 + his fare $20 = $34.50. Cost if she hitchhiked - $7 for share of gas cost + $20 her fare = $27. Either way, it is cheaper to go with Nate for $25. (A), (B) and (D) ignore parts of the expenses. (E) assumes, incorrectly, grandpa's offer is good before Chicago—he agreed to pay the fare from Chicago to Florida only.

25. **(D)** In base two there are only two symbols, 0 and 1. The basic collection is two ⟍. Every time we have two sticks, two bundles of sticks, two of anything, they become *one* collection so the two ⊘ ⊘ should be ⊘ ⊘ (Similar to one bunch of ten bundles of ten — which is one hundred, 100 base ten.) Thus (A) is incorrect. (B) is incorrect since five is not a symbol of base two. 101 base two in (C) is correct but that isn't what Figure B shows! (E) is using incorrect symbols just as (B) is.

Section 3: Literature and Fine Arts

1.   **(E)**   The costuming shown is Elizabethan dress and would be appropriate for most Shakespearean plays (E). The puffing and slashing sleeves, the farthingale skirt and the male's gartered hose are all indicative of this period. Choice (E) is correct.

2.   **(D)**   You are asked to view the setting of a play and determine which style of scene design has been used. Symbolism (B) is the visualization of a play's idea through special scenic treatment. Expressionism is exaggerated symbolism. It usually distorts the scenic elements (A). Impressionism (C) attempts to enable the audience to see through the character's eyes. It is usually expressed through exaggeration and contrasts. Since the setting pictured does not use distortion or exaggeration, but is a realistic presentation of a drawing room or living room, we realize it is a realistic setting. Choice (D) is correct.

3.   **(D)**   John is described by the speaker as "practical in the extreme." We are also told that he has "no patience with faith, an intense horror of superstition, and scoffs openly at any talk of things not to be felt and seen and put down in figures." John is concerned with concrete reality, not "romantic felicity" as is the speaker. Choice (D) is the correct answer.

4.   **(B)**   The speaker says of her story that she "would not say it to a living soul, of course, but this is dead paper and a great relief to my mind." Writing is, for her, an outlet, a way for her to address her problems. Choice (B) is the correct answer.

5.   **(C)**   When not used to signal direct discourse, quotation marks indicate that the speaker or writer is being sarcastic and that the word being used has a different meaning than its dictionary definition. The fact that "work" (line 26) is in quotation marks tells us that the speaker is being sarcastic about her "occupation." Choice (C) is the correct answer.

6.   **(D)**   The building pictured in the example, an 11th century Norman church in the north of France, shows the typically massive masonry construction of these early Romanesque churches. These buildings, which did not yet have the advantage of Gothic arches and flying buttresses, relied for strength and stability on thick, blank walls which were pierced only by small window openings. Stone masonry bonded by mortar was, therefore, the architects' fundamental material. Oak timbers were probably used here also, although they were likely restricted to roof and ceiling framing and to construction scaffolds. All of the other materials listed in the answer choices are industrial-age materials which were unavailable to the medieval architect.

7.   **(C)**   The second century Chinese bronze horse shown in the example effectively exploits the unexpected contrast between the huge massive animal and its graceful, almost delicate pose and action. The horse is elegantly poised on one rear hoof and seems to be flying or swimming through the air, rather than merely trotting. It therefore expresses lightness and motion, not massiveness and stability, and completely denies any suggestion of physical decay. Additionally, although the horse in Chinese art was a symbol of majestic power, this sculpture does not allude in any specific way to either military prowess or moral fortitude.

8.   **(B)**   Phaethon was (in classical myth) the son of Helios, the Sun, who at one time undertook to drive his father's chariot. Persephone was (in classical myth) queen of the underworld and the reviving crops. Thus, their names (I) as well as Phaethon's occupation (II) characterize them as "gods"; choice (B) is correct.

9.   **(E)**   This city view by the French Impressionist Camille Pissarro is one of many in which the artist painted the scenes he saw beneath his second- or third-story Paris hotel windows—the correct answer is (E). The tilted perspective, with diagonal street axes and no horizon line, may owe a debt to photography, to Japanese prints, or to the example of his Impressionist peers. The resulting composition lacks not only a central focal point, but any single focal point at all; likewise, the only architecture visible does not dominate the scene, but, rather, acts as incidental local detail. The anonymous figures in the crowds below the artist's window share this lack of focus: they are busy in normal daily activity, without the least suggestion of drama. Finally, the idea that this scene was recorded from the window of a train lacks evidence: the scene is distinctly urban, not rural, and it is unlikely that a train would either pass through the crowded centers of a city or that it would be elevated to this height.

10.   **(C)**   In the work pictured, the American sculptor David Smith used power tools to cut, weld, and polish industrial-strength steel to create an ensemble in which the heavy, cubic forms balance in arrested motion. The sculptor obviously neither modelled the materials with his hands nor poured them into a mold: these forms have a rigid, machine-like, technological perfection to them and lack any such irregularities as those resulting from the molding action of human fingers. This same cubic perfection, and the gleaming, reflective surfaces, refute the idea of chisel work as well. And, finally, the erroneous suggestion that the artist merely joined ready-made industrial forms as he found them stems from this same sense of rigid, cubic perfection in the work's individual components.

11.   **(A)**   In this passage, the speaker tells of how he is everywhere and a part of everything in the natural world. This is done by example: "Where the bee sucks, there suck I," "In a cowslip's bell I lie," and, "Merrily, merrily shall I live now/Under the blossom that hangs on the bough" are all examples of how the speaker makes himself a part of nature.

12.   **(C)**   A dramatic monologue is a speech or narrative spoken by a single character, designed to sound more like everyday speech than lyrical poetry. (A), (C), and (E) are all lines of poetry, but (C) is considered an example of dramatic monologue because of the way in which it sounds more like words spoken by a specific character as opposed to simply "the poet" or "the speaker" of (A) and (E).

13.   **(D)**   The passage begins with a character crying, so we know that it is most likely a moment of high emotion. Next we are told that the character, "had never felt like that himself towards any woman, but he knew that such a feeling must be love." The character, Gabriel, has just discerned, through what he has heard about "that" (as in "he had never felt like that himself"), the meaning of love. Once this happens, his own identity begins "fading out into a grey impalpable world"; his state of consciousness, and even existence, is being altered because of his recent discovery.

14. **(A)** The 17th century Japanese ink-on-paper scroll painting shown in the example relies almost exclusively on the qualities of line to convey the graceful forms of two leaping deer. In this painting, called *Deer and Calligraphy*, both the animals and the scripted characters share the same quality of fluid, rhythmic, spontaneous "writing." Gradations of tone are unimportant here, since the images are defined by black line on white, and volume, too, is absent, since these forms show no shading or modulation of tone. Color, and its modifying term *hue*, are likewise missing from this black-and-white drawing.

15. **(D)** The arch, whether rounded or pointed, is completely absent from the building pictured in the example, even though the alternating use of windows with rounded pediments in the lower story seems to suggest the presence of arches. Otherwise, all of the other features listed in the answer choices do help regularize the design of this 17th century English Renaissance structure. The uniform second-story windows assert a regularity over the alternating window designs below them; they also emphasize a strong horizontal thrust across the building's facade, which is repeated in the balustrade at roof-level. The nearly-flush front surface of the building is broken only by the window openings and by the engaged columns at the building's center and the pilasters at the outer corners. Both of these features project just enough to establish a vertical contrast to the horizontal facade, but not enough to create a system of alternating solids and voids.

16. **(D)** The late 18th century Neoclassical painting shown in the example illustrates an episode from ancient Roman legend and attempts to simulate the static, balanced, monumental character of much Classical relief sculpture. The men in the main figure group, therefore, are represented in statuesque, absolutely motionless poses, and the correct answer choice here is (D). The compositional devices listed in all of the other answer choices are important to the painting. The figures stand within a shallow pictorial space, which is marked off by the arches in the background; these arches also serve to focus the man in the center. This shallow space, however, is modified somewhat by the checkerboard floor, which creates a slight perspective recession into the background and makes the figures' space seem logical and convincing. The strong highlighting on the foreground figures accentuates their static, sculptural quality, even as it pulls them to the absolute front of the picture. The intersecting lines of arms and swords establish the central focal point of the composition.

17. **(A)** This question asks you to consider both geographical proximity and some general characteristics of Eastern architecture in order to logically determine who would have the most direct influence on Japanese style. Of the answer choices, Greece and Nigeria fall well outside the Asian sphere both in distance and in building styles, while Easter Island, a Pacific site, is not known for a distinctive native architecture. Indonesian temple buildings may share something of the exotic, heavily-ornamented character of the structure pictured but the most representative Indonesian buildings are both much larger and are constructed of stone. The seventh century building pictured, in fact illustrates the strong dependence of Japan on the arts of China. The Chinese character of the structure is visible in the distinctive silhouette of the roof, with its long sweeping pitch and upturned corners in the heavy tiled roof, and in the wealth of elaborate brackets which support the dramatically projecting eaves.

18. **(E)** An oxymoron is an apparent contradiction in terms, such as "jumbo shrimp," "cruel kindness," or (as some would say), "military intelligence." Passage (E) contains an oxymoron because it mentions flames which give "No light, but rather darkness." Choice (E) is the correct answer.

19. **(B)** Assonance is the repetition of vowel sounds in a single line of poetry. Passage (D) contains three examples of assonance: the words "Rocks" and "bogs," the words "caves," "lakes," and "shades," and the words "fens" and "dens." Thus, passage (B) is the correct answer.

20. **(A)** Iambic pentameter refers to the meter, or rhythm, of a line of poetry composed of five feet, each of which is an iamb, having one unstressed syllable followed by a stressed syllable. A line of poetry written in iambic pentameter is ten syllables long. Passage (A) contains two lines of poetry written in iambic pentameter. When read aloud, the unstressed-stressed pattern emerges: "For SHADE to SHADE will COME too DROWsiLY, / And DROWN the WAKEful ANGuish OF the SOUL." Thus, choice (A) is the correct answer.

21. **(B)** The passage serves to introduce an upcoming story to be told by the narrator. He begins by exclaiming, "there may as well be an end of this!" and then gives a list of reasons why he has finally decided not to "keep my trouble to myself." He is about to relate an event, or series of events, to his friend, because keeping silent has been "burning [him] rather violently." He is very excited about what he has to say; choice (B) is correct. There is no evidence that the speaker feels guilty, ashamed, sorrowful, or relieved, so (A), (C), (D), and (E) are all incorrect.

22. **(C)** The speaker gives, as one of the reasons for telling his story, "if confession were not good for the soul, though harder than sin to some people, of which I am one," showing that he regards confession as a healthy, although difficult activity. (C) is the correct answer. He never speaks of confession as being unnecessary, nonsensical, impossible, or comical, so (A), (B), (D), and (E) are all incorrect.

23. **(A)** Three of the answer choices—(A), (C) and (D)—show groups of figures engaged in activities which might be interpreted as ceremonial. Choice (C) illustrated a column of soldiers marching across the midsection of a ceramic vessel: while they may be marching in a ceremonial function such as a parade or assembly, they are most likely intended to be shown advancing into battle, and, in any case, their primary function on this vase is decorative. Choice (D) shows figures engaged in music-making activities in formally arranged groups, but here, too, the illustrations serve the secondary purpose of amplifying the accompanying text. Only answer Choice (A), an ancient Persian relief sculpture, uses a rigidly schematized, formal composition and style to record an actual ceremonial event. Here, the clear-cut, well-defined figures are strictly arranged in three horizontal tiers, and each carries an accessory or attribute which identifies his role within this state occasion.

24. **(C)** Only answer choices (A) and (C) repeat the simplified forms of the human figure within a sculptural or ceramic context. Choice (A) appears to continually repeat a series of nearly-identical figures arranged on three horizontal levels, but close inspection reveals several types of figures here, each marked by a variety of detail in posture, costume, accessories, etc. Further, the figures are sculpted in a softly-rounded, convincing style. The figures in choice (C), in contrast, are grouped in a horizontal sequence which appears to show variety and movement; close examination, however, shows that the artist here has simply repeated figures whose clothing, weapons, postures, positions, and facial features are identical. While this serves to illustrate an anonymous mass of marching soldiers, it is even more important in helping the group of figures fit neatly, conveniently, and decoratively into its allotted space on the round "belly" of the vase.

25. **(D)** Calligraphy, or "fine writing," implies a two-dimensional or graphic format. Three of the possible answer choices, (A), (B) and (E), are forms of sculpture or sculptural relief, and therefore contain no drawn, calligraphic elements. Choice (C) presents a flat, two-dimensional illustration painted in black and white and minimal color. However, the images here are rigidly formalized and static, and display none of the rhythmic curves or flourishes of artistic penmanship. Only choice (D), a ninth century manuscript illustration, links calligraphy with figure drawing in the same rhythmic, linear style. In this illustration of the Bible's Psalm 150, the text written in ink above accompanies the figures below. Each is drawn in the same bold, agitated black and white line, with a sketchy spontaneity that creates an animated, nervous tension.

26. **(B)** The rose has, for centuries, been a symbol of virginal love and beauty. By calling the rose "sick," the poet is implying that somehow this virginal beauty has been lost. This is due to, as the poet states, an "invisible worm," that has found the rose's "bed/Of crimson joy." The loss of virginity has been equated with "sickness," and the sex act causing the loss is alluded to in terms of "worms" and "beds of crimson joy."

27. **(D)** Because of the "worm," the "rose" is "sick"; choice (D) is the best answer because it addresses the archetypical symbol of the rose as virginal love and beauty. Since the rose is "sick," this beauty is gone. Some of the other choices may adequately answer the question, but not as well as (D).

28. **(C)** In the example shown, the *Bull's Head* of 1943, the Spanish artist Pablo Picasso joined a bicycle seat and a set of handlebars in a clever, unexpected combination to produce a sculptural analogy to an actual bull. Thus, the artist was concerned here with form and substance, not with a contrast of line and tone and, even though the resulting artwork resembles a hat- or coat-rack the sculptor's first purpose was not to produce a functional device. Likewise, even though the bull has mythological connotations and figures prominently in many ancient religions, the artist was intent not on creating a religious symbol, but in exploring the visual unity of common objects brought together in new ways. The result is a strictly visual, sculptural effect, and in no way provides a metaphor for human experience.

29. **(B)** The passage describes large pieces of machinery coming toward two characters in a boat. The pieces of machinery are propelled by the water, a force of nature, making (B) the correct answer. None of the other conflicts are present in this passage.

30. **(B)** Three of the answer choices, (A), (C) and (E), illustrate Impressionist paintings, which tend to suppress or eliminate secondary or decorative detail in the search for a quick, spontaneous, and optically "true" impression of the subject. None can be said to concentrate on details in the figure's dress. Choice (D) shows a work of exhaustive detail, in which each tree branch, leaf, and grass stem, and the details and textures of clothing, stand out with stark realism. The main figure subject, however, far from merging into the background detail, is dramatically set off against it, especially in the face, neck, and arms. Only choice (B), by the American James MacNeill Whistler, accentuates decorative detail at the expense of the subject. In this case, the details of tiny flowers running up the back of the woman's dress connect visually to the delicate floral details in the wallpaper to the left, while the pale form of the woman's figure shades and merges into the background and almost reduces her to a flat pattern.

31. **(C)**   Two of the answer choices crop, or cut off, the main subject, much as the arbitrary framing of a photograph might do. Choice (E) a study of two women and a child by the American Impressionist Mary Cassatt pulls the figures to the very front of the picture plane, and cuts them off abruptly at the bottom edge and right side of the picture. The result seems to be an unposed, accidental image produced by a moment's glance. These figures, however, are firmly centered within the picture's borders, with a definite focal point in the image of the child with the book at center. Choice (C), by contrast, presents an extremely random composition in which the human subject is so far off-center and so dramatically cropped that she barely retains pictorial "presence" in the composition. This picture by the French Impressionist Edgar Degas produces an effect of seemingly unplanned, immediate realism which resembles a casually-aimed photographic snapshot.

32. **(D)**   Only two of the answer choices, (C) and (D), create their desired effect by positioning the primary subject noticeably off-center, thereby undermining the pictures formal visual balance. Choice (C), by the French painter Degas, shows a woman seated at a table on which rests an enormous bouquet of flowers. Even though the woman, apparently the main subject or sitter, glances out of the picture to the right and invites the viewer's gaze to follow, the huge bunch of flowers dominates the picture and calls the viewer's eye continually back to the painting's focal center. Answer choice (D), however, by the French Realist Bastien-Lepage clearly positions the primary subject off-center, as she stares and steps to the right with her arm outstretched. The figure seems to have just left the empty center of the picture and is about to exit the painting at the right. Her glance, her pose, and her position create a strongly directional thrust which draws the viewer's eye out of the picture as the figure moves.

33. **(E)**   India's famous Taj Mahal, pictured in the example, is laid out according to strict rules of symmetry: the main, central mass of the building, capped by a large dome, is buttressed by balanced pairs of smaller structures, each of which is topped by its own small dome. The four slender outlying towers mark off the corners of a square, while the whole complex is bisected by the long axis of the reflecting pool. This symmetry, however, though it creates balance and order, is less important to the building's weightless appearance than are the other answer choices. The repeated domes are graceful, balloon-like shapes which seem to rise and lift the building. Likewise, the four high towers create a strong, repeated vertical thrust which visually pulls the building upward. The white marble gleams and reflects the light, making the enormous mass of the building seem airy, delicate, and insubstantial. Finally, the pool in the foreground denies the solidity of the earth beneath the building and creates a reflection which seems to suggest that the building floats on water or clouds.

34. **(C)**   The way in which the passage describes, in detail, the setting, as well as the way in which the focus narrows as the passage proceeds (it moves from an entire neighborhood to a single man) marks it similar in tone and style to the opening stage directions of a play. Choice (C) is correct.

35. **(B)**   The fact that this character is known only as "the old man with the hempen beard who sleeps where nobody knows" lends him an air of insignificance—he is a type, not an individual, and is thus unworthy of a specific name. Choice (B) is correct.

Section 4: Science

1.   **(A)**   Neither a moving automobile (I), nor expanding gas (II), have potential or stored up energy; rather, the two have kinetic (moving) energy. The other items have potential or stored up energy. When the potential energy is set free, they too will then have kinetic energy. (A) is the correct answer since it enables the reader to choose both the moving automobile and the expanding gas. Since the other items are examples of potential energy, they cannot be chosen; notice that the reader is looking for the ones which do NOT have potential energy.

2.   **(D)**   Answer (D) is the correct answer. This answer enables the reader to choose all the phrases for the best answer. Matter and energy cannot be destroyed; (A) is therefore true. Matter or energy can be changed into other forms of matter or energy. (B) is also a correct answer. Energy can be changed from one form to another (C). For example, electrical energy may be converted to light energy in the case of an electric light bulb. Again, (D) enables the reader to choose all three correct answers. (E), none of the above, should not be chosen.

3.   **(E)**   Answer (E) enables the reader to choose both (A) and (B) which are correct answers. In answer (A), e (energy) equals m (mass, the amount of matter in a body) times c^2, (the speed of light squared). (B) is also a true statement for it states that the total amount of matter and energy in the universe remains the same. Answer (E), again, enables the reader to choose both. Answer (C) is incorrect because matter can be changed into energy and energy can be changed into matter. (C) should not be selected since it is false. Answer (D) should not be selected since it allows the reader to choose (A) which is true, (B) which is true, and (C) which is a false statement.

4.   **(C)**   The body does not "rob" materials from the skeleton when calcium is in short supply (B). Neither does it convert carbon to calcium (A). Rather, the body fails to replace atom for atom the normal withdrawal of calcium (C). A simple exchange has become a one-sided situation; as a result the skeleton (the support mechanism) may be seriously weakened. All of the above (D) and none of the above (E) also are incorrect. Only (C) is the correct answer.

5.   **(C)**   Sound energy is a type of wave energy so (C) is correct. Mechanical energy (A) is the most common form of energy about us. All moving bodies produce mechanical energy. The energy produced from machines is also mechanical energy. It is apparent that sound energy does not fit in this category. (A) is not the correct answer. Electrical energy (B) is the energy produced by the moving of electrons through a substance; electrical energy runs motors, lights homes, and makes telephones work. Sound energy is not a type of electrical energy. Answer (B) is incorrect. Nuclear energy (D) comes from the nucleus of an atom when it splits into two parts or when nuclei of atoms are fused together. Clearly sound waves do not fit into this classification. (D) is incorrect. Heat energy (E) is a form of radiant energy; sound energy does not fit under the category of heat energy. Sound energy would not fit under the category of radiant energy since radiant energy (another form of wave energy) includes light rays, infrared rays, radio waves, cosmic rays, radiant heat, X-rays and ultraviolet rays. (E) should not be selected. (C) is the correct answer.

6. **(D)**   Since the reader is looking for the one answer that is incorrect, (D) must be chosen. Photosynthesis is the process by which plants create their own food. The other answers (A), (B), (C), and (E) are correct statements and should not be chosen.

7. **(A)**   Since a meter is 39.37 inches or about the height of a five-year-old child, (A) is the best choice. A liter (B) is a measure of volume; it is slightly more than a quart. It is not the best unit to use to measure the height of a doorknob. A gram (C) is about the weight of a paper clip; since a gram is a measure of weight (mass) and not length, gram is not the best unit to use. A decimeter (D) is one tenth of a meter; a personal reference for a decimeter is about the distance between the end of the thumb and the end of the middle finger. This distance is a little more than 3" in an adult—about the length of a new piece of chalk. A decimeter could be used to measure the height of a doorknob from the floor but is not the measurement closest to the height . (D) is not the right answer. (E) is 1000 meters; since a meter is a little more than 3 feet, a measure of a little more than 3000 feet is not the best measure to apply to the height of a doorknob. (E) should not be chosen.

8. **(C)**   In a taproot system there is a primary taproot that grows until it is the major root in the system. An example of a plant that has a taproot system would be a carrot. (A) is a false statement; roots generally help to hold the plant in the ground. In a diffuse root system there is a network of roots. The primary root lives only for a short time so (B) is false. Both diffuse and taproot systems may be used to store food in the roots; (D), therefore, is false. (E) is partially true; roots do help with absorption, support, storage; roots, however, also help with reproduction. For instance, a gardener would plant dahlia bulbs (roots) to grow new dahlias.

9. **(A)**   The symbol for hydrogen is H. The other items are not symbols for hydrogen. No element on the periodic table of the elements is represented by Hy (B). He (C) is the symbol for helium, not hydrogen. Hi is not a symbol on the periodic table; (D) should not be chosen. Since Hn is not a symbol on the periodic table, it should not be selected as a symbol for hydrogen.

10. **(E)**   A shark (E) is not not a mammal; rather it is classified as a fish. Since it is NOT a mammal, a shark (E) is the correct answer for the question asking for the item which is not a mammal. All the other items (a bat, a whale, a gibbon [ape], and an elephant) are mammals; (A), (B), (C), and (D) may not be chosen.

11 . **(C)**   Most people are omnivorous (both plant- and animal- eating) so (C) is the correct answer. Herbivorous (A) or plant-eating (vegetarianism) does not describe most people. Carnivorous (B) or meat-eating does not describe most people. People do not generally migrate (D) or move from one area to another according to the season. Hibernating (E) or sleeping during the winter is not an activity typical of people. (A), (B), (D), or (E) should not be chosen.

12. **(E)**   Vitamin K (E) is the vitamin physicians may use to help blood to clot during a surgical operation. Vitamin K may also be obtained through certain foods and may also aid in blood clotting. The other vitamins are not useful in blood clotting. Vitamin A (A) is generally associated with healthy skin, not blood clotting. There are several B vitamins, so answer (B) is not clear; none of the B vitamins, however, are noted for their blood-clotting properties. (B) should not be chosen. Vitamin C (C) is needed for the prevention of scurvy,

preventing bleeding of the gums, and helping to prevent bruising. (C) is not the right choice. Vitamin D (D) is necessary for the proper utilization of calcium; it is not noted especially for clotting of the blood. (D) is a wrong answer and should not be chosen.

13. **(B)** The two, long, pointed teeth near the front of the human mouth are properly called canines (B). The central incisors are the two front teeth; they are straight across the bottom. (A) is not a correct answer. The premolars (C) are located behind the canines; they are broad and flat for chewing. (C) could not refer, then, to the long, pointed teeth. Molars, like premolars, are broad, flat teeth for chewing. Molars (D) are located to the back of the mouth; (D) could not be the long, pointed teeth referred to in the question. Lateral incisors (E) are located to each side of the central incisors. Lateral incisors are flat across the bottom. They are not the sharp, pointed teeth referred to in the question. (E) is a wrong answer and should not be chosen.

14. **(D)** The question asks for the false statement about the protozoans. (D) is false. A slipper-shaped protozoan is the paramecium, not the euglena. (D) is the correct choice for this question seeking a false statement. The other answers (A), (B), (C), and (E) are true statements and should not be selected.

15. **(E)** Using nuclear fusion to destroy colonies of insects seems drastic at this time. It is doubtful that such means would be used in the near future just to control insects! (E) is an incorrect answer, but since the statement asks for the false answer, (E) should be chosen. The other statements (A), (B), (C), and (D) are all true methods being used to control insects. None of them should be chosen since the instructions are to pick a means not used for controlling insects. (A) might be an answer picked by some respondents. In that case, the reader needs to remember that draining swamps was a means used in some countries to eliminate the mosquito, which was causing disease.

16. **(D)** The correct answer for the definition of energy is (D). All three answers (A), (B), and (C) are acceptable definitions of energy and may be chosen by using the answer (D). (E) is an incorrect answer since the reader would be selecting none of the answers given above.

17. **(D)** (D) is the correct answer because it allows you to choose radiant energy, of which light and radio waves are examples. Radiant energy is a form of wave energy. Mechanical energy (A) is the energy form seen most. All moving bodies produce mechanical energy; energy produced machines of all kinds is mechanical energy. Radio waves do not fit this category. Heat energy (B) is produced by the movement of molecules; the faster their rate of movement, the hotter the substance becomes. Since radio waves do not fit under the heat energy category, (B) is not appropriate. Electrical energy is the energy produced when electrons move through a substance; radio waves do not fit this category so (C) should not be chosen. Nuclear energy is a result of the splitting of the nucleus of the atom or from the fusion of the nuclei of atoms; (E) is not an appropriate answer since radio waves are not the result of this fusion or fission.

18. **(E)** There are normally 32 permanent teeth in the adult mouth. Answer (E) allows the reader to choose this answer. Without the wisdom teeth, there are 28 teeth (B). A child has about 28 teeth from the time the 12-year molar is cut until the cutting of the wisdom teeth at age 18; (B) is an incorrect choice. The other answers (A), (C), and (D) are inappropriate numbers of teeth to select.

19. **(D)**   Three statements about chemical energy in question 19 are true: I, III, and IV. Only answer (D) allows the reader to choose these three items. II [which is included in (A), (B), and (E)] is a false statement since chemical energy is really a form of potential—not kinetic—energy. V is a false statement; the definition given is really the definition of nuclear fission—a form of energy. V is included in (E). Since both II and V are included in (E), (E) should not be chosen. It is apparent then that (A), (B), (C) and (E) are erroneous statements and should not be selected.

20. **(C)**   Only one statement given is false; item (C). It is not the drone bee that is the largest but the queen bee. Since (C) is the only false statement, you should choose it. (A), (B), (D) and (E) are true statements, and therefore incorrect.

21. **(C)**   Only one statement is false about stems, item (C). Girdling a tree or plant will kill it. (C) is the answer to be chosen since a false answer is needed. You should not choose (A), (B), (D), or (E) because they are true as they are written.

22. **(D)**   Getting the nucleus of the atom to break up is called fission. Since the reader is to choose the answer which pertains to *fission* and not *fusion*, (D) is the only possible choice. The other answers (A), (B), (C) and (E) pertain to nuclear fusion and should not be chosen.

23. **(A)**   Since heat energy is produced by moving molecules I, since the faster the movement the more heat energy the substance has II and the hotter the substance becomes III, answer (A) is the correct one. Answer (B) omits III which is true and must be included; (B) should not be selected. Answer (C) omits I which is true and must be listed; (C) should not be chosen. A substance is not cooler as a result of the movement of its molecules. The movement results in a hotter substance. IV is false and should not be selected. Since (D) contains IV it is an inappropriate choice. (E) cannot be chosen because it not only omits I, II, and III but also includes V, which is an erroneous statement. Slow moving molecules do not produce heat in a substance; V and, therefore, (E) is false.

24. **(E)**   A nymph hatches from an egg and looks just like an adult except it has no wings or mature sex organs. A nymph is not one of the stages in complete metamorphosis but is rather a stage in incomplete metamorphosis. (E) should not be selected. Egg (A), the larva stage or stage in which the insect looks like a segmented worm (B), the pupa stage or stage which is called the resting or changing stage (C), and adult stage (D) are the four stages in complete metamorphosis.

25. **(E)**   To change normal body temperature (98.6° F) to Celsius, subtract 32 from the Fahrenheit; this gives 66.6. The result is multiplied by 5/9. The result is 37.7° C; (E) is the closest answer of the five to 37.7° C. (E) should be chosen. Normal body temperature is 98.6° F. This is not listed. If the you do not know how to convert Celsius to Fahrenheit, you can perhaps reason out the answer. For instance, most of us know that 100° C is about 212° F. Half of this would be 50° C, or 106° F. The temperature 106° F is above 98.6° F; (C) is too high. The next possible answer would be (E), or 37° C; this is the correct answer. 100° C—answer (A)—is too high since that equals 212° F 32° F is freezing; (B) could not be the correct choice. Since 212° F is the boiling point of water, (D) could not be the correct answer

26. **(C)** Heat normally causes a solid to expand; cold normally causes a solid to contract. Hot water would cause the outside tumbler to expand; if the inside tumbler is cooled, it would contract. This procedure should cause the two tumblers to slip apart. Allowing the two tumblers to cool would probably not result in their slipping apart. (A) should not be chosen. Heating both tumblers would cause both to expand and the result would probably be a tighter fit. (B) is incorrect. Cooling both tumblers (D) would result in a contracting of the two and a probably tightening of the fit; (D) is inappropriate. Contracting the outside tumbler by the use of cold and expanding the inside tumbler by the use of heat would only result in a tighter fit. (E) is incorrect.

27. **(E)** If the refrigerator is working properly, the Freon never leaves the refrigerator since the system is sealed. Warm air is discharged into the air, not Freon. (E) is the false answer and is the choice to be selected. All the other answers (A), (B), (C), and (D) are true and cannot be selected since a false answer is needed.

28. **(E)** Conifers do not have leaves which drop off during the fall season usually; the conifers are often called evergreens and have needles, not leaves. (E) is a false answer and is, therefore, the one to be selected. All the other answers (A), (B), (C), and (D) are true and cannot be chosen.

29. **(D)** It is not vacuoles which carry out all the activities that living things do in order to live; it is cells that do this. (D) is, therefore, a false answer and is the correct choice for question 29. All the other answers (A), (B), (C), and (E) are true and cannot be chosen. Vacuoles are spaces in the cytoplasm; they are sometimes used to store waste products, water, or even food. It is very evident, then, that (D) is a false answer.

30. **(E)** The earth behaves as a huge magnet; it has a north pole and a south pole. Answer (E), therefore, is false. It is the correct answer because it is a false statement. All the other answers (A), (B), (C), and (D) are true and cannot be chosen.

NTE Test of Professional Knowledge

TEST 4 – ANSWER SHEET

Section 1	Section 2	Section 3
1. Ⓐ Ⓑ Ⓒ Ⓓ Ⓔ	1. Ⓐ Ⓑ Ⓒ Ⓓ Ⓔ	1. Ⓐ Ⓑ Ⓒ Ⓓ Ⓔ
2. Ⓐ Ⓑ Ⓒ Ⓓ Ⓔ	2. Ⓐ Ⓑ Ⓒ Ⓓ Ⓔ	2. Ⓐ Ⓑ Ⓒ Ⓓ Ⓔ
3. Ⓐ Ⓑ Ⓒ Ⓓ Ⓔ	3. Ⓐ Ⓑ Ⓒ Ⓓ Ⓔ	3. Ⓐ Ⓑ Ⓒ Ⓓ Ⓔ
4. Ⓐ Ⓑ Ⓒ Ⓓ Ⓔ	4. Ⓐ Ⓑ Ⓒ Ⓓ Ⓔ	4. Ⓐ Ⓑ Ⓒ Ⓓ Ⓔ
5. Ⓐ Ⓑ Ⓒ Ⓓ Ⓔ	5. Ⓐ Ⓑ Ⓒ Ⓓ Ⓔ	5. Ⓐ Ⓑ Ⓒ Ⓓ Ⓔ
6. Ⓐ Ⓑ Ⓒ Ⓓ Ⓔ	6. Ⓐ Ⓑ Ⓒ Ⓓ Ⓔ	6. Ⓐ Ⓑ Ⓒ Ⓓ Ⓔ
7. Ⓐ Ⓑ Ⓒ Ⓓ Ⓔ	7. Ⓐ Ⓑ Ⓒ Ⓓ Ⓔ	7. Ⓐ Ⓑ Ⓒ Ⓓ Ⓔ
8. Ⓐ Ⓑ Ⓒ Ⓓ Ⓔ	8. Ⓐ Ⓑ Ⓒ Ⓓ Ⓔ	8. Ⓐ Ⓑ Ⓒ Ⓓ Ⓔ
9. Ⓐ Ⓑ Ⓒ Ⓓ Ⓔ	9. Ⓐ Ⓑ Ⓒ Ⓓ Ⓔ	9. Ⓐ Ⓑ Ⓒ Ⓓ Ⓔ
10. Ⓐ Ⓑ Ⓒ Ⓓ Ⓔ	10. Ⓐ Ⓑ Ⓒ Ⓓ Ⓔ	10. Ⓐ Ⓑ Ⓒ Ⓓ Ⓔ
11. Ⓐ Ⓑ Ⓒ Ⓓ Ⓔ	11. Ⓐ Ⓑ Ⓒ Ⓓ Ⓔ	11. Ⓐ Ⓑ Ⓒ Ⓓ Ⓔ
12. Ⓐ Ⓑ Ⓒ Ⓓ Ⓔ	12. Ⓐ Ⓑ Ⓒ Ⓓ Ⓔ	12. Ⓐ Ⓑ Ⓒ Ⓓ Ⓔ
13. Ⓐ Ⓑ Ⓒ Ⓓ Ⓔ	13. Ⓐ Ⓑ Ⓒ Ⓓ Ⓔ	13. Ⓐ Ⓑ Ⓒ Ⓓ Ⓔ
14. Ⓐ Ⓑ Ⓒ Ⓓ Ⓔ	14. Ⓐ Ⓑ Ⓒ Ⓓ Ⓔ	14. Ⓐ Ⓑ Ⓒ Ⓓ Ⓔ
15. Ⓐ Ⓑ Ⓒ Ⓓ Ⓔ	15. Ⓐ Ⓑ Ⓒ Ⓓ Ⓔ	15. Ⓐ Ⓑ Ⓒ Ⓓ Ⓔ
16. Ⓐ Ⓑ Ⓒ Ⓓ Ⓔ	16. Ⓐ Ⓑ Ⓒ Ⓓ Ⓔ	16. Ⓐ Ⓑ Ⓒ Ⓓ Ⓔ
17. Ⓐ Ⓑ Ⓒ Ⓓ Ⓔ	17. Ⓐ Ⓑ Ⓒ Ⓓ Ⓔ	17. Ⓐ Ⓑ Ⓒ Ⓓ Ⓔ
18. Ⓐ Ⓑ Ⓒ Ⓓ Ⓔ	18. Ⓐ Ⓑ Ⓒ Ⓓ Ⓔ	18. Ⓐ Ⓑ Ⓒ Ⓓ Ⓔ
19. Ⓐ Ⓑ Ⓒ Ⓓ Ⓔ	19. Ⓐ Ⓑ Ⓒ Ⓓ Ⓔ	19. Ⓐ Ⓑ Ⓒ Ⓓ Ⓔ
20. Ⓐ Ⓑ Ⓒ Ⓓ Ⓔ	20. Ⓐ Ⓑ Ⓒ Ⓓ Ⓔ	20. Ⓐ Ⓑ Ⓒ Ⓓ Ⓔ
21. Ⓐ Ⓑ Ⓒ Ⓓ Ⓔ	21. Ⓐ Ⓑ Ⓒ Ⓓ Ⓔ	21. Ⓐ Ⓑ Ⓒ Ⓓ Ⓔ
22. Ⓐ Ⓑ Ⓒ Ⓓ Ⓔ	22. Ⓐ Ⓑ Ⓒ Ⓓ Ⓔ	22. Ⓐ Ⓑ Ⓒ Ⓓ Ⓔ
23. Ⓐ Ⓑ Ⓒ Ⓓ Ⓔ	23. Ⓐ Ⓑ Ⓒ Ⓓ Ⓔ	23. Ⓐ Ⓑ Ⓒ Ⓓ Ⓔ
24. Ⓐ Ⓑ Ⓒ Ⓓ Ⓔ	24. Ⓐ Ⓑ Ⓒ Ⓓ Ⓔ	24. Ⓐ Ⓑ Ⓒ Ⓓ Ⓔ
25. Ⓐ Ⓑ Ⓒ Ⓓ Ⓔ	25. Ⓐ Ⓑ Ⓒ Ⓓ Ⓔ	25. Ⓐ Ⓑ Ⓒ Ⓓ Ⓔ
26. Ⓐ Ⓑ Ⓒ Ⓓ Ⓔ	26. Ⓐ Ⓑ Ⓒ Ⓓ Ⓔ	26. Ⓐ Ⓑ Ⓒ Ⓓ Ⓔ
27. Ⓐ Ⓑ Ⓒ Ⓓ Ⓔ	27. Ⓐ Ⓑ Ⓒ Ⓓ Ⓔ	27. Ⓐ Ⓑ Ⓒ Ⓓ Ⓔ
28. Ⓐ Ⓑ Ⓒ Ⓓ Ⓔ	28. Ⓐ Ⓑ Ⓒ Ⓓ Ⓔ	28. Ⓐ Ⓑ Ⓒ Ⓓ Ⓔ
29. Ⓐ Ⓑ Ⓒ Ⓓ Ⓔ	29. Ⓐ Ⓑ Ⓒ Ⓓ Ⓔ	29. Ⓐ Ⓑ Ⓒ Ⓓ Ⓔ
30. Ⓐ Ⓑ Ⓒ Ⓓ Ⓔ	30. Ⓐ Ⓑ Ⓒ Ⓓ Ⓔ	30. Ⓐ Ⓑ Ⓒ Ⓓ Ⓔ
31. Ⓐ Ⓑ Ⓒ Ⓓ Ⓔ	31. Ⓐ Ⓑ Ⓒ Ⓓ Ⓔ	31. Ⓐ Ⓑ Ⓒ Ⓓ Ⓔ
32. Ⓐ Ⓑ Ⓒ Ⓓ Ⓔ	32. Ⓐ Ⓑ Ⓒ Ⓓ Ⓔ	32. Ⓐ Ⓑ Ⓒ Ⓓ Ⓔ
33. Ⓐ Ⓑ Ⓒ Ⓓ Ⓔ	33. Ⓐ Ⓑ Ⓒ Ⓓ Ⓔ	33. Ⓐ Ⓑ Ⓒ Ⓓ Ⓔ
34. Ⓐ Ⓑ Ⓒ Ⓓ Ⓔ	34. Ⓐ Ⓑ Ⓒ Ⓓ Ⓔ	34. Ⓐ Ⓑ Ⓒ Ⓓ Ⓔ
35. Ⓐ Ⓑ Ⓒ Ⓓ Ⓔ	35. Ⓐ Ⓑ Ⓒ Ⓓ Ⓔ	35. Ⓐ Ⓑ Ⓒ Ⓓ Ⓔ

NTE CORE BATTERY–Test 4
TEST OF PROFESSIONAL KNOWLEDGE
Section 1

TIME: 30 Minutes
35 Questions

DIRECTIONS: Each of the following questions and incomplete statements is followed by five answer choices. Select the choice which best answers each question.

---

1. New teachers may have a more difficult time learning to identify potentially gifted children. This is due primarily to
   - (A) conflicting research data.
   - (B) pressure from parents who think their child is gifted.
   - (C) unreliable or invalid test scores.
   - (D) lack of teaching experience.
   - (E) classroom mood and/or environment.

2. If you are conducting a laboratory experiment in science class you would be implementing which means of instruction most?
   - (A) Deduction
   - (B) Unitization
   - (C) Discrimination
   - (D) Automaticity
   - (E) None of the above.

3. When the teacher wants a higher order response from the students he will probably
   - (A) not accept all short responses.
   - (B) make the statement lengthy with more sophisticated vocabulary.
   - (C) restate the question and ask a left-brain preference student.
   - (D) ask students to write down their responses and then read them aloud.
   - (E) ask for additional information.

4. Bloom's taxonomy represents six levels of thinking opportunities for students. Each level gives teachers opportunities to formulate summative and formative, convergent and divergent questions. The first level (knowledge) questions are primarily
   - (A) summative and divergent.
   - (B) memory.
   - (C) divergent.
   - (D) convergent.
   - (E) synthesis.

5. There are some isolated situations, in which, despite conscientious planning and good lesson presentation, the students are unable to learn certain material. This is especially true in the lower grades. When this occurs,

   (A) the teacher should re-evaluate the entire lesson plan and re-introduce it at a later time.

   (B) the objective was inappropriate.

   (C) they are not ready for the concept developmentally, so the teacher should give up.

   (D) the learners have insufficient previous knowledge.

   (E) the strategies and methods were inappropriate.

6. Teachers who receive merit pay have

   (A) taught ten years or more in the same school district.

   (B) evidence of higher achievement scores for their students.

   (C) greater enthusiasm and fewer discipline problems in the classroom.

   (D) attended many in–school workshops for staff.

   (E) demonstrated excellent performance consistently.

7. The emphasis on correlating studies is a concept in understanding the relationship of

   (A) a child's development to curriculum.

   (B) the amount of financing to literacy.

   (C) social life to economic level.

   (D) economics to literacy.

   (E) teachers of one discipline to teachers of another.

8. When we consider behavioral objectives we are looking at

   (A) what the teacher should do to see that learning occurs.

   (B) the lesson plan that is taught.

   (C) what a student should be able to do upon completion of instruction.

   (D) a statement of what students and teachers should do.

   (E) None of the above.

9. The adverse reaction of educators toward merit pay says it will reduce

   (A) effort by average teachers.

   (B) cooperation and communication of teachers.

   (C) salaries of the rest of the teachers.

   (D) respect for all colleagues whether on merit pay or not.

   (E) students' respect for teachers.

10. Low income minority students may be difficult for teachers to understand and motivate because of

   (A) disinterested parents.   (D) too difficult a curriculum.

   (B) high absenteeism.   (E) outside peer pressure.

   (C) language and cultural differences.

11. The learning process used by teachers which is capable of molding our responses without any direct reinforcement is referred to as
     (A)   operant extinction.   (D)   modeling or imitating.
     (B)   operant conditioning.   (E)   None of the above.
     (C)   operant shaping.

12. The United States Supreme Court has held that students may
     (A)   not be subject to corporal punishment.
     (B)   be expelled from school but for no longer than 10 days.
     (C)   withdraw from school at age 15 if employed.
     (D)   have their driver's license suspended if under 18 years old and they drop out of school.
     (E)   wear buttons that promote political issues.

13. John Dewey's philosophy of education would have stated that the purpose of education is
     (A)   the personal and social growth of the individual.
     (B)   that all the time should be spent on academic development.
     (C)   that science should have the major emphasis in the curriculum.
     (D)   that morals should be taught extensively.
     (E)   that the humanities should have the major emphasis in the curriculum.

14. Objectives, supplementary materials, teaching strategies, and activities are part of the
     (A)   short-term plan.   (D)   unit plan.
     (B)   daily plan.   (E)   curriculum.
     (C)   calendar plan.

15. Citizen advisory committees are sometimes used in local schools. Which of the following would be the most appropriate function for a high school advisory committee?
     (A)   evaluate teachers for tenure.
     (B)   screen complaints about school library books.
     (C)   raise money for school athletics.
     (D)   encourage the school board to increase the percent of the school district budget spent on the high school.
     (E)   review the school curriculum and suggest priorities for curriculum improvement.

16. Planning procedures are an important part of the science teacher's skills. When he/she directs a pre-teaching activity it is intended to
     (A)   reflect the student's product and process skills for science.
     (B)   provide information for writing the science objectives.
     (C)   motivate the students to study science.
     (D)   All of the above.

17. An integral part of teleconferencing is
    (A) direct teaching.
    (B) achievement scores.
    (C) distance education.
    (D) strategic teaching.
    (E) group discussion.

18. Research of John Goodlad indicated student talk in the classroom takes up less than what percentage of the instructional time?
    (A) 50%
    (B) 6%
    (C) 20%
    (D) 2%
    (E) 10%

19. Critiquing language arts lessons is a culminating step in the planning procedure. Lesson critiques are most beneficial for
    (A) the teacher to plan more effectively.
    (B) the teacher and the students to determine goal achievements.
    (C) the students to determine what they learned.
    (D) the students to determine heir goal achievements.
    (E) the students to determine their teacher's methods.

20. Teachers have to deal with the many pressures children face in the world which lead to
    (A) high interest in school work.
    (B) having knowledge of a particular subject.
    (C) readiness to set new goals and challenges.
    (D) having knowledge of the world.
    (E) lowered self esteem.

21. If a teacher has determined that punishment is necessary, which of the following are appropriate guidelines for punishing students?
    I.   Let students know what behavior will be punished before administering any punishment.
    II.   Punish only about every third time the behavior occurs so the students being punished won't believe you are making an example of them.
    III. Punish immediately following the inappropriate behavior.
    IV.   The teacher should explicitly identify for the student the behavior that is to change as a result of the punishment.
    (A) I and II only.
    (B) III and IV only.
    (C) I, II and III only.
    (D) I, III and IV only.
    (E) II, III and IV only.

22. During June, 1990, the United States Supreme Court ruled that which of the following groups could use public school facilities to hold meetings?
    (A) Prayer groups
    (B) Science clubs
    (C) Chinese students
    (D) Young Republicans
    (E) Junior Acheivement

23. To facilitate learning a teacher must
    (A) properly use different forms of teaching strategies.
    (B) be able to successfully use direct and indirect teaching.
    (C) be successful working with group and individual students.
    (D) All the above.
    (E) Only (A) and (B).

24. The learning stations approach allows many students to experience many materials in a given period of time. From a behavioral standpoint, which student would need the most teacher reinforcement to be successful?
    (A) An auditory learner
    (B) A learning disabled student
    (C) A student who is chronically off-task
    (D) The student who does average work
    (E) A quiet, yet gifted, student

25. United States educators have decided that Japanese education
    (A) should be a model for U.S. education.
    (B) is of better quality than U.S. education.
    (C) should not be a model for the U.S.
    (D) doesn't place enough pressure for students.
    (E) is "on par' with U.S. education.

26. Which of the following are characteristics of norm-referenced test?
    I. Students are compared to a set of standards.
    II. Students must demonstrate skills on the test at some predetermined level.
    III. Students compete against other students.
    IV. Used to determine if students are in the top 20% of a class.
    (A) I only.   (D) III and IV only.
    (B) I and II only.   (E) II, III and IV.
    (C) III only.

27. Public Law 95-56 (1978) makes provisions for the gifted and talented, since the law states that schools will identify and provide them with appropriate education. Yet some schools do not because
    (A) it would mean additional trained staff, facilities, testing and identifying efforts, and establishing objectives and goals for their program.
    (B) parents may complain if their child is not identified as gifted.
    (C) administrators think it will cost them extra money and they have teachers that do not want the gifted pulled from their rooms.
    (D) it is easier to ignore the gifted and let them read library books or help the slow learner.
    (E) gifted students often teach themselves and therefore require less teacher interaction

28. In order for a teacher to identify the distinguishing characteristics of at-risk students, he/she must recognize their
    (A) high self-esteem.
    (B) low education grades and scores.
    (C) good home environment and support.
    (D) high interest in all courses.
    (E) hostile behavior.

29. The career ladder concept is based upon the assumption that
    (A) teachers stay too long in the classroom and need to move on to other jobs in the school system.
    (B) good teachers should be rewarded at a level that would make them want to stay in the classroom.
    (C) teachers will use and support most of the present teacher evaluation systems.
    (D) good teachers will make good administrators so a career path into school administration should be made available.
    (E) persons with college degrees, but not teacher certification, should be given a shorter route to become certified and start a teaching career.

30. Teachers group students for many reasons, and they use different types of groups. Which of the following would be the best placement for a student from a culturally deprived situation who also has a language barrier?
    (A) A panel with low achievers
    (B) A project group
    (C) A research group
    (D) A group which has the teacher as a member
    (E) A discussion group that is heterogeneous

31. When Thorndike developed the stimulus-response theory of learning, it helped to derive his Law of Effect. A student receives an A on a math test. Receiving the good grade serves as
    (A) a stimulus.
    (B) a sign that the student studied.
    (C) a sign that learning has occurred.
    (D) an effect.
    (E) Only (A), (B) and (C).

32. Poor teachers will use only the curriculum guide and textbooks provided by the school because
    (A) it is a sign of being a cooperative teacher.
    (B) they lack motivation, enthusiasm, and love for teaching.
    (C) they may be accused of teaching the wrong thing if they add enrichment materials or knowledge.
    (D) they feel it gives adequate material and knowledge for the age they are teaching.
    (E) they must be accused of subjecting students to an "information overflow".

33. New teachers are encouraged to follow the text closely the first few years of teaching. This is recommended
     (A) to build self-confidence in teaching.
     (B) to establish the pattern of teaching the required curriculum.
     (C) to build an awareness of and appreciation for established skills.
     (D) All the above.
     (E) None of the above.

34. A major advantage identified in support of team teaching at the high school level is that
     (A) it allows teachers to better understand individual children.
     (B) it will reduce school instructional costs.
     (C) it utilizes the special competencies and strengths of teachers.
     (D) it is easier to build into the master schedule.
     (E) it has consistently resulted in students having higher achievement test scores.

35. It was in 1837 that kindergarten was founded by
     (A) Piaget.   (D) Froebel.
     (B) Hutchins.   (E) Montessori.
     (C) Herbart.

Section 2

TIME: 30 Minutes
35 Questions

DIRECTIONS: Each of the following questions and incomplete statements is followed by five answer choices. Select the choice which best answers each question.

---

1. What approach has been successful for student-centered teaching?
    (A)   Team-teaching
    (B)   An authoritarian teacher in the control
    (C)   Small group activities with little guidance or supervision by the teacher
    (D)   Provide structured activities so the students do not have to use their abilities in applying concepts
    (E)   Promoting development of higher cognitive growth

2. A student with severe behavior problems may be able to be successful in the regular classroom. What special modifications may be needed?
    (A)   Modifications are not needed.
    (B)   More frequent praise and reinforcement is needed.
    (C)   Instruct other students to intentionally ignore their peer.
    (D)   Focus the attention of other students on the peer.
    (E)   Distance the student.

3. When a teacher is the center of the classroom activity, what approach is being used?
    (A)   Discovery approach   (D)   Small group activity
    (B)   Unfocused discussion   (E)   Direct instruction
    (C)   Indirect instruction

4. Approaches to gifted education does not include which one of the following?
    (A)   Advance at a rate that everyone in class can master
    (B)   Group students by ability so they can achieve and be challenged
    (C)   Provide enriched learning experiences in one or more subjects
    (D)   Emphasize accelerating students' progress in special programs or special in-class activities
    (E)   Provide opportunities for out-of-class learning

5. Excellent student involvement occurs when
    (A)   administrators decide a plan.
    (B)   the teacher decides on a plan.

(C)   the students decide on a plan.

(D)   the teacher and students decide on a plan and its implementation.

(E)   the teacher and administrators decide on a plan and its implementation.

6.   When writing a daily lesson plan you should include

(A)   questions you want to ask to check for comprehension.

(B)   anticipatory activity or lesson opener.

(C)   objectives and means to obtain them.

(D)   All the above.

(E)   Only (B) and (C).

7.   Obtaining background information is necessary to determine what knowledge the student already possesses. This is which step of the lesson critique stage?

(A)   Teacher activities   (D)   Teacher preparation

(B)   The objectives   (E)   Means of closure

(C)   Instructional procedures

8.   A developmentally appropriate curriculum for young children would include a major emphasis upon

I.   learning experiences that include physical activity.

II.   questions emphasizing convergent thinking.

III.   students learning to be quiet, orderly and attentive.

IV.   using manipulative materials.

(A)   I and II only.   (D)   II and III only.

(B)   I and III only.   (E)   II, III and IV only.

(C)   I and IV only.

9.   The pay of most teachers in the United States is determined by the single salary schedule. Which of the following items are considered in determining each individual teacher's salary on the single salary schedule?

(A)   Test performance of pupils and years of teaching experience

(B)   Years of teaching experience and the teacher's level of education

(C)   Pupils' test performance and principal's ratings of teachers

(D)   The teacher's level of education and peer ratings

(E)   Principal's ratings and peer ratings

10.   Horace Mann is recognized as

(A)   the leading advocate of private schools for religious education.

(B)   an advocate of westward expansion.

(C)   the founder of the common school movement to fund free elementary schools open to all students.

(D)   the founder of academy schools which were located in the southern states and provide free schools for former slaves.

(E)   the first U.S. Secretary of Education.

11. The kindergarten was designed to
    (A) teach children to read early.
    (B) develop social skills and know the self.
    (C) develop good relationship with parents.
    (D) correlate the curriculum better.
    (E) foster a love of learning.

12. While developing inductive reasoning, the teacher will first
    (A) introduce the generalizations to be learned.
    (B) state the objectives.
    (C) present specific data from which a generalization is to be drawn.
    (D) state a trial hypothesis.
    (E) predict a tentative set of results.

13. A learning center is designed to include
    (A) uninteresting materials.
    (B) play things, only .
    (C) difficult tasks designed to make students work and learn.
    (D) buysy work.
    (E) various levels of reading and interest.

14. Within a career ladder plan, teachers seeking a promotion are evaluated by
    (A) colleagues.
    (B) students.
    (C) student achievement scores.
    (D) classroom observation.
    (E) amount of material covered in a certain time span.

15. Which classroom management skill would adaptations and accommodations for the left- and right-brain preference students be a function of?
    (A) Lesson plans   (D) (A) and (B).
    (B) Strategy   (E) All of the above.
    (C) Assertive discipline plan

16. Goals are written for a school by
    (A) the federal government board and Secretary of Health, Education and Welfare.
    (B) curriculum committees chosen by the local school system.
    (C) a combination of teachers and parents.
    (D) the State Commissioner of education and his staff.
    (E) individual disciplines' departments.

17. Formative questions are typically used
    (A) to determine the students' understanding and applications of the objectives.
    (B) periodically throughout the lesson sequence.

(C)   to give the teacher specific information and assessment.

(D)   All of the above.

(E)   Only (A) and (B).

18.   In order for teachers to integrate technology into the classrooms, the principals should

(A)   observe what teachers already know.

(B)   include knowledge of technology on teacher evaluations.

(C)   check with state department on technology.

(D)   channel available funding into the purchasing of equipment.

(E)   plan staff seminars on using technology.

19.   If a teacher is willing to increase wait time after asking a question he/she is likely to encounter

(A)   improved student response.

(B)   an increase in the number of appropriate responses.

(C)   an increase in the number of accurate responses.

(D)   more restlessness in his students.

(E)   Only (A), (B) and (C).

20.   Educating the whole child is a concept emphasized by

(A)   concentrating on the core curriculum.

(B)   observing the psychological behaviors of the student.

(C)   growth and development of the entire child.

(D)   stressing your value system to the students.

(E)   the teaching of ethics.

21.   Which of the following is the least effective method of determining the level of a student's reading ability?

(A)   Report cards from previous years   (D)   Using test results

(B)   Teacher judgment   (E)   Vocabulary drill

(C)   Consulting with last year's teachers

22.   During a classroom discussion the teacher said, "Amy and Joe appear to be arguing that the Civil War started because of the fear of some southern state residents of economic domination by the North, while most of the class thinks slavery was the sole cause of the Civil War." The teacher is perfoming what important function in a class discussion?

(A)   Providing new information

(B)   Orienting the students to the objective of the lesson

(C)   Putting together a final consensus

(D)   Reviewing and putting together opinions into a meaningful realtionship

(E)   Using prompting techniques

23. If you are required to teach a unit on a subject for which you have little background studies or knowledge and feel you do not have adequate resources available or ample time to prepare, perhaps the best introductory activity for you would be

    (A) to tell what you know and skip to another subject.

    (B) to assign independent projects to the students.

    (C) a bulletin board display that a student or volunteer made.

    (D) to substitute the subject with one you know.

    (E) to have a resource person speak.

24. As a result of educational policy reports in the 1980s there have been changes in

    (A) higher education, teacher preparation programs.

    (B) teacher certification requirements.

    (C) high school requirements.

    (D) All of the above.

    (E) Only (A) and (C).

25. Questions can be used to

    (A) allow for creativity.

    (B) check student comprehension.

    (C) review the material previously covered.

    (D) All of the above.

    (E) Only (B) and (C).

26. Teachers who expect to have low-achieving students reach higher levels of cognitive understanding should use

    (A) cooperative learning.   (D) indirect teaching.

    (B) reasoning skills.   (E) lecture-format instruction.

    (C) achievement scores.

27. The high school history teacher asked the American History class, "What was the effect of the Great Depression upon the attitude of Americans?" The teacher paused for about four or five seconds, then said, "John, would you please answer the question?" The procedure described above is an example of

    (A) low level question.   (D) wait-time.

    (B) anticipatory set.   (E) convergent questioning.

    (C) prompting.

28. Jean Piaget's principles of learning are based on

    (A) children's cognitive development. (D) children's moral instruction

    (B) individualized instruction.   (E) children's self-conceptions

    (C) children's physical development.

29. The Madeline Hunter model includes a step designed to focus student attention upon the topic of the lesson. This step is known as

    (A) modeling.   (D) anticipatory set.

    (B) input.   (E) divergent questioning.

    (C) withitness

30. "On the worksheet are economic characteristics of ten countries we have not studied. Using what you know about capitalism and socialism, what countries do you believe have a socialistic system?" The teacher has asked a(n)

    (A) knowledge question.
    (B) comprehension question.
    (C) application question.
    (D) evaluation question.
    (E) redireted question.

31. The primary reason for instructional planning is

    (A) to have a plan for a substitute if you are out unexpectedly.
    (B) because it is required by administrators.
    (C) to focus your instructional methods, and skills, as well as the student's learning skills.
    (D) to accomplish state requirements.
    (E) to allow you to move from topic to topic with ease and without delay.

32. Rousseau believed that students could learn best if they experienced

    (A) library resources such as books and periodicals.
    (B) the teachers having a vital role.
    (C) field trips with direct experiences.
    (D) their parents' or caretakers' moral lessons.
    (E) Both (A) and (D).

33. Teaching strategies are necessary to

    (A) keep the long-term curriculum goals in sight.
    (B) direct the administrator's attention to right emphasis.
    (C) keep the teacher on task with the least amount of time.
    (D) keep the students on task with no distractions.
    (E) direct both the students and teacher toward accomplishing a goal.

34. Student instruction using individualized plans is not often used because

    (A) it takes too much time and money to implement.
    (B) achievement scores are not considered.
    (C) students do not like it.
    (D) sequence and structure in the subject are not considered.
    (E) All of the above.

35. A usable definition of an objective is

    (A) a statement of students' expectations.
    (B) a goal for the teacher and the students.
    (C) a statement of learner outcomes.
    (D) a statement of teaching methods.
    (E) an inventory of questions to be asked, materials to be used, and information to be covered.

Section 3

TIME: 30 Minutes
35 Questions

> **DIRECTIONS**: Each of the following questions and incomplete statements is followed by five answer choices. Select the choice which best answers each question.

1. The time needed to learn is a consideration in mastery instruction. Another factor to consider is

   (A) teacher's attitude.
   (D) student's attitude.
   (B) school environment.
   (E) teacher's knowledge.
   (C) student's characteristics.

2. Assertive Discipline involves all of the following EXCEPT that

   (A) the students establish clear guidelines for their behavior.
   (B) the teacher creates and establishes clearly defined rules.
   (C) the teacher establishes clear consequences for violating the rules.
   (D) the teacher establishes a reward for appropriate behavior.
   (E) the teacher should be in charge of the classroom.

3. Classroom teachers are concerned that the special-needs students in their rooms achieve academic goals. Perhaps the greatest tendency is to

   (A) set goals lower for the special-needs students.
   (B) not give clear explanations that the students can understand.
   (C) provide too much guidance and assistance.
   (D) spend too much time preparing special materials for one student.
   (E) treat the student as an "average" one and hope he will feel comfortable enough to let learning take place.

4. Segregation that occurs as a result of school policies, laws, or government actions is

   (A) dejure segregation.
   (D) semi-integration.
   (B) controlled choice.
   (E) None of the above.
   (C) integration.

5. Recent research on the relationship of time and student learning defined engaged time. Which definition is correct?

   (A) Engaged time is that part of allocated time in which students are actively involved with academic subject matter.
   (B) Engaged time is the amount of time a student spends in independent study.
   (C) Engaged time is the amount of time allocated for each subject, for example, 45 minutes for math.

    (D)   Engaged time is the allocated time in which students are involved with academic subject matter and have a high rate of success (80% or higher).

    (E)   Engaged time is the average time the teacher spends on the core subjects in the curriculum.

6.   Wait-time is important when planning a questioning strategy. Which of these is not true?

    (A)   It discourages thoughtful risking

    (B)   It facilitates comprehension

    (C)   It allows assimilation of information so that rapid guessing does not occur

    (D)   It gives the teacher time to formulate the next question

    (E)   It allows students time to reword any new found information

7.   After asking a question, the amount of time a teacher waits for a response should

    (A)   depend on how uncomfortable and humiliated the student may appear to be.

    (B)   bring a negative response from the student called on to answer.

    (C)   serve to stimulate improved student responses.

    (D)   not vary according to the student's intellectual ability.

    (E)   depend on the time remaining in the lesson.

8.   Integration and desegregation are different, since integration includes

    (A)   voluntary student isolation according to race.

    (B)   students are isolated in the school according to race.

    (C)   students of different races go to the same school.

    (D)   students attending the same school, but separation existing.

    (E)   development of positive interracial contact.

9.   Which type of planning by teachers is the most important and effective planning?

    (A)   Yearlong plans   (D)   Weekly lesson plans

    (B)   Daily lesson plans   (E)   Monthly lesson plans

    (C)   Unit plans

10.   Summative questions are typically used for which purpose?

    (A)   For pre-introductory

    (B)   For one-word answers

    (C)   For closure and evaluation

    (D)   To determine the progress toward goals and objectives

    (E)   Attention-getting devices in the anticipatory set

11.   When you use cognitive memory questions, it requires that students

    (A)   form a hypothesis.   (D)   recall information.

    (B)   solve a problem.   (E)   criticize an idea.

    (C)   compare and contrast information.

12. In the past few years, we have seen a movement of the Hispanic population into the inner-city in large urban areas, which has resulted in a form of
    (A) ability grouping or tracking. (D) controlled choice.
    (B) magnet programs. (E) integration.
    (C) segregation.

13. What is the proper sequence of the four major steps of class planning?
    (A) Evaluate the lesson, establish purpose, select the learning material, and organize the lesson
    (B) Establish teacher and student goals, choose appropriate materials, plan the lesson presentation and evaluate the lesson
    (C) Establish teacher goals, organize the lesson, select learning material and equipment, and evaluate the lesson
    (D) Establish goals, evaluate the lesson, organize the lesson and select materials
    (E) Organize lesson, establish goals, select materials, evaluate the lesson

14. Removing external stimuli is the reading teacher's attempt to increase
    (A) positive behavior. (D) class discussion.
    (B) attention. (E) test scores.
    (C) motivation.

15. Praise brings positive results in the classroom. While it is effective on the average, teachers praise students in class less than
    (A) 40% of the time. (D) 20% of the time.
    (B) 10% of the time. (E) 50% of the time.
    (C) 2% of the time.

16. The student will identify the various parts of a dictionary entry during class discussion.

    The objective listed above may have one or more deficiencies. Select the statement that is the best answer.
    (A) The behavior is not specified.
    (B) The condition is not specified.
    (C) The degree of mastery is not specified.
    (D) All requirements for an objective are met.
    (E) Neither the behavior nor the condition are specified.

17. When answering convergent questions, students must
    (A) make a prediction. (D) make a judgment.
    (B) criticize a statement. (E) solve some types of problems.
    (C) give "yes" or "no" answers.

18. Bilingual education for single-language proficient students consists of instruction in
    (A) their native language and one other.
    (B) English.

(C)   two extra foreign languages.

(D)   only English and their native language.

(E)   None of these.

19.   *A Nation At Risk*, written in 1982, called for school reform in several areas. Which of the following area/areas was listed as needed reform?

(A)   That state and local officials assume a more active role in promoting educational excellence

(B)   To raise the standards and difficulty levels of textbooks, grading systems and tests

(C)   To allow more autonomy for teachers

(D)   (A) and (B) only.

(E)   (B and (C) only.

20.   Which of the following most influenced the desegregation of schools?

(A)   Governors

(B)   Department of Education Commissioners

(C)   The U.S. Supreme Court

(D)   U.S. Presidents

(E)   Pressure groups and lobbyists

21.   Working one-to-one with a student at any age is a nearly perfect example of

(A)   instruction.   (D)   guided practice.

(B)   strategy.   (E)   integration.

(C)   motivation.

22.   Self-discipline includes the ability and desire to

(A)   see that other peers behave appropriately.

(B)   see that one's own behavior is corrected when identified as inappropriate.

(C)   behave without any adult supervision.

(D)   All the above.

(E)   (A) and (B) only.

23.   A teacher should meet the needs of ethnically diverse students matching teaching activities to

(A)   school curriculum guides.

(B)   children's experiences.

(C)   materials and resources available.

(D)   state instructional guides.

(E)   individual textbook guides.

24.   What are the purposes for lesson planning?

(A)   School administrators require plans

(B)   Teachers can more effectively remember and implement what they and the students need to do

    (C)   Teachers reduce their anxieties by thinking through what they believe students should learn

    (D)   All of the above.

    (E)   (A) and (B) only.

25.   Discovery lessons require the teacher to assume which of these roles?

    (A)   Resource person, manager, receptor

    (B)   Facilitator, manager, sage

    (C)   Receptor, facilitator, sage

    (D)   Sage, resource person, manager

    (E)   Facilitator, resource person, manager

26.   Individual Educational Plans were required under Public Law 94-142 for

    (A)   disadvantaged and handicapped children.

    (B)   handicapped children.

    (C)   school age handicapped children who require special education or other special services.

    (D)   gifted and handicapped children.

    (E)   disadvantaged and gifted children.

27.   Which is NOT a reason to rely upon nonverbal communication?

    (A)   Verbal messages are likely not to be genuine

    (B)   The forcefulness of nonverbal signals

    (C)   Feelings too offensive may be easier stated or displayed nonverbally

    (D)   More than one means of communication may be needed to give a complex message

    (E)   Even non-active students may become non-verbally involved in class

28.   Questioning strategy is part of

    (A)   teaching methodology.   (D)   instructional objective.

    (B)   teaching strategy.   (E)   All of the above.

    (C)   data processing.

29.   Public Law 94-142 states that education for all disabled children

    (A)   should be restricted learning environment.

    (B)   should be an equal educational opportunity.

    (C)   should be performed in the home.

    (D)   should be accomplished through the provision of self-contained classrooms.

    (E)   should be accomplised through the provision of at-home tutors.

30.   Public school teachers are accountable for all of the following areas EXCEPT

    (A)   legal laws pertaining to schools.

    (B)   social development of the students.

    (C)   personality development of the students.

(D)   academics for that subject or grade level.

(E)   religious teaching.

31.   Refusing to grant points due to misbehavior in a classroom where the teacher gives students points for positive behavior is a form of

(A)   withholding reinforcement.   (D)   averting control.

(B)   positive reinforcement.   (E)   None of these.

(C)   reinforce-ignore strategy.

32.   Evaluative questions require that students

(A)   give yes or no answers.   (D)   make inferences.

(B)   define the word.   (E)   judge and defend.

(C)   recall facts.

33.   Which of the following statements concerning teacher tenure are true?

I.   Generally, tenured teachers can only be fired for specific reasons outlined in state law.

II.   Without tenure, teachers might avoid teaching controversial topics.

III.   Tenured teachres may not be replaced by lower paid beginning teachers to reduce a school district's payroll.

IV.   Tenure protects the academic freedom of teachers.

(A)   I, II and III are true.   (D)   I and III are true.

(B)   I and II are true.   (E)   I, II, III and IV are true.

(C)   I and IV are true.

34.   Merit pay is an educational issrue across the United States. Teacher groups generally oppose merit pay for all of the following reasons EXCEPT

(A)   standardized tests of pupils are not a complete measure of teacher performance and should not be used as the basis for merit pay.

(B)   ratings of teachers by principals may be biased.

(C)   the percent of high ability students vary in each classroom.

(D)   merit pay decisions may be politically influenced.

(E)   years of service and education level can be determined without bias.

35.   A "foundation program' for school finance refers to

(A)   a specific amount of money per classroom provided to local school districts by the state government.

(B)   a specific amount of money per student enrolled in each school provided to local school districts by the state government.

(C)   the amount of the local tax rate multiplied by the assessed property values in a school district.

(D)   state funding for local school districts which provides a minimal level of educational services regardless of the taxable value of property in a local district.

(E)   a minimum tax rate established in a local shcool district.

TEST OF PROFESSIONAL KNOWLEDGE

ANSWER KEY

SECTION 1

1.	(D)	10.	(C)	19.	(B)	28.	(B)
2.	(A)	11.	(D)	20.	(E)	29.	(B)
3.	(E)	12.	(E)	21.	(D)	30.	(E)
4.	(D)	13.	(A)	22.	(A)	31.	(A)
5.	(A)	14.	(D)	23.	(D)	32.	(B)
6.	(E)	15.	(E)	24.	(C)	33.	(D)
7.	(A)	16.	(D)	25.	(C)	34.	(C)
8.	(C)	17.	(C)	26.	(D)	35.	(D)
9.	(B)	18.	(C)	27.	(A)		

SECTION 2

1.	(E)	10.	(C)	19.	(E)	28.	(A)
2.	(B)	11.	(B)	20.	(C)	29.	(D)
3.	(E)	12.	(C)	21.	(A)	30.	(C)
4.	(A)	13.	(E)	22.	(D)	31.	(C)
5.	(D)	14.	(D)	23.	(E)	32.	(C)
6.	(D)	15.	(D)	24.	(D)	33.	(E)
7.	(B)	16.	(B)	25.	(D)	34.	(A)
8.	(C)	17.	(D)	26.	(A)	35.	(B)
9.	(B)	18.	(E)	27.	(D)		

SECTION 3

1.	(C)	10.	(C)	19.	(D)	28.	(B)
2.	(A)	11.	(D)	20.	(C)	29.	(B)
3.	(C)	12.	(C)	21.	(D)	30.	(E)
4.	(A)	13.	(B)	22.	(D)	31.	(A)
5.	(A)	14.	(B)	23.	(B)	32.	(E)
6.	(A)	15.	(C)	24.	(D)	33.	(E)
7.	(C)	16.	(C)	25.	(E)	34.	(E)
8.	(E)	17.	(E)	26.	(C)	35.	(D)
9.	(C)	18.	(A)	27.	(A)		

DETAILED EXPLANATIONS OF ANSWERS
NTE CORE BATTERY–Test 4

TEST OF PROFESSIONAL KNOWLEDGE
Section 1

1.   **(D)**   The correct answer is(D), lack of teaching experience. With experience a teacher will learn to look for certain skills and abilities more readily. Answers (A), (B), (C) and (E) may all confuse the issue of identifying potentially gifted children, but with added teaching experience, most teachers learn to weed through this information successfully. (D), lack of teaching expeience, is what hinders most new teachers in this task inititally.

2.   **(A)**   The correct answer is (A), deduction, which is the process of thinking in which a set of specific data is presented or observed and a generalization is drawn from the data. Choice (B), unitization, is incorrect since it is the learning of individual facts or rules. You are not looking at data to analyze. (C) discrimination, is incorrect as it is defined as distinguishing examples from a concept of non-examples. (D), automaticity, is also incorrect as it is putting facts or rules together in an action sequence and being able to execute the sequence rapidly and automatically; for example, learning to read.

3.   **(E)**   The correct response is (E). A positive approach to getting a student to respond in more detail is by phrasing the question to get additional information. (A), not accepting all short responses, will cause students to hesitate or to not answer at all. Choice (B), make the statement lengthy with more sophisticated vocabulary, is incorrect, because the students would not understand what you are asking. Questions need to be stated so that all students are able to respond. Consequently, (C), to ask left-brain students only, is incorrect. Finally, (D) is incorrect because the writing down of responses creates a test-like environment and may hamper spontaneity.

4.   **(D)**   Bloom's taxonomy was designed with levels of the teaching process. Summative and divergent responses are conflictive, which makes (A) incorrect. Response (B), an example of memory is not first level questioning. Choice (C) is incorrect, since divergent questions should cause students to ask further questions, carry out experiments, or do library or other research. These responses are not completely determined by convergence, which is a process causing students to move toward closure, to summarize and draw conclusions, or to recall information. Synthesis (E) is incorrect because it involves both creation and criticism of ideas.

5.   **(A)**   This is a question which requires you to carefully read and think about each choice. The first and best choice is (A) as it indicates good teaching procedure as reevaluating the entire plan and reteaching the concept. Response (B), the objective was inappropriate, is incorrect as the objective is not necessarily wrong but the approach of teaching the objective

is not appropriate. It is not that students are not ready for the material; instead it is the approach you use for their developmental level, so (C) is incorrect. It is possible that the students have the previous knowledge, but the means you use may affect their responses, so (D) is not the appropriate choice. There are many factors involved in the learning and teaching processes, so it is not always (E), the strategies and methods were inappropriate.

6.   **(E)**   Merit pay is not based on how many years of teaching, whether in the same or different school districts, so response (A) is not correct. It is great for students to score higher on achievement tests. However, there could be several variables to consider, such as higher ability level, conducive environment for learning, highly innovative, creative and motivating lessons; and good teacher– student relations. Response (B) lacks proof that the teacher is the only factor, so it is not correct. Certainly, to receive merit pay a teacher must have consistently exhibited high qualities of excellent teaching. Thus (E) is correct. Response (C) is a blanket statement which is obviously not always true. Teachers should all attend school workshops for staff, but since it does not warrant merit pay on that basis, choice (D) is not correct.

7.   **(A)**   When we are looking at educating the whole child, we must consider the child's developmental stage and the curriculum designed for the child. Thus (A) is correct. The amount of financing may be important, but many have prevented literacy occurring with little money available, so response (B) is not correct. In correlating studies, we look at the curriculum offered, not social life or economic level. Thus (C) is not correct. Neither does comparing economic level to literacy become the real issue in the concept of understanding the relationships for correlating studies, so (D) is not correct. Choice (E) is incorrect because the practice of correlating studies is designed to help students link *material* from one discipline to another, not teachers.

8.   **(C)**   Behavioral objectives should consider what students should be able to do after the teacher has completed well-prepared and presented instruction, so response (C) is correct. It cannot be based solely on the teacher's follow-up to see that learning occurred, so response (A) is not correct. Behavioral objectives do look at lesson plans and statements of what should be accomplished, but they are not complete within the part given. Thus responses (B) and (D) are not correct.

9.   **(B)**   Merit pay has been a controversial issue for several years. However, one of the more often heard concerns is that it breaks down cooperation and communication between the teachers, so (B) is the correct choice. The person classed as an average teacher, but who feels he deserves higher credit or evaluations may decide "what is the use," and thus exert less effort. Effort and salaries may be reduced for those not included in merit pay, so responses (A) and (C) are incorrect. Respect for all colleagues needs to be there to work in the best interest of the students. Merit pay, however, seems to build a barrier so (D) is not correct. The average student is not interested in his teacher's salary, so (E) is also incorrect.

10.   **(C)**   Teachers draw so much from their own environment and experiences. Accordingly, language and cultural differences may exist. If differences occur, it may be difficult for a teacher to identify a means of motivating the student, so response (C) is correct. The other choices may be detrimental factors: disinterested parents, high absenteeism, outside peer pressure and the student's finding the material too difficult to master, but these issues can be dealt with. You must first understand where the student is and his/her background. Responses (A), (B), (C) and (D) are incorrect.

11. **(D)** Response (A) is incorrect, as extinction means to end. Therefore, extinction is not a learning process. Response (B) is incorrect, since operant conditioning is usually considered a learning process in which actions are strengthened or weakened by their consequences, so there would be direct reinforcement involved. Again, response (C) is incorrect since operant shaping would have direct reinforcement. The correct response is (D), modeling or imitating, which are both without any direct reinforcement in the learning process.

12. **(E)** The United States Supreme Court has left the issue of corporal punishment to lower courts. The Supreme Court has extended due process rights to students who are suspended or expelled, but has not limited the length of explusions. The Court has not identified an age for leaving school, not has it yet been asked to rule on the issue of withholding the driver's licenses of dropouts. The Court has ruled that students have the right to wear buttons dealing with political issues.

13. **(A)** John Dewey was interested in the personal and social growth of individuals as stated in response (A). He felt the others would evolve if your concern was on the individual's personal and social progress. Dewey was not as concerned with academic development so response (B) is incorrect. Neither was Dewey's accent on science's or humanities' being taught in the curriculum nor the morals being elaborated on. Thus (C), (D) and (E) are all incorrect.

14. **(D)** When looking at the first three choices, the time element is stressed rather than content. Short-term and daily plans do not necessarily tie in with long-term or calendar plan, or content continuity. Thus, (A), (B) and (C) are incorrect. Response (D) is correct, since a unit plan's content should consist of the objectives, to be implemented; supplementary materials you plan, to utilize; and a variety of activities you plan to use to make it innovative, interesting, highly motivating, and informative. The unit plan gives unity to a series of lesson plans. The unit plan may vary according to the amount of materials, objectives and depth you are to teach (usually 2 to 6 weeks with an hour per day.) Response (E) is incorrect because a curriculum involves much more long-term and general planning, which leaves the choices of strategies and activities up to individual teachers.

15. **(E)** The advisory committee for an individual school should not be involved in the evaluation of teachers. While the advisory committee might review selection policies for the school library, the initial screening of complaints would normally be done by a professionally trained person. Advisory committees should not assume the function of school booster clubs. A school advisory committee might become involved in the district-wide budget appropriations process, but major change would probably have to be accomplished by increasing the percent of the budget allocated to one high school at the expense of other schools. If this was done, the advisory committee would not be able to function in an impartial manner. Curriculum review is an important function of school advisory committees, so choice (E) is the best answer.

16. **(D)** The pre-teaching activity should be a reflection of (A), (B) and (C). It is vital to identify the product and process skills the students have acquired; to provide information for the level of writing the objectives, and to motivate the students. If these factors are not acquired in the pre-teaching the rest of your plans will not be effective. Response (D) is the correct answer, since it includes all in (A), (B) and (C).

17. **(C)** Teleconferencing may provide education in an isolated area. It also may be cheaper to teleconference than to hire extra faculty in a particular school. Appropriate education may be offered from a distance as (C), the correct choice, indicates. The loss of direct teaching on a personal basis occurs with teleconferencing, so response (A) is not correct. Response (B), achievement test scores would not be a factor to consider either. Neither would response (D), strategic teaching be correct. For teleconferencing you would need lectures, and the direct approach would be used; thus (E) is incorrect.

18. **(C)** John Goodlad did research to see how much time in the classroom the teacher spent talking, in relation to the ratio of students' talking. Unfortunately, he did not find a 50% participation rate for students. In fact, the student participation rate was less than 20% according to his data, so response (C) is correct. (B), (D) and (E) are incorrect too.

19. **(B)** First, consider the reasons for critiquing before considering who should be involved in the process. As in response (A), which is incorrect, a teacher may be biased in planning and not see things objectively. Response (B) is correct. The teacher and students should give input to determine the goal achievements. When you have the teacher and students involved the output should be more objective and beneficial in the planning procedure. Choice (C) is incorrect, as students should not be the ones to determine what they should learn and have not been taught enough critiquing skills to be effective alone. Again, (D) and (E) are incorrect based on the fact that students have not acquired nor do they have access to what are appropriate goal achievements or methods for their particular lesson. Nor do they have the means to acquire the culminating step in the planning procedure. Lesson critiques require a cooperative effort from teacher and students to be the most beneficial.

20. **(E)** Teachers must deal with the pressures the students have experienced before they arrived at school. Many of the students have been abused, humiliated, and insulted to the point that their self-esteem has been affected. Thus, (E) is the correct response. Usually, because of high stress, there is not a high interest in school or anything involved with school, so response (A) is incorrect. There is not the energy or desire to set new goals or challenges when the social pressures are too great for the students to face, so response (C) is incorrect too. When students are lost in the stresses and pressures of their own lives, they are not interested in acquiring knowledge of the world, or a particular subject, so (B) and (D) are incorrect. The task the teacher has to work on first is to get the students to feel good about themselves, and to reduce the pressures of their environment as much as possible. Low self-concept must be improved before other types of learning can take place.

21. **(D)** Guideleines for punishment include a clear statement to students indicating which behaviors will result in punishment. Generally, punishment is assigned immediately after the offense, with the intent to make the association of the behavior and the punishment clearly understood. The teacher should identify the offense being punished and explain the proper behavior. Punishing on an irregular basis will indicate to students that the teacher is inconsistent and unfair. Response II is incorrect, so choice (D) is the best answer,

22. **(A)** The Supreme Court examined an upheld the right of prayer groups to meet using public schools. The right of prayer groups to meet had been questioned on the basis of separation of church and state. The science club, Junior Achievement, and other groups were already permitted to meet, provided they followed school regulations.

23. **(D)** There are many factors that facilitate learning. You need make use of variations in teaching strategies, and comfortably use direct and indirect teaching. A teacher has to be able to interrelate with individuals, small groups and entire classes to expect learning to occur effectively. Thus, (A), (B) and (C) are all correct responses so (D) is the correct answer.

24. **(C)** Response (A) is incorrect, as, although the auditory learner may encounter some difficulty learning on the paperwork activities, some activities at a learning station may have a cassette to listen to for comprehension or directions. Choice (B) is incorrect, for the fact that the student may have learning disabilities does not necessarily prevent her from staying on task. It may simply mean she will complete the work at a slower rate. A student who is chronically off-task (C) would need the most teacher reinforcement at a learning station. Thus, choice (C) is the correct answer. Choices (D) and (E) the student who does average work and the quiet, yet gifted, student are probably content at that rate, so they would stay on task to produce their usual quality work. Thus (D) and (E) are incorrect.

25. **(C)** United States educators have decided that Japanese education should not be a model for the U.S., as stated in response (C). Some of the concerns about Japanese education that educators have expressed include too much emphasis on high academic performance, too much pressure on students, and too much emphasis on testing, thus resulting in high percentages of suicide of Japanese students. These facts rule out choices (B),(D) and (E) as correct answers. Response (A) is not correct as educators would not consent to Japan's having the model for U.S. educational system.

26. **(D)** A norm-referenced test can be used to compare students to other students, while a criterion-referenced test compares a student to a predetermined standard. On a criterion-referenced test an acceptable score or standard is determined prior to the test. Students competing against each other and using test scores to determine the top group in a class are characteristics of norm-referenced tests. Responses III and IV are correct so choice (D) is the best answer.

27. **(A)** Public Law 95-561 has not received large funding, which means more effort has to be exhibited at the local level by providing staff, facilities and effort. Response (A) is correct. Response (B) is incorrect, as most parents do not feel adequate enough to identify a gifted student. Nor would they take the time to complain. Choice (C) is incorrect, as administrators' cost and teachers' feelings are not criteria for consideration when complying with a law. (D) is incorrect, since many schools do ignore gifted students, feeling that they will be motivated to learn on their own; however, asking the students to read a library book or help slower students is the easy way out for teachers. (E) is incorrect, because while it is true that many gifted students teach themselves, this does not mean that they require less teacher interaction.

28. **(B)** The most obvious and concrete characteristics of at-risk students would be their low education grades and scores. So, response (B) would best reflect the identification of at-risk students. Choices (A) and (D) are not correct, as high self-esteem and high interest parallels high success, and at-risk students do not experience high success. The home environment and support are usually not the best for at-risk students. There is lack of encouragement or a non-conducive learning environment in the home. Thus, response (C) is not correct either. (E) is incorrect because a student who is at-risk is not necessarily hostile.

29.   **(B)**   Career ladder programs are designed to provide sufficient rewards to keep good teachers in their classrooms. The programs are not designed to develop administrators or personnel for other school positions. Career ladder programs usually require some form of evaluation, but there is no assumption that teachers support very many of the present evaluation systems. Teachers are concerned that evaluation systems are not objective and are open to bias. Choice (E) is incorrect because the description refers to alternative certification, not career ladder programs.

30.   **(E)**   It is obvious that the culturally deprived student needs special attention. If the student has the two disadvantages of culture and a language barrier, choice (A) would not be the best group. The low achievers are struggling themselves; thus, encouragement and assistance would not be provided by the peers in the group. Response (B) would not help the struggling student, since the student would have communication barriers and could not contribute effectively to a project or group. That student would probably hamper progress for the groups in choices (B) or (C). The student may be intimidated by the presence of a teacher in his group, so (D) is incorrect. Response (E) would be the best placement for a culturally deprived student with a language barrier, so that he/she could hear discussion from a heterogeneous group of students. The student would feel more comfortable and could possibly be an asset to that discussion group.

31.   **(A)**   A student is motivated by an excellent test score, so the test score serves as the stimulus. Thus, response (A) is correct. Receiving a good grade does not prove that the student studied, as he/she may have already had the knowledge, so response (B) is incorrect. Response (C) is incorrect because a test score does not prove that learning has occurred. Choice (D) is incorrect. Receiving a good grade does not serve as an effect.

32.   **(B)**   Response (A) is incorrect, since using only the curriculum and textbook does not reveal whether a teacher is a cooperative teacher or not. It probably reveals laziness. Choice (B) is correct, as a good teacher will use the curriculum guide and textbooks only as starters. If he/she is motivated, enthusiastic and loves teaching, he would not settle for the minimum of just those two sources. Response (C) is incorrect, for, using the excuse, "I might teach the wrong thing" is not a logical rationale. Choice (D) is incorrect since they have not identified enough with the age they are teaching to add the extra materials. Thus, you can see from this question that good teachers use textbook curriculum guides and other supplemental materials to enrich the class and make learning more meaningful.

33.   **(D)**   Even though new teachers are well trained in most institutions, there is much to learn in the actual classroom during the first few years of teaching on your own. Thus, your self-confidence level may rise as you teach and feel you are covering all areas the text has suggested, so (A) is a correct response. A new teacher has to establish her own pattern or personality in teaching, while covering the required materials in the curriculum, so (B) is a correct statement too. As you become aware of the skills you are building within the students and develop an appreciation for how you have been able to acquire those skills, you, as a new teacher, will be encouraged. Since (A), (B) and (C) are correct statements, your response should be (D), all of the above.

34. **(C)** Team teaching provides the opportunity for the teachers in the team to use their individual expertise and strengths to the fullest extent. There is no substantial body of evidence to indicate that it is cheaper, easier to schedule, or in any way related to higher achievement test scores. It is possible that teachers in a team might use the team to study, and as a result better understand children, but this has not generally been identified by the advocates of team teaching at the high school level as a major advantage.

35. **(D)** Froebel was the founder of the first kindergarten. (D) is the correct response. Responses (A), (B), and (C) are educators, but are not involved in the kindergarten movement directly.

Section 2

1. **(E)** The student-centered activity should promote development of higher levels of thinking, and cognitive growth should occur. Thus, response (E) is correct. You would not have a student-centered activity with an authoritative teacher remaining in control and thinking for the student, or a team of teachers, so responses (A) and (B) are incorrect. A small group activity, to be effective and productive, needs some guidance from the teacher or it may turn to chaos. (C) is not a correct response. If activities are too structured by the teacher and the students do not have to use their own thinking abilities, it is not a successful student-centered approach, so (D) is incorrect.

2. **(B)** Modifications will definitely be needed, so (A) is incorrect. Praise and positive reinforcement are important to all students. However, a severe behavior problem student will respond more favorably with frequent positive praise, so (B) is correct. Often students in a class have low tolerance for inappropriate behavior so they will ignore a classmate. This should not be encouraged by the teacher, as it affects the problem student negatively, often increasing the problem behavior. (C) is incorrect. Conversely, if all of the student's peers' attention is focused on him, this will also cause behavior problems, so choice (D) is also incorrect. Response (E) is incorrect, as the student needs to be near the teacher so that he/she can frequently give the praise needed for appropriate behavior.

3. **(E)** When the teacher is in charge she is using direct instruction. The teacher may lecture, explain or discuss, but basically, the teacher is directing the class, so (E) is correct. Response (A) is incorrect, since the discovery approach lends to students' investigation or experimental skills and activities. An example of the discovery approach would be a science lab class. (B) is incorrect because there is no center of activity in an unfocused discussion. Response (C) is incorrect, as it is the same as the discovery approach. Response (D) is incorrect, as a teacher may give some guidelines for a small group, but the actual small group activity would be in the form of reflection, discovery, or discussion.

4. **(A)** It is defeating the goals of gifted education to try to advance the gifted student at a rate everyone else in class can master, so (A) is the correct response. The advantages of a gifted educational program are found in choices (B), (C), (D) and (E). If you have the gifted students grouped with others of high ability then you can challenge them to achieve more. Also, enrichment materials may be provided, rather than the students' feeling there is

redundancy of material they have already mastered. The accelerating student may be more challenged at a higher level of thinking, by special activities designed for them. Responses (B), (C), (D) and (E) are incorrect.

5.　**(D)**　As you look at this question, keep in mind what research has found. When students have a part in planning, with the teachers guidance, there will be more involvement and enthusiasm. Interest and motivation levels which leads to icreased involvement, so response (D) is correct. If only (A) administrators, (B) teachers, (E) teachers and administrators together, or (C) students made plans, there would not be an appropriate plan or activity, with the necessary and appropriate goals and objectives.

6.　**(D)**　A good teacher will have a lesson plan, so when looking at this question, you need to consider the segments that make the plan. Response (D) is correct, as you need to have anticipatory activities, objectives stated, instructional techniques, and comprehension checks, to see that all the students understand the concepts. Thus (A), (B) and (C) are correct, but are included in response (D).

7.　**(B)**　The teacher's activities would be designed after background information is determined, so response (A) is incorrect. One of the steps in the lesson is to state your objectives, which would be determined by knowledge of the students' background and what you need to teach next. (C), (D) and (E) are not correct, as the instructional procedures, teacher preparation, and means of closure are made after the background information of the students' knowledge is determined. Thus, (B) the objective, is the only choice that is a part of the lesson critique stage.

8.　**(C)**　In a developmentally appropriate curriculum major emphasis would be placed upon the inclusion of physical activities and using manipulative materials. Activities leading to divergent thinking would be emphasized. The curriculum would promote activity, so less emphasis might be placed upon quiet and orderly conduct. This question is related to devlopmental patterns.

9.　**(B)**　In most single salary schedules the two factors used are the years of teaching experience and the level of education. While some educators recommend using pupils' test performance or peer ratings, these items are generally not considered as complete measures of teacher performance. Principals' ratings are frequently used to determine if teachers will continue to be employed or recommended for tenure, but are not used as a factor in the single salary schedule.

10.　**(C)**　Horace Mann, the secretary to the Massachusetts State Board of Education, was the leading 19th century advocate of free public elementary schools. The schools were for all students or the "common man." He is generally recognized as "the father of the public school."

11.　**(B)**　The original intent of kindergarten was not the same as it is today. It was not designed for early mastery of reading, so response (A) is not correct. It was designed to help younger children develop social skills and to know him/herself before beginning school. Developing social skills early helps children to adjust to the learning environment and to see success from the beginning of first grade, so (B) is correct. A good relationship with parents is important, but not the purpose of kindergarten, so response (C) is incorrect. At kindergarten there should not be a concern for correlating reading, math, science, etc., but social skills should be the emphasis, so choice (D) is not correct. While it would be ideal to foster a love of learning in all students, this was not the original intent of kindergarten, so (E) is incorrect.

12. **(C)** When presenting a lesson which has as a goal the development of inductive reasoning, the teacher should first present specific data which can serve as the basis for generalization. In an inductive lesson you would not introduce the generalization or the objectives as the best first step in the lesson. Answer (D) is incorrect because an hypothesis is not the first step, and if used at a later stage, would probably be stated by the students. Predicting a tentative set of results could be an interesting teaching technique, but it would not be the first step on the inductive process. The best answer is (C).

13. **(E)** Learning centers are designed to arouse the interest of students, expand their knowledge in a certain area, give reinforcement of material taught, and meet individual needs at the various level of reading and interest in a classroom. Thus, response (E) is correct. If the materials are uninteresting the students will not stay with it long, so (A) is certainly not a correct choice. Response (B), only play things, would not entertain nor encourage learning since the students would leave it quickly, as a sense of satisfaction of learning would not be occurring. If the tasks are too difficult, a student may become frustrated and give up, so (C) is incorrect. Students are aware whether there are appropriate objectives and goals for what they are asked to do, so response (D), busy work, would not suffice.

14. **(D)** In most schools, the principal or building supervisor is the only person designated to evaluate the teachers. Thus, the recommendations for promotions are made based on classroom observations, so response (D) is correct. School administrators may observe the interaction of colleague and students, but there usually is not a formal observation paper filled out, so (A) and (B) are incorrect. In the past, student achievement scores were weighed heavily with regard to whether or not someone was released from their contract, but it has not been a factor for career ladder progression, so response (C) is incorrect. Response (E) is incorrect because "amount of material covered" does not always equal "amount of material learned."

15. **(D)** The responses (A) and (B), lesson plans and strategy are both important to consider in order to meet the individual needs of the left- or right-brain student. Thus, choice (D) is the correct response. Response (C), assertive discipline plan, is an incorrect answer. It is important to have behavior management in the classroom, which may be acquired by using the assertive discipline plan. However, fairness to all students, whether right- or left-brain is important. Thus, the consideration has to be on how to best adapt the lesson to accommodate each individual student.

16. **(B)** Appropriate goals are developed for a particular locale in connection with the state curriculum guide. The best method is to choose a committee within the local school district, so (B) is the correct response. The federal government board and Secretary of Health, Welfare, and Education do not write specific goals, but instead, give general goals, leaving the rest to the state. Thus, (A) is not the correct response. Parents' input can be helpful, but many parents do not have adequate educational knowledge to sufficiently write goals, so response (C) would not be a good choice. Neither the State commissioner, nor his board, write specific goals for any particular school, so (D) is incorrect.

17. **(D)**   Comprehension of the student's understanding of the objectives for a particular lesson and the application of the concepts should be checked throughout a lesson. Thus, formative questioning is used to determine the student's understanding and applications of the objectives so that the teacher may check for specific information and assessment. Response (D) is the correct choice, since all of the above responses are true.

18. **(E)**   Principals' attitudes, beliefs, levels of motivation and enthusiasm can influence teachers and the amount of involvement in which they will contribute to new ideas or concepts. If staff seminars are planned to expose and inform about the use of technology in teaching. Then it can be integrated. Response (E) is correct. Observation of what teachers already know does not necessarily help to integrate technology in the classroom, so choice (A) is incorrect. Response (B) is not correct because a teacher should not be evaluated on technology if appropriate training has not first been provided. Checking with the state department does not assure the principal that teachers have integrated technology. Thus, response (C) is in error. Purchasing equipment does not necessarily mean that it will be used effectively in the classroom, so (E) is incorrect.

19. **(E)**   Keep in mind that a teacher's response and attitude affect student response in the future. If wait time is increased it will improve student responses, as well as the number of accurate and appropriate responses that will be given. Thus, the partial statements of (A), (B) and (C) are correct, so response (D) should be your choice. (E) is incorrect, because restlessness is a result of frustration, which occurs less with appropriate wait time.

20. **(C)**   Educating the whole child is a concept referring to the growth and development of the entire child. Thus, response (C) is correct. To only look at curriculum, in (A), behaviors, in (B), your value system, in (D), or ethics, in (E), would not educate the entire child, so (A), (B), (D) and (E) are incorrect.

21. **(A)**   Report cards are not a good indicator of the readability level of a student, since grades are determined on the material on their level. The least effective method, and the correct answer, is (A). Since good teachers work closely with students, they can be good judges of a student's reading level, so response (B) is incorrect. Certainly, last year's teacher and test results would be good resources to utilize in identifying the reading level. Thus, responses (C) and (D) are incorrect. While vocabulary drills may not be entirely effective, they may lend some insight into a student's reading abilities certainly more than (A), so (E) is incorrect.

22. **(D)**   The teacher has been reviewing what appear to be two conflicting opinions and has identified the relationship of those opinions. Since the information apparently came from the students, the teacher is not providing new information, so response (A) is incorrect. The teacher statement may be related to the objective(s) of the lesson, but the statement was not an orienting statement. Since the statement is a review of two major ideas discussed by the class, it is not a final consensus, as suggested in choice (C). Prompting is the providing of clues to improve a students' incomplete response, so it is not related to the summary of opionions found in the teacher's statement. Response (D) is the correct answer.

23. **(E)**   Required curriculum is a teacher's responsibility to teach. A teacher should not try to cut studies short, so response (A) is incorrect. Resource persons can be valuable in

sharing their expertise with a class of students. An introduction by a resource person can establish background information, as weel as, motivate and inspire the student to learn more. Therefore, response (E) is your best choice. A bulletin board display may be an asset to use in the unit, but they are not as valuable as a resource person. Thus, choice (C) is incorrect. Response (D) is definitely not correct, because ignoring instruction on any objectives or materials would only leave a gap in the students' education. Response (B) is incorrect because the teacher will be unable to answer student questions which arise on completion of the project. Teachers must always be prepared and willing to give extra time to research the subject, if needed.

24. **(D)** As a result of the emphasis on improving education in the mid 1980s, some changes have occurred. Improvements have occurred in higher education, teacher preparation programs, teacher certification requirements and high school requirements. All the choices are correct, so the correct response is (D).

25. **(D)** Using questioning strategies appropriate for the particular grade level is an important part of the teaching process. Questions may be used to allow for creativity of the students by improving communication skills. An important step in teaching any lesson is to check comprehension so that you, as a teacher, know that the students understand the concept. Questioning students is a good review technique of the material previously covered. Thus, (A), (B) and (C) are correct responses, so, (D) is the correct answer.

26. **(A)** Cooperative learning strategy may be defined as establishing working groups, organizing and implementing useable procedures for students to follow, and allowing for student input. Interactions with others in the group, and having the teacher as a facilitator, will assist low achievers in reaching higher levels of cognitive understanding. Thus, response (A) is correct. Reasoning skills are at a higher level of thinking. The low achiever would not necessarily be ready for this, so response (B) is incorrect. Achievement scores would not be indicators of low achievers' cognitive understanding level. Thus, (C) is not correct. Low achievers do not usually perform well when indirect teaching strategy is used, as many have difficulty with the inquiry or discovery approach, so (D) is incorrect. Low achievers usually benefit more from group work than from a one-sided lecture, so (E) is incorrect.

27. **(D)** The question asked by the history teacher required a response at a higher level on the cognitive taxonomy and does not lead to a single correct answer. It is, therefore, not a low level or a convergent question. There is nothing in the brief description to suggest that the question was used to focus student attention, or that prompting behavior was involved. There is an indication that the recommended 3-5 seconds of wait-time was allowed between the question and asking a specific student to respond.

28. **(A)** Piaget's principles of learning are based on children's cognitive development. Response (A) is correct, as the learning of a specific concept can occur only if a child is cognitively ready to learn. Individualized instruction, physical development, moral instruction, and children's self-conceptions are important, but Piaget did not feel that they are basic to learning , so responses (B), (C), (D) and (E) are incorrect.

29. **(D)** The Hunter model includes several steps. Modeling behavior is focused upon the teacher illustrating the new content or skill. Input is related to the new information taught. Withitness refers to the ability of the teacher to recognize student behavior problems. Divergent questioning is a teaching technique that may be used in many classes, but is not necessarily an attention focusing technique. Anticipatory set refers to teaching behaviors that will focus students' attention upon the lesson. Response (D) is correct.

30. **(C)** The question requires students to use economic characteristics and apply that information to determine the type of economic system. The question requires more than recall or comprehension in responses (A) and (B), but does not ask for a student evaluation as in response (D). There is no indication that the teacher is redirecting student discussion, so the best answer is (C).

31. **(C)** Instructional planning is important and will be consistently implemented by a good teacher. However, to practice it solely to provide plans for substitutes in times of unexpected absences is not a primary reason. Most schools do require lesson plans and a substitute folder when a teacher is absent, but instructional planning has a more vital function, so response (A) is not correct. The plan allows the substitute to continue with as normal a day as possible. Some school administrators do require a copy of the instructional plans to be submitted so that they can verify what is being taught, as well as see that state curriculum requirements are being met. Responses (B) and (D) are true, but not the primary reasons, so they are not correct. The reason for the instructional planning is to focus on your methods and skills, as well as to look at the students' learning skills. Thus, response (C) is correct. While instructional planning does allow one to smoothly move from topic to topic and without delay, this is not the primary reason for planning, so choice (E) is incorrect.

32. **(C)** Rousseau believed that direct experiences, such as field trips, were the best learning experiences for students, so, response (C) is correct. Library resources, teachers, and morals are important, but Rousseau did not feel they were as important. Thus (A), (B) and (D) are not correct. Response (E) is incorrect, since (C) is correct.

33. **(E)** Teaching strategies are necessary to benefit both the students and teachers in accomplishing their goals. Choice (E) is correct. Daily teaching strategies have little effect on long-term curriculum issues. Thus, (A) is incorrect. When considering teaching strategies, the administrators are usually not as concerned about the strategy as they are the end results, so response (B) is incorrect. It is not solely the student nor just the teacher who must be considered in planning the strategies to be utilized. Consequently (C) and (D) are not correct.

34. **(A)** Student instruction needs to be appropriately designed for the individual students. However, an individual plan takes extra time and money to implement, so choice (A) is correct. Often, achievement scores are a criterion used in determining the level of the individual plan necessary for each student to start working toward and maintaining success. Thus, response (B) is incorrect. It is a fallacy to think that students do not like the individualized approach within logically sequenced and structured program, so (C) and (D).

35. **(B)** When writing objectives you should be establishing goals for the teachers and students. Thus, (B) is correct. An objective should not include only student expectations and outcomes; the teacher must be considered as well. Thus, responses (A) and (C) are not

correct. Objectives should be the goals or accomplishments for teachers and students and not just the teachers' chosen method. So, (D) is the incorrect response. Keep in mind that objective may be defined as the specific observable skill that the teacher expects the student to demonstrate as a result of her/his lesson presentation. While questions, materials, and the information to be covered are all critical to the success of a lesson, they are not part of the goal-setting objective, so (E) is incorrect.

Section 3

1.   **(C)**   Mastery instruction time is not based on teachers' and students' attitudes, school environment or teaching knowledge. (A), (D) and (E) are incorrect. The students' characteristics are the greatest factor to consider in mastery learning, as well as the time needed, so, the correct response is (C).

2.   **(A)**   Assertive Discipline does not mean that students can do whatever they want and establish the guidelines for however they want to behave. Thus, response (A) is the exception and correct answer. Assertive Discipline is a plan to establish appropriate rules for the classroom, with consequences for violating rules, or rewards for appropriate behavior, with the teacher in charge. The plan does include (B), (C), (D) and (E), so they are not the exception and are incorrect responses to the question.

3.   **(C)**   Classroom teachers are concerned about meeting the individual needs and academic goals of special students. Probably the greatest tendency is wanting to assist too much in giving guidance. Thus, response (C) is correct. A classroom teacher may have a tendency to set lower goals for the special needs students, not give clear explanations, or spend extra time preparing materials for one student, but the question says the greatest *tendency*. It is highly unlikely that a teacher would ignore a special-needs student in the hope that he would "mainstream himself." Thus, responses (A), (B), (D) and (E) are not the best responses.

4.   **(A)**   De jure segregation is defined as resulting from laws, school policies, and/or government actions that are designed to specifically bring about separation, so response (A) is correct. Controlled choice and integration may occur, but they do not cause segregation, so choices (B) and (C) are incorrect. Response (D) is incorrect, since (A) is a correct choice.

5.   **(A)**   An important part of the research on academic learning time is the amount of student engaged time. Engaged time is the time the student is actively engaged with academic subject matter. Engaged time might include independent study, but is not limited to independent study. The total amount of time a teacher spends on each subject is allocated time. Including a level of achievement, as in response (D), has changedd the statement to a definition of academic learning time. The average amount of time the teacher spends on core subjects is not related to engaged time.

6.   **(A)**   When planning your questioning strategy, if wait-time is considered, thoughtful risking is encouraged. Thus, response (A) is correct. Responses (B), (C), (D) and (E) are correct statements about wait-time. However, the question was which of these is NOT true, so responses (B), (C), (D) and (E) would be incorrect choices. Wait-time does facilitate

comprehension; it allows students to assimilate information and not guess; it helps teachers to formulate the next question they want to ask and it allows students to record information. Wait-time is valuable in successful teaching.

7.   **(C)**   By waiting for responses, a teacher will motivate and stimulate the students to improve these responses. Thus, response (C) is correct. If a teacher causes the students to feel uncomfortable and humiliated, they will not want to respond next time, so (A) is incorrect. Wait-time could bring a positive or correct answer, while not allowing wait-time may bring a negative response. Thus, response (B) is incorrect. Wait- time after asking a question must vary according to the student's intellectual ability, so response (D) is incorrect. The amount of time left in the lesson is irrelevant to the theory here, so response (E) is incorrect.

8.   **(E)**   Integration and desegregation are different since integration includes development of positive interracial contact so response (E) is correct. Students are never allowed to voluntarily isolate themselves according to race, so (A) is incorrect. When students are isolated in the school according to race, it is de jure segregation and would not be included in integration, so response (B) is incorrect. If students of different races go to the same school, but a separation exists, it is not desegregation nor integration, so choices (C) and (D) are incorrect .

9.   **(C)**   A unit plan is the most effective plan, since you have thoroughly thought through the unit in terms of goals, objectives, a variety of teaching techniques, prepared materials, and resources for the subject. A unit may cover several days or weeks so that more continuity in teaching and the learning process exists, so response (C) is correct. You may have a general guide for the yearlong plans, but they are probably not specific. Thus, (A) is not correct. A daily lesson plan developed in isolation does not bring continuity to the lessons being presented, so choice (B) is incorrect. A weekly lesson plan may not completely cover a particular subject. Thus, you may feel restricted, with not enough, or too much, time for a particular subject. You can see response (D) is not an appropriate choice. (E) is incorrect for the same reason as (A).

10.   **(C)**   Summative questions are used to summarize, pull all points or thoughts together, and for closure and evaluation of what has been taught. Thus, response (C) is correct. Summative questions would have to be at the end, so pre-introductory could not be a consideration. (A) is incorrect. Summative allows for explanations or details, so one word answers would not suffice. Thus, (B) is incorrect. As you go over the goals and objectives, you would not use summative questions to evaluate progress. (D) is incorrect too. You would not expect an entire, involved summary at the beginning of a lesson, so (E) is incorrect.

11.   **(D)**   Cognitive memory questions require a student to recall information when needed. Thus, (D) is the correct choice. Making a hypothesis, solving a problem, comparing and contrasting information, or criticizing an idea do not depend on total recall of information. Thus, responses (A), (B), (C) and (E) are incorrect.

12.   **(C)**   As a result of Hispanics moving to inner-cities, a segregation of students has occurred. Those who previously lived in the inner-city have relocated to areas outside of the large urban locations. Thus, segregation has evolved in a natural way, so response (C) is correct. The fact that Hispanics have moved to the inner-cities does not affect whether there is ability grouping or tracking, magnet programs, or controlled choice, so responses (A), (B),

and (D) are incorrect. Since the correct answer is (C), response (E), the opposite of (C), is incorrect.

13. **(B)** The four major steps in proper sequence are: first, establish teacher and student goals; then, choose appropriate material for the grade level or ability level; third, plan the lesson presentation; and, finally, after teaching the lesson, evaluate it. Thus, (B) is the correct choice. Responses (A), (C), (D) and (E) are not in the correct order.

14. **(B)** If a teacher removes anything from the classroom environment that distracts from learning, she/he will have the students' attention, thus reading will increase so response (B) is correct. Positive behavior is not a factor that external stimuli would affect reading class improvement, so (A) is not a correct choice. External stimuli being removed may not alter the motivation level for reading class, or cause less attention to occur in reading, increase motivation, foster class discussion, thus responses (C) and (D) are not correct.

15. **(C)** Praise brings positive results in a classroom. Unfortunately, the average teacher praises the students less than 2% of the time, thus, response (C) is correct. The percentages of 40%, 10%, 20% and 50% are incorrect, so (A), (B), (D) and (E) are incorrect.

16. **(C)** A properly written objective should identify the behavior expected of the student, the degree of mastery to be demonstrated, and the conditions for demonstrating mastery. For the objective in question, the behavior is identifying the various parts of a dictionary entry, so response (A) is not correct. The general condition of displaying this behavior during a classroom discussion is identified. The objective has no indication of the degree of mastery or level of performance that is expected. Since the degree of mastery is not specified, answer (D) cannot be correct.

17. **(E)** Convergent questions are usually related to direct instruction and the arrival at a definite answer. Convergent questions require that students solve some types of problems to get a definite answer. Thus, (E) is correct. Predictions may be made and worked through in non-direct instruction and in divergent questions, so (A) is incorrect. Yes or no answers do not suffice for convergent questions. Making a judgment does not answer a convergent question, so responses (C) and (D) are not correct.

18. **(A)** Bilingual education refers to a student speaking his own native language and one other language. Thus, response (A) is correct. English may not be one of the languages of a bilingual student, so responses (B) and (D) are not correct. Adding two extra foreign languages would not offer students a bilingual education, but would simply overwhelm them with too much at once, thus, response (C) is incorrect. If they had two foreign languages, English and their native language to learn, it would be difficult to become proficient in all. Another factor to consider is that supporters of bilingual education believe that teaching children in their native language will help build or maintain a sense of identity among ethnic or racial minorities.

19. **(D)** The book *A Nation At Risk* was written to encourage reform in the involvement of state and local officials, and to raise the standards in education. Responses (A) and (B) were two of the areas on the list for reform, so response (D) is the correct choice. Some of the areas of the reform dealt with teachers, but not with more autonomy for teachers. Thus, response (C) is incorrect.

20.   **(C)**   The U.S. Supreme Court had the most influence on the desegregation issue. When a group of white citizens tried to delay the implementation of the *Brown v. Topeka Board of Education* ruling, the U.S. Supreme Court intervened. Each time there arose conflict issues on desegregation, the federal court was involved. Thus, response (C) is correct. More recently, the U.S. President has called governors to meetings aimed at better education, but not specifically concerning desegregation, so responses (A) and (D) are incorrect. The Department of Education Commissioners has not been directly involved in desegregation as the U.S. Supreme court has been. Thus, choice (B) is incorrect.

21.   **(D)**   Guided practice helps you to identify the students' individual weaknesses and strengths. It allows one student to work on his/her low skills area, while another works on his/her own weakness. Thus, response, (D), guided practice, is the correct choice. Instruction, strategy, and motivation are factors to consider with groups as well as individuals, but guided practiced is more nearly a perfect example of one-to-one. Thus, responses (A), (B) and (C) are incorrect.

22.   **(D)**   Self-discipline concerns a person's intrinsic desire to control his/her own behavior in an appropriate way. Certainly, responses (A), (B) and (C) are true concerning self-discipline, so response (D) is correct. A person who has self-discipline will be in control of him/herself, as well as seeing that other peers respond appropriately without adult supervision.

23.   **(B)**   Good teaching occurs when a teacher first identifies the background of the students, whether they are from ethnic groups or others. Planning for teaching should then match teaching activities which would coincide with the children's past experiences. Thus, response (B) is correct for considering ethnically diverse students. With regard to individual differences, the greatest criteria is not school curriculum guide, materials and resources or state instructional guides. Therefore, responses (A), (C) and (D) are incorrect.

24.   **(D)**   Some of the purposes for lesson planning are that school administrators may require them to be on file; the teachers will be more effective in the implementation of their presentations; and stress and anxiety will be reduced by having a detailed plan to meet all the objectives. Thus, choices (A), (B) and (C) are all correct, and (D) is the right answer.

25.   **(E)**   The teacher who is using discovery approach in presenting a lesson assumes the roles of facilitator, resource person, and manager of class activity. When using a non-direct or inquiry approach, the teacher's role changes from the direct approach of lecturing, to allowing investigations, experiments and research. Thus, (E) is the correct response. In response (A), the word "receptor" makes it incorrect. The teacher is a resource person and manages the class activity, but he is not a receptor or receiver. In (C), the words "receptor" and "sage" make the choice incorrect, as the teacher is not the receiver, nor is it necessary for the teacher to show wisdom or to pass judgment. The word "sage" makes responses (B) and (D) incorrect.

26.   **(C)**   Individual Educational Plans are required for each handicapped child or others needing special services, according to Public Law 94-142. These children are tested at school age, so the correct response is (C). The disadvantaged, handicapped and gifted children mentioned in (A), (B), (D) and (E) may be pre-school age, or beyond public school age, since it isn't indicated, so the choices of (A), (B), (D) and (E) are incorrect.

27. **(A)** Nonverbal communication is vital for teachers to ensure good classroom management. However, the one that is not a reason for nonverbal communication is response (A). Response (A) is the correct choice as verbal messages are likely to be genuine. Nonverbal communication is forceful and may be an appropriate means of displaying feelings or conveying a complex message. Nonverbal communication is an effective means of keeping from interrupting the train of thought in a class or embarrassing someone, and it does allow nonactive students to become involved in a class, so responses (B), (C), (D) and (E) are incorrect.

28. **(B)** Part of a good teaching strategy is the skill of questioning to check for previous knowledge, comprehension of what is being taught, or summarizing the knowledge acquired, so (B) is the correct answer. The methodology, data processing, and instructional objectives are not part of the questioning strategy. Thus responses (A), (C) and (D) are incorrect. Methodology is the correct sequence of events. Data processing is gathering information or data in a systematical approach. The instructional objective states what you hope to teach the students.

29. **(B)** When Public Law 94-142 was passed it decreed that "all" children be given an appropriate education. Equal opportunities are to be provided to the handicapped so that their education is on par with other students. Response (B) is correct. Education for the handicapped should be in an unrestricted learning environment. Thus, response (A) is incorrect. The law requires an appropriate education at school, so having a handicapped child educated at home is not sufficient. (C) is not the correct choice. What is appropriate for a handicapped child may be a self-contained classroom, but the best method may be for a student to be mainstreamed for part of the school day, so (D) is not correct. Public Law 94-142 does not provide for at-home tutors, so (E) is incorrect.

30. **(E)** Public school teachers are accountable to know and comply with the legal laws pertaining to schools, as noted in response (A). Social development of the students is part of a teacher's educating the whole child, so (B) is a true statement. The academics for the subject or grade level are also a vital consideration for a public school teacher, and the students' personalities are involved in the idea of developing the whole child. Thus, religious teaching is the exception, as public school teachers are not accountable for this type of education. Response (E) is the correct choice.

31. **(A)** When points are not given for inappropriate behavior, but points are given for positive behavior, it is known as withholding reinforcement from the negatively reacting student. Thus, response (A) is the correct one. If you gave positive reinforcement, it would encourage the student to continue with the misbehavior, so response (B) is incorrect. You cannot use reinforce-ignore strategy if you plan to withhold points for misbehavior. Thus, choice (C) is incorrect. Averting control is not the answer either. It needs to be clear why points are given and why they are taken away in the classroom, so response (D) is also incorrect.

32. **(E)** Evaluative questions require a student to think and sort out information in order to arrive at a sound evaluation or judgment. This cannot be arrived at with just a yes or no answer, so (A) is an incorrect choice. imply defining a word does not give any indication that you have evaluated the information. Thus, (B) is not correct. After looking at the different

points of view or ideas, when given an evaluative question, you can judge the information and arrive at an answer, so response (E) is correct. Evaluative questions do not lead students to make inferences, so (D) is not correct.

33. **(E)** Tenure is controlled by state law. State laws generally identify incompetence, insubordination, and immorality as some of the reasons that may be used to dismiss a tenured teacher. Because the tenured teacher may be dismissed only for specific reasons, teachers do have academic freedom and may be more prone to deal with controversial topics. Tenured teachers may not be randomly dismissed and replaced by lower paid, beginning teachers. This question deals with educational law.

34. **(E)** Merit pay is often proposed as a possible reform of teaching. The idea of paying more to the best teacheres has floundered on the objection by teachers and teacher organizations that teaching cannot be precisely evaluated. Standardized pupil tests do not measure all aspects of student learning and were not designed to evaluate teachers. The percent of high- and low-ability students in a class will influence standardized test scores and this fact makes comparison of teachers based upon pupil test scores difficult. Rating systems are viewed by teachers as unreliable and open to bias and manipulation. Variables such as years of service and the education level of teachers are easily determined and accepted by teachers. They are not included in most merit pay plans. This question deals with school system policy.

35. **(D)** Foundation programs provide a minimum of state funding to local school districts, regardless of the taxable wealth of the local school district. In practice, this often means that poorer school districts receive a higher percent of their funding from the state government than do other school districts in the state. Responses (A) and (B) provide for state funding based upon "flat grant" for either number of classrooms or number of students. These funding methods are used, but do not by themselves provide for any variation in funding to local school districts. Foundation programs often establish a minimum tax rate that local schools must enforce it they are to be eligible to receive foundation funding. However, local taxes and tax rates do not define the foundation program.

National Teachers Examination

SPECIALTY TESTS

- Art Education
- Biology and General Science
- Business Education
- Chemistry
- Early Childhood Education
- Educational Leadership: Administration and Supervision
- Education of Mentally Retarded Students
- Elementary Education
- English Language and Literature
- French
- Guidance Counselor
- Home Economics
- Mathematics
- Physical Education
- School Psychologist
- Social Studies
- Spanish
- Special Education

National Teachers Examination

SPECIALTY TESTS – ANSWER SHEET

1. Ⓐ Ⓑ Ⓒ Ⓓ Ⓔ	1. Ⓐ Ⓑ Ⓒ Ⓓ Ⓔ	1. Ⓐ Ⓑ Ⓒ Ⓓ Ⓔ
2. Ⓐ Ⓑ Ⓒ Ⓓ Ⓔ	2. Ⓐ Ⓑ Ⓒ Ⓓ Ⓔ	2. Ⓐ Ⓑ Ⓒ Ⓓ Ⓔ
3. Ⓐ Ⓑ Ⓒ Ⓓ Ⓔ	3. Ⓐ Ⓑ Ⓒ Ⓓ Ⓔ	3. Ⓐ Ⓑ Ⓒ Ⓓ Ⓔ
4. Ⓐ Ⓑ Ⓒ Ⓓ Ⓔ	4. Ⓐ Ⓑ Ⓒ Ⓓ Ⓔ	4. Ⓐ Ⓑ Ⓒ Ⓓ Ⓔ
5. Ⓐ Ⓑ Ⓒ Ⓓ Ⓔ	5. Ⓐ Ⓑ Ⓒ Ⓓ Ⓔ	5. Ⓐ Ⓑ Ⓒ Ⓓ Ⓔ
6. Ⓐ Ⓑ Ⓒ Ⓓ Ⓔ	6. Ⓐ Ⓑ Ⓒ Ⓓ Ⓔ	6. Ⓐ Ⓑ Ⓒ Ⓓ Ⓔ
7. Ⓐ Ⓑ Ⓒ Ⓓ Ⓔ	7. Ⓐ Ⓑ Ⓒ Ⓓ Ⓔ	7. Ⓐ Ⓑ Ⓒ Ⓓ Ⓔ
8. Ⓐ Ⓑ Ⓒ Ⓓ Ⓔ	8. Ⓐ Ⓑ Ⓒ Ⓓ Ⓔ	8. Ⓐ Ⓑ Ⓒ Ⓓ Ⓔ
9. Ⓐ Ⓑ Ⓒ Ⓓ Ⓔ	9. Ⓐ Ⓑ Ⓒ Ⓓ Ⓔ	9. Ⓐ Ⓑ Ⓒ Ⓓ Ⓔ
10. Ⓐ Ⓑ Ⓒ Ⓓ Ⓔ	10. Ⓐ Ⓑ Ⓒ Ⓓ Ⓔ	10. Ⓐ Ⓑ Ⓒ Ⓓ Ⓔ
11. Ⓐ Ⓑ Ⓒ Ⓓ Ⓔ	11. Ⓐ Ⓑ Ⓒ Ⓓ Ⓔ	11. Ⓐ Ⓑ Ⓒ Ⓓ Ⓔ
12. Ⓐ Ⓑ Ⓒ Ⓓ Ⓔ	12. Ⓐ Ⓑ Ⓒ Ⓓ Ⓔ	12. Ⓐ Ⓑ Ⓒ Ⓓ Ⓔ
13. Ⓐ Ⓑ Ⓒ Ⓓ Ⓔ	13. Ⓐ Ⓑ Ⓒ Ⓓ Ⓔ	13. Ⓐ Ⓑ Ⓒ Ⓓ Ⓔ
14. Ⓐ Ⓑ Ⓒ Ⓓ Ⓔ	14. Ⓐ Ⓑ Ⓒ Ⓓ Ⓔ	14. Ⓐ Ⓑ Ⓒ Ⓓ Ⓔ
15. Ⓐ Ⓑ Ⓒ Ⓓ Ⓔ	15. Ⓐ Ⓑ Ⓒ Ⓓ Ⓔ	15. Ⓐ Ⓑ Ⓒ Ⓓ Ⓔ
16. Ⓐ Ⓑ Ⓒ Ⓓ Ⓔ	16. Ⓐ Ⓑ Ⓒ Ⓓ Ⓔ	16. Ⓐ Ⓑ Ⓒ Ⓓ Ⓔ
17. Ⓐ Ⓑ Ⓒ Ⓓ Ⓔ	17. Ⓐ Ⓑ Ⓒ Ⓓ Ⓔ	17. Ⓐ Ⓑ Ⓒ Ⓓ Ⓔ
18. Ⓐ Ⓑ Ⓒ Ⓓ Ⓔ	18. Ⓐ Ⓑ Ⓒ Ⓓ Ⓔ	18. Ⓐ Ⓑ Ⓒ Ⓓ Ⓔ
19. Ⓐ Ⓑ Ⓒ Ⓓ Ⓔ	19. Ⓐ Ⓑ Ⓒ Ⓓ Ⓔ	19. Ⓐ Ⓑ Ⓒ Ⓓ Ⓔ
20. Ⓐ Ⓑ Ⓒ Ⓓ Ⓔ	20. Ⓐ Ⓑ Ⓒ Ⓓ Ⓔ	20. Ⓐ Ⓑ Ⓒ Ⓓ Ⓔ

Each of the 20-question answer blanks above can be used for any of the Specialty Tests which follow.

ART EDUCATION

This test measures knowledge of the history of world art, art analysis, the materials, tools and techniques, processes of art, and theories of art education. It also covers teaching and learning, educational objectives, and evaluations. There are three major subject areas in this test: survey and analysis of world art; the materials, tools, techniques, and processes of art; and professional practices.

The test questions may aim at particular grade levels or may be generally applicable to different levels.

DIRECTIONS: For each question or incomplete statement, choose the best answer which answers the question or completes the statement.

---

1. The great ziggurat at Ur was produced by a Mesopotamian civilization known as the
    - (A) Egyptians.
    - (B) Sumerians.
    - (C) Assyrians.
    - (D) Babylonians.
    - (E) Minoans.

2. Flying buttresses, pointed arches, and stained glass windows are characteristic of which historic style of architecture?
    - (A) Romanesque
    - (B) Byzantine
    - (C) Renaissance
    - (D) Gothic
    - (E) Baroque

3. Of the following painters, choose the one NOT usually associated with the French Impressionists.
    - (A) Mary Cassatt
    - (B) Edgar Degas
    - (C) Auguste Renoir
    - (D) Claude Monet
    - (E) Eugene Delacroix

4. Jackson Pollack's *Lucifer* of 1947 is an example of what post World War II artistic movement?
    - (A) Fauvism
    - (B) Futurism
    - (C) Cubism
    - (D) Abstract Expressionism
    - (E) Mannerism

5.   Caravaggio's *The Conversion of St. Paul* (above) exhibits all of the following char-
      acteristics EXCEPT
      (A)   a contrast of deep shadows and bright highlights.
      (B)   a sense of drama.
      (C)   a preference for soft contours and loose brushwork.
      (D)   a strongly foreshortened figure.
      (E)   a composition with very little negative space.

6.   A printmaking process that involves the use of a limestone block is
      (A)   lithography.   (D)   woodcutting.
      (B)   engraving.   (E)   serigraphy.
      (C)   etching.

7.   One of the leaders in the USA of art education reform, the author of *Educating Artistic
      Vision*, is
      (A)   Ralph Nader.   (D)   Elliot Eisner.
      (B)   Mortimer Adler.   (E)   Edward Hirsch.
      (C)   Bill Honig.

8.   In art education circles, the acronym DBAE stands for
      (A)   Design Basics for Aesthetic Education.
      (B)   Design By Advanced Education.

(C)   Discipline-Based Art Education.

(D)   Developing Brainpower through Arts Education.

(E)   Don't Blame Art Educators!

9.   Which of the following is a complementary color pair?

(A)   Blue and green   (D)   Purple and red

(B)   Yellow and red   (E)   Yellow and blue

(C)   Red and green

Questions 10 through 12 are based on the following works of art.

(A) *Venus of Willendorf*, Naturhistorisches Museum, Vienna.

(B) Alexander Archipenko,
    Woman Combing Her Hair,
    Museum of Modern Art, New York

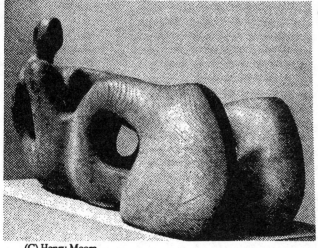

(C) Henry Moore,
    Reclining Figure,
    Detroit Institiute of Art

(D) Henri Matisse, *Back I*, Tate Gallery, London.

(E) Canova, *Pauline*   ,
Galleria Borghese, Rome

10. Which of the above figures seems to best embody the compositional principles of Cubism?

11. Which of the above was produced during the Neoclassical period?

12. Which of the above may have served as a Paleolithic fertility idol?

13. The illustration above is of a Buddhist burial mound located in India. Completed in the first century A.D., structures like this one are among the most important ancient architectural monuments of southern Asia. They are called

(A) stupas.   (D) mandorlas.

(B) pagodas.   (E) basilicas.

(C) mastabas.

Museum of Natural History, New York

14. This Pacific Northwest Indian blanket, shown on the previous page, created by the Chilkat Indians in the 19th century, possesses all of the following characteristics EXCEPT
    (A) a tendency to round off corners.
    (B) symmetry.
    (C) rhythmic repetition of forms.
    (D) the appearance of abstracted animal parts.
    (E) an emphasis on deep perspective.

15. Which of the following is NOT considered by artists to be a technique of forming clay "by hand"?
    (A) Pinching
    (B) Coiling
    (C) Slab building
    (D) Modeling
    (E) Throwing

16. "Form Follows Function" is an expression coined by
    (A) Frank Lloyd Wright.
    (B) Louis Sullivan.
    (C) Le Corbusier.
    (D) Miles van der Rohe.
    (E) Walter Gropius.

17. The painting above, entitled *Nude Descending a Staircase #2* was painted by
    (A) Marcel Duchamp.
    (B) Pablo Picasso.
    (C) George Braque.
    (D) Piet Mondrian.
    (E) Fernand Léger.

18. Of the following questions that an art educator might ask a student, choose the one most likely to encourage critical rather than aesthetic thinking.

    (A) Will it matter if some of the figures in the drawing are not as detailed as the others?

    (B) What color should the border of the painting be?

    (C) What sort of line would produce the greatest effect of motion?

    (D) Would it be better to fill up the space with many colors or leave some space empty?

    (E) Which painting has the most impact?

19. According to the National Art Education Foundation, all of the following assumptions are incorrect, except one. Choose the "correct" assumption.

    (A) The production of art is an enrichment activity, like visiting a museum or seeing a play. As such there is no need for sequential instruction.

    (B) The purpose of art education is to get students involved in the creation of objects in a variety of media. Experiences with a variety of media can't be made sequential.

    (C) Art has significant content, and it demands sequential instruction.

    (D) Although there are few teaching aids available, and although most teachers are forced to make up lesson plans with limited resources, successful results are often obtained; sequential art instruction is not important.

    (E) Given proper materials, children will produce art. Sequential art education is undesirable since it might upset a child's innate understanding of art.

20. In a perspective drawing, the lines that appear to be perpendicular to the picture plane and which intersect at the vanishing point are called

    (A) epigones.   (D) imagines.

    (B) orthogonals.   (E) lintels.

    (C) hatchings.

ANSWER KEY

1.	(B)	6.	(A)	11.	(E)	16.	(B)
2.	(D)	7.	(D)	12.	(A)	17.	(A)
3.	(E)	8.	(C)	13.	(A)	18.	(E)
4.	(D)	9.	(C)	14.	(E)	19.	(C)
5.	(C)	10.	(B)	15.	(E)	20.	(B)

DETAILED EXPLANATIONS OF ANSWERS

1. **(B)** The ziggurat at Ur is the finest extant example of Sumerian architecture; actually, it is the best preserved ancient temple tower in all of Mesopotamia (present-day Iraq). To be specific, the ziggurat at Ur was built about 2100 BC by a group known as the Neo-Sumerians, the last civilization to embrace the customs and language of the earlier Sumerians (active from about 3000 to 2350 B.C.). The Egyptians neither lived in Mesopotamia nor built ziggurats, although their pyramids (which served as royal tombs not temple platforms) are sometimes confused with ziggurats. The Assyrians and Babylonians lived in Mesopotamia, but these civilizations had nothing to do with the great ziggurat at Ur, built centuries before the Assyrians and Babylonians came along. The Minoans lived on the Island of Crete and did not build ziggurats.

2. **(D)** Flying buttresses, pointed arches and stained glass windows appear together only on Gothic style buildings, most of which were built between 1150 and 1500. Buildings of the Romanesque period (c.1050-1150) usually employ wall buttresses and rounded arches; only a few employ pointed arches. The flying buttress was a device invented specifically to support the high vaults of Gothic churches. Byzantine buildings, like the famous Hagia Sophia in Istanbul, are characterized by domes and rounded arches, among other things. The same is true for Renaissance and Baroque architecture.

3. **(E)** Delacroix was a painter from the Romantic era, perhaps best known for his large paintings of subjects taken from Romantic literature, such as his *Death of Sardanapolis* of 1826. He worked a half century before the Impressionists had their first exhibitions. Degas, Renoir, and Monet are the three best known Impressionists, most active from about 1865 to 1895. They painted existing landscapes, cities, and people (subjects that would have had little appeal to the earlier Romantics), all done in their characteristically bright colors and loose brushwork. Mary Cassatt was an American painter who moved to France in the 1870s and became an outstanding Impressionist in her own right, though her work is most closely associated with that of her colleague, Degas.

4. **(D)** Pollack's *Lucifer* is monument of Abstract Expressionism, one of the most influential artistic movements of the 20th century. Pollack's work is characterized by drips

and splotches of paint arranged in rhythmic patterns on large canvases. Pablo Picasso is the best known practitioner of Cubism, an early 20th century style characterized by fractured, though straight, lines, and, at least at times, recognizable subject matter. Henri Matisse was the leader of the Fauvists, a group of French artists active in the early 20th century and known for their use of intensely bright colors. Mannerism is a 16th century style associated mostly with Italian artists.

5.   **(C)**   St. Paul (or Saul as he was known at this point) has just been knocked from his horse and blinded by the light of God. Caravaggio renders the scene with a dark background strongly broken by a beam of light coming from above. It is a dramatic scene, a climactic moment in the life of the apostle. The figure of Paul has been foreshortened such that his head is closer to the viewer than the rest of his body. The artist has filled the composition almost completely; there is very little unoccupied, or "negative," space. He has also used clear, precise contour lines and detailed brushwork.

6.   **(A)**   In conventional lithography a limestone block, obtained preferably from quarries in Bavaria, is used as the support for the crayon marks, acids, and inks needed for a lithograph. The support for woodcuts is wood. Serigraphs are produced on silkscreens. Metal plates, usually of zinc or copper, serve for engravings and etchings.

7.   **(D)**   Elliot Eisner became one of the leaders in art education with his book *Educating Artistic Vision* (1972). This was followed by other seminal books like *The Arts, Human Development and Education* (1976). Ralph Nader is a consumer advocate and author of *Unsafe at Any Speed*. Mortimer Adler is a nationally recognized philosopher, author and educator, author of *The Paideia Program*, and advocate of learning through the great books. Bill Honig is an educational administrator for the state of California, noted for his reform of grade school textbooks and for his own book *Last Chance for Our Children: How You Can Help Save Our Schools*. Ed Hirsch is the author of *Cultural Literacy*, an outline of some of the names, concepts, expressions, etc. that every educated American should know.

8.   **(C)**   Discipline-Based Art Education is an approach to the teaching of art that integrates art history, art criticism, aesthetics, and art production. Teachers versed in DBAE have their students do much more than traditional arts and crafts; they also encourage the reading, writing, and critical analysis of art.

9.   **(C)**   Red, yellow and blue are the primary colors. Their respective complements are green, purple, and orange.

10. **(B)**   Produced in 1915 at the height of the movement known as Cubism, Archipenko's *Woman Combing Her Hair* is composed of the facet-like planes and displaced body parts typical of Cubist art.

11. **(E)**   Antonio Canova's *Pauline Borghese as Venus*, 1808, is a portrait of an early 19th century woman dressed (somewhat) in classical attire, on a classical couch, in a classical pose, complete with a classical hairstyle. The piece was produced during the Romantic era, when it was fashionable to emulate all things Greco-Roman.

12. **(A)**   One of best known artifacts of the Paleolithic or Old Stone Age era, the so-called *Venus of Willendorf*, was made around 20,000 B.C. The statue's emphasis on genitalia and breasts suggests its purpose had something to do with human reproduction.

13. **(A)** Pagodas are tower structures found in Buddist temples in China and Japan. Mastabas are tombs built by Egyptians during the Old Kingdom. Basilicas are large buildings, rectangular in plan, which were used by the ancient Romans for public assemblies, and by Christians as the basic form for churches. A mandorla is an almond-shaped halo surrounding medieval images of Christ.

14. **(E)** Like most two-dimensional art produced by pre-modern American Indians, there is little evidence (at least to "Western" eyes) of any attempt to create an illusion of three dimensions.

15. **(E)** Pinching, coiling, slab building, and modeling are all methods of forming clay strictly by hand. "Throwing" clay involves the use of a potter's wheel, and thus is not technically considered a method of hand-forming clay.

16. **(B)** Louis Sullivan, an architect best known for his late 19th century skyscrapers, promoted the idea that a building's form should follow its function. His slogan "form follows function" became one of the Great Truths for modern architects of the 20th century, among them Gropius and Mies van der Rohe.

17. **(A)** Exhibited in 1913 at the famous Armory Show in New York City, Duchamp's *Nude Descending a Staircase* became one of the most vilified (and celebrated) paintings of the 20th century. For many Americans this painting represented everything that was perverse about modern European painting. Stylistically, Duchamp's work relies on the slightly earlier Cubist compositions of Picasso and Braque. However, unlike the static figures of Picasso and Braque, Duchamp's nude is captured in the process of moving.

18. **(E)** Aesthetic questions involve the objective consideration of the effects of line, color, shape, etc. Critical thinking, best encouraged through the comparison of works of art, results from attempts to gauge a work's artistic merit.

19. **(C)** It is the position of the NAEA that quality art education should be sequential. Like any science, art includes a body of knowledge that is best learned a bit at a time and in a logical, progressive order. See the booklet "Quality Art Education: Goals for Schools: An Interpretation," The National Art Education Association, Reston, Virginia, 1986.

20. **(B)** Imagines are wax ancestor portraits favored by the ancient Romans. Hatching is a drawing and printmaking technique in which fine lines are placed close together to achieve an effect of shading. Epigones are members of any generation that is less distinguished than the one before, e.g., the artists who followed Giotto were epigones. Lintels are beams used to span openings, as in post-and-lintel architecture of the Greeks.

BIOLOGY AND GENERAL SCIENCE

This test assesses the preparation for teaching biology at the secondary level. It covers not only factual material but also knowledge of the techniques and processes of teaching biology. About 60% of the test is comprised of questions related to the biological sciences, with the remaining 40% divided between chemistry, physics, earth and space sciences, and history, philosophy, methodology, and science technology.

DIRECTIONS: The group of questions below is based on a classroom situation. First read the description and the students' comments. Then identify the appropriate student for each question. A comment may be used once, more than once, or not at all.

Questions 1-2 are base on the following passage

In discussing types of organisms, a teacher comments that parasites and saprophytes thrive in the environment. She asks the class to describe what distinguishes parasites and saprophytes. Five students respond as follows:

(A) Student A: Saprophytes are an example of mutualism; parasites are an example of commensalism.

(B) Student B: Both saprophytes and parasites are examples of commensalism.

(C) Student C: Saprophytes thrive on decaying vegetation; parasites live on animals.

(D) Student D: Saprophytes thrive on decaying vegetation; parasites live on another organism at the expense of that organism.

(E) Student E: Saprophytes are plants; parasites are animals.

1. Which student has given the most accurate answer?

2. Which students seemed to have confused the kingdoms?

Listed below are blood types of the parents and the blood types and genetic constituents possible in children.

BLOOD TYPE OF ONE PARENT	BLOOD TYPE OF OTHER PARENT	GENETIC CONSTITUENTS AND BLOOD TYPES POSSIBLE IN CHILDREN
O	O	Only as aa (Type O)
O	A	Aa (Type A) or aa (Type O)
O	B	a^B a (Type B) or aa (Type O)
A	B	

3. With one parent with Type A and another parent with Type B, the possible blood type(s) would be which of the following?

(A)   A, B   (D)   AB, A, B, 0
(B)   A, B, 0   (E)   AB, A, B
(C)   AB

4.   The general features of the Phylum Arthropoda include which of the following?
      I.   A complete digestive tract.
      II.   Constitute approximately 80% of the known kinds of animals.
      III.   The only flying invertebrates.
      IV.   Possession of 3 or more pairs of jointed legs.
      V.   The process of molting, a characteristic of all arthropods.
      (A)   I, II, III, IV, V   (D)   III, IV, V
      (B)   I, III, V   (E)   None of the above.
      (C)   II, IV, V

5.   In comparing mankind with other organisms and looking toward the future, which of
      the following are important differences noted?
      (A)   Many humans who would have been eliminated in previous centuries by
            disease and by deformities now live to have their own children.
      (B)   Only human beings tax the more vigorous and productive members for support
            of the less vigorous.
      (C)   Only humans have released agents increasing the natural environmental level
            of radioactivity.
      (D)   All the above.
      (E)   (A) and (B) only.

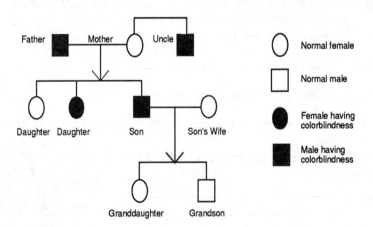

6.   From the above pedigree chart for red-green colorblindness, which conclusions can
      you reach?
      I.   The blindness is a sex-linked trait.
      II.   A colorblind man cannot pass it to his son.
      III.   A daughter can be a carrier.

IV.   The trait crisscrosses from female to male.

V.   The trait appears more frequently in males than females.

(A)   I, II, III, IV, V   (D)   III, IV, V

(B)   I, III, V   (E)   None of the above.

(C)   II, IV, V

7.   Segmented and unsegmented worms are similar in that both

I.   are elongated.   V.   are small in size when compared to the size of an insect.

II.   are soft-bodied.   IV. have rounded bodies.

III. are of only casual importance.

(A)   I, II, III, IV   (D)   IV, V

(B)   II, III, IV   (E)   II, IV, V

(C)   III, IV, V

8.   In countries where medical skill and a public understanding about health and disease are widespread, which of the following changes are evident?

I.   Accidental deaths have been decreased.

II.   The communicable disease death rate has decreased.

III. The infant mortality rate has decreased.

IV.   More people live out a full life.

V.   People live long enough to succumb to degenerative disease.

(A)   I, II, III   (D)   II, III, IV, V

(B)   I, II, III, IV   (E)   III, IV, V

(C)   I, II, III, IV, V

9.   Which of the following clearly distinguishes gymnosperms and angiosperms?

(A)   Both gymnosperms and angiosperms are similar in that they both reproduce asexually.

(B)   In the angiosperms the seeds are enclosed in a fruit, whereas in a gymnosperm the seeds are naked.

(C)   Only the tissue surrounding the developing sporophyte in the gymnosperm is used for food; in the angiosperm the food for the developing sporophyte must come from the immediate environment.

(D)   In the angiosperm the pollen grain germinates inside the pollen chamber and is in direct contact with the ovule.

(E)   Angiosperms are geologically old.

DIRECTIONS: The questions below consist of an incomplete scientific analogy followed by five suggested completions. The analogy, when properly completed, would be suitable for use in explaining the scientific terms in the incomplete analogy. Select the pair of terms that best completes the analogy.

10. PEPSIN:PROTEIN::

    (A)   amylase:starch
    (B)   bile:sugar
    (C)   lipase:carbohydrates
    (D)   maltase:nucleic acid
    (E)   nucleases:sucrose

11. RED CORPUSCLES:OXYGEN::

    (A)   white corpuscles:clotting
    (B)   platelets:infection
    (C)   plasma:carbon dioxide
    (D)   fibrin:clot
    (E)   hormones:plasma

DIRECTIONS: The group of questions below consists of five lettered headings followed by a list of numbered sentences. For each numbered sentence, select the one heading that is most closely related to it. Each heading may be used once, more than once, or not at all.

Questions 12-14

    (A)   Lens
    (B)   Cornea
    (C)   Pupil
    (D)   Iris
    (E)   Conjunctiva

12.   Protection is the purpose of this membrane.

13.   This structure is used to focus light on the retina.

14.   This is the clear, front part of the eye.

Questions 15-16

    (A)   Right ventricle
    (B)   Capillaries
    (C)   Left atrium
    (D)   Aorta
    (E)   Right atrium

15.   Blood from the pulmonary veins enters here.

16.   Blood from the right atrium goes here.

17.   Plant tissues or bacteria subjected to solutions behave differently from animal cells/ tissues because of the presence of a cell wall in plants and bacteria. Which of the following best describes the results?

(A)   Plant cells placed in a hypertonic solution absorb water from the solution and swell considerably.

(B)   Plant tissues placed in a hypotonic solution lose fluid immediately since water molecules move from greater concentration to lesser concentration.

(C)   Through a process known as active transport, the cell can work to make molecules go from low concentration to high concentration; for instance, certain seaweeds are able to accumulate concentrations of iodine a million times greater than the surrounding sea water.

(D)   A solution of the same concentration as that inside a plant cell is said to be osmotic.

(E)   The movement of water molecules through a semipermeable membrane like a cell wall is called diffusion.

18.   Which of the following terms best describes a plant which contains two seed leaves in the embryo, netted venation in the leaves, and vascular strands in a single circle?

(A)   Biennials.   (D)   Dicotyledons.

(B)   Annuals.   (E)   (A) and (D) only.

(C)   Monocotyledons.

19.   Which of the steps below is not a proper part of the scientific method?

(A)   Form the hypothesis.   (D)   Alter the data.

(B)   State the problem.   (E)   Communicate the findings.

(C)   Test the hypothesis.

DIRECTIONS The group of questions below concerns a laboratory situation. First study the description of the situation. Then choose the answer which would best fit the results of test tube #3.

Test Tube	Contents	Time	Results
#1	Lime and water combined	Immediately	Cloudy
#2	Lime and water combined	After 24 hours	Clear water at top
#3	Blow into clear limewater from #2 with a straw	Immediately	

20.   The result of blowing into the clear limewater with a straw is which of the following?

(A)   The water remains clear.

(B)   The limewater turns milky when CO_2 is mixed with it; the powder formed is limestone.

(C)   The water turns a black color if the person is a smoker or remains unchanged if the person is a nonsmoker.

(D)   The water turns pink to show it is an acid.

(E)   The water turns blue to show it is a base.

ANSWER KEY

1.	(D)	6.	(A)	11.	(D)	16.	(A)
2.	(E)	7.	(A)	12.	(E)	17.	(C)
3.	(D)	8.	(D)	13.	(A)	18.	(D)
4.	(A)	9.	(B)	14.	(B)	19.	(D)
5.	(D)	10.	(A)	15.	(C)	20.	(B)

DETAILED EXPLANATIONS OF ANSWERS

1. (D)   2. (E)

The student who states that saprophytes live on decaying vegetation and that parasites live on another organism at the expense of that organism has given an accurate description of saprophytes and parasites. (D) is the correct answer for question 1.

The student who stated that saprophytes are plants and that parasites are animals (E) seems to have confused the definition of *parasite*, *saprophyte*, *plant*, and *animal*. (E), then, correctly answers question 2 which asks which student confused the kingdoms. Student A states that saprophytes exhibit mutualism (benefits accrue to both partners) and parasites exhibit commensalism (benefits accrue to one partner without detriment to the other). This is not a true statement. Parasites live on another organism at the expense of that organism. Saprophytes thrive on decaying vegetation. (A) is inaccurate. Student B states that both saprophytes and parasites are examples of commensalism. This is certainly not accurate. Saprophytes thrive on decaying vegetation and parasites live on another organism at the expense of that organism. Student B is in error. Since parasites do not necessarily live just on animals, Student C is in error.

3. (D)   Due to an inherited character there are several different blood groups—O, A, B, and AB. These groups are due to an inherited character of which there is one recessive form (which has the symbol a) and two different dominant forms (with symbols A and a^B). Neither of the dominant conditions is recessive to the other; both are dominant to a. Genetically, the blood group O can be represented by the symbols aa, group A by either AA or Aa, group B either $a^B a^B$ or $a^B a$, and group AB by Aa^B. It is easy to see that only certain blood types are possible among the children of definite parents. With A and B parents the possible blood types are types AB, A, B, and O. The genetic constitutions are Aa^B , Aa, $a^B a$ or aa. Only answer (D) allows the reader to choose these possible types.

4. (A)   (A) is the best answer since all the possibilities (I, II, III, IV, and V) given are characteristics of Arthropoda. None of the other choices [(B), (C), (D), and (E)] allow this choice.

5. (D)   Only (D) allows the reader to select (A), (B), and (C)—all of which are true and accurate statements. (D) is the correct answer. (E) only allows (A) and (B) to be selected and (C) would have to be omitted. Since (A), (B), and (C) are correct, (D) is the only appropriate answer.

6.   **(A)**   All the statements (I, II, III, IV, and V) are correct. Choice (A) allows the reader to select all of these statements. The other answers allow the reader to choose none or just a partial selection of the correct answers. Choice (A) is correct because the evidence that the trait is sex-linked (I) is that a colorblind man can never pass the colorblindness on to his sons (II). Statement (III) is also correct, because there is a colorblind daughter in the first filial generation. The trait appears to be passed from female to male, therefore statement (IV) is true. Finally, the fact that colorblindness appears in 8% of the males and less than 1% of the females is evidence that (V) is correct.

7.   **(A)**   All the statements about segmented and unsegmented worms are true except for the statement that the worms are small in comparison with insects (V). Some worms are up to 12" long. Answer (A) allows the reader to choose all the answers except for V. (B), (C), (D), and (E), then, should not be selected.

8.   **(D)**   Only one of the statements is false. Accidental deaths (I) have not been decreased as a result of medical skill and public understanding. Answer (D) allows the reader to choose (II, III, IV, and V). (D) is the best answer since all the statements (except I) are true.

9.   **(B)**   Only (B) is a true statement. Gymnosperms and angiosperms do not reproduce asexually (A); rather the two reproduce sexually. (A) is false. In the angiosperm the surrounding tissue, the endosperm, and sometimes the cotyledons which are part of the embryo are used for food. (C) falsely states that the food must come from the environment. (D) is false. The pollen grain germinates a distance from the ovule; the long pollen tube carries the grain to the ovule of the flower. (E) is false also. Angiosperms are not considered geologically old; they are only 130-140 million years old. Only (B) is a true statement and the correct answer.

10.   **(A)**   Pepsin is used to digest protein. Since amylase is used to digest starch, the analogy is the same. (A) is the right answer. Bile from the liver contains no digestive enzymes; it is not used to digest starch. (B), then, is an incorrect answer. Lipase (C) is used to digest fats, not carbohydrates as answer (C) implies. (C) is an incorrect answer. Maltase is used to change maltose to glucose—not to change nucleic acids as answer (D) suggests. (D) is an incorrect answer. The nucleases are used to digest nucleic acids—not sucrose. (E) is incorrect and should not be chosen.

11   **(D)**   The red corpuscles are important in that they carry oxygen. The red corpuscles, then, are important to oxygen. Fibrin is important to forming a clot; the analogy is the same and (D) should be selected . White corpuscles are used to fight infection—not clotting. (A) is incorrect. Platelets help with blood clotting, not fighting infection; it is the white corpuscles which fight infection. (B) is incorrect. The plasma is the liquid portion of the blood which contains the corpuscles and other important parts of the blood. It is not responsible for carrying carbon dioxide. (C) is wrong. The blood plasma does contain hormones, but the order is incorrect. *Plasma* should come before *hormones*.

12.   **(E)**   13.   **(A)**   14.   **(B)**   The conjunctiva (E) is a protective membrane which covers the eye. It answers correctly question 12. The lens (A) is used to focus light on the

retina; it correctly answers question 13. The clear, front part of the eye is the cornea (B). It is an appropriate answer for number 14. Two answers were left unused. The pupil (C) is the opening in the eye . The iris (D) is the colored part of the eye.

15. **(C)**   16. **(A)**
    Blood from the pulmonary veins enters the left atrium (C) of the heart. (C) correctly answers number 15. Blood from the right atrium goes into the right ventricle of the heart. (A) is the correct answer for number 16. Three items were not selected. Blood from the left atrium enters the aorta (D); (D) was not the correct answer to either question 15 or question 16. Capillaries (B) are the very tiny blood vessels in the body; (B) does not answer any of the questions. The right atrium is the upper right portion of the four-chambered heart; (E) does not answer any question.

17. **(C)**   Only statement (C) is true. The rest of the statements are false. For instance, plant cells placed in a hypertonic solution (A) lose rather than absorb water. (A) is incorrect. Plant tissues placed in a hypotonic solution gain rather than lose fluid. (B) is incorrect. A solution of the same concentration as that inside a plant cell is said to be isotonic—not osmotic. (D), then, is false. The movement of water molecules through a semipermeable membrance like a cell wall is called osmosis—not diffusion. (E) is false.

18. **(D)**   Two seed leaves, netted venation, and vascular strands in a single circle are characteristic of dicotyledons. (D), then, is the best answer. A monocotyledon (C) has one seed leaf, does not have netted leaves, and has vascular strands scattered throughout rather than arranged in a single circle. (C) is incorrect. A biennial plant lasts two years and may or may not possess these characteristics. (A) is incorrect. An annual plant lives but one year or one season, and may or may not possess these characteristics. (B) is inappropriate. (E) which allows the reader to select biennial (A) and dicotyledon (D) couples a right and a wrong answer together. (E) should not be selected.

19. **(D)**   Altering the data (D) is not a step in the scientific process. Data should not be altered or changed. If this is done, the results of the experiment cannot be proved as accurate. The rest of the items are steps in the scientific process. (D) should read, "Collect the data."

20. **(B)**   Blowing into the limewater results in a milky liquid. The powder which is formed is limestone. (B) is correct. The limewater does not remain clear when CO_2 is blown into it; (A) is incorrect. The water does not turn black if a person has been smoking; (C) is a false statement. If litmus paper is placed in the limewater, the paper will turn blue to show that the limewater is a base. The experiment, however, makes no mention of adding the litmus paper. (E) should not, therefore, be chosen. Likewise, (D) should not be chosen because no mention of litmus paper is made and because the pink color resulting from an acid would not occur with a base.

BUSINESS EDUCATION

This test measures the business and economic literacy of prospective business teachers. It is wide in scope because of the variety of facets of business, but it can be divided into the following categories: Business Information—mathematics, communications, and consumer education (37.5%); Professional Business Education—organization, objectives, methodologies, and planning of business education (25%); Areas of Specialization within Business Education—office procedures, shorthand, data processing, etc (37.5%). Many other topics are included under each category.

DIRECTIONS: Each of the questions or incomplete statements below is followed by five suggested answers or completions. Select the one that is best in each case.

PART I.

1. Because of decreasing enrollment in shorthand courses, shorthand should be
    (A) integrated as part of the business communications course.
    (B) taught on three levels: beginning, intermediate and advanced.
    (C) taught as an alphabetic system rather than using the present symbolic system.
    (D) taught so that most students would persist with the subject long enough to attain high speeds.
    (E) taught by machines.

2. In teaching business communications for the modern office, the teacher should place the greatest emphasis on
    (A) sales letters.
    (B) short memos.
    (C) formal reports.
    (D) collection letters.
    (E) specialized letters.

3. Keyboarding should be taught for some degree of computer fluency at what level?
    (A) Kindergarten
    (B) First grade
    (C) Ninth grade
    (D) Sixth grade
    (E) Third grade

4. In teaching Beginning Accounting at the four year college/university level,
    (A) no microcomputer is needed; manual accounting teaching is preferred.
    (B) intensive use of microcomputer software is needed, but it should be limited mainly to that which correlates with the textbook.
    (C) intensive use of microcomputer software is needed, but it should go beyond the textbook.
    (D) extensive microcomputer usage is preferred.
    (E) mainframe computer usage is preferred.

5. Which of the following is the most accurate statement regarding machine shorthand?
    (A) It is used in the average office.
    (B) It is a relatively new device.
    (C) It is relatively easy to learn.
    (D) It is easier for shorthand-machine writers to transcribe one another's notes than it is for writers of handwritten shorthand.
    (E) It is the wave of the future.

6. Which of the following statements is FALSE?
    (A) The accounting clerk need not be proficient in programming, but should understand how data fed into the computer is processed and how to interpret the data emerging from the computer.
    (B) The challenge of the computer frequently activates students who normally display little motivation.
    (C) The computer is more than an accounting tool and will gradually replace accountants themselves.
    (D) The basic question of whether it is preferable to follow accounting instruction with a course in data processing or to integrate data processing with accounting from the beginning is unresolved.
    (E) Most business teachers today believe that computer instruction should go "hand-in-hand" with accounting instruction.

7. Dvorak has invented a typewriter keyboard which places the vowels and most used consonants in the "home row." Should we keep the present keyboard or change to Dvorak's keyboard?
    (A) Keep the present keyboard, otherwise current employees will need to be changed.
    (B) Change to Dvorak to increase production.
    (C) Encourage business people to change to Dvorak in their offices to cut expenses.
    (D) Encourage business people to change to Dvorak because it will be favored by the educational establishment.
    (E) Allow students to learn on either keyboard.

PART II.

8. Which of the following is FALSE?
    (A) Microcomputers provide a process of text revision and editing.
    (B) The emphasis in business communication at the four year college/university rarely focuses on the final product.
    (C) Most business educators do not feel comfortable with computers.
    (D) Machine shorthand is now available that allows for direct text editing from the dictation, and immediate transcription of the dictated document.
    (E) The modem translates information to be written on the microcomputer from one foreign language to another.

9. The doctorate in business education should include mostly
   (A) practical details of teaching.   (D) ancient and modern languages.
   (B) highly refined scientific research.   (E) computer programming.
   (C) administration and supervision.

10. In the future, business education will most likely include
    (A) more use of standard textbooks.
    (B) more typewriting so that it will become a common tool of communication, as common as the pen is now.
    (C) fewer instructional machines for independent study.
    (D) the business teacher more as a technician and less a professional.
    (E) more use of card files in record keeping.

11. Which of the following is TRUE?
    (A) It is no longer possible to find a decent job without a college education.
    (B) Schools fail to educate 50% of the young men and women each year who turn eighteen for the eight out of ten job opportunities which do not require a college education.
    (C) The number of jobs which unskilled workers can fill is increasing rapidly.
    (D) The number of jobs requiring a liberal arts education is growing more rapidly than is the number of jobs demanding a technical skill.
    (E) The federal government invests fourteen dollars in the nation's universities for every dollar it invests in vocational education programs.

12. The professional business teacher
    (A) works by the hour.
    (B) regards himself or herself as an employee.
    (C) requires close supervision or direction.
    (D) needs certification.
    (E) acts according to his/her judgment only.

13. Which of the following business education research topics is probably the LEAST VALUABLE in terms of deriving accurate statements?
    (A) To determine the optimal class size for learning
    (B) To determine whether students learn better or faster through use of specialized equipment than traditional classroom methods
    (C) To determine the most effective and efficient building layout for the most effective learning
    (D) To determine which business teacher's organization provides the most inspiration for business teachers
    (E) To determine the master's program for business teachers

PART III.

14. Working capital is
    (A) money which does not have to be paid back but earns the supplier the right to share the profits.

     (B)   money used by the corporation to pay interest to its bondholders.

     (C)   money used to purchase fixed assets.

     (D)   money used by the corporation to pay dividends to its stockholders.

     (E)   money needed for the day-to-day operation of business, over and above cash generated by the business.

15. Which of the following is deductible by a corporation before figuring income tax on net income?

     (A)   Interest payments to corporation bondholders

     (B)   Dividend payments to corporation preferred stockholders

     (C)   Dividend payments to corporation common stockholders

     (D)   Dividend payments to corporation preference stockholders

     (E)   None of these.

16. Britain's Poll Tax is considered by economists to be

     (A)   progressive.

     (B)   regressive.

     (C)   socialistic.

     (D)   helpful to the poorer classes rather than to the richer classes.

     (E)   a "sin tax."

17. Which nation is now the world's principal supplier of new investment capital?

     (A)   United States of America   (D)   West Germany

     (B)   The United Kingdom   (E)   Japan

     (C)   The Soviet Union

18. When the Federal Reserve Board fears that greater inflationary pressures are being placed on the economy, it tends to

     (A)   encourage the government to borrow more money.

     (B)   encourage the government to spend more money.

     (C)   raise the interest rates.

     (D)   decrease member bank reserve requirements.

     (E)   use federal reserve dollars to purchase more government bonds.

19. How could an end to the federal budget deficit affect the economy?

     (A)   It will cut inflation.

     (B)   It will hurt the competitiveness of U.S. business abroad.

     (C)   It will raise interest rates.

     (D)   It will increase America's dependence on foreign capital.

     (E)   It will force us into socialism.

20. Higher interest rates tend to

     (A)   encourage recessions.   (D)   increase the money supply.

     (B)   increase inflation.   (E)   increase housing starts.

     (C)   ease monetary policy.

| ANSWER KEY |

1.	(C)	6.	(C)	11.	(E)	16.	(B)
2.	(B)	7.	(A)	12.	(D)	17.	(E)
3.	(E)	8.	(E)	13.	(D)	18.	(C)
4.	(B)	9.	(C)	14.	(E)	19.	(A)
5.	(D)	10.	(B)	15.	(A)	20.	(A)

DETAILED EXPLANATIONS OF ANSWERS

1.   **(C)**   Choice (A), integrating shorthand as part of the business communications course, is not correct because shorthand requires extensive practice in order for a student to gain expertise. Choice (B), teaching beginning, intermediate, and advanced shorthand in the same class period, is impractical because it would require dictation at varying speeds to each of the three groups at the same time. Choice (C), teaching an alphabetic system of shorthand is the best choice because students learn it more easily and can reach speeds of 80-100 words per minute more readily than with symbolic shorthand. Choice (D) is not a good selection because students must study shorthand diligently for 3 or 4 semesters in order to attain high speeds, and few of them are willing to put in enough time and effort to accomplish this. (E) is not a good choice, because machine shorthand is too difficult for the average shorthand student.

2.   **(B)**   Choice (A) is not the best, because only secretaries in sales-related offices might spend time on sales letters. Choice (B) is the best, because today, short memos in response to day-to-day situations are the quintessential form of office communications. Choice (C) is not the best answer, because today, few secretaries spend much of their time on formal reports. Choice (D) is not the best, because only a small portion of the secretary's time in most offices is spent on collection letters. (E) is not the best choice, since in most offices, the specialized letters do not occupy a great deal of the secretary's time.

3.   **(E)**   Choice (A) is not a good answer, because kindergarten students would use computers mainly to identify letters and perhaps a few words. Choice (B) is not a good answer, because first grade students would use the computer just to identify letters and words. Choice (C) is not the best answer, because surveys show that students can learn adequate keyboarding skills many years earlier than the ninth grade level. Choice (D) is not the best answer. Students can learn keyboarding prior to the sixth grade level, since writing fluency has already been developed. Choice (E) is the best answer. A survey done in 1983 by the Shoreham-Wading River School Districts in Long Island revealed that third grade students have adequate reading skills to bring about fluency in writing, and so they can be taught touch typing successfully.

4. **(B)** Choice (A), which favors teaching manual accounting without the microcomputer is not the best answer, since manual accounting is a thing of the past. Choice (B), combining textbook instruction with intensive use of microcomputer software is the best answer since the students need to learn the principles well, but he/she also needs to see how these principles are implemented on the computer. Choice (C) is not the best, because at the beginning stage of accounting instruction, emphasis must be placed on principles, not on computer instruction beyond the scope of the textbook. Choice (D) is not the best, because extensive microcomputing instruction is the subject of a course on computers, not beginning accounting. Choice (E) is not the best, since microcomputers are more useful to accounting students than are mainframe computers.

5. **(D)** Choice (A) is not a good answer, because machine shorthand is not found in use in the average American business office today. Choice (B) is not the best. The use of machine shorthand is not new. The keyboard for machine shorthand was first developed in Ireland in the late nineteenth century. Choice (C) states that machine shorthand is relatively easy to learn. This is a poor choice, because on the average, most people find machine shorthand difficult, frustrating, and time consuming. Choice (D) is the best answer. Machine shorthand letters are printed on a continuous tape, and people who do shorthand-machine writing and know the brief forms do fairly well at reading one another's tapes (in fact much better than do writers of handwritten shorthand). Choice (E) is not the best, because machine shorthand is a specialty mainly for dictation at high speeds.

6. **(C)** Choice (A) is not a false answer, because accounting clerks need to know how the data is fed into the computers and processed, and how to interpret the output. It is not necessary for accounting clerks to be good at programming since this is done by programming specialists. Choice (B) is not the false answer since computers today seem to motivate students who otherwise might show little interest in business subjects. Choice (C) is the false answer that should be checked. Computers are only accounting tools. They bring speed and accuracy to the printouts as long as accurate information is inputted. Accountants are the brains of the input and will never be replaced by computers. Choice (D) is not the false answer, because professional business teachers do not yet agree as to whether manual accounting instruction should be followed by a data processing course or whether both should be taught at the same time in one integrated course. Choice (E) is not the false answer, because with the advent of microcomputers, business teachers realize that they must now teach accounting with hands-on microcomputer usage.

7. **(A)** According to the thinking of leading business educators, choice (A) is the best answer. Most business educators think we should keep the present typewriter (computer) keyboard so that current employees do not need to be retrained. Choice (B) is not the best answer. If everyone knew the Dvorak keyboard, there might be some increase in production. However, most business educators do not think this increase is worth the time it would take to retrain all employees. Choice (C) is not the best, because there is too much opposition to relearn the keyboard. This condition-response situation has been "automated" into the minds of most people since youth, and most are not willing to change. Choice (D) is not the best because, according to the 1987 National Business Education Yearbook, business educators do not favor the change to the Dvorak keyboard. Choice (E) is not the best, because the entrance into business of some people knowing only the present keyboard and others knowing only the Dvorak keyboard would require businesses to buy more typewriters, some with one keyboard, and some with the other.

8. **(E)** Choice (A) is not the false statement, because one of the important benefits of microcomputers is text revision and editing. Choice (B) is not the false statement, because

business communication courses at the college level do not stress the final product. Choice (C) is not the false statement, because most business educators do their best to learn about new computers as they reach the market. Choice (D) is not the false statement, because technology has improved greatly, and it is now possible for machine shorthand experts to edit their texts, and to have material printed in machine shorthand on the tapes get transcribed and printed on paper, in a language readable to the general public. Choice (E) is the false choice which should be marked, because a modem is used to send information from the computer over the telephone wires, not to translate information from one language to another.

9. **(C)** Choice (A) is not the best, because practical details of teaching should be mastered by prospective teachers taking undergraduate work. Choice (B) is not the best, because highly refined scientific research should be accomplished by doctoral students in fields other than business education. Choice (C) is the best, because a person studying for a doctorate in business education will be planning to do administrative or supervisory work in the educational system. Choice (D) is not the best, because there is usually no foreign language requirement for the doctorate in business education. Choice (E) is not the best, because computer programming should be studied as undergraduate work, not as doctoral work.

10. **(B)** Choice (A) is not the best, because future teaching and learning in business education will probably include a much greater use of the computer, at the expense of standard textbooks. Choice (B) is the best, because with the advent of greater use of the computer by almost everyone, and with input to the computer mainly by the keyboards similar to those used on the typewriter, probably everyone will use the computer in the future. Choice (C) is not the best, because machines for instructional use will probably increase rather than decrease. Choice (D) is not the best, because the expanding need for business instruction should require the services of more professional business teachers rather than technicians. Choice (E) is not the best, because future record keeping will probably include placing more information in computers as data base rather than placing information on card files.

11. **(E)** Choice (A) is not correct. It is still possible to get ahead without a college education. Choice (B) is not the best, because the number of unskilled jobs is not increasing rapidly. Choice (D) is not the best choice, because the number of technical job openings is increasing more rapidly than the number of openings for people with an education in the liberal arts. Choice (E) is correct. The National Advisory Council on Vocational Education reports that the federal government spends only 1/14 as much on vocational education programs as it invests in the nation's universities.

12. **(D)** Choice (A) is not the best, because most business teachers work by the month on a salaried basis, not on an hourly basis. Choice (B) is not the best, because most business teachers regard themselves as professionals, not as employees. Choice (C) is not the best, because most business teachers work independently of administration and usually know more about their subject than do their supervisors, so they do not usually need close supervision or direction. Choice (D) is the best. Business teachers on the elementary and high school levels do need to be certified by the state. Choice (E) is not the best, because business teachers must keep up with the important changes in the modern office, including computers. This requires constant learning, ability to change, and humility, not self importance.

13. **(D)** Choice (A) is not the least valuable choice in terms of deriving accurate statistics, because a research topic regarding optimal class size for learning could be made

into a statistical study for comparison. Choice (B) is not the least valuable choice in terms of deriving accurate statistics, because a research topic regarding the use of specialized equipment in contrast to the traditional classroom would be both measureable, and of immeasureable value, in the education field. Choice (C) is not the least valuable choice in terms of deriving accurate statistics, because a research topic regarding the most effective learning could be turned into a comparative study analyzing student-learning results in various building-layout situations. Choice (D) is the least valuable choice in terms of deriving accurate statistics because "inspiration" is a difficult product to measure quantitatively. Choice (E) is not the least valuable choice for deriving accurate statistics. It would be possible to send surveys nationwide to a random sample of business teachers and administrators to derive their ideas regarding the best master's program for business teachers.

14. **(E)** Choice (A) is not the best definition for working capital, because money which does not have to be paid back, but which earns the supplier of the money (the investor) the right to share in the profits, can only be the original invested capital that usually is used by the company to buy land, buildings, trucks and other assets to get the business started. Choice (B) is not the best definition for working capital, because interest pay to bondholders should come from earnings. Choice (C) is not the best definition for working capital, because money used to purchase fixed assets cannot be used on the day-to-day operation of the business. It is already spent for fixed assets. Choice (D) is not the best definition for working capital, because money to pay dividends to stockholders should come from earnings. If it is paid out to stockholders, it can no longer be used for the day-to-day operation of the business. (E) is the best answer, because working capital is the cash needed in the day-to-day operation of the business.

15. **(A)** Choice (A) is the best, because income tax, according to the present federal laws, is paid on net income. This net income is computed by deducting all business expenses from business gross income, and one of the legally deductible business expenses is bond interest expense. Choice (B) is not the best, because preferred dividend payments can be made only AFTER income tax is paid to the federal government. Choice (C) is not the best, because common dividend payments, too, can be made only AFTER income tax is paid to the federal government. Choice (D) is not the best, because preference stock dividend payments can be made only AFTER income tax and preferred dividends are paid. Preference stock is a type of stock between preferred and common on corporate books. Choice (E) is not correct because answer "A" is correct.

16. **(B)** Choice (A) is not the best, because a progressive tax increases proportionately as the base of the tax increases. For instance, the income tax increases as a person's income increases. However, a poll tax is the same amount collected from everyone, from queen to kitchen maid. Choice (B) is the best answer, because a poll tax is considered by economists to be regressive. As a person's income increases, the percentage of the income paid as a poll tax decreases in relation to the person's total income, since dollars paid for poll tax remains the same for all people, no matter what their incomes. Choice (C) is not the best answer because socialists usually tend to want to tax the rich, while the poll tax proportionately taxes the poor more heavily. Choice (D) is not the best answer because, contrary to the statement, the poll tax falls on the poor more heavily than the rich; therefore it is not "helpful to the poorer classes." Choice (E) is not the best answer, because a so-called "sin tax" is usually one levied on liquor and cigarettes.

17. **(E)**   Choice (A) is not the best because the people of the United States today are not willing to save much; they would rather spend. Therefore, they do not have much in the way of savings to supply the world with new investment capital. Choice (B) is not the best, because the people of the United Kingdom are not willing to save much in the way of savings to supply the world with new investment capital. Choice (C) is not the best, because the Soviet Union's economy is in serious trouble. Choice (D) is not the best, because the people in West Germany do not save and invest as much as do the people of Japan. Choice (E) is the best, because the people of Japan today are willing to save a great deal and forego spending until the future. They supply the world with the most new investment capital.

18. **(C)**   Choice (A) is not the best, because the government borrowing more money would add to inflationary fires, rather than decrease them. Choice (B) is not the best, because increased government spending, also, would add to inflationary fires. Choice (C) is the best answer, because raising interest rates by the government would make it more difficult for people to borrow and then spend money, and this would slow down the rate of spending, and thus cut inflation. Choice (D) is not the best, because if the member bank reserve requirements decreased, the member banks would have more money to lend, and this would fire up inflation. Choice (E) is not the best, because if the government sold its bonds to the Federal Reserve system, this would give the government more money to spend, and thus increase inflation.

19. **(A)**   Choice (A) is the best answer here. If the federal government could balance the budget, there would be no deficit. The government would no longer have to borrow new money. This would tend to cut the interest rate, which in turn would slow down and perhaps completely stop inflation. Choice (B) would not be the best answer. An end to the deficit would not hurt U.S. competitiveness abroad. On the contrary, the U.S. would be more competitive, because interest rates would be lower and the dollar stronger, thus making for a favorable balance of payments. Choice (C) would not be the best answer. A balanced budget would not raise interest rates. On the contrary, it would tend to lower interest rates, because the government would no longer be competing with private industry in trying to borrow more money. So with demand for borrowed money decreasing, interest rates should decrease also. Choice (D) would not be the best answer. With a balanced budget, the U.S. government would no longer need to borrow new money. Therefore, it would be free from borrowing foreign capital. Choice (E) would not be the best answer. An end to the deficit would lower interest rates and help reduce the balance of payments deficit. In turn, this should improve business and make the free-market economy work better, thus decreasing the need to resort to socialism.

20. **(A)**   Choice (A) is the best answer. High interest rates do tend to cause recessions, because they prevent many people from borrowing money. So there is less money in circulation, and it moves around more slowly. There is less business then, and less investment; this eventually causes fewer jobs and more unemployment—and the vicious cycle continues. Choice (B) is not the best answer. High interest rates do not increase inflation; they tend to decrease inflation, because there is less borrowing. Choice (C) is not the best answer. High interest rates do not ease monetary policy. On the contrary, they toughen monetary policy. It is the low interest rates that are considered to ease monetary policy. Choice (D) is not the best answer either. High interest rates do not increase the money supply; they tend to decrease the money supply, because they discourage people from borrowing money, so there is less money in circulation. Choice (E) is not the best answer. Most prospective buyers do not have the entire amount of money needed to buy a house. They usually need to borrow a large sum of money. Any increase in interest rates greatly multiplies the ultimate cost to the prospective purchaser, discouraging many prospects from buying. Therefore, an increase in interest rates decreases housing starts.

CHEMISTRY

Like the Biology test, this test assesses the preparation for teaching chemistry at the secondary level. The major ideas of chemistry are covered. These questions test not only scientific facts but also the ability to teach chemistry to secondary school students.

DIRECTIONS: Each of the following questions and incomplete statements is followed by five answer choices. Select the choice which best answers each question.

---

1. An unbuffered solution of pH 2.00 is mixed with an equal volume of an unbuffered solution of pH 6.00. The pH of the resultant solution is

   (A) 2.00

   (B) 2.30

   (C) 4.00

   (D) 8.00

   ((E) More information needs to be given.

2. The polyatomic ion, SO_4^{-2} is called

   (A) Sulfite.

   (B) Sulfide.

   (C) Sulfate.

   (D) Sulfur-tetroxide.

   (E) Phosphate.

3. The best source of a culture of *Paramecium* would be

   (A) Stagnant water infused with straw or hay.

   (B) Fresh sea water.

   (C) Water from a rapidly flowing mountain stream.

   (D) Blood.

   (E) (A), (B), and (C).

4. If $_{53}^{131}I$ decays by beta emission, the daughter atom is:

   (A) $_{54}^{131}Xe$

   (B) $_{53}^{130}I$

   (C) $_{52}^{130}Te$

   (D) $_{52}^{131}Te$

   (E) $_{50}^{127}Sb$

5. If the rest mass of an object is m_o, what is its mass when traveling at 0.95 times the speed of light?

   (A) $m_o\sqrt{1-0.95}$

   (B) $m_o\sqrt{0.95-1}$

   (C) $m_o/\sqrt{1-0.95}$

   (D) $\sqrt{0.95}/m_o$

   (E) $m_o/\sqrt{0.95-1}$

6. AMPLITUDE:BRIGHTNESS::

   (A) frequency:pitch

   (B) wavelength:intensity

(C)   speed of light:speed of sound   (D)   frequency:loudness

(E)   wavelength:color

The five choices below are for the next three questions.

(A) $13 \, C, 12 \, C$
      $6 \quad 6$

(B) O_2, O_3

(C) $Cu^{+1} Cu^{+2}$

(D) Co, CO

(E) H_2O, H_2O_2

7.   Which of the above show two allotropes of the same element?

8.   Which of the above shows two different compounds of the same elements?

9.   Which of the above shows two different isotopes of the same element?

10.   An example of a strong base would be

(A) $Cs(OH)$

(B) NH_4OH

(C) $Fe(OH)_2$

(D) $Fe(OH)_3$

(E) $Cu(OH)_2$

11.   To the proper number of significant figures, the solution to the equation $\log_{10} (7.8500 \times 10^{28})$ is

(A)   28.8

(B)   28.9

(C)   28.895

(D)   28.89487

(E)   Significant figures are not used in logarithmic terms.

12.   An example of a monocot would be

(A)   Corn

(B)   Beans

(C)   Oak

(D)   Pine

(E)   Fern

13.   Which of the following is a type of igneous rock?

(A)   Shale

(B)   Sandstone

(C)   Coal

(D)   Granite

(E)   Magma

Questions 14 and 15 are based on the following passage.

Students were asked: "What volume of 0.200 M sulfuric acid (M.W. = 98.07340) is needed to neutralize 5.00 grams of calcium carbonate (M.W.= 116.08860)?" Below are five of their answers.

(A) $2HSO_4 + CaCO_3 \rightarrow H_2O + CO_2 \uparrow + Ca(SO_4)_2$
[(5.00 gm/116.08860 gm/mole) x (1 mole HSO_4/2 moles $CaCO_3$)]/
0.200 moles/litre = 0.10768 litres

(B) $H_2SO_4 + CaCO_3 \rightarrow CaSO_4 + CO_2 \uparrow + H_2O$
[(5.00 gm/116.08860 gm/mole) • (1 mole H_2SO_4/1 mole CaO_3)]/
0.200 moles/litre = 0.215 litres

(C) $3H_2SO_4 + CaCO_3 \rightarrow CaH_2 + 2CS_2 + 10 O_2\uparrow$

[(5.00 gm/116.08860 gm/mole) • (3 moles H_2SO_4/mole $CaCO_3$)]/
0.200 moles/ litre = 0.646 litres

(D) $2HSO_4 + CaCO_3 \rightarrow CO_2 \uparrow Ca(SO_4)_2 + H_2O)$

[(5.00 gm/116.08860 gm/mole) • (1 mole HSO_4/2 moles $CaCO_3$)]/
0.200 moles/litre = 0.108 litres

(E) $H_2SO_4 + CaCO_3 \rightarrow CaSO_4 + H_2O + CO_2 \uparrow$

[(5.00 gm/116.08860 gm/mole • (1 mole H_2SO_4/mole $CaCO_3$)]/
0.200 moles/litre = 0.21535 litres

14. Which student got the correct answer, but needs to be reminded of significant figures?

15. Which student understands significant figures, but must be reminded that the sulfate ion has a minus two charge?

16. The charge of one electron is
(A) equal in magnitude, but opposite in sign as that of the proton.
(B) equal to one volt.
(C) varies, depending upon the type of atom the electron is orbiting.
(D) one Coulomb.
(E) one amphere.

Questions 17 and 18 refer to the five choices below:

(A) Nucleus   (D) Ribosome
(B) Mitochondria   (E) Chloroplast
(C) Endoplasmic reticulum

17. Which of the above would one find in a blue-green algae?

18. Which of the above is considered the "powerhouse" of eukaryotic cells?

19. ANGULAR VELOCITY : RADIANS/SECOND::
(A) linear velocity : centimeters/second
(B) radian : degree
(C) degree/second : radian/second
(D) rotational inertia : rotational kinetic energy
(E) linear velocity : kinetic energy

20. What is the concentration of a solution in which 20.0 millilitres contains 5.0 millimoles of solute?
(A) 5 x 20 = 100 M   (D) 0.02/5 = 0.0040 M
(B) 20/5 = 4.0 M   (E) 5/0.02 - 250 M
(C) 5/20 = 0.25 M

ANSWER KEY

1.	(B)	6.	(E)	11.	(D)	16.	(A)
2.	(C)	7.	(B)	12.	(A)	17.	(D)
3.	(A)	8.	(E)	13.	(D)	18.	(B)
4.	(A)	9.	(A)	14.	(E)	19.	(A)
5.	(C)	10.	(A)	15.	(D)	20.	(C)

DETAILED EXPLANATIONS OF ANSWERS

1. **(B)** Remember that pH is a logarithmic term (pH = -log $[H_3O^+]$). Hence, a solution with a pH of 2.00 would have a hydronium ion concentration ($[H_3O^+]$) of 1.0^2 x 10^{-2} M, and with a pH of 6.00 $[H_3O^+]$ = 1.0 x 10^{-6} M. For convenience, it is easiest to take a volume of one litre, although any volume will work. In one litre of each solution we will have 1.0^2 x 10^{-2} + 1.0 x 10^{-6} = 1.00010 x 10^{-2} moles of H_3O^+. However, the new volume is now two litres (1 + 1 = 2). This gives a $[H_3O^+]$ = 1.00010 x 10^{-2}/2 = 5.00050 x 10^{-3} M. Taking the log of this term and changing the sign, gives a value of 2.30. If one forgets to divide the total number of H_3O^+'s by the new volume one gets the -log (1.00010 x 10^{-2}) = 1.999956572, which rounds off to 2.00 which is (A). If one simply tries to average the pH values, they get (2 + 6)/2 = 4, which is (C). If one simply adds the pH values, they get 2.00 + 6.00 = 8.00, which is (D).

2. **(C)** The correct answer is (C), sulfate. Sulfite, (A), is SO_3^{-2}. Sulfide, (B), is S^{-2}, and is not a polyatomic ion. Sulfur-tetroxide, (D), is SO_4, and is not an ion. Phosphate, (E), is PO_4^{-3}.

3. **(A)** *Paramecia*, and cilliates in general, can be found in hay infusions, hence their old name "infusoria." Protozoans can be found in any of the mentioned sources, but (A) is the best environment for this particular genus.

4. **(A)** When an atom decays by beta emission, the atomic number increases by one, and the atomic mass remains the same. In the case of iodine, atomic number 53, the new atomic number is 54, which is that of xenon; the mass remains unchanged. Answers (B) and (C) show a change in mass, which cannot happen with beta decay. Answer (D) shows an increase in atomic number with no change in mass, which would happen with positron decay. (E) shows a decrease by two in atomic number, and decrease by four in mass that would occur with alpha decay.

5. **(C)** The other answers do not make any sense.

6. **(E)** The amplitude of a light wave determines how bright the light is. The wavelength of a light wave determines the color of the light. (A) is wrong, although the frequency of a

sound wave does determine the pitch of the sound, this analogy is with light. (B) and (D) are both wrong, as wavelength has nothing to do with intensity, nor does frequency with loudness. (C) is also incorrect, as this analogy has nothing to do with comparing the speed of light to that of sound.

7. **(B)** Allotropy is used to designate the existence of an element in two or more forms in the same physical state, in this case oxygen gas and ozone. Another example of allotropes would be carbon in the form of graphite and diamond.

8. **(E)** Water is made of hydrogen and oxygen in a 2:1 molar ratio. Hydrogen peroxide is made of hydrogen and oxygen in a 1:1 molar ratio.

9. **(A)** Isotopes have the same atomic number (hence they are the same element), but differ in atomic mass. In this case it is carbon of mass 12 and 13 (both have atomic numbers of 6). Another example would be oxygen of mass 16 and 18 (but both would have an atomic number of 8).

10. **(A)** All hydroxides of group 1A elements make strong bases. The strength of the bases increases as one moves down the table. Francium hydroxide would be the strongest base, but it is radioactive, and no isotopes of it exist with long enough half-lives to be practical. Hence, cesium is the next element up, and is stable, so cesium hydroxide is the strongest base.

11. **(D)** Remember, in a logarithmic term, the digits to the left of the decimal are simply place-holders, those on the right are significant. Since there are five significant figures in the original number, there need to be five significant figures in the answer.

12. **(A)** A monocot has only one cotyledon (primary leaf) on the developing embryo in its seed. Corn is such a plant. Bean plants and oak trees are dicots, which mean they have two cotyledons on the developing embryo in their seeds. Pine trees have many cotyledons (polycots) on the developing embryo in their seeds. Ferns have no seeds, therefore, they cannot be considered at all in this question.

13. **(D)** Igneous rock is formed by cooling magma, which is molton rock. This explanation rules out choice (E). All other choices are sedimentary rocks.

14. **(E)** There are only three significant figures in the mass given (5.00 grams), hence, there can be only three in the answer.

15. **(D)** The significant figures are correct, but sulfate is incorrectly treated as if it had a charge of minus one, hence the stoichiometry is incorrect.

16. **(A)** Although an electron has only 1/1832 the mass of a proton, it has just as much charge, only it is negative, and a proton is positive. (C) is incorrect because all electrons have the same charge irrespective of their environment. (D) is incorrect, although charge is measured in coulombs. An electron actually has a charge of 1.60×10^{-19} Coulombs. (B) is incorrect, as a volt is a measure of the work done per Coulomb of charge. An electron-volt (eV) is the energy required to excite an electron to a potential of one volt, and is a common unit of energy in particle physics. (E) is incorrect, as the amphere is a measure of the number of Coulombs passing a point during a given period of time. This is called the current.

17. **(D)**   Blue-green algae are prokaryotes, hence they lack all of the organelles listed except ribosomes. Ribosomes are found in both prokaryotic and eukaryotic cells and are the site of protein manufacture.

18. **(B)**   The Krebs Cycle occurs in the mitochondria.

19. **(A)**   Angular velocity can be measured in radians/second, and linear velocity can be measured in centimetres/second. Radians and degrees both measure angles (B), degrees/second and radians/second both measure angular velocity (C), rotational inertia is related to rotational kinetic energy (D), and linear velocity is related to kinetic energy (E), but these lack the relationship with the first comparison that choice (A) maintains.

20. **(C)**   5.0 millimoles/20 millilitres = 0.25 moles/litre = 0.25 M.

EARLY CHILDHOOD EDUCATION

This test is for those who have completed their undergraduate studies in this field. The test measures the student's knowledge of the growth cycle, development of children, teaching behaviors curriculum development, and development-related activities for young children. The two main parts of the test cover 1) the nature of growth and development and 2) the appropriateness of teaching behaviors.

DIRECTIONS: Each of the following questions and incomplete statements is followed by five answer choices. Select the choice which best answers each question.

---

1. Children who are not aware that lines of objects continue to have the same number when objects are rearranged
    (A) have developed an awareness of irreversibility.
    (B) are considered "disadvantaged."
    (C) have not developed an awareness of conservation of number.
    (D) are lacking contingency management.
    (E) lack an understanding of the phoneme-grapheme relationship.

2. A kindergarten teacher is working with the students on *-ed, -ing,* and *-s*. He was most likely teaching a lesson on
    (A) syllabication.
    (D) digraphs.
    (B) phonics.
    (E) structural analysis, particularly prefixes.
    (C) suffixes.

3. The ordering of objects or events according to a given dimension is which of the following?
    (A) One-to-one correspondence
    (D) Anticipating
    (B) Equivalency
    (E) Seriation
    (C) Classification

4. Which of the following quotations is the best for a teacher to use in her classroom?
    (A) "Notice Mary is lazy again today. Let's all try to be good workers so she can see how smart we are and learn from us."
    (B) "John has painted a picture in art today. Come by to see his picture so you can see what a good boy he is."
    (C) "John, let me add some eyes to the face on your picture so your parents will be proud of you when they come to open house."
    (D) "All of you take out your coloring books and color page 3 like the sample on the board."
    (E) "I like the way Jane is sitting. She is using good posture. Let's try to sit the same way."

5. Which of the following activities is least appropriate for young children?
   (A) Painting with a sponge
   (B) Painting with oils
   (C) Painting with tempras
   (D) Painting with finger paints
   (E) Using templates of the letters for tracings

6. As the music books are used, the students are becoming aware of musical symbols. The children are most likely in which of the following?
   (A) Nursery school   (D) First grade
   (B) 4-year-old class   (E) Above first grade
   (C) Kindergarten

7. Using function as a criterion for sorting is
   (A) common for young children at the age of three or above.
   (B) a task children of four commonly do well.
   (C) a task children of five usually accomplish.
   (D) a task only a few children, even at age five, can perform.
   (E) a task commonly dealt with during the sensorimotor period.

8. When giving directions on how to cut a snowflake, a third grade teacher should do which of the following?
   (A) Give out printed directions.
   (B) Give out pictured directions.
   (C) Give directions orally.
   (D) "Walk" the students through cutting a snowflake.
   (E) (B), (C), and (D) only.

9. Which of the students are demonstrating the most sophisticated behaviors?
   (A) Jane is playing with dolls while Bill is playing with building blocks.
   (B) Jane is painting while Bill is drawing.
   (C) Jane is building a tower while Bill is preparing a snack of raisins and bananas.
   (D) Jane is pretending to be a lion and Bill a lion tamer.
   (E) All of the above are of equal sophistication.

10. The method which makes use of daily living, sensory, academic, and cultural and artistic materials was developed by which of the following?
    (A) Bruner   (D) Montessori
    (B) Maslow   (E) Piaget
    (C) Bereiter

11. Two children are fighting. The best approach for the teacher to take first is which of the following?
    (A) Separate the two, deal quickly with the aggressor to remove him from the scene, and then check on the victim.

(B)   Separate the two and take both to the guidance counselor for a conference.

(C)   Separate the two and attend first to the victim.

(D)   A teacher of young children should not attempt to separate the two unless an adult witness is present.

(E)   Send another person for an administrator, separate the two, turn the aggressor over to the administrator, and then deal personally with the victim.

12.   The teacher shows the children a comb, combs her hair with it to remind them of its function, and then shows them how the comb can attract some bits of paper. The children then try to find out why this unexpected event occurred. This is an example of which of the following?

(A)   Expository teaching   (D)   The discovery approach

(B)   The phonic approach   (E)   Individualized instruction

(C)   The unit method

13.   Which of the following principles of child development is false?

(A)   Development occurs in a regular fashion.

(B)   Development proceeds from general to specific.

(C)   Growth and development vary among individuals.

(D)   Development proceeds from specific to general.

(E)   Development is influenced by nature and nurture.

14.   Students in Pygmalion Primary School have studied the home and family, the school and community, the state and nation, and are now studying regions of the world. The approach being used is probably which of the following?

(A)   Expanding horizon approach   (D)   Open classroom

(B)   Spiral curriculum   (E)   Hidden curriculum

(C)   Learning centers

15.   Which of the following punishments is probably LEAST effective in dealing with a second-grader who constantly has tantrums at the least provocation?

(A)   The teacher might prohibit the child's participation in the situation that caused the child to have a tantrum; after a discussion with the child indicates that the child is again ready to attempt a board game with the other members of his group, she may allow the child to try again.

(B)   The child should have an opportunity to realize that the teacher has more power than he; the teacher might demonstrate this by arranging a situation where the teacher does not achieve the results he wants and the teacher can enter into a tirade or tantrum much worse than the child's to demonstrate the adult's power.

(C)   The teacher might continue with the class activities and ignore the pouting child.

(D)   The teacher might isolate the child from the rest of the class in a time-out room.

(E)   The parents should be called in to confer with the teacher about how the situation is handled at home.

16. The children in your class have difficulty expressing the order of events, understanding numbers and their relations, and remembering rules. Which of the following is probably the stage of their development according Piaget's developmental stages?

    (A) Formal operations   (D) Sensorimotor

    (B) Concrete operations   (E) None of the above.

    (C) Preoperations

17. A teacher of young children has spent a lot of time having her students focus on the activities below.

    I. Sorting objects by shape.

    II. Finding letters which are alike and different.

    III. Printing the letters *m*, *s*, and *d*.

    IV. Recognizing and interpreting pictures.

    In which order did she work with the children on these skills?

    (A) IV, I, III, II   (D) II, III, IV, I

    (B) I, II, III, IV   (E) II, I, III, IV

    (C) I, IV, II, III

18. Which of the methods below does not involve active participation by the student?

    (A) Inquiry learning   (D) Scientific method

    (B) Discovery learning   (E) None of the above.

    (C) Process approach

19. Which of the following is not one of the steps in the scientific method?

    (A) Form the hypothesis.   (D) Alter the data.

    (B) State the problem.   (E) Communicate the findings.

    (C) Test the hypothesis.

20. Which of the following objectives is stated in behavioral terms?

    (A) The student will be able to comprehend the meaning of the picture.

    (B) The student will be able to appreciate the work done by community helpers.

    (C) The student will be able to read aloud all the words from the Primer List of the Dolch Popper Words.

    (D) The student will be able to understand the reasons for the change in seasons.

    (E) All the above.

ANSWER KEY

1.	(C)	6.	(E)	11.	(C)	16.	(C)
2.	(C)	7.	(D)	12.	(D)	17.	(C)
3.	(E)	8.	(E)	13.	(D)	18.	(E)
4.	(E)	9.	(D)	14.	(A)	19.	(D)
5.	(B)	10.	(D)	15.	(B)	20.	(C)

DETAILED EXPLANATIONS OF ANSWERS

1. **(C)** The child who is not aware that lines of objects continue to have the same number when the objects are rearranged has not yet developed an awareness of conservation of number. (C) is the correct answer, then, and should be selected. (A) could be selected if the words *not* and *reversibility* (not *irreversibility*) were used. As it is written, (A) is incorrect and not an appropriate choice. Students who have not reached a stage in their development to allow them to recognize conservation of number are not usually referred to as "disadvantaged"; that term is usually associated with children who are lacking the experiences needed to perform successfully in a school situation. (B) is not the best answer. Contingency management is the control of reinforcements to affect the frequency of desirable or undesirable behaviors. (D) is not an appropriate choice. Not understanding conservation of number does not necessarily mean that a child lacks an understanding of the letter-sound relationship. (E), then, is not appropriate.

2. **(C)** All the letters given were endings or *suffixes*. (C) is the best answer. Syllabication (A) involves more than just suffixes; (A) is not the best choice. Phonics (B) has to do with the phoneme (sound) grapheme (letter) relationship. It—like syllabication—involves more than just the three suffixes listed; (B) is not the best choice. Digraphs (D) are two consonants or vowels coming together with one sound; the sound of the individual letters is not heard. All the suffixes given do not even have two consonants or vowels coming together; (D) could not be the correct choice. (E) states that particularly prefixes were emphasized; none of the items given were prefixes. (E) is not the best choice.

3. **(E)** The definition of *seriation* is the ordering of objects or events according to a given dimension; (E) is the best choice. One-to-one correspondence involves taking two sets or groups of items and pairing or matching them one-on-one. This is a totally different task than seriation. (A) is not the best choice. Equivalency (B) has to do with two groups or sets which have the same number of elements but not necessarily the exact same elements. (B) is not an acceptable answer. Classification (C) is the act of systematically grouping objects or events according to identifiable common characteristics. (C), then, is not the correct answer. Answer (D), which has to do with anticipating or predicting, is not an acceptable answer for the task described.

4. **(E)** (E) is the best answer. It praises the child who is sitting correctly and gives the others a model for a good behavior. (A) is a poor statement. It makes Mary look bad to the others in the class; it involves a subjective judgment of *lazy*. There is no specific task to be remedied and it causes the rest of the class to appear *smart*. No hope is given that Mary will improve; chances are the self-fulfilling prophecy is already at work here! (B) is not the best choice because it uses the words "good boy." John, then, has drawn a good picture and is a good boy; this means that if he does not succeed next time he will be a bad boy. Praise should be centered around the task and not the personality of the child. The teacher should not add some features to the child's creative masterpiece; (C) is a poor choice. Instructing children to color from a coloring book and even giving directions on the colors to use is not a very creative art lesson. (D) is an inappropriate choice.

5. **(B)** Oil paints are not water-based. They are not as safe for young children as water based materials. Oil paints are difficult to remove and often involve the use of turpentine and linseed oil. (B) is the correct answer since the least appropriate material is sought. Sponge painting (A) uses larger muscles than would painting with a small, detail brush; sponge painting is very appropriate for young children. Since (A) is appropriate, it should not be chosen for a question which asks for the least appropriate answer. Tempras (C) are water-based and appropriate; finger paints (D) are appropriate for young children since they are water-based and do not necessitate fine motor skills. Using templates (stencils) for tracings (E) is appropriate. Since (A), (C), (D), and (E) are appropriate, they should not be selected.

6. **(E)** Musical symbols involve very abstract reasoning. Reading the symbols also is an advanced skill. The use of music books is typically above the first grade level. (E) is the best answer. Answers (A), (B), (C), and (D) would introduce this abstract material before most students are ready.

7. **(D)** Using function as a criterion for sorting is a task only a few children, even at the age of five, can perform. (D) is the best answer. Children of age three (A), four (B), or five (C) do not usually do this task well. (A), (B), and (C), then, should not be selected. According to Piaget, the sensorimotor period (E) is the period from birth to 24 months; this is certainly not an appropriate time to introduce sorting. (E) is an inappropriate answer.

8. **(E)** Since children learn in various ways, the best approach would be to give directions in visual or "pictured" form (B), in oral form (C), and kinesthetically (D) for the kinesthetic/tactile learner. (E) allows the reader to select (B), (C), and (D) . None of the answers alone would be sufficient. Giving printed directions alone (A) may not be appropriate for the reading level of most third grade children; diagrams would be helpful for this task.

9. **(D)** Only (D) involves cooperative play, which is more sophisticated than parallel play. Answers (A), (B), and (C) all involve parallel play, in which children engage much earlier than cooperative play. Stating that all of the examples of play are of an equal sophistication (E) is an inappropriate answer for question 5.

10. **(D)** The question describes best Marie Montessori's materials. (D) is the best answer. Bruner (A) is noted for his theory of the structure of the discipline. Maslow (B) states that there is a hierarchy of needs with the basic needs of food and shelter at the bottom and self-actualization at the top. Bereiter (C) with others developed an academic program for early childhood education; this academic program (DISTAR) is frequently used with

disadvantaged children. Piaget is best known for his work in identifying developmental stages of young children.

11. **(C)**   The teacher should attend first to the victim after separating the two. (C) is the best answer. If the teacher responds first to the aggressor, it conveys that he/she is more important. (B), then, is incorrect. After separating the two, the teacher should attend to the victim and, if possible, deal with the situation himself/herself; the guidance counselor may be consulted if it is a school rule, but the teacher may handle the situation more easily. The teacher should not wait for a witness before separating the two children; harm could come to either or both. (D) is not an appropriate answer. Again, the teacher should separate the two—not send someone for the administrator first as (E) states. Separating the two by having the aggressor dealt with by the administrator and the victim dealt with by the teacher is not the best approach. (E) is not the best answer.

12. **(D)**   Solving a problem presented by the teacher is most likely an example of the discovery approach. (D) is the best answer. Expository teaching (A) is another name for the teacher-centered (lecture) method; it is certainly an inappropriate answer. The phonic approach is a way of teaching reading; it is clearly an inappropriate answer. (B) should not be chosen. The unit method is a method of teaching which involves planning in advance for a 2-3 week period; the exercise mentioned here does not imply several weeks of activities will develop. (C) is inappropriate. Individualized instruction (E) is not implied by question 12; rather whole-group work was involved as an introduction. (E) is inappropriate.

13. **(D)**   Except for (D) all the statements about child development [(A), (B), (C), and (E)] are true. (D) is false because development proceeds from general to specific, not specific to general as (D) states.

14. **(A)**   The scope and sequence of social studies given here is a direct example of the expanding horizon or widening horizon approach developed originally in the 1920's and still used by many textbook companies, school systems, and teachers. The spiral curriculum (B) enables the children to build progressively on information learned previously; (B) does not fit the sequence described in question 14. Learning centers (C) is a type of classroom organization; the sequence described in question 14 seems to relate more to the vertical organization of the school than to the horizontal organization suggested by learning centers; (C) is not the best answer. The open classroom (D) is based on the British primary schools and involves much pupil freedom and choice. Like centers (C), the open classroom (D) relates to horizontal school organization while the question concerns vertical organization. The hidden curriculum includes all the experiences that a child has in school—particularly those experiences which were not intended by the teacher.

15. **(B)**   Having the teacher herself/himself enter into a temper tantrum would hardly be beneficial to the child who has tantrums or to the other children in the classroom. (B) is probably the least effective choice. Prohibiting the child's participation in the activity that caused the tantrum until the child is ready to attempt the activity again (A) might be a reasonable course to follow. Ignoring the pouting child (C) might be a reasonable policy to follow—particularly if behavior modification is being employed. (C) is a reasonable answer and therefore not the poor answer the question seeks. Using a time-out room for a tantrum seems a logical procedure to follow. (D), therefore, cannot be used. Talking with parents (E) is also reasonable and should not be selected.

16. **(C)**   Each of the characteristics given is one which is descriptive of the preoperational stage, typical of 2-7 year old children. (C) is the best answer. Formal operations (A) is a stage when children use abstractions and form theories about everything; it is typical of children of ages 11-15. (A) is not the best answer. In the concrete operational (B) stage children develop concepts of numbers, relations, understanding what others say, and understanding and remembering rules; children in this stage are ages 7-11. (B) does not fit the characteristics given in question 16. The sensorimotor period is the stage in which children learn from sensory experiences and from motor activities; it corresponds to the ages 0-2 years. Clearly (D) is not the best answer. (E), which states that none of the above is appropriate, is incorrect since (C) is the correct answer.

17. **(C)**   The teacher who has the students sort objects by shape first has begun with the concrete level of learning; by proceeding next to work with pictures, the teacher has moved to the semi-concrete level. Since reading precedes writing, the teacher who has the students discriminate before writing is following the correct sequence. (It should be noted that both II and III are at the abstract level.) The best sequence, then, is I, IV, II, and the same sequence the reader can select with answer (C). The other answers [(A), (B), (D), and (E)] are incorrect.

18. **(E)**   Since all the methods given—inquiry (A), discovery (B), process (C), and scientific (D)—involve active participation by the student, (E) is the best answer. (E) allows the reader to select "None of the above" as the correct answer.

19. **(D)**   Altering the data (D) is not a step in the scientific process. Data should not be altered or changed. If this is done, the results of the experiment cannot be proved as accurate. The rest of the items are steps in the scientific process. (D) should read, "Collect the data."

20. **(C)**   Being able "to read aloud" (C) is an observable behavior and the best choice for the behavioral objective. Being able to comprehend (A), to appreciate (B), and to understand (D) are open to many interpretations and are not clearly observable. (A), (B), (D), and (E) are not appropriate answers. "None of the above" (E) is not to be chosen since one of the above answers (C) is correct.

EDUCATIONAL LEADERSHIP:
Administration and Supervision

This Specialty Test measures knowledge of the functions of an administrator or supervisor. This test is intended for those who are candidates to receive master's degrees or have already attained a master's degree and are seeking appointment as administrators or supervisors. The test is broken down into instructional leadership (37%), administrative leadership (33%), and individual and group leadership skills (30%). Some topics include curriculum design, program evaluation, staff development, business and fiscal features of school management, and school-community relations.

DIRECTIONS: Each of the following questions and incomplete statements is followed by five answer choices. Select the choice which best answers each question.

---

1. Implementation of curriculum revision calls for the effective administrator to provide
   - (A) strong top-down leadership to minimize opportunity for objections from teachers to be heard.
   - (B) freedom of choice for teachers because those who resist change will be alienated by administrative pressure.
   - (C) minimal publicity, especially to parents, to prevent those who might oppose reform from learning about changes.
   - (D) staff development and administrative influence to promote the new curriculum.
   - (E) strong commitment to the curricular change but no intrusion on the instructional methods of teachers.

2. Administrators may be described according to whether their style is *Task Oriented* or *Relationship Oriented*. Which of the following describes the attitude of the Relationship-style leader in respect to the least preferred co-worker?
   - (A) Favors the least-preferred co-worker
   - (B) Favors the most-preferred co-worker
   - (C) Sees little difference between least-preferred and most preferred co-worker
   - (D) Gives special attention to the least-preferred co-worker to improve her/his interpersonal skills
   - (E) Avoids the least-preferred co-worker to reduce conflict

3. School leaders who adapt their behavior according to the situation they encounter embrace which of the following theories of leadership?
   - (A) Theory Y
   - (B) Human relations theory
   - (C) Theory X
   - (D) Contingency theory
   - (E) Conceptual theory

4. Which of the following most accurately describes the role of the local school principal?

   (A) She performs tasks similar to those of the superintendent but does so within the policy limits of the district.

   (B) She sets school policy that matches the needs of the individual school.

   (C) She is limited to the management of the educational program and personnel (teachers and pupils).

   (D) She is a facilitator and does not exert any more influence than does any other professional in the school.

   (E) Since she is responsible for all school activities the principal retains veto power over all student and faculty recommendations.

5. Which of the following actions by a school principal is a necessary component of "clinical supervision"?

   (A) Preparing written reactions to teachers regarding student evaluations of the teacher's performance

   (B) Discussing new teaching methods with teachers

   (C) Comparing achievement scores of pupils with national norms and discussing these results with teachers

   (D) Observing and recording teachers' performances in classrooms and conferring with them about their teaching

   (E) Discussing teacher effectiveness with the teacher's department chairperson or a peer teacher to identify strengths and weaknesses

6. The autocratic school leader whose actions cause subordinates to be dependent will develop a staff that tends to be

   (A) supportive of the strong leadership provided.

   (B) motivated to assert their individuality.

   (C) frustrated, apathetic, and disinterested.

   (D) friendly towards one another but distant from the school leader.

   (E) loyal to the school administrator.

7. The primary purpose of the school district budgeting process is to

   (A) translate the district's priorities into programmatic and financial terms.

   (B) provide rewards and incentives to personnel and to implement programs which have been judged to be most successful.

   (C) determine the local tax rate for school support.

   (D) establish a basis for soliciting financial support from business and industry.

   (E) compare per-pupil costs with other districts to monitor the economic efficiency of the schools.

8. When objects of expenditure such as personnel, supplies, and capital outlay are the focus of analysis and budget authorization, the approach is called

   (A) contingency budgeting.   (D) zero-based budgeting.

   (B) program budgeting.   (E) line-item budgeting.

   (C) program planning and budgeting systems (PPBS).

9. The powers not delegated to the United States by the Constitution are reserved to the individual states, and Congress may collect taxes to provide for the general welfare of the United States. In regard to education this means that

   (A) Congress is authorized to support and control public schools.

   (B) Congress may levy taxes to support education and the local school districts are empowered to control education.

   (C) Congress may levy taxes to support education but is not authorized to control education.

   (D) states are authorized to set school policy without regard to the articles of the Constitution.

   (E) Congress may not levy taxes to support education except for categorical funding of special programs.

10. The Fourth Amendment protects citizens from unreasonable search and seizure. Student possession of drugs and other contraband has led to searches of students and student lockers. These searches are most likely to be considered legal if the court considers

   (A) school officials to be private persons.

   (B) school officials to be acting *in loco parentis.*

   (C) school officials to be officers of the state.

   (D) school officials to be equivalent to police officers.

   (E) all students to be minors.

11. School administrators often interview applicants. Which of the following is a legally acceptable question to ask in an interview?

   (A) Where were you born?

   (B) Have you ever been arrested?

   (C) What schools have you attended?

   (D) Where can you be reached in an emergency?

   (E) How long have you been a resident of this city?

12. Which of the following categories of conditions must be met in establishing school staffing practices?

   (A) Public advertisement of positions, clear job description, and specific salary offered for the vacancy.

   (B) Due process, curriculum goals, collective bargaining agreements.

   (C) Treatment of minorities, collective bargaining agreements and school district tradition.

   (D) Curriculum goals, school district tradition, and collective bargaining agreements.

   (E) Due process, treatment of minorities, and collective bargaining agreements.

13. In contrasting *Summative* with *Formative* evaluation, which of the following is the more dominant purpose of *Formative* evaluation?

   (A) Decide on salary   (D) Document reasons for dismissal

   (B) Determine tenure   (E) Improve instruction

   (C) Basis for retention

14. The administrator who evaluates teacher effectiveness on the basis of "process variables" examines which of the following elements to assess teacher performance?

    (A) The behavior of pupils in the classroom

    (B) The actions of the teacher in carrying forth the planning and delivery of instruction

    (C) The performance of students on school district and national examinations

    (D) The success of students after leaving school as determined by follow-up studies of graduates

    (E) The credentials of the teacher and pupil evaluation of the instruction provided

15. Academically effective schools are lead by principals whose behavior towards teachers is dominated by which of the following characteristics?

    (A) They emphasize teaching, learning, and high standards.

    (B) They focus on creating and maintaining a positive personal relationship.

    (C) They leave teachers alone in respect to their teaching and other professional actions.

    (D) They delegate responsibility for the instruction and curriculum of the school to chairpersons and supervisors.

    (E) They give the highest priority to the establishment and maintenance of positive student conduct.

16. The highest priority and first order of business for school administrators is to

    (A) develop and maintain high employee morale.

    (B) promote the highest possible level of instruction.

    (C) assure the financial stability of the organization.

    (D) develop and maintain productive relationships with the political entities that control education.

    (E) develop and maintain community and media support for schools.

17. Which of the following is most often the preferred strategy for changing educational practice?

    (A) Advocate and persuade

    (B) Mandate and coerce

    (C) Provide financial inducements

    (D) Change agent approach (agricultural model)

    (E) External pressure from media and community

18. Whether in business or in school, the system that functions most effectively is one in which

    (A) evaluation of results is accurate and provides feedback to members of the group for improvement.

    (B) the leaders establish clear goals so everyone knows what is expected of them.

    (C) participation of the group members is valued.

(D)   division of responsibility is arranged to make each person's task as simple as possible.

(E)   leaders are changed frequently to encourage new ideas.

19.   Which of the following systems of leadership most strongly enhances professional performance in school organizations?

(A)   Consultative System

(B)   Exploitive-Authoritative System

(C)   Benevolent-Authoritative System

(D)   Participative-Group System

(E)   Laissez-Faire System

20.   Though policy-making occurs throughout the educational system, the agency to which constitutional authority grants the responsibility for educational policy is

(A)   the office of the state commissioner of education.

(B)   the school board of the local school district.

(C)   the state boards of education.

(D)   the office of the governor of each state.

(E)   the individual state legislature.

ANSWER KEY

1.	(D)	6.	(C)	11.	(C)	16.	(B)
2.	(C)	7.	(A)	12.	(E)	17.	(A)
3.	(D)	8.	(E)	13.	(E)	18.	(C)
4.	(A)	9.	(C)	14.	(B)	19.	(D)
5.	(D)	10.	(B)	15.	(A)	20.	(E)

DETAILED EXPLANATIONS OF ANSWERS

1.   **(D)**   Curriculum revision will most likely occur when the staff is provided with initial and continuing preparation and support to sustain the intended reforms. Furthermore, the principal who continues to support the changes through the influence of his/her position provides the leadership to counteract the negative reactions that will inevitably arise from those who resist change and look for reasons to revert to previous behavior. Curriculum reform cannot be evaluated unless it is implemented, and after the school leader has agreed to the changes, that leader has a responsibility to give strong support to the changes to give them a fair chance to be implemented and evaluated. Choices (B) and (E) represent a weak leadership position either in respect to the content of the curriculum revision or the teaching methods necessary to implement the changes. Choices (C) and (A) minimize the importance of broadening the base of support and shared decision making as an element necessary to determine the appropriate changes and to bring about reform.

2.   **(C)**   The relationship-oriented style leader accepts people and tends to treat and view everyone the same. People are not "favorites" or "enemies" but are human beings with a right to their own feelings and deserve to be treated consistently by their leaders. The relationship-oriented leader is most comfortable treating others consistently, regardless of behavior that may cause them to be viewed as less-preferred than others in the workplace. To be consistent with this view, alternatives (A), (B), (D) and (E) are not appropriate responses.

3.   **(D)**   The contingency theorist supports the view that any single theory will not necessarily work in all the different situations a school leader encounters. The action of the leader is "contingent" on the circumstances in any given situation. Contingency based administrators will lead by adapting their actions to the circumstances. In some cases they may be task oriented, in others human relationships are most important, and in others a group process or autocratic approach may seem best. Thus any specific theory, such as those listed in choices (A), (B), (C) and (E) are too restrictive to be the proper choice.

4.   **(A)**   The school principal performs duties related to instructional leadership, community relationships, staff personnel, pupil personnel, facilities, finance, business management and myriad of other duties that are also performed by the district superintendent.

School district policy determines the limits and responsibilities of the principal and he or she cannot set individual school policy without board approval, which makes (B) an incorrect answer. Answer (C) defines the role too narrowly. Answer (D) is incorrect; it would be an impossible situation because a school would be paralyzed if all recommendations required compromise and consensus—there are too many cases in which the principal must be decisive and "take charge." (E) is too controlling to provide a school atmosphere in which faculty and/or students can assume responsibility for helping with the successful operation of the school.

5. **(D)**   The fundamental idea that determines the correct answer to this question is that systematic classroom observation and feedback must be included in clinical supervision. Other forms of supervision may be useful but when they are limited to student performance, lesson plans of teachers, or discussion of teaching methods, they fail to include the critical and core idea of classroom observation.

6. **(C)**   Autocratic leadership has been shown in almost all research studies, beginning with the research of Kurt Lewin in the 1930's, to be counterproductive in respect to employee performance. Such leadership tends to promote antagonism by subordinates towards their leaders, low morale, and dissension. Choices (A), (B), (D) and (E) all have some element of employee performance that is *not* likely to occur under the autocratic leader.

7. **(A)**   Budgeting is more than financial planning—it is a reflection of the priorities for which funding is required. Budgeting is an outgrowth of decisions that are made about the school program and the elements that support that program. These elements include such factors as personnel, materials, support services, and facilities. The budgeting process must take these prior decisions into account to allot resources appropriately. Thus, the primary goal of budgeting is to translate program priorities into resource allocations—including decisions about the amount and distribution of the funds to support the school district. The remaining alternatives provided in this question are either components of the correct answer or consequences and by-products of the budgeting process.

8. **(E)**   The correct response to this item simply calls for an understanding of the terms used in school finance. Line-item budgeting is defined in the question and (E) is the correct definition. Program budgeting is tied to programs rather than to specific items. PPBS is similar to program budgeting but is thought of in terms of a broader system in which programs are included. Zero-based budgeting calls for an annual "fresh start" to justify the existence of each program and its expenditures. Contingencies are allocations to a category as a "safety net" or back-up to cover unexpected costs. It does not provide for the categories listed in the question.

9. **(C)**   Answer (C) is consistent with the conditions described in the question. Answer (B) grants control to local districts when the states actually hold this power. Answer (A) says Congress may control schools when they are not authorized to do so. Answer (D) provides for states to depart from the articles of the Constitution and it has been ruled that states may not interpose state laws between citizens and the United States Constitution. Congress does legislate financial support for schools and includes both categorical funding and more general support through their bureaus.

10. **(B)**   This question can be answered by eliminating alternatives that are incorrect and by understanding the role of parents, protection of minors, and responsibilities of officers of the state. Choice (C) grants to private citizens a right they clearly do not have, and choice

(E) denies constitutional protection to minors. Neither of these is acceptable. Police officers and other state officials may not search without probable cause. Though the issue is not totally clear, the most acceptable response is that parents have the right to monitor the behavior of their children and if teachers are acting in place of the parents (*in loco parentis*), they also may have the right to search for contraband.

11. **(C)** The essential criterion to be applied in the interviewing process is whether or not the questions relate to a BFOQ (bona fide occupational qualification). Responses (A), (D) and (E) are clearly not job related and could even be regarded as prejudicial, depending on the applicant's circumstances. Choice (B) is not acceptable because people are sometimes falsely arrested. A more acceptable question would be to ask if the applicant had ever been *convicted* of a felony—if that is a concern of the prospective employer.

12. **(E)** The correct answer to this question is determined by isolating those components that focus directly on staffing. In each of the incorrect answers [(A), (B), (C) and (D)] one variable that is indirectly related to staffing is listed. These variables include the curriculum goals, school district tradition, and specific salary (a salary range may be advertised).

13. **(E)** The contrast between summative and formative evaluation includes the expectation that formative evaluation will help to "form" or develop the ability of the supervisee, and summative evaluation includes assessment at a more final or later stage of performance. Because of this distinction, formative evaluation would not be appropriately used to make decisions about tenure, retention, or salary. However, formative evaluation can be diagnostic and provide supervisees with recommendations that might later become the basis for employment decisions.

14. **(B)** The term "process variable" is different from the term "product variable." Product variables are those variables that could be considered the results of teaching or the actions of students. These include such factors as students, test scores, student behavior, and student evaluations. Process variables are those actions, or processes, which the teacher uses in instruction. The assumption is that if the teacher performs according to the recommended practices of the profession, then the teacher has done the right things to promote learning. Thus, supervision by the administrator or supervisor which is directed at teacher performance, is supervision based on "process variables."

15. **(A)** The research on effective schools is consistent in reporting that leadership in effective schools includes attention to the delivery of effective instruction. Principals in effective schools can be friendly and warm but the thrust of their efforts and the use of their conversational and leadership time when interacting with teachers is on the improvement and/or maintenance of instruction. Choices (B)-(E) include behaviors that may contribute to high morale, good working relationships, or mutual respect, but they do not include the unique mission of schools to emphasize learning.

16. **(B)** The reason for all other activities of the school administrator is to support instruction and learning. Though it is sometimes tempting to address problems such as employee morale or public relations in isolation from instruction, unless the administrator has clearly recognized the ultimate goal of schools as serving pupils, the other "problems" will often be resolved for the wrong reasons and in the wrong way. All organizations need goals that serve as guides to action, and the goal to provide instruction serves as the school's beacon. Choices (A), (C), (D) and (E) are helpful activities but they are part of the support system to meet the more important and pervasive goal of instruction.

17. **(A)**   Educational change requires cooperation from many participants. It also requires that these participants share in the decisions for change and believe in the beneficial results of change. Cooperation, belief, and shared decisions can be developed best by a leader who expresses confidence in the proposed changes and then persuades those who may disagree by providing information and an opportunity for debate. This combination can be described as advocating and persuading. The other choices in this question identify dictatorial tactics (mandate and coerce) bribery (financial inducements), top-down (agricultural agent), or high-pressure tactics which violate the premise on which change in a professional bureaucracy is most likely to occur.

18. **(C)**   Organizations increase their chances for success when all members of the organization share the responsibility for success. Whether the leadership is prone to top-down or shared decision-making, the role of all members of the organization can be considered and valued. When group members can participate in those decisions that affect them, the potential for the organization to succeed is increased. This participation is especially critical for schools because they are a *professional* bureaucracy in which many of the employees are professionally trained. Their contribution to school success can be based on experience and training that represents knowledge of their field of work and also includes an expectation that the conditions of employment will include opportunities to use their knowledge to influence the conditions under which they work. Choices (A), (B), (D) and (E) fail to give central concern to the role of group members and are less likely to create the optimal circumstances for organizational success.

19. **(D)**   The basic concept of empowerment and shared leadership is included in choice (D). The other systems listed in alternatives (A), (B), (C) and (E) either describe authoritarian approaches or indifferent leadership. The team building and cooperative spirit that creates attractive and motivating work conditions are enhanced through a system that calls for group participation. These conditions further promote the dedicated performance of professionals.

20. **(E)**   The Tenth Amendment of the Constitution provides that "The powers not delegated to the United States by the Constitution, nor prohibited by it to the States, are reserved to the States respectively, or to the people." Since education is not mentioned in the Constitution nor delegated to the federal government, it becomes one of those powers reserved to the states or the people. This interpretation has been the basis on which state legislatures have become responsible for the establishment of policy for the system of schools within their state.

EDUCATION OF MENTALLY RETARDED STUDENTS

This test assesses the knowledge of prospective teachers of the mentally retarded. This test is not intended for those who specialize in behavior disorders or learning disabilities. The test focuses on the mildly retarded (educable), moderately retarded (trainable), and severely retarded. The questions range from preschool through high school. Knowledge of developmental growth is also tested. Topics covered include: principles of child development (10%), understanding exceptional students (7%), understanding mentally retarded students (25%), knowledge of assessment principles and practices (13%), delivery of services (13%), design and implementation of instruction (25%), and professional responsibilities (7%).

DIRECTIONS: Each of the following questions and incomplete statements is followed by five answer choices. Select the choice which best answers each question.

---

1. No. 21 Trisomy syndrome is characterized by oval-shaped eyes, thick eyelids, a flat face and nose, a large tongue, and retardation. Another term for this condition is
    (A) Turner's syndrome.
    (B) Klinefelter's syndrome.
    (C) Down's syndrome.
    (D) Bilirubin encephalopathy.
    (E) Phenylketonuria (PKU).

2. Most states have laws that require a person to be institutionalized if they
    (A) have obvious physical deformities.
    (B) have an IQ below 90.
    (C) show evidence of organic brain dysfunction.
    (D) have an IQ below 90 and deformities.
    (E) have an IQ below 70 and show social incompetence.

3. In addition to the Wechsler Intelligence Scale for Children (Revised), the test that is frequently used to diagnose mental retardation or learning disabilities is the
    (A) Wide Range Achievement Test.
    (B) Stanford-Binet Intelligence Scale.
    (C) Thematic Apperception Test.
    (D) Slosson Intelligence Test.
    (E) Department of Mental Health Assessment Battery for Children.

4. A ten-year-old moderately retarded client has a history of frequently speaking out. Although talking behavior is desirable, you wish to reduce the frequency of these outbursts. Which behavioral technique would be the best to use?
    (A) Extinction
    (B) A DRL schedule
    (C) A DRH schedule
    (D) Over-training
    (E) Punishment

5. The American Association on Mental Deficiency defines mental retardation in terms of

    (A) physical abnormalities.   (D) level of behavioral performance.
    (B) genetic damage present.   (E) All of the above.
    (C) verbal skills.

6. You are trying to establish reliable eye contact with a moderately retarded four-year-old. You are using applesauce as a reinforcer. In order to produce the fastest results, you should reward the child on a(n) _____ reinforcement schedule.

    (A) intermittent   (D) partial
    (B) DRL   (E) secondary
    (C) continuous

7. Physical guidance has been shown to be an effective technique for use

    (A) only with normal clients.
    (B) with mildly retarded individuals.
    (C) with mild and moderately retarded subjects.
    (D) even with severely retarded students.
    (E) only with sighted clients.

8. A ten-year-old that scores a mental age of five on the Stanford-Binet Intelligence Scale would be classified as _____ retarded.

    (A) moderately   (D) profoundly
    (B) mildly   (E) extremely
    (C) severely

9. An infant born with phenylketonuria (PKU) is at high risk for the development of mental retardation. The effects of this genetic defect can be minimized

    (A) by ritalin and similar drugs.
    (B) by a restricted diet.
    (C) with corrective surgery.
    (D) by an intense behavior modification program.
    (E) by the appropriate antitoxin.

10. For classroom management, a teacher places an uncooperative, disruptive student in a small room by himself for five minutes. The technique that the instructor is using is called

    (A) punishment.   (D) overcorrection.
    (B) extinction.   (E) timeout.
    (C) negative reinforcement.

11. When conducting a preliminary assessment of a new student, the most comprehensive and detailed data is available from

    (A) school records.
    (B) the parents.

(C)   the Wechsler Intelligence Scale for Children (Revised).

(D)   Leiter International Performance Scale.

(E)   medical records.

12.   A program emphasizing self-help competency, language development, vocational potentials, and social development could be designed for a _____ retarded individual.

(A)   mildly   (D)   (A) and (C).

(B)   moderately   (E)   (A) and (B).

(C)   profoundly

13.   The use of aversive control, i.e., electric shock as a punisher, to control a retarded client

(A)   is legal in all states.

(B)   requires only parental permission.

(C)   should be used only as a last resort.

(D)   seldom produces long-term effects.

(E)   can cause permanent neural damage.

14.   Jean Piaget gauged intelligence as a matter of

(A)   psychosexual development.   (D)   scores on standardized IQ tests.

(B)   cognitive development.   (E)   All of the above.

(C)   moral development.

15.   Profoundly retarded individuals function at which one of Piaget's stages of development?

(A)   Preoperational   (D)   Sensorimotor

(B)   Concrete   (E)   None of the above.

(C)   Formal

16.   An instructional system in which poker chips are earned by engaging in appropriate behavior, and are later exchanged for privileges, is called

(A)   discrimination training.   (D)   generalization training.

(B)   a token economy.   (E)   an honor point system.

(C)   overtraining.

17.   The observational technique wherein the teacher observes the subject for 30-minute intervals, scheduled irregularly throughout the week, is called

(A)   random sampling.   (D)   time sampling.

(B)   continuous recording.   (E)   interval sampling.

(C)   interval recording.

18.   Which of the following techniques is most beneficial for a moderately retarded student who attends school but resides at home with his/her parents?

(A)   Weekly written reports to the parents

(B)   Consultations with other experts for advice

    (C)   Weekly parent teacher conferences

    (D)   Semiannual review by the entire staff of detailed progress reports

    (E)   A token economy

19.   The "twin studies," cognitive appraisal of identical twins separated at birth, suggest that environment can influence IQ by as much as _____ points.

    (A)   5   (D)   20

    (B)   10   (E)   30

    (C)   15

20.   A form of retardation in which the fetal brain stops developing during the fourth or fifth month of pregnancy is known as

    (A)   Hydrocephalus.

    (B)   Turner's syndrome.

    (C)   Korsakoff's syndrome.

    (D)   Klinefelter's syndrome.

    (E)   Microcephalus.

ANSWER KEY

1.	(C)	6.	(C)	11.	(B)	16.	(B)
2.	(E)	7.	(D)	12.	(E)	17.	(A)
3.	(A)	8.	(A)	13.	(C)	18.	(C)
4.	(B)	9.	(B)	14.	(B)	19.	(C)
5.	(D)	10.	(E)	15.	(D)	20.	(E)

DETAILED EXPLANATIONS OF ANSWERS

1.   **(C)**   Trisomy 21, or Down's syndrome, is the most common form of retardation. It was first described by Langdon Down in 1866. At the turn of the century, the life expectancy was less than 10 years of age. Today, due to advances in antibiotics and surgical techniques, most Down's syndrome patients live to adulthood.

2.   **(E)**   By law, individuals with an IQ below 70 who exhibit social incompetence, including antisocial behavior, can be classified mentally retarded and institutionalized. However, if the condition does not manifest itself until the person is an adult (18 years of age or older), the condition is considered a mental illness and not mental retardation.

3.   **(A)**   The Wide Range Achievement Test developed by J. Jastak and S. Jastak in 1978 is used frequently as a diagnostic tool. It enables the user to gage frustration tolerance, performance anxiety, achievement motivation, and impulse control.

4.   **(B)**   A differential reinforcement of low rate (DRL) schedule would be the best strategy. A DRL schedule rewards the subject if a minimum amount of time has passed between responses. Premature responses reset the clock. For example, on a DRL 10 minute schedule, the client is rewarded for speaking out if at least 10 minutes have passed since their last remarks. If only seven minutes had transpired, the client must wait another 10 minutes before verbal behavior would rewarded.

5.   **(D)**   The American Association on Mental Deficiency (AAMD) defines retardation in terms of behavioral performance or lack thereof, on a variety of tasks. This definition does not include biological, psychological or sociological factors that produce the conditions.

6.   **(C)**   Continuous reinforcement is recommended when establishing any behavior for the first time. Every occurrence of the desired behavior should be rewarded with social praise (a secondary reinforcer) as well as with the primary reinforcer, applesauce in this example.

7.   **(D)**   Physical guidance has been demonstrated to work effectively even with severely retarded individuals. It is the preferred technique to use in order to establish imitative behavior.

8. **(A)** The formula for assessing IQ is (mental age divided by chronological age) X 100. A 10-year-old who scores a mental age of five has an IQ of 50. Mild retardation is indicated by a score of 52-67. The range for moderate retardation is 36-51. Severe and profound retardation ranges are 20-35, and below 20, respectively.

9. **(B)** Phenylketonuria (PKU) is the result of a genetic defect that produces a deficiency in the production of an enzyme that transforms phenylalanine into another amino acid. Without the enzyme, phenylalanine produces damage to the nervous system. A diet low in phenylalanine minimizes or prevents the damage.

10. **(E)** Timeout is a technique wherein a student is momentarily deprived of privileges, in this case, social contact. Punishment requires the presentation of an aversive stimulus, not the removal of positive reinforcer conditions.

11. **(B)** The parents usually have had the most contact with the subject. They can provide detailed information about abilities, or lack thereof, that are not necessarily evident or measured by tests. Medical and school records provide limited information about cognitive and social skills.

12. **(E)** Both the mildly and moderately retarded individual would benefit from such a program. The profoundly retarded (IQ less than 20) would not be able to develop the target behaviors.

13. **(C)** The use of aversive methods involving pain or discomfort for the client is not legal in all states. Those that permit it have strict guidelines. It is usually used as a short-term last resort for self-abusive clients. Self-abuse is punished by mild electric shock, while more appropriate behavior is positively reinforced. No tissue damage is produced.

14. **(B)** Piaget's life work explored the cognitive development of humans. His research demonstrated that humans had to be a minimum age in order to grasp certain concepts and to reason abstractly. Psychosexual and moral development represent the views of Freud and Kohlberg, respectively.

15. **(D)** Humans develop different cognitive abilities as a function of maturity and brain development. A profoundly retarded human would function at the lowest level of cognitive development—the sensorimotor stage, where their abilities are comparable to a two-year-old.

16. **(B)** A token economy enables subjects to earn tokens as rewards for engaging in cooperative behavior. At specified times, these tokens are exchanged for rewards (e.g., candy, combs), or privileges (e.g., access to television, video games).

17. **(A)** Random sampling is an observational technique wherein the observer records data at randomly selected intervals. Interval recording refers to observing the client at the same specified time interval every day. Continuous recording (which is the best method) has someone observing the subject at all times.

18. **(C)** One of the biggest problems with the moderately retarded is retention of learned behavior. Behavior modification works best if the parents continue the program at home,

particularly on weekends. Keeping the parents involved reduces the likelihood that extinction of established behavior patterns will occur.

19 **(C)** Studies of identical twins separated at birth and tested as adults suggest that the environment, ranging from enriched to average to impoverished, can influence IQ up to 15 points. Since the standard deviation on the Stanford-Binet scale is 15, environment is very influential in cognitive development.

20. **(E)** Autopsies of patients afflicted with microcephalus indicate that their brains stopped developing early in the pregnancy. The condition is believed to be caused by infections or exposure to radiation. The head typically reaches only 17 inches in circumference, compared to the normal adult who has a head circumference of about 22 inches. Consequently, the microcephalic's head appears to be cone shaped. These clients are frequently profoundly retarded.

ELEMENTARY EDUCATION

The Elementary Education Specialty Test is designed for students preparing to teach grades 1-8. Eight subject areas are dispersed among the test. These include language arts, reading, mathematics, science, social studies, music, art, and physical education and health. The majority of the questions are based on the first five areas respectively. Every question relates either to the child as the focus of teaching or to the process of teaching. There are 150 questions total taken within a time limit of 120 minutes. Below are 20 examples.

> **DIRECTIONS**: Each of the following questions and incomplete statements is followed by five answer choices. Select the choice which best answers each question.

1. The realm of teaching social studies encompasses all of the following topics EXCEPT
   - (A) human behavior
   - (B) safety procedures
   - (C) governments
   - (D) economics
   - (E) geography

2. Which figure(s) and/or theme(s) are teachers most likely to encounter in the art work of elementary school children?
   - (A) Foreign countries
   - (B) Bodies of water
   - (C) Beings from outer space
   - (D) Animals
   - (E) People

3. A third-grade student is having trouble grasping the concepts of grouping and regrouping numbers. The best instructional strategy to employ in this case would involve
   - (A) a ditto sheet with pictures of groupings.
   - (B) a videotape on grouping and regrouping.
   - (C) chalkboard illustrations.
   - (D) manipulatives.
   - (E) math textbook examples.

4. A teacher should refrain from rigid correction of a young child's mechanics of grammar in writing because such staunch criticism will
   - (A) cause the child to be rebellious.
   - (B) damage the child's natural drive to write in descriptive, complex language which may be more difficult for them to correctly spell and punctuate.
   - (C) cause a child's writing vocabulary to closely resemble his speaking vocabulary.
   - (D) interfere with punctuation, grammar, and spelling being taught as it should be, by drill only.
   - (E) generate an overload of work for the instructor.

5. All of the following paired techniques are tools used to enhance creative writing in the classroom EXCEPT

   (A) practice through Basal readers and letter writing.

   (B) playing background music and maintaining a relaxed atmosphere.

   (C) writing poems and keeping simple diaries.

   (D) using photographs, transparencies, and pictures as springboards for ideas.

   (E) writing captions for pictures and paintings.

6. Contemporary approaches to music instruction stress the following activities as appropriate for helping children develop a foundation of musical skills:

   (A) Singing, playing, moving, creating, listening, reading

   (B) Singing, folk dancing, public performance, listening

   (C) Singing, playing, listening, reading, dancing

   (D) Singing, attending concerts, movement, creative activities

   (E) Singing, moving, listening, reading

7. A social studies lesson which involves the use of maps, dictionaries, encyclopedias, and world almanacs can be said to simultaneously teach skills in social studies and

   (A) art.   (D) mathematics.

   (B) science.   (E) home economics.

   (C) reading.

8. Which of the following is the best example of a science classroom activity incorporating seriation—a typical task given to early elementary school children?

   (A) Students formulate and evaluate their own hypothesis.

   (B) Students chart the foods according to the food group to which they belong.

   (C) Students arrange pictures of a cat from birth to adulthood.

   (D) Students predict the results of adding ink to cold and warm water.

   (E) Students write up the results of their experiments.

9. Children in the early elementary grades confuse which of the following musical concepts and terms most frequently?

   (A) High, fast, and loud   (D) Low and loud

   (B) Fast and slow   (E) Slow and loud

   (C) Fast, soft, and low

10. Joshua is able to decode words like *forest, squirrels*, and *thicket* without any trouble; however, he has no idea what the words mean. What would be the best reading readiness activity for Joshua?

    (A) Ask Joshua to use the dictionary to determine the meanings of the words. He should then make his own personal dictionary containing these words.

    (B) Either administer, or ask the Reading Specialist to administer, a reading comprehension test to Joshua.

    (C) When Joshua has a list of these words, tell him the definitions and have him write them down. Encourage Joshua to practice these words both with and without the worksheet.

(D) Place emphasis on enhancing Joshua's background of experience throughout the use of fieldtrips, films, pictures, or other experiences, until he has a grasp on the concepts.

(E) Ignore the problem for now. Joshua will understand as he gets a little older.

11. A child who is confused about the right and left sides of his body is lagging in

(A) gross motor coordination.   (D) locomotor skills.

(B) perceptual-motor development.   (E) gross visual motor control.

(C) body awareness development.

12. The teacher is asking the children to examine a copy of the local newspaper and find several advertisements on political candidates. The students are asked to find examples of leading statements that may sway the reader. What type of reading comprehension skill is this learning activity reinforcing?

(A) Identifying figurative language

(B) Identifying propaganda techniques

(C) Recognizing common sentence patterns and expansions

(D) Detecting/following a sequence of ideas

(E) Creatively responding to the reading passage

13. The value of addition and subtraction, in connection with the concept of money exchange, could be most comprehensively taught to young students through the hands-on approach of

(A) interactive math software.

(B) a token economy integrated into the classroom system, wherein students can earn certain amounts of "money," which can then be exchanged for actual goods and services.

(C) a field trip to a local bank.

(D) the solving of a massive puzzle, which requires the addition and subtraction of money in order to assemble it.

(E) flash cards.

14. Sponge printing is an especially appropriate art activity for three to eight-year-old children because

(A) it is less messy to clean up than other activities.

(B) it allows for greater depiction of detail.

(C) it compensates for perceptual problems.

(D) it relies mostly on gross motor skills, as opposed to fine motor skills which young children may not yet have mastered.

(E) it doesn't involve much imagination.

15. Which of the following techniques is least effective in teaching a new dance to an elementary school class?

(A) Giving verbal descriptions throughout the demonstration

(B) Having students practice steps without music

(C)   Clapping to the rhythm

(D)   Stepping in place to the music

(E)   Familiarizing children with the music

16.   The music above represents the first phrase of which of the following songs?

(A)   Yankee Doodle   (D)   America

(B)   Twinkle, Twinkle, Little Star   (E)   Pop Goes the Weasel

(C)   Old MacDonald

17.   In a physical education class, which of the following statements is least effective for positive reinforcement?

(A)   "Good job."

(B)   "You're not the only student who ever finished last."

(C)   "Good, I see that you are bending your knees."

(D)   "Watch the ball as you did before."

(E)   "Good, keep going one step at a time."

18.   Which of the following science activities requires students to seek their own solutions to a problem?

(A)   Diagramming the oxygen cycle

(B)   Determining the variables that deter the growth of a plant

(C)   Labeling the parts of an earthworm

(D)   Constructing a graph of the amount of rainfall for a month

(E)   Constructing a model of a rocket

19.   From the following, choose the best question a teacher would ask a student in order to stimulate scientific investigation.

(A)   How do seeds sprout?

(B)   Why does nature abhor DDT?

(C)   Why do electrons want to leave the metal?

(D)   Karen, can you tell us about light?

(E)   What do you think will happen to the plants if they are moved to a dark area?

20. Following is a brief interaction between a student and a teacher. Indicate which term best illustrates the sample interaction.

Robbie: "The word is 'narrative'."

Teacher: "Susan, is Robbie correct?"

(A) Positive reinforcement   (D) Extinction

(B) Negative reinforcement   (E) Feedback

(C) Mastery learning

ANSWER KEY

1.	(B)	6.	(A)	11.	(C)	16.	(A)
2.	(E)	7.	(C)	12.	(B)	17.	(B)
3.	(D)	8.	(C)	13.	(B)	18.	(B)
4.	(B)	9.	(A)	14.	(D)	19.	(E)
5.	(A)	10.	(D)	15.	(B)	20.	(E)

DETAILED EXPLANATIONS OF ANSWERS

1. **(B)** Answer choice (B) is the exception in this case. The area of social studies involves the understanding of human behavior (A), the variations of government systems (C), geography (E), and the workings of economics (D), in addition to other specialty areas, such as communication and technology. Safety procedures, (B), are generally studied under the subject heading of Physical Education and Health, and involve safety in the classroom, home, and playground, as well as safety in all physical activities.

2. **(E)** School-age children draw the human figure far more often than any other theme. Although the themes mentioned in (A), (B), (C), and (D) do appear, they are not nearly as common.

3. **(D)** The most appropriate and concrete manner in which to teach the concepts of grouping and regrouping involves the use of manipulatives. Sticks or beads may be used to represent individual numbers which can, in turn, be grouped into larger groups of 5 or 10. Hands-on manipulatives will aid the child in grasping the concept concretely, as she interacts with the objects directly. Once the child understands the concept comfortably, more pictorial, abstract approaches such as those mentioned in choices (A), (B), (C) and (E) can be used to practice and reinforce that knowledge.

4. **(B)** A child will be more likely to acquire a love of writing if content is valued over mechanical correctness. His writing vocabulary will develop in a manner similar to his speaking vocabulary, (the opposite of what is stated in (C)), in that he will write more vividly and fluently if he is not in fear of criticism. Staunch criticism could possibly make a child rebellious, as stated in (A), but it could also cause him to be withdrawn, insecure, or react in any number of different ways. Choice (D) is incorrect, as the teaching of punctuation, grammar, and spelling should be intricately woven into the curriculum, as opposed to just "drilled" into a child's memory. Choice (E) is not relevant to the question.

5. **(A)** All of the answer choices listed in (B), (C), (D), and (E) are legitimate techniques used in connection with creative writing. Although letter writing is also a legitimate strategy, Basal readers tend to stifle creativity, rather than enhance it, making choice (A) the exception and the correct answer.

6. **(A)** Answer choice (A) is the most inclusive. All other answers omit at least one of the modes of musical activity and expression in which children can be engaged. Folk dancing and public performance (B), dancing (C), and attending concerts (D), are all included in the broader categories of answer choice (A).

7. **(C)** Although the subject of social studies is capable of overlapping with art (A), science (B), mathematics (D), and home economics (E) in a myriad of ways, the particular lesson cited most emphasizes social studies in connection with reading, (C).

8. **(C)** Seriation has to do with ordering; arranging the pictures of the cat exercises this skill. Only (C) is correct. Formulating a hypothesis (A) is not necessarily related to seriation. Charting foods (B), and predicting results (D) are not related to seriation. Writing up the results of an experiment (E) is not related to seriation. Therefore, (C) is the best choice.

9. **(A)** Both research and the experience of many teachers indicates that children in the early elementary grades confuse the concepts high, fast, and loud, and use the terms incorrectly when describing music. For example, a child may describe music performed loudly as "high," regardless of its pitch. While the concepts and terms listed in the other answer may also be confused or inappropriately used by some children, the terms in choice (A) represent the most frequent examples of confusion.

10. **(D)** By implementing the strategy suggested in (D), the teacher endeavors to broaden Joshua's schemata which, in turn, will enhance his understanding of both oral and written language. Rarely should a teacher ignore a breakdown in comprehension. (E), (A) and (C), pencil and paper activities, are very low on the hierarchy of effective teaching techniques (Dale's Cone of Experience). Finally, before a Reading Specialist is called in, the teacher should strive to broaden the base of experiences for Joshua. One more test (B) will in no way solve Joshua's problems.

11. **(C)** Body awareness involves identification of body positions, proportions, and movement. The three aspects of body awareness include: body image (how it looks and functions), body insight (the relationship between body parts), and body concept (verbal explanation of body parts and functions). Choice (A), gross motor coordination involves sequenced and rhythmic use of large body muscle groups. (B), perceptual-motor development as a general term describing the growth of one's basic abilities to enable more complex forms of learning. Locomotor skills are those active skills necessary to move the body from one place to another. (D) is not the answer. Finally, gross visual motor control (E) involves visual tracking in conjunction with movement of large body muscles. Confusion of the left and right sides of the body does not fall under this category. Only choice (C) properly answers the question.

12. **(B)** The teacher is asking the students to locate several political ads and identify the words that might sway the reader. The best response is (B), identifying propaganda techniques. Choices (A), (C), (D), and (E) are in no way connected to the mentioned activity.

13. **(B)** Young children learn best through the repetition of concepts relevant to their everyday lives. A token economy involving "money," goods, and services, which is integrated into the curriculum and implemented throughout the course of the school year, would best teach students these particular concepts. Incidental learning of related concepts would occur, as well. While the strategies listed in (A), (C), (D), and (E) would all be useful

in teaching the general concepts of math and money exchange, they are isolated lessons whose application is limited. In comparison, a token economy contains much more potential for variety in learning, as well as for continual and varied reinforcement of learned concepts.

14. **(D)** Sponge printing is appropriate for very young children because the fine motor skills required for more detailed types of art work have not yet been mastered at this age. Gross motor skills, however, are carried out with relative ease, making activities like sponge printing good practice for the young child. All other answers, (A), (B), (C), and (E) are not relevant or correct. An art activity that is imaginative and will benefit children should be implemented regardless of the degree of clean-up required. Although sponge printing does not allow for a great deal of detail, nor does it compensate for perceptual problems, it does allow for a good deal of imagination on the part of the child.

15. **(B)** Children's interest will not be sustained if they are made to continually practice steps without accompanying music. The other choices, (A), (C), (D), and (E) are all effective teaching techniques which heighten children's success with, and enjoyment of, new dances.

16. **(A)** The musical score portrayed is from the song "Yankee Doodle." None of the other choices match up correctly.

17. **(B)** Sympathizing or consoling a student can actually be a roadblock to communication. Positive reinforcement should also be constructive. Choice (A) is also a less than adequate statement for positive reinforcement, as it does not provide feedback as to which behavior is being reinforced. The other choices, (C), (D), and (E), are statements of positive reinforcement.

18. **(B)** Determining variables that deter the growth of a plant (B), would involve students seeking solutions to a problem. Diagramming (A), labeling (C), graphing (D), and constructing (E), do not involve seeking individual solutions to a problem. (B) is the best choice.

19. **(E)** The question which tends to stimulate thinking and investigation is (E). (A) is a knowledge level question. (B) is misleading, since it suggests that nature has a mind of its own and can think. (C) implies that electrons have human qualities. (D) is an extremely vague and unfocused question. (E) is the only high-level question provided.

20. **(E)** The teacher is using other students in the class to provide feedback. In this manner the teacher is involving the entire class, rather than maintaining a closed dialogue between teacher and student. Positive reinforcement (A) refers to a situation in which an action leads to the appearance of something good or positive for the person involved. Negative reinforcement (B), occurs with the removal or termination of something negative. The teaching concept of mastery learning (C) provides for students to be given as much time and instruction as is necessary to master the majority of intended objectives. Finally, the practice of extinction (D) within a classroom setting involves placing a student in a situation which generally causes them anxiety, while ensuring that unpleasant events do not follow. After several uneventful exposures to such a situation, the student's fear should be extinguished. Clearly, the provided dialogue supports evidence only for answer choice (E), feedback.

ENGLISH LANGUAGE AND LITERATURE

This test is designed for prospective high school English teachers. The test covers literature, composition, and language. Approximately 50% of the test will focus on literature, both analytical and factual. It tests knowledge of time periods, genres, major authors, and major movements. The questions will also test knowledge of literary devices. Approximately 40% of the test focuses on composition, which consists of rhetorical strategies, arguments, types of writing, and research materials. Approximately 10% of the test will be on language: the history and structure of English, syntax, and semantics.

DIRECTIONS: Each of the following questions and incomplete statements is followed by five answer choices. Select the choice which best answers each question.

---

1.   Which of the lines below begin a poem by Walt Whitman?
 (A)   I celebrate myself, and sing myself,
       And what I assume you shall assume,
       For every atom belonging to me as good as belongs to you.
 (B)   Because I could not stop for Death—
       He kindly stopped for me—
 (C)   Hog Butcher for the World,
       Tool Maker, Stacker of Wheat,
       Player with Railroads and the Nation's Freight Handler;
       Stormy, husky, brawling,
       City of the Big Shoulders.
 (D)   Let us go then, you and I,
       When the evening is spread out against the sky
       Like a patient etherized upon a table
 (E)   Two roads diverged in a yellow wood

2.   Which would be the best source of information for the following items: periodic sentence, *deux ex machina*, conceit, fabliau, ottava rima?
 (A)   *Books in Print*   (D)   Handbook of literary terms
 (B)   Dictionary   (E)   *Reader's Guide*
 (C)   *Contemporary Literary Criticism*

Questions 3-4 refer to the pairs of sentences below.
 I.   Pauline planned to quickly and efficiently finish the cost analysis report.
       Pauline expected to just barely meet the Friday deadline.
 II.   The career that I thought would interest my son totally bored him.

The career that I thought would interest my son bored him totally.

III.   Hiram Bingham discovered the ruins of Machu Picchu in 1911.

The ruins of Machu Picchu were discovered by Hiram Bingham in 1911.

IV.   Moviegoers wishing to carefully save money often go to the dollar cinemas.

Moviegoers wishing to be careful in spending their money often go to the dollar cinema.

V.   She had only ten dollars in her purse.

Only she had ten dollars in her purse.

3.   Which would be useful in discussing split infinitives?

(A)   I only.   (D)   II and III.

(B)   I and IV.   (E)   V only.

(C)   III and V.

4.   Which would be useful in a lesson on acceptable and unacceptable use of passive voice?

(A)   I and II.   (D)   III only.

(B)   I and IV.   (E)   V only.

(C)   II and IV.

Questions 5-6 refer to the lines below.

> So Grendel ruled, fought with the righteous,
> One against many, and won; so Herot
> Stood empty, and stayed deserted for years,
> Twelve winters of grief for Hrothgar, king
> Of the Danes, sorrow heaped at his door
> By hell-forged hands. His misery leaped
> The seas, was told and sung in all
> Men's ears.

5.   The lines above are from

(A)   *Beowulf.*   (D)   *Morte D'Arthur.*

(B)   *Everyman.*   (E)   *The Divine Comedy.*

(C)   *The Faerie Queen.*

6.   What two literary devices are used in line 6?

(A)   Simile and synecdoche   (D)   Epithet and contrast

(B)   Metonomy and assonance   (E)   Kenning and alliteration

(C)   Personification and caesura

Questions 7-9 refer to the poem and the student paper below.

Follower

My father worked with a horse plow,
His shoulders globed like a full sail strung

Between the shafts and the furrow,
The horses strained at his clicking tongue.

An expert. He would set the wing
And fit the bright steel-pointed sock.
The sod rolled over without breaking.
At the headrig, with a single pluck

Of reigns, the sweating animal turned around
And back into the land. His eye
Narrowed and angled at the ground,
Mapping the furrow exactly.

I stumbled in his hobnailed wake,
Fell sometimes on the polished sod;
Sometimes he rode me on his back
Dipping and rising to his plod.

I wanted to grow up and plow,
To close one eye, stiffen my arm.
All I ever did was follow
In his broad shadow round the farm.

I was a nuisance, tripping, falling,
Yapping always. But today
It is my father who keeps stumbling
Behind me, and will not go away.

Seamus Heaney

Student Paper

The poem examines the relationship of a boy with his father. The boy appears to be quite young, perhaps about six years old, and awed by the expertise of his father at the plow. The use of specific terms related to farming underscores the authenticity of the poem. Aware of the hard work involved in the father's craft, the son would follow in the wake of his father's furrows and sometimes ride on his father's shoulders. Even though he wanted to grow up and plow the land as well as his father, the author feels he has not lived up to his father's image and remains in the father's "broad shadow."

7. Which of the following is the most appropriate comment for a teacher to make on the student's paper?

(A) I don't really like your paper because you seem to be summarizing the poem rather than analyzing it.

(B) The first three sentences begin with "the," and "the" is overused in other places in these sentences. Please note that sentence variety is necessary to create and maintain the reader's interest.

(C) You are sensitive to the plight of the little boy, but you need to reevaluate your position on the attitude of the author toward his father now. Consider carefully the last three lines.

(D) This paper could be made better by including details about the author's life that pertain to the poem.

(E) Your interpretation of then poem is largely correct. However, you only have one quotation from the poem. Why don't you strengthen your paper by adding more specific details and quotations from the poem?

8. The major division in the poem occurs between lines

    (A) 4 and 5.   (D) 16 and 17.
    (B) 7 and 8.   (E) 18 and 19.
    (C) 12 and 13.

9. The title of this poem is made effective through the use of

    (A) paraphrase.   (D) stereotype.
    (B) ambiguity.   (E) analogy.
    (C) allusion.

10. The Reverend Kumalo seeks his sister Gertrude and his son Absalom in the city of Johannesburg. Absalom is tried and condemned for murder. Kumalo returns to his country home with Gertrude's daughter. The novel discussed above is

    (A) Alan Paton's *Cry, the Beloved Country.*

    (B) Thomas Mann's *Death in Venice.*

    (C) James Baldwin's *Go Tell It on the Mountain.*

    (D) Alice Walker's *The Color Purple.*

    (E) Maya Angelou's *I Know Why the Caged Bird Sings.*

11. Which of the following tribes names the original inhabitants of England?

    (A) Angles   (D) Frisians
    (B) Saxons   (E) Celts
    (C) Jutes

12. Which of the following would form a unit dealing with stories of initiation?

    (A) *Swan's Way, The Turn of the Screw, Candide*

    (B) *Evelina, The Rise of Silas Lapham, Look Homeward, Angel*

    (C) *The Old Man and the Sea, Emma, The Plague*

    (D) *Great Expectations, The Red Badge of Courage, Ulysses*

    (E) *Tom Jones, The Sound and the Fury, Maggie: A Girl of the Streets*

Questions 13-14 refer to the student papers below.

I.   Linda knows that she is expected to care for her men. Devoted to Willy, Linda never utters a negative word about him. She refuses to confront Willy with evidence that he is considering, and has attempted, suicide. Linda spends the play mending stockings rather than upset Willy by asking for new ones. When her sons abandon Willy in the restaurant bathroom, Linda attacks Biff and Happy with vicious honesty.

II.   Willy Loman has an unrealistic view of success. His father, whom Willy considers a great success at making and selling flutes, irresponsibly abandoned the family. Willy's brother Ben followed the father's example and made money through shady ventures in distant places. Therefore, Willy thinks the only way he can get positive strokes is by exaggerating or escaping the truth.

III. Being adventuresome and well-liked comprise only a part of Willy's dream. Although money is often gained through daring speculation, it can easily be lost in the same manner. The important thing is to be rich by any method. Willy also believes that a handsome appearance will open all doors because if one has personal attractiveness, then money will be easy to make through cooperation of others.

IV.   Ben's world is an alternative world in that whenever anything goes wrong in life, Willy has an escape from the reality of his problem into Ben's world, which is a Utopia. Willy does not ever distinguish between the two, and so he believes that he could actually succeed in Ben's world if given the break, but he really would not succeed and this is just another part of Willy's escape from reality.

V.   The other women in the play can be dismissed as the dumb "floozies" who please the man through physical gratification. Willy, while on sales trips, has an affair with a woman he thinks can get him through to the buyers, but who is really using him to get stockings. Happy has a series of affairs with women engaged to other men, and, toward the end of the play, Happy and Biff pick up two women who fake a knowledge of professional sports.

13.   Which student paper is a commentary on values held to be important in American society?

(A)   I.   (D)   IV.

(B)   II.   (E)   V.

(C)   III.

14.   Which pair of student papers discusses stereotyped roles?

(A)   I and II.   (D)   II and V.

(B)   II and IV.   (E)   I and V.

(C)   III and IV.

15.   Which student paper is weakened by stringy sentences?

(A)   I.   (D)   IV.

(B)   II.   (E)   V.

(C)   III.

16.   I.   Call me Ishmael.

II.   Marley was dead, to begin with.

III.   When Gregor Samsa woke up one morning from unsettling dreams, he found himself changed in his bed into a monstrous vermin.

IV.   It was the best of times, it was the worst of times.

V.   It is a truth universally acknowledged, that a single man in possession of a good fortune must be in want of a wife.

Which two of the previous are opening lines of novels written by Charles Dickens?

(A)   I and V   (D)   II and V

(B)   I and III   (E)   III and V

(C)   II and IV

17. Which of the following would form a unit dealing with magical realism?

    (A) "A Clean, Well-Lighted Place," *A Clockwork Orange*, *The Way to Rainy Mountain*

    (B) "A Very Old Man With Enormous Wings," *In the House of Spirits*, *One Hundred Years of Solitude*

    (C) "The Bear," *Invisible Man*, *Brave New World*

    (D) "Average Waves in Unprotected Waters," *The Guest*, *The Golden Notebook*

    (E) "The Lagoon," *Don Quixote*, *The Loved One*

1	2
beget	procreate
home	domicile
blessing	benediction
doggish	canine
fatherly	paternal

18. Which of the following accurately describes the words listed above?

    (A) 1 includes Anglo-Saxon equivalents for the Latin terms listed in 2.

    (B) 1 includes substandard equivalents for the standard terms listed in 2.

    (C) 1 includes the less descriptive equivalent for the more descriptive terms listed in 2.

    (D) 1 includes common terms for the obsolete equivalents listed in 2.

    (E) 1 includes headings in a thesaurus, and 2 the synonyms.

19. At his birth an oracle prophesied that he would kill his father and marry his mother. His parents abandoned him to die on a mountaintop, but he was saved and adopted by a distant king and queen. As a man, he heard the prophesy and tried to escape his fate by running to another country. He ended up in the land of his birth and unknowingly fulfilled the dire prediction.

    The above passage describes

    (A) Theseus.   (D) Prometheus.

    (B) Orpheus.   (E) Oedipus.

    (C) Perseus.

20. Which of the following is NOT considered a traditional folk or literary epic poem?

    (A) "Gilgamesh"   (D) "Song of Roland"

    (B) "Rape of the Lock"   (E) *Paradise Lost*

    (C) "El Cid"

ANSWER KEY

1.	(A)	6.	(E)	11.	(E)	16.	(C)
2.	(D)	7.	(C)	12.	(D)	17.	(B)
3.	(B)	8.	(C)	13.	(C)	18.	(A)
4.	(D)	9.	(B)	14.	(E)	19.	(E)
5.	(A)	10.	(A)	15.	(D)	20.	(B)

DETAILED EXPLANATIONS OF ANSWERS

1. **(A)** These are the opening lines of Walt Whitman's "Song of Myself."

2. **(D)** Although these terms for literary analysis could be found in a dictionary, the best source is a handbook of literary terms.

3. **(B)** The following phrases insert one or more adverbs in an infinitive: "to quickly and efficiently," "to just barely meet," and "to carefully save."

4. **(D)** If the discovery were a more important concept in a particular context, then the passive construction in the second sentence of III would be acceptable.

5. **(A)** These lines depicting Grendel's reign of terror before the coming of the hero Beowulf are from the Old English poem named after the hero.

6. **(E)** The line contains the kenning "hell-forged" and alliterates the "h" sound in three words.

7. **(C)** This comment is the most appropriate because the student has not considered the last three lines: the author and his father have effectively reversed roles because the father now stumbles behind the son.

8. **(C)** Lines 1-12 concern the father, and lines 13-24 primarily concern the son.

9. **(B)** The title is ambiguous in that both the son and the father fulfill the role of follower: the child followed his father, and later the father follows his son.

10. **(A)** Alan Paton is a native of South Africa who wrote this novel about the injustices and mercies that happen to Kumalo.

11. **(E)** The original inhabitants of England were the Celts. All the other tribes listed were invaders.

12. **(D)** All three novels have as one of the main characters a boy or young man who grows into awareness of and an acceptance of the realities of adult life.

13. **(C)** The American dream includes being rich, handsome, adventurous, and well-liked. In this play, *Death of a Salesman,* Willy Loman dies because he adheres too closely to the standards of the American dream and cannot fulfill those standards himself.

14. **(E)** The first and last paragraphs discuss the stereotypical roles of women—the madonna/whore extremes.

15. **(D)** This student sample is composed of just two sentences. The second sentence in particular is three independent clauses strung together by conjunctions. This sample would benefit from subordination of ideas, eliminating needless repetition, and varying sentence structure.

16. **(C)** Sample opening II comes from *A Christmas Carol,* and sample opening IV comes from *A Tale of Two Cities.*

17. **(B)** "A Very Old Man with Enormous Wings" and *One Hundred Years of Solitude* are both written by Gabriel Garcia Marquez, and *In the House of Spirits* was written by Isabel Allende. These two writers from South America are noted for their stories of magical realism.

18. **(A)** The terms in column 1 are Anglo-Saxon words. The terms in column 2 are Latin equivalents brought to England by the Norman Catholic conquerors.

19. **(E)** The Greek legend of Oedipus is of a man who kills his father and marries his mother.

20. **(B)** Alexander Pope's "The Rape of the Lock" is a mock epic, a humorous burlesque of the traditional epic.

FRENCH

The French test has five sections: listening comprehension; reading comprehension; written expression; phonetics, morphology, and syntax; and cultural background. Varied topics and different levels of difficulty appear in each section. The test also assesses the prospective French teacher's knowledge of the differences between English and French, learning problems which may occur, and instructional approaches.

Listening Comprehension

In this section of the test, you will listen to native French speakers on a tape recording. The recording consists of single utterances, short dialogues, and other types of spoken material, such as talks and news items. From the four choices in the test book, select the response most likely to be made in each situation presented, or the best answer to each question asked.

The questions are designed to test phonemic discrimination and comprehension of idiomatic expressions, vocabulary, and structure typical of conversational French. They may also test comprehension of important facts or ideas contained in the passage. Following are some sample questions that are representative of this section. The listening parts are transcribed in this case, since a tape will not be provided.

DIRECTIONS: You will now hear a series of questions or statements. Next to each number in your test book you will find four sentences, one of which is the most appropriate response to the spoken question or statement. In each case, select the best choice.

---

1. *You will hear:* Pourriez-vous me dire où se trouve la rue de Sèvres?

   You will read:

   (A) Débrouillez-vous tout seul.

   (B) Elle est perdue depuis des années.

   (C) Je regrette. Je ne suis pas du quartier non plus.

   (D) Elle est toujours à côté du roi.

2. *You will hear:* Il n'y a pas de biscuits pour le goûter?

   You will read:

   (A) Non, parce qu'elles sont toujours trop amères.

   (B) Si, il y en a. Je viens d'en acheter.

   (C) Non, je ne veux pas les nettoyer.

   (D) Mais pas pour le petit déjeuner, voyons!

DIRECTIONS: For each question in this part you will hear a short conversation between two people and will read a question about the conversation in your test book. From the four choices following each question, choose the most appropriate response.

3. *You will hear:*

Man A: Tout `a coup un cycliste a heurté ma camionnette. Je ne l'avais pas vu venir. Heureusement il portait un casque.

Man B: Oui, il a eu de la chance, celui-là.

You will read: De quoi s'agit-il?

(A) D'un cambriolage   (C) D'une course `a vélo

(B) D'une livraison de vin   (D) D'un accident de route

DIRECTIONS: In this part you will hear a number of spoken selections. Each selection is followed by a series of spoken questions. In the pause following each question, you are to choose the most appropriate answer from the four choices printed in your test book.

You will hear:

Avec ses vingt-cinq kilomètres carrés, Saint-Bartélémy, l'une des plus minuscules petite Antilles, est à 210 kilometres de la Guadeloupe dont il dépend administrativement.

Elle semble protéger sa spécificité par les remparts de mer bleue qui bordent ses plages de sable blanc. C'est un avenir croissant à l'ombre des souvenirs d'un passé mouvementé. Ici, le passé et le présent se rencontrent dans des contrastes fascinants.

You will read:

4. De quoi s'agit -il dans ce passage?

(A) D'une lutte politique

(B) D'une ancienne ville du moyen âge

(C) Du regret du passé

(D) D'une petite île caraibe

5. Quel est le rapport entre la Guadeloupe et Saint-Barthélémy?

(A) Saint-Barthélémy en est la capitale.

(B) Saint-Barthélémy cherche `a en maintenir une grande distance.

(C) La Gaudeloupe dépend administrativement de Saint Barthémély.

(D) Saint-Barthémély dépend administrativement de la Guadeloupe.

Reading Comprehension

This section consists of short selections dealing with varied topics on several levels of difficulty, each followed by questions about its content, mood, or principal ideas.

DIRECTIONS: Read the following passage carefully for comprehension. It is followed by a number of incomplete statements. Select the completion that is best according to the passage.

Du Mont Saint-Michel au Château d'If, du Beffroi de Lille à la cité de Carcassonne, quatre-vingts des plus beaux sites de l'Hexagone sont à vos pieds dans le parc Minifrance de Brignoles dans le département du Var. Vitesse de croisière conseillée pour ce tour de France en miniature: quatre-vingts minutes! Soixante-dix architectes, chimistes, sculpteurs et décorateurs ont accumulé 150,000 heures de labeur pour la réalisation de ces petites merveilles.

6. Pour visiter ce parc, il faut
   (A) près d'une heure et demie.
   (B) au moins deux jours.
   (C) moins d'une heure.
   (D) plus d'une matinée.

7. Ce parc en miniature a été réalisé par
   (A) plus de mille spécialistes.
   (B) une poignée d'hommmes.
   (C) moins de cent professionnels.
   (D) près de trois cents personnes.

8. L'expression "à vos pieds" pourrait être remplacée par
   (A) à l'horizon.
   (B) à votre portée.
   (C) dans vos chaussures.
   (D) souterrains.

9. Le parc Minifrance se trouve
   (A) à Paris.
   (B) dans un château.
   (C) près d'un beffroi.
   (D) à Brignoles.

Written Expression

This section consists of two parts, A and B. In Part A, the candidate is asked to identify the correct structure and lexical completion for a sentence. Part B tests the candidate's ability to distinguish between appropriate and inappropriate styles for various types of writing.

DIRECTIONS: This part consists of a number of incomplete statements, each having four suggested completions. Select the most appropriate completion and blacken the corresponding space on the answer sheet.

---

10. Quand tu _____ ton travail, tu pourras regarder la télévision.
    (A) finis
    (B) as fini
    (C) auras fini
    (D) finirais

11. Là, vous verrez une place au milieu de _____ est une grande statue.

    (A)   laquelle   (C)   qu'

    (B)   quoi   (D)   quelle

12. Je l' _____ depuis une bonne demi-heure quand elle est arrivée.

    (A)   attends   (C)   ai attendue

    (B)   attendais   (D)   avais attendue

13. J'espère que tu _____ venir demain.

    (A)   puisses   (C)   pourras

    (B)   as pu   (D)   aies pu

DIRECTIONS: The paragraphs in this part are drawn from various types and styles of written text, such as formal and informal letters, newspaper accounts, and other materials. Each contains numbered blanks, indicating omissions in the text. Following each paragraph are four suggested completions for each numbered blank. All four completions are grammatically correct, but one of them is stylistically INAPPROPRIATE to the paragraph. Read the entire paragraph carefully, and then for each question select the ONE choice that is NOT APPROPRIATE to the style of the paragraph as a whole.

---

14. Excusez-moi de vous déranger, Madame. Il y a _____ en bas qui m'a dit qu'il vient de la part de Monsieur Naudé et qu'il aimerait bien vous parler.

    (A)   un jeune homme   (C)   un agent de police

    (B)   un mec   (D)   un monsieur

15. Vous êtes très aimable , mais je regrette de ne pas pouvoir y participer. Pour autant que ceci me gêne, il faut avouer que

    (A)   je suis fauché.   (C)   je suis au chômage.

    (B)   je manque d'argent.   (D)   j'ai tout perdu au jeu.

Language Learning Problems

The emphasis in this section is on those differences between English and French that are important in teaching. The questions involve the identification of both typical learning problems and instructional approaches the teacher can take in dealing with these problems. The following examples are representative of the questions in this section.

16. The student who writes or says: "Le musée est une bonne place à visiter" has

    (A)   made a gender mistake.

    (B)   made a mistake with a false cognate.

    (C)   chosen an incorrect preposition.

    (D)   made a mistake in word order.

17. Which of the following would not be understood as a question if the students failed to say "moi" with a rising intonation ?

    (A) Il veut venir avec moi?

    (B) Veut-il venir avec moi?

    (C) Est-ce qu'il veut venir avec moi?

    (D) Crois-tu qu'il tienne à venir avec moi?

Cultural Background

This section of the test is designed to measure the knowledge of culture and civilization needed by teachers to introduce their students to the cultural context of the language they are studying. Questions touch on behavior patterns and lifestyles as well as on such aspects of civilization as history, geography, literature, and the arts.

> **DIRECTIONS:** Each of the incomplete statements below is followed by four suggested completions. Select the completion that is best in each case.

18. Which of the following sights in Paris was not constructed in the twentieth century?

    (A) Le Centre Pompidou   (C) La Place de la Concorde

    (B) La Pyramide du Louvre   (D) La Tour Montparnasse

19. Le Tour de France is

    (A) a famous bicycle race.

    (B) a tour of the French chateaux.

    (C) a tour of all the francophone countries.

    (D) the colonial period of French history.

20. Le Maréchal Pétain

    (A) was a famous royalist during the French Revolution

    (B) was head of the French government during the Second World War.

    (C) a hero of the Algerian War.

    (D) the Prime Minister under De Gaulle.

ANSWER KEY

1.	(C)	6.	(A)	11.	(A)	16.	(B)
2.	(B)	7.	(C)	12.	(B)	17.	(A)
3.	(D)	8.	(B)	13.	(C)	18.	(C)
4.	(D)	9.	(D)	14.	(B)	19.	(A)
5.	(D)	10.	(C)	15.	(A)	20.	(B)

DETAILED EXPLANATIONS OF ANSWERS

1.   **(C)**   The person is looking for a street, "la rue de Sèvres." The only likely response is: "I'm sorry. I'm not from this neighborhood either." It would be unlikely for someone to say: "Débrouillez-vous tout seul," or "Get along by yourself."

2.   **(B)**   You would need to know that the word "goûter" means a snack eaten in the late afternoon. "Si" is the response given to answer "yes" to a question framed in the negative. So the only possible response is "Yes, there are. I just bought some."

3.   **(D)**   The first man says that a cyclist collided with (a heurté) his small truck (camionnette.)

4.   **(D)**   Saint Barthélémy is a Caribbean island, one of the smallest of the Antilles ("une des plus petites Antilles"), and 210 kilometers from Guadeloupe ("distante de la Guadaloupe de 210 kilomètres.")

5.   **(D)**   You would need to undersand the relative pronoun "dont". "(Elle) est distante de la Guadeloupe *dont* elle dépend administrativement", *upon which* it depends.

6.   **(A)**   "Vitesse… pour ce tour de France en miniature: quatre-vingt (80) minutes." Eighty minutes is almost ("près de") an hour and a half ("une heure et demie.")

7.   **(C)**   Seventy ("Soixante-dix architectes, chimistes, sculpteurs et décorateurs ont accumulé plus de 150,000 heures…") is fewer than one hundred ("moins de cent.")

8.   **(B)**   "A votre portée" means "within your reach," an expression almost interchangeable with "à vos pieds," which means "at your feet."

9.   **(D)**   The phrasing "le parc Minifrance de Brignoles dans le departement du Var" would make us understand that Brignoles is the name of the town in which the park was built. In any case, none of the other choices is possible.

10. **(C)** "Le futur antérieur" is used to express the idea that the future action of "finishing your work" will be accomplished before the future action of "being able to watch television." "(Tu) pourras" is the future tense of pouvoir.

11. **(A)** A form of the relative pronoun "lequel" is used as the object of a prepositon, in this case "au milieu de." The form "laquelle" is feminine singular to agree with the antecedent "place."

12. **(B)** The imperfect is used to express an action that began in the past and continued until another time, also in the past. English uses the progressive form of the pluperfect (had been + present participle, or "had been") to express this idea.

13. **(C)** "(Tu) pourras" is the future tense. "Demain" means "tomorrow." Note that the verb "espérer does *not* take the subjunctive.

14. **(B)** The style here is polite, if not deferential. "Un mec," "un gars," and "un type" are familiar words that mean "a man" or "a guy."

15. **(A)** The tone here is formal, distant. In the current argot, (B), (C) and (D) are expressions that mean "to be broke" and are not in keeping with the level of speech here.

16. **(B)** The French word "une place" is "un faux ami", and does not mean "place" in the sense intended in the sentence. The correct word would be "un endroit" or "un lieu."

17. **(A)** There are three ways to form a question that has a "yes or no" answer. 1. by placing "est-ce que" in front of the declarative sentence, 2. by inverting the subject pronoun and the verb, and 3. by raising the voice at the end of the declarative sentence. In answer (A) the form is identical to that of the declarative sentence, and intonation alone will convey that it is a question.

18. **(C)** The obelisque, in the center of la Place de la Concorde, was erected in 1836. The other buildings and sights, la Tour Montparnasse, le Centre Pompidou, and the new pyramid structure of the Louvre are very recent additions to the tour guides of Paris.

19. **(A)** "Le Tour de France" is the most famous French bicycle race. Begun in 1903, it takes place every summer along a circuit organized across France.

20. **(B)** Between July 10, 1940, and August 20, 1944, the French government was headed by the Maréchal Pétain and was moved from Paris (which was then occupied by the Germans) to the famous spa of Vichy. The Vichy government has remained a very controversial period in French history because of its policy on cooperation and collaboration with the Nazis.

GUIDANCE COUNSELOR

This test is intended for those who are completing or have already completed their master's degree in programs for guidance counselors. The test focuses mostly on the secondary level, although there are some questions which involve elementary and junior high school. The test covers four areas: counseling, consulting, coordinating, and professional. Topics of counseling skills include: ego, interpersonal, moral/ethical values, career/leisure, sexual, and academic/cognitive. The test has two sections, one of which is taped.

DIRECTIONS: Each of the following questions and incomplete statements is followed by five answer choices. Select the choice which best answers each question.

---

1. Each of the following characteristics are essential in a guidance counselor except
    - (A) the ability to appreciate individual differences.
    - (B) an understanding of the value of learning.
    - (C) a real interest in people.
    - (D) the ability to remain emotionally insulated from the client's problems.
    - (E) the belief that all people can make a contribution.

2. A guidance counselor would suspect that a client may be a gifted student if they exhibit
    - (A) a rapid rate of learning.
    - (B) superior reading ability with a great degree of retention.
    - (C) insatiable curiosity.
    - (D) a preference for difficult tasks.
    - (E) All of the above.

3. A client comes in to see you. She is very upset and informs you that she is pregnant and doesn't know what to do. You should
    - (A) encourage her to go discuss her problem with her parents.
    - (B) send her to see her minister.
    - (C) allay her fears and then inform her of her options.
    - (D) send her to the school nurse or other female authority figure.
    - (E) find out who the father is.

4. Which of the following is not one of the responsibilities of a guidance counselor?
    - (A) Encourage clients to conform to society's norms for acceptance
    - (B) Help clients develop self esteem
    - (C) To help the student select a career
    - (D) To necessarily provide information in a friendly manner
    - (E) All of the above are expected of counselors.

5. During the first interview with a client, the guidance counselor should do all the following except

    (A) inform the client about confidentiality.

    (B) realize that silence indicates the interview isn't going well.

    (C) refrain from excessive talking.

    (D) try to relate to the client's perceptions.

    (E) assign any significance to the topics chosen, or order in which the client discusses them.

6. A police officer informs you that there has been a rash of burglaries within the vicinity of the school. He asks you for the names of some clients that you believe might have been involved. Your response should be

    (A) to provide him with the names of likely suspects.

    (B) to send him/her to the principal for the information.

    (C) to remind the officer that legally you cannot divulge file information without the client's permission.

    (D) to promise to ask your most trusted clients for any information about these crimes.

    (E) All of the above.

7. All of the following would be appropriate data to collect during the intake interview except

    (A) parents' ages and occupations.

    (B) medical history.

    (C) history of mental illness in the family.

    (D) the nature and number of sexual relationships the client has had.

    (E) prior experiences with counselors.

8. Fear of the counselor, or dislike of the topic at hand is suggested by

    (A) evidence of frustration.   (D) frequent emission of petty remarks.

    (B) avoidance of eye contact.   (E) the presence of tears.

    (C) the expression of negative feelings.

9. Confrontation should be used when

    (A) there is a discrepancy between the client's statements and his/her behavior.

    (B) an accusation is necessary.

    (C) the counselor suspects that the client is a liar.

    (D) the client is acting immature.

    (E) All of the above.

10. John, a college sophomore, seeks counseling because he has trouble getting dates. The correct approach of the counselor would be to

    (A) give him a pep talk designed to bolster his ego.

    (B) provide statistics on the success/failure dating rate of college students to prove he's exaggerating his failures.

(C)   set realistic goals and help him reach them.

(D)   encourage him to develop friendships and mimic popular male students.

(E)   suggest he try to date only women who have a reputation for dating anyone.

11.   The typical guidance counselor holds a _____ degree, and works in (a)n _____ setting.

(A)   B.A., elementary school   (D)   Master's, secondary education

(B)   B.A., secondary education   (E)   Ph.D., college

(C)   Master's, elementary school

12.   When selecting strategies, the guidance counselor should

(A)   suggest a number of possible strategies.

(B)   suggest strategies based on the client's selected goals.

(C)   provide information about the advantages and disadvantages of each strategy.

(D)   allow the client to decide on the best strategy to use.

(E)   All of the above.

13.   All of the following are cognitive behavior modification techniques recommended by guidance counselors except

(A)   modeling.

(B)   discussions of ego-defense mechanisms.

(C)   thought stopping.

(D)   behavior rehearsal.

(E)   self management.

14.   When evaluating a client's strategy, the guidance counselor should do all of the following except

(A)   alter his/her tenets without verbal justification.

(B)   list the people who will be involved.

(C)   suggest how the client should evaluate his/her strategy.

(D)   explain why strategy evaluation is important.

(E)   teach the client how to collect data.

15.   Guidance counselors should do all of the following except

(A)   not hurry when deciding on a counseling strategy.

(B)   not try to learn about every little facet of the client's life or history.

(C)   not expect to succeed every time.

(D)   subscribe to and read professional journals.

(E)   have a clear, precise idea of how people should act, and guide the client to that style.

16.   A student comes to you and informs you that if he cannot be a doctor, life isn't worth living. Your response should be

(A)   "Why not discuss it with your parents?"

(B)   "There are plenty of suitable alternatives."

(C) "Your youth makes you say a crazy thing like that."

(D) "Let's discuss what a career in medicine involves."

(E) "I know exactly what you mean. When I was your age, I used to want to be an engineer."

17. Cathy is a high school sophomore. She makes an appointment to see the guidance counselor because she thinks that she wants to be an architect. Cathy would like advice on courses to take during the next two years. The best response from the guidance counselor would be

(A) to tell her the truth. Few women become architects. Most shift to interior decorating.

(B) to act impressed that she has already chosen a profession, and help her find out about college programs.

(C) tell Cathy her career choice is premature, and offer to talk to her about it next year, if she is still interested.

(D) inform her that most people don't pick a profession until they are in college.

(E) suggest that she take calculus and physics courses to see if she has the talent.

18. Roger is a muscular high school junior with failing grades. During his first appointment with the guidance counselor he states that he is going to go into professional football and sees no value in school subjects. How should the guidance counselor respond?

(A) "Few people succeed at making the pros, so you'll need something to fall back on."

(B) "We're here to discuss your grades, and how to improve them."

(C) "Sounds great, they make a lot of money. Let's talk about how to get to the pros."

(D) "Why don't you go talk to the football coach about your chances."

(E) "Most football draft picks are in colleges, and you won't get into one with these grades."

19. All of the following guidance counselor characteristics would be perceived as gestures of sincerity except

(A) rehearsed answers.   (D) caution.

(B) openess.   (E) availability.

(C) spontaneity.

20. The primary difference between a paraphrase and a perception check is

(A) to paraphrase is to restate the client's remark while perception check attempts to gage the accuracy of your interpretations.

(B) when paraphrasing we tell the client what they meant to say, and when perception checking, we ascertain whether or not they understand us.

(C) paraphrasing means to condense their remarks while a perception check tests their sense of reality.

(D) paraphrasing refers to quoting famous sayings while perception checks refers to consulting with other counselors.

(E) paraphrasing is done only in individual meetings while perception checks are best used in group settings.

ANSWER KEY

1.	(D)	6.	(C)	11.	(D)	16.	(D)
2.	(E)	7.	(D)	12.	(E)	17.	(B)
3.	(C)	8.	(B)	13.	(B)	18.	(C)
4.	(A)	9.	(A)	14.	(A)	19.	(A)
5.	(B)	10.	(C)	15.	(E)	20.	(A)

DETAILED EXPLANATIONS OF ANSWERS

1.   **(D)**   The competent guidance counselor accepts individuality in their clients, and doesn't try to shape conformity. They continually update their knowledge base because they appreciate the value of learning. They must have a real interest in people and the ability to get involved. Emotional insulation and inflexibility are not admirable traits in a guidance counselor.

2.   **(E)**   All of the descriptions are characteristics of a potentially gifted student. Others include novel applications of knowledge, the use of comprehensive and forceful logic in their arguments, and the ability to produce comprehensive planning.

3.   **(C)**   An emotionally upset client doesn't attend very well to any discussion. Your first efforts should be to calm her down. Your next responsibility is to provide her with her options. The ultimate decision has to be hers and made after she is well informed.

4.   **(A)**   Guidance counselors are not expected to preach the dominant moral, sexual, and social norms of their culture. They are expected to aid clients in making up their own minds on these issues.

5.   **(B)**   Silence is a form of communication, and doesn't necessarily mean that the meeting is failing.

6.   **(C)**   Without the written consent of a client, a guidance counselor cannot divulge file information no matter how altruistic the cause. Besides being illegal, it would undermine their credibility with, and ability to be trusted by, other clients.

7.   **(D)**   Appropriate sexual history includes questions about marriages, engagements, knowledge of birth control, and reasons that previous relationships didn't work out. Asking for details about personal sexual acts isn't appropriate.

8.   **(B)**   Avoidance of eye contact, foot tapping, furrowed eyebrows, and playing with a ring or other jewelry suggest fear and apprehension. The other choices are indicative of anger in the client.

9.   **(A)**   Confrontation, which isn't aversive if it is handled right, is useful when a client's statements are contradicted by their behavior. For example, a student may claim that they find school very dissatisfying but their grades are excellent. Or they claim they want to change but then blame their parents for their behavior.

10.   **(C)**   The best approach is to set specific realistic goals, and describe in detail the behavior that will lead to success. A discussion of various situations and how the client will respond to them is beneficial.

11.   **(D)**   Most licensed guidance counselors hold a Master's degree in Guidance and Counseling, and work in a secondary (junior and senior high school) education setting.

12.   **(E)**   All of the choices are recommended courses of action for a guidance counselor. It is best not to decide on the client's course of action and then try to convince them of the merit of your decision.

13.   **(B)**   Ego-defense mechanisms are found in the Freudian approach to personality. The other four choices are behavioral in nature because they stress the influence of environment on behavior.

14.   **(A)**   Counselors should never dictate to clients. They shouldn't act as if they are older and wiser, and therefore, will dictate client policy. Their job is to guide the client to make their own decisions. To alter or veto a plan without justification is unacceptable.

15.   **(E)**   There is enormous variability in people. A guidance counselor should resist developing a narrow point of view concerning what is appropriate behavior.

16.   **(D)**   Value judgment statements negating a client's feelings should be avoided. The other four choices suggest condescension, mockery, or omniscience, all of which can alienate a client. Better to discuss what medicine really is, and the client's suitability for a career in it. Many students select vocations based on TV and film stereotypes without any factual knowledge of what is really involved.

17.   **(B)**   Any other choice would be discouraging. The guidance counselor's job is to help students make informed decisions.

18.   **(C)**   Although choices (A) and (B) are true, choice (C) is the better response. The other four choices would probably produce hostility. By agreeing with him from the onset, you are likely to gain his trust. Under the guise of helping him to the pros, you can explain the value of an education and grades.

19.   **(A)**   Clients may perceive rehearsed answers as indicative of mediocrity, or indifference. They believe that they are unique people, and expect individualized treatment. Students often compare experiences they have had with a counselor. If they discover that the counselor essentially told both of them the same thing, they suspect the counselor of not really caring.

20.   **(A)**   When we paraphrase a client, we restate what they just said as a means of proving that we are listening to them, and to encourage additional statements from them. Counselors do perception checks on themselves to verify that they are judging the situation correctly. The counselor usually asks qualifying questions that confirm or deny their interpretation of the situation.

HOME ECONOMICS

This test assesses the knowledge of home economics and the methods of teaching home economics. The test covers a broad range of subject areas, but is broken down into the following: family and human development, management, consumerism, nutrition and food, clothing and textiles, housing, and home economics education. All of the questions relate to both the individual and the family.

> **DIRECTIONS**: Each of the following questions and incomplete statements is followed by five answer choices. Select the choice which best answers each question.

1. The increase in the number of women in the United States who are gainfully employed has influenced the family by
    (A) removing the division of labor at home.
    (B) increasing the divorce rate since women who are gainfully employed are more likely to divorce.
    (C) decreasing the number of goods and services produced at home.
    (D) assigning household tasks along sex lines.
    (E) increasing family dependence upon the extended family for support and child care.

2. The term the "sandwich generation" refers to
    (A) middle-aged persons who are caring for their children and their elderly parents.
    (B) the children who are part of blended families.
    (C) divorced individuals attempting to fit into the singles world and be a single parent in charge of a family.
    (D) adolescents who waver between the adult independent state and child-parent dependence.
    (E) young working couples accepting job responsibilities, care of young children and managing the family and home.

3. Which of the following statements about communication within the family is NOT true?
    (A) Communication requires a sender, a receiver and a message.
    (B) All family communication begins with a strong verbal message which makes the sender's intentions clear.
    (C) Good communicative skills require attention to context, timing, clarity, respect, listening and feedback.
    (D) Quarreling is a form of family communication which can be either constructive or destructive.
    (E) Family communication may be hindered by fear, feelings of insecurity, and differing expectations of family members.

4. The American diet is undergoing a change. Dietary guidelines published by the government have encouraged dietary modifications to reduce the incidence of diet-related diseases. Listed below are some changes suggested by USDA. Choose the only change which Americans as a whole have made in the last ten years.

    (A) Eat fewer saturated fats from sources such as eggs, beef and whole milk
    (B) Eat less total fat in the daily diet
    (C) Eat fewer foods high in sugar
    (D) Increase consumption of low-fat dairy products
    (E) Decrease consumption of alcoholic beverages

5. School children are encouraged to reduce the amount of sugar in their diets. Several reasons are given for doing this, but only a few are based upon scientific research. Choose the correct reason from those stated below.

    (A) Eating too many sugar-rich foods can cause a child to become diabetic.
    (B) Hyperactive behavior in young children is caused by eating too many sugar-rich foods
    (C) Overconsumption of sugar-rich foods has been shown to cause heart disease.
    (D) Eating too many sugary foods throughout the day can result in tooth decay.
    (E) Overconsumption of sugar-rich foods throughout life is associated with colon cancer.

6. Several facts about dietary fiber are listed below. Choose the one which is NOT TRUE.

    (A) Most foods are not labeled for total dietary fiber content.
    (B) Dietary fiber is the part of plants that humans can't digest.
    (C) There is no reason to take fiber supplements or to add fiber to foods that do not already contain it.
    (D) Foods high in fiber are often high in starch, and therefore are calorie dense.
    (E) The exact amount and type of fiber needed in a person's daily diet is not known.

7. Knowing that food labels are sources of important information, John examines the label on mayonnaise to determine the ingredients. Specifically, he wants to determine if eggs and palm oils are used. He cannot find an ingredient label even though he feels it is required to be there by law. Why is it not present?

    (A) The formula for the product is protected by a patent.
    (B) The producer has the formula on file with the FDA and therefore does not need to put it on the jar.
    (C) The product is made according to a strict government formula and meets a Standard of Identity.
    (D) Ingredient labeling is not required because the product makes no dietary claims.
    (E) The food is Kosher and exempt from label requirements because it adheres to Jewish dietary laws.

8. Maximum death benefits for the most minimal monthly or yearly premiums may be obtained through which form of life insurance?

(A) Term insurance   (D) Variable universal life insurance

(B) Whole life insurance   (E) Credit life insurance

(C) Universal life insurance

9. Specific guidelines have been set by the USDA for the sodium content of foods. Which term listed below is used for a food which by definition "contains 35 mg of sodium or less per serving"?

(A) Low Sodium   (D) Reduced Sodium

(B) Very Low Sodium   (E) No Salt Added (Unsalted)

(C) Sodium-Free

10. Although open dating on food items is mandatory in very few states, it is helpful when it appears because it

(A) indicates the last day when it is safe for the consumer to eat the food.

(B) helps the consumer know how long and under what conditions the food has been stored.

(C) assures that the food will taste fresh and be safe to eat.

(D) provides some information concerning the food's freshness and allows the consumer to save money by buying items "past their date" at lower prices, knowing that they are still fresh enough to eat.

(E) assists the consumer in making a purchase decision because it is a guideline, furnished by the manufacturer, for product freshness and refers to the last suggested sale date.

11. According to the law of supply and demand, when there is an orange freeze in Florida, orange juice will be

(A) low in price because people will switch to tomato juice to avoid price increases.

(B) in short supply, and therefore high in price.

(C) not affected in price or supply.

(D) not available.

(E) in short supply, and the price will not change.

12. A teaching method which might be chosen to encourage learners to examine their attitudes and feelings toward an issue, as, for example feeding a two-year-old at family meal time, and which would be within the Affective Educational Domain is

(A) use of a cartoon depicting a child eating with the family and creating an "amusing scene" followed by discussion using valuing and "what if you" questions.

(B) use of a textbook on the young child for reading, notetaking and discussion.

(C) teacher-delivered lecture with chalkboard or transparencies on feeding practices of young children and adult interventions.

(D) a guest speaker who directs a local day care center speaking about "feeding the toddler."

(E) a computer program, used by individual students, which presents material textbook-fashion, and then includes questions and case studies.

13. When choosing a piece of computer software to use with a curriculum unit, the teacher's first consideration should be

(A) the number of routines or options on the menu of the software.

(B) copyright regulations of the company producing the software.

(C) the publishing company's age, location and reputation.

(D) the length of time it will take for students to use the software.

(E) whether use of the software as a teaching method meets the stated specific educational objectives.

14. Many housing options are available to American consumers. Which one of the following offers freedom from maintenance tasks, greater mobility and most control of expenses?

(A) Condominium apartment ownership

(B) Cooperative apartment membership

(C) Single family home ownership

(D) Townhouse condominium ownership

(E) High-rise apartment rental

15. Mortgages are used for several purposes. Which one of the following might be sought by an elderly homeowner needing current income from an existing frozen asset?

(A) Reverse-Annuity Mortgage (D) Rollover Mortgage

(B) Variable Rate Mortgage (E) Price-Level-Adjusted Mortgage

(C) Graduate Payment Mortgage

16. The term "Smart House," as used by the housing industry, refers to a model house being built to meet future consumer needs relative to safety, security, entertainment, costs, convenience, comfort, and communications. This house is

(A) a house with system integration that uses a single wiring cable to supply AC power, low voltage DC, telephone, audio, video, and high-speed data communication.

(B) a house made entirely of recycled materials such as plastic, glass, metals, and paper.

(C) a house where all of its own energy needs are self-generated through solar power, wind power, recycled wastes, etc.

(D) a house designed using systems and material that provide completely for home care and cleaning through vacuum, steam cleaning, etc.

(E) a house containing a computerized network that monitors all systems of the house such as heating, plumbing, electricity, etc. to be sure they are operating at maximum efficiency.

17. Which of the following statements contain descriptive information found on the hangtag and label of a suit being purchased for style, durability, resiliency, drapability and easy care? If tailoring and fit are comparable, which choice adheres to these criteria most fully?

(A) 25% wool, 75% polyester, medium-weight pin stripe worsted

(B) 65% rayon, 35% polyester, light-weight sharkskin-type weave

(C)   100% wool, light-weight worsted gabardine

(D)   65% polyester, 35% combined cotton natural blend, medium-weight gabardine

(E)   100% wool, medium-weight woolen flannel plain weave

18.   Complementary colors appear more intense with sharper contrasts when used in full strength (high chroma) next to each other than when used with other colors. This phenomenon is called

(A)   Split Complement Harmony.   (D)   Monochromatic Harmony.

(B)   Triad Harmony.   (E)   Analogous Harmony.

(C)   Simultaneous Contrast.

19.   Due to uncertainty about needs, time and resources, careful family resource management and establishment of goals is most difficult for which group listed below?

(A)   Expanding family   (D)   Middle-aged

(B)   Elderly   (E)   Teenagers

(C)   Young married

20.   Students in the high school Family Living class recognize that garbage in the school cafeteria, physical education areas, and laboratories (including home economics laboratories) is not being collected with care for recycling. Working in groups, each group seeks to solve the problem. Which group uses the problem-solving process?

(A)   Recognizing the problem, group A contacts two neighboring schools to determine their solutions. One is chosen and presented to the principal. It is put into action.

(B)   Group B recognizes the problem and discusses it with the teachers involved, the principal and the school food service manager. Using their suggestions, a plan is put into action.

(C)   Group C does a survey of the students involved. Using their suggestions, a plan is devised and put into action. A few weeks later, changes are made based upon a second series of student interviews.

(D)   Group D brainstorms and thinks about possible outcomes. They are creative and choose a method to reach the desired outcome. Working with the principal they implement their plan. Results are observed and some changes made.

(E)   Group E writes down the problem and discusses it, considering possible solutions. They gather information from others involved in (teachers, staff) or experienced with (other school personnel, state department officials) the problem. Solutions are defined and tested. The plan is implemented and results are evaluated.

ANSWER KEY

1.	(C)	6.	(D)	11.	(B)	16.	(A)
2.	(A)	7.	(C)	12.	(A)	17.	(C)
3.	(B)	8.	(A)	13.	(E)	18.	(C)
4.	(A)	9.	(B)	14.	(E)	19.	(B)
5.	(D)	10.	(E)	15.	(E)	20.	(E)

DETAILED EXPLANATIONS OF ANSWERS

1.   **(C)**   Although (A), (B), (C) and (D) are sometimes true, data indicate that most working women are still responsible for the traditional "women's roles" of child care, cleaning, laundry, cooking, etc. Some are unable to rely upon the extended family due to the lack of proximity and increased interests of retired grandparents. All families, however, are buying more convenience foods, house and lawn services, have decreased home construction of clothing and goods, and use more appliances. (C) is correct.

2.   **(A)**   The term "sandwich generation" has been used to describe the generation between one's children and one's parents, as in (A). All other responses do not describe varied generations.

3.   **(B)**   The response (B) is incorrect since nonverbal communication is frequently as important or more important than verbal communication. In fact, some communication may be very effective and be only nonverbal, as in raising one's eyebrows or shaking one's fist at someone. Children are particularly sensitive to recognizing parental feelings through parental actions.

4.   **(A)**   Americans have changed dietary intake to lower consumption of saturated fats as in (A) (the correct response), but they have replaced these fats with unsaturated forms such as margarine and oils, thereby keeping total fat in the diet high. Although artificial sweetener consumption has increased, sugary food consumption remains high. Low-fat milk consumption has increased, but increased consumption of high-fat cheeses and ice creams offsets any benefit. Alcoholism remains a big problem in our nation.

5.   **(D)**   Sugar consumption is associated with an increased risk of diabetes mellitus and heart disease, and for a small percentage of children, hyperactivity, but it does not cause these disorders, according to current scientific evidence. It has not been associated with cancer. However, response (D) is a proven fact, more so if these foods are consumed constantly, not just at meals.

6.   **(D)**   Dietary fiber which comes from plants consists of many types, all of which are not included on labels which give "crude fiber" values. A balanced diet containing foods high in fiber negates the need for fiber supplements. Specific fiber needs are not known, but people can safely eat such high-fiber foods as grains, pasta, fruits and vegetables, which contain only 4 calories per gram, providing they do not add calorie rich sauces, gravies, and fats. (D) is not true.

7.   **(C)**   Some food products, such as mayonnaise, are exempt from ingredient label requirements because they meet a Standard of Identity which includes using a formula specified for that product. All other products are required to list ingredients on the label in descending order of amount, but the specific amount need not be listed. Response (C) is correct.

8.   **(A)**   Term insurance provides death benefits only, and since it has no savings element and does not build cash values as do responses (B)-(D), it provides larger death benefits for lower cost. Response (E) is a life insurance designed to pay one's credit debts upon death.

9.   **(B)**   The correct response is (B). (A) refers to a food with 140 mg or less per serving; (C) foods have less than 5 mg per serving. Reduced sodium foods (D) have at least a 75% reduction in sodium from the usual amount, and (E) foods are foods normally processed with salt, but in this case no salt was added.

10.   **(E)**   Open dating only provides a guide for the consumer, provided by manufacturer, suggesting the last sell date for freshness. The storage conditions can influence the food's freshness; these are unknown. Therefore open dating is only a source of information and cannot guarantee the freshness or safety of the product.

11.   **(B)**   Even though all orange juice does not originate in Florida, a freeze there affects supply. Many people will not switch to another juice, since orange juice is an American favorite. Supplies will be short. Therefore producers will charge more, and consumers will pay more (response (B) is correct).

12.   **(A)**   Response (A) is the only one which allows students to be involved by responding in a non-threatening way to an amusing non-personal scene, allowing them to express their own feelings regarding how they would feel and react. All other responses are listening to or reading cognitive material, and reacting based on factual learning, as opposed to one's own feelings.

13.   **(E)**   Although (A) and (D) are considerations, no software should be chosen unless it will help learners meet educational objectives as well as, or better than, other possible educational methods. Computer software should not be used just to keep students busy or occupied.

14.   **(E)**   Only in (E) is the resident free to move without a sale taking place. The lease, if present, is the only limiting factor. Control of expenses under the lease period is known, and maintenance is the owner's concern.

15.   **(E)**   In responses (B)-(E) the borrower (homeowner) makes mortgage payments according to a specified schedule, which in some cases is open to change or renegotiation. Response (E) provides income for the homeowner by taking money out of the existing asset (the house).

16. **(A)** The Smart House, now being built as models in the U.S. and Canada, features the single wiring cable as described in (A). All services are available at every outlet.

17. **(C)** A wool fabric resists wrinkles wears well and has the soft drape that suit-tailoring requires. Worsted fabrics are smooth and more tightly woven than woolens, meaning they hold their shape and crease best. A twill weave such as the gabardine will wear longer than a plain weave, as found in the pin stripe. Although synthetics such as polyester are durable, they often lack the drape of wool and can be difficult to mold and shape (a blend containing a lower percentage of polyester is desirable). (C) gives a choice that meet all criteria based upon fabric, weight, and weave.

18. **(C)** The correct term for the definition is (C) and is true when choosing either clothing or home furnishings. In (A) and (B) the colors are located in other locations on the color wheel than in a complementary position. In (D) only one hue is used, and in (E) colors appear next to each other on the color wheel.

19. **(B)** For group (B), the elderly, planning is difficult due to uncertainties concerning death of self or a spouse, health, retirement needs, and actual date of retirement. Although the other groups have variable resources and uncertainties, they are not as great.

20. **(E)** Only response (E) includes each step in the problem-solving process: identify the problem, determine possible outcomes, gather data, choose best possible solution from possible outcomes, implement the plan and evaluate the results.

MATHEMATICS

This specialty test is designed for prospective teachers of mathematics at the secondary level. The questions are divided into two main areas: mathematical content and mathematics education. These questions emphasize pedagogy but also include knowledge of various organizations, trends, and curricular developments. The following topics are covered on the test: numeration systems; number concepts; structure of matematical systems; arithmetic algorithms; conditional algebraic statements and identities; elementary functions; measurement and approximation; two- and three-dimensional geometry; trigonometry; exponential and logarithmic functions; probability and statistics; calculus; and mathematics education.

DIRECTIONS: Each of the following questions and incomplete statements is followed by five answer choices. Select the choice which best answers each question.

---

1. One mile equals approximately
   (A) 160,934 centimeters.
   (B) 14,311 centimeters.
   (C) 160,000 centimeters.
   (D) 106,934 centimeters.
   (E) 160,034 centimeters.

2. If $a^2 - b^2 = 0$, then which of the following is necessarily true?
   (A) $ab^{-1} = -1$
   (B) $ab^{-1} = 1$
   (C) $ab = 0$
   (D) $a = 0$ and $b = 0$
   (E) $|a| + |b| = 2|a|$

3. For $0 \leq \theta < \dfrac{\pi}{2}$, if $(\sin 2\theta + \cos 2\theta)^2 = 1$, then $\theta =$
   (A) 0
   (B) $\dfrac{\pi}{2}$
   (C) $\dfrac{\pi}{4}$
   (D) A and B
   (E) (A) and (C)

4. If $y = (ax^2 + bx)^c$, c is an integer, and $\dfrac{dy}{dx} = c\,(ax^2 + bx)\,(2x + 1)$, then a, b and c are elements of
   (A) $\{2\}$
   (B) $\{1\}$
   (C) $\{1, 2\}$
   (D) $\{1, 3\}$
   (E) $\{2, 3\}$

5. If a, b, c, a′, b′, c′ are integers where $d > 1$ and $\dfrac{ax^2 + bx}{cx + d} = \dfrac{a'x^2 + b'x}{c'x + 1}$, then
   (A) d divides a and c only.
   (B) d divides a, b and c.
   (C) d is the greatest common divisor of a, b and c.
   (D) d divides a and b only.
   (E) d divides b and c only.

6. $(x^2 + 1)(x^2 - 3) \le -2(x^2 + 1)$ if and only if

   (A) $x \le 1$ (D) $x \ge 2$

   (B) $1 \le x \le 2$ (E) $x \ge 1$

   (C) $1 < x < 2$

7. If $y = \dfrac{(3x^2 + 5)^2}{x^2 + 7}$ which of the following is a rational approach to solve for dy/dx?

   (A) Product Rule   (D) Addition Rule

   (B) Quotient Rule   (E) $\dfrac{dy}{dx} = \lim_{h \to 0} \dfrac{f(x + h) - f(x)}{h}$

   (C) Chain Rule

8. If the determinant of the matrix $M = \begin{pmatrix} a & b \\ b & a \end{pmatrix}$ is 1, then which of the following is NOT true?

   (A) M has an inverse   (D) $|a| = \sqrt{2}$ if $|b| = 1$

   (B) 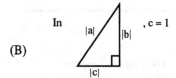   (E) $b = 0$ if $|a| = 1$

   (C) M may not have inverse

9. If $x + \sqrt{2}$ is a rational number, then

   (A) x is necessarily rational.   (D) (A) or (C).

   (B) x is necesssarily irrational.   (E) $x = 0$.

   (C) x is necessarily an integer.

10. The above figure is used to illustrate

    (A) possible way of two circles with common tangent line.

    (B) two concentric circles.

    (C) two circles with disjoint interior.

    (D) two circles with disjoint exterior.

    (E) (C) and (D).

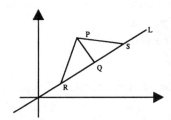

11. In the figure above, if Q is a point on L closest to P, then

    (A) $\overline{PQ} \perp L$.

    (B) $\triangle PRQ \cong \triangle PSQ$ for any points R, S on L

    (C) there is a point Q' on L so that $Q \neq Q'$ and $|PQ| = |PQ'|$.

    (D) if $|PR| = |PS|$, then $\triangle PRQ \cong \triangle PSQ$.

    (E) (A) and (D).

12. A and B are independent events; the probability that not both A and B will occur is $\frac{6}{7}$. If the probability that B occurs is $\frac{2}{7}$, then the probability that A occurs is

    (A) $\frac{2}{7}$.

    (B) $\frac{1}{7}$.

    (C) $\frac{1}{2}$.

    (D) $\frac{3}{14}$.

    (E) $\frac{2}{21}$.

13. Which of the following is NOT true about the number of roots of a quadratic equation $ax^2 + bx + c = 0, a \neq 0$?

    (A) If it's a perfect square the quadratic equation has only one real root.

    (B) The quadratic equation may have more than one real root.

    (C) If the graph of the $f(x) = ax^2 + bx + c$ does not intersect the real axis then the equation can still have a real root.

    (D) If the discriminant is negative the quadratic equation cannot have a real root.

    (E) (A) and (D).

14. If N is an orthogonal complement of a subspace M of a finite dimensional vector space V, then one of the following is false.

    (A) $V = M + N$

    (B) If N is orthogonal to every element of M, then $n \in N$.

    (C) If N is orthogonal to every element of N, then $n = 0$.

    (D) If m is orthogonal to every element of N, then $m \in M$.

    (E) If $m \in M$ and $n \in N$, then m and n are orthogonal.

15. Which of the following is true about $f(x) = \log(x^2 + 1)$
    (A) $\sqrt{f}$ may be undefined
    (B) f is always positive
    (C) Domain of $\dfrac{1}{f} = (-\infty, \infty)$
    (D) Domain of $f = (0, \infty)$
    (E) f is an even function

16. If the graph of $2 + ae^x$ has an x intercept, then
    (A) $a^3 < 0$
    (B) $a = 0$
    (C) $a > 0$
    (D) $a^2 = 0$
    (E) $a^3 > 0$

17. The first four terms of two sequences are $1, -\dfrac{1}{6}, \dfrac{1}{(4)(9)}, -\dfrac{1}{(8)(27)}, \ldots$ and $-1, \dfrac{1}{2}, -\dfrac{1}{6},$

    $\dfrac{1}{24} \ldots.$ The sum of the 16th term of the first sequence and the 6th term of the 2nd sequence equals

    (A) $\dfrac{-1}{\left(2^{16}\right)3^{16}} + \dfrac{1}{720}$

    (B) $\dfrac{1}{\left(2^{16}\right)3^{16}} + \dfrac{1}{720}$

    (C) $\dfrac{-1}{\left(2^{15}\right)3^{15}} + \dfrac{1}{720}$

    (D) $\dfrac{-1}{\left(2^{15}\right)3^{15}} - \dfrac{1}{720}$

    (E) $\dfrac{-1}{\left(2^{16}\right)3^{16}} + \dfrac{1}{120}$

18. Which of the following is NOT a way of finding convergence of an infinite series?
    (A) Geometric series test
    (B) Geometric mean
    (C) P-series test
    (D) Alternating series test
    (E) Integral test

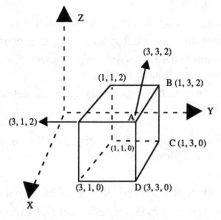

19. A cube in the X - Y - Z space is shown in the figure above. Which of the following vectors is perpendicular to the face ☐ ABCD?

(A) (-2, -2, 0)   (D) (0, -2, 0)

(B) (0, 0, -2)   (E) (-2, 0, 0)

(C) (0, -2, -2)

20. If $f(x) = \dfrac{(x + 3)^2 - (x - 1)^2}{x + 1}$ and $g(x) = 8$, then

(A) $f(x) = g(x)$ for every x   (D) $f(x) = g(x)$ for every x except x = -1

(B) Domain f = Domain g   (E) (A) and (C).

ANSWER KEY

1.	(A)	6.	(B)	11.	(E)	16.	(A)
2.	(E)	7.	(B)	12.	(C)	17.	(C)
3.	(E)	8.	(C)	13.	(C)	18.	(B)
4.	(C)	9.	(B)	14.	(C)	19.	(D)
5.	(B)	10.	(A)	15.	(E)	20.	(D)

DETAILED EXPLANATIONS OF ANSWERS

1. **(A)** 1 mile = 5,280 feet, 1 foot = 12 inches and 1 inch $\approx$ 2.54 centimeters. $\therefore$ 1 mile = 5,280 ft/mile x 12in/ft x 2.54 cm/in $\approx$ 160, 934 cm.

2. **(E)** If $a^2 - b^2 = 0$ then all we can conclude is that a - b = 0 or a + b = 0. In other words, a = b or a = -b. But this is the same as |a| = |b| since (E) says |a| + |b| = 2|a| which is the same as |a| = |b|, then (E) is the correct answer. When $a^2 - b^2 = 0$, ab may or may not equal 1, so (B) is not the answer. Similarly, (A), (C) and (D) don't give the correct answer.

3. **(E)** $(\sin2\theta + \cos2\theta) = 1$ is the same as $\sin^2 2\theta + 2 \sin2\theta \cos2\theta + \cos^2 2\theta = 1$. $\sin^2 2\theta + \cos^2 2\theta + 2\sin \cos2\theta = 1$. $1 + 2\sin2 \cos2\theta = 1$, since $\sin^2 \propto + \cos^2 \propto = 1$ or $2\sin2\theta \cos2\theta = 0$. $\sin 4\theta = $, since $2\sin \propto \cos \propto = \sin2 \propto$. So $4\theta = 0$ or $4\theta = \pi$ or $4\theta = 2\pi$. $\sigma = 0$ or $\theta = \dfrac{\pi}{4}$ or $\theta = \dfrac{\pi}{2}$. Since $0 \le \theta < \dfrac{\pi}{2}$, then the answer is (E).

4. **(C)** On the one hand, for $y = (ax^2 + bx)^c$. $\dfrac{dy}{dx} = c (ax^2 + bx)^{c-1} (2ax + b)$. But, its given that $2a = 2$, $b = 1$ and $c-1 = 1$. $\therefore$ a = 1, b = 1 and c = 2.

5. **(B)** It's given that
$$\dfrac{ax^2 + bx}{cx = d} = \dfrac{a^1x^2 = b^1x}{c^1x + 1} \text{ and } d > 1$$
If d divides a and c only or a and B only or b and c only the constant term of the denominator of the right hand side wouldn't have been 1. So, d must divide a, b and c, and this is all we can conclude. We can't be sure if d is the greatest common divisor of a, b and c. So, the answer must be (B).

6. **(B)** Moving all expressions in $(x^2 + 1) (x^2 - 3x) \le -2 (x^2 + 1)$ to the left hand side we will get: $(x^2 + 1) (x^2 - 3x) + 2 (x^2 + 1) \le 0$ or $(x^2 + 1) (x^2 - 3x + 2) \le 0$, factoring out x2 + 1 i.e., $x^2 - 3x + 2 \le 0$, dividing both sides by $x^2 + 1$, since $x^2 + 1$ is always positive or (x -

2) $(x - 1) \leq 0$, factoring the left hand side so $1 \leq x \leq 2$. If $x < 1$ or $x > 2$ then $(x - 2)(x - 1) > 0$. As a result (A) and (D) cannot be answers. In (C) 1 and 2 are not included and (E) contains numbers that do not satisfy the inequality. So, the answer must be (B).

7. **(B)** Since, $\dfrac{(3x^2 + 5)^2}{x^2 + 7}$

is a rational function the natural approach is to use the quotient rule, although the product rule does apply after rewriting the function as $(3x^2 + 5)^2 (x^2 + 7)^{-1}$. The chain rule may be used at some stage, but it is not the natural approach. The same is true about the addition rule. The definition form of finding a derivative, as given in (E), also works. But, we don't usually approach such a problem through the definition unless instructed to do so.

8. **(C)** It is given that the determinant of $M = \begin{pmatrix} a\ b \\ b\ a \end{pmatrix}$ is 1.

This means $a^2 - b^2 = 1$.
Therefore, if $|b| = 1$, then $a^2 - 1 = 1$ i.e., $a^2 = 2$ or $|a| = \sqrt{2}$. So, (D) is true similarly (E) is true.

Since $a^2 - b^2 = 1$, then $a^2 = b^2 + 1$. ∴ In $\triangle$ $|a|^2 = |b|^2 + c^2, c > 0$ and so $c = 1$. As a result

(B) is also true. It is a fact that if the determinant of a matrix is different from zero, then the matrix is invertible and this makes (A) true. So, (C) is the answer.

9. **(B)** $x + \sqrt{2} = p/q$, p and q are integers and $g \neq 0$. This is given. If x is rational then $\sqrt{2} = p/q - x$ is rational, which cannot be, since $\sqrt{2}$ is irrational. So, (A) is false. Similarly (C) is false and consequently (D) is false. Also, if $x = 0$, then we will get $0 + \sqrt{2}$ is rational, which is not true, so x cannot be zero. So the answer is (B).

10. **(A)** If two circles are concentric and have an intersection point, then they are the same. So, (B) is not true. Since these two circles have common interior points and common exterior points then (C) and (D) are false too. This figure illustrates one possibility of the way two circles may have a common tangent point.

11. **(E)** If Q is a point on L closest to P then, from Euclidean geometry, we know that $\overline{PQ} \perp L$. In addition, if $|PR| = |PS|$, then by the right angle hypotenuse side theorem we know that $\triangle PRQ \cong \triangle PSQ$. So, (D) is also true. But, since Q is unique (C) is false. (B) obviously is false. Hence, the answer is (E).

12. **(C)** The probability of the opposite of the event that both A and B occur is 6/7.

Therefore, the probability that both A and B occur $= 1 - \dfrac{6}{7} = \dfrac{1}{7}$. On the other hand we are told

that A and B are independent and that probability of B $= \dfrac{2}{7}$. So, we have

(Probability A) (Probability B) $= \dfrac{1}{7}$ i.e., (Probability A) $(\dfrac{2}{7}) = \dfrac{1}{7}$ which means that Prob-

ability A $= \dfrac{1}{2}$.

13. **(C)** If $ax^2 + bx + c = 0$ is a perfect square, then it can be rewritten in the form $(x + d)^2 = 0$, i.e., $x = -d$ is the only root. This makes (A) true. If the discriminant is positive it will have two real roots. So, (B) is true too. (D) is also true. But, since the x intercept of $f(x) = a^2 + bx + c$ is at exactly the roots of $ax^2 + bx + c = 0$, then (C) is not true.

14. **(C)** If M and N are orthogonal complements and V is finite dimensional space, then from a fact in linear algebra, $V = M + N$. (B) is also true, since N is a collection of all vectors that are perpendicular to M. Similarly, (D) is true, obviously (E) is true since vectors in M and vectors in N are perpendicular to each other. But, (C) is false. For example if you take $V = P^2$ i.e., the vector space of all ordered pairs of real numbers, M = the line Y = X and N = the line Y = -X, then M and N are perpendicular. Moreover, the vector (1, -1) is in N and it's perpendicular to all vectors in M, but it is not zero.

15. **(E)** For every x, $x^2 + 1 \geq 1$ and $\log(x^2 + 1)$ is defined and $\log(x^2 + 1) \geq 0$, i.e., $\sqrt{\log(x^2 + 1)}$ is always defined. So, (A) is false. When x = 0, $\therefore (0) = \log(0 + 1) = 0$. Therefore, $1/f$ is undefined at x = 0 which means Domain $\dfrac{1}{f} \neq (-\infty, \infty)$. So, (C) is false. Since Domain $f = (-\infty, \infty)$ then (D) is false. However, for every x, $f(x) = \log(x^2 + 1)$ and $f(-x) = \log(-x^2 + 1) = \log(x^2 + 1)$, which shows that $f(x) = f(-x)$ and consequently f is an even function which makes (E) true.

16. **(A)** If a = 0, then $2 + ae^x$ is simply the constant function $f(x) = 2$ and its graph is parallel to the x axis and has no x intercept. If a > 0, then $ae^x > 0$ and this means $2 + ae^x > 2$ and $f(x) = 2 + ae^x$ has no x intercept. If $a^3 > 0$, then a > 0 and by the above reasoning $2 + ae^x$ can't have x intercept. If $a^2 = 0$, then a = 0 and therefore $2 + ae^x = 2$ with no x intercept. But, if $a^3 < 0$ then a < 0. Setting $f(x) = 0$ to find the intercept, $2 + ae^x = 0$ or $2 = -ae^x$. Furthermore, $e^x = -2/a$ and $-2/a > 0$ since a < 0. As a result $x = \ln(-2/a)$ is the x intercept of the graph of $f(x) = 2 + ae^x$ and this makes (A) the only true choice.

17. **(C)** In the first sequence:

1st term $= \dfrac{1}{2^0 3^0}$, 2nd term $= -\dfrac{-1}{2^1 3^1}$, 3rd term $= \dfrac{1}{2^2 3^2}$, ...observe that the even terms are

negative and according to the above pattern the 16th term is $\dfrac{-1}{2^{15} 3^{15}}$.

In the 2nd sequence:

1st term $= \dfrac{1}{1}!$, 2nd term $= \dfrac{-1}{2}!$, 3rd term $= \dfrac{-1}{3}!$, 4th term $= \dfrac{1}{4}!$, since $1 = 1!, 2 = 2!, 6 = 3!$

and $24 = 4!$. Also the odd terms are negative and the even ones positive. So, if we follow this

pattern the 6th term of the 2nd sequence is $\dfrac{1}{6}! = \dfrac{1}{720}$. Hence (C) i.e., $\dfrac{-1}{2^{15} 3^{15}} + \dfrac{1}{720}$ is true and

the rest are false.

18. **(B)** All but (B) are well known tests of convergence of a given series. Geometric mean is irrelevant to the discussion of series, since it deals with only finite collections of numbers.

19. **(D)** The face $\square$ ABCD is parallel to the X-Z plane. So, all vectors perpendicular to this face have to be parallel to the Y axis, and (0, -2, 0) is the only such vector among the five given choices.

20. **(D)** $f(x) = \dfrac{(x+3)^2 - (x-1)^2}{x+1} = \dfrac{[(x+3) + (x-1)][(x+3) - (x-1)]}{x+1}$ by difference

of two squares $= \dfrac{(2x+2)(4)}{x+1} = \dfrac{2(x+1)(4)}{x+1} = 8$ for $x + 1 \neq 0$ or $x \neq -1$. Recall that

$\dfrac{8(x+1)}{x+1} = 8$ only if $x \neq -1$, since if $x = -1$ the left hand side is (8) $0/0$ which is undefined.

So, (A), (B), (C) and (E) are false and (D) is true.

PHYSICAL EDUCATION

This test is very broad in its areas of testing because of the variety of programs available. The test is divided into several sections and subsections, as follows. Physical education (human movement): activities (fundamental motor skills, games and sports, outdoor leisure pursuits, dance, exercise and physical fitness); science of human movement (exercise physiology, human anatomy, mechanics of human movement, development, and motor learning). Physical education as a profession: role; professional organizations; curriculum; teaching/learning process (implementing and evaluating).

DIRECTIONS: Each of the following questions and incomplete statements is followed by five answer choices. Select the choice which best answers each question.

1. The handicapping conditions represented by Public Law 94–142 includes children defined as
   I. Mentally retarded
   II. Hard of hearing
   III. Learning disabled

   (A) I and II.
   (B) I.
   (C) III.
   (D) I, II, and III.
   (E) II and III.

2. Most children with a history of epileptic seizures
   (A) can take part in physical education programs with non-epileptics.
   (B) may participate in limited activities, depending on the type of seizure experienced.
   (C) may experience minor motor seizures during physical activity.
   (D) will have an abnormal increase in heart rate and blood pressure during physical activity.
   (E) have poor eye-hand coordination.

3. Activities that develop gross motor-visual skills almost always involve the use of a
   (A) ball.
   (B) balance beam.
   (C) trampoline.
   (D) exercise mat.
   (E) racquet.

4. A volleyball game scores for
   (A) 12 points, and the serving team must win by 1 point.
   (B) 11 points, and the serving team must win by 1 point.
   (C) 15 points, and the serving team must win by 2 points.
   (D) 14 points, and the serving team must win by 2 points.
   (E) 14 points, and the serving team must win by 1 point.

5. Exercise systems commonly used to develop muscular strength include

 I.   Weight training   III. Isometric training
 II. Interval training   IV.   Isokinetic training
 (A) I, II, and III.   (D)   III and IV.
 (B) I, III, an IV.   (E)   I, III, and IV.
 (C) I and II.

6. During prolonged exercise in the heat, fluid balance is reestablished by

 (A) consuming salt tablets.   (D) taking mineral supplements.
 (B) taking vitamins.   (E) drinking orange juice.
 (C) drinking water.

7. Most of the calories in an athlete's diet should be derived from

 I.   Fats   III. Proteins
 II. Carbohydrates
 (A) I and II.   (D)   III.
 (B) I.   (E)   I and III.
 (C) II.

8. Of the following, which test does NOT measure muscular strength and endurance in children?

 (A) Pull ups   (D) Sit and reach test
 (B) Flexed arm hang   (E) Abdominal sit ups
 (C) Grip strength test

9. Dance steps most appropriate for younger children (grades 1–2) are

 (A) walk and/or skip.   (D) skip and step-hop.
 (B) run and/or skip.   (E) All of the above.
 (C) skip and slide.

10. A "safety" awarded in a football game counts for

 (A) 6 points.   (D) 1 point.
 (B) 5 points.   (E) 3 points.
 (C) 2 points.

11. In aquatic instruction, flotation belts are best used to teach children how to

 (A) float.   (D) surface dive.
 (B) dog paddle.   (E) frog kick.
 (C) flutter kick.

12. Which of the following symptoms is characteristic of heat stroke?

 (A) Muscle cramping   (D) Dry skin
 (B) Shallow breathing   (E) Thirst
 (C) Profuse sweating

13. Inflammation of the musculotendinous unit of the lower leg that is caused by an overexertion of muscles during weight-bearing activity is called

    (A) shin splints.
    (D) muscular sprain.
    (B) stress fracture.
    (E) compartment syndrome.
    (C) muscular strain.

14. Lifetime physical activity protects against

    (A) coronary heart disease.
    (D) obesity.
    (B) diabetes.
    (E) All of the above.
    (C) hypertension.

15. The term "learning disability" excludes learning problems traceable to

    (A) minimal brain dysfunction.
    (D) auditory handicap.
    (B) brain injury.
    (E) None of the above.
    (C) dyslexia.

16. Which of the following vitamins is fat-soluble?

    (A) Vitamin A
    (D) Vitamin B-1
    (B) Vitamin C
    (E) Vitamin B-12
    (C) Vitamin B-6

17. The *least* desirable method of teaching children a new dance is

    (A) lining children up in the formation of the dance.
    (B) clapping to the beat of the music.
    (C) giving a verbal description to accompany the music.
    (D) long practice sessions without the music.
    (E) long practice sessions with the music.

18. A motor disorder caused by brain dysfunction is termed

    (A) arthritis.
    (D) epilepsy.
    (B) cerebral palsy.
    (E) paralysis.
    (C) rheumatic heart disease.

19. You are instructing a tennis class. Of the following statements, which is the *least* effective form of feedback to your student?

    (A) "You hit the ball at the right time."
    (B) "Well done."
    (C) "Bend more at the knees; you'll get more power."
    (D) "Watch Joe's backhand stroke."
    (E) "You're not watching the ball."

20. Physical activity contributes to the development of which of the following cognitive behaviors?

    (A) Perceptual awareness
    (D) All of the above.
    (B) Problem-solving strategy
    (E) (A) and (B).
    (C) Creativity

ANSWER KEY

1.	(D)	6.	(C)	11.	(B)	16.	(A)
2.	(A)	7.	(C)	12.	(D)	17.	(D)
3.	(A)	8.	(D)	13.	(A)	18.	(B)
4.	(C)	9.	(A)	14.	(E)	19.	(B)
5.	(B)	10.	(C)	15.	(D)	20.	(D)

DETAILED EXPLANATIONS OF ANSWERS

1.   **(D)**   Public Law 94-142 provides a legal definition for the term "handicapped children." It includes children who have been evaluated as being mentally retarded, hearing impaired, deaf, speech impaired, visually handicapped, seriously emotionally disturbed, orthopedically impaired, having other health impairments (e.g., anemia, arthritis, etc.), deaf-blind, multi-handicapped, or with specific learning disabilities. P.L. 94–142 states that these children need special education and services.

2.   **(A)**   Epilepsy refers to different kinds of seizures. Most epileptic children can participate in regular physical education classes, regardless of the type of seizure previously experienced (B). Seizures are caused by an electrochemical imbalance in the brain. A minor motor seizure (C) causes localized contractions of muscles on one side or in one part of the body. Sweating and rapid heart rate (D) are characteristic of an autonomic seizure. Poor hand-eye coordination (E) is not caused by seizures.

3.   **(A)**   Gross visual-motor skills involve movement of the body's large muscles as visual information is processed. A ball is always used to perfect these skills. In some cases a bat or racquet will also aid in developing these skills.

4.   **(C)**   A volleyball game ends with 15 points, as long as the serving team has won by 2 points. One point is scored by the serving team if the receiving team cannot return the ball that was propelled across the net within the boundaries.

5.   **(B)**   Interval training (A), (C) and (E) is associated with the development of cardiovascular endurance and performance of aerobic activities (e.g., swimming, running, and cycling). Weight training involves a progressive increase in workload to develop muscular strength. With isometric exercise, the muscle does not change its length as a person exerts force against a resistance. In this case the force is static. However, with isokinetic exercise, the resistance pushes back with force equal to the one that the person exerts.

6.   **(C)**   Fluid is always reestablished by drinking water. A common practice is to drink before, during and after an event. It is not necessary to take salt tablets (A) since normal

salting of food is adequate to replenish the salt lost with sweat. Sugared drinks and juice (E) draw water to the gastrointestinal tract and cause cramps. Vitamin (B) and mineral supplements (D) will not replenish water.

7. **(C)** Roughly 60% of the calories consumed should be derived from carbohydrates. These should mostly include complex carbohydrates that come from foods such as bread and pasta.

8. **(D)** The grip strength test (C), pull ups (for boys) (A), and flexed arm hang (for girls) (B), as well as abdominal sit ups (E) are all tests to measure muscular strength and endurance. The sit and reach test measures flexibility.

9. **(A)** The skills required to master a certain dance will determine the suggested grade level for that dance. The simplest steps used are "walk and/or skip" and are therefore appropriate for grades 1–2. The steps "run and/or skip" (B), and "skip and slide" (C), are more difficult, and therefore suggested for grades 2–3. Even more difficult is the "step-hop" (D), and it is incorporated in dances appropriate for grades 3–6.

10. **(C)** A "safety" in a football game goes to the offensive team player when he or she is touched by the ball while standing behind the goal line. It counts for 2 points.

11. **(B)** A flotation belt is used to help children learn to dog paddle and should fit snugly across the waist. The device should be used for a limited amount of time to avoid dependence, which can lead to delay of swimming skill development.

12. **(D)** A heat stroke is characterized by dry skin. It is the most dangerous of all heat injuries and demands immediate medical care.

13. **(A)** Shin splints involve inflammation of the musculotendinous unit of the lower leg. They are caused by an overexertion of muscles during weight-bearing activity (e.g., running).

14. **(E)** Researchers have found that a lifetime commitment to physical activity, especially aerobic sports, will protect against coronary heart disease, diabetes, hypertension (high blood pressure), and obesity.

15. **(D)** The term "learning disabilities" excludes any learning problems caused by retardation. It also excludes auditory, visual, and motor handicaps. The term refers to perceptual handicaps, dyslexia, developmental aphasia, brain injury and brain dysfunction.

16. **(A)** Vitamins A, D, E, and K are considered fat-soluble. This means that the body will store them if they are taken in excess of the body's normal requirement, and consequently may cause illness. An excess of water-soluble vitamins (Cs and Bs) is released in the urine.

17. **(D)** It is not advisable to have long practice sessions without music since the teacher can hold the students' attention if they hear the music. Also, they can feel its pattern so that they can incorporate the dance steps. The other choices for this question offer desirable methods for teaching dance.

18. **(B)** Cerebral palsy is a motor disorder caused by brain dysfunction. Arthritis (A) involves joint inflammation and is often due to rheumatic fever which may also cause rheumatic heart disease (C). Epilepsy (D) involves different types of seizures that are caused by chemical imbalances in the brain. Paralysis (E) is loss of the power of voluntary movement. All are handicapping conditions.

19. **(B)** A comment such as "well done" does not provide effective feedback since it does not give specific comment or what the student did well.

20. **(D)** Perceptual awareness (e.g., the location of the ball in relation to the bat), problem-solving strategy (e.g., learning how to solve a movement problem), and creativity (e.g., games that are not predesigned and will incorporate new skills), are all cognitive behaviors of physical education.

SCHOOL PSYCHOLOGIST

This test is designed for those who have completed master's degrees who wish to become school psychologists. The test assumes that the candidates has had practical experience in the field. Key topics include assessment, intervention, evaluation, professional practice, psychological foundations, and educational foundations.

DIRECTIONS: Each of the following questions and incomplete statements is followed by five answer choices. Select the choice which best answers each question.

1. When offering guidance to a teacher concerning problems with a particular student, the school psychologist is likely to suggest all of the following possibilities except
   (A) cultural language disabilities.
   (B) emotional problems.
   (C) physiological problems.
   (D) problems at home.
   (E) intelligence differences between races.

2. Mary is a bright student but she is constantly disrupting the class by trying to draw the teacher into a power struggle for control. The school psychologist might advise the teacher to do all of the following except
   (A) not show Mary the anxiety she is causing.
   (B) ignore the student's disruptive behavior.
   (C) verbally embarrass the student until she is more cooperative.
   (D) suggest psychotherapy to the parents.
   (E) reinforcing the student when she engages in more productive behavior.

3. One of the major contrasts between the suburban and urban school settings that a school psychologist should be aware of is
   (A) less interest in the education of children in urban settings.
   (B) there is more diversity among students in suburban schools.
   (C) there is more peer pressure to conform in urban schools.
   (D) crime, delinquency, and similar problems are more prevalent in urban schools.
   (E) teachers tend to be more experienced in urban schools.

4. Each of the following are primary responsibilities of a school psychologist except
   (A) alerting the local police force about the problems of certain students.
   (B) being aware of the variance in attitudinal and cultural values of different racial and religious groups.
   (C) a familiarity with basic research design and statistic analyses.

(D) the responsibility of persuading parents to avail themselves of community and school services.

(E) counselling teachers about behavior modification techniques.

5. Test scores and data analyses of group intelligence tests employ all of the following methods of data presentation except

(A) letter ratings.   (D) sigma scores.

(B) standard error of the mean.   (E) stanine scores.

(C) percentile values.

6. School psychologists are trained in, and are expected to perform all of the following responsibilities except

(A) reviewing the records of teachers to determine if they are qualified to teach certain subjects.

(B) administering tests to assess student abilities.

(C) designing specialized programs for particular students.

(D) familiarizing staff members with out-of-school services available to them or their students.

(E) updating their expertise by reading the professional journals in their area.

7. One of the reasons that school psychologists as a group publish little research relative to the other disciplines in applied psychology is

(A) the complexity of the legalities that have to be honored.

(B) the fact that most research requires the use of teacher and class time.

(C) the cost of conducting research and data analyses.

(D) their heavy work loads leave little time for research.

(E) All of the above.

8. Which of the following is not a primary difference between dealing with an adolescent student and an elementary school student?

(A) The tendency to act out

(B) The necessity to get consent from the student to be treated

(C) The advantages of using group therapy

(D) The potential advantages of being counselled

(E) The severity of the inappropriate behavior they engage in

9. The most difficult and trying problem for a school psychologist to deal with is

(A) a reading disability.   (D) language deficits.

(B) a physical impairment.   (E) shyness.

(C) acting out.

10. The primary purpose of a psychological report is

(A) to amass data on students.

(B) to serve as the basis for publications.

(C) to enable the principal to report school status to the school board.

(D)   communication.

(E)   to determine student placement.

11.   The school psychologist should have a prominent place in the school administration for all of the following reasons except

(A)   having the ability to get things done.

(B)   personal freedom.

(C)   having power and authority.

(D)   independence of the administrative structure.

(E)   making recommendations.

12.   The basis of the relationship between school psychologists and the teaching staff

(A)   is based on being polite but distant.

(B)   requires the teachers to defer to the psychologist in all matters.

(C)   expects the school psychologist to restrict their activities to student interactions.

(D)   is often one of suspicion because the psychologist is the intermediary between teachers and the administration.

(E)   involves mutual efforts to improve the effectiveness of the educational process.

13.   The better "intelligence," "mental ability," and "learning aptitude" tests attempt to assess students across a(n) _____ year interval.

(A)   one-   (D)   six-

(B)   two-   (E)   eight-

(C)   four-

14.   The Wechsler Intelligence Scale for Children differs from the Revised Stanford Binet test in

(A)   the age groups that can be tested.

(B)   the distribution of verbal and nonverbal tasks.

(C)   its applicability with psychotic students.

(D)   is accounting for cultural background differences.

(E)   All of the above.

15.   All of the following are commonly used personality tests except the _____ test.

(A)   Rorschach   (D)   Sica Personality Inventory

(B)   Children's Apperception   (E)   Bender Motor Gestalt

(C)   Michigan Picture Story

16.   A third grade transfer student scores a 66 on the Revised Stanford Binet test. They would be placed in

(A)   an advanced class.

(B)   a class appropriate for their age.

(C)   a special education class.

(D)   a program for remedial visual motor training.

(E)   a program emphasizing math.

17.   When writing a paper for publication in an APA journal describing a student with psychological problems, the school psychologist would probably use the technical terms available in

(A)   the DSM III-R.

(B)   Freeman Category Scales.

(C)   WISC Rating Scales.

(D)   Terman's Disorder Classification system.

(E)   legal texts.

18.   In a staff meeting, a neurologist states that a particular hyperactive student must have brain damage and will therefore benefit little from attempts at a normal education. The correct response from the school psychologist should be to

(A)   agree with the diagnosis of this other professional because it is their area of expertise.

(B)   promise to personally inform the parents.

(C)   seek information on special schools that help students with this problem.

(D)   ask the neurologist to support his statement with data.

(E)   recommend that the student be suspended from regular classes immediately.

19.   The longest running philosophical trend in the education of children with behavioral problems has been the _____ approach.

(A)   structured school

(B)   behavioral

(C)   conservative

(D)   gestalt

(E)   permissive-sentimental

20.   One primary difference in the way a school psychologist would administer IQ tests to second grade and tenth grade students is in the

(A)   size of the groups.

(B)   type of tasks.

(C)   number of proctors necessary.

(D)   time limits.

(E)   All of the above are differences.

ANSWER KEY

1.	(E)	6.	(A)	11.	(D)	16.	(C)
2.	(C)	7.	(E)	12.	(E)	17.	(A)
3.	(D)	8.	(D)	13.	(B)	18.	(D)
4.	(A)	9.	(C)	14.	(B)	19.	(E)
5.	(B)	10.	(D)	15.	(D)	20.	(E)

DETAILED EXPLANATIONS OF ANSWERS

1. **(E)** The school psychologist would suspect that the student's problems could stem from any of the choices except (E). There is no convincing evidence of the superiority or inferiority of any race.

2. **(C)** Power struggles with authority figures occur for a variety of reasons. Depending on verbally abrasive responses to punish usually results in alienation of the student and deterioration of class atmosphere.

3. **(D)** Due to the greater density of people, wide range of economic bases, overcrowding and understaffing, and acceptable community norms, urban schools have more problems with teen gang behavior and criminality. There is less variability in race, religion, and family income, in suburbs. Teaching posts in suburban schools are frequently earned after a teacher has spent years in an urban school.

4. **(A)** It is unethical to provide any state agency with information about particular students without expressed written permission. The other choices are all responsibilities expected of a competent school psychologist.

5. **(B)** Letter ratings are often assigned. For example an "A" to represent all IQ scores above 118. "B" would refer to scores between 110 and 117. Sigma scores refer to a measure of standard deviation. The stanine system places scores in one of nine categories, stanine 9 (the highest 4%) to stanine 1 (the lowest 4% of the scores).

6. **(A)** Review of teaching credentials and teaching assignments are the responsibility of the school principal.

7. **(E)** Research guidelines require the school psychologist to acquire written permission from numerous sources. Research often takes away from instruction time so some teachers are reluctant to get involved. Work loads (meetings, conferences, assessments, etc.) often leave little time to conduct research.

8.   **(D)**   Adolescents are more likely to act out, be hostile, or suspicious, relative to a younger student. Adolescents usually band together in groups or gangs, making group therapy less personally threatening to them. Younger students tend to benefit more from individualized treatment. Because they are older, adolescents may have problems (e.g., sex, drugs) that the younger student wouldn't have. They also are not considered children, and must, therefore, consent to treatment. The answer is (D). People of all ages can benefit positively from counselling.

9.   **(C)**   Acting out may stem from emotional problems, faulty home environment, the desire to support a sense of omnipotence or superiority, or other complex variables. This client tends to be much less cooperative than any of the other four problems listed.

10.   **(D)**   Communication is the primary purpose of psychological reports. Their purpose is to inform teachers, present diagnostic assessments, and make recommendations. They are sometimes used for research and student placement but these uses are inclusive of choice (D)—communication.

11.   **(D)**   A school psychologist depends on the support of administration and will alienate them if they act totally independent and indifferent to administrative concerns. However, an upper level administrative position is essential in order to get things done, command the respect of the staff, and to make recommendations in matters not necessarily in his/her area of responsibility.

12.   **(E)**   Both teachers and the school psychologist have common goals. They include improving the quality of the instruction offered, helping students with problems that interfere with the education process, and advising administration on program development. These goals necessitate the development of a relationship based on mutual trust and acknowledging that each person has expertise that others can benefit from.

13.   **(B)**   Assessment tests should be designed to encompass a two-year period. If test items cover too broad an age range, the easier items may falsely raise the grades of older students while the more difficult items would be beyond the range of the younger students tested.

14.   **(B)**   The Stanford Binet test has a heavy emphasis on verbal skills while the WISC uses verbal and nonverbal tasks equally. Neither test is appropriate for psychotic students or students with limited command of the English language.

15.   **(D)**   The Sica Personality Inventory test doesn't exist. All of the other tests are frequently used to assess personality. Other useful tests include the Make-A-Picture-Story, Blacky, and the House-Tree-Person tests.

16.   **(C)**   The average score on the test is 100. A score below 70 suggests mental retardation. The low IQ may not necessarily be due to visual motor problems. The student would be expected to have problems keeping up in a class appropriate for their age.

17.   **(A)**   The Diagnostic and Statistical Manual, Version III-revised, provides the standardized categories of mental illness used by both the American Psychiatric Association and the American Psychological Association.

18.   **(D)**   This diagnosis cannot be made without the benefit of neurological tests. These tests cannot always indicate brain damage. Some students function quite well even if brain

surgery has been performed. The belief that a hyperactive child must have brain damage has more support from folklore than science.

19. **(E)** This approach dates back to the late 19th century. G. Stanley Hall, a pioneer in education was very influenced by Freud's psychoanalytic approach. Children were expected to have to drain off hostilities, act out aggressive and sexual themes as a means of maturing. Hence, unrestricted permissive environments were recommended.

20. **(E)** All four variables would differ depending on the age of the students. Younger students take tests with more pictorial tasks. Group testing of young students should be limited to ten or less due to their tendency to get distracted or attempt to innocently help friends. Because of the differences in tasks, verbal content, ages of the students, the number of proctors and test duration will vary.

This test is intended for those who wish to teach history and social sciences in the secondary school. It is divided into three main sections: history and social sciences; inquiry, critical thinking and information processing; and professional dimensions of social studies education. The topics covered include professional education (18%), history—United States and World (25%), government/civics (16%), sociology (16%), geography (15%), and economics (10%).

DIRECTIONS: Each of the following questions and incomplete statements is followed by five answer choices. Select the choice which best answers each question.

---

1. The war of 1812 was important to America because
   - (A) it opened the territory west of the Mississippi.
   - (B) it allied the colonies with the mother country, Great Britain.
   - (C) it gave the new nation the respect of other foreign nations for the first time.
   - (D) it led to the rebuilding of the South and the end of slavery.
   - (E) it resulted in the rise of the capitalistic system in America.

2. During a social studies lesson, the teacher asked the students to pause and consider the topic as to how they felt, their beliefs about the subject and how it may have affected them as individuals. This is an example of
   - (A) discovery learning.
   - (B) inquiry learning.
   - (C) exploration.
   - (D) reflective thinking.
   - (E) sociodrama.

3. A primary reason that France aided America in her war for independence from Great Britain was rooted in which of the following?
   - (A) France's love for the new nation, America
   - (B) France's continuing and ongoing struggle with Great Britain
   - (C) The struggle between Spain and France over control of the seas
   - (D) The belief France held in democratic ideals
   - (E) Louis XVI's religious beliefs

4. The Industrial Revolution created a new social class which were mainly landless and who were termed the
   - (A) Utilitarians.
   - (B) Proletariat.
   - (C) Republicans.
   - (D) Elitists.
   - (E) Democrats.

5. Bicameral refers to which of the following?
    (A) The way by which the system of checks and balances works
    (B) A two-party system in which each party nominates candidates for elections
    (C) A legislature which consists of two houses
    (D) A national policy consisting of foreign and domestic
    (E) The agency responsible for formulating governmental contracts on imports

6. A basic concept from history is that human conflict is often the source of social change. Which of the following is not an example of this concept?
    (A) Religious persecution in Europe in the 18th century led to settlement in America
    (B) The Civil War led to the end of slavery in America
    (C) The revolutions of the middle 16th century in Europe led to the establishment of more democratic states
    (D) The discovery of gold in California led to the gold rush
    (E) American civil rights clashes of the 20th century led to equal opportunities for blacks and minorities

7. Which of the following statements best describes the final step in the inquiry process?
    (A) The framing of the hypothesis
    (B) The gathering and evaluating of the sources of evidence
    (C) The generalizing statement about how well the hypothesis has given meaning to undertaking the problem
    (D) The cataloging of all sources used and an evaluation of each
    (E) The conclusion in which all arguments are summarized and evaluated

8. On June 28, 1914, in Sarajevo, a town in the Austro-Hungarian empire, the Archduke and Archduchess were assassinated. What was the result of this event?
    (A) The start of World War I   (D) The start of the French Revolution
    (B) The fall of the Bastille   (E) The start of World War II
    (C) The formation of the United Nations

9. All of the following contributed to the growth of mass production except
    (A) hand tools.   (D) machine tools.
    (B) standard parts.   (E) the rotary engine.
    (C) the wheel.

10. A social studies teacher has asked the students to internalize the ideas, concepts, and data learned and put them together in new ways which are meaningful to them. This is an example of
    (A) comprehension.   (D) synthesis.
    (B) values orientation.   (E) application.
    (C) sociodrama.

11. Democracy refers to the involvement of all the citizens in its control of government, while an oligarchy
    (A) relegates control of government to the mother country.
    (B) relegates control of government to male citizens only.
    (C) relegates control of government to a select few.
    (D) relegates control of government to a religious group.
    (E) relegates control of government to an autocrat.

12. The Protestant Reformation brought about which of the following?
    (A) A call for a more humanistic system in society
    (B) A feeling of hopelessness with society
    (C) A more trade-oriented system in society
    (D) A call for a democratic system in society
    (E) A demand for equality for women

13. The enlightenment theorists perceived human beings as being
    (A) deprived.
    (B) inherently good.
    (C) perfectible through good works.
    (D) non-educable.
    (E) liabilities to the state.

Questions 14-15 refer to the following passage.

As the 1880's progressed, Americans began to give more attention to the idea that the United States should obtain colonies overseas. The patriotic pride of America embraced the idea of possessions that stretched around the world. The spread of American political and economic control moved from overland to overseas and changed the United States from a continental to a world power.

14. Which term below best describes the policy reflected in the passage?
    (A) Mercantilism
    (B) Progressivism
    (C) Liberalism
    (D) Manifest Destiny
    (E) Imperialism

15. What was taking place during this time which caused America to look from over land to overseas?
    (A) The Spanish-American War
    (B) The Boxer Rebellion
    (C) The Industrial Revolution
    (D) The Mexican Revolution
    (E) The sinking of the *Lusitania*

16. In his "Social Contract," John Locke emphasized the importance and sanctity of
    (A) the state's rights.
    (B) the church's rights.
    (C) the individual's natural rights.
    (D) the rights of a collective group.
    (E) the rights of the citizens.

17. A culture may briefly be described as
    (A) a given way of life for a given people in a given geographic location.

    (B)   a society of people with an organized government.

    (C)   an ethnic group of people living together.

    (D)   a nation of ethnic groups within a given boundary.

    (E)   a given society of people embracing one religious belief.

18.   According to the Constitution, which of the following powers does the President not have?

    (A)   The power to veto

    (B)   The power to appoint Supreme Court Justices

    (C)   The power to establish voting qualifications

    (D)   The power to sign treaties with foreign countries

    (E)   The power to serve as Commander-in-Chief

19.   In 1932 Franklin D. Roosevelt was elected president of the United States. Which statement below describes one of his primary tasks?

    (A)   To make peace with Germany

    (B)   To cure America's economic depression

    (C)   To make peace with Mexico

    (D)   To correct a foreign trade imbalance

    (E)   To sign the Panama Canal treaty

20.   Which of the following statements is most generally true during a period of inflation?

    (A)   Your money buys more than before

    (B)   The prices of goods generally rise

    (C)   Savings accounts usually benefit by increased interest gained

    (D)   Labor costs usually go down

    (E)   Farmers generally benefit from high profits

ANSWER KEY

1.	(C)	6.	(D)	11.	(C)	16.	(C)
2.	(D)	7.	(C)	12.	(A)	17.	(A)
3.	(B)	8.	(A)	13.	(B)	18.	(C)
4.	(B)	9.	(E)	14.	(E)	19.	(B)
5.	(C)	10.	(D)	15.	(C)	20.	(B)

DETAILED EXPLANATION OF ANSWERS

1. **(C)** This question requires that you have a knowledge and understanding of American history. You are asked to choose the answer which tells why the War of 1812 was important to America. You may recall that the War of 1812, sometimes referred to as the Second War for Independence, established the new nation as a world power for the first time and brought respect from Great Britain and France. Therefore choice (C), "it gave the new nation the respect of other foreign nations for the first time," is correct.

2. **(D)** This question requires that you have a knowledge and understanding of social studies teaching theory and methodology. The setting is a social studies lesson. The teacher is basically asking the students to pause and reflect on the topic being presented. Thus, choice (D) is the correct answer as this methodology used by the teacher is reflective thinking, a methodology designed to cause students to evaluate information in a personal manner and to relate it to their lives.

3. **(B)** Here you must apply your knowledge of American history. The question calls for the primary reason for France's aiding America in 1776. France's continuing struggle with Great Britain for colonial dominance had suffered a severe setback with the treaty of Paris in 1763. Here she lost virtually all of her interests in the Western Hemisphere to Great Britain. France was further afraid that the American colonies under strong British control would make England even more powerful, Therefore, France allied herself with the colonists against Great Britain in their struggle against the mother country. The correct choice therefore is (B).

4. **(B)** In this question you are required to have a knowledge of world history. The question asks for the name of the new social class created by the Industrial Revolution. The Industrial Revolution in the 19th century caused a population move to the cities, near the factories, where there were jobs. These factory workers held no land and were dependent largely on factory wages for survival. The term for this working class was the Proletariat. Therefore, choice (B) is the correct answer.

5. **(C)** This question requires that you have a knowledge of government and, more specifically, an understanding of a republican form of government such as that of the United States. The question calls for you to identify the statement which refers to a bicameral system. As you should have recalled, a bicameral system is a legislature consisting of two houses. An example is the U.S. Congress, which is divided into the Senate and the House of Representatives. Therefore, choice (C) is correct.

6. **(D)** The question calls for you to choose the statement which is NOT an example of human conflict leading to social change. Choices (A), (B), (C), and (E) all represent human conflicts in history which resulted in social change. The discovery of gold in California was not an example of a human conflict. Therefore, choice (D) is the correct answer.

7. **(C)** This question requires that you have an understanding of teaching theory and methodology in the social studies, more specifically an understanding of the inquiry process. All of the choices reflect various steps in the inquiry process; however, you are asked which statement best describes the final step. In the final step of the inquiry process, one must provide a generalizing statement about how well the hypothesis has given meaning to understanding the problem. Choice (C) is the correct answer.

8. **(A)** This question requires that you possess a knowledge and understanding of world history. The question requires more specifically that you be familiar with the causes of World War I. As you should have recalled, the assassination of the Austrian Archduke and Archduchess, heirs to the Austro-Hungarian throne, resulted in the beginning of World War I. Thus, choice (A) is the correct answer.

9. **(E)** In this question you are required to have an understanding of economic movements in American history. More specifically, you are asked to identify the one choice which did not contribute to the growth of mass production. Choices (A), (B), (C), and (D) all present instruments which contributed greatly to mass production. The rotary engine, however, a concept used in automobile engines today, did not contribute to the growth of mass production in general. Therefore, choice (E) is correct.

10. **(D)** To answer this question correctly, you must have a clear understanding of *Bloom's Taxonomy*. Choices (B) and (C) are not a part of this *Taxonomy*. Choices (A), (D), and (E) are all levels of this *Taxonomy*, but the question asks for the specific level of the *Taxonomy* which requires the students to organize ideas, concepts, and learned data in a new, personally meaningful and creative manner. This is the synthesis level. Choice (D) is therefore correct.

11. **(C)** Here you must have a knowledge of the evolution of governmental forms. The question requires you to simply choose the statement which best describes an oligarchy. All the choices refer to forms of government, but only choice (C) correctly describes an oligarchy, which relegates control of government to a select few.

12. **(A)** This question requires that you have a basic knowledge of world history, especially those basic socio-political and religious movements which shaped man's current situation. Each of the choices (B), (C), (D), and (E), while presenting resulting changes in human society, do not reflect a change in society brought about by the Protestant Reformation, which called for a more humanistic societal system. Choice (A), therefore, is the correct answer.

13. **(B)** In your knowledge of world history, you may recall that the Age of Reason, or The Enlightenment, was dominated by intellectuals such as Rousseau, Voltaire, and Diderot, who felt that man was basically and inherently good and through reason and cooperation with one another could make great progress in building a happier social community. Choice (B) is therefore the correct answer.

Questions 14-15 require that you have a knowledge and understanding of American history. also, you must apply this knowledge and understanding to the passage.

14. **(E)** Here you are asked to choose the statement which best describes the policy of holding overseas colonial possessions for the interests of the mother country. Only choice (E), Imperialism, is correct.

15. **(C)** In this question you are to recall the most significant event taking place during the 1880's that caused America to look beyond, from America to overseas. You may recall that the most significant event taking place in the mid-19th century which was driving America to seek overseas markets and possessions was the Industrial Revolution. Choice (C) is, therefore, the correct answer.

16. **(C)** Your understanding of world history is brought into play in this question, which calls for a knowledge of John Locke's philosophy on government and the natural rights of man. More specifically, you are asked to determine what important concept Locke was emphasizing in his "Social Contract" from among the choices presented. In his "Social Contract" Locke was concerned with the state's rights, choice (A), as well as the rights of citizens and the collective group, choices (E) and (D). He is not particularly concerned with the church's rights, choice (B). However, he is concerned with and emphasizes the importance and sanctity of the individual's natural rights, choice (C), the correct answer.

17. **(A)** In understanding the social sciences, you must have a knowledge of the meaning of culture, society, ethnic groups, and nationalities. In this question, you are simply asked to choose the statement which describes a culture. Only choice (A) is correct as a culture may briefly be described as a given way of life for a given people in a given geographic location.

18. **(C)** This question requires that you have a knowledge and understanding of American government and the Constitution. More specifically, you are asked to identify the statement which depicts a constitutional power that the President of the United States does NOT possess. The President possesses all of those powers set forth in choices (A), (B), (D), and (E). However, he does not have the power to establish voting qualifications, choice (C), which is the correct answer.

19. **(B)** This question requires a knowledge and understanding of American history, more specifically of our Presidents and their times. You are asked here to choose the statement which describes one of Franklin D. Roosevelt's primary tasks in 1932 upon his election. If you recall your American history, in 1932 America was in the grip of an economic depression. Roosevelt's primary task was to cure America's economic depression. Thus, choice (B) is the correct answer.

20. **(B)** A general knowledge of basic economics is required to answer this question. You are asked to choose the statement which is most generally true during a time or period of inflation. After reading all of the choices, you should have found that (B), "the prices of gods generally rise," is correct. Choices (A) and (D) are incorrect. Choice (C), while possibly true, is not generally true of an inflationary period. Choice (E) is irrelevant here.

SPANISH

The Spanish test has five sections: listening comprehension; reading comprehension; written expression; phonetics, morphology, and syntax; and cultural background. Varied topics and different levels of difficulty appear in each section. The test also assesses the prospective Spanish teacher's knowledge of the differences between English and Spanish, learning problems which may occur, and instructional approaches.

I. Listening Comprehension

In this part of the test you will listen to native speakers of Spanish on a tape recording. The listening passages will be single utterances, brief dialogues, newscasts, etc. From the four possible responses, you should choose the one which is most likely to be made in each situation or the best answer to each question. This part seeks to evaluate your ability to discern phonemic contrasts, your understanding of idiomatic expressions, vocabulary and conversational Spanish. In addition, questions may also test your comprehension of important facts or ideas. The listening parts are transcribed in this case, since a tape will not be provided.

DIRECTIONS: You will now hear a series of questions and statements. Next to each number in your test booklet you will find four sentences, one of which is the most appropriate response to the spoken statement. In each case, select the best choice.

1. *You will hear:* ¿Qué traje me va mejor, éste o aquél?
    You will read:
    (A) No te traje ése.   (C) Te traigo aquél.
    (B) Ése te va mejor.   (D) Creo que se va a mejorar.

DIRECTIONS: For each question in this part you will hear a short conversation between two people and will read a question about that conversation in your test booklet. Choose the best answer from the four responses given.

2. *You will hear:*
    Man: ¿Qué número calza usted?
    Woman: Calzo número treinta y cinco.
    Man: ¿Por qué no se prueba este par?
    Woman: No, gracias. Prefiero un par de tacón alto.

    You will read: ¿Dónde se encuentran las dos personas?
    (A) En una confitería   (C) En una librería
    (B) En una estación   (D) En una zapatería

In this part of the test you will hear a number of spoken passages. Each will be followed by a series of questions. During the pause after each question you should select the most appropriate response from the four choices given in your test booklet.

Se acaba de saber que el nuevo satélite será lanzado al espacio el mes entrante si no aparecen más desperfectos o fallas en el mecanismo del cohete como sucedió la semana pasada. En su misión, dicho satélite sacará fotos de los principales desiertos del hemisferio norte con el propósito de averiguar si existen yacimientos de minerales importantes en estas regiones áridas todavía no explotadas por la industria minera.

3.   ¿Qué quieren descubrir con el lanzamiento de este satélite?

    (A)   Si hay seres inteligentes en el espacio

    (B)   Si existen desiertos no descubiertos hasta ahora

    (C)   Si hay minerales importantes bajo los desiertos

    (D)   Si ha habido explosiones de bombas atómicas en los desiertos

4.   ¿Cuándo será lanzado el satélite?

    (A)   El mes que viene

    (B)   Cuando se manifiesten más fallas

    (C)   Cuando descubran los yacimientos

    (D)   Cuando se averigüe su propósito

II. Reading Comprehension

In this section of the test there are short reading passages on a wide variety of topics and on several levels of difficulty. Following each passage there are several questions about its content, mood or principal ideas.

DIRECTIONS: Read the following passage carefully, trying to comprehend as much as possible. Each selection is followed by questions or incomplete statements. Choose the best answer or completion according to the passage.

Habiendo traspasado la barrera pirenaica al norte, los árabes llegaron hasta la ciudad de Poitiers en su guerra de conquista religiosa. No tuvieron éxito con su plan para apoderarse de lo que hoy es Francia ya que fueron rechazados hacia el sur por el héroe cristiano Carlos Martel. En la Pennísula Ibérica se concentraron los musulmanes en la actual región de Andalucía donde floreció su cultura mucho más adelantada que la del resto de Europa. Los pocos cristianos refugiados en el norte de la península empezaron su lenta guerra de reconquista que tardó siglos en realizarse.

5.   Según el pasaje, los árabes

    (A)   fueron más allá de los Pirineos en su cruzada islámica.

    (B)   no atravesaron los Pirineos.

(C)   tomaron posesión de Francia.

(D)   repulsaron al héroe Carlos Martel.

6.   ¿Cómo progresó la Reconquista cristiana?

    (A)   Rápidamente   (C)   Aceleradamente

    (B)   Fácilmente   (D)   Despacio

De semblante altivo y desdeñoso, se colocó en medio de la estancia mirando a todos con cara de reto y menosprecio, sabiendo que ninguno de sus vituperadores se atrevería a desafiarlo a pesar del general enojo que sentían por él. Cobardes todos ellos. Gente vil y mal nacida que no captaba lo que significaba ser noble y castellano.

7.   El personaje central del párrafo se muestra muy

    (A)   misericordioso.   (C)   orgulloso.

    (B)   humilde.   (D)   tímido.

8.   El personaje central inspiraba en los demás un profundo sentimiento de

    (A)   valor.   (C)   cariño.

    (B)   enfado.   (D)   compasión.

III. Structure and Written Expression

This section is divided into two parts, A and B. In Part A you are to identify the proper structural form to complete correctly the sentences of a brief paragraph. Part B seeks to evaluate indirectly your writing skills by asking you to identify grammatical errors in a given sentence.

Part A

> **DIRECTIONS:** In the sentence below, the blank spaces indicate omissions. You are to select from the four options given the one which fits structurally and grammatically in the sentence. Be sure to read the entire passage before attempting to answer.

_____(9)_____ el almuerzo, la criada fue a su cuarto _____(10)_____ que _____(11)_____ muy cansada.

9.   (A)   Acababa   (C)   Acabó

    (B)   Acaba   (D)   Acabado

10.   (A)   ya   (C)   hasta

    (B)   desde   (D)   antes

11.   (A)   fue   (C)   estaba

    (B)   era   (D)   estuviera

Part B

DIRECTIONS: The sentence below contains ONE grammatical error. Choose the underlined portion of the sentence which you consider grammatically or stylistically incorrect. Remember that in this part of the test you are to select an INCORRECT word or phrase.

12. El ama de casa se quejaba de que subieran tan mucho los precios.
          A   B   C   D

IV. Language Analysis (16%)

This section of the test emphasizes those linguistic elements which are important in the teaching of Spanish, especially those which are significantly different from English usage.

DIRECTIONS: Select the best of the four choices offered as answers to the following questions.

13. Which of the following verbs has the same pattern as *dormir* for the present subjunctive tense?

    (A)   volver   (C)   almorzar

    (B)   pedir   (D)   poder

14. In which of the following words does the *s* sound differ from the same letter in the remaining three words?

    (A)   rosa   (C)   Castilla

    (B)   desde   (D)   semanal

15. Which of the following phrases refers to something nearer to the listener than to the speaker?

    (A)   Aquellos zapatos   (C)   Aquel pañuelo

    (B)   Estos trajes   (D)   Ese sofá

16. Which of the following verbs is often followed by the preposition *de* when there is a complement after it?

    (A)   Enamorarse   (C)   Tardar

    (B)   Casarse   (D)   Asistir

V. Cultural Background

This portion of the test seeks to evaluate one's knowledge of Hispanic culture and civilization necessary for teachers to acquaint their students with the cultural background of the peoples whose language they are studying. Questions deal with such things as customs, history, geography, literature and the arts.

> **DIRECTIONS:** Complete each of the statements below by choosing the best answer from the four options.

17. The running of the bulls through the streets of the Spanish city of Pamplona is part of the celebration of
    (A) la Pascua Florida.
    (C) la fiesta de San Fermín.
    (B) la Fallas.
    (D) el dos de mayo.

18. The political philosophy which was officially espoused by the Franco regime in Spain was
    (A) Communism.
    (C) Socialism.
    (B) Fascism.
    (D) Republicanism.

19. At the time of the Spanish conquest an aboriginal people *not* found in Mexico were the
    (A) Guaraníes.
    (C) Toltecs.
    (B) Mayans.
    (D) Aztecs.

20. The literary movement which first appeared in Spanish America and was later transplanted to Spain was
    (A) Modernism.
    (C) Neoclassicism.
    (B) Romanticism.
    (D) Realism.

ANSWER KEY

1.	(B)	6.	(D)	11.	(C)	16.	(A)
2.	(D)	7.	(C)	12.	(D)	17.	(C)
3.	(C)	8.	(B)	13.	(B)	18.	(B)
4.	(A)	9.	(D)	14.	(B)	19.	(A)
5.	(A)	10.	(A)	15.	(D)	20.	(A)

DETAILED EXPLANATION OF ANSWERS

1.   **(B)**   Answer (B) is correct. It means "That suit (near you) fits you the best or is the most becoming to you." This would be the proper response to the question, "Which suit fits me the best or is the most becoming to me, this one or that one (over there)?." Notice the idiomatic use of the verb *ir* in this expression. This item tests not only your comprehension of the idiomatic expression, but also seeks to ascertain whether you realize that "traje" in the question is a noun and not the first person singular of the preterite tense of the verb *traer*. Answer (A) ("I didn't bring you that one.") would be wrong because it assumes that the verb in the question is *traer* and not *ir*. The same would be true of answer (C) ("I'll bring you that one"). Finally, answer (D) ("I believe that he [she,it, you] is [are] going to improve") is wrong because it completely misses the point of the question and assumes that the verb is ir a; *mejorarse*, is going to improve or is going to get better.

2.   **(D)**   Answer (D) is right. The conversation between the man and woman takes place in a shoe store, *zapatería*. You should know this if you can recognize several words and expressions from the conversation: *calzar*, ("to wear a certain size"), *número*, ("size"), *par*, ("pair"), *tacón alto*, ("high heel"). None of the above words would normally be used in a confectionery shop, "confitería," answer (A), in a station, "estación," answer (B), or in a bookstore, "librería," answer (C).

3.   **(C)**   The correct answer is (C), "if there are important minerals beneath the deserts," "si hay minerales importantes bajo los desiertos." In the second sentence of the comprehension paragraph we learn that on its mission the satellite, "satélite," will take pictures of the principal deserts of the Northern Hemisphere, "sacará fotos de los principales desiertos del hemisferio norte," for the purpose of verifying if there exist, "con el propósito de averiguar si existen," deposits of important minerals, "yacimientos de minerales importantes," in those areas. Answer (A), "if there are intelligent beings in space," is incorrect because the focus of the satellite's mission is terrestrial. Answer (B), "if there exist any deserts not thus far discovered," is wrong. The discovery of new deserts is not the purpose, but rather the investigation of those which are already known. Finally, answer (D), "if there have been any atomic bomb explosions in the deserts," is also erroneous, for this is not a military surveillance satellite.

4.   **(A)**   Answer (A) is correct. The satellite will be launched next month, "el mes entrante." If you knew that "el mes entrante" is the same as "el mes que viene," you would have gotten this answer right. Answer (B), "when more defects become evident," certainly is wrong because those problems would only delay the launch even more. Answer (C), "when they discover more deposits," is also illogical because the deposits will be discovered following the launch, not prior to it. Answer (D), "whenever its purpose is ascertained," is obviously in error because the purpose of the satellite's mission has already been determined.

5.   **(A)**   The best answer is (A), i.e., that the Arabs went beyond ("más allá de") the Pyrenees in their attempt to conquer the Christians. It is the first phrase of the reading passage which establishes this fact: "Habiendo traspasado la barrera pirenaica al norte" ("Having crossed the barrier of the Pyrenees to the north..."). Answer (B) is clearly in error because it maintains that the Arabs did not cross, "No atravesaron," the Pyrenees. Answer (C) is also incorrect, for it asserts that the Arabs took possession of France, "tomaron posesión de Francia." The selection indicates, however, that the Arabs failed in their plan to seize, "no tuvieron éxito en su plan de apoderarse de...," that region. Response (D) is wrong, for the Arabs did not repulse or drive back the Gallic hero Charles Martel. In fact, the paragraph states the very opposite, that the Arabs were driven out of that area by Charles Martel.

6.   **(D)**   The proper choice is (D), "despacio," "slowly." We know this from the use of the word "lenta," "slow," in the final sentence, which refers to the progress of the Christian reconquest of Spain from the Arab invaders. The same sentence asserts that that struggle took centuries to be fulfilled. In fact, if we count from the time of the first invasion in 711 to the final defeat of the Arabs by Fernando and Isabel in 1492, it lasted just short of eight centuries. For that reason, answer (A), "rápidamente," "rapidly," and answer (C), "aceleradamente," "speedily," are wrong. Also answer (B), "fácilmente," "easily," is incorrect. Since the reconquest was so prolonged, it could hardly be characterized as easy.

7.   **(C)**   Answer (C) is the best choice. The central character of the paragraph is proud or haughty, "orgulloso." There are numerous words and expressions in the paragraph which reveal this attitude: "altivo," (arrogant), "desdeñoso," (disdainful), "con cara de reto y menosprecio," (with an expression of challenge and scorn). This individual, obviously a Spanish nobleman, considers himself superior to his adversaries. He is certainly not the least bit compassionate, answer (A), "misericordioso," humble, answer (B), "humilde," or shy, answer (D), "tímido."

8.   **(B)**   The proper answer is (B), "enfado," anger, which is a synonym for "enojo," which appears in the comprehension passage, where we learn that the main character inspires general anger, "general enojo" among his adversaries. Although he himself may possess courage, "valor," answer (A), it is not clear that he necessarily inspires this attitude in others. Answer (C), tenderness, "cariño," and answer (D), pity, "compasión" are incorrect also. In fact, he inspires emotions which are quite the contrary.

9.   **(D)**   Answer (D) is correct. In this phrase we need an adjective which will modify the noun *almuerzo*. Among the list of possibilities given, only *Acabado* is an adjectival form derived from the verb *acabar*. The first part of the sentence, up to the comma, means "The luncheon completed" or "The luncheon having been completed." Answers (A), (B) and (C) do not fit structurally into the context of the sentence, for they are not adjectives, but rather verb forms: "Acababa" the first or third person singular of the imperfect tense, "Acaba," the third person singular of the present tense, "Acabo," the third person singular of the preterite tense.

10. **(A)**   The correct answer is (A), *ya*. To have chosen this answer correctly you would have needed to know that *ya que* is an idiomatic expression which means "since" in the sense of "because." Answer (B) would have been incorrect because *desde que* means "since" when we refer to time only. For example, we can say "Estoy más tranquila desde que llegó mi padre," which means "I am calmer since my father arrived." Answer (C), *hasta*, and answer (D), *con tal*, which signify "until" and "provided that," respectively, would not make sense in the context of this sentence

11. **(C)**   Answer (C), "estaba" is the right choice. We need to use the verb *estar* in this context because we are referring to a temporary or transitory state expressed by the adjective *cansado*. The options give you two different forms of the verb *estar*: *estaba* and *estuviera*. The latter is the imperfect subjunctive form of the verb and should not be used here because there is nothing in the sentence requiring the subjunctive mood. The expression *ya que*, for example, does not cause a subjunctive because it does not express purpose, but rather consequence. We would want to use the imperfect tense of the indicative mood of *estar* in this instance because that tense is most often used for description in the past. Answers (A) and (B), *fue* and *era*, are the preterite and imperfect tenses, respectively, of the verb *ser*. Neither of them is right in this context because *ser* is not generally used to express passing or temporary states.

12. **(D)**   You were right if you chose (D) as the incorrect form in the sentence. To express the idea of the adverbial phrase "so much" in Spanish we simple say *tanto*, *tanta*, etc. These forms are never directly followed by any form of *mucho*. This is a mistake which is made very frequently by those whose first language is English. You may have erroneously chosen (A) as the incorrect form just because we have used the masculine article *el* in front of the feminine noun *ama*. This is not a mistake, however, because we use *el* in front of *feminine singular* nouns if they begin with stressed *a* or stressed *ha*. Examples: *el arca, el haba*, but *La Alhambra*. In the last instance the stress in *Alhambra* is not on the first syllable. Note that in the plural the regular feminine plural article is used. Examples: *las amas, las arcas, las habas*. The expression *se quejaba de que*, answer (B), is not wrong. *Quejarse de* is an idiomatic expression which means "to complain about." It is used here in the imperfect tense to place emphasis on the fact that the housewife *was in the process* of complaining about how much the prices were rising. If we had wished to show that the action of complaining was finished, we would have used the preterite form of the verb: *se quejó*. Note that this verb is generally followed by the preposition *de* when it means to complain *about* something. Also, if *quejarse de* is followed by a subordinate clause, that clause must be introduced by the pronoun *que* as happens in our sentence. Answer (C), *subieran* is not in error. It is the third person plural of the imperfect subjunctive mood of the verb *subir*. Here the subjunctive must be used because of the preceding phrase *se quejaba de que*. Expressions like *quejarse de, alegrarse de*, etc., which express a subjective, emotional attitude regarding the idea which follows them usually require the subjunctive in the subordinate clause which follows. Here we have used the imperfect subjunctive because the preceding verb, *quejaba*, was in a past tense, the imperfect indicative. On the other hand, had the sentence used the present indicative in the main clause, the verb in the resulting subordinate clause has to be expressed in the present subjunctive. In other words, we usually try to preserve that natural sequence of tenses. For example, compare the following sentences as to their use of the subjunctive: *Se quejaba de que lloviera.* (She/He was complaining about it raining...because it *was* raining.); *Se queja de que llueva.* (She/He is complaining about it raining...because it *is* raining.)

13. **(B)**   The proper answer is (B), the verb *pedir*. Only vowel-changing verbs of the third conjugation, i.e., verbs whose infinitive ends in -ir, experience a change in the forms for

nosotros and *vosotros* in the present subjunctive. In such cases, the change is the same as that which occurs in the third person singular and plural of the preterite tense. As *pedir* is the only third conjugation verb among the possible answers, it is, therefore, the only possible correct response. Answers (A), (C) and (D) are incorrect because they are not third conjugation verbs and, therefore, cannot experience vowel changes in the first and second person plural of the present subjunctive as happens with the verb *dormir*.

14. **(B)** The correct choice is (B), "desde." Most commonly in Spanish the letter *s* has a hissing sound similar to that of the double *s* in the English word "kiss". This is exactly how it should sound in "rosa," answer (A), in "Castilla," answer (C), and in "semanal," answer (D). If, however, the letter *s* immediately precedes a *d* as in "desde," or an *m*, as in "mismo," for example, it then has a buzzing or voiced sound as the *s* in the English word "rose."

15. **(D)** The correct response is (D), *ese sofá*. The demonstrative adjectives (*este, ese, aquel*, and their various singular, plural, masculine and feminine forms) are used to point out *which* objects or persons a noun refers to. Depending on which one is used, they usually indicate the general proximity of the person or object either to the speaker or the listener. The demonstrative *ese* and its forms indicate proximity to the listener and mean "that"/"those" near the person to whom we are speaking. The word *este* and its forms mean "this"/"these" and refer to something near to the speaker. Therefore, answer (B) is wrong. The demonstrative *aquel* and its forms mean "that"/"those" and refer to something at some distance from *both* the speaker and the listener. Consequently, both (A) and (C) are incorrect.

16. **(A)** If you answered (A), *enamorarse*, you are right. In Spanish there are certain verbs which require that very specific prepositions be used following them if a complement appears immediately afterwards. There seems to be no very easy way to remember which prepositions go with which verbs. Nevertheless, the more you read and hear authentic Spanish, the more familiar you will be with which prepositions are used in any given case. The verb *enamorarse* is the only verb of the choices which takes the preposition *de* following it. Example: *Don Quijote se enamoró de Dulcinea del Toboso.* (Don Quijote fell in love with Dulcinea del Toboso.) The verb *casarse* is followed by the preposition *con* when it would have a direct object after it in English. Example: *Romeo no se casó con Julieta.* (Romeo didn't marry Juliet.) The verb *tardar* is followed by the preposition *en* when there is an infinitive directly after it. Example: *Tardaste mucho tiempo en llegar.* (You were a long time in arriving.) Finally, the verb *asistir* is followed by the preposition *a* when a place is indicated immediately afterwards. Example: *Asistían a la Universidad de Madrid.* (They were attending the University of Madrid.)

17. **(C)** (C) is the correct answer. The running of the bulls through the streets of Pamplona, (region of Navarra), Spain is part of the festival of San Fermín, celebrated from July 6 through 15. The event takes place each morning during that period. The bulls are released from their corrals and are headed in the direction of the bullring as the city's youth and foreign tourists run ahead of them, trying to avoid being gored. Occasionally there are tragic mishaps along the way. Participants usually wear the typical regional costume: white pants and shirt, red neckerchief. Answer (A) is incorrect, for it simply refers to Easter Sunday. The Fallas, answer (B), in the city of Valencia, Spain celebrates the feast of San José, March 12-19. As a climax to this festival, gigantic cardboard figures of a satirical nature are set afire in the streets and squares. Answer (D) is also incorrect. El dos de mayo, May 2, is Spain's national independence day commemorating Madrid's popular uprising in 1808 against Napoleon's army of occupation.

18 **(B)** The correct answer is (B), Fascism. In July of 1936 the Spanish general Francisco Franco led a rebellion against the Second Spanish Republic and thereby started the Spanish Civil War, 1936-1939. During the war Franco was supported by the Fascist Italy of Mussolini and the Nazi Germany of Hitler. Following his victory in 1939 Franco established himself as *Caudillo*, supreme leader. During a large part of his dictatorial regime he allowed only one political party, La Falange Española, the Spanish Fascist party, which was originally founded by José Antonio Primo de Rivera in 1933. Answer (A) is wrong because Franco was a lifelong foe of Communism and felt that his mission was to save Spain from the Communist threat. The same was true of his attitude toward Socialism, answer (C). Answer (D) is likewise incorrect, for we know that it was Franco who chose to overthrow the Spanish Republic in 1936.

19. **(A)** Answer (A), the Guaraníes, is correct as they are the only indigenous people among the four choices given who did not live in Mexico. The Guaraníes, in fact, were concentrated in an area extending from what is today northern Argentina through Paraguay and into the Amazon region. On the other hand, the Toltecs, (C), and the Aztecs, (D), were peoples whom Cortés encountered as he undertook the conquest of Mexico. (See *Las cartas de relación* of Cortés and *La verdadera historia de los sucesos de la conquista de Nueva España* by Bernal Díaz del Castillo.) Finally, the Mayans, answer (B), a large family of Indian peoples, were concentrated in Central America and parts of Mexico, especially the Yucatan Peninsula, where we still find the monumental remains of their great civilization in places such as the ruins of Chichén Itzá, Uxmal and Palenque.

20. **(A)** Answer (A), Modernism, is correct. This literary movement of the last decades of the nineteenth century and the early twentieth century was initiated by, among others, the Nicaraguan poet, Rubén Darío. It was a very eclectic movement which drew upon various earlier literary and artistic schools, Romanticism, Symbolism, the French Parnasians, for much of its inspiration. In poetry, it experimented with poetic forms and themes used during Medieval and Renaissance times. Modernism was the first literary trend to arise in Latin America and later be adopted by Spanish peninsular authors, in this case, Valle-Inclán and Antonio Machado, for example. Prior to the advent of Modernism and from the time of Spanish domination of Latin America, Spanish American authors tended to imitate the literary trends popular in Spain or other European countries. This was the case with Neoclassicism, answer (C), Romanticism, answer (B), and Realism, answer (D), all of which, consequently, are incorrect responses.

SPECIAL EDUCATION

This test is very broad because it covers all areas of exceptionality. It measures basic knowledge required of all special education teachers. Some questions focus on development from ages three to twenty-one. Others concentrate on common characteristics between various learning-disabled children. The main topics include: understanding exceptionalities (15%), legal issues and compliance (10%), assessment/evaluation in special education (20%), service delivery and instruction (33%), and classroom management (22%).

DIRECTIONS: Each of the following questions and incomplete statements is followed by five answer choices. Select the choice which best answers each question.

---

1. Which behavior modification technique would best benefit a student diagnosed with microcephalus?

    (A) Shaping

    (B) A token economy

    (C) Intermittent reinforcement

    (D) Verbal skill development

    (E) Vocational skill development

2. Which of the following approaches in psychology provides the majority of the teaching techniques used with the retarded?

    (A) Psychoanalytic

    (B) Humanistic

    (C) Behavioral

    (D) Neurobiological

    (E) Phenomenological

3. Which of the following factors is responsible for the difficulty that mentally retarded individuals have in acquiring basic academic skills?

    (A) Expectancy of failure

    (B) Deficits in attending to relevant stimulus cues

    (C) Poor retention level

    (D) Inefficient prior learning

    (E) All of the above.

4. Each of the following conditions is caused by a genetic defect except

    (A) Tay-Sach's disease.

    (B) Rubella.

    (C) Trisomy 21 syndrome.

    (D) Turner's syndrome.

    (E) Klinefelter's syndrome.

5. Which of the following causes of retardation is produced by endocrine gland imbalance?

    (A) Trisomy 18 syndrome

    (B) Bilirubin encephalopathy

    (C) PKU

    (D) Cretinism

    (E) Rubella, congenital

6. Precaution must be exercised when assessing a subject. Studies have shown that labelling a person mentally retarded (whether it is true or not) can
    (A) radically alter the child's self concept.
    (B) lead to erroneous institutionalization.
    (C) convince the parents to provide less than a rich environment because they believe that their child needs simplicity.
    (D) alter the ways in which the child interacts with other children, and is treated by others.
    (E) All of the above.

7. In general, mentally retarded children will most benefit from which environment?
    (A) A supportive home environment
    (B) An institutional setting
    (C) A private school
    (D) A community-oriented residential care facility
    (E) All of the above are equally good.

8. Public Law 94-142, the Education of All Handicapped Children Act, guarantees all mentally retarded individuals
    (A) the right to attend any public school.
    (B) the right to be educated at public expense.
    (C) below the age of 12 an education.
    (D) adequate foster care.
    (E) All of the above.

9. The MORC program differs from the ENCOR approach in that the MORC program _____, while the ENCOR program _____.
    (A) trains clients to work in the home, trains clients to work in the community.
    (B) is an alternate approach to institutionalization, returns clients to a state facility after training.
    (C) places clients in foster homes, rents houses for the clients to share with staffers.
    (D) is designed for mildly retarded children, is geared for the profoundly retarded.
    (E) All of the above.

10. Which of the following is not necessarily a characteristic of gifted children?
    (A) They acquire reading at an early age
    (B) They have a large vocabulary
    (C) They like to experiment with new ideas
    (D) They are exceptionally good looking
    (E) They ask many questions and expect detailed answers

11. The gifted make up _____ percent of the population and have an IQ above ____.
    (A) 2-4, 132   (D) 1, 160
    (B) 0.1, 148   (E) 15, 116
    (C) 10, 100

12. Each of the following conditions is legally considered a handicap except
    (A) speech impairment.　　　(D) mental retardation.
    (B) deafness.　　　(E) loss of a limb.
    (C) emotional disturbance.

13. A speech pathologist would engage in all of the following except
    (A) providing a classroom environment with unpressured verbal exchange.
    (B) elimination of any possibility of mockery or embarrassment.
    (C) providing varied opportunities for speech.
    (D) reinforcing any instances of the use of new speech patterns.
    (E) consultations with other language pathologists.

14. A teacher with a visually impaired student should do all of the following except
    (A) accept the child as a regular member of the class.
    (B) consult with the school psychologist or resource teacher about their assessment of the student's level of visual functioning.
    (C) have lower expectations of this student relative to the rest of the class.
    (D) expect the student to organize and maintain their personal desk materials.
    (E) encourage the use of low vision in your selection of instructional materials.

15. Which of the following is not a recommendation for teachers with a hearing impaired student?
    (A) Don't assign a buddy to help communicate class activities
    (B) Assign a favorable seat away from radiators, fans, and other distracting noises
    (C) Speak naturally but always face the child when addressing him or her
    (D) Verbally check the hearing aid daily and encourage the student to report its failure to you
    (E) Increase blackboard use to enable written information to supplement verbal classroom instruction

16. A student experiences an epileptic seizure during class. The teacher should do all of the following except
    (A) ease the child to the floor while reassuring the other students.
    (B) force an object between the teeth to prevent biting of the tongue.
    (C) place a cushioning object under the back of the head.
    (D) loosen any tight clothing.
    (E) allow the seizure to run its course.

17. Which of the following statements is false?
    (A) The range of learning environments is greater for handicapped children relative to normals.
    (B) The quantitative degree of the handicap is as important as its qualitative nature when designing instruction.
    (C) Learning doesn't proceed well if the student's behavior is not under stimulus control.

(D) Handicapped children exhibit a greater range of behaviors than non-handicapped children.

(E) All of the above are true statements.

18. *Remedial* education stresses _____, while *compensatory* education involves _____.

(A) reading skills only, a wide range of improvements.

(B) establishment of new skills, acceptance of partially developed abilities.

(C) individual performance, group performance.

(D) the strengthening of an existing skill, replacement of one skill for another.

(E) All of the above.

19. Each of the following techniques are behavior modification strategies except

(A) modeling.   (D) negative reinforcement.

(B) positive reinforcement.   (E) physical guidance.

(C) dream analysis.

20. All of the following are primary differences between "normal" and retarded children except

(A) rate of learning.   (D) the need for acceptance.

(B) level of learning.   (E) rate of forgetting.

(C) transfer of learning.

ANSWER KEY

1.	(A)	6.	(E)	11.	(A)	16.	(B)
2.	(C)	7.	(A)	12.	(E)	17.	(E)
3.	(E)	8.	(B)	13.	(B)	18.	(D)
4.	(B)	9.	(C)	14.	(C)	19.	(C)
5.	(D)	10.	(D)	15.	(A)	20.	(D)

DETAILED EXPLANATIONS OF ANSWERS

1.   **(A)**   Microcephalus is a condition caused by arrested development of the brain during the fourth or fifth month of pregnancy. The client is usually profoundly retarded. Shaping, the reinforcement of approximations of a desired behavior, would be the best technique to use to establish rudimentary skills such as eye contact and self-feeding behavior.

2.   **(C)**   The behavioral approach, with its emphasis on the influence of environment on behavior, provides the bulk of the training techniques used with the retarded. Because of their limited cognitive abilities, the psychoanalytic (Freudian) and humanistic (phenomenological) approaches have limited application to the training of the retarded.

3.   **(E)**   All of these factors are relevant. Many retarded subjects attend to irrelevant stimuli concomitant to the learning situation. For example, while attempting to learn shapes, they may attend more to the color of the stimuli. rather than the differences in shapes. Many new skills require that prior acquisition of antecedent abilities. Prior faulty learning will undermine the acquisition of new skills. Unless the training situation is structured for frequent success, making many errors while learning leads to frustration, expectation of failure, and avoidance of new learning situations. Finally, poor retention levels reduce the likelihood of sustained performance without frequent repetitious exercises.

4.   **(B)**   Rubella defects, such as retinal problems and deafness, are caused by the mother's contraction of German measles during the first trimester of pregnancy. The other choices are caused by chromosomal anomalies.

5.   **(D)**   Cretinism is produced by a malfunction in thyroid gland function. The result is typically an individual short in stature with short limbs and a curved spine (dwarfism). Treatment with thyroid gland extract, before age one, reduces the chances of retardation and physical abnormalities.

6.   **(E)**   The answer is self-explanatory. Documented studies have suggested that labels often produce self-fulfilling prophecies. One troubling study demonstrated that teachers that are provided the IQ test scores of their students give more attention to the higher scoring

students. This differential treatment could result in performance differences that would erroneously appear to support the test results.

7. **(A)**   Studies indicate that a supportive home environment produces the best chance of maximizing emotional and mental development. A one-to-one relationship with familiar people provides the most comfortable and profitable environment for the child. The other choices listed are all useful but the President's Committee on Mental Retardation (1970) reported that these facilities tend to have overcrowding, high teacher-student ratios, and not enough money to provide adequate programs.

8. **(B)**   Public Law 94-142 guarantees all mentally retarded individuals the right to an education. Furthermore the training should be provided in the "least restrictive environment" possible. The law enabled the establishment of alternatives to massive state institutions. These alternatives included halfway houses, group homes, and foster home care.

9. **(C)**   Both the MORC and ENCOR programs have been shown to be successful alternatives to state institutional care. In both programs, the clients range from mild to moderately retarded. Both programs are designed to prevent the client from returning to an institution.

10. **(D)**   Exceptional children exhibit all the cognitive characteristics listed. Exceptional looks are not always present. Many an intellectual giant was physically lacking with less than average features, e.g., Mozart, Steinmetz, and Edison.

11. **(A)**   The gifted represent 2-4% of the population and have an IQ above 132. The highly gifted have an IQ above 148. The average IQ is 100, while genius starts above 160. An IQ above 116 indicates an academically talented student.

12. **(E)**   Loss of a limb is considered a disability and not a handicap. In addition to the other choices, the United States Office of Education has defined a "legal handicap" to include: deaf-blind, hard of hearing, multi-handicapped, orthopedically impaired, and specific learning disabilities.

13. **(B)**   All of the choices except (B) are employed by speech pathologists. Children with speech handicaps often suffer frustration, low self-esteem, fear of mockery and impatience from others trying to understand them. These factors produce avoidance behaviors in children, i.e., they avoid using language in order to avoid these aversive outcomes. An atmosphere of patience, acceptance, and an abundance of positive reinforcement is essential for these children to develop their verbal skills.

14. **(C)**   The majority of the approximately 70,000 school children who have a visual handicap have a low-vision problem. Most classroom tasks may be more difficult for them, but not unattainable. A teacher that does not treat them differently than the other students in the class is setting an example of acceptance for the other students.

15. **(A)**   Having another student act as a buddy who monitors performance and communicates classroom activities instructions is beneficial to a hearing-impaired student. It saves the student the embarrassment of frequently asking the teacher to repeat instructions.

16. **(B)** Pushing an object such as a pencil between the teeth may damage them, the gums or tongue. If the student has a history of tongue biting a handkerchief may be placed between the molars but only if the mouth is already open.

17. **(E)** All the statements ar true. Additionally, there is no single technique, teaching style, or philosophical orientation that will work for every handicapped student.

18. **(D)** Remedial training refers to exercises designed to raise a person's abilities to normal levels. Compensatory training refers to the establishment of one skill to replace another skill. For example, teaching a blind student to read Braille is compensatory training.

19. **(C)** Dream analysis comes from the psychoanalytic (Freudian) approach. Dreams are believed to reveal subconscious wishes, desires, and conflicts.

20. **(D)** Retarded children, particularly the mildly retarded, are as sensitive as "normal" children.

REA's **Problem Solvers**

The "PROBLEM SOLVERS" are comprehensive supplemental text-books designed to save time in finding solutions to problems. Each "PROBLEM SOLVER" is the first of its kind ever produced in its field. It is the product of a massive effort to illustrate almost any imaginable problem in exceptional depth, detail, and clarity. Each problem is worked out in detail with a step-by-step solution, and the problems are arranged in order of complexity from elementary to advanced. Each book is fully indexed for locating problems rapidly.

ADVANCED CALCULUS
ALGEBRA & TRIGONOMETRY
AUTOMATIC CONTROL
   SYSTEMS/ROBOTICS
BIOLOGY
BUSINESS, ACCOUNTING, & FINANCE
CALCULUS
CHEMISTRY
COMPLEX VARIABLES
COMPUTER SCIENCE
DIFFERENTIAL EQUATIONS
ECONOMICS
ELECTRICAL MACHINES
ELECTRIC CIRCUITS
ELECTROMAGNETICS
ELECTRONIC COMMUNICATIONS
ELECTRONICS
FINITE & DISCRETE MATH
FLUID MECHANICS/DYNAMICS
GENETICS
GEOMETRY

HEAT TRANSFER
LINEAR ALGEBRA
MACHINE DESIGN
MATHEMATICS for ENGINEERS
MECHANICS
NUMERICAL ANALYSIS
OPERATIONS RESEARCH
OPTICS
ORGANIC CHEMISTRY
PHYSICAL CHEMISTRY
PHYSICS
PRE-CALCULUS
PSYCHOLOGY
STATISTICS
STRENGTH OF MATERIALS &
   MECHANICS OF SOLIDS
TECHNICAL DESIGN GRAPHICS
THERMODYNAMICS
TOPOLOGY
TRANSPORT PHENOMENA
VECTOR ANALYSIS

If you would like more information about any of these books,
complete the coupon below and return it to us or visit your local bookstore.

RESEARCH & EDUCATION ASSOCIATION
61 Ethel Road W. • Piscataway, New Jersey 08854
Phone: (908) 819-8880

Please send me more information about your Problem Solver Books

Name _____

Address _____

City _____ State _____ Zip _____